The Pivotal States

THE
PIVOTAL STATES

*A New Framework for U.S.
Policy in the Developing World*

Robert Chase, Emily Hill, and
Paul Kennedy, Editors

W. W. NORTON & COMPANY
New York · London

Copyright © 1999 by Robert Chase, Emily Hill, and Paul Kennedy

All rights reserved

Printed in the United States of America

First Edition

For information about permission to reproduce selections from this book, write to
Permissions, W. W. Norton & Company, Inc., 500 Fifth Avenue, New York, NY 10110.

The text of this book is composed in Perpetua
Desktop composition by Gina Webster
Manufacturing by The Maple-Vail Book Manufacturing Group
Book design by Charlotte Staub
Cartography by Jacques Chazaud

Library of Congress Cataloging-in-Publication Data

The pivotal states : a new framework for U.S. policy in the developing world /
Robert Chase, Emily Hill, and Paul Kennedy, editors.
p.   cm.
Includes bibliographical references and index.
ISBN 0-393-04675-3
1. United States—Foreign relations—1989– . 2. Developing countries—Foreign relations—
United States. 3. United States—Foreign relations—Developing countries. I. Chase, Robert.
II. Hill, Emily. III. Kennedy, Paul M., 1945– .
E840.P4   1998
327.73—dc21   98-29490
CIP

W. W. Norton & Company, Inc., 500 Fifth Avenue, New York, N.Y. 10110
http://www.wwnorton.com

W. W. Norton & Company Ltd., 10 Coptic Street, London CW1A 1PU

2 3 4 5 6 7 8 9 0

CONTENTS

NOTES ON CONTRIBUTORS

EILEEN F. BABBITT is an assistant professor of international politics and the director of the International Negotiation and Conflict Resolution Program at the Fletcher School of Law and Diplomacy at Tufts University. Prior to joining the faculty of Tufts, Dr. Babbitt was the director of education and training at the United States Institute of Peace in Washington, D.C., and deputy director of the Program on International Conflict Analysis and Resolution at the Center for International Affairs, Harvard University. She has authored and coauthored many articles and book chapters on international mediation and conflict resolution, including "Overcoming the Obstacles to Effective Mediation of International Disputes," coauthored with Lawrence Susskind in *Mediation and International Relations*, edited by J. Bercovitch and J. Rubin (1992), and "The Power of Moral Suasion in International Mediation: A Profile of Jimmy Carter," in *When Talk Works: Profiles of Master Mediators*, edited by D. Kolb and Associates (1994).

JOHN BRESNAN is a senior research scholar of the East Asian Institute of Columbia University. He also has been the executive director of the university's Pacific Basin Studies Program. He is the author of *Managing Indonesia: The Modern Political Economy* (1993) and the editor of *Crisis in the Philippines: The Marcos Era and Beyond* (1986). Mr. Bresnan is most recently the author of *From Dominoes to Dynamos: The Transformation of Southeast Asia* (1994). Mr. Bresnan has held executive positions with the Ford Foundation, including assistant representative in Indonesia (1961–1965), representative in Indonesia (1969–1973), and head of the Office for Asia and the Pacific (1973–1981).

ROBERT CHASE is an assistant professor of economics at the Johns Hopkins School for Advanced International Studies (SAIS) in Bologna, Italy. At Yale University, he received his Ph.D. in economics and was Olin Post-Doctoral Fellow of international security studies. In addition to his work on the pivotal states, he served as the Secretariat economist for the Independent Working Group on the Future of the United Nations, whose report, *The United Nations in Its Second Half-Century*, was presented to U.N. Secretary-General Boutros Boutros-Ghali in June 1995. Prior to his graduate study, he worked for the World Bank, negotiating with the governments of Zambia and Cameroon to design and implement innovative projects to address structural adjustment's social effects.

STEPHEN P. COHEN is the director of the Program in Arms Control, Disarmament and International Security (ACDIS) and is a professor of history and political science at the University of Illinois. He has written, coauthored, or edited eight books, including *India: Emergent Power?* (1978), *The Indian Army* (revised, 1990), *Nuclear Proliferation in South Asia* (1990), *The Pakistan Army* (revised, 1992), *South Asia after the Cold War: International Perspectives* (1993), and *Brasstacks and Beyond: Perception and Management of Crisis in South Asia* (1995).

DONALD C. F. DANIEL is the Milton E. Miles Professor of International Relations and the director of the Strategic Research Department of the Center for Naval Warfare Studies at the Naval Warfare College, Newport, R.I. He has been a Ford Foundation Scholar at the Brookings Institution in Washington, D.C., a research associate at the International Institute for Strategic Studies in London, England and a researcher-in-residence at the Disarmament and Conflict Resolution project in the United Nations Institute for Disarmament Research in Geneva, Switzerland. Dr. Daniel has also served as a consultant for numerous governmental and private organizations in the United States and abroad. He coedited *Beyond Traditional Peacekeeping* (1995), his latest published book, and, with two colleagues, he is presently completing a new book for the United States Institute of Peace, entitled *Talons of the Dove*, that deals with the application of coercive inducement in United Nations peace-support operations.

DANIEL C. ESTY is the director of the Yale Center for Environmental Law and Policy and an associate professor at Yale's School of Forestry and Environmental Studies and the Yale Law School. He previously served in a variety of positions with the U.S. Environmental Protection Agency (EPA), including deputy chief of staff and deputy assistant administrator for policy, planning and evaluation. He negotiated on behalf of the EPA the 1992 Climate Change Convention, the environmental provisions of the North American Free Trade Agreement (NAFTA), and the accords that emerged from the Rio Earth Summit. Dr. Esty is the author or editor of four books and numerous articles on the linkages between the environment and trade, competitiveness, development, international governance and national security. His book *Greening the GATT: Trade, Environment, and the Future* was released in June 1994.

SUMIT GANGULY is a professor of political science at the graduate school and Hunter College of the City University of New York and is also an adjunct professor of political science at Columbia University. A specialist on the politics of South Asia, he is the author of *The Origins of War in South Asia: The Indo-Pakistani Conflicts Since* 1947 (second edition, 1994) and *The Crisis in Kashmir: Portents of War, Hopes of Peace* (1997). He has also edited *Mending Fences: Confidence and Security Building Measures in South Asia* (1996). Dr. Ganguly's publications have appeared in a number of scholarly journals including *Asian Affairs*, *Asian Survey*, *Current History*, *Foreign Affairs*, *International Security*, *The Journal of Asian and African Affairs*, the *Journal of International Affairs*, *The Journal of Strategic Studies*, *Survival*, and the *Washington Quarterly*.

JACK A. GOLDSTONE is a professor of sociology and international relations at the University of California, Davis. He is author of the award-winning *Revolution and Rebellion in the Early Modern World* (1991), and editor-in-chief of the forthcoming *Encyclopedia of Political Revolutions*. Dr. Goldstone has published widely on the issues of population change and domestic conflict, and served on the Foreign Policy Studies Committee of the Social Science Research Council and the Committee on Science and International Security of the American Association for the Advancement of Science.

JEFFREY HERBST is the acting associate dean and an associate professor of politics and international affairs at Princeton University's Woodrow Wilson School. He has also taught at the University of Zimbabwe, the University of Ghana, the University of Cape Town, and the University of the Western Cape. His current research focuses on the politics of economic and political reform in South Africa, the politics of boundaries, and the evolution of self-determination. Dr. Herbst is the author of *State Politics in Zimbabwe* (1990), *U.S. Economic Policy Toward Africa in the 1990s* (1992), and *The Politics of Reform in Ghana, 1982–1991* (1993).

EMILY HILL is a research associate at International Security Studies at Yale University. She is a Ph.D. candidate in the Department of History at Yale and is completing her dissertation, "The Myth of American Idealism: Intellectuals and International Relations 1928–1945." In 1993–1994, she served on the Yale Secretariat for the Independent Working Group on the Future of the United Nations, which published the report *The United Nations in Its Second Half-Century* (1995). Ms. Hill is an associate at the consulting firm McKinsey & Company.

PAUL KENNEDY is J. Richardson Dilworth Professor of History and the director of International Security Studies at Yale University. He is internationally known for his writings and commentaries on global political, economic, and strategic issues. He is on the editorial board of numerous scholarly journals and writes for the *New York Times*, the *Los Angeles Times*, the *Atlantic*, and many foreign-language newspapers and magazines. Dr. Kennedy is the author or editor of thirteen books, including *Pacific Onslaught 1941–43* (1972), *The Rise and Fall of British Naval Mastery* (1976), *The Rise of the Anglo-German Antagonism 1860–1914* (1980), *The Realities Behind Diplomacy* (1981), *Strategy and Diplomacy 1870–1945* (1983), and *The Rise and Fall of the Great Powers* (1988). His latest book is *Preparing for the Twenty-first Century* (1993).

JEAN KRASNO holds a Ph.D. in international politics from the City University of New York, where she wrote her doctoral dissertation on Brazil. She joined Yale in June 1995 as a post-doctoral associate in United Nations Studies and as a lecturer in the Department of Political Science. She is also the deputy director of the Oral History Project at Yale, which is dedicated to interviewing participants in key events of the history of the United Nations. While continuing her role in United Nations studies, Dr. Krasno has also been the coordinator of the Pivotal States Project at International Security Studies at Yale. Her article "Democratization and Reforming the United Nations" appeared in the summer 1996 edition of *Democratization*, and she also published an article entitled "Brazil's Secret Nuclear Program" in the summer 1994 edition of *Orbis*.

ALAN O. MAKOVSKY, a senior fellow at the Washington Institute for Near East Policy in Washington, D.C., is a specialist in Middle Eastern and Turkish affairs. He joined the Washington Institute in 1994 after eleven years in the U.S. Department of State, where he served in a variety of capacities, including Turkey analyst and division chief for southern Europe in the Bureau of Intelligence and Research, and as a political adviser to Operation Provide Comfort, a Turkey and northern Iraq–based multinational military operation; and adviser to the Special Middle East Coordinator. He is the author of several articles on Turkey, including most recently "Israeli-Turkish Relations: A Turkish 'Periphery Strategy'?" in Henry J. Barkey, ed., *Reluctant Neighbor: Turkey's Role in the Middle East* (1996), and "How to Deal with Erbakan" in *Middle East Quarterly* (March 1997).

CHARLES H. NORCHI is a fellow at International Security Studies and a lecturer in international studies and political science at Yale University. He is cochair and cofounder of the International Centre for Humanitarian

Reporting based in Geneva, Switzerland. He serves on the advisory board of the Robert F. Kennedy Human Rights Center and is a contributing editor for *Crosslines Newsjournal.* Mr. Norchi's recent publications include "Letter from Aden," *Crosslines* (February–March 1997); "The National Human Rights Commission of India as a Value Creating Institution" in John Montgomery, ed., *Human Rights Policy in the Pacific Basin* (forthcoming); and "The Circum-Mediterranean: Clashing Civilizations or Common Interests?" in *Middle Sea: Mediterranean Sea Power in the Past, Present and Future* (forthcoming).

ROGER OWEN is A. J. Meyer Professor of Middle East History at Harvard University and the director of the Harvard Center for Middle Eastern Studies. He previously taught at Oxford University, where he was several times director of the Middle East Centre at St. Antony's College. He is the author of *Cotton and the Egyptian Economy 1820–1914* (1969), *The Middle East in the World Economy 1800–1914* (1981), and *State, Power and Politics in the Making of the Modern Middle East* (1992). Dr. Owen has just completed a coauthored economic history of the Middle East in the twentieth century.

WILLIAM B. QUANDT is Harry F. Byrd Jr. Professor of Government and Foreign Affairs at the University of Virginia. From 1979 to 1994, he was a senior fellow in the Foreign Policy Studies Program at the Brookings Institution. His many publications include *Saudi Arabia in the 1980s: Foreign Policy, Security and Oil* (1981), *Camp David: Peacemaking and Politics* (1986), and *Peace Process: American Diplomacy and the Arab-Israeli Conflict Since 1967* (1993). An expert on the Middle East, U.S. policy toward the Arab-Israeli conflict, and energy policy, Dr. Quandt served as a staff member on the National Security Council (1972–1974, 1977–1979). He was actively involved in the negotiations that led to the Camp David accords and the Egyptian-Israeli peace treaty.

HASAN-ASKARI RIZVI is Quaid-i-Azam Professor of Pakistan Studies, Southern Asian Institute, Columbia University, New York, and a professor of political science, Punjab University, Lahore, Pakistan. He holds a Ph.D. from the University of Pennsylvania and, in addition to several research papers, his books include *Pakistan and the Geostrategic Environment* (1993) and *The Military and Politics in Pakistan* (revised, 1987).

ANDREW L. ROSS is a professor of national security affairs in the Department of National Security Decision Making, U.S. Naval War College. He is the editor of *The Political Economy of Defense* (1991), coeditor of *Strategy and Force Planning* (1995), and the author of numerous articles and book chapters on grand strategy, defense planning, regional security, weapons proliferation, the international arms market, defense industrialization, and security and development. Dr. Ross has held research fellowships at Cornell, Princeton, and Harvard and taught in the political science departments at the University of Illinois and the University of Kentucky.

PETER H. SMITH is a professor of political science, Simón Bolívar Professor of Latin American studies, the director of the Center for Iberian and Latin American Studies, and the director of Latin American Studies at the University of California, San Diego. He is a specialist in comparative politics, Latin American politics, and U.S.–Latin American relations. His publications include *Politics and Beef in Argentina: Patterns of Conflict and Change* (1969), *Argentina and the Failure of Democracy: Conflict among Political Elites, 1904–1955* (1974), and *Labyrinths of Power: Political Recruitment in Twentieth Century Mexico* (1979) Dr. Smith's most recent book is *Talons of the Eagle: Dynamics of U.S.–Latin American Relations*, published by Oxford University Press in April 1996.

MICHAEL S. TEITELBAUM is a demographer at the Alfred P. Sloan Foundation in New York. He presently serves as one of nine commissioners of the U.S. Commission on Immigration Reform. He publishes extensively in scientific and popular journals and in national op-ed pages. His books include *The British Fertility Decline: Demographic Transition in the Crucible of the Industrial Revolution* (1984), *Latin Migration North: The Problem for U.S. Foreign Policy* (1985), *The Fear of Population Decline* (1985, coauthor), *Population and Resources in Western Intellectual Traditions* (1989, coeditor), *Threatened Peoples, Threatened Borders* (1995, coeditor), and *Broken Boundaries: Low Fertility, High Immigration, and Rising Nationalisms* (forthcoming, coauthor).

ACKNOWLEDGMENTS

In the course of preparing this book, we have become indebted to a vast number of people who have played key roles in making this effort possible. Although only a few can be mentioned here, we would like to express our gratitude to Susan Sechler, the director of the Global Stewardship Initiative, whose faith in the concept encouraged us to launch the entire project, and to the Pew Charitable Trust for their generous grant and support. Our staff at Yale was headed by Jean Krasno, the coordinator of the pivotal states project. They did an excellent job of planning all the events associated with the project and keeping track of all the inevitable details. Special thanks to those at Yale go to Genevieve Drewes as researcher to the project, and to Susan Hennigan, Cindy Huang, and Andrew Levine. The dedicated efforts of Ann Carter-Drier always ensured that we stayed within our grant budget and guidelines. We are particularly indebted to Sheila Klein, whose careful word processing and editing aided us in coordinating the final drafts.

A number of people and organizations deserve our heartfelt thanks for helping us formulate our ideas and develop the thesis in greater depth. First, we want to thank the Council on Foreign Relations, which sponsored a series of round table discussions on the pivotal states thesis and whose journal *Foreign Affairs* published the first article on the idea. Jane Wales participated in a number of our discussions and added her creative analysis to the formation of the thesis. At the U. S. Department of State, we would like to thank Undersecretary of State Timothy Wirth for his thoughtful input and Alan Lang, chair of the Secretary's Open Forum, who organized two panel presentations on pivotal states at the State Department. Our gratitude also goes to Jeffrey Meer of the Department of Global Affairs, who organized a discussion of the issue.

P. J. Simmons and Michael Vaden put together an all-day round table discussion on pivotal states at the Woodrow Wilson Center in Washington, D.C. Professor Stephen Szabo of the School for Advanced

International Studies (SAIS) in Washington also sponsored a panel discussion for the school's students and faculty. A special thank-you also goes to Moreen Steinbruner of the Center for National Policy for bringing together a high-level group of policy thinkers who devoted a day to a dialogue on our ideas. We would like to give a warm thanks to our Congresswoman, Rosa deLauro of Connecticut, and her chief of staff, James John, who sponsored an excellent workshop on pivotal states for members of Congress. Other members of Congress who offered their interest and support for the idea were Senator Christopher Dodd and Senator Joseph Lieberman, both of Connecticut.

Robert Chase
Emily Hill
Paul Kennedy

The Pivotal States

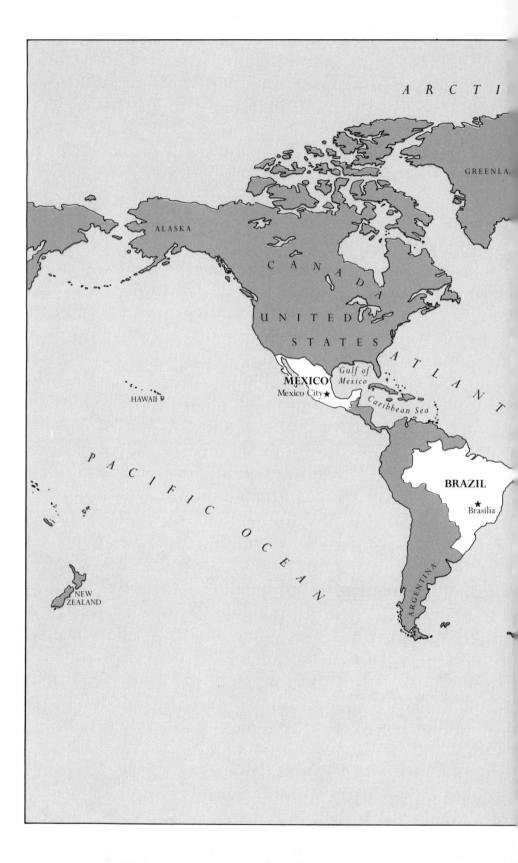

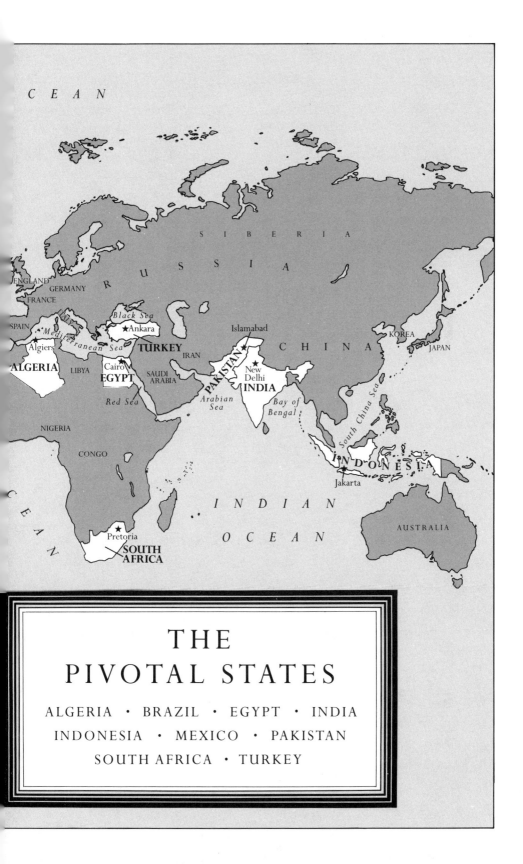

THE
PIVOTAL STATES

ALGERIA · BRAZIL · EGYPT · INDIA
INDONESIA · MEXICO · PAKISTAN
SOUTH AFRICA · TURKEY

INTRODUCTION

Robert Chase, Emily Hill,
and Paul Kennedy

As the twentieth century draws to a close, the nature and purposes of American foreign policy have become matters of intense debate and great confusion. The United States, as the world's only superpower, is pressed to play a leading role in all matters of international conflict, from Bosnia to the Spratly Islands. In the face of this pressure, the American public and the Congress remain wary of overseas commitments. Even many foreign-affairs experts are calling for strategic disengagement.[1] Similarly, few are certain of what implications will follow from the crisis in Asia, or what lessons to draw from this crisis. It appears that the Cold War's end has resulted in not the hoped-for new world order, but a fractured interna-tional landscape that both policy makers and scholars have difficulty under-standing and describing. Given this basic uncertainty, it is unsurprising that America's external policies often appear contradictory and haphazard. It is also not surprising that this period of intellectual confusion has produced a plethora of sloganlike interpretations of how the world is changing.[2]

The intellectual inquiry that produced the following collection of essays—hereafter referred to as the "pivotal states" project—focuses on one dimension of the search for a coherent post–Cold War U.S. foreign policy by suggesting a strategy of selectivity and setting priorities regard-ing the developing world. This project does *not* address traditional Great-Power issues, such as the expansion of NATO, the future of Russia, or how to handle China—problems at the top of any Secretary of State's agenda.[3]

1. For a good recent example, see Eugene Gholz, Daryl G. Press, and Harvey M. Sapolsky, "Come Home America: The Strategy of Restraint in the Face of Temptation," *Inter-national Security* 21, no. 4 (spring 1997).
2. One thinks here, for example, of the "end of history" (Fukuyama), the "coming clash of civilizations" (Huntington), the "unipolar moment" (Krauthammer), the "coming anar-chy" (Kaplan), and the like.
3. For example, Secretary of State Madeleine Albright visited the "northern capitals" in her first official tour of February 1997 but not any states in the developing world.

1

We take it for granted that the U.S. government will always give top priority to its Great-Power relationships with Europe, Russia, Japan, and China, and that it will be attentive to special clients such as Israel, Saudi Arabia, Kuwait, and South Korea, plus a few "rogue" states such as North Korea, Iraq, Iran, and Libya, which threaten those special clients.

But what strategy should the United States pursue toward the remaining 130 or 140 countries of the world? After all, some of these states are already important players in their regions and have the potential to become Great Powers themselves during the century ahead. A strategy that clearly identifies these emerging states now, and extends special relations to them, could ease American foreign-policy concerns in the future.

Crudely put, one can conceive of American governments having to face three types of foreign-policy problems: handling friends, handling foes, and handling the rest. On the whole, we feel that U.S. foreign policy since 1945 has successfully supported its allies, through NATO and a variety of other pacts and bilateral arrangements. It also has had a good record of deterring the Soviet Union and of containing foes such as Saddam Hussein. But its record in dealing with "the rest" is much less impressive, in part because Americans for years tended to view the so-called Third World through Cold War glasses. With the global struggle against communism over, there is a real prospect that U.S. policy toward Third World regions will be one of neglect, interrupted by occasional demands for humanitarian interventions, for the opening of markets, or for helping to ease financial turmoil as in the current crisis in Asia. Our call is for policy makers to refashion American strategy vis-à-vis the developing world along more coherent lines.

We therefore begin this investigation with a question: If the secretary of state were to plan a tour of world capitals *not* among the Great Powers, taking into account changes in the distribution of global power and paying heed to the importance of stability and prosperity in the developing world for America's future, which countries would appear on the itinerary? Obviously, in a diplomatic trip of this nature, that official could not possibly visit all of the world's 140 developing states. Yet, equally clearly, some of these states are more important to U.S. national interests than others, and this importance should earn them the consideration of American strategists. American policy makers need a concept or framework that will allow them to select and support those states in the developing world that are important to U.S. security, broadly defined.

Such a policy of discrimination would resemble those applied by many Great Powers, including the United States, in the past. When there is dramatic change in the international order, major nations must reassess their foreign policies in order to maintain their favorable strategic positions and protect their national security. For example, at the end of World War II, the United States had to overhaul its foreign policy. The power vacuum in Europe, the disintegration of an exhausted British Empire, and aggressive Soviet policies prevented the United States from retreating back into isolationism, as it had in the aftermath of World War I. Indeed, the end of World War II provided a historic moment in which the burgeoning American internationalist movement finally saw its beliefs manifested in policy. The United Nations, the Marshall Plan, and NATO, among other initiatives of the Roosevelt and Truman administrations, marked the triumph of internationalism in the United States. Such policies would have been inconceivable just ten years earlier.

If the global landscape transformed by the end of the Cold War provided a similar opportunity for a reassessment of foreign policy, most Americans did not seem to notice. Dramatic gestures such as the Truman Doctrine or the "X" article in the 1947 *Foreign Affairs* were absent. Intellectuals have debated U.S. policy options at considerable length, but neither the White House nor the Congress appears to have paid much attention. Domestic issues and scandals have taken center stage. Furthermore, many Americans have embraced the theory of triumphant capitalism—they see the collapse of the Soviet Union and the recent weakening of many Asian economies as proof of the West's superior social, political, and economic system. Not only does the United States not seem in decline, as pundits warned in the 1980s, but it has emerged as the sole remaining superpower. The American survival instinct, which drove foreign policy after World War II, has instead been sublimated into the enthusiastic purchase of mutual funds. Meanwhile, the long shadow cast by Vietnam and, twenty years later, by the Mogadishu debacle, inhibits serious discussion of which U.S. interests in the developing world are most important, and what should be done to preserve them.

After the tensions and expense of the Cold War, much can be said for a "strategy of restraint"[4] during the present circumstances. But this period of apparent peace and prosperity is exactly when American leaders should be taking the long view and using the time to reconsider their grand strategy. As Sir Halford Mackinder once noted, democracies have a hard time thinking strategically in the years of peace;[5] yet it is such times that best afford fruitful contemplation and a healthy, periodic reassessment. Moreover, some of the challenges to international stability that the world faces in the early twenty-first century—challenges arising from demographic and environmental pressures on developing societies—are

---

4. See Gholz, Press, and Sapolsky, "Come Home America."
5. H. J. Mackinder, *Democratic Ideals and Reality* (London: Constable and Company, 1919), 23.

different from those confronted after World War II. They require not only an altered understanding of global trends but also a new kind of preparation to meet them.[6]

Finally, it is precisely because the United States is the one remaining superpower that it is so important to carefully set and calibrate American strategic priorities across the globe. America is expected in some circles to police the world; yet that won't happen, partly because it hasn't the political will, and partly because (for all its strengths) it lacks the resources. Moreover, the long-term global balance of power, despite the recent turbulences in Asia, are probably tilted against both Europe and the United States.[7] All this suggests that an intelligent strategy must be found that avoids both the perils of American overstretch and the folly of ignoring the developing world altogether.

Assuming that America's relations with the Great Powers and special client or rogue states will always receive adequate notice in the State Department and Congress, what attention does the rest of the world require? What strategic priorities should be identified within those vast regions? This was the background to our "Pivotal States and U.S. Strategy" article, first published in *Foreign Affairs* in January 1996. The article suggested focusing American attention and energies on a select group of developing countries—the "pivotal states"—whose futures were poised at critical turning points, and whose fates would significantly affect regional, and even international, stability. The article argued that although all developing nations are no doubt important in their own right, from America's viewpoint some are a lot more important than others. We need a clearer and more comprehensive policy toward a part of the world that the United States has misunderstood and mishandled through much of its history.

At the time we wrote that article, there were several reasons to examine such a strategy. As noted above, the new world order was proving more difficult to manage than optimists had predicted, and the end of the bipolar world had created confusion in both policy-making and academic circles over how to devise an American foreign policy for the 1990s. As a subpart of a revised post–Cold War grand strategy, the pivotal states idea provided a means to organize at least one set of American relationships—those with the developing world.

Second, the strategy offered a way to counteract the resurgent neoisolationism that threatened to dictate congressional policy toward foreign

6. Paul Kennedy, *Preparing for the Twenty-First Century* (New York: Random House, 1993).
7. See the tables about changing shares of world GDP, as illustrated in David Marsh, "Balance of Economic Power Begins to Shift," *Financial Times*, March 9, 1994, p. 14.

affairs following the November 1994 elections. A policy that could be sold as a rigorously discriminate means to prevent instability and promote prosperity in the developing world could also appeal to legislators who believed that those regions no longer warranted the attention or money they merited during the Cold War. This was a very secular and realist argument, not a humanitarian or idealistic one; yet in forcing a debate about how the social and political disintegration of particular pivotal states would affect U.S. interests, this argument could possibly draw attention to what was happening more broadly in the developing world.

Third, a pivotal states strategy offered a means to reshape the enduring and somewhat sterile debate between those who regarded traditional military (or "old security") issues as the greatest threats to U.S. interests and those who viewed the "new security" issues—including environmental degradation, overpopulation, and underdevelopment—as the biggest dangers. When we were writing the article, the mainstream in policy circles still considered these new security issues to be peripheral; conversely, the school of thought led by authors such as Jessica Tuchman Matthews had challenged the entrenched, realist emphasis on military and political security.[8]

In truth, as our article argued, neither the old nor the new approach will suffice. The traditional, state-centered approach to foreign policy, which stresses the importance of military security, does not adequately attend to the newer threats to American national interests. A country such as Egypt, for example, could become unstable, not just because of military threats from Libya's Muammar Qadaffi but also through excessive demographic and environmental change, which might weaken the Egyptian state and create serious security threats for the United States and its allies. On the other hand, the "new" conception of security, which emphasizes the primary importance of such nonmilitary pressures, stresses the need to take a global or holistic approach to addressing them, through (for example) UN conferences, NGOs (nongovernmental organizations), and "civil society" actors. This universalist approach makes a strategy based on the newer conceptions of security impractical because it does not sufficiently acknowledge the necessity of working with national governments. Nor does it adequately recognize the most important task of foreign policy—protecting the national interest—and for this reason it shies away from secular arguments about U.S. security needs.

Our hope was that a pivotal states strategy would encourage the traditional, state-centered policy-making structures (for example, the NSC, the State Department, the Pentagon) to consider new security issues seri-

---

8. Jessica Tuchman Matthews, "Redefining Security," *Foreign Affairs* 68, 2 (spring 1989).

ously, thereby lending a greater clarity to the making of foreign policy. This strategy would confirm the importance of working chiefly through national governments to ensure stability and progress, since it poses the question, How can the United States best help South Africa (or Turkey or Indonesia) improve its condition? At the same time, such a question would call attention to the serious nonmilitary security issues that threaten national and international stability in the developing world; it might have the indirect effect of reminding Americans of what Dan Esty terms "pivotal issues" (population, migration, environment) affecting the future of our planet.

Finally, a pivotal states strategy would force American policy makers to *anticipate* the future rather than relying on the comfortable but outdated strategies and relationships of the Cold War. This strategy is proactive rather than reactive, for it is based on the consideration that these countries need our best attention and support now, not when they encounter future troubles. We believe that relationships with many of the pivotal states will gain importance as the twenty-first century unfolds. The repercussions of rapid change in the developing world, including population growth, disruptive migration, and popular fundamentalist movements, are increasingly affecting industrialized countries, and even the United States can no longer isolate itself from them. Because it argues for both bilateral (and, in a complementary form, multilateral) cooperation to mitigate such pressures, a pivotal states strategy would encourage American policy makers to face these challenges before they directly threaten U.S. national security.

As our investigation deepened, we came to see that a developing state could be pivotal for a variety of reasons. A confluence of factors, not all of which have to be present, make the future of these states critical for both regional and international stability. First, some of them are geostrategically important to the United States and its allies; severe social and political turbulences in countries such as Indonesia, Turkey, Egypt, and Mexico would certainly affect American security interests. These are "pivots" in the traditional, Mackinderian sense, as would be understood by, say, British defense planners at the turn of the twentieth century.

Second, as modernizing countries that still face Third World challenges, pivotal states have uncertain futures. Our pivots are "wobbly" or "tippy," admittedly some much more so than others. Looking at any one, optimistic analysts could legitimately predict a rosy future. They could envision the state enhancing political and social stability through respect for democratic, participatory principles and human rights, and achieving steady, stable economic growth through prudent internal and external economic policies. For the same state, however, more pessimistic analysts could doubt the government's ability to maintain order. In some cases, they might fear that financial instability could disrupt economic flows into, out of, or within the country, and that it might effectively lapse into chaos. In other words, each of the pivotal states is poised between potential success and possible failure, and it is not clear which scenario will prove the more accurate.

Third, pivotal states have the potential to work a significant beneficial or harmful effect on their regions. These are not desperately poor, war-stricken countries such as Rwanda and Haiti. All of them are large, populous states with a growing (often very substantial) middle class, considerable infrastructural and educational investments, and an "emerging markets" potential that involves increasing integration into the global economy. In our view, it makes sense to give them special attention. Such a suggestion is controversial. Many critics are disturbed that this strategy focuses not on the poorest of the poor, but on countries with considerable resources and economic prospects—but that is *precisely the point* behind our hypothesis. Each pivotal state, we argue, influences its neighbors through extensive economic and/or political linkages. These linkages suggest that if a pivotal state grows smoothly and equitably, its success would nurture other states in the region. Conversely, chaos in a pivotal state such as Indonesia would generate transboundary mayhem in the form of severed trade links, increased migration, communal violence, pollution, disease, and so on. It is worth noting that this select group of states—there are only nine of them—alone constitutes *one-third* of the earth's population. Where they go in the early twenty-first century, we feel, goes much of the rest of the developing world.[9]

Finally, pivotal states can play a key role in global negotiations on such crosscutting issues as environmental accords, human rights, and population issues. Despite the temptation to walk away from the world's problems, most Americans sense that this is no longer possible. Yet preserving the rain forests and animal species of the globe requires negotiating with Brazil and Indonesia and India. In order to achieve further progress in reversing the trend toward global warming, certain of our pivotal states (India especially) must play a vital role. If we want to encourage the spread of democracy and human rights across our globe, it is important—as Charles Norchi argues in this book—to have large "platforms," such as

9. It should also be noted that, in calling for U.S. strategy to focus on these key players, we do not assume that the really poor and smaller countries will be neglected; rather, assisting them is a charge to the entire international community, to be carried out by UN agencies, the World Bank, NGOs, and charities—which is, after all, what they do best. See our Conclusion.

South Africa, in the developing world. If we want the World Trade Organization (WTO) regime to function well and the global economy to open further, the pivotal states must be involved. If the American export economy needs to rely ever more on "big emerging markets," our pivotal states provide most of the latter.[10]

Keeping all these aspects in mind, we argued that serious consideration of a pivotal states strategy would require a U.S. policy toward the developing world that pays special attention to a discrete number of countries. On the basis of the criteria listed above, we identified the following states as pivotal: Mexico, Brazil, Algeria, Egypt, South Africa, Turkey, India, Pakistan, and Indonesia. Given their size, population, geostrategic position, economic potential, capacity to affect global and regional issues, and the related criteria, they demand focused American attention.[11]

Readers should not fixate on this particular list. Some of our nine are more pivotal than others. In the decades ahead, the list could change, either because some of them become full Great Powers, or because new candidates arise. Similarly, it is wise not to fixate on states missing from our list, such as Ukraine (which is closely tied to questions about the future of Russia and the expansion of NATO) or Nigeria (because it presently lacks the educational and infrastructural capital to prosper) or Iran (because it is, from the U.S. standpoint, in the special "rogue states" category). The very fact that commentators ask, "Why not country X?" indicates that they, too, think some developing states are more important than others. Above all, they should remember that this is a list based on considerations of U.S. strategy, not on OXFAM assessments of social need.

Focusing on pivotal states offers the possibility of concentrating limited American foreign-policy attention and resources to their greatest, salutary effect on U.S. interests.[12] Furthermore, a well-developed policy toward a pivotal state could affect an entire region through spillover effects on neighboring states. Such a policy might also persuade these substantial regional actors to play constructive roles in international issues, such as building stability in sub-Saharan Africa, or dissuade them from acting as "spoilers" who might block international accords on the environment or intellectual property rights.

10. See Jeffrey Garten, *The Big Ten: The Big Emerging Markets and How They Will Change Our Lives* (New York: Basic Books, 1997).
11. Robert S. Chase, Emily B. Hill, and Paul Kennedy, "Pivotal States and U.S. Strategy," *Foreign Affairs* 75, no. 1, (January/February 1996).
12. To be sure, the circumstances in a pivotal state such as Pakistan or Algeria may become so turbulent that there is little that America or the international community can do but let events run their course. Still, if a country really is wobbling and external assistance could swing the balance, a focused and helpful U.S. policy could help to ensure a more promising future.

What we are calling for is, of course, not new. Indeed, the idea of a "pivotal state"—a key country whose future may not only determine the success or failure of its region but also significantly affect international stability—has a long and distinguished pedigree reaching back through history. The classic example of a pivotal state throughout the nineteenth century was Turkey, the epicenter of the so-called Eastern Question. Because of Turkey's strategic position on the Straits of Constantinople, the disintegration of the Ottoman Empire posed a perennial problem for British and Russian policy makers. Whether the sultan's government swung toward Britain or Russia was critically important to both powers; each attempted to wield influence over the region. The fate of this pivot remained indisputably more important to both empires than the fate of Tunis and Samarkand, and it consequently demanded the greatest attention of foreign ministers.

Similarly, American policy makers in the twentieth century have employed their own versions of a pivotal states theory. Statesmen from Acheson to Eisenhower to Nixon and Kissinger continually referred to countries whose fall to communism would act like a rotten apple in a barrel or a falling domino. Although the domino theory as applied to American policy was never a successful policy of discrimination—indeed it worsened the problem of American strategic overextension—the theory at its core was about supporting pivotal states in order to prevent their "fall" and the consequent fall of neighboring states. Again, in the late 1970s, U.S. strategists endeavored to identify and work with "regional influentials" in order to advance American interests in certain parts of the globe. All of these frameworks had mixed success, which must be a caution to those advocating any new variant. Still, the concept of a pivotal state seemed to offer a means of testing the degree to which current policies actually reflect American strategic priorities. Are these important countries receiving adequate American attention?

The publication of "Pivotal States and US Strategy" attracted a considerable response from both scholars and policy makers. It was debated at the Council on Foreign Relations and in various forums in Washington, D.C., during 1996 and 1997. Among the groups interested in this idea was the Global Stewardship Initiative of the Pew Charitable Trusts, which tracks global issues of population, migration, and development. To encourage further exploration of our ideas, the foundation offered to sponsor a series of discussions and presentations on the pivotal states. By so doing, it hoped to increase the awareness of the American public and their representatives about global trends. It recognized that any serious discussion about U.S. policies toward the developing world necessarily raises questions about whether America understands, or has a coherent strategy for dealing with, global "new security" issues.

In order to assess fully the prospects of the pivotal states, the project enlisted the help of prominent experts on each pivotal state. These scholars were asked to identify the main challenges facing their states over the next ten to fifteen years. We also charged them to confront directly the question of whether, by the definitions discussed above, their state actually qualifies as "pivotal." Could their significance for the United States be captured in a paragraph for a midwestern senator or radio station? How seriously would the long-term success or failure of their state affect regional and international stability? Is it at a crossroads of development—could its possible futures include notable success as well as disappointing failure? How possible was achieving "healthy" stability in, say, Egypt or Indonesia, as opposed to merely authoritarian rule, and how would one define the former condition? Did the global crosscutting issues we identified pose a problem for this state, and if so, did it take a leadership position in attempting to confront these issues?

At the same time, we asked the country experts for proposals regarding American policy. What mixture of strategies did the scholars recommend to help the pivotal states move along a favorable path and away from disaster? How could the United States best assist these countries, whether directly or indirectly, in a secondary role, or through regional and/or international agencies? How focused, if at all, was American official attention on these countries? Most important of all, what improvements could be instituted to give greater coherence and consistency to American strategy toward each of these pivotal states? The results of this "litmus test" lie in the following pages.

These questions, among many others, produced the nine substantive essays that form the first part of this book. Regardless of how readers judge the practicality of America's implementing a global "pivotal states" strategy in the near future, these essays contribute to understanding transformations in key parts of the developing world and assessing whether or not American policies can help.

Our basic assumption was that the stability and future prosperity of these key developing states were being challenged, less by traditional military threats (though some of those still exist), than by transnational and local pressures affecting their social fabrics and political stability. Whether it was resource depletion or too-rapid population growth, human-rights abuses or turbulent financial flows, the problems were great. If our pivotal states could not overcome these tests, it was unlikely that the rest of the developing world could do so either. As a "check" of whether we or our country-case experts fully understood these nonmilitary forces for change, therefore, we also invited a number of other scholars to contribute essays on these crosscutting matters.

Ultimately, these analyses proved to be invaluable, partly because they assessed each pivotal state and its current problems and prospects from a global and comparative perspective. The essays reveal how each pivotal state fits into the patterns and dynamics that are driving global trends, and they evaluate the practicality of confronting these challenges by working through state governments as a pivotal states strategy recommends. They are designed to complement the essays on the nine pivotal states by emphasizing the global nature of the "new security" threats rather than the centrality of each state. These essays are included in the second part of this collection.

One final remark worth making is about the intellectual nature of this exercise. This post–Cold War condition of ours sees many a theory, and many a slogan, attempting to capture what is happening in the world at large. Frequently, a "trial balloon" article is followed by a book, elaborating on the author's original arguments and responding to criticisms of them.[13] Although initially tempted to write further in defense of the pivotal states notion, we decided to do something different. We would leave the original *Foreign Affairs* article unaltered, warts and all, and turn to scholars from widely varying fields of expertise for detailed feedback. We expected both to modify our initial analyses of the states substantially and to refine our ideas about American strategy further, which we have done. As we will discuss in the Conclusion, some of what we learned was unexpected—and the more intriguing for being so.

What we are convinced of, however, is the utility of this intellectual process. Having floated a "trial balloon" before our scholarly peers, policy makers, strategists, and country experts, we are pleased to bring the results of this endeavor to the reader. Our own view is that, with modifications, our pivotal states idea will be extremely useful in focusing American policies toward the developing world and in drawing the public's attention to the challenges that those countries, and our entire global community, will confront in the years to come.

---

13. This applies, for example, to the authors and theses listed in note 2.

THE

CASE STUDIES

$\big($ INDONESIA $\big)$

John Bresnan*

The United States announced a major new policy with regard to Indonesia in the last months of 1997. As financial panic spread from Thailand to the rest of Southeast and East Asia, the U.S. Treasury Department announced that it would commit $3 billion to an international effort to rescue the Indonesian economy. U.S. Treasury Secretary Robert E. Rubin said in a statement that the action was "critical to the national security and economic interests of the United States." Indonesia was among those countries, he said, that "are not only key markets for U.S. exporters, but are also crucial to our efforts to promote growth, peace and prosperity throughout the world." Off the record, officials defended the action in terms of arresting the spreading "market contagion": the United States could not regard the growing crisis in Indonesia as a "confined event, like a civil war." At a minimum, continued turmoil in Asian markets could have a dampening effect on American exports and threaten the opening of world markets, one of the central foreign policy goals of the Clinton presidency. More ominous was the fear that market instability in Indonesia could lead to a violent leadership transition in a country in which the last such event, in 1965, involved the deaths of up to half a million people.[1]

These statements were the strongest expressions of a positive U.S. interest in Indonesia in many years. They also came in the wake of considerable distancing between Washington and Jakarta following allegations of Indonesian meddling in the U.S. presidential election of 1996. There also had been increasingly strong U.S. congressional criticism of Indonesian behavior in East Timor, which led to the ending of long-standing forms of coopera-

---

* [Editors' note: Since Dr. Bresnan composed this prophetic essay on Indonesia's future in late 1997/early 1998, much of what he anticipated has come to pass, most notably the spring 1998 regime crisis that culminated in President Soeharto's resignation. The editors have tried to indicate this change of power at certain places in the text.]

1. David E. Sanger, "The Economic Stakes in Asia: Clinton Hopes $3 Billion for Indonesia Will Help Dull Panic," *New York Times*, November 1, 1997.

tion between the armed forces of the two countries. Fashioning a coherent set of U.S. policies on Indonesia would thus require more than a stroke of the Treasury pen. Yet the principal condition underlying relations between the political elites of the two countries was mutual ignorance. The financial crisis in East Asia had moved the United States and Indonesia to enter into a complex and sensitive relationship for which neither was prepared.

Moreover, the crisis added urgency to a host of issues that were much broader than Indonesia: the nature of the East Asian "miracle," the applicability of the Japanese model of development to other societies, the roles of the United States and Japan in the regional economy, the future of the International Monetary Fund, and the prospects for unfettered international private debt in the new global economy. This new agenda was a burden that U.S.–Indonesian relations were ill equipped to bear.

CURRENT DOMESTIC CONDITIONS

After acceding to power in March, 1966, General (later President) Soeharto led a political system that prized stability. Power was centered in the presidency. Soeharto was supported by the army, which has its roots in the national revolution, and by a Western-educated technocracy. Together these forces produced policies over the past thirty years that had much in common with the rest of the East Asian region. Economic development was rapid, and social change widespread.

Indonesia's gross national product (GNP) per capita in U.S. dollars in 1994 was $880, just enough to place it above the range of what the World Bank classifies as a low-income economy. Yet when GNP is converted from local currency, using purchasing-power parities instead of exchange rates as conversion factors, its per capita income rose to the equivalent of $3,600, near that of the poorer Latin American and East European states.[2]

Indonesia achieved this level of economic development through high annual rates of growth over the past thirty years. Real per capita gross domestic product has more than trebled in just a little over a generation.[3] Indonesia's GNP grew in real terms between 1985 and 1994 at an average annual rate of 6.0 percent per capita, which compared favorably with the average *decline* of 1.2 percent experienced by all lower-middle-income countries as a group.[4]

Infant mortality fell from 127 per one thousand live births in the early

2. World Bank, "Selected World Development Indicators," in *From Plan to Market: World Development Report 1996* (New York: Oxford University Press, 1996), Table 1, 188–189.
3. Hal Hill, *The Indonesian Economy since 1966: Southeast Asia's Emerging Giant* (Cambridge: Cambridge University Press, 1996), 4.
4. World Bank, "Selected Indicators," Table 1, 188–189.

1960s to 53 in 1994, a reduction of 58 percent.[5] Life expectancy at birth has increased 44 percent since the early 1960s, reaching 63 years by 1994. Secondary school enrollment went from a total of 12 percent of the age group in the early 1960s to 48 percent for boys and 39 percent for girls in 1993.[6]

Indonesia in 1996 had a per capita gross national product that was higher than that of either China or India. But the levels of infant mortality, life expectancy and education are only somewhat better than India's, and they are uniformly and significantly lower than China's. It might be thought that Indonesia has less equitable patterns of income distribution than China and India, but this is not borne out by studies monitored by the World Bank. The bank recently estimated that Indonesia has a relatively low, and equitable, Gini index of 31.7, whereas India has an index of 33.8 and China an index of 37.6.[7]

It is more likely that Indonesia's level of social development, compared with those of the Asian giants, reflects its extremely low starting point in the political turbulence of the late Sukarno years. From 1960 to 1965, Indonesia's per capita income was estimated to be $30 per annum—by far the lowest in Asia, and a third of China's or India's.[8] Indonesia's medical and educational services reflected this extremely low income. Whereas China had one doctor for every 1,600 people in 1960–1965, and India had one for every 4,880, Indonesia had only one for every 31,700. China enrolled 89 percent of its primary-school-age population in school, and India had 74 percent in school, whereas Indonesia had 72 percent there.[9]

The Indonesian economy recovered rapidly after Soeharto assumed power. His government was instrumental in this process, but not because Soeharto imposed a new economic philosophy. A deep-seated mistrust of market forces, economic liberalism, and private (especially Chinese) ownership remains in Indonesia.[10] Soeharto did, however, make economic development a priority. And his conservative management of the economy shared several basic features with the "miracle" economies of East Asia and the booming economies of neighboring Singapore, Malaysia, and

5. World Bank, "Selected Indicators," Table 6, 198–199.
6. World Bank, "Selected Indicators," Table 7, 200–201.
7. World Bank, "Selected Indicators," Table 5, 196–197. The Gini index measures the extent to which the distribution of income (or, in some cases, consumption expenditures) among individuals or households within an economy deviates from a perfectly equal distribution. A Gini index of zero percent represents perfect equality.
8. World Bank, *Social Indicators of Development: 1990* (Baltimore: The Johns Hopkins University Press, 1991),63, 143, and 145.
9. World Bank, *Social Indicators*, 62–63, 142–143, and 144–145.
10. Hill, *The Indonesian Economy* , 93.

Thailand in Southeast Asia. Fiscal and monetary policy was cautious and predictable. When pressed, policies favored openness to the international economy. And strong emphasis was placed on reducing poverty and social inequity.[11] The results "validated for many Indonesians [Soeharto's] vision of a strong, insulated, paternalistic, developmental state."[12]

Even before the financial crisis of 1997, however, presidential succession was looming large. Soeharto was seventy-six years of age, and his wife had died in the previous year. His current five-year term in office was scheduled to be up for renewal in March 1998. Soeharto had permitted nepotism and corruption to reach very large proportions in recent years; he was widely seen as out of touch with public opinion; and outbreaks of communal violence suggested that his regime was losing its power to command the support of ordinary, especially younger, citizens. As the financial crisis grew in late 1997, Soeharto was obliged to cancel public appearances on grounds of illness. There was widening doubt that he was up to the demands of his office. By early 1998, critics were calling publicly for him to stand down, which he finally did later in the year. Some intellectuals called for an end to the entire political regime.

Any change in the regime will likely involve three separate but overlapping elements in Indonesian society: the army, devout Muslims, and the new middle class.

The army has long claimed the right to participate directly in Indonesia's domestic political affairs. It will be in a position to dominate the succession process after Soeharto dies. Whether or not the next president is another army officer, he will certainly be a much weaker president than Soeharto is today. The power Soeharto has accumulated over thirty years will not likely transfer to another individual. And an army controlled less fully than Soeharto controls it would potentially threaten stability, especially if it was torn between the president and its own base of legitimacy in the opinion of society. The Jakarta press has already raised this issue as a result of the Megawati affair—the heavy-handed removal of the popular daughter of Sukarno, the country's first president, from the leadership of a political party. Nor is army unity a given. Religion and academy class divide the officer corps, and although these divisions are not well understood, they could facilitate either peaceful or violent political change, depending on the circumstances, in a crisis.

Islam has enjoyed a revival in Indonesia in the past decade. Soeharto

11. Hal Hill, *Towards a Political Economy Explanation of Rapid Growth in Southeast Asia*. Working Papers in Trade and Development, No. 96/2. (Canberra: Department of Economics, Research School of Pacific and Asian Studies, The Australian National University, 1996).
12. R. William Liddle, "Indonesia's New Order: A Stable Authoritarian Regime" (unpublished conference paper, 1996), 2.

effectively removed Islamic organizations from the political stage, yet at the same time he acknowledged the strength of Muslim opinion in social and cultural terms: He has altered the dress code for female students in state schools, established a national lottery, sanctioned the establishment of a new Indonesian Association of Muslim Intellectuals headed by a prominent cabinet officer, and appointed devout Muslims to top army posts. On the other hand, any incident that aroused Muslim opinion to the point of violence in the capital city might have the potential to split the army between these officers (known as "green," a color associated with Islam) and others who identify themselves with national unity (known as "red and white," the color of the Indonesian flag).[13]

By the standards of its neighbors, the middle class of Indonesia remains small. It is urban, yet the urban population of Indonesia is still relatively small. Newspaper circulation in Indonesia is only one-third to one-half the rate of the Philippines or Thailand. University students are fewer in number relative to the size of the population. Juwono Sudarsono has estimated that it would take another decade of very rapid economic growth to create an Indonesian middle class comprising 25 percent of the population[14]—roughly that of the Philippines in 1986 or Thailand in 1992, when middle-class demonstrators brought down authoritarian governments.

The Indonesian middle class is also predominantly a dependent middle class. Many members belong to the civil or military service, and they include employees of powerful state enterprises that dominate such industries as rice, oil, and banking. Private businessmen in these and other sectors depend heavily on bureaucratic patronage in order to succeed. Moreover, a disproportionate share of the private business community is composed of ethnic Chinese, whose minority status has invited harassment during times of social stress. Although their increasing strength could potentially balance the civil and military bureaucracies, the Chinese instead generate envy and suspicion. Discussions in Indonesia of inequitable income distribution usually refer to the extraordinary concentration of wealth in a relatively small number of Chinese families. Indonesians widely believe that ethnic Chinese own around 75 percent of the country's corporate wealth, of its top two hundred business houses, and of the Jakarta stock exchange's listed companies.

As the financial crisis deepened in the first months of 1998, sporadic outbursts of violence occurred over rising food prices in many places.

13. R. Willim Liddle, "The Islamic Turn in Indonesia: A Political Explanation," *Journal of Asian Studies* 55, no. 3 (August 1996): 613–634.

14. Juwono Sudarsono, "Demokrasi Lapisan Menengah," *Gatra*, January 4, 1997, p. C.

Workers in the cities were laid off, especially in construction and light manufacturing, and told to go home to their villages. But a prolonged drought had depressed the rural economy. Food was in short supply. Programs of public works were hastily devised to provide temporary employment. But whether a social safety net of sufficient size could be created was uncertain. Soeharto began to speak of unnamed enemies as being behind the economic collapse. Voices were raised accusing the Chinese of being unpatriotic. Army leaders said they were prepared to cope with any eventuality.

Indonesia had already experienced a series of outbreaks of communal violence in late 1996 and the first half of 1997 that shook the confidence of the regime and moved analysts to raise fundamental questions about the social costs of economic progress and political repression. Four incidents stood out, although many others, smaller in scale, occurred as well. In a town in East Java in October 1996, rioting broke out over a perceived slight to Muslims in a court case. In a town in West Java in December 1996, Muslims rioted in reaction to police violence. In both cases, the rioters attacked government buildings, destroyed Chinese shops, and burned Christian churches. Several people lost their lives and many were injured in each instance.[15] In West Kalimantan (Borneo) in December 1996, a fight among teenagers after a concert led to large-scale violence between native Dayaks and migrants from the island of Madura; by the end of February 1997, the army was reporting that three hundred people had died in the fighting, while independent sources counted the total at well over one thousand. In South Kalimantan, on the last day of campaigning before parliamentary elections in May 1997, members of rival political parties clashed, and rioting broke out. The rioters looted a shopping complex and caused a fire in the complex that killed 130 people. In spite of the government party's record victory at the polls, it was evident that large numbers of Indonesians are alienated from the regime.

The process of changing regimes will be equally fraught with difficulty. The army will likely resist any diminution of its political role, suggesting a possible future of coups and threatened coups, such as Thailand and the Philippines have experienced. Devout Muslims may insist on increasing their political role, calling into question the Indonesian political system's capacity to sustain its present pluralism. The uncommitted middle class, shaken by the recent rioting, is likely to push for a continuation of the status quo. For these reasons, the evolution of a political regime that better represents the widely varying interests of Indonesian

15. "Indonesia: Signs of Danger," *Economist*, January 4, 1997, p. 40; John McBeth and Margot Cohen, "Indonesia: Tinderbox," *Far Eastern Economic Review*, January 9, 1997, pp. 14–15.

society, and one that can also maintain public order, cannot be assumed. A large amount of good fortune will be needed. It will help very much if the international rescue effort enables the economy to begin to turn around. If the effort fails, the prospect is very grim indeed.

What happens to Indonesia will affect not only the rest of Southeast Asia, but also the rest of the wider Asia-Pacific region.

INDONESIA AS A PIVOTAL STATE

Indonesia is first among equals of the ten states of Southeast Asia and a significant actor in the wider region of East Asia and the Pacific. It bulks large in Southeast Asia partly because Indonesians make up 40 percent of the entire region's population. Neither Brazil nor Nigeria comes anywhere near to occupying the demographic position in Latin America or Africa that Indonesia holds in Southeast Asia—a region roughly equal to Latin America or sub-Saharan Africa in total population.

Indonesia also looms large because of the size and diversity of its economy. Indonesia's gross domestic product has been the largest in the region. Moreover, the Indonesian economy is more broadly based than any other in Southeast Asia, in part because of its rich mineral resources. These include, in addition to oil and natural gas, deposits of tin, iron, bauxite, nickel, copper, silver, and gold, all of which Indonesia exports in significant quantities through working arrangements with major multinational corporations from East Asia, North America, and Western Europe.

Indonesia's geographic position also makes it a leader in Southeast Asia. The relative remoteness of the Indonesian archipelago protects it from external threats. Only domestic subversion by the one-time Communist party of Indonesia, with the support of China and Russia, has posed a serious threat in fifty years of independence. At the same time, its geography has given Indonesia potential rights over sea lanes that are essential to the survival of Singapore and Malaysia, to the foreign trade of Australia, and to the supply of Middle Eastern oil to Japan, Korea, and Taiwan. Indonesia's strategic location explains the keen interest in Indonesian affairs on the part of these regional and extraregional powers.

Indonesia's diplomatic history further increases its significance to Southeast Asia. The volatility of the country's domestic politics in the early 1960s was reflected in its foreign policy. Affronted because Malaysia had federated without consulting him, Sukarno initiated a campaign of "confrontation" against the new neighboring state. When Malaysia joined the UN Security Council in 1963, Sukarno withdrew from the United Nations and attempted to form a parallel Conference of New Emerging Forces, comprising Asian and African nations and members of the Soviet bloc. By 1965 Sukarno was declaring a Beijing-Hanoi-Jakarta axis. "Confrontation" against Malaysia was moving toward invasion when Sukarno fell from power in 1966.

Soeharto has, in contrast, emphasized good neighborly relations. In 1967 Indonesia joined Malaysia, the Philippines, Singapore, and Thailand in founding the Association of Southeast Asian Nations (ASEAN), in order, as Michael Leifer has put it, "to expunge the legacy of confrontation and also to promote a willing acceptance of Indonesia's political primacy" in the region.[16] Acting largely by consensus, ASEAN has kept territorial disputes among member states under reasonable control, enabled the members to give priority to their own internal security and economic development, and provided a means for members to act in concert should external powers intervene in the region's affairs. When Vietnam invaded Cambodia at the end of 1978, the former supported by the Soviet Union and the latter by China, ASEAN began a campaign of diplomatic opposition that eventually obliged the Vietnamese to withdraw.[17] Under the new strategic exigencies of the 1990s ASEAN admitted Vietnam in 1995, and Laos and Myanmar (Burma) in mid-1997. The enlargement of ASEAN, its sponsors reckon, will give it a larger voice in forums beyond Southeast Asia.

Indonesia already has led ASEAN in demonstrating its major stake in designing the international architecture for peace and prosperity in the wider Asia-Pacific region. The ASEAN states were crucial to the creation in 1989 of Asia Pacific Economic Cooperation (APEC), the first intergovernmental association in history linking North America, Northeast Asia, Southeast Asia, and Oceania. This was in spite of Malaysia's strong preference for an economic grouping that would exclude North America and Oceania. The ASEAN states also were crucial to the agreement to hold regular summit meetings of APEC members, which has increased their political investment in the organization. This was again in spite of the resistance of Malaysia, which boycotted the first such meeting in Seattle. Indonesia is widely credited with moving ASEAN members to override Malaysian opposition to these developments. Indonesia also inspired the principal APEC commitment to date by lobbying before the 1994 meeting in Bogor, Indonesia to generate agreement on creating a tariff-free environment for trade in the Pacific by the year 2020.

Indonesia also led the ASEAN states in taking a further significant step in July 1993, when their foreign ministers voted to launch the ASEAN

16. Michael Leifer, *Indonesia's Foreign Policy* (London: George Allen & Unwin, 1983), 142.
17. Evelyn Colbert, "Southeast Asian Regional Politics: Toward a Regional Order," in *Dynamics of Regional Politics: Four Systems on the Indian Ocean Rim,* ed. W. Howard Wriggins (New York: Columbia University Press, 1992), 211–274.

Regional Forum (ARF), which aims to address the security of the entire Asia-Pacific region, the first intergovernmental effort ever to do so. The original member states included, in addition to the ASEAN states, the United States and Canada, Japan and South Korea, Australia and New Zealand, and Russia and (most important) China. India and Myanmar were subsequently added. It has become clear that the absence of North Korea and Taiwan from the membership severely limits ARF's ability to play a useful role with respect to the Korean peninsula and the Taiwan strait. Interest in ARF has tended to focus as a result on its utility with regard to overlapping claims to areas in the South China Sea that involve China, Taiwan, Vietnam, the Philippines, Malaysia, Brunei, and potentially Indonesia. But ARF also provides a point of contact among the major Pacific powers, which could ameliorate future disputes.

Given this diplomatic creativity, Indonesia's neighbors must hope that the process of leadership and regime change will not significantly modify its present policy orientation. No one anticipates a return to the volatility of the Sukarno period, but a weaker leader than Soeharto could rely on the domestic appeal of a more nationalistic agenda. Furthermore, in the new interdependence of East Asia and the Pacific, such an Indonesian agenda could be unsettling to the region's peace and prosperity. Not a stronger Indonesia but a weaker one is to be feared. The Indonesian armed forces lag far behind those of Singapore and Malaysia in their modernization, particularly with respect to their naval and air arms; no threat to Indonesia's neighbors is seen from this direction. The threat, if there is one, lies in an Indonesia in disarray, unable to maintain its internal security, failing to meet its international obligations, and jeopardizing the orderly development of its own large economy and society and of its region.

An Indonesia in disarray would be damaging to the interests of many other countries. A suggestion of this prospect was already evident in the haze of smoke from the Indonesian forest fires that blanketed much of Southeast Asia in 1997. The Indonesian press reported that fires were burning in more than six hundred locations on the islands of Sumatra, Kalimantan, and Java between March and August, according to satellite images of the National Oceanic and Atmospheric Administration of the United States. The fires were attributed to the clearing of new areas for corporate tree plantations and to an Indonesian government response that was seen as ineffectual and hampered by corruption. The persistence of the fires was caused by a delay in the arrival of monsoon rains as a result of the El Niño weather pattern. Smoke from the fires, mingling with urban pollution, spread from Indonesia to Malaysia, the Philippines, Singapore, Thailand, Brunei, and Papua New Guinea. Airports were closed and flights canceled around the region. Hundreds of thousands of people were reported ill with respiratory ailments. Foreign business travel and tourism to the region fell—just when the region, in the early stages of the monetary crisis, could least afford it. The smoke also delayed delivery of relief supplies to remote locations on the island of New Guinea, where hundreds were reported to have died from starvation and illnesses associated with a shortage of drinking water.[18]

But the environmental disaster was only one aspect of the potential costs of an Indonesia in disarray. Singapore and Malaysia have extensive political, economic, and military ties with Indonesia that are the closest in the region. Thailand, the Philippines, and Vietnam also are united with Indonesia in growing bonds of common political and economic purpose, including a free-trade area in which Indonesia represents far and away the largest future market. Japan, South Korea, Taiwan, and Australia all have extensive economic and security interests in Indonesia as well, not the least of which is the passage through Indonesian waters of much of their vital international trade. All these nations and the United States too would be affected, some perhaps profoundly, if Indonesia were unable to take the necessary steps to restore confidence in its economic management.

There is one addendum to this assessment of Indonesia's international role. Indonesia has incurred criticism, intense at times, of its management of East Timor, the former Portuguese colony that gained increased international attention as a result of the 1996 Nobel Peace Prize. The eastern half of the island of Timor was a Portuguese colony for four centuries, until political turmoil in Lisbon led the Portuguese administration to withdraw abruptly in August 1975. A Marxist party unilaterally declared independence, and Indonesian troops stormed ashore in December with much loss of life. U.S. President Gerald Ford and Secretary of State Henry Kissinger had met with Soeharto just before Indonesia acted. It has been widely reported that they received advance notice of Indonesia's intention to intervene; the fall of Saigon to Communist troops only months before, along with Timor's remoteness, undoubtedly contributed to Kissinger's saying that he understood the Indonesians had to do what they had to do.[19]

But it is evident that a large number of people in East Timor continue

---

18. See, for example: "Terpantau Satelit: Ratusan Lokasi Kebakaran Hutan," *Kompas,* August 6, 1997; Seth Mydans, "Southeast Asia Chokes on Indonesia's Forest Fires," *New York Times,* September 24, 1997; Margot Cohen, "Unlucky Country," *Far Eastern Economic Review,* December 25, 1997, and January 1, 1998.

19. James Dunn, "The Timor Affair in International Perspective," in *East Timor at the Crossroads: The Forging of a Nation,* ed. Peter Carey and G. Carter Bentley (Honolulu: University of Hawaii Press, 1995), 59–72; Paul F. Gardner, *Shared Hopes, Separate Fears: Fifty Years of U.S.–Indonesian Relations* (Boulder: Westview Press, 1997), 285–289.

to resist Indonesian authority and resent Indonesian economic and cultural encroachment. Armed attacks on Indonesian troops took place as recently as May and June 1997. And any number of visitors to East Timor have reported the widespread Timorese desire for the Indonesians to withdraw. The United Nations continues to view Portugal as the administering authority. The European Union is holding off a major economic agreement with ASEAN until Portugal's interests in the matter are satisfied.[20] The 1996 Nobel Peace Prize, awarded to Bishop Carlos Ximenes Belo and José Ramos Horta for their championing of the rights of the people of East Timor, helped put the issue on the U.S. congressional agenda.[21] Until an acceptable international settlement of East Timor's status is reached, it appears likely to be an added burden on Indonesia's international agenda.

AMERICAN AMNESIA

Until Treasury Secretary Rubin's statement on the monetary crisis, the official view of American interests in Indonesia's future was not easily discovered. The White House, when it issued *A National Security Strategy of Engagement and Enlargement* in February 1996, described American interests around the world at some length—the document is forty-five pages long—but it did not once mention Indonesia by name.[22] Indeed, there has been a pattern of such official amnesia. Winston Lord, the Assistant Secretary of State for East Asian and Pacific Affairs in the first Clinton administration, in his confirmation hearings in March 1993, delivered a prepared text of fifteen pages on the goals of U.S. policy in the Pacific without mentioning Indonesia.[23] The same was true when the Department of Defense issued its report of February 1995, *United States Security Strategy for the East Asia–Pacific Region*; Indonesia was not mentioned except in a list of the members of ASEAN and a table that listed even the smallest Pacific island grouping.[24]

The invisibility of Indonesia to Americans is of long standing. Toward the end of World War II, when General Douglas MacArthur's proposal to

20. Stephen Sherlock, "Political Economy of the East Timor Conflict," *Asian Survey* XXXVI, no. 9 (September 1996): 835-851.
21. Philip Shenon, "Timorese Bishop and Exile Given Nobel Peace Prize: Award Panel Criticizes Indonesia on Rights," *New York Times*, October 12, 1996, p. 6.
22. Office of the President of the United States, *A National Security Strategy of Engagement and Enlargement* (Washington, D.C.: U.S. GPO, February 1996).
23. Winston Lord, "A New Pacific Community: Ten Goals for American Policy" (opening statement at confirmation hearings, March 31, 1993).
24. Department of Defense, *United States Security Strategy for the East Asia–Pacific Region* (Washington, D.C.: Department of Defense, February, 1995).

liberate the Dutch East Indies was rejected in favor of racing up the island chain of the western Pacific to the home islands of Japan, Americans lost the opportunity to be the liberators of this large and consequential nation. After the war, the academic study of Indonesia had barely begun when the United States became involved in Vietnam, polarizing the nation's campuses and leading to a sharp decline in academic interest in Southeast Asia—a decline that has begun to reverse only recently. Meanwhile, in the U.S. government, the bureaucratic efficiencies gained by combining Southeast Asia in a single unit with China and Japan in the Department of State and elsewhere have been offset by the continued absence of senior officials with Indonesian experience in the executive branch. One result is that, in the words of Paul Wolfowitz, a former senior official of the State and Defense departments, as well as a former ambassador to Jakarta, "even relatively well-informed Americans are unaware of the facts that make Indonesia one of the most important countries of the Pacific region."[25]

Against this background of ignorance, a series of events in the second half of 1996 put Indonesia in the pages of American newspapers and triggered discussion of policy toward Indonesia in American circles for the first time in a generation. On July 27, rioting broke out in the streets of Jakarta, the worst in more than twenty years. Crowds of young people protested the forcible eviction, from the headquarters of the "opposition" Indonesian Democratic Party, of followers of Megawati, who had been deposed not long before from her position as party chairman by a government-instigated party gathering.[26] On October 11, the two Timorese received the Nobel Peace Prize. And on October 14, it was charged that the Clinton presidential campaign had received illegal contributions from sources close to James Riady, a member of a prominent Chinese-Indonesian family.[27]

These events led to a cascade of negative commentary in the American press and pressure for punitive action from both in and out of Congress. Matters came to a head in mid-1997. The State Department criticized the May 29 elections in Indonesia for severely limiting competition. Moving to preempt action by the U.S. Congress, Indonesia on June 6 canceled plans to buy nine F-16 fighter planes from the United States, as

25. Paul Wolfowitz, Testimony Before the U.S. Senate Committee on Foreign Relations, Subcommittee on East Asian and Pacific Affairs, Hearings on Indonesia, September 18, 1996.
26. Seth Mydans, "Protesters Angered by Raid Battle Police in Indonesia," New York Times, July 28, 1996, p. 8.
27. Eric Schmitt, "Gingrich Vigorously Assails Democrats' Fund Raising," New York Times, October 14, 1996.

well as participation in a U.S.-funded program of military training. The U.S. House of Representatives approved unanimously on June 10 an amendment to the Foreign Relations Authorization Act criticizing Indonesia's abuses of human rights in East Timor. A Republican congressman reported on June 12 that the United States had evidence that John Huang, a former employee of the Riady family's Lippo Group, while working at the Commerce Department, had passed classified economic information to his former employer. The Clinton Administration announced on June 13 that it would ask the World Trade Organization to rule against Indonesia's national car project, "a program run by Mr. Suharto's son that puts foreign companies at a disadvantage in the country's potentially huge automobile market."[28] In New York City, it was reported on June 15 that the speaker of the city council had introduced a measure that would bar the city from doing business with companies that operate in Indonesia, among other countries, apparently for abusing the rights of Christians in East Timor. Measures to take similar action against Indonesia were reportedly under consideration in other American cities and some states.

Against this background of negative domestic opinion, any U.S. role in the effort to halt the collapse of the Indonesian economy was bound to encounter criticism. As events unfolded, the U.S. role in the affair became quite prominent. In January 1998, as Mr. Soeharto continued to drag his feet about taking actions agreed on with the International Monetary Fund, and as fear grew that the regional crisis might become a global one, the U.S. Treasury deputy secretary, Lawrence Summers, issued a public warning that the international support to Indonesia was in imminent danger of being withdrawn.[29] President Clinton telephoned Mr. Soeharto to say, first, that the United States would do all it could to help the Indonesian economy; and second, that it was urgent that the IMF agreement be implemented.[30] With the Indonesian currency still falling, a rush of other foreign government leaders telephoned Soeharto, urging him to bend. Mr. Summers called on President Soeharto in person. The head of the IMF, Michel Camdessus, did the same and extracted a detailed set of undertakings signed by Soeharto personally. On a regional tour, U.S. Secretary of Defense William Cohen added his support. The United States had by now inserted itself deeply into the Indonesian crisis. And it had some reason to be hopeful; the new IMF terms called for the rapid

28. David E. Sanger, "In the Shadow of Scandal, U.S. Challenges a Suharto Project," *New York Times*, June 14, 1997.
29. David E. Sanger, "U.S. Warning to Indonesia: Comply on Aid: Funds Could Be Cut Off If Terms Are Ignored," *New York Times*, January 8, 1998.
30. Senior State Department Official, January 9, 1998.

stripping away of monopolies and cartels that were among the most objectionable instruments of Mr. Soeharto's political control.

But the economic crisis showed no sign of easing. On the contrary, Mr. Soeharto continued to demonstrate a lack of resolve to carry through on reforms, and the Indonesian economy continued to suffer in consequence. The value of the Indonesian currency fell when Mr. Soeharto indicated in February 1998 that his candidate for vice president and potential successor was B. J. Habibie, the leading figure in the bloated state-enterprise sector of the Indonesian economy and singularly lacking in private-sector support. The value of the currency fell again a few days later when Mr. Soeharto indicated he was preparing to risk a confrontation with the IMF and the United States over monetary policy, and Messrs. Camdessus and Clinton were moved to repeat their earlier warnings that international support was in peril.[31]

Clearly patience with Mr. Soeharto was running out. On February 16, *the New York Times* in an editorial called on Washington to "register its objections" to Mr. Soeharto's plan "to have himself re-elected to a new five-year term next month."[32] On February 20, Mr. Clinton phoned for the second time in a week. A White House spokesman said Mr. Clinton had told the Indonesian president that it was important for Mr. Soeharto to "demonstrate his political commitment to economic reform."[33]

Indonesians had long asked American friends what they had to do to be taken seriously by Americans. By 1998, they had one answer to that question. Three months later, the Indonesian leader resigned and the Soeharto era came to an end.

AMERICA'S INTERESTS

President Clinton stated early in 1996 that the new era in world affairs calls for the United States to pursue a national strategy which, focusing on new threats and new opportunities, has three central goals:

> To enhance our security with military forces that are ready to fight and with effective representation abroad.
>
> To bolster America's economic revitalization.
>
> To promote democracy abroad.[34]

---

31. Richard W. Stevenson, "I.M.F. Opposing Indonesia's Plan for Currency," *New York Times,* February 14, 1998; David E. Sanger, "Clinton Tells Indonesia to Stick to Reform," *New York Times,* February 15, 1998.
32. "Mr. Suharto's Extended Run," *New York Times,* February 16, 1998.
33. "Clinton and Suharto Talk," *New York Times,* February 22, 1998.
34. Office of the President, *A National Security Strategy,* I.

How do these broad goals apply to a country such as Indonesia? Clearly they do not apply equally. Indonesia was hardly mentioned in the most recent Defense Department study of U.S. security in the East Asia–Pacific region; one must assume that it is not a high priority from the point of view of the U.S. military. And it should be clear from the foregoing discussion of domestic conditions in Indonesia that democracy is not a likely prospect for that country in the foreseeable future, even after Soeharto's resignation. One of the problems with American policy, then, is the large gap that exists between the ringing statements of policy expressed in global terms and the reality of practical cases to which those policies must be applied.

Reduced to more credible terms, the American security interest in Indonesia appears to be of two kinds. The White House and the Department of Defense are still focused on what one might call "hard" security: the use of the armed forces of the United States in major regional contingencies. The White House devoted half its 1996 national strategy paper to explicitly military aspects of security; the Defense Department in its 1995 report had ranged beyond them only in a brief digression, acknowledging the significance of Asia's new economic success and concluding that, for this very reason, "maintaining a credible security presence in Asia is vital to the post–Cold War international system now taking shape."[35] Neither the White House nor the Department of Defense seems inclined yet to set much store by what one might call "soft" security: the promotion of conditions that contribute to U.S. security without the need to bring U.S. armed forces into play.

This is a useful distinction to make as one considers U.S. security interests in Indonesia. From the point of view of "hard" security, Indonesia is not a locus of the credible American security presence that is required in the East Asia–Pacific region. Indonesia is important to the United States military primarily, as Deputy Assistant Secretary of Defense Kurt Campbell has testified, "in terms of international transit rights through sea lanes."[36] Indonesia's vast span of thousands of islands forms a gateway between the Pacific and Indian Oceans through which U.S. naval forces periodically need to pass, particularly en route to and from the Persian Gulf. And it is of primary importance to the United States that its "rights of passage through this strategic archipelago not be infringed."[37]

From the point of view of "soft" security, Indonesia is important to the

35. Department of Defense, *United States Security Strategy*, 7.
36. Kurt M. Campbell, Statement for the Senate Foreign Relations Committee Hearing on Indonesia, September 18, 1996 (Washington, D.C.: United States–Indonesia Society, n.d.).
37. Campbell, statement on Indonesia.

United States as "a positive force for promoting regional and global goals that are in the U.S. interest," to use the words of Assistant Secretary Lord.[38] The principal interest the United States has in East Asia and the Pacific, as our behavior over the past sixty years attests, is that no other power or concert of powers should dominate the region. At present, the state that has the greatest potential to fill the role of regional hegemon is undoubtedly China, which is currently enjoying a very rapid rise in its economic output, in its foreign export earnings, and in its capacity to finance the modernization of its armed forces. China's rising position in the region will be moderated to mutual benefit to the extent that it is balanced by the rise of other states, of which Indonesia is a prominent example. This is the principal "soft security" interest the United States has in Indonesia, and it has implications for American policy. In a nutshell, it has made no sense for the United States to be concerned about Chinese aggressive behavior in the South China Sea and, at the same time, to deny Indonesia the ability to purchase U.S. F-16 fighter aircraft. Nor will the United States keep Indonesia from acquiring aircraft from other sources to fill its needs; Russia quickly offered to sell advanced fighter aircraft to Indonesia with no political strings attached.

The U.S. "soft security" interest in Indonesia, in its entirety, is considerable. We have already seen the role that Indonesia has played in the founding of ASEAN, in moving APEC to reach agreement on long-term trade liberalization, and in founding the ASEAN Regional Forum. Indonesia also has recently brokered a peace agreement between the government and a Muslim separatist group in the southern Philippines, completed a decade of providing a safe haven for thousands of refugees from Vietnam, and sponsored a series of workshops to help resolve the long-standing territorial disputes in the South China Sea. Indonesia has become a significant global actor as well in recent years, chairing the Nonaligned Movement and the Organization of the Islamic Conference and sitting on the Security Council of the United Nations. Indonesia also has supported recent U.S. efforts in extending the Treaty on the Nonproliferation of Nuclear Weapons, in attempting to negotiate a comprehensive test ban treaty, and in developing an acceptable nuclear energy regime in North Korea. On this record, it would seem that Assistant Secretary Lord was not overstating the case when he concluded that "Indonesia is a critically important nation in a region of vital significance to the U.S."[39]

Some might doubt that Indonesia could meet President Clinton's standard of an economic partner that can help "bolster America's economic

---

38. Winston Lord, Statement for the Senate Foreign Relations Committee Hearing on Indonesia, September 18, 1996 (Washington, D.C.: United States–Indonesia Society, n.d.).

39. Lord, statement on Indonesia.

revitalization," but it was approaching that level before the financial crisis. Bilateral trade between the United States and Indonesia grew rapidly over the previous five years to more than $12 billion in 1996.[40] The World Bank estimated that growth rates prior to the crisis would put Indonesia among the world's twenty biggest economies by 2005.[41] This growth, and the fact that its economy was already the region's largest, caused the U.S. Department of Commerce in 1994 to select Indonesia as one of its "10 Emerging Markets" for priority attention. Another reason for Commerce Department attention was the high level of U.S. investment in Indonesia. Direct investment by American business totaled more than $7 billion in 1995, excluding the petroleum and natural gas sector. This reflected an increase of 118 percent since 1990 and made Indonesia the second largest locus of such U.S. investment among the ASEAN economies.[42] U.S. investment in Indonesia's oil and gas industries is not quantifiable in the same terms, but former Assistant Secretary Lord has described it as "massive."[43] Caltex produces annually almost half of all Indonesia's crude oil and condensate, and ARCO and Mobil are its third and fourth top producers. Moreover, new fields of natural gas to be exploited by Exxon and ARCO are expected to be worth tens of billions of dollars.[44] There seems no question that, when oil and gas are included, Indonesia leads the ASEAN economies in total U.S. investment. It is not too much to say that key sectors of the American economy now depend to an unprecedented degree on the continuing rise of Indonesia's economy.

If these were the only interests of the United States in Indonesia, one could possibly say, as President Clinton does in his national strategy statement of 1996, that "our goals . . . are mutually supportive."[45] Enhancing security and bolstering economic prosperity do tend to go hand in hand. It is the addition of "promoting democracy" that has introduced a conflict of interest. Part of the problem lies in a confusion of terms. The White House strategy statement describes "promoting democracy" in various ways. One formulation is "working with new democratic states to help preserve them as democracies committed to free markets and respect for human rights.[46] Another is that "we seek to increase respect for funda-

40. U.S. Department of Commerce. International Trade Administration. U.S.–Indonesia Trade Statistics, Doc. 4306, automated fax retrieval system, June 27, 1997.
41. K. T. Arasu, "Indonesia future bright if policy right—World Bank," Reuters, Jakarta, June 18, 1997. Available at Clarinews, C-Reuters@clarinet.
42. Lord, statement on Indonesia.
43. Lord, statement on Indonesia.
44. Embassy of the United States of America, Jakarta, Indonesia, *Petroleum Report: Indonesia: 1993* (Jakarta Embassy of the United States of America, August 1993).
45. Office of the President, *A National Security Strategy*, ii.
46. Office of the President, *A National Security Strategy*, 32.

mental human rights in all states and encourage an evolution to democracy where that is possible."[47] A third formulation speaks of "enlargement of the community of market democracies respecting human rights and the environment."[48] The most extensive formulation in the White House statement says:

> The core of our strategy is to help democracy and free markets expand and survive in other places where we have the strongest security concerns and where we can make the greatest difference. This is not a democratic crusade; it is a pragmatic commitment to make freedom take hold where that will help us most. Thus, we must target our effort to assist states that affect our strategic interests, such as those with large economies, critical locations, nuclear weapons or the potential to generate refugee flows into our own nation or into key friends and allies. We must focus our efforts where we have the most leverage. And our efforts must be demand-driven—they must focus on nations whose people are pushing for reform or have already secured it.[49]

How does this apply to Indonesia? Secretary of State Warren Christopher, speaking before the Senate Foreign Relations Committee on August 1, 1996, said:

> I think there's a strong interest in seeing an orderly transition of power there that will recognize the pluralism that should exist in a country of that magnitude and importance. So we will be encouraging a transition there that expresses the popular will.[50]

Assistant Secretary Lord, speaking before the same committee on September 18, 1996, said:

> Administration officials, including President Clinton, repeatedly made clear that our relationship, as strong as it currently is, cannot reach its full potential until Indonesia improves its human rights performance.[51]

What do these statements mean? Mr. Christopher seems to have stated a highest-expectation position: that the United States has a "strong interest" in a more pluralist or populist government in Jakarta. Is this true? Would a more pluralist or populist government be in the U.S. interest? One feels obliged to suggest that this need not necessarily be the case. On the contrary, it is likely that almost any successor regime will be more problematic for U.S. interests. We have seen that the Soeharto regime,

47. *Office of the President, A National Security Strategy,* 32.
48. *Office of the President, A National Security Strategy,* 32.
49. *Office of the President, A National Security Strategy,* 32.
50. Lord, statement on Indonesia.
51. Lord, statement on Indonesia.

with all its limitations, acted in ways that are consistent with U.S. interests across a wide range of regional and global issues. There is no basis for believing that a more pluralist or populist government in Indonesia would be certain or even likely to improve on this performance. We also have seen that the domestic conditions in Indonesia give us every reason to expect that the political transition in Indonesia will be fraught with difficulty. Many members of the Indonesian elite would settle for an orderly transition. Nor is it clear that a more pluralist or populist regime would be their first priority for change; a less corrupt regime would almost certainly be the preference of many. In any event, to say that the United States has a view on what direction this process should take also ignores the White House dictum that the United States put its efforts where it can make the greatest difference. To suggest that this would be in the democratization of Indonesia is surely wishful thinking.

Assistant Secretary Lord indicated that his statement also was intended to cover a broad range of political activity. He discussed conditions of detention, accusations of torture, the people's inability to change their government, and limitations on freedoms of expression, association, assembly, and the press. He expressed special concern for the human rights situations in East Timor and Irian Jaya, noted progress in response to abuses by troops, and reviewed reports of mistreatment of political detainees in the aftermath of July, 27 1996.[52]

It is unfortunate that the Clinton administration has developed neither a sense of priorities as it confronts its ambitious political agenda abroad, nor some sign that it is capable of judging when and where it is timely for the administration to put its energies to work. We have already indicated that freely contested elections do not appear likely in Indonesia for some time to come. Nor is there any reason to suppose that elections would produce a democratic regime. On the other hand, the president's dictum that the United States must be pragmatic, demand driven, and focused where it has the greatest interest and the most leverage seems to us eminently sensible. From this perspective, the United States has the greatest interest in the peaceful evolution of the Indonesian political regime. And the United States has the most leverage in the context of the IMF agreement. Ending the numerous monopolies and preferential arrangements as called for in that agreement would go a long way toward removing significant obstacles to evolutionary political change in Indonesia.

Yet the greatest danger in Indonesia is that leadership change, as it unfolds, will not be peaceful. The United States has an interest in making clear that a peaceful transition is essential to continued international

---

52. Lord, statement on Indonesia.

financial support. Any reading of the past behavior of the U.S. Congress would lead one to this conclusion. So would any reading of the international financial markets. The financial crisis thus presented the United States with an opportunity to approach Indonesia with a coherent set of goals for the first time in years.

Whether the United States will be able to pursue these goals consistently, however, remains in question.

NEEDED POLICY CHANGES

It is fruitless to attempt to offer any but the most fundamental policy prescriptions in a situation as volatile as that of Indonesia in 1998. Civilian demonstrators were protesting unemployment, food shortages, and rising prices. Riots had occurred in many places; Chinese-owned shops in particular were targeted. Students in Jakarta called on the president to step down, which Soeharto refused to do for several months. It is feared that the Indonesian army might in time find itself firing on unarmed civilians. If this occurs the Clinton administration will find itself under strong congressional pressure to respond. The international program to stabilize the Indonesian economy would be in jeopardy. And if that program collapses, the law and order situation in Indonesia can only grow worse. Thus, much depends on the course of events in Indonesia, and over this the United States has only limited influence.

U.S. ability to influence events in Indonesia through the Indonesian armed forces is minimal. Kurt Campbell of the Pentagon had told the Senate Foreign Relations Committee that "in any scenario one can imagine for Indonesian political transition, the armed forces will remain one of the most important institutions in the country for some time." Many analysts would agree. However, Mr. Campbell also told the Committee that "it is unrealistic to assume that any U.S. policies or actions taken toward the Indonesian military will produce fundamental change in the military's behavior."[53] That also was probably correct. So there should be no illusions; the ability of the United States to influence events in Indonesia was not great, and there was a good chance that, rather than improving, the situation in that country might grow even worse before it could get better.

The Asian financial collapse had already provided the U.S. government with some valuable experience in crisis management. After some initial tendency on the part of the U.S. Treasury to act on its own, the White

53. Campbell, statement on Indonesia.

House took a more active role in coordinating U.S. action, particularly prior to the telephone calls initiated by Mr. Clinton. A loose coalition of governments with major interests in Indonesia was formed, including Japan, Germany, Singapore, and Australia. How well this coalition would hold up as the focus of concern moved from economic to political matters was uncertain, but the lesson was clear that Washington could not hope to influence developments in Jakarta without its being part of a wider multilateral effort.

The White House had rarely become involved on Indonesian matters in the years preceding the financial crisis, and was ill prepared to deal with the financial crisis when it broke. Not a single person in the senior ranks of the executive branch had significant Indonesian experience. Fortunately, the new assistant secretary of state for East Asia and the Pacific, Stanley Roth, who was appointed only after the post had been allowed to remain vacant for half a year, was knowledgeable about Indonesia and concerned about giving more attention than his predecessor to Southeast Asia. But the institutional weakness remained. One prescription that could be drawn from these observations is that, at a minimum, the National Security Council staff should include one individual designated to hold the Indonesia brief and to know where to find expertise when needed. Another conclusion one might draw is that something seriously needs to be done to bring senior U.S. officials, including members of the Cabinet and leading members of the Congress, into more regular contact with the elites of countries such as Indonesia and with Americans in business, academia, and the NGO community who monitor their affairs without the distorting filter of the Washington Beltway. At this writing neither the secretary of the treasury nor the secretary of state had taken this obvious step to acquaint themselves with independent opinion on Indonesia.

The increasing difficulty in communicating with Mr. Soeharto, and the decline in his predictability, suggested that the United States finds it hard to make clear to foreign client regimes that its own actions are meant to benefit the foreign society as a whole, in this case Indonesia, and not for the benefit of Mr. Soeharto and his family and cronies. This would call for the United States to go beyond its focus on the reforms that were a condition of its financial support. It has to begin to speak up when fundamental political rights are abused. The United States needs to use its limited political influence in Jakarta with deliberation, but that does not mean that it must speak critically only in private, as it has tended to do in the past. For the foreseeable future, the best hope for Indonesia lies in the gradual evolution of the political system and a transitional Indonesian regime that respects the fundamental rights of its nonviolent domestic critics. When these rights are violated, the United States will have to respond, or it will fail to support the very elements in Indonesian society that are working for evolutionary change. When and how the United States responds are issues for well-informed judgment, but it is reasonable to expect that it will be doing so more frequently in public as the crisis deepens.

It also appears that the time has come for the United States to give more active attention to East Timor. Assistant Secretary of State John Shattuck was reported on January 30, 1998, as saying, "There was little progress on international efforts to find a solution to the problem of East Timor and security forces continued extra-judicial killings, disappearances and torture."[54] The official U.S. position has been that "the United States accepts the incorporation of East Timor without maintaining that a valid act of self-determination has taken place" and believes that "an internationally accepted comprehensive settlement is the best way to achieve lasting improvements in the situation."[55] It had been left to the United Nations to take action to promote such a settlement. UN Secretary General Kofi Annan initiated fresh Indonesian-Portuguese-Timorese talks, and a distinguished Pakistani diplomat was understood to have made a vigorous effort to achieve some progress. In the light of the Shattuck statement, however, it appears that the United States can no longer leave the matter there. The East Timor issue has the potential to derail U.S. involvement in the IMF effort to stabilize the Indonesian economy. The United States thus has reason to make East Timor a matter for bilateral discussion.

Meanwhile, having played a role in the design of the international rescue plan, the United States has a role to play in its implementation. In particular, the United States needs to press, as a matter of high priority, for greater transparency in Indonesian economic decision making. That goal now has the support of independent-minded leaders of the Indonesian business community. Success in this area would help reduce the corruption indicated by U.S. business leaders as the principal obstacle to greater U.S. exports to Indonesia. It also would contribute to the peaceful transition of the Indonesian political system.

The United States thus faces a complex and sensitive agenda with respect to Indonesia, which is made all the more daunting by the problem of leadership on both sides

54. Reuters, "U.S. Slams 'Authoritarian' Indonesia over Rights," *Yahoo Finance*, January 30, 1998. Available at http://biz.yahoo.com/finance.
55. Lord, statement on Indonesia.

THE PROBLEM OF LEADERSHIP

Problems of leadership weighed heavily on relations between the United States and Indonesia at this writing in mid-1998.

In Indonesia, a crisis of confidence in President Soeharto's management of the economy swept the domestic and foreign markets. Long regarded as a man who could be counted on to make hard decisions when they were recommended by his senior advisers as essential to the long-term health of the economy, Soeharto in late 1997 and early 1998 gave every appearance of being an elderly man preoccupied with the financial interests of his children. It was not just that his leadership suffered growing disapproval as the costs of the financial crisis began to become evident in rising unemployment and prices. The reliability of his word was cast in doubt by his delay in implementing his agreements with the International Monetary Fund and by his actions, which were seen as risking the future of the economy in order to provide benefits for his family.

The first agreement with the Fund, on October 31, 1997, called for the closure of sixteen banks; they were closed, but two of them, owned by Soeharto family members, were back in business in a matter of days. No action was taken on other steps called for by the agreement. In January 1998, Mr. Soeharto made public a budget for 1998–1999 that the markets viewed as unrealistic; the currency fell to a record low, and the United States issued its first public warning that the IMF rescue program was in jeopardy. Pressed by Mr. Clinton and other heads of government, Mr. Soeharto signed a more explicit agreement with the IMF that set dates by which certain monopolies, cartels, and other preferential arrangements favoring his family and friends were to be stripped away. But Mr. Soeharto's commitment to the agreement was left in doubt by the failure of either Mr. Soeharto or his economic ministers to explain to the nation what was going on.

In February 1998, Mr. Soeharto announced that he intended to stand for reelection the following month; he also indicated that his choice as vice president and potential successor was B. J. Habibie, a controversial figure in the state-owned sector of the economy. The currency market reacted unfavorably to this news. Then Mr. Soeharto all but committed himself to a controversial plan to establish a currency board that would peg the Indonesian currency to the U.S. dollar at a rate almost twice the prevailing market value. The plan was presented to Mr. Soeharto by an American economist introduced to him by his children. It was widely observed that the plan would enable Mr. Soeharto's children to move large amounts of money abroad while putting the Indonesian economy at considerable risk. The IMF threatened to withdraw its support; so did Mr. Clinton during another telephone call, the contents of which were made public. The Indonesian minister of finance issued a statement indicating the establishment of the currency board might be postponed. By this time, Mr. Soeharto's reputation for probity was in shreds.

Yet Mr. Soeharto controlled the assembly that was to reelect him. He also continued to have the support of the armed forces leadership, which was largely composed of former aides and included a son-in-law in a key command in Jakarta. And in what was seen by many as an attempt to divert attention away from the Soeharto family, the armed forces took the extraordinary step of announcing allegations that tied two internationally prominent members of the Chinese minority, Jusuf and Sofyan Wanandi, to a small left-wing political organization and a bomb threat. Inasmuch as the Wanandi brothers had supported Soeharto in his rise to power, but had recently made public statements critical of the government, the message seemed to be that it was not safe for anyone to speak his mind.

With Soeharto's resignation, this farcical state of affairs is over; but who can predict what next will happen in Jakarta?

Meanwhile, in Washington, an embattled president had scant time for attention to the Asian financial crisis. He was under investigation by the Whitewater prosecutor for possible subornation of perjury in the case of a young female White House intern with whom he was alleged to have had a sexual relationship (which Mr. Clinton denied). He faced a major decision whether or not to bomb Iraq in an effort to reduce the prospects of that nation's developing weapons of mass destruction (international support for bombing was weak). Mr. Clinton also had looming the start of a trial in Arkansas on charges of sexually propositioning a state employee, and continuing investigations of potentially illegal campaign fund-raising (which linked Mr. Clinton to Indonesia).

Never seen as a president with particular interest in Asia, Mr. Clinton had nevertheless established a good personal relationship with Mr. Soeharto through meetings in Tokyo, Seattle, Bogor, and Washington between 1993 and 1996. Then charges surfaced just before the U.S. elections in 1995 that Chinese-Indonesians had traded campaign funds for talks with the U.S. president on U.S. Asia policy, and the Clinton-Soeharto relationship fell apart. When the two leaders attended the Asia Pacific Economic Cooperation (APEC) summit of November 1997, Mr. Clinton avoided even a chance meeting with Mr. Soeharto. It was against this background that Mr. Clinton began his series of telephone calls to the Indonesian president in January 1998. Rather than an old friend, Mr.

Clinton was now the distant and distracted leader of the lone superpower, and so a caller to be taken seriously on policy but not one to be listened to on more fundamental matters.

Thus to the institutional weaknesses in both governments for resolving the financial crisis of 1997–1998 were added the personal weaknesses of the two presidents. Such a combination held little promise for the future.

CONCLUSION

If anything positive could be said to have come out of the financial crisis of late 1997 and early 1998, it was the recognition of mutual dependence between the United States and Indonesia. There seemed to be little question that either country could any longer proceed on the assumption that it need not take the other into account. This realization was not likely to be a source of unalloyed satisfaction in either capital. Washington and Jakarta harbored considerable ignorance and suspicion of each other. Much now depends on whether the IMF program can be sustained and whether it will prove effective. If it were to collapse in a chorus of mutual recrimination, the relationship would be more troubled than it had been before the U.S. Treasury acted. Even if it were to succeed, its success probably would be measured in terms that would attract little political support on either side. The longer-term impact on Indonesian opinion of financial austerity that was associated with the United States, and the potential impact on American opinion of law-and-order action by the armed forces of Indonesia, can only be imagined.

That Indonesia is a pivotal state for U.S. policy was thus established by the events of late 1997 and early 1998. That the United States faces a large task in learning how to deal with this pivotal state seems the surest lesson to be drawn from the experience.

INDIA

Stephen P. Cohen and Sumit Ganguly*

One would expect that a state that: (1) comprises 20 percent of the world's population and is likely to surpass China's in the next twenty-five years; (2) is located adjacent to a region of great importance to the United States (the oil-rich Persian Gulf); (3) has long-standing strategic and cultural links to energy-rich and newly accessible Central Asia; and (4) had, seven hundred years ago, colonized and transformed much of Southeast Asia would be regarded as "pivotal," or at least important to the United States. Add to this the fact that the state in question—India—has maintained, against all odds and all predictions, a functioning democracy for most of its fifty years of independence. Indeed, most of the world's citizens living under democratic rule reside in India,[1] and every time India goes to the polls it becomes, on that date, history's largest single organized human activity. Further, India maintains powerful military forces and manufactures a wide range of advanced military equipment for its million-man army, its forty-five-squadron air force, and its small but expanding navy. Finally, though estimates vary, most analysts would agree that India's middle class numbers in the neighborhood of one hundred million, and the U.S. Department of Commerce has designated India as one of the ten "big emerging markets." It also has the world's third largest pool of scientifically and technically trained personnel.

Despite this (and, one might add, despite India's historical, cultural, and civilizational impact on the West, on China, and on much of Asia) India has not for the past thirty years been counted among the "pivotal" or even most important states in the world. True, India's smaller neighbors regard it with a mixture of envy and fear, but China, most Western states, Japan, and many other economic and political *arrivistes* tend to dis-

---

* [Editors' note: As this book goes to print, the news of the nuclear testing by India and Pakistan re-emphasizes the need for a more focused U.S. strategy toward South Asia.]

1. Which is not to say that India's citizens enjoy their democratic rights equally, or at a level comparable with that of most Western industrialized democracies.

miss India as a no-show. Singapore's political leaders and business community regularly visit India to deliver scathing lectures on India's need to pull itself together politically, move ahead economically, and generally follow the "tiger" model of East and Southeast Asia. For reasons to be discussed, this advice is unlikely to be accepted.

Is India destined to be always "emerging" but never actually arriving? Will it again be relegated to the second division of international politics, despite the remarkable qualities described above and despite the slow transformation of its economy now under way? Or does it face the prospect of extreme chaos and disintegration? India is still beset by population pressure, the demands of its nearly fifty thousand castes, and the self-evident inability of its urban areas to cope with an influx from the countryside, where conditions in many of its five hundred thousand villages ensure that India will continue to count over half the world's poor among its citizens. Add to this mixture the growing environmental damage to the ecosphere, and one wonders if the question might be not whether India will emerge, but whether it will collapse, bringing down much of South Asia with it.

Our short answer to the last question is a firm "no." India may be a "pivotal" state for America in the future, but it will not be one that is important because of *failure*. Yet there is no assurance that it will exactly "succeed" along a number of dimensions—strategic, economic, and social. Of course, whether India emerges as a strong, viable, and independent state will be determined largely by Indians themselves, but we believe that not only will the fate of India be important for American policy makers, but that America can, in a number of ways, shape India's potential emergence as a more stable, more coherent, and more strategically sympathetic great power.

This chapter explores India's weaknesses and its strengths and comes to a net assessment of India's social, economic, and strategic importance to the United States. Our chief conclusion is that certain factors, not always apparent to the outside world, explain much of India's paradoxical appearance: a state with considerable potential and considerable accomplishments, yet one that has perpetually disappointed.

INDIA AS A "DEVELOPING" STATE: ECONOMIC AND SOCIAL FACTORS

South Asian experts tend to preface their answers to questions about India with the caveat "Well, it depends." India is a backward, impoverished country, racked by political instability. It is also a rich and powerful country (especially when viewed from the perspective of its smaller neighbors) that has shown surprising political resilience over the past fifty years. Distance tends to magnify both capabilities and vulnerabilities, making the task of situating India on the developing-developed continuum especially tricky.

Because of this geocultural, economic, and political complexity, India is more like a continent than a state. A comparison with all of Europe or all of Latin America is appropriate—India's population exceeds those of Latin America and Africa combined. Large areas of India are among the most backward in the world—India has nearly half of the world's poorest people, largely concentrated in the states of central and eastern India: Madhya Pradesh, Bihar, Uttar Pradesh, and Orissa. It is in these regions that literacy and economic growth are the lowest, with absentee landlordism and caste and religious violence the greatest. They also generate the largest numbers of economic refugees, most of whom head toward the booming cities of modern India.

Yet large areas of India are politically orderly, economically thriving, and socially quite "modern." Western and southern India, especially the states of Gujarat, Maharashtra, Karnataka, and Tamil Nadu, are doing very well, and some of these have literacy rates comparable with parts of the Western world and the "tigers" of East Asia; they also possess a highly mobile, talented work force and have produced émigré populations that give Indian businessmen and traders a strong foothold in Africa, the Middle East, parts of Central Asia, and even the United States and Canada. If Karnataka were an independent state, it would be the international counterpart of Malaysia or even Taiwan.

Although India, considered in terms of gross figures and percentages, falls into the category of economically "less developed," it is also a state that has managed to gather together resources for specific *national* purposes. At the time of writing, India is the only country in the world with a functioning commercial space satellite; it has been able to manufacture, under license, a whole range of medium-technology military equipment; and its schools and universities pump out thousands of world-class scientists and engineers (as well as many mediocre ones). Above all, it has a level of political coherence that far exceeds its economic development and is greater than that of most African states, many countries in Central and Latin America, large parts of Southeast Asia, Central Asia, and even Europe (the former Yugoslavia comes to mind, but also Italy and, until recently, Spain).

Finally, it is necessary to take into account India's enormous *potential* for rapid economic growth despite important institutional and infrastructural constraints that are all too familiar. Despite fitful attempts to reform the hidebound Indian economy after a fiscal crisis in 1991, no government has yet to develop an explicit policy framework. Antiquated labor laws, continued policy differences among decision-making bodies, high governmental subsidies, and an unwillingness to divest sections of the loss-making public sector all remain important constraints on economic growth. An inadequate and sagging infrastructure has simultaneously limited the inflow of foreign investment and hobbled economic growth.[2] Three areas in particular pose serious problems: telecommunications, transport, and power.

All these obstacles notwithstanding, India has successfully overcome its "Hindu growth rate," to borrow the late Indian economist Raj Krishna's memorable words. Over the past five years India's economic growth has hovered around 5 percent or better, a far cry from the 3 percent of the 1970s. In 1996 the Indian economy grew more than 6 percent. In the 1997 budget Finance Minister P. Chidambaram set a target of 7 percent. If the country can sustain the pace of its reforms and move to the next phase, India's national income could double in a decade.

INDIA'S DISINTEGRATIVE POTENTIAL

How does India's patchwork quilt of economic progress—some states rich, some poor—correlate with India's overall disintegrative potential? Here the record is very impressive. Although some argue that India is an artificial country,[3] the record of political cohesion is now fifty years old, despite a plethora of separatist and internal revolutionary movements.

Historically, the most significant political failure is represented by the creation and continuing existence of Pakistan itself. Fifty years ago, on the eve of partition, most Indian political leaders came to the conclusion that it was preferable to deny major political concessions to the "Pakistan" movement, allowing a fragmented Pakistan to come into being. Nehru and others believed the unprepared state would collapse in a matter of months or years and would then be reintegrated into India proper. They

2. Between 1991 and May 1996 India attracted $22 billion worth of foreign direct investment. Currently, the United States is the largest foreign investor in India, with a stake of $5.4 billion. These figures are from the government of India.

3. The argument, heard both in the West and in Pakistan, is that there has never been a "Hindu" civilization that governed India—the only significant empires being those of Indian Buddhists, Muslims (the Mughals, who had their roots in Central Asia), and Christians (the Portuguese, French, and British). Further, Pakistani theoreticians claim that the creation of Pakistan itself was only the first partition of India, that others will follow, and that the giant, unnatural India will eventually be reduced to a series of minor, bickering Hindu states—which would give Pakistan, backed by the Islamic world, strategic superiority in the region. This belief is not widely held in Pakistan, in part because it is Pakistan, not India, that has been unable to quash separatist movements and that faces a somewhat greater prospect of such movements in years to come.

guessed wrong, which may have made the central government of India even tougher on subsequent separatist or autonomist movements.

There have been plenty of these. Two princely states, Hyderabad in the south and Jammu and Kashmir in the north, either sought or were tempted by independence; the former was forcibly kept within the Indian union, the latter was incorporated into India after an initial promise that the Kashmiris would be allowed to vote on their future. No other region has been granted even this opportunity. In the northeast alone there have been four or five separatist groups. The Nagas (many of whom were Christians, with strong foreign links to both China and Christian missionaries[4]) were eventually beaten down in the mid-1970's after a ten-year insurrection. More recently, separatist Mizos and Bodos, Assamese, Manipuris, and tribal guerrillas in Tripura have taken up arms and train bombs against New Delhi (with assistance, in several cases, from other states). Since these movements were in a distant corner of India, public and international access could be tightly controlled, and since the numbers involved were relatively small, they never received much publicity in the human rights community. This was certainly not the case in the agriculturally rich Punjab, where a full-fledged separatist movement seeking a Sikh state (Khalistan) led to virtual warfare from 1984 onward and indirectly led to the assassination of Indira Gandhi and many other Indian politicians and officials, as well as heavy police repression in the Punjab.

India faces other challenges to its statehood. Significant Maoist-inspired movements have persisted in Andhra Pradesh, West Bengal, Assam, and Bihar. In some cases the movements are no less motivated, led, and armed than similar groups in Central America, Latin America, and Africa, yet no serious observer of India expects them to succeed. Why not?

There are at least four reasons why the disintegration of India is an improbable event: capabilities, strategies, elite integration, and sheer size.

First, the Indian state has the *capacity* to acquire, organize, and apply the full resources of a continent-size region to any particular local area. As poor as it is, the Union Government maintains one of the world's largest armies and a vast panoply of paramilitary forces, aside from the regular state police, and has several very experienced intelligence agencies. The Indian state has a history that spans, in various forms, well over several hundred years. The British Raj was built on the British East India

---

4. In one of the more unusual examples of "civilizational clash" these Southern Baptist Nagas (some of whom were recently headhunters) are converting to Judaism and have staked a claim as the lost tribe of Israel.

Company, which in turn borrowed some of its institutions from the Moguls, who themselves had built on Turkic and Persian as well as Hindu and Buddhist models. If nothing else, states have institutionalized memories; the government of India and the various state governments know what to do when faced with a militant, violent, or separatist movement.[5]

Crudely put, the *strategy* followed at both the state and national levels is, in the words of a senior Indian Police Service officer, "hit them over the head with a hammer, then teach them to play the piano." Translated: The government of India will apply massive, and sometimes brutal, force to contain any group that proclaims that it wants to leave the Union; but after that it will willingly deal with the leadership in whatever way is necessary—which often means bribing or coopting them. When the former rebels are themselves faced with successor separatist movements they in turn will apply the same techniques. This is most evident in the northeast, where yesterday's student radicals are today's government and have to cope with their own revolutionary successors.

The key element in this strategy is *accommodation*. The Indian government will partially accede to the demands put forth by the most extreme separatist groups. Gradually, the lesson has sunk in: Political patronage grows out of the barrel of a gun. The most recent and sensational example is Phoolan Devi, the "Bandit Queen," now an important politician in India's largest state, Uttar Pradesh. Although she was not a separatist, her surrender and political rehabilitation followed the model precisely. In India, much political violence, even in the name of separatism, grows out of the failure of democratic politics, and the inevitable solution in such a case is more democracy. Most Indian Sikhs, for example, were not, even at the height of the Khalistan movement, as interested in a separate state as they were in obtaining justice within the Indian one.[6] This is also true of the separatist movement in Kashmir. It had Kashmiri rather than Islamic roots, and it would not have burst into armed opposition in 1989 had Kashmir been handled more wisely in the preceding years.[7]

5. For an excellent discussion of the role of information and intelligence gathering under the British Raj see C. A. Bayly, *Empire and Information: Intelligence Gathering and Social Communication in India, 1780–1870* (Cambridge: Cambridge University Press, 1996).
6. One look at a map shows how improbable Khalistan would have been as a state—without access to the sea, and with two hostile and far more powerful neighbors.
7. Indian Muslims are not, as a rule, "militant," and most are content to live within a more or less secular India. The one place where "Islamic" extremism has taken root is in Kashmir, but there it rests on a long history of Kashmiri (i.e., ethnic and linguistic) separatism, which includes Hindus as well as Muslims. For an extended discussion of the origins of the Kashmir insurgency, see Sumit Ganguly, *The Crisis in Kashmir: Portents of War, Hopes of Peace* (Cambridge: Cambridge University Press; Washington, D.C.: Woodrow Wilson Center Press, 1997).

The success of the pressure-cooption strategy is made possible by two inter-related factors: the vastness of India and the inability of separatist movements to work together. Indian separatist movements have usually arisen one at a time in different regions of the country, enabling the government to apply overpowering resources in each instance. India *appears* to be perpetually in chaos, and there has been a general increase in social and political violence over the last two decades, but the major separatist threats have been fairly regularly spaced (first the Tamils in the 1950s, then the Nagas, then the Sikhs, now the Kashmiris). If dissident and separatist groups were able to unite or mount simultaneous attacks on the Indian state, then some might succeed, but so far that has not happened, despite some outside support and encouragement.

THE ENVIRONMENTAL "THREAT"

Some have argued that India's alarming environmental degradation might undermine political stability and hobble India's prospects of development. Although the more alarmist scenarios[8] can be discounted, India's environmental problems—sometimes in combination with particular resource scarcity—at times do precipitate social tensions and culminate in violence. For example, the water quality of India's principal rivers poses a severe environmental hazard. Most of the thirteen river basins in India that constitute close to 80 percent of the total water surface are acutely polluted. The growth of bacteria in these river basins has passed danger levels in many locales. More specifically, the Ganges, India's sacred river, is among the worst polluted in the subcontinent. Despite the much-vaunted Ganga Action Plan that was launched in 1985, the river still absorbs as much as 1,340 liters of raw sewage every day along its 2,525 kilometers.[9] These alarming statistics are closely linked to the rise of a variety of waterborne diseases.

Environmental degradation also threatens other areas of human activity in India. Parts of India have seen an alarming reduction in forest cover. Excessive, and frequently illegal, logging has led to the destruction of evergreen forests in the states of Uttar Pradesh, Himachal Pradesh, Madhya Pradesh, and Jammu and Kashmir—although it must be noted that because of extensive reforestation programs India has more forest cover now than it did thirty years ago. Despite the protests of local and

8. See, for example, Sandy Gordon, "Resources and Instability in South Asia," *Survival* 35, no. 2 (summer 1993); Arthur Bonner, *India: Averting the Apocalypse* (Durham, N.C.: Duke University Press, 1990).

9. Samar Halarnkar, "Rivers of Death," and Ramesh Menon, "Ganga Clean-Up: Monumental Failure," *India Today*, January 15, 1997, pp. 102–105, 104.

regional politicians, the Indian Supreme Court has recently responded to a number of public-interest litigation petitions to stop such clear-cutting of the evergreen forests. The court has, at least temporarily, suspended many of the logging and cutting operations in the most affected states.[10]

Although the environmental lobby—which has indigenous Gandhian roots and linkages to Western environmental activists—has offered a number of gloomy scenarios, its pessimism does not seem to be shared by the average Indian citizen. Repeated public opinion polling indicates a low level of interest in environmental issues, but more important politically, a high level of satisfaction with the present overall state of Indian politics and economic progress. On the crucial question, "Are you better off now than your parents?" the polls show a resounding "yes" response. The views of most outsiders about India's poverty, environmental degradation, and so forth may not be shared by the people who count the most—India's voters. This is because another transformation is occurring in India, more important politically than environmental issues, security issues, or even the problem of political corruption, which is growing so rapidly that India, along with Pakistan, is ranked among the most corrupt countries in the world.

INDIA'S SECOND REVOLUTION

India's independence in 1947 was hailed as a revolutionary event: the acquisition of self-government by a fifth of the human race. For over thirty years Indian politics was both democratic and stable, with the ruling Congress party (like Mexico's PRI) dominating at both the center and in India's twenty-plus states.

However, in the 1990s India has been plunged into political instability at the center and in many of its most important states, especially those in the conservative, relatively backward "Cow Belt"—Uttar Pradesh, Bihar, and Madhya Pradesh. Finally, in the eleventh general election, held in 1996, no party emerged with a majority in the Indian parliament. Eventually, a coalition government, composed of some thirteen parties under the banner of the United Front, assumed office. This minority government survived an important challenge to its existence in April 1997, when its principal parliamentary ally, the Congress party, briefly withdrew support. The coalition finally collapsed in late November 1997 as the Congress party again withdrew its support for the United Front government.

This new instability is the direct result of a second revolution in

10. Subhadra Menon, "A Legal Blow," *India Today,* January 31, 1997, p. 80.

India—what V.S. Naipaul has termed "a million mutinies now."[11] This is a revolution dictated by the logic of democratic politics and should be familiar to American readers.[12]

Before independence, India had the greatest gap in the world between rich and poor, between high status (e.g., high-caste Brahmins) and low status (e.g., India's millions of untouchables, backward castes, and tribes). It also had regions of very high income and literacy, and relatively emancipated women, and regions of appalling poverty and very low literacy, especially among girls and women.[13] Slowly at first, but accelerated by state intervention and quota systems, a second revolution has taken place in India—one in which the very lowest untouchable castes (now called Dalits) can aspire to government and private jobs, administrative positions, and political power.

This second revolution has been characterized by Indian scholars and journalists as a "churning" whereby the lowest castes and social groups aspire to higher positions, toppling old political alignments, creating mass migrations (as they move in search of better jobs and living conditions), and generally being drawn into the political process. The instability and incoherence, let alone the corruption, of sequential governments at the center and in important states is directly due to this social revolution. New, rude groups have come to power, unschooled in the niceties of parliamentary debate or the laws against corruption. Parts of India resemble America's Wild West or some of the most corrupt southern states during the height of Jim Crow. Many of India's cities no longer resemble the orderly cantonment-dominated British Indian metropoles so much as the corrupt, violent, machine-dominated cities of nineteenth-century Britain or early twentieth-century America.

The functioning and composition of Delhi's current United Front (UF) coalition is shaped by this second revolution. As the UF government demonstrated, Indian high-caste elites, drawn primarily from north India, no longer dominate national governments. In effect, parliament and the Cabinet are now genuinely representative of India's linguistic, cultural and religious diversity. With individuals from every corner represented in the Cabinet, the nation has been bound together in a fashion that significantly reduces its disintegrative potential. In contrast to the era of a Congress party government dominated by high-caste Brahmins, the UF government did not have a single Brahmin Cabinet minister. In contrast to an era when the Congress party, under Indira Gandhi, meddled in the

11. V.S. Naipaul, *India: A Million Mutinies Now* (New York: Penguin Books, 1992).

12. If the reader can imagine an America where, simultaneously, the civil rights movement was at its height in the South and the urban North had to accommodate a massive inflow of immigrants, he or she would have some idea of the second or "cultural" revolution underway in India right now.

13. The most prosperous areas of India included some of the princely states, others of which were some of the most backward and regressive.

most trivial affairs in the states, the states' chief ministers now influence the center's policies.

Further, the extraordinarily smooth transition in 1997 from one United Front prime minister (the rustic H.D. Deve Gowda) to another (the suave but politically vulnerable I. K. Gujral) showed the underlying robustness of some of India's political institutions. A minority government has continued the economic reform strategies begun by P. V. Narasimha Rao; it has pursued a significant new strategic initiative toward India's neighbors (the "Gujral Doctrine"); and it has defied the United States on the Comprehensive Test-Ban Treaty (CTBT). These foreign-policy steps have received wide support from other parties, indicating that a broad consensus remains on foreign and security policies among Indian politicians, although foreign policy has lost its importance, compared with trade and investment policy, for all political parties. Far more significant than this defiance of the West was the United Front's elevation of India's vice president, the distinguished ex-diplomat K. R. Narayanan, born a Dalit, to the presidency of the country.

STRATEGY AND SECURITY

These momentous internal developments preoccupy India's political elite, both at the center and, emphatically, in the state capitals. However, an important strategic elite, concentrated almost entirely in New Delhi, does continue to discuss India's larger role in the world, its relations with the United States, and its possible emergence as a great power.

The pivotal state model suggests that after the end of the Cold War, security threats to pivotal states have shifted from external to internal sources. This is not quite true of India, which has always faced a powerful combination of genuine external and internal threats. The possibility of an India-Pakistan conflict remains fairly significant (and the regional consequences of war would be graver than in 1965 or even than in 1971, when Pakistan was split in two). Further, despite adroit diplomacy, most of the Indian strategic community shares the view of many others along China's periphery that the massive economic transformation of the People's Republic of China (PRC) has threatening foreign-policy implications. After Taiwan, India has the most significant border/territorial disputes with the PRC of any of its neighbors.[14] Exacerbating India's strategic vulnerability to China is the collapse of a quasi-ally, the Soviet

14. Despite recent improvements in relations with the PRC, which have included the adoption of a series of confidence- and security-building measures (CSBMs), some Indian elites have considerable misgivings about the PRC. For a discussion of CSBMs along the Sino–Indian border, see Sumit Ganguly and Ted Greenwood, eds., *Mending Fences: Confidence- and Security-Building Measures in South Asia* (Boulder: Westview Press, 1996).

Union, a source of military technology as well as diplomatic support.

Although this chapter focuses on India as a pivotal state in terms of American interests, it must also be noted that India has its own pivots. Nepal is seen as a critical buffer between India and China, and Indian strategists worry that a weak or collapsing Nepal might provide opportunities for direct Chinese interference in South Asia. They hold the same view of Bangladesh. In the case of Nepal, Bangladesh, and Sri Lanka, it is widely appreciated in India that the collapse of any one of these states, or a spell of instability, would be detrimental to vital Indian interests. These concerns, first and foremost, stem from the fact that almost all of India's neighbors have overlapping ethnic, linguistic, and cultural ties with India itself. The Sri Lankan conflict has created enormous problems for India in the southern state of Tamil Nadu. The Bhutan-Nepal conflict over Nepali-speaking Bhutanese resulted in the expulsion of one hundred thousand Nepali-speakers into north India. Bangladeshis pour into eastern India in vast numbers seeking work and have even been formed into vote banks in such distant cities as New Delhi, where they are registered by local politicians.[15] Moreover, the vulnerability of these states invites outsiders: Chinese "meddling" in Nepal; American, Israeli, and Pakistani "meddling" in Sri Lanka; and so on.

The one case where some Indians might welcome political disintegration would be that of Pakistan. Although Indian strategists proclaim that they would not want to incorporate a state of 110 million Muslims into India itself, Pakistan is the only regional military rival of India. A Pakistan disassembled into its constituent linguistic components would present no direct military threat to New Delhi. Such a strategy might have been feasible before 1990 (and may have been part of the near-war crisis of 1987), but Indian leaders now understand that a broken Pakistan might still have access to nuclear weapons and the incentive to use them against New Delhi. Like North Korea or Iraq, a collapsing Pakistan could create unimaginable horrors for its immediate neighbors.

India's strategic importance beyond its own region has been debated for decades. The Indian strategic community, of course, tends to hold Indocentric perceptions of the strategic importance of the state and the region. They argue that India is not only a Central Asian power, but that since it abuts two of the richest regions of the world—the oil-generating and unstable Middle East and the immensely productive Southeast Asia—

---

15. This is exactly the way in which illegal Mexican immigrants are integrated into Chicago's economy and politics.

it must be treated as a major state.[16] However, many Americans have been less convinced of India's (and South Asia's) strategic importance. India was seen as part of a larger containment strategy during the Cold War, and neither the China-firsters (such as Dean Rusk, who had served in the China-Burma-India theater during World War II), nor the Europe-firsters (such as Dean Acheson, George Kennan, or Henry Kissinger) thought much of India or South Asia. The Indo-Pakistani crisis of 1990 has somewhat altered that perception, because the world's second post-Hiroshima nuclear crisis may have taken place in South Asia in the spring of that year.[17] The recent official American view has been that the Kashmir dispute could lead to a significant conventional war between India and Pakistan and that since both have, or could soon assemble, nuclear weapons, the region could be the site of a nuclear war between the two states. South Asia is the only region where two hostile, nuclear-armed pivotal states confront each other. Our estimate is that the risks of a nuclear war are considerably greater (and in American terms, the interests at stake are somewhat higher) in Northeast Asia than in South Asia.

However, although these concerns preoccupy India's Delhi-centered strategic community, they are somewhat peripheral for most politicians and most voters. The typical Indian politician is quick to assert his or her patriotism and support a "strong" India—one that does not yield to pressure or give up one ounce of its sovereignty—but most Indian political leaders are consumed by domestic politics. At best, they realize that the new economic reforms and the move toward a market economy will increase their piece of the economic pie and make their state or caste somewhat better off. Thus, the typical political leader in India is disinterested in foreign policy—but, significantly, is also uninterested in breaking away from India itself. As noted above, there have been separatist movements in the country earlier, but these have tended to arise among minorities located in a border area where there was sympathy or active support coming from the other side.

16. They argue that the continent-size India is a strategic prize in itself; this view was held by Walt W. Rostow, who in the 1960s and 1970s put forward the proposition that the United States had to resist communism in Vietnam because if it fell, then other "dominoes" would fall, one by one, until India, the greatest prize of them all in Asia, would succumb to communism.
17. We now have two very different accounts of the crisis: One by Seymour Hersh, "On the Nuclear Edge" (*New Yorker,* March 29, 1993), quotes senior CIA officials to the effect that this was the most serious crisis involving nuclear weapons since the Cuban Missile Crisis. The other is a Stimson Center report, in which several individuals associated with the crisis play it down. A study in progress by an international team of scholars is likely to conclude that the former view is closer to the truth, although for reasons which the U.S. government was unaware of at the time.

Thus, although it is self-evident that a breakdown in India would have a profound impact on all of South Asia, India is not likely to disintegrate, plunging South Asia and adjacent regions into crisis.[18] It is not a "tippy" state, even though it appears at times to be in chaos. If anything, the two most likely scenarios follow different paths: One would be the collapse of one of India's neighbors, triggering a race between India and other powers for influence among the ruins of a failed state; the second would be the gradual escalation of tension and conflict between India and Pakistan (or India and China), leading to a regional and perhaps wider conflict—but this would not stem from the key factors suggested by the idea of a pivotal state.

To summarize, our estimates of India's economic, political, social, and strategic capabilities are, on balance, sanguine. In terms of economic levels and gross developmental indicators, India is a "weak" pivotal state; its fragility is also emphasized by its high levels of social violence, migration, environmental degradation, and so forth. However, this ignores the very uneven way in which development takes place in this megacountry. It is as if Mexico and the United States were one state; gross levels would be averaged out, but the total capacity of the state to project power or to retain control over dissident or separatist regions might well be maintained at a very high level. To extend the comparison a bit further, imagine a U.S.–Mexico state that had a powerful but hostile Canada to the north as well as a powerful and hostile enemy to the south, and that was undergoing a domestic social revolution at the same time. There has been no radical shift in the source of threat (as seen from New Delhi), nor can we conclude that the capacity of the Indian state to deal with threats from either direction has diminished. The crucial factor in India's case is the coherence of its politics and institutions, not its gross levels of economic development or air pollution.

India is not a "hot spot," but perhaps it is a "hot subcontinent." Its regions are in a state of social revolution, but it is a revolution framed by a set of well-understood rules of the game. Until now, skillful political management has been able to keep antagonistic or separatist forces in check; Indian politics is becoming even more complex as the "churning" process continues, but this is oddly stabilizing also. Many groups are now entering the political arena for the first time, but their expectations are quite modest, and it is evident that they are satisfied with a slow but steady expansion of the economy. It is unlikely that in the next

18. And even if it did, one could ask, as some have, "What difference would that make to vital or important American interests?" We will return to this question later in this essay.

five to ten years the accommodative, marginally expanding Indian political system will not be able to cope with these new demands and pressures, but it is also unlikely that the country as a whole will be inclined to move outward, so consumed will it be with internal changes.

AMERICAN PERCEPTIONS AND POLICY

India is a strong, or at least potentially strong, pivotal state in terms of the dimensions set forth in this project. However, American policy has usually treated India in terms of its weaknesses and disintegrative potential. Although there were brief spells of strategic cooperation (just after the Sino-Indian war of 1962) and moments when India was thought to be strategically hostile (in the 1980s, when Delhi was seen by some as Moscow's strategic partner), administration after administration has supported India's economic and social development, invariably arguing that massive foreign and technical assistance was necessary to promote economic growth; in turn, this growth was important for the sustenance of Indian democracy. Even though India was a chronic nuisance to the United States in the United Nations and stood aloof or was hostile to American policies in Korea, Vietnam, Europe, the Middle East, and various disarmament forums, it was the largest recipient of developmental assistance for many years. It was India's collapse, not the possibility of strategic cooperation, that generated American interest.

This was not the view of the *Indian* strategic elite for more than fifty years.[19] In their view (quite similar to Samuel Huntington's notion of civilizational entities), India is destined to play a great role in the world.[20] Although India had to accept economic assistance for many years, the goal of this elite has been economic and strategic autarky, rooted in the belief that great states are not dependent states. Indians have always been less worried about the integrity of their own country than about the weakness and vulnerabilities of their neighbors and how outside powers may use those weak states to undercut India. Since the United States has often had large economic and military assistance programs in Pakistan, as well as

19. One of the authors of this chapter is writing a book on different perceptions of South Asian security; two chapters are devoted to India. For a summary see the relevant sections in Stephen P. Cohen, "America and India: A New Approach," *American Defense Annual, 1996–1997*, ed. Williamson Murray and Allan R. Millett (Washington D.C.: Brassey's, 1996), ch. 7.

20. The *locus classicus* of the Indian view is in Nehru's writings, but the same theme of a great Indian civilization-state has been a central tenet of conservative Hindu political groups. For Huntington's view of civilizations see Samuel P. Huntington, *The Clash of Civilizations and the Remaking of World Order* (New York: Simon and Schuster, 1997).

economic aid programs in other regional countries, American regional goals are suspect; Indians fear that the United States is a false friend because it continues to support states (China and Pakistan in particular) that resist India's natural regional dominant position.

Further, the Indian strategic community's view of the United States and China is quite at variance with the self-image of these two states as they approach South Asia. The United States in particular falls into the category of a state that is politically hostile, militarily and economically powerful, but physically distant. Washington is at best careless, at worse malevolent, and usually unpredictable—it can influence South Asia without even intending to. Yet it is very difficult for Indians to influence the United States.[21]

In the abstract, classical realpolitik (and rational choice theory) would suggest that it does not matter what the elite of a state such as India thinks about its Great Power status or whether they believe their country to be a failing state or a successful one. *American* policy makers should be able to come to an objective assessment of the importance of a state and assign it a position in the hierarchy of nations and within its region. This assessment is determined by American interests and concerns—not by the self-image of foreign leaders. Such an approach should avoid the pitfalls of clientitis—an excessive identification with the perspective and views of another state and the consequent warping of judgment about the importance of that state.

In practice, the objective measures used by many American analysts and policy makers—income, military power, economic and strategic capabilities, and so forth—provide at best a bare-bones framework and at worst a misleading basis for prediction. The American assessment of where India stands in relation to its neighbors, and with other important countries, often differs from the assessment by India's strategic elite. That elite's self-image may be unrealistic, or wrongheaded, or incapable of achievement—but it is what drives India. This has been especially the case in recent years, when vital domestic political considerations have become a significant factor in India's foreign policy. India's opposition to the CTBT, for example, was not predicted by any American expert, but after the fact it was clear that the United Front coalition was willing to reverse forty-five years of professed foreign policy to accommodate alliance partners and significant opposition parties.

Perceptions are important. Distance and unfamiliarity with a foreign culture exacerbate the problem of understanding India, as does the prick-

---

21. The Indians are trying to learn the game. Recently, one distinguished Indian-American was jailed as a result of an Indian Embassy attempt to illegally influence American congressmen.

ly independence of the Indian strategic elite.[22] American and Indian perceptions of India's "rightful" place in the world have not been congruent for most of the past fifty years, and the end of the Cold War did not improve the situation.

POLICY IMPLICATIONS

Americans need to understand what Indians are very much aware of: that, despite India's considerable military and strategic capabilities and the significant economic reforms now in place that will ultimately enhance those capabilities, India is likely to be distracted by its internal revolution for the near future. This revolution is deceptive because it conveys an impression of chaos and weakness, but India has demonstrated a remarkable capability for accommodation and change. Its political elites understand that force can be counterproductive, and its own political history teaches that accommodation and adjustment can in the long run create a stronger whole.

This suggests that the United States will not have many opportunities for a "grand coalition" with India and that India's foreign and strategic policies will continue to be made with one eye on domestic consequences, especially if there continues to be a series of weak governments in power in New Delhi. Indian prime ministers are likely to look for areas of cooperation with the United States, but not at the risk of angering coalition partners. Nor, however, are they likely to engage in adventures of the sort that characterized Indian policy in the 1980s under Indira Gandhi and Rajiv Gandhi.

India thus only partially matches up with the pivotal state model. It is not likely to fail economically and thus does not need foreign aid: It has become a major aid donor in its own right, though it does need foreign investment and access to foreign, especially American, markets. It is not likely to fail politically, creating chaos in South Asia and adjacent regions. Nor, however, is it likely to "emerge" as a major international player as long as it is highly dependent on foreign investment and as long as its domestic political revolution is underway.

Further, the Cold War–derived American policies of the more distant and even the recent past do not "fit" the region, nor do they further the diverse American interests in South Asia.[23] Up to 1990 South Asia was

22. Similarly, it was difficult for Americans to appreciate European resistance to various doctrines of "limited nuclear war" and fighting the first round of a war with the Soviet Union on European territory.
23. For a totally honest discussion of the impact of the Cold War on American policy with the Third World see Peter Rodman (a former aide to Henry Kissinger and a high-level American policy maker in the Reagan and Bush administrations), *More Precious than Peace: The Cold War and the Struggle for the Third World* (New York: Scribner's, 1994).

largely seen as an adjunct to the Cold War. America intermittently supported Pakistan in an attempt to balance Soviet influence; in turn, this led
India to explore a Soviet connection, although India was in virtual alliance
with both Moscow and Washington against Beijing after the Sino-Indian
war of 1962. All through the Cold War, quite apart from the strategic
approach to India and Pakistan, the United States sustained interest in the
economic development of the region, and India in particular received
massive amounts of economic grant aid and technical assistance.

These twin concerns, strategic partnership and economic development, changed dramatically after the end of the Cold War. With the withdrawal of the Soviet Union from Afghanistan, the region's strategic value
plummeted to zero. American thinking on economic issues came around
to the view that the reform of the Indian and Pakistani economies was
more likely to bear fruit than mere aid—which in any case was dwindling
rapidly. Thus, the value of India and Pakistan was much lower after the
end of the Cold War than during it, indirectly *heightening* the risk of a
regional conflict.

Indeed, one striking fact about recent American policy is that there
was no coherent policy review toward India after the end of the Cold
War. There was no comprehensive survey of the several American interests embedded in India, let alone a strategy that might determine which
was more important and how more pressing or urgent interests could be
optimized without sacrificing less urgent but perhaps equally important
long-term interests. Instead, by default, a very few "global" issues with
regional manifestations came to dominate American policy almost to the
exclusion of all other concerns. The chief issue was nonproliferation,
although it was sometimes supplanted by assaults on regional states for
their human rights violations. From 1990 to 1994, American policy
toward India was on autopilot—steered almost entirely by global nonproliferation concerns and fanned by the fear that the spread of nuclear
weapons to South Asia (first made evident in the 1990 crisis) would lead
to a nuclear war.

If regional conflict alone were the stimulus for American policy, then
this would have led to very different policies than were attempted. Except
for a few failed efforts to get India and Pakistan to discuss their differences
over Kashmir and a very large, private NGO effort to promote confidence-building measures in the region,[24] American policy from 1994
onward has been driven mainly by the attempt to get India and Pakistan

---

24. There have been dozens of these, including two inconclusive efforts by the United States
    Institute of Peace; neither the Bush nor the first Clinton administration thought that
    there was much prospect for a more active American policy on Kashmir.

to adhere to the permanent extension of the Nuclear Nonproliferation Treaty (NPT) and then (in 1996) to the CTBT.

Of course neither effort had much chance of success, since both Islamabad and New Delhi see nuclear weapons (or the option to build and deploy them at short notice) as central to their national security. This basic fact was consciously dismissed as irrelevant or inconvenient by senior U.S. policy makers for four years, and only recently has some understanding of the linkage between treaty adherence and actual regional security problems penetrated into the senior levels of the American policy community. In the words of the recent Council on Foreign Relations Task Force, "the time has come to rethink the U.S. approach to the Indo-Pakistani nuclear rivalry."[25] However, American officials were less concerned with promoting regional stability, or influencing regional strategic decisions over the long run, than with getting treaty adherence in the short run.

Several terms introduced by American policy makers in this period indicate how badly they understood the region and how inept they were in formulating a policy for influencing India. For example, the Pentagon's "counterproliferation" strategy, developed after the war with Iraq, seemed to put India and Pakistan in the category of "rogue states."[26] No better excuse could be provided to hawks in New Delhi to argue for the acceleration of India's nuclear program, nor was there a better way of putting those who opposed proliferation in India on the defensive. Subsequently, the administration (again, with one eye on congressional critics) invented the phrase "cap, reduce, and eliminate" to describe its long-term strategy for Pakistan and India. Here, again, Americans seemed to be saying that eventually the two countries would have to give up their nuclear capabilities and that the present policy was merely a way station on the road to complete regional nuclear disarmament (without any commitment to applying such a policy to existing nuclear-weapons states).[27] Finally, American policy toward India (and Pakistan) frequently referred to the strategy of developing incentives and disincentives, "carrots and sticks," that would get the two countries to both roll back their nuclear programs and sign both the NPT and CTBT. As one Indian minister has suggested,

25. Richard N. Haass, chairman, and Gideon Rose, project director, *A New U.S. Policy Toward India and Pakistan*, Task Force Report, Council on Foreign Relations, 1997.

26. The remarks, at this time, of the former director of Central Intelligence that the dragon enemy of the United States had been supplanted by a world of "poisonous states" expressed this mindset perfectly.

27. Of course, the real audience for such statements was the American arms-control community, especially the nonproliferation true believers, and Congress, which made considerable funds available for the nonproliferation and counterproliferation efforts.

such language implies that you are dealing not with proud, sovereign people but with animals that need to be rewarded or beaten.

Indeed, if one wanted to encourage regional states to go nuclear, it would be harder to devise a more successful strategy than that promulgated after the triumph of American arms over Iraq. Not a few Indian and Pakistani observers noted that if Iraq had only waited until it had a nuclear weapon ready, then the United States would never have been able to put the alliance together. Both India and Pakistan need nuclear weapons for the same reason the United States needed them during the Cold War: to offset a hostile state whose conventional forces were superior. The shoe is now just on the other foot.

Fortunately, key American interests in South Asia have not been seriously damaged by these inept policies. It is not in the strategic interest of either India or Pakistan to overtly deploy a fabricated nuclear weapon or even to deploy provocative missiles, although both have the capability to do so.[28] Both sides have been very cautious in Kashmir: The Indians have refrained from hot pursuit, and Pakistan has pulled back on its support for Kashmiri militants. Both states are fighting a low-intensity war with each other through their respective intelligence agencies. Neither seems ready to escalate to regular conventional conflict. Indeed, the military establishments of both states have never been in worse shape: Equipment purchases have been cut back, defense spending on both sides is static, training is reduced, and block obsolescence has caught up with their air, naval, and ground forces.

Human rights issues remain a matter of concern, but primarily to the many regional human rights groups. India, faced with armed separatist movements that have turned New Delhi into the bomb capital of the world, has not been gentle with accused terrorists when they have been caught and has persuaded such groups as Amnesty International to change their one-sided assessments to include terrorist acts as violations of human rights. (Previously Amnesty International merely catalogued government deeds, on the grounds that such separatist groups were not "responsible," a policy that led many Indians to conclude that AI and other human-rights groups were anti-Indian.)

---

28. The present situation is one of a more or less stable plateau, or "nonweaponized deterrence." For discussions of the stability and wisdom of this arrangement, and what the United States might do to preserve stability, see the Council report cited in note 25, but also the several critical dissenting opinions by task force members. The issue was discussed in earlier reports by the Asia Society (especially *Preventing Nuclear Proliferation in South Asia*, 1994), and a report by the Carnegie Endowment for International Peace; for a book-length treatment see Stephen P. Cohen, ed., *Nuclear Proliferation in South Asia: The Prospects for Arms Control* (Boulder: Westview, 1991).

The human rights issue, particularly as it played out in Kashmir, often put India at loggerheads with the United States. The two countries still have sharp differences on other human rights issues, including the abolition of child labor. A recent Indian Supreme Court decision enjoining the central government to start enforcing existing child-labor laws may alleviate some of the tensions on this score.

The human rights arena was not the only area where the United States and India were at odds over the creation and enforcement of universally applicable regimes. U.S. efforts to forge new global regimes on such issues as world trade and environmental protection brought the two nations into conflict. U.S. negotiators were quite distressed with India's initial and strenuous objections to many features of both these regimes. Eventually, despite initial acrimonious exchanges, bilateral discussions and multilateral diplomacy have narrowed the differences. More to the point, India has, with some reservations, joined the formal multilateral arrangements in both these areas.[29] As the Indian economy modernizes and the country becomes more closely integrated with the global trading system, greater convergence between Indian and American positions is entirely likely. Differences, however, are sure to persist in the environmental arena. For most Indian decision makers, despite India's staggering problems of environmental degradation, the imperatives of rapid industrialization and economic growth have higher priority. Other issues are also important, for example the production of narcotics (40 percent of the heroin consumed in the United States comes from Afghanistan and Pakistan), the further reform of the Indian economy, and so forth.

However, America's strategic interests in the region have yet to be fully explored—so busy have officials been with persuading or coercing adherence to the NPT and CTBT.[30] The most important of these issues is the relationship of India with the People's Republic of China. They have, still, the longest contested border in the world, and neither side has shown any indication that it is ready for major compromises on its own territorial claims. (China claims all of India's northwest state of Arunachal Pradesh, although Indian forces occupy it today; Chinese

29. On the issue of global trade, in particular intellectual property rights , see Meheroo Jussawalla, *The Economics of Intellectual Property in a World without Frontiers* (New York: Greenwood Press, 1992). On the question of ozone depletion and the Montreal Protocol see Richard Elliot Benedick, *Ozone Diplomacy* (Cambridge, Mass.: Harvard University Press, 1991), and Peter M. Haas, Robert O. Keohane, and Mark A. Levy, eds., *Institutions for the Earth* (Cambridge, Mass.: MIT Press, 1993).

30. On this question, the Council Task Force wisely took an eclectic approach and refused to rank various American interests in South Asia.

forces occupy a major section of the Aksai Chin region to the west, claimed by India.) Although the two states have come to a limited accommodation on the pulling back of forces from the line of control, each holds considerable leverage against the other. China can resume support for separatist groups in India, or it can improve its relations with India's neighbors (above all, Pakistan—which it has supplied with nuclear and conventional military technology enabling Islamabad to contain India— but also Bangladesh, and, in an emerging contest, Myanmar). In turn, though still a weak power economically, India has provided a safe haven for hundreds of thousands of Tibetan refugees, many of whom would like to take up arms against the People's Republic and create an independent Tibet.

TOWARD A NEW POLICY

America's strategic absentmindedness after the end of the Cold War is quite impressive. Washington managed both to ignore and to alienate the second-largest country in the world for a good five years, although there are a few signs that the second Clinton administration will attempt a fresh start. If that is the case, then the following suggestions seem to flow from our analysis of India's position as neither a weak pivot nor a powerful global state. It is somewhere in between, of central importance to South Asia (a region with one-fifth of the world's population), but not yet of vital importance to the United States.

South Asia is probably the most important test of whether the United States can develop a foreign policy that gives proportionate attention to regions and states of differing interest. The pattern in the past has been that the biggest threats (North Korea, Iraq) get disproportionate attention, leading to the neglect of areas of opportunity or regions where a low-key, low-cost policy might advance a variety of lesser but still important U.S. interests. The following proposals build on several recent studies of American policy toward India—and the apparent emergence of a consensus, at least among the nonofficial observers of the region.

First, the United States needs to organize itself in such a way that middle powers such as India receive the appropriate level of attention and interest. Although the Department of State has granted South Asia its own separate bureau, no other government agency has followed suit; *in every other case the region is tucked into a Near East bureau.* On any given day, the Israel-Arab-Palestine problem, or Iraq, or Iran, or inter-Arab issues will absorb virtually all of the attention of senior officials in such a bureau or division.[31] South Asia receives high-level attention only when it appears to be on the verge of a crisis. Those who "work" the region are sometimes tempted to exaggerate the risk of a nuclear or conventional war to attract the attention of otherwise uninterested policy makers. The best place to begin organizational reform would be in the National Security Council, with the appointment of a full-time staff member to watch over the India (and Pakistan) portfolio.

Second, the ability of the United States to deal with India "normally" is constrained by a very complex web of legislation designed to prevent India from becoming a nuclear-weapons state or to punish it if it were to take that step. Much of this legislation is irrelevant to our attempt to influence India (and Pakistan, for that matter) and needs to be adjusted systematically so that policy makers can provide assistance to the Indian civilian nuclear power program (one of the most dangerous on earth), to sell dual-use technology, and to expand military-to-military cooperation. This adjustment could be undertaken in a series of legislative exemptions, in amendment form, to present legislation. This, however, presupposes intensive legislative-executive discussions on such changes.

This would help clear the air for the exploration of long-term strategic commonalities between Washington and New Delhi. The Council on Foreign Relations Task Force advocated a closer strategic relationship between the two countries. This could involve their policies toward China, international peacekeeping activities, or even the problem of a failing, nuclear-armed Pakistan. However, one dissent to that report suggested that India might not be ready for such strategic cooperation. This is something that can be determined only by dialogue and discussion, and by actual cooperation when the opportunity arises. (India did break with past policies during the gulf war by providing military refueling rights to American aircraft and has recently been engaged in extensive military-to-military cooperation with the United States—unimaginable ten years ago.)

The United States could prepare itself to assume a more active role in helping India and its neighbors, especially Pakistan, reach an accommodation on their apparently central dispute over Kashmir. We have used the term "apparently" because the India-Pakistan conflict rests on other factors as well. Kashmir is the source of conflict, but it also symbolizes deeper differences between the two countries. The United Front government did not attempt a rapprochement with Pakistan because of the latter's

31. On the other hand, the Pentagon has compounded the problem of developing a coherent regional strategy by making Pakistan the responsibility of CENTCOM (located in Florida), whereas India falls within the coverage of CINCPAC (located in Hawaii). Thus, to some American officials, India lies on the western frontier of the Pacific basin; to others it is a southern appendage to the Middle East region.

inchoate politics, although it did announce a more liberal visa policy for Pakistani scholars and journalists. However, the United Front government moved boldly to accommodate Bangladeshi concerns on the sharing of river water (exploiting the agreement to move ahead to cooperation on antiterrorism); it also normalized relations with Nepal and Sri Lanka.

The United States has applauded these small steps, but it can do more. It has been reluctant to enter the Kashmir conflict directly, but it should be ready, in cooperation with other major powers, when and if the moment comes, to offer its services to both sides, perhaps as a guarantor of a final agreement on Kashmir, perhaps by providing satellite and other forms of verification of an agreement, perhaps by offering economic inducements should the two sides reach an accommodation. The American experience with peace processes elsewhere is a useful asset.

What the United States need not do in enhancing its relationship with India is sacrifice a long-standing relationship with Pakistan. Precisely because the latter has been in political chaos, and may well conform to this project's definition of a pivotal state, important American interests are at stake in Pakistan. Many of these overlap with vital Indian interests, not least the risk that India would face from a last-ditch Pakistani "Masada"-style nuclear attack. Indian interests, and those of the United States, are best served by a long-term strategic accommodation with Pakistan. An American connection with Islamabad, even including military sales, can be of value to India. However, those sales would need to be judged carefully to avoid the impression in India and Pakistan that the United States is either balancing these states (they are not equal, and America has different interests in each) or using one to undercut the other.

Finally, American policy makers, who have for so long ignored India and India's potential as a limited partner in a variety of strategic or international circumstances (especially peacekeeping), must not expect too much too soon from a country that is groping economically and in the throes of a domestic political revolution. South Asia has attracted fresh American attention. The undersecretary of state and the secretary of state have already visited India, and at the time of this writing (February 1998) a presidential visit was being planned. Such visits force serious consideration of a region, with the concomitant risk that after ignoring South Asia for many years (or paying attention to it because of peripheral or secondary reasons), the United States might come to expect too much by way of strategic cooperation. What the United States can expect is limited cooperation in a number of international forums where American and Indian interests intersect. For example, India's willingness to accede to the Montreal Protocol of 1985 was deemed crucial to the success of the multilateral negotiations on the protection of the global environment. Currently, the success of ongoing global negotiations on trade liberalization depends, in no small measure, on India's acquiescence. The United States and India (and Pakistan) have a shared interest in maintaining the status quo in the vital oil-producing areas of the Persian Gulf and in ensuring stability in Central Asia, where there is the prospect of vast new energy sources. Yet it would be wrong for American officials to travel to New Delhi with the expectation that they will find a willing and eager partner. It will take several years of dialogue, of getting to know one another, before serious cooperation can be contemplated. India is likely to remain, for the duration of the current Clinton administration, a state that has not yet realized its potential. But looking beyond the next few years to the time when India's economy grows to world-class size and it has passed through its domestic political revolution, India may turn out to be a strong candidate as America's chief economic, strategic, and even ideological partner in southern Asia.

PAKISTAN

Hasan-Askari Rizvi*

Pakistan can be viewed as a pivotal state for U.S. purposes on a number of counts. The first reason is that it forms one side of a critical strategic duo in the international arena. As East and West Germany were to each other, as South and North Korea are to each other, and as Russia and Ukraine are to each other, Pakistan and its subcontinental "twin," India, are coeval; moreover, they contain one-fifth of humanity. It would therefore be impossible for America to have a coherent and focused "Pakistan policy" without an equally sensible "India policy," and vice-versa. This, at least, has long been recognized by professional diplomats and strategists (if not by politicians) in Washington, who see that Pakistan's strategic location and proximity to regions traditionally important to U.S. foreign-policy considerations assign considerable weight to this pivotal state.

Second, Pakistan has successfully employed its Islamic identity to establish political, economic, and security linkages with the Muslim world, especially the Middle East and the Persian Gulf region, which has added to its diplomatic clout. At a time when extremist Islamic movements are threatening many regimes in the Muslim world and there is often talk of Islamic "fundamentalism" or "orthodoxy," Pakistan represents a relatively moderate and democracy-oriented face of Islam, and it has traditionally maintained cordial relations with the West. Pakistan can facilitate a dialogue between the Islamic world, especially the Islamic movements, and the West.

Third, Pakistan is one of the populous countries of the world, with an annual population growth of 2.8 to 3 percent. From the viewpoint of reducing the increases in global population totals, Pakistan is third in importance only to China and India. Yet if due attention is not given to social development, and if natural resources are not effectively managed, the population "bomb" can threaten peace and stability in Pakistan, with ramifications for other countries. By the same token, however, this large

* [Editors' note: see note at the beginning of the India essay.]

population offers a market that becomes ever more important as trade and investment drive increasing global interaction. Pakistan also has a highly professional, qualified, and skilled work force that has performed excellently inside the country and elsewhere.

Fourth, Pakistan is directly relevant to urgent U.S. agendas concerning narcotics control, containment of transnational terrorism, and nuclear weapons nonproliferation, the last especially so in the aftermath of Pakistan's nuclear tests in the spring of 1998. In all these respects, a pro-American Pakistan could play a positive role, whereas a disgruntled and alienated Pakistan might be a major "spoiler." This also has a bearing on neighboring territories. Pakistan stands as a bulwark against the unrest and instability that have engulfed southern Tajikistan and Afghanistan. If Pakistan collapses for one reason or another, the whole region will be overwhelmed by chaos and disorder, thereby threatening U.S. policy on narcotics and terrorism.

Finally, given the ongoing adversarial relationship between India and Pakistan, a constant engagement between the U.S. and Pakistan on socioeconomic issues and security affairs can help to moderate Pakistan's India policy and keep its tensions with India within manageable limits. This would facilitate the general U.S. goal of promoting peace and stability in the region which, in turn, would give a boost to participatory governance and the liberalization of the economy in both Pakistan and India. Finding ways, whether direct or indirect, to assist this more favorable outcome is clearly in America's best interests.

GEOGRAPHIC LOCATION

Pakistan shares frontiers with two important Asian states, China and India, and before the disintegration of the Soviet Union it was separated from that country by a narrow strip of Afghanistan. Pakistan inherited its northwestern border with Afghanistan from the British Indian empire. Afghanistan attracted British attention due to Britain's distrust of Russia, going back to the nineteenth century. A combination of a strong military posture, the use of Afghanistan as a buffer, and constant diplomatic maneuvering ensured the security of the British Empire vis-à-vis imperial Russia and later the Soviet Union. This territory was not just the Indian frontier, but the most vulnerable frontier of the whole Empire.[1]

1. The Simon Commission (1930) appointed by the British government to make recommendations on constitutional and political changes in India refused to hand over the control of defense affairs to Indians on the ground that the defense of the Indian empire, especially its northwestern frontier (the India-Afghan border), was crucial to the security of the empire as a whole. The northwestern frontier was, in the opinion of the Commission, a frontier of "the first importance from the military point of view for the whole empire." See *Report of the Indian Statutory Commission, 1930*, vol. II, 173–175.

The northwestern frontier continued to be important in the context of the Cold War due to its proximity to the Soviet Union. Pakistan's participation in U.S.–sponsored alliances in the mid-1950s was therefore viewed as directly relevant to American containment policy. Pakistan's geographic location gained additional strategic importance with the Soviet military intervention in Afghanistan in December 1979. Pakistan played a key role in implementing the Western policy of countering Soviet attempt to subdue Afghanistan. It offered sanctuary to Afghan resistance groups; facilitated material support for these groups by the West and by conservative Arab states; cooperated with the U.S. in security affairs, including the sharing of intelligence on Afghanistan; and extended humanitarian assistance to Afghan refugees in Pakistan with the support of the international community.

The end of the Cold War and the disintegration of the Soviet Union have changed the geostrategic environment, but Pakistan continues to be important due to its proximity to the newly independent states of Central Asia and post-Soviet Afghanistan. Independence came to the states of Central Asia suddenly and in the absence of a popular movement with that goal. These states are now engaged in forming their independent identities and are endeavoring to address their socioeconomic problems, both of which are proving to be uphill tasks. Pakistan, being a neighboring state, could possibly contribute to the efforts of these countries to achieve prosperity and peace.

Pakistan also shares an important four-hundred-mile-long frontier with China in the Kashmir-Xinjiang region. The first road link between the two countries was inaugurated in 1971. It was later upgraded to international standards and an all-weather road, the Karakoram Highway (KKH), which passes through the most rugged mountainous terrain along the traditional silk route.[2] It connects China's Xinjiang Province with Pakistan's northern areas, thereby providing a road link from Xinjiang to the Middle East and the Arabian Sea. Though the KKH was designed to improve communication and trade, its strategic importance cannot be ignored. It can be used for troop movement and, with some upgrading, could also take heavy armor and large-size container trucks. In addition to trade and passenger traffic, the mail from Xinjiang to Saudi Arabia and Turkey comes to Pakistan though this route. A good number of Chinese Muslims take this road to Islamabad, Pakistan, then continue by air to Saudi Arabia for the annual pilgrimage.

2. For an in-depth study of road construction in Pakistan's northern areas, see Mahnaz Z. Ispahani, *Roads and Rivals: The Political Uses of Access in the Borderlands of Asia* (Ithaca, N.Y., and London: Cornell University Press, 1989).

Pakistan and China have maintained cordial relations since the early 1960s and have generally been supportive of each other's foreign-policy goals. Pakistan served as a useful link between China and the rest of the world at a time when the United States was bent on isolating China. The political and economic relations that China cultivated with Pakistan helped to ease the rigors of isolation, and China cited its ties with Pakistan to demonstrate its desire to develop mutually beneficial relations with non-Marxist states. This also gave Pakistan a counterweight against India and Russia, which obviously comforted successive governments in Islamabad but deepened Indian mistrust.

Proximity to the gulf region and the multifaceted political, economic, and security links that Pakistan has cultivated with those Arab states have added to its diplomatic clout, and connect it to issues of security and stability in that vital region. Though one can talk of historical and cultural bonds between Pakistan and the gulf area, effective economic and security ties really developed only in the 1970s, making Pakistan perhaps the only non-Arab developing state with influence in these countries.

THE NATIONAL IDENTIFICATION WITH ISLAM

This proximity factor has been reinforced by Pakistan's projection of its Islamic identity in foreign policy. This fits well with the consciousness that has now developed among the Muslim states to assert their "Islamic-ness" in global affairs, enabling Pakistan to build relations with these countries at both bilateral and multilateral levels. Pakistan's importance here can be measured by the fact that, despite various disputes among themselves, all Muslim states are equally supportive of Pakistan's independence and territorial integrity. Their diplomatic and material support certainly helped Pakistan to recover from the military debacle and dismemberment of 1971. Since then, Pakistan has maintained close interaction with these states, and their overall diplomatic support has been a source of strength for Pakistan in its problems with India. Some of the oil-rich countries such as Saudi Arabia, Kuwait, the United Arab Emirates (UAE), Libya, and prerevolution Iran have extended material assistance to Pakistan in the form of grants, interest-free loans, investment in joint industrial projects, financial contribution to health care and educational projects, and humanitarian-relief assistance. Pakistan is a founder-member of, and very active in, the Organization of the Islamic Conference (OIC), the largest and the most important forum of the Muslim states. On March 23, 1997, the OIC held an extraordinary summit conference in Islamabad to commemorate the fiftieth anniversary of Pakistan's independence. Pakistan is also a member of the Economic Cooperation Organization (ECO), which includes Iran, Turkey, Afghanistan, and the states of Central Asia.

Pakistan's Islamic identity has great significance when one examines its security-related linkages with a number of Muslim states, including the gulf sheikhdoms, Saudi Arabia, Jordan, Libya, and Syria. Security relations with countries such as Saudi Arabia and Jordan go back to the mid- and late 1960s, when bilateral protocols of cooperation were signed. Pakistan cultivated similar relations with the others in the 1970s. Since then Pakistan has offered varying degrees of support in the security field to most gulf states. It has provided training facilities for their military personnel in Pakistan; made Pakistani military personnel available to these states for training and support assignments, and in certain cases for active security duties; and sold weapons.

Until the early 1980s, the sultanate of Oman recruited Baloch youths directly by sending its recruiting teams to Baluchistan, a province of Pakistan.[3] This practice has now been discontinued, but a large number of Baloch are serving in the Oman army. Libya used to have a strong Pakistani presence in the military and civilian sectors, although this has since been drastically reduced due to Libya's unstable foreign policy and its financial problems. However, Pakistan continues to maintain a reasonably comfortable relationship with Libya, including a limited presence of Pakistani personnel.

In addition, Iran and Turkey are two non-Arab Middle Eastern states with which Pakistan has had close interaction, dating back to the early years of its independence. The present-day Islamic leadership in Iran periodically gets perturbed both by Pakistan's relations with the United States and Islamabad's support to the Taliban in Afghanistan. However, both Iran and Pakistan recognize geographic and economic realities and continue to seek smooth and cordial interaction. Finally, Pakistan has maintained economic and trade relations, including cooperation in scientific and technological fields, with the Muslim states of Africa and Southeast Asia.

Pakistan's important place in the Muslim world thus adds a new dimension to the idea of its being a pivotal state. It also has significant linguistic, commercial, and historic relations with Europe and North America, giving it the potential to serve as a bridge between the West and the Muslim world. This could be an asset at a time when the Muslim world is endeavoring to carve out an autonomous role for itself in the international system, and while a host of conflicts and misunderstandings exist between some Muslim states and the West. Moreover, it is likely that the grass-

3. For details of Pakistan's interaction with the gulf region and the Middle East, see Hasan-Askari Rizvi, *Pakistan and the Geostrategic Environment: A Study of Foreign Policy* (New York: St. Martin's, 1993), 12, 70–84.

roots and populist Islamic movements will become more important in the twenty-first century, since they have already developed strong ties among the common people and are actively building nonstate institutions. This makes them an important element in civil society, capable of influencing, if not dominating, the state. To prevent such movements from taking a strongly anti-Western direction, a constant engagement with the outside world is needed that will cultivate mutual understanding and smooth interaction. Because of its Islamic credentials and connections on the one hand, and its link with the West on the other, Pakistan can be instrumental in facilitating such a dialogue.

Consistent and positive policies can be expected to emanate from Islamabad, however, only if the country makes progress in three different (though related) areas: improving its security parameters, nourishing democracy, and dealing with its social and demographic challenges.

THE SECURITY PARAMETERS

Pakistan's eastern neighbor India, with which it shares a border of about 2,250 kilometers, looms large in Pakistan's security perspective. Their bilateral relations have been marked by mutual distrust and antagonism, although there have been periods of relative cordiality in their interaction. This pattern is shaped by a host of factors which include, among other things, the legacy of the quarrels of the preindependence period; the compounding impact of the negative developments in the postindependence period, especially in the early years; the wars of 1948, 1965, and 1971; and a sharp divergence in their viewpoints on the regional power structure. Pakistan's security perceptions have also been shaped by Afghanistan's irredentist claims on Pakistani territory and the intermittent border clashes between the two countries in the 1950s and the 1960s. Their diplomatic relations were severed twice, in 1955 and 1962.

Pakistan thus developed a deep sense of insecurity from the early years, and the search for security from external threats emerged as *the* cardinal concern of its foreign and defense policies, with ramifications also for domestic politics.[4] Pakistan adopted two strategies to deal with the security dilemma: first, the augmentation of military security against the perceived external threats, and the strengthening of Pakistan's long-term security arrangements; and, second, the use of diplomacy to offset India's

---

4. For studies of problems and difficulties in Pakistan's relations with India and Pakistan's defense problems, see Pervaiz Iqbal Cheema, *Pakistan's Defence Policy, 1947–58* (London: Macmillan, 1990); Sumit Ganguly, *The Origins of War in South Asia: Indo-Pakistan Conflicts Since 1947* (Boulder: Westview, 1988); and G. W. Choudhury, *Pakistan's Relations with India* (New York: Praeger, 1968).

military superiority. The allocation of more resources for defense, procurement of weapons from abroad, and the strengthening of extraregional and Muslim-world ties were high on Pakistan's list of priorities. It
was due to these reasons that Pakistan willingly joined the U.S.–sponsored security arrangements of the 1950s, hoping this would facilitate the
transfer of much-needed weapons and secure American diplomatic support in its disputes with India and Afghanistan.

Security issues have shaped all the subsequent shifts in Pakistan's foreign policy. Whether it was the decision to cultivate expanded relations
with China and improvement of ties with the Soviet Union in the sixties,
or the decision to pursue an independent and nonaligned approach in
foreign policy by loosening connections with the West and expanding
ties with the developing world in the early seventies, or a return to the
West (including the revival of security ties with the U.S.) after the Soviet
military intervention in Afghanistan, these moves reflected the perceptions of policy makers as to how best to ensure security in a changing
regional and international environment. Thus, the importance Pakistan
attaches to its relations with China can be attributed to the latter's cooperation in the defense field, that is, supply of weapons and military hardware, establishment of defense-related industry, and cooperation in the
nuclear and missile programs. Similarly, the changes in Pakistan's interaction with the United States can partly be explained with reference to
periodic divergences in their views on security issues in South Asia, the
question of U.S. weapons supply, and American pressure on Pakistan's
nuclear program.[5]

External security is still the major concern of the state. That is the reason that all Pakistani governments, civilian and military, have allocated the
largest portion of national resources to defense and security. Only recently has debt servicing taken a lead over defense allocations in shares of the
national budget; yet despite strong IMF pressures to reduce defense
expenditures further in order to overcome the ongoing economic crisis,
the government has refused to do so.

Pakistan's controversial nuclear and missile programs have also to be
seen in the context of its security predicament with regard to India. These
programs acquired a prestige dimension only when the West in general,

5. For Pakistan's security perceptions and weapons procurement policy, see Hasan-Askari
   Rizvi, "Pakistan's Threat Perception and Weapons Procurement," in *The Diffusion of
   Advanced Weaponry: Technologies, Regional Implications and Responses*, ed. Thomas Wander,
   Eric Arnett, and Paul Bracken (Washington, D.C.: American Association for the
   Advancement of Science, 1994), 193–210; Stephen P. Cohen, "U.S. Weapons and
   South Asia: A Policy Analysis," *Pacific Affairs* (spring 1976): 49–69; and Shirin Tahir-
   Kheli, *United States and Pakistan* (New York: Praeger, 1982), 81–114.

and the United States in particular, applied pressure to compel Pakistan to reverse its nuclear program and place it under strict international safe-guards—demands which were viewed in Pakistan as discriminatory. No matter how one plays up the prestige dimension of the nuclear program or describes it as the "Islamic bomb," the primary considerations shaping Pakistan's nuclear and missiles programs are its feelings of insecurity aris-ing from a sharp power asymmetry in South Asia, periodic disruptions of its weapon supply from the external sources, and India's own nuclear and missile programs, which have a clear edge over their counterparts in Pakistan. One may question the degree of insecurity entertained by Pakistan's policy makers, but the fact remains that as long as it is not addressed by some form of regional or global nonproliferation arrange-ments that also involves India, the current profile of Pakistan's nuclear and missile programs is not likely to be altered drastically.

DOMESTIC POLITICAL CONTEXT

The restoration of democracy in Pakistan in 1985 after a long spell of military rule has expanded the scope of political freedoms, and the infra-structure of civil society is sprouting. An attempt is being made to assign some priority to socioeconomic development, environmental issues, and deregulation of the economy and international trade. However, it is pre-mature to assume that the participatory political process has developed strong roots and become an irreversible phenomenon. The ideological commitment to participatory political governance is strong at the popu-lar level, where a fair and free electoral process, socioeconomic justice, and the accountability of those exercising power are recognized as estab-lished norms of political order. However, the track record of the polity has been marked by frequent breakdown of constitutional order, military rule, absence of elections at regular intervals, a selective enforcement of the rule of law, and a poor tradition of accountability of rulers. The authoritarian traditions inherited from the colonial period persisted with the rise of a bureaucratic-military elite, which maintained a patron-client relationship with political leaders, institutions, and processes. The elite consciously discouraged the growth of autonomous political activity and viable political organizations by engaging in constitutional and political engineering, selective consensus building, coopting a section of political elite, and using the coercive apparatus of the state.

Democratic political forces and institutions could not develop into viable and autonomous entities, since the establishment could easily set them aside at will. This gave rise to palace intrigues, threats, and shrewd manipulation of divergent interests, with complete disregard for any principles of democracy and constitutionalism. A web of nonofficial groups and organizations and informed public opinion that could articulate civic demands was either too feeble or missing altogether. The political process was also monopolized directly, or through client political organizations, by the establishment. Those who found themselves excluded from the political process (not coopted or refusing to be coopted) had no stake in it, and politics became a zero-sum game: the "out" groups and the "in" groups engaged in a brute struggle for power. Thus, the Bengalis of East Pakistan (1947–1971), despite constituting a majority of the population, found themselves excluded from the political process and obtaining a minimal share of the economic pie. As they pressed hard for their political and economic rights, they developed a confrontation with the "in" group, that is, the West Pakistan–dominated establishment. The latter's decision to use military force to cow the Bengalis pushed them out of the federation.

This authoritarian tradition was incorporated in the constitution by the military government of General Mohammad Zia ul-Haq in 1985, when it tilted the balance of power in favor of the president (he himself held that office at that time) rather than the prime minister and equipped the president with discretionary powers to dismiss the prime minister and dissolve the elected National Assembly. This diluted the parliamentary character of the constitution and weakened the elected assembly and the political government.[6] Four governments and National Assemblies were dismissed (in May 1988, August 1990, April 1993, and November 1996) by the president at his discretion with the backing of the top brass of the military. Only recently has this ability been reversed. In April 1997, the parliament rescinded the powers of the president to dismiss the government. However, it is too early to know if this change has actually shifted the balance of power in favor of the prime minister and the National Assembly.

6. The Constitution of the Islamic Republic of Pakistan, 1973, Article 58 (2)(b). The Constitution, as originally adopted by the National Assembly in 1973, did not contain this clause; the president could not dissolve the National Assembly except on the recommendation of the prime minister. General Zia ul-Haq amended this clause along with several other sections of the Constitution in March 1985 under martial law. Later, these amendments were approved by the National Assembly and labeled as the Eighth Amendment, before General Zia ul-Haq withdrew martial law. Pakistan has experimented with six constitutional arrangements: the Interim Constitution, 1947; the 1956 Constitution, abrogated after the military takeover in October 1958; the 1962 Constitution, which replaced martial law in 1962, and was abrogated in March 1969 when the military again assumed power; the Interim Constitution, 1972, which replaced martial law; the 1973 Constitution, which was held in abeyance when the military assumed power in July 1977; and the (amended) 1973 Constitution, which was revived in 1985 and is currently operational in Pakistan.

Several other developments have kept democratic political forces weak and divided and have adversely affected the development of viable participatory institutions and processes. First, General Zia ul-Haq's martial law government (July 1977–December 1985) and his civilianized regime (December 1985–August 1988) pampered nonpolitical entities and highly conservative Islamic groups as part of their cooption efforts and to undercut the support of their political adversaries. In this way, Zia ul-Haq created a large group of beneficiaries, chiefly scornful of democracy, who were promoted to the national level under the protective cover of martial law.

Secondly, orthodox Islamic groups also put pressure on the democratic process and endeavored to dictate the political agenda. These elements gained strength against the backdrop of the Afghan war, 1979–1989, as material resources became available to them and they obtained sophisticated weapons, which they often used to show their strength in the domestic context. However, despite greater activism on their part and an increase in religion-oriented violence, these groups have little chance of overwhelming the state due to their own denominational differences and personality clashes. Moreover, since the state itself pursues an Islamic agenda, it is difficult for these groups to project themselves as the sole defenders of Islam. They are unlikely either to have a head-on collision with the state (as is the case in Algeria) or to overwhelm the state (as was the case in Iran). The Islamic groups are successful in influencing policy making to the extent that they join hands with other "nonreligious" groups, or when the state has its own reasons to pursue Islamization. Still, it is probably wise for the state to use a carrot-and-stick policy as well as to incorporate some elements of Islam in its agendas in order to deflect their street power.

The third major cause that has contributed to the problem of governance and thus poses a threat to stability and orderly political change relates to Pakistan's failure to accommodate ethnic, linguistic, regional, and cultural diversity in a plural and democratic framework. The Pakistani power elite were strongly convinced that the Islamic identity would override regional and ethnic identities, and therefore they dealt with diverse groups and their demands in an abrasive manner, employing authoritarian and administrative solutions that complicated the nation-building process. What they overlooked was that "Pakistanis had twin identities: they were both a Muslim and a Punjabi, or Bengali, or a Sindhi or a Baluch or a Pathan."[7] The breakup of Pakistan and the establishment

7. Gowher Rizvi, "Pakistan: The Domestic Dimensions of Security," in *South Asian Insecurity and the Great Powers*, ed. Barry Buzan and Gowher Rizvi (New York: St. Martin's Press, 1986), 84; see also Rounaq Jahan, *Pakistan: Failure in National Integration* (New York: Columbia University Press, 1972).

of Bangladesh in 1971 were the consequence of their failure to recognize this reality. In the post-1971 period, the Pakistan government revised its strategy by adopting a more flexible and accommodating approach toward ethnic identities, resorting to coercion only selectively. The restoration of the democratic process in 1985 further defused tension. The government and the opposition have alternated in the exercise of power, and some of the hitherto extreme nationalist-separatist groups have returned to the electoral process. The moderation of political conflict due to the revival of the electoral process makes one optimistic that Pakistan no longer faces another breakup, despite the twin challenges of urban decay and weapons proliferation that will be discussed below.

These problems and weaknesses of the political order make it convenient for the military to maintain its centrality to the political process. Pakistan's highly professional and disciplined military is a guarantee of the stability and continuity of the political system. However, the military, with its highly skewed ethnic composition, cannot satisfy ethnic-linguistic pressures. Additionally, direct military rule has always faced a serious crisis of legitimacy, no matter how long a military ruler stays in power or how carefully tailored a political system he outlines for the postwithdrawal period.

The current power arrangement of constitutional rule—an elected government with a relatively powerful president, and the top brass of the military in the background—moderates the authoritarian tradition with democracy. It is a triangular power equation comprising the president, the prime minister, and the chief of army staff, locally known as the Troika. These arrangements have enabled the military to participate in the political process without actually assuming power, which has facilitated the functioning of the electoral process and the management of state affairs by the political leadership. However, political stability still depends on the smooth functioning of the Troika. If strains develop in the Troika, political confusion and uncertainty abound; very often the prime minister, who represents the weak and divided political forces, finds it difficult to hold on to power.[8] During Nawaz Sharif's second government, he amended the constitution to reduce the powers of the president and to strengthen the position of the prime minister. However, this did not improve the prime minister's position to the extent that he could alone command the political system. The military's clout was intact, and the

---

8. The elected governments were dismissed and the assemblies were dissolved in May 1988, August 1990, April 1993, and November 1996 by the president. New general elections were held in November 1988, October 1990, October 1993, and February 1997.

prime minister still needed to work in harmony with the president and the army chief for effective political management. The Sharif government was paralyzed when a confrontation developed between the president and the chief justice of the Supreme Court in November 1997. But for the support of the army chief the government could not redeem its position. The current power sharing arrangement, which is likely to continue in the future, helps to ensure stability and continuity with a semblance of democracy *despite* the preeminence of the establishment, sharp economic disparities, ethnic and linguistic diversity, religious-sectarian cleavages, a frail democratic culture, and an underdeveloped civil society.

POPULATION, SOCIO-ECONOMIC AND ENVIRONMENTAL ISSUES

Pakistan's population in 1996 was estimated at 133 million, the seventh largest in the world and still growing fast. Such a high population is a liability as well as an asset, depending on the social indicators. The literacy rate of 36–37 percent includes anybody who can read a sentence or a headline in a newspaper. In real terms, literacy is much lower. Female literacy in particular is very low; in certain parts of Balochistan, it is less than 1 percent. Educational facilities are limited in the rural areas, especially in the remote regions, and the dropout rate at the primary level (grades 1 to 5) is high. Almost half of Pakistan's population is under twenty-one, which means that it faces a larger "youth bulge" than any one of the other pivotal states. Most young people are entering the job market without sufficient education and skills, thereby building serious pressures on the social and political system. The most ironic aspect is that Pakistan cannot gainfully employ even those who manage to get college and university educations.

The high annual growth rate of Pakistan's population (ranging from 2.8 to 3 percent), coupled with legal and illegal immigration, explains the rapid increase in population. Refugees from Afghanistan are the largest group and, according to the United Nations High Commissioner for Refugees (UNHCR), their population touched the figure of 3.272 million in 1990 before dropping to 1.20 million in the beginning of 1997.[9] As civil strife persists in Afghanistan, a two-way movement of Afghans continues. Other sizable groups of foreign migrants include Iranians (mostly dissidents), Kurds from Iraq, Muslims from Mynmar (Burma), Bangladeshis (Biharis and Bengalis), and Sri Lankans who have come to Pakistan either to escape from a hostile domestic political situation or to seek employ-

9. *Dawn* (Karachi), February 24, 1997.

ment and thereby support their families back home. This growing population pressure jeopardizes planning for social and environmental development and poverty alleviation. It thus poses a major threat to stability and orderly political and social change and makes unemployed and alienated youth vulnerable to extremist religious calls.

This socioeconomic crisis has been exacerbated by the military-dominated view of security, which focused attention and resources on external threats. As a consequence, Pakistan's socioeconomic, cultural, and ecological needs were given a lower priority.[10] In addition, the social sector suffered from a development strategy of the 1960s that aimed at a high GNP growth rate with strong incentives for the private sector but neglected the distributive aspects of economic development. A nationalization policy, introduced in the early 1970s, could not rectify socioeconomic imbalances and widespread poverty. The increased bureaucratic control of the economy under the cover of nationalization further aggravated the socioeconomic crisis. As population pressure increased in rural areas where basic facilities were lacking, internal migration led to rapid and unplanned urbanization. The cities were unable to cope with the influx of population, and ghettos sprang up rapidly in all major, especially industrial, cities. As a result, the number of localities lacking minimum civic facilities increased, accentuating social and environmental challenges. If anything, these pressures are increasing today.

The depletion of natural resources and the environmental degradation that pose serious threats to stability and security are the result of, among other causes, rapid population growth, immigration, and a neglect of the social sector. Waterlogging and high salinity have traditionally been menaces to agriculture. Governmental efforts to control these problems in the 1960s reclaimed some land. However, the pressures persist as a major danger both to agriculture and to public health. Pakistan's scarce forest reserves are being depleted at a faster pace than their replacement. Unplanned and unauthorized tree cutting is a major threat, which has increased after the influx of the Afghan refugees into the North West Frontier Province (NWFP). Similar pressure is mounting on grazing fields for animals and on water resources in the NWFP and Balochistan. Other issues that require attention include desertification of some areas in Sindh, Punjab, and Balochistan; a shortage of water generally; and the rising toxic levels of rivers due to the dumping of untreated industrial and

10. For a treatment of different aspects of security, see Marvin G. Weinbaum, "Security Regimes in South Asia: Definitions and Priorities," in *South Asia Approaches the Millennium: Reexamining National Security*, ed. Marvin G. Weinbaum and Chetan Kumar (Boulder: Westview, 1995), 1–16; see also Rasul Bakhsh Rais, "Security, State and Democracy in Pakistan," *ibid.*, 63–78.

other waste in them.[11] Air pollution is easily noticeable in most urban areas, which have witnessed a population influx and the deterioration of civic amenities.

This situation is also worsened because existing laws, and their enforcement, are not stringent enough to hold industry and others responsible for the damage they cause to the environment. The government of Pakistan and the UNHCR have launched a program of tree plantation and for the development of water resources and grazing areas in the regions where the Afghan refugees were settled. But a more comprehensive approach is needed to address these problems, which threaten societal stability elsewhere in Pakistan as well. This will require the reordering of priorities on the part of the policy makers as well as fresh legislation for environmental protection. However, the major constraint on the government's policy is the sheer scarcity of resources, which can only partly be surmounted by seeking the cooperation of the nongovernmental organizations (NGOs) and international agencies working on socioeconomic development and environmental security.

There is a brighter side to the population factor. Pakistan also has a highly educated, professionally qualified, and skilled work force that has performed excellently within the country and elsewhere. Over 3 million Pakistanis are living mainly in three large communities overseas: the gulf and the Middle East, the United Kingdom, and North America.[12] They have built some goodwill in their adopted countries and, after becoming established in the United Kingdom and the United States, have started participating in the politics of their adopted countries; they often lobby for the cause of their ancestral country. Overseas Pakistanis send funds back home either to support their families or for investment purposes, an important source of foreign exchange for a country that is perennially short of that item. A substantial population also means a large market that will attract international (including American) business attention as trade barriers are gradually removed. There are also reasonable prospects for investment, as production costs are relatively low. The question remains, therefore, whether Pakistan can modify its population increase, handle its other problems, and get through the next fifteen to twenty years to enjoy prosperity and sustainable human development.

11. Akmal Hussain, "The Dynamics of Power: Military, Bureaucracy and the People," in *Internal Conflicts in South Asia*, ed. Kumar Rupesinghe and Khawar Mumtaz (London: Sage Publications, 1996), 39–54.
12. Shahid Javed Burki, "Role of Overseas Pakistanis," *Friday Times* (Lahore), August 15–21, 1996, p. 6.

INTERNATIONAL PROCESSES
AND PAKISTAN'S VULNERABILITY

As if these challenges were not serious enough, various international processes in the post–Cold War period are putting stresses and strains on the Pakistani polity. As socioeconomic issues and participatory political management gain greater importance, Pakistan is finding the adjustment process to be rather painful, especially when it is increasingly difficult to obtain economic assistance from abroad. Like all the pivotal states, it is under pressure to initiate free-market reforms. The first wave of deregulation of the economy has, however, adversely affected the political credibility and the regulatory capacity of the state, because a host of corruption scandals have surfaced, for example, the sale of industrial units or their shares at throw-away prices to politically connected people and kickbacks for the state functionaries. Similarly, fears are being expressed that the privatization process may produce some powerful industrial groups that could then use their economic clout to dominate the political process. Various financial scandals since 1990–1991, when deregulation and privatization were initiated, have tainted the credibility of the political government and created a strong perception that economic liberalization has increased corruption in the society.

There is a serious dichotomy in the economic landscape of Pakistan: On the one hand are deals of billions of dollars for the sale of state industries and the high-profile life-style of the wealthy power elite. On the other hand, the common people, shocked by financial dealings at the top, growing corruption, and the rise of consumerism as multinationals penetrate the market, are under growing economic stress. Added to their plight is the withdrawal of subsidies for foodstuffs, fertilizers, and utilities under pressure from the International Monetary Fund. This has caused price hikes, thereby causing more distress for the poor. Moreover, the lowering of tariffs threatens inefficient middle- and small-level local industry, placing the employment of a large number of people in jeopardy. As elsewhere, international agencies and the West are stressing the need to give greater attention to the social sector and human development so as to enable the common person to absorb the initial shocks of the ongoing economic restructuring. However, the fate of these programs depends to a large extent on the international "dole" because the government suffers from a serious shortage of domestic resources, especially when its options for diverting resources from debt reservicing and defense are very limited. When such a scarcity of resources is coupled with rapid population growth and problems of political and economic management, the prospects of the government's providing tangible relief to the common people appear bleak.

Pakistan has borrowed heavily from domestic and international sources over the years, causing a heavy debt burden. In early 1997, the total foreign debt was $30 billion and domestic debt stood at $23 billion. When debt servicing and defense are put together, hardly any budgetary resources are available to the national government, which has to borrow for the salaries of civil servants, administrative expenditures, and development work,[13] thereby adding to its debt burden. So far, the government has managed to repay its debts on time, but unless Pakistan is able to put its economic house in order, control high spending and the trade deficit, and improve its foreign-exchange reserves, it faces the threat of being a loan defaulter, which would undermine its prospects for attracting investment and financial support from abroad. Given such a difficult economic situation, Pakistan will find it hard to make more resources available for coping with socioeconomic pressures and environmental and other societal challenges. It is caught between a rock and a hard place, a situation familiar to many developing societies today.

Another illustration of how international processes can cause problems is the impact of Pakistan's participation in the Afghanistan war of 1979 to 1989. Ten years of active involvement in the Afghan war, with the full support of the West, have changed the social profile of Pakistan to such an extent that any government faces serious problems in effective governance. Pakistani society is now more fractured, inundated with sophisticated weapons, brutalized due to growing civic violence, and overwhelmed by the spread of narcotics mainly due to the spillover of the Afghan war. Weapons siphoned off from supplies for resistance groups and others manufactured in the tribal areas are easily available to those pursuing partisan objectives or criminal activities. Afghanistan and Pakistan have become major centers of poppy cultivation, processing and exporting heroin that threatens the social fabric of Pakistan, the United States, and Europe.[14] In addition to increased drug addiction in Pakistan over the last decade, the drug and weapons trade has made great profits for individuals and groups who use their wealth to buy political influence, neutralize the authority of the state, and engage in violence against their adversaries.

The Afghan war also witnessed the growth of a close interaction

13. See Mahbub ul Haq, "A Search for Solutions," *Newsline* (Karachi), March 1997: 36–39.
14. For an in-depth analysis of the rise of narcotics production and export from Afghanistan and Pakistan since 1979, see Ikramul Haq, "Pakistan Afghan Drug Trade in Historical Perspective," *Asian Survey* 36, no.10 (October 1996): 945–963.

between a number of Islamic militant groups of the Arab world and the Afghan resistance movement. A large number of Arab volunteers joined the Afghan resistance movement to fight against the Soviet Union. After the withdrawal of Soviet troops from Afghanistan, they stayed on in Afghanistan, using it and adjacent Pakistani territory as a sanctuary and training base for their activists. These militant elements (often described as the Afghan war veterans) returned home periodically and resorted to violence against their governments, which they viewed as corrupt and un-Islamic. They also targeted American interests in the Arab world and elsewhere in retaliation for American support to their governments or for what they described as anti-Islam policies of the U.S. administration.[15]

These transnational factors combine with the domestic political and economic predicaments—and with the security dilemmas vis-à-vis India—to compound the problems of governance. The consequence is that the state of Pakistan often finds itself under serious constraints while attempting to perform its basic duties towards its citizenry, all of which causes apprehension about the prospects for its future stability. In sum, its future is uncertain and wobbly.

OPTIMISTIC AND PESSIMISTIC SCENARIOS

The most optimistic future scenario visualizes Pakistan as having adopted a participatory political process that offers ample opportunities to diverse interests to accommodate each other within the constitutional and democratic framework. In the economic domain, Pakistan will make rapid strides as it addresses its debt problem, discovers new natural resources, and gradually moves to further industrialization by mobilizing domestic resources and international cooperation. These developments will make it possible to devote resources to the improvement of the social

15. The U.S. intelligence functionaries associated with the Afghan war were aware of the connections between the militant Islamic groups from the Arab world and Afghan resistance; they encouraged this collaboration. After the withdrawal of Soviet troops from Afghanistan, when the Afghan war veterans embarked on their own agenda, which threatened American interests, they were labeled terrorists. In 1992–1993, the United States threatened to declare Pakistan a terrorist state because these militant Islamic elements continued to operate, in collaboration with the Afghan groups, from the Pakistani territory adjacent to Afghanistan. Pakistan, desperately in need of international economic and diplomatic support, adopted a number of measures to discourage such activity, which saved it from being designated as a terrorist state. However, it is neither advisable nor possible for Pakistan to declare a war on Afghan groups and their allied Arab elements because this would have serious implications in the Pakistani domestic context. The Afghan groups continue to enjoy connections and support in Pakistan, and it is also widely known that the connection between militant Islamic elements and the Afghans once enjoyed the blessings of the United States.

sector and to help strengthen civil society. Higher living standards could bring a diminution in population growth and more attention to the environment. Such a Pakistan would be better placed to play a stabilizing role in the region and strengthen moderate and democratic Islamic elements. Significant improvements in relations with India, and the settlement of the Afghan and Kashmir conflicts, would also be part of this favorable scenario.

In a pessimistic future scenario, Pakistan will increasingly become ungovernable. The writ of the government will be limited as socioeconomic pressures mount, and ethnic and regional cleavages threaten the political process. Since weapons are easily available, the competing groups will use them to settle their scores as well as to challenge the tottering government's authority. These developments will further undermine the economy and cause greater frustration, alienation, and insecurity in society. The result will be a situation of near anarchy. This in turn could trigger the rise of an authoritarian/dictatorial regime that would find it difficult to establish its authority over the entire country. The military is the most likely candidate for establishing such a rule, although it will have to negotiate with the civilian groups to build a support base. Were such an internally threatened regime to seek to divert attention elsewhere— or were it alleged that India was abetting certain groups—peace on the subcontinent might again be in jeopardy.

Another scenario visualizes civil strife in some parts of the country— conflict among groups and between the government and some groups, or both—which would threaten peace and stability in the strife-ridden areas. Chaos and confusion will strengthen the position of the Islamic groups, which are likely to attract a large number of people as offering an alternate solution to the political and economic ailments. However, no monolithic Islamic movement or leadership is likely to surface. A host of Islamic groups will compete and cooperate with one another or with "nonreligious" groups. In their drive for supremacy, these Islamic groups may invoke their transnational Islamic linkages to mobilize support from other Muslim countries. This would further increase the role of external actors in Pakistan. It would be difficult to negotiate compromises if the situation settled into an Afghan-like civil conflict.

The most likely scenario, however, is that the present-day slow progress to democracy will continue, although periodic setbacks cannot be ruled out. If the problems of economic and political management are brought under control, though not necessarily resolved, and some degree of participatory and transparent governance is sustained, Pakistan will be in a position to function as a relatively coherent political unit and play an active role in the international system. But those are considerable "ifs."

U.S. INTERESTS AND POLICY

A stable Pakistan is in the interest of the United States because it can contribute to achieving American foreign policy goals of peace and stability in the region, democracy and social development, market economy and free trade, control of narcotics, containment of international terrorism, and nonproliferation of weapons of mass destruction.

Pakistan is an important bridgehead to Central Asia for trade and economic interaction. It offers relatively short transit routes from Central Asia to the sea via its port of Karachi. If Pakistan's port of Gwadar in Balochistan, situated close to Iran and almost at the mouth of the Persian Gulf, is developed, the distance to the coast can be reduced further in the case of Turkmenistan, Uzbekistan, and Kazakhstan. These transit routes offer the states of Central Asia much-needed opportunities for expanding international trade and commerce and reducing their dependence on the Russian Federation for transit facilities.

Pakistan is also important as an outlet for oil and gas from Turkmenistan, Uzbekistan, and Kazakhstan. Some Western multinational corporations are currently working on an oil and gas pipeline from Turkmenistan to Pakistan via Afghanistan for supply to Pakistan and elsewhere.[16] Much importance is being given to this route as it can reduce the dependence of Central Asia on the Russian Federation as well as making Iran a less attractive oil and gas transit route. Pakistan is already offering technical know-how and professional skills in banking, public administration, educational, and technical fields to some of the states of Central Asia and since 1996 has provided military training facilities to Turkmenistan. There is much scope for expansion of this relationship.

The ongoing civil strife in Afghanistan also makes it imperative that Pakistan continue to operate as a coherent political entity so as to contain turmoil in that country. Though Pakistan has not had much success in resolving the intra-Afghan feud, the fact remains that without the cooperation of Pakistan there is hardly any prospect of a settlement in Afghanistan. Pakistan continues to maintain ties with most Afghan groups and is still host to Afghan refugees. However, Pakistan's role as a facilitator of peace in Afghanistan depends to a great extent on its own internal stability and cohesion.

Tajikistan faces an insurgency in its southern region. Afghanistan is

16. Ahmed Rashid, "Central Asia Power Play" and "Pipe Dreams," *Far Eastern Economic Review*, April 10, 1997, pp. 22–25,28.

already in the grip of intense internal strife. If Pakistan descends into chaos and turmoil like that in Afghanistan and cannot continue as a political entity, the whole region from the southern parts of Tajikistan to the shores of the Arabian Sea and the Indian Ocean will be in turbulence. This would not be a good omen not only for the neighboring states but also for the international system. During the years of the Afghanistan war, Pakistan was described as a bulwark against Soviet expansionism and the frontline state for the "free" world. Now, Pakistan is a bulwark against the turmoil that is spilling over from Afghanistan. It is still a frontline state as far as the fight against chaos, narcotics trafficking, and international terrorism are concerned. Pakistan and the United States are already cooperating in checking narcotics production and trafficking, although the latter is not fully satisfied with the former's counternarcotics efforts.[17] Pakistan has also adopted measures to discourage Arab/Islamic militant elements from operating from Afghanistan-Pakistan under the cover of or in association with Afghan groups and some NGOs extending humanitarian assistance to the refugees.[18] If Pakistan slips into chaos and confusion, it will become extremely difficult to contain drug trafficking and Afghan-linked transnational terrorism.

Ethnic entities in Pakistan have their counterparts in neighboring India, Afghanistan, Iran, and some gulf states. A weakened Pakistan, coupled with Afghanistan in turmoil and strife-ridden Tajikistan, could give a boost to ethnic upheaval, which would pose serious challenges to the state system in the region. Such instability could send a stream of refugees to other countries and especially the West, putting pressure on their economies and generating social tensions. Instability and ethnic turbulence in Pakistan and neighboring states are likely to draw in major powers such as China, India, and Russia, which have traditionally maintained interests in this region; they will be jockeying for influence, if not a foothold. The United States will not be able to stay aloof from such a power game. It is therefore imperative from the U.S. standpoint that the

17. See the narcotics control report on Pakistan released by the U.S. Department of State, which expressed dissatisfaction with Pakistan's performance. Pakistan received $2.5 million as assistance for narcotics control in 1995. There was no change in the narcotics control–related assistance in 1996. See *Dawn*, March 2, 1996.

18. Since 1993, the police have been launching raids on militants' hideouts in refugee camps or elsewhere from time to time. Militants are deported if their documents are not in order. However, a large number of them are based in Afghanistan or cross over from Pakistan to Afghanistan when Pakistani authorities move against them. On several occasions, there have been armed clashes between the police and the Arab volunteers; in March 1997, an armed encounter near Peshawar involved some Egyptians and Algerians. The Islamic groups and parties in Pakistan are very critical of the government's strict policy on these elements.

existing state structures in the region do not crumble. The United States should work toward strengthening Pakistan, which has so far demonstrated some semblance of order and stability and has a sufficiently developed state apparatus.

Pakistan's geographic proximity to the Middle East and its historical, cultural, economic, and, above all, security ties with gulf states have great significance for U.S. policy makers, who have an abiding interest in the stability of the region—a goal shared by Pakistan for its own considerations. Major U.S. interests in the gulf region include an uninterrupted flow of oil to the West and Japan, trade and investment, the recycling of petrodollars, and the sustenance of pro-West regimes. Pakistan's policies toward the gulf region are helpful to these U.S. goals. By making its troops available to Saudi Arabia and other gulf states in the past, Pakistan helped them to manage their security problems.

Pakistan's military presence had two advantages. First, the military was professional and disciplined, with sufficient experience in handling the American weapons and equipment that the Gulf states were using. Second, the shared religious background of the Pakistani personnel made them more acceptable in the gulf. A large number of Pakistanis were already working in the civilian sector, so the introduction of Pakistani military personnel did not evoke negative reaction. The latter feature has acquired greater significance in view of the experience of U.S. troops in Saudi Arabia in the aftermath of the war with Iraq (1991). The continued presence of American troops has evoked much resentment among fundamentalist Islamic groups. There have been a couple of instances of attacks on American installations and personnel in Saudi Arabia. The tension caused by the presence of American troops can be reduced by stepping up Pakistani's security role in the region and especially by replacing a large number of American troops with Pakistani troops. However, Pakistan will not like to be seen as playing the U.S. game in the gulf and cannot be expected to allow the use of its troops against any Muslim country.

Pakistan's importance for U.S. goals in the Gulf can also be gauged from another angle. Pakistan's Makran coast and especially the port of Gwadar have strategic importance. Their control by a hostile power could adversely affect U.S. interests in the Persian Gulf and Indian Ocean region.

The United States cannot pursue its agenda on nonproliferation of weapons of mass destruction in South Asia without cultivating Pakistan, which has acquired nuclear weapons capability. U.S. economic assistance and military sales in the 1980s dissuaded Pakistan from making a bomb. Pakistan also suspended the production of weapons-grade uranium, although it refused to surrender its nuclear weapons option unilaterally. A stable and secure Pakistan will be more willing to cooperate on the nonproliferation issue because Pakistan's perceived insecurity had led it to work on nuclear weapon capability. These weapons are viewed as the last-resort defense mechanism. If Pakistan's survival is not at stake, it will be responsive to proposals for the ultimate elimination of weapons of mass destruction. The United States can evolve a nonproliferation regime for South Asia by engaging in simultaneous dialogue with India and Pakistan. However, a credible nonproliferation policy must address Pakistan's security concerns and must apply equally to India.

A stable and secure Pakistan can contribute to stemming the conflict and chaos that threaten to overwhelm the region, and it can be instrumental to the realization of a new global agenda. Therefore, economic and political support to Pakistan to enable it to overcome its domestic socioeconomic problems facilitates international peace and stability. There is much scope for cooperation between Pakistan and the United States as they have overlapping interests. The experience of the 1950s and the 1980s shows that the two countries can work together for the promotion of peace and stability. Though they diverged on some issues during that period, they generally maintained a favorable disposition toward one another. One cannot expect the two states to have a unanimity of views on all issues in the post–Cold war period. Divergence in perspectives should be recognized as normal, just as is the need to build on the points of convergence; the relationship can vary from one issue to another. Such an approach can promote a sound and stable relationship and will save the two sides from developing undue expectations, thus avoiding the "fatal flaw" of their relationship in the 1950s.[19]

POLICY RECOMMENDATIONS

Any revival of an active relationship calls for removal of the ban on military sales and economic assistance to Pakistan imposed in October 1990 under the Pressler amendment as a retaliation against Pakistan's nuclear program. This has caused damage to their bilateral relations, although a

19. Thomas Perry Thornton, *Pakistan: Internal Developments and the U.S. Interests*, FPI Policy Briefs (Washington, D.C.: Foreign Policy Institute, SAIS, The Johns Hopkins University, March 1987), 11.

one-time waiver was given under the Brown amendment in 1995.[20] If the objective of the Pressler amendment was to warn Pakistan in a loud and clear manner, this purpose was served. Pakistan did slow down its nuclear program, but it is more determined than ever not to give up the weapons option unilaterally. As a matter of fact, the imposition of the Pressler amendment has strengthened the "bomb" lobby in Pakistan and has reinforced anti-American sentiments there, making it more difficult for the government to yield more ground on the nuclear issue. Nonproliferation should be pursued in a pragmatic manner; the whole relationship cannot be put at stake on this question. A dialogue and normalization of relations, rather than punitive measures, are needed for developing a nonproliferation regime in South Asia. Similarly, there is a need to explore prospects of greater cooperation in the economic, trade, investment, cultural, and security domains. In view of Pakistan's pivotal situation in the region, the United States "must bolster its influence in that country and must assist in every way in stabilizing its political structure."[21]

Any review of Pakistan's relevance to U.S. interests and goals is incomplete without looking at its implications for India–U.S. relations. U.S. policy makers maintain that they do not see their relations with Pakistan and India in either-or terms; rather, the relationship is based on mutually advantageous considerations for each state. However, U.S. policy is not always interpreted in this manner by Pakistan and India, which view this relationship in the context of their mutual rivalry and distrust. This creates a dilemma for U.S. policy makers: How can the United States maintain equally good relations with Pakistan and India? Additional problems arise because a section of U.S. academia and others with an interest in South Asia argue that, in view of India's uninterrupted democratic track record, size, resources and military power, it should be the natural ally of the U.S.; Pakistan has a precarious existence and suffers from so many internal contradictions that it is not a promising state.

Pakistan is no doubt smaller and weaker than India. However, given its strategic location, population, Islamic identity, international linkages

20. Under the Brown amendment (1995) the U.S. administration released weapons and military equipment that Pakistan had ordered and paid for before the embargo was imposed in October 1990 under the Pressler amendment. The United States will also refund Pakistan's money, which it had paid for F-16 aircraft, by selling these aircraft to some third country. This is only a one-time waiver, and the embargo imposed in October 1990 stays intact. There has also been a partial restoration of relations between the military establishments of the two countries since 1995, when the Pakistan–U.S. Consultative Group was revived, and Pakistan improved its interaction with the U.S. CENTCOM. The two countries also conduct joint exercises of the special groups of their armies.

21. Ralph Braibanti, "Strategic Significance of Pakistan," *Journal of South Asian and Middle Eastern Studies* XX, no. 1 (fall 1996): 1–19.

(especially with the Muslim world), and economic potential, Pakistan cannot be sidelined. Any attempt to develop a "strategic partnership"[22] with India that is insensitive to Pakistan's concerns or is perceived in Pakistan as being anti-Muslim or anti-China would not be conducive to stability and peace. The United States should maintain active interaction with Pakistan and India, as each is important in its own right. American objectives regarding nuclear and missile nonproliferation, drug trafficking, terrorism, and transborder migrations can be better achieved if India and Pakistan are equally involved in the process. Neglecting one for the sake of the other would be counterproductive.

The major policy dilemmas for the United States are caused by the conflict and distrust that exists between Pakistan and India. It is in the American interest to work toward reducing tensions between these two countries. The United States can act as a facilitator for the initiation of a dialogue on their contentious issues and lend them a helping hand in the course of such a dialogue. It can also encourage the two states to adopt measures for conflict reduction and confidence building so that the overall environment improves. Some significant moves have been made in confidence building between Pakistan and India at official and unofficial levels over the last eight to ten years. More work is required so that South Asia, like other regions, moves in the direction of reconciliation and cooperation. The improvement of relations between Pakistan and India will make policy management less problematic for the United States.

---

22. See *A New U.S. Policy Toward India and Pakistan*, a report of an Independent Task Force (New York: Council on Foreign Relations, 1997), 35.

TURKEY

Alan O. Makovsky

Abutting several regions of high priority in U.S. foreign policy, Turkey is of demonstrated importance to American security interests. But notwithstanding a dynamic private sector and a colorful, often vibrant democracy, Turkey is a politically troubled nation. Turkey's ability to effectively play the role of Western security partner will be determined by how it resolves the fundamental political problems that threaten its stability and call into question its future as a member of the Western family of nations. U.S. policy can help Turkey resolve these issues in a manner that preserves and perhaps strengthens its ties with the West.

Turkey is a "pivotal state" in more than one sense. First, Turkey is a state susceptible to ideological pivots. Before the emergence of the anticlerical Republic of Turkey founded as a result of the Ataturk revolution in the 1920s, the Ottoman empire was the world's leading Islamic state, with its ruler, the sultan, widely recognized as the titular leader, or caliph, of the Islamic world. During the nineteenth century, the Ottoman empire itself veered between secular and Islamist tendencies. Now, at the end of the twentieth century, steadily growing religious consciousness has once again brought Islam to the fore as a political movement, boosting an Islamist to the prime ministry for one year and hinting that Turkey may forsake its decades-old quest for integration with the West.

Second, Turkey is pivotal because it is vital to U.S. interests in many of the regions that it borders, including the Balkans, the Persian Gulf, the Arab-Israeli arena, the former Soviet Union, and the Mediterranean, Aegean, and Black Seas. Were Turkey to turn decidedly away from its alignment with the United States and the West, serious harm to American interests and greater instability would likely result in all these areas.

In perhaps a third aspect of the term "pivotal"—as a state whose neighbors look to it for leadership—Turkey's qualifications are currently minimal though potentially greater. If Turkey succeeds in building its economy and resolving the issues that trouble its own democracy, the bloc of formerly Soviet Turkic-language states might come to see Turkey's Westernizing/secularizing example as a role model, as was once hoped, and Turkey itself as a regional leader.

Turkey is potentially pivotal in yet two other respects as well: as a "paradigm of the possible" for both relations between Western Europe and a Muslim state, and for the adaptability of a Muslim-majority state to Western-style democracy. Among the Islamic states of the traditional Middle East, Turkey has always enjoyed a privileged position in its relations with the West. It is the only Muslim-majority state in NATO. It is the only Muslim-majority state that has a customs union agreement with the European Union (EU) and observer status in the EU's military wing, the Western European Union. Although Turkey's hopes for positive action on its 1987 application for full-membership status in the EU now appear forlorn, Turks feel their long-time commitment to Western defense through NATO merits them membership in the EU, which they see as the body that now certifies "Western-ness" in the way NATO formerly did. In that regard, many other Muslim states may gauge Western Europe's attitudes toward Muslims generally by its treatment of Turkey.

As a regime, Turkey has been the Islamic world's foremost democratic example for decades. Its democratic ride has been bumpy, but should it reach its destination of Western-style democracy, it will have achieved more than a national success. It will have effectively challenged the contention of skeptics who say that democracy and Muslims do not easily mix. So far Turkey, although coming close, has not quite achieved this goal.

Turkey is not easy to categorize. It is not only NATO's only Muslim-majority state. It is also one of NATO's largest states (population 63 million[1]) as well as its poorest, the only NATO state ranked by the World Bank as less than an "upper-middle-income" nation[2]. Although Turkey aspires to membership in the EU and recognition as a fully "European" state, and although most Western foreign-affairs bureaucracies group Turkey with European states—primarily because of its NATO membership—only 3 percent of Turkey's land mass actually lies in Europe. The remaining 97 percent sits east of the Dardanelles-Marmara-Bosphorus sea lane, classically considered the dividing line between Europe and Asia. Differing culturally from its Western allies and differing politically and in foreign-policy orientation from most of the rest of the Islamic world,

---

1. According to the results of a 1997 census, Turkey's population is 62,610,252. The results were released in February 1998, too late for analysis in this paper. "Türkiye kesin nufüsü 62,610,252," *Sabah* (daily newspaper, Internet version), February 7, 1998.
2. World Bank, *From Plan to Market: World Development Report 1996* (New York, 1996), 188–189.

Turkey is a hybrid that generally feels misunderstood by its allies and targeted by its neighbors. Despite a constitution that enshrines secularism as a state principle and a foreign policy establishment firmly committed to alignment with the West, questions about its future direction, east or west, perennially abound.[3]

Politically, Turkey still is probably the most democratic state in the Islamic world.[4] However, its experiment in multiparty democracy, generally considered to date from the 1950 elections, has been interrupted by two outright military coups, one overtly threatened coup that led to the collapse of an elected government and, in 1997, a military-initiated public-pressure campaign—in effect, an unstated but widely perceived coup threat—that created the conditions for the downfall of a government that took office through democratic procedures.

Turkish military regimes and civilian courts have closed many political parties over the years, including, most strikingly, the pro-Islamist Refah Party in early 1998. The Refah Party, the largest party in Parliament and the senior government coalition partner from mid-1996 to mid-1997, was accused of trying to subvert Turkey's constitutionally mandated "secular order."[5]

In economic terms, Turkey defies the experts.[6] Its inflation rate has

3. Polling data usually suggest that Turks are roughly evenly divided in thirds as to the category which best describes them, "Western," "Islamic," or "both." That divided sentiment is of less immediate policy relevance than one might think. The Turkish elite that dominates foreign-policy decision making is overwhelmingly committed to a vision of their nation as a Western state. Over the longer term, however, the ambivalence reflected in the polls could prove significant. (A recent United States Information Agency–sponsored survey showed a dramatic tilt toward Turks' seeing their country more as part of the Muslim world (47 percent) than the European world (27 percent), with less than a fifth (15 percent) seeing Turkey as part of both worlds. The survey was conducted in the first months of the pro-Islamist Necmettin Erbakan's prime ministry, however, possibly skewing the results. U.S. Information Agency, "Turks Shift Toward Islamist Orientation, Staunch Secularism Declines," September 12, 1996, p. 1.

4. The Freedom House annual survey for 1996 actually gives Jordan a somewhat higher democratic rating than Turkey. This seems to me unjustified. The monarchy in Jordan, for example, can more easily override popular will than can the military or any comparable body in Turkey; the monarchy also appoints and dismisses governments.

5. The party's leader, former Prime Minister Necmettin Erbakan, and four other members were expelled from Parliament. Most of the remaining Refah parliamentarians joined the newly formed Virtue Party. As of this writing, it was unclear if the public prosecutor would seek to close the Virtue Party, which is generally seen as merely a renamed version of Refah. Under Turkish law, banned parties cannot simply reopen under a new name, though this law has not always been enforced.

6. The following discussion of Turkey's economy draws considerably from William Hale, "Turkey: Economic Issues and Foreign Policy" (paper presented at "The Domestic Context of Turkish Foreign Policy," seminar at Washington Institute for Near East Policy, Washington, D.C., July 28–29, 1996).

topped 70 percent annually every year for over a decade, hitting a high point of 106.3 percent in 1994 and again topping triple figures, at 101.6 percent, in 1997. Average inflation for 1992–1997 was 85.4 percent, making the Turkish lira one of the world's most worthless monetary units. As of January 1, 1998, one U.S. dollar was the equivalent of 205,000 Turkish liras and rising fast; this compared with a 1993 average exchange rate of 11,000 lira to the dollar and a controlled exchange rate of 3.5 lira to the dollar in the mid-1970s. For 1996, the government-announced consolidated budget deficit was at 8.8 percent of GNP and the public sector borrowing requirement (PSBR) at 9.6 percent of GNP. Long-discussed privatization remains mainly on the drawing board. Delegations from international financial institutions regularly urge Turkish governments to cut spending and undertake major structural reforms, but they have met with little success.

Foreign direct investment is disappointingly low—only $612 million, or 0.33 percent of GNP, in 1996. In conversations with London businesspeople and bankers interested in the Turkish market, the British scholar William Hale found political instability, the inflation rate, and uncertainty about government economic policies to be the primary disincentives to investment. U.S. businesspeople often cite administrative and legal impediments as the leading problems, particularly the Turkish courts' rejection of the international arbitration of disputes.

Turkey has other problems as well. It boasts the least equitable income distribution in the OECD, aside from Mexico's.[7] The illiteracy rate of the six-years-and-older population was 19.5 percent, according to the 1990 census, a relatively high figure for an OECD country (though a marked improvement over the 1950 rate of 70 percent). Worse, nearly one-third of the adult female population remains illiterate—a tribute to a lingering, if receding, belief among those in the countryside (and particularly in the predominantly Kurdish southeast) that education for girls is an unnecessary luxury. That, in turn, contributes to an ongoing population problem, since illiterate women proportionately bear far more children than literate women.[8] Aside from the growth rate, major population-related problems include rapid urbanization, fueled by wide-scale displacement in the countryside as a result of the war with the Kurdish separatist PKK, and

---

7. Economist Intelligence Unit, *Country Report: Turkey, 2nd Quarter 1997* (hereafter EIU:CR2/97), 21; Economist Intelligence Unit, *Country Profile: Turkey 1995–96* (hereafter EIU:CP95–96), 17.

8. EIU:CP95–96, 18. Overall, however, Turkey appears to be getting its population growth under control; the birthrate has fallen from 4.7 percent to an estimated 2.3 percent over the past four decades, thanks in large part to educational gains.

the "youth bulge"; as of 1991, roughly 52 percent of Turks were between five and twenty-nine years of age.[9] Some fear that severe youth unemployment will create political instability and a ready constituency for Islamic fundamentalism. Officially, unemployment stood at 7.5 percent in 1995, but Turkey's leading trade union estimates the real figure at 27 percent.[10]

Yet the Turkish economy continues to display dynamism, producing hope that its job-creation potential (spiked by a 1996 customs union agreement with the European Union) is up to the challenge of the "youth bulge." The Turkish economy registered gains of 8 percent in 1995, 7.9 percent in 1996, and an expected 5 percent in 1997. Despite a negative growth rate of –6 percent following the collapse of the lira in 1994, Turkey regularly has produced one of the highest average growth rates among OECD states over the past two decades. GDP increased, in real terms, by an annual average of 4.6 percent between 1980 and 1993. Per capita GNP increased, in real terms, by an annual average of 1.5 percent during roughly the same period (1985–1994).[11] Since undertaking major reforms to open its economy and encourage exports in 1980, Turkey has seen its exports increase nearly eightfold, from $3 billion in 1980 to $23.5 billion in 1996.[12] Although its total foreign debt is roughly $80 billion, or 44 percent of GNP, Turkey has not had great problems borrowing the funds to service its debt, probably because of its record of growth and its good repayment record. As of 1995, GNP was roughly $160 billion and per capita income approximately $2,650.[13]

On the basis of 1994 per capita GNP, the World Bank categorizes

9. In comparison, the figures for France and Portugal were 36 percent and 44 percent, respectively. EIU:CP95–96, 18. Some Turkish demographers, such as the former World Bank official Baran Tuncer, dismiss the severity of the population growth rate. Citing the downward trend in the rate, Tuncer argues that Turkey will reach near-zero growth before the end of the second decade of the twenty-first century. Interview, July 29, 1997.

10. EIU:CR1/97, 24.

11. *The Europa World Year Book 1996*, Volume II (hereafter *Europa*) (London: Europa Publications, 1996), 3178.

12. Hale estimates the 1996 figure at $32.3 billion, if the "gray economy"—in particular, the "suitcase trade" with visitors from the former Soviet Union and Eastern Europe—is factored in.

13. Figures vary widely, depending on sources. These figures are derived from those in *Europa*, p. 3178. The *Financial Times'* "Survey: Turkey," estimates 1996 total GDP (nominal) at $182.9 billion. *Financial Times*, May 26, 1997, p. 23. EIU:CR2/97 gives a per capita income figure of $2,928 for 1995. *World Factbook 1996*, produced by the Central Intelligence Agency, uses a "purchasing power equivalent" methodology to arrive at a figure of $345.7 billion of "national product" in 1995 and an estimated $5,500 per capita income.

Turkey as a "lower-middle-income" economy. This puts it in the same category as, though slightly better off than, countries such as Uzbekistan, Kazakhstan, Macedonia, Jordan, Morocco, Tunisia, and Algeria.[14] Perhaps more noteworthy as a sign of Turkey's growth pattern is that the World Bank also calls Turkey one of the developing world's ten "emerging giants."[15]

A likely explanation of Turkey's ability to "muddle through" economically is its huge "gray economy," estimated variously at 40 to 70 percent of its official economy. Turkey clearly needs to get its fiscal house in order; economic structural problems discourage foreign investment and prevent Turkey from realizing its potential as a regional powerhouse. Nevertheless, most experts believe economic collapse or disaster to be unlikely.

TURKEY: HOW PIVOTAL FOR THE UNITED STATES?

The case for Turkey's regional "pivotalness" is straightforward. From the time it joined NATO in 1952 until the demise of the Soviet Union in 1991, Turkey anchored NATO's southern flank. It presided over one of the world's key choke points, the Straits of the Bosphorus and the Dardanelles—Moscow's major sea outlet to the world—and straddled 530 kilometers of southwestern Soviet border, where it provided the United States and NATO with invaluable listening posts. In the post-Soviet era, though it no longer shares a border with Russia, Turkey nevertheless serves as a valuable insurance policy against the possibility of resurgent Russian imperialism and aggression.

In the Middle East, Turkey was an important ally for the United States during the 1991 gulf war. Motivated mainly by a desire to strengthen ties with Washington, Turkish president Turgut Ozal contacted U.S. president George Bush one day after the Iraqi invasion, pledging to close down the Iraqi-Turkish oil pipeline and link Turkey to the anti-Iraq sanctions effort,[16] thus anticipating actions that would be required by U.N. Security Council

14. By way of comparison, Greece, Mexico, Saudi Arabia, Oman, and Korea are labeled "upper-middle-income" economies. All EU and NATO countries except Greece and Turkey are "high-income" economies. Among Middle Eastern states, only the United Arab Emirates, Kuwait, and Israel are "high income."

15. The other nine, in order of GNP, are China, Brazil, Russia, India, Mexico, Argentina, Indonesia, Thailand, and Pakistan. Turkey's GNP ranks eighth in this group, just after Indonesia's. World Bank News Release 97/1296S, "World Bank Offers New Yardstick to Measure Development," April 6, 1997, press release on issuance of new World Bank publication, *World Development Indicators: 1997* (Washington, D.C., 1997).

16. Interview with Morton I. Abramowitz, U.S. ambassador to Turkey at the time of the Iraqi invasion of Kuwait, October 17, 1997.

resolutions several days later. Again at Ozal's initiative, U.S. bombers were granted permission to launch raids on Iraq from Incirlik Air Force Base in southern Turkey. Even without fighting, Turkish troops stationed along the Iraqi border during the war tied down nine Iraqi divisions, roughly 100,000 troops,[17] diverting them from action in the south. After the war and still today, Incirlik has remained essential to the anti-Saddam coalition as the base of operations for Operation Provide Comfort (renamed Operation Northern Watch in 1997), the U.S.-led, multinational force that enforces the "no-fly" zone above the thirty-sixth parallel in northern Iraq and seeks to deter Iraq from attacking its Kurdish population.

Elsewhere in the Middle East, Turkey has been a useful supporter of the peace process and a pacesetter in Muslim-world normalization with Israel. Its good relations with both Israel and the Palestinians were highlighted early in 1997 when, following the Israeli-Palestinian agreement on redeployment in Hebron, both signatories invited Turkey to send troops to serve in a temporary international monitoring force. Turkey was the only Muslim state to receive such a request. Drawing on its European experience in the Conventional Armed Forces in Europe (CFE) agreement, Turkey was also an active member of the Arms Control and Regional Security (ACRS) Working Group in the Middle East multilateral peace talks before the work of that group essentially ground to a halt as a result of Israeli-Egyptian disagreements about nuclear arms.

For thirty years, from 1949 to 1979, Turkey was the only Muslim state to recognize Israel. (In 1979, Egypt became the second.) At least on a formal level—rumors of a close Turkish-Israeli intelligence connection persisted whatever the state of visible relations—Turkish-Israeli ties had more downs than ups until the 1990s, but Ankara, in deference to its allies in the West, consistently rejected Arab importuning to break relations with the Jewish state. Since the Madrid peace conference of 1991, and particularly since the Israel-PLO Declaration of Principles in 1993, Turkish-Israeli relations have warmed rapidly, taking on the appearance of a "strategic relationship" and exciting concern in neighboring Iran, Iraq, Syria, and some other Arab States. Trade and tourism have surged. Joint agricultural projects were undertaken in Turkmenistan and Uzbekistan. In 1996, Turkey and Israel signed a free-trade agreement as well as several military agreements. To support this growing relationship, the United States joined Israel and Turkey in a trilater-

---

17. Sabri Sayari, "Between Allies and Neighbors: Turkey's Burden Sharing Policy in the Gulf Conflict," in *Friends in Need: Burden Sharing in the Persian Gulf War*, ed. Andrew Bennett, Joseph Lepgold, and Danny Unger (1997),197–217.

al naval search-and-rescue exercise in the Mediterranean in January 1998.

Turkey is the only state in the world to border three states on the list of state sponsors of terrorism—Iran, Iraq, and Syria. As such, it serves as a bulwark against the spread of that activity. Its military's traditional commitment to secularism makes it particularly dogged in its opposition to Islamic fundamentalist terror. In 1997, the Turkish military openly accused Iran of trying to use fundamentalist terrorism to undermine the Turkish regime.

Turkey's historical, ethnic, linguistic, cultural, and religious ties to peoples in the region—reinforced by the ethnic presence of these peoples in the mix of Turkish citizenry—gives Ankara long-term opportunities for special influence in the region, particularly among Muslims of the Balkans, the Caucasus, and Central Asia.

In Central Asia and the Caucasus, Turkey offers a pro-Western diplomatic, economic, and transport alternative to Moscow and Tehran. Were a solution reached to the Nagorno-Karabagh problem (involving a disputed Armenian-populated enclave within the borders of Azerbaijan, a Turkic-language state) and strains between Armenia and Turkey thereby eased, Turkey's ability to play the role of outlet for Central Asian and Caucasian states would be greatly improved. Even now, largely as a result of U.S. diplomacy, at least some of the Azerbaijani oil extracted from the Caspian Sea may make its way westward through Turkey (rather than entirely through Russia), which would greatly enhance Turkey's role in the region. Turkey thus could be a beneficiary of Washington's desire to break Moscow's monopoly on Central Asian energy routes.

Turkey enjoys growing economic ties with the states of the former Soviet Union, facilitated by linguistic and cultural affinities. Turkey's early post-Soviet hopes to immediately develop a sphere of influence among the Turkic-language states of the region proved unrealistic. Similarly, Turkey's once much touted "role-model" status for the Muslim states of the former Soviet Union met a general lack of receptivity on the part of the newly independent states[18] and has been further undermined by Ankara's problems with its own democratic development, including the 1996 accession to power of a pro-Islamist party that tarnished Turkey's image as a secular state. But Turks are among the leading economic players in the region, and, over time, Turkey's natural linguistic and cultural advantages are likely to pay economic and diplomatic dividends—partic-

18. Gareth Winrow, *Turkey in Post-Soviet Central Asia* (London: Royal Institute of International Affairs, 1995), 24.

ularly as local Turkic tongues replace Russian as the language of the elite in the new states, as seems inevitable.[19]

Other regional Muslim peoples of the former Soviet Union, including those in Russia, also have special relations with Turkey. This is notably true, in the case of Russia, of the Chechens and Tatars. During the Chechen rebellion, Turkish sympathies for Chechnya were evident— Turkey was the only state to host a Chechen public information office— but stopped short of open or significant material support.[20]

In the Balkans, Turkey has provided forces for all of the UN and NATO monitoring and peacekeeping forces, land, sea, and air, including the UN Protection Force (UNPROFOR) and its follow-up Stabilization Force (SFOR), the UN-sponsored International Police Task Force (IPTF), and NATO's implementation force (IFOR), designed to enforce the cease-fire established by the Dayton peace accords. At U.S. behest, Ankara also took a leading role in training and equipping forces of the Bosnian-Croat Federation army.

A constructive Turkish role in the Balkans is especially useful to the U.S. because of Turkey's potential for influencing fellow Balkan Muslims. Turkish involvement provides important reassurance not only for Bosnian Muslims, but also for Albanians and others. Turkey has established economic and military training ties with Albania. It also exerts influence over the ethnic Turkish and non-Turkish Muslim minorities in Greece and Bulgaria, both of which groups (particularly the Bulgarian Turks) live in sometimes hostile and potentially explosive environments. Turkey also has good relations with Macedonia, a strategically placed (albeit non-Muslim) state whose mere existence is an irritant to Greece.

Were Turkey to turn decidedly away from the West, U.S. interests in each of the regions discussed here would suffer. For example, a Turkey sympathetic with Iran, as the pro-Islamist former prime minister Necmettin Erbakan envisioned, could become an important base for the spread of fundamentalism and terrorism. Moreover, the loosening of Turkish-Western ties would harm U.S. and European interests in other

19. Regarding Turkey's goals, prospects, and early experiences in ties with Central Asia, see Philip Robins, "Between Sentiment and Self-Interest: Turkey's Policy Toward Azerbaijan and the Central Asian States," *Middle East Journal*, vol. 47, no. 4 (1993): 593–610; Heinz Kramer, "Will Central Asia Become Turkey's Sphere of Influence?" *Perceptions* 1, no. 1 (1996): 112–127; Martha Brill Olcott, *Central Asia's New States: Independence, Foreign Policy, and Regional Security* (Washington, D. C.: United States Institute of Peace Press 1996); Graham E. Fuller, "Turkey's New Eastern Orientation," in *Turkey's New Geopolitics*, ed. Graham E. Fuller and Ian O. Lesser (Boulder: Westview Press, 1993), 39–97; and Winrow, *Turkey in Post-Soviet Central Asia*.

20. See Robert Olson, "The Kurdish Question and Chechnya: Turkish and Russian Foreign Policies since the Gulf War," *Middle East Policy* 4, no. 3 (1996): 106–118.

ways. In particular, an important source of restraint on Turkey in its rivalry with Greece, as played out both in the Aegean and in Cyprus, would be lost, enhancing the likelihood of war. The United States, as needed, has exercised a similarly restraining influence in Turkish-Armenian relations.

That is not to say, however, that Turkey reflexively sees its regional interests as fully congruent with those of the United States and the West. For example, Turkey tends to view the possibility of renewed Russian nationalism and imperialism as far more likely than does the United States. Russia's unwillingness to comply with CFE-mandated troop and materiel levels in the Caucasus was particularly upsetting to Ankara, whereas Washington was more willing to accommodate it. In response to a U.S. request, Turkey unhappily agreed to go along with an increase in Russia's allowable levels in 1996.

Turkey's attitude toward Iran—even before Erbakan became prime minister—is more akin to Europe's than to that of the United States. Despite Turkish accusations of Iranian support for terrorism in Turkey, Ankara traditionally views Iran as an important trading partner, and has been loath to confront the Iranians publicly.[21] And whereas the Turkish establishment objected to the warmth Erbakan displayed toward Iran, it fully shared his desire for close economic relations with Iran. When Erbakan signed a $23 billion gas-pipeline deal with Iran in August 1996, just days after President Clinton signed the Iran-Libya Sanctions Act intended to impede foreign investment in Iran, most analysts interpreted it at the time as deliberate slap in the face to Washington. That is not the whole story, however. The Turkish establishment, including the military, likely knew in advance about Erbakan's plans to sign the agreement and supported it. With energy demands growing at over 5 percent per year, Turkey feels pressed to find new sources; the Iranian gas-pipeline plan enjoyed support across the Turkish political spectrum.

Turkey has been similarly unsettling, at times, to U.S. policy aims regarding Iraq in recent years. Ankara has at times called for a unilateral easing of sanctions on Iraq or even indicated that it prefers a return of Saddam Hussein's control in northern Iraq rather than the current situation of Iraqi Kurdish control. Moreover, Turkish political leaders have often criticized Operation Northern Watch and its predecessor, Operation Provide Comfort, as a threat to Turkish security, claiming that

---

21. The military's accusations leveled against Iran in 1997, noted above, were an exception to this rule. Even the military, however, acknowledges Iran's commercial potential for Turkey.

it contributes to a "power vacuum" in northern Iraq that allows anti-Turkish PKK terrorists to thrive.

Regarding the Middle East peace process, some in the U.S. administration were unhappy in 1995–1996 when Turkey made clear that it was not willing to "subsidize" a prospective Israeli-Syrian peace by agreeing to provide Syria with extra water to compensate it for whatever would have been lost to Israel. With so much U.S. senior-level attention focused on achieving Israeli-Syrian peace, Washington often seemed to view with annoyance Turkish complaints about Syrian behavior—such as its support for the PKK—and particularly any Turkish hints that Syrian-Israeli peace should be held hostage to Syrian compliance with Turkish concerns.

Not surprisingly, Turkey has frequently taken tougher positions than Washington would have preferred on issues in its immediate region where it sees its interests directly at stake. This has been true regarding Cyprus, Greece, Armenia, and even Bosnia, where Turkey covertly supplied arms and military assistance, apparently without the backing of Washington. Despite these divergences, Turkey has usually been supportive of and often pivotal to key U.S. interests in the region.

HOW PIVOTAL IN THE REGION?

The proposition that Turkey is regionally pivotal not only geostrategically but also politically—that other regional states look to it for leadership and seek to emulate its example—is questionable. Turkey is a regional power, to be sure. But unlike Egypt, Turkey does not play a leadership or, indeed, a crucial role on behalf of any bloc of states. In the immediate aftermath of the breakup of the Soviet Union, Ankara hoped to play such a role for the newly independent Turkic-language states. Turkey still believes this will someday be the case—an annual Turkic summit initiated by Ankara in 1992 reflects that long-term hope—but for now it is not.

Turkey's democratic, free-market policies have not inspired much imitation in the region. Indeed, when surveying Turkey's neighbors, it is quite obvious that Turkey's weighty presence has little effect on their regime orientation. As noted, three of Turkey's neighbors—Iran, Iraq, and Syria—are on the U.S. list of state sponsors of terrorism and generally promote policies hostile to U.S. aims. Their autocratic regimes are the virtual antitheses of Turkey's.

Moreover, among Turkey's immediate Islamic neighbors—that is, Iran and the Arab world—Turkey evokes little warmth. The backwardness and oppressiveness of Ottoman rule has assumed mythic proportions in

Arab national histories, serving as both an ongoing inspiration for Arab nationalism and a scapegoat for contemporary Arab problems. Resultant ill will toward the Turks of history is often directed toward contemporary Turkey. Even Turkey's relations with most of those Arab states with which it seemingly shares a community of interests—such as pro-Western Egypt and Saudi Arabia—are both unsentimental and surprisingly undeveloped. Turkey carries its own historical baggage regarding the Arab world, with attitudes colored by lingering resentment over the defection of the Arabs from the Ottoman side in World War I and by a post-Ottoman focus on Westernism and secularism that has often bred disdain for Arab culture among the Turkish elite.

Turkey (like the Ottoman Empire before it) has rarely enjoyed good relations with Iran. Each state has tended to be respectfully wary of the other, and that is the case today. Even as Turkey seeks to build economic ties with Tehran, the two states face several points of friction in their bilateral relations: rivalry in Azerbaijan and Central Asia; Iranian suspicions of Turkish support for Azerbaijani pan-Turkists who would favor union with what is now Iranian Azerbaijan; and Turkish suspicions of Iranian support for the PKK and for Islamic radicals.

Azerbaijan, the neighboring state seemingly most amenable to Turkish influence, has been careful (like other Turkic-language states) to balance its relations with Russia, Turkey, and Iran.[22] The only elected leader of Azerbaijan, the strongly pro-Turkish Ebulfaz Elchibey, held office no more than one year before being pushed out by a 1993 coup that installed the present ruler, Haydar Aliyev, whose ability to work effectively with the Russians is seen as one of his strongest suits.

On diplomatic matters, Azerbaijan treats Turkey as first among equals because of Ankara's strong backing of its position in the Nagorno-Karabagh issue; for example, Azerbaijan has called for a prominent role for Turkey in the Minsk Group, the primary framework for negotiations on Nagorno-Karabagh, and publicly backed Ankara's bid to be the primary export route for Caspian Sea oil. However, Turkey gets little in the way of direct diplomatic return on the issue it sees as most vital to its own national interest and international prestige: Cyprus. Neither Azerbaijan nor any other Turkic-language state has joined Turkey in recognizing the Turkish Republic of Northern Cyprus. This northern, Turkish Cypriot–inhabited portion of Cyprus, under Turkish protection,

22. Interestingly, Azerbaijan's foreign trade figures reflect that balance. Its three leading trade partners in the first seven months of 1996 were Iran ($158 million), Russia ($135 million), and Turkey ($132 million). *Eurasian File* no. 66 (Turkish International Cooperation Agency, Republic of Turkey Ministry of Foreign Affairs, Ankara, Turkey), October 1996.

declared independence in 1983. Turkey alone extends diplomatic recognition to it.[23]

Nor is Turkey pivotal as a bridge between cultures, as it has traditionally claimed. Turkey has rarely, if ever, acted as any sort of intermediary between the United States and another regional state, Arab or Turkic, each of which has its own independent set of interests and relationships with the United States and the West that are unaffected by Turkey. Nevertheless, Turkey's proximity and its linguistic and cultural affinity to the Turkic-language states of the former Soviet Union do at times facilitate Turkish entree and make Turks useful business partners for Westerners in that region. Although it is a plausible prospect that Turkey will eventually gain greater political influence with the Turkic-language states, particularly as the current Russia-oriented elites in those states pass into history, it is difficult now to foresee Turkey's approaching the kind of leadership role Egypt plays in the Arab world.

TURKISH PIVOTALNESS AND U.S. POLICY

This distinction between two types of "pivotalness"—geostrategic and political—may offer a partial explanation for a complaint frequently heard from Turks. Why, they ask, is Turkey always a function of U.S. policy toward somewhere else, such as Iraq, Iran, or the Soviet Union? Why is there no integrated Turkey policy?

In fact, U.S. policy makers tend to appreciate Turkey mainly for its real estate value—that is, its proximity to real and potential trouble spots—not for its more questionable regional leadership value.

On the whole, then, U.S. policy makers tend to take Turkey for granted, convinced that Turkey has little choice but to align itself with the West. In that sense at least, the era of Prime Minister Necmettin Erbakan may ultimately prove helpful to U.S.–Turkish relations. For the first time in years, Turkey became the object of sustained senior-level attention from the U.S. administration, which feared that the pro-Islamist prime minister might lead Turkey out of the Western orbit. High-level bureaucrats from throughout the government met regularly to evaluate the implications for U.S. interests of Islamist rule in Turkey. A policy battle raged among senior government officials over how much and what type of contact the United States should pursue with Turkey's pro-Islamist government officials.

This much more senior-level focus on Turkey is unusual. Although President Bush and Turkish president Turgut Ozal spoke regularly during

---

23. See Winrow, *Turkey in Post-Soviet Central Asia*, 20.

the 1990–1991 gulf crisis and war, this crisis-specific focus did not result in broad or enduring senior-level attention for Turkey. For years, Turkey has received scant attention from officials above the office director or, occasionally, the deputy assistant secretary level. A rare assistant secretary for European affairs such as Richard Perle at the Pentagon in the 1980s or Richard Holbrooke at the State Department in the mid-1990s has taken a deep personal interest, resulting to some extent in a more sustained policy interest, in U.S.-Turkish relations. Only two presidents, Eisenhower and Bush, have visited Turkey. Setting aside the extraordinary circumstances of 1990–1991, official visits by the secretary of state have been exceedingly few. Although Warren Christopher visited the Middle East over twenty times in his peace-process efforts, he never made an official visit to neighboring Turkey—and that despite well-known Turkish anxiety that the U.S., in its rush for Middle East peace, would fail to remonstrate with President Hafiz al-Assad over Syrian support for the anti-Turkey PKK.

There are many reasons for the U.S. tendency over the years to give Turkey less than its policy due. First, the bureaucratic structure of U.S. foreign-policy agencies militates against policy prominence for the Turks. Largely at is own request, Turkey was moved into the Bureau of European Affairs at the State Department (and into equivalent Europe bureaus in other policy and intelligence agencies) in the 1970s. That move, from its previous home as part of a Greece-Turkey-Iran office in the Bureau of Near Eastern and South Asian Affairs, left Turkey somewhat of a bureaucratic orphan. Although the U.S. policy community's European experts appreciated its geostrategic importance as a bulwark against Soviet expansion, it was usually seen as a low priority, marginal to the bureau's primary concerns. Moreover, diplomatic postings in Turkey or on Turkish-related affairs in Washington were not generally regarded as stepping stones to higher positions in European affairs. Ambitious "Europe-track" diplomats aspiring to deputy assistant secretaryships or assistant secretaryships or higher fought for jobs in Brussels (where NATO is headquartered), Bonn, London, Paris, Rome, and Moscow, not Ankara. This was all the more the case since Turkey was linguistically, politically, and policy-wise in a class by itself; professional experience in Turkey, though a NATO country, did not transfer well to other Europe-related jobs. No other Cold War–era country (aside from Cyprus) used Turkish, or anything remotely like it, as an official language. A tour as a political officer in Bonn might make one an expert on high-profile issues such as European integration, evolving mainland attitudes toward arms control, or other mainstream East-West issues. A tour in Ankara was more likely to leave one an expert on nonmainstream issues such as Cyprus, Aegean disputes, Turkish ties with the Middle East, or human rights.

Second, U.S. domestic politics probably have caused executive branch leaders to shy away from high-profile association with Turkey, which is frequently the object of criticism from powerful pro-Greece, pro-Armenia, pro-Kurd, and human rights lobbies and constituencies. No meaningful pro-Turkey constituency or citizens' lobby exists. Controversial issues involving Turkey, such as arms sales, tend to take on an "administration-versus-Congress" coloring, generating battles that political-level officials in the administration usually wish to avoid, lest they be forced to assume a highly visible pro-Turkish posture that could impede their longer-term political aspirations. Thus, responsibility for arguing for U.S. support for Turkey tends to fall to officials below the seniormost levels.

In striving for politically dictated "balance" in its relations with Turkey and Greece, the United States tends to demean Turkey's value. Turkey has six times Greece's population and has potential impact on a far wider array of U.S. foreign policy issues than does Greece. Yet Greece has traditionally received seven-tenths as much U.S. military aid as Turkey, and aid to both parties is scheduled to end in fiscal year 1999. Linkage of Turkey policy to Greece policy extends further. U.S. officials rarely visit one state without visiting both, and senior officials from the two states tend to be invited to Washington in roughly equal proportion.

Third, some participants in post–Cold War policy debates have maintained that post-Soviet Turkey has little strategic value for the United States. This line of argument is gradually losing out in a U.S. government that remains wary of possible resurgent Russian expansionism, as exemplified not only by its advocacy of NATO expansion, but also its emphasis on developing non-Russian routes for transporting energy resources in the Caspian Sea region. Turkey is obviously a bulwark against potential Russian aggression and a natural alternative energy route. Other U.S. regional initiatives, already discussed, in which Turkey plays an important-to-crucial role—such as those in Bosnia and northern Iraq—have also enhanced Ankara's standing as a post–Cold War U.S. strategic asset. Nevertheless, debate over Turkey's importance has not been fully put to rest among policy analysts or policy makers.

Fourth, policy makers have tended to deal with Turkey piecemeal, to see it as a fractured set of separate policy problems deriving from various regional issues. This, in a sense, is a structural problem. If, as supporters of Turkey's "pivotalness" contend, Turkey derives its importance primarily from being at the geographic center of a large circle of important but often unconnected policy problems, it is perhaps to be expected that U.S.

policy toward Turkey will be mainly a function of those surrounding problems. When Turks complain, as they often do, that the U.S. lacks an integrated Turkey policy, they mean that there is no consistent policy of U.S. support for building Turkey into a strong regional power. This lack of a "Turkey policy" is in part a result of the constraints on U.S. resources and the domestic political considerations cited above. It also reflects concern about Turkey's human rights shortcomings, and a certain wariness among some officials about whether a strong Turkey acting as an independent regional force would necessarily enhance U.S. interests. Nevertheless, Turkey has consistently supported crucial U.S. interests, and a stronger Turkey could play that role more effectively.

The Erbakan era, and the concern over Turkey's future that it generated, raised Turkey's profile in policy circles. Now that Erbakan has left office, it remains to be seen whether the United States will revert to its previous back-burner approach regarding Turkey, or whether Turkey will continue to benefit from sustained high-level attention from senior policy makers. Auguring for the latter course is the unprecedented appointment in 1997 of a recent ambassador to Turkey, Marc Grossman, to the slot of assistant secretary of state for European affairs. Unlike previous incumbents of that position, who generally arrive at the job with a resume dominated by experience in Bonn, London, Paris, or Brussels, Grossman spent six of the eight years previous to his appointment in Ankara, has been deeply involved in every key decision involving U.S.–Turkish ties in the post–Cold War world, and has a keen appreciation of Turkey's importance to U.S. global objectives and a deep understanding of Turkish politics and policy making. Grossman's appointment to the crucial post of the State Department's chief Europe watcher suggests that the Clinton administration sees Turkey as one of the important issues on its European agenda and that its interest in Turkey is not a passing phenomenon.

CHALLENGES TO STABILITY

Turkey's democracy is no longer young by world standards; its first competitive, multiparty election took place in 1950. Nevertheless, that democracy has not succeeded in establishing its own equilibrium or in bringing stability to Turkish society.

Three sets of overlapping problems cloud Turkey's future: (1) civilian versus military control; (2) ethnicity, in particular the integration of the Kurdish minority; and (3) the role of Islam in politics and society. These call into question Turkey's ability to achieve the standards of other Western European democracies, its long-term desire to remain part of the West, and the willingness of the West to view it as a true partner.

Success in resolving these three issues would fully qualify Turkey as a Western democracy and almost certainly would firmly bind Turkey to the West as a security and diplomatic partner. Resolution of the first of these problems alone is important but not crucial to a healthy Turkish security relationship with the West; failure to resolve it would impede full integration into Western Europe, however. Failure to resolve the second problem, or at least to progress toward its resolution, would not only block Turkey's full integration, but may also over time erode Turkey's status as a desirable partner for the West in security-related matters. Turkey's future relationship with the West will probably be most determined by the third issue: If Turkey remains a predominantly secular state, it will almost perforce remain pro-Western and a relatively reliable partner for the West. If it turns increasingly to religion as its state-organizing principle, it will almost certainly be lost as a reliable Western ally.

Civilian-Military Relations.

The role of the military in Turkish politics and policy making remains significant, and often paramount. Although the military's power is not all-embracing, few major decisions are implemented in Turkish foreign policy or security policy without the military's concurrence. The military also asserts itself in what it deems important internal security issues, such as the Kurdish issue or, more recently, political Islam. Two critical developments in very recent Turkish history—one in foreign policy, one in domestic affairs—resulted primarily from military initiatives. These were, respectively, the initiation of military ties with Israel in February 1996 and the fall of the pro-Islamist prime minister Necmettin Erbakan's coalition government in June 1997.

In a formal sense, the military exercises its influence through a constitutionally mandated body called the National Security Council (NSC). Under the chairmanship of the president of the republic, it consists of the top five military and the top five civilian leaders. All important security and foreign policy issues are reviewed, discussed, and usually decided by the NSC. Although constitutionally merely an advisory body that makes recommendations to the cabinet, its decisions are rarely overruled.[24]

In an informal sense, military influence over policy derives from a combination of public mystique and ability to intimidate politicians. The military sees itself as the guardian not only of the constitution and the

---

24. A significant exception to this general rule was the 1990–1991 gulf crisis and war, when President Turgut Ozal led Turkey into the anti-Iraq coalition, despite the reticence of the Turkish military. A bold and experienced politician with a commanding majority in Parliament, Ozal used this rare combination of assets to assert the civilian government's prerogative.

republic but also of the republic's Ataturkist, i.e, secularist and pro-Western, heritage. It is also seen this way by much of the nation. Poll results in Turkey consistently show the military to be by far the most respected of all Turkish institutions.[25] Its officers are generally viewed as honest, self-sacrificing, and motivated by patriotism, not personal gain. Few military officers have been implicated in scandal; advancement in the military is generally meritocratic, rarely the result of nepotism.[26]

The "intimidation factor" is a direct result of the fact that the military has inserted itself directly into Turkish politics three times (1960, 1971, 1980) since Turkey's first democratic elections in 1950. As a result, although Turkey's democracy is nearly a half-century old, its current skein of democratic civilian rule, fifteen years, is the longest in its history. With intended irony, Andrew Mango wrote recently that three times "the military stepped in to reestablish the social order that democratically elected governments had disturbed."[27]

Each time the military has intervened in Turkish politics, it has sought to correct what it saw as imperfections in the political order and then to return as quickly as possible to the barracks. In so doing, it has dramatically swayed the course of Turkish democracy while avoiding long tenures in office. The leftist-oriented 1960 coup resulted in a relatively liberal constitution (though one which also institutionalized the role of the NSC) and an election law based on pure proportional representation. The 1971 "coup by memorandum"[28] was intended as a right-wing corrective to the 1960 coup. The 1980 coup was an attempt to restore order to a society that had broken down into virtual anarchy as a result of massive political terrorism and a fractionalized and paralyzed parliament; it brought a more politically and socially conservative constitution (including enhanced powers for the presidency and an unprecedented requirement that religion be taught in the schools) and a new election law

25. A USIA–sponsored poll in Turkey at the end of 1995 showed 85 percent of Turks expressing confidence in the army, with only 14 percent lacking confidence. A similar result was obtained in 1994. "Turks Disappointed in Domestic Political Institutions," USIA Office of Research and Media Reaction (February 27, 1996).

26. For two important studies of the Turkish military, including its value-formation process, see Mehmet Ali Birand, *Shirts of Steel* (London and New York: I. B. Tauris, 1991), and William Hale, *Turkish Politics and the Military* (London and New York: Routledge, 1994).

27. Andrew A. J. Mango, "Testing Time in Turkey," *Washington Quarterly* 20/1 (winter 1997): 3–20 (quote is on p.3).

28. The military did not directly take over in 1971. Instead, it sent a written warning ("memorandum") to the elected government, made public over state-run media, that it would take over if the government did not resign. The government complied with the threat, and the military appointed a civilian "technocratic, above-parties" government to run the country.

requiring parties to win at least 10 percent of the national vote in order
to gain admission to Parliament. The 1982 constitution and the 10 percent "barrier," a well-conceived but ultimately unsuccessful effort to
reduce fractionalization of the political spectrum, remain the law of the
land today.

Many of today's political leaders are among those who felt the full
impact of the coups. President Suleyman Demirel was displaced as prime
minister in both the 1971 and 1980 coups; political parties led by the former prime minister Necmettin Erbakan were banned after each of those
coups, and Erbakan was tried (and acquitted) following the latter coup.
The current deputy prime minister Bulent Ecevit and his party, as well as
many other politicians and parties, were also banned from political life for
several years after the 1980 coup. In the most drastic action of all, following the 1960 coup, the prime minister, foreign minister, and finance
minister were tried on dubious charges and executed. The net effect of
this history is that few Turkish politicians are inclined to challenge the military directly on fundamental issues.[29]

Turkish military influence, which appeared to recede in the 1980s, has
visibly increased in the 1990s as a result of several factors, including weakened civilian leadership. However, two main factors stand out: the emergence of the battle with the Kurdish separatist PKK into a full-blown
insurgency and the 1996 accession to power of Erbakan's Refah (Welfare)
party, which is believed to favor political Islam. In fighting the PKK, the
military is widely perceived as determining the political as well as the military direction of the struggle. At various times over the past five years,
Turkish political leaders have publicly bruited the possibility of allowing
the Kurds greater freedom of cultural expression; their rapid retreat from
this position in most cases has fueled speculation that the military leadership forced them to back down.

The military sees the emergence of political Islam as an assault on
Ataturk's secularist heritage and on Turkey's pro-Western foreign policies. After Erbakan became prime minister in June 1996, the military
leadership flooded the Turkish public with on-the-record and background
affirmations of its uncompromising commitment to secularism, all clearly intended as warnings to the Erbakan government. This culminated in a
late February 1997 demand by the NSC, clearly at military initiative, for
the implementation of eighteen measures intended to minimize Islamist

29. According to various statements by the military and leaks (apparently military inspired)
    following meetings between top-level military brass and the then newly installed
    Erbakan government, the issues that the military considers fundamental are democra-
    cy, the secular structure of the state, territorial integrity, respect for Ataturk, and rela-
    tions with the United States, NATO, and Israel.

influence in politics, government, and society.[30] The centerpiece of these demands was a call to abolish the increasingly popular religious junior high schools. Under pressure, Erbakan signed his consent to the demands but avoided implementing them.

The military stepped up the pressure. In April, the military declared Islamism Turkey's "number one" problem, ahead of Kurdish separatism and terrorism. In June, a military briefer assailed "reactionaries" (understood by all to mean Erbakan and his party) for undermining Ataturk's legacy, ignoring the constitution's secular requirements, infiltrating Islamists into the bureaucracy, using government funds to support political Islam, and even cooperating with Kurdish terrorists. Islamists, the military charged, had "created a climate that encourages and rewards those who raise a green [i.e., Islamist] banner instead of the sacred flag of the Turkish Republic and who are disrespectful toward the spiritual identity of Ataturk."[31] In effect, the military accused the Erbakan government of treason, and Ankara again was rife with coup rumors.

Although Erbakan tried to hold out, his government finally collapsed in June 1997 and was replaced by an all-secular government. Erbakan attributed his resignation to "tension" created by the military's antigovernment campaign and implicit coup threat. Erbakan had badly miscalculated the military's willingness to tolerate his efforts to increase Islam's role in Turkish society. With its successful effort to undermine the Erbakan government, the military affirmed its own crucial position in Turkish political life. That it toppled the government without leaving the barracks inspired one Turkish writer to label the change in government "a post-modern coup."

The military also dominates foreign policy when it chooses to. The fact that Erbakan's government took several foreign policy-initiatives—agreements with Israel, renewal of Operation Provide Comfort—that ran directly counter to its long-proclaimed principles suggested that the military, not Erbakan, was pulling the strings. When the military staged a major anti-terrorist operation in northern Iraq in May 1997, it did not inform the prime minister until after the action was under way, reportedly for fear he might compromise the mission.

Even before Erbakan took power, in February 1996 the military deputy chief of staff, Cevik Bir, went to Israel to sign a first-ever military training agreement with Israel, which, among other things, allows Israeli aircraft to train in Turkish airspace. The agreement marked a dramatic

---

30. For a complete list of the eighteen demands, see *Turkish Times*, March 15, 1997, pp. 1–2.
31. "TURKEY: General Saner's Speech to Turkish General Staff," *Sabah*, June 12, 1997, as reported in FBIS-WEU-97-114, from the Internet.

tightening of relations between the two most militarily powerful states in the Middle East. That the military initiated so significant an agreement clearly testifies to that institution's broad sway in foreign policy matters.

Whatever the give-and-take between the civilian and military branches of government, the military's political priorities remain intact. Although supportive of democracy, the military sees its guardianship of the traditional values of the Ataturkist state, namely, secularism and Western orientation, as its paramount obligation.[32]

Implications

If Turkey is to qualify as a true democracy in the eyes of Western Europe, the relationship of the Turkish military to Turkish politics ultimately will have to alter decidedly in favor of civilian control. However, even with the current arrangement, Turkey could continue to have productive security and nonsecurity relations with Western powers. Other than in times of direct military intervention into government, Western European institutions never cite civilian-military relations among their inventory of Turkey's main human rights shortcomings. Western European governments were notably silent regarding the military's role in goading the Erbakan government from office, at least partly because they were happy to see it go. Nor has NATO contested the level of civilian control in Turkey, even as it insisted on clear civilian control as a criterion for new NATO members. Particularly at a time when an Islamist with a history of anti-Western rhetoric was at the helm of the Turkish government, most Western governments were probably quietly grateful for the presence of the Turkish military as a firewall against a potential Islamist effort to subvert Turkish secularism and to back Islamist movements in Europe.

ETHNICITY

Since 1984, Turkey has been engaged in a struggle with a Kurdish separatist organization—originally, at least, of Marxist-Leninist orientation—called the Workers Party of Kurdistan (PKK, by its commonly used Kurdish acronym). The PKK relies on both terrorist and guerilla tactics. With a training base in the Syrian-controlled Lebanese Bekaa Valley and with the support of Syria and other regional states, the PKK fight against Turkey consisted largely of cross-border attacks in the 1980s. Since 1991,

---

32. Birand, *Shirts of Steel,* p. xx; Hale, *Turkish Politics,* drawing on the typologies and terminologies of others, describes the Turkish military's role in Turkish politics as "an arbitrator or guardian role" (322).

however, PKK success in infiltrating its fighters into Turkey has transformed its insurgency into an internally based one, while drawing heavily on its bases in Kurdish-controlled northern Iraq. In response, the Turkish military assumed a more aggressive posture, attacking PKK bases rather than merely responding to attacks as it did in the initial stages of the PKK campaign. One element of this approach since 1992 has been a steady aerial pounding, coupled with occasional ground incursions, against PKK bases in northern Iraq. Another has been the razing and/or depopulation of some twenty-five hundred to three thousand villages and hamlets in the Turkish southeast to rob the PKK of sustenance and support.[33] In 1996, the delivery of food to an entire province in central eastern Turkey was carefully controlled for weeks as part of an effort to, in effect, starve out the PKK.

Despite the Turkish military's relative gains against the PKK in the mid-1990s and its success in easing PKK pressure in southeastern cities and towns, the PKK has refused to fold. In part, that is because of its seemingly limitless resources; in addition to support from neighboring states, it reportedly profits mightily from the international drug trade and receives vast sums (both extorted and voluntary) from Turkish-Kurdish and Turkish-Turkish guest workers in Europe. But pressures of this sort do not explain the PKK's hold over at least a significant minority of the Kurdish population. Rather, the PKK feeds off widespread dissatisfaction among Turkey's Kurds. Although Turkish officials have acknowledged the need to deal with the problem by "nonmilitary means," usually meaning economic and social reforms, policy makers have generally resisted political reform to meet Kurdish demands. Understandable concerns about giving in to violence and deeply ingrained traditional Turkish state practice both contribute to this reluctance.

As to traditional state practice, through most of its modern history Turkey has fostered the notion that it is a "unitary" state "without ethnic minorities." The amalgam of various Muslim groups that remained in (or made their way to) Anatolia after the Ottoman Empire's breakup were deemed, without differentiation, "Turks." Thus, Turkey did not recognize Kurds or any other Muslim group as a separate ethnicity.

This emphasis on the states's unitary nature has roots both in historical trauma and perceived political reality. The historical trauma was the collapse of the Ottoman Empire and the tough stance of the Western allies toward the rump Ottoman state after World War I. The long-time Turkish refusal to acknowledge ethnicity or formally to accept the use of

33. U.S. Department of State, *Turkey Country Report on Human Rights Practices for 1996*, January 30, 1997.

languages other than Turkish reflects the Turkish establishment's professed fear that Turkey, like the Ottoman Empire before it, could
be balkanized by ethnic separatism. For over seventy years the Turkish
establishment has held that unrestricted expression of ethnic and linguistic differences would rapidly lead to separatism and political disintegration.[34]

The "unitary state" approach has generally succeeded with the non-
Kurdish groups, which are individually too small in size and too geographically scattered to present a serious separatist threat, even were any of them
so inclined. Only the Kurds, large in number and inhabiting a geographically contiguous area in southeastern Turkey, create a serious problem.

For even the most liberal Turkish policy makers, the struggle with the
PKK presents a dilemma. They could make concessions and possibly whet
the separatist appetite, or fight on, conceding nothing, and possibly fuel
the resentment that fosters separatism.

In 1991, Turkey opted for change, taking a significant step toward recognizing the Kurds, first when President Ozal convinced Parliament to
repeal a 1983 law banning use of the Kurdish language and later when
newly elected Prime Minister Suleyman Demirel, on a visit to the southeast, announced that "we recognize the Kurdish reality." These efforts
failed to ease the PKK insurgency; far from satisfied, the separatists
stepped up their attacks. Since that time, and particularly since Ozal's
death in 1993, attitudes in Ankara have hardened.

But there are some signs that the process of accepting Kurdish distinc-
tiveness is tentatively moving forward. Since 1991, newspapers have
freely used the term "Kurd"; the euphemisms of former days, such as
"people of the southeast" or "regional people," appear to be on the way
out. Parties formed mainly to support Kurdish rights have been allowed
to participate in elections, notwithstanding Turkish constitutional pro-
scriptions on ethnically based parties. Still, these parties have been seriously encumbered by Turkish legal restrictions—two have been closed
down entirely—and subjected to harassment, both official and nonofficial. Turkish officials now often refer to their state as "pluralistic";[35] the

34. According to one scholar, there are some 47 ethnic groups in Turkey. (Peter Alford
Andrews, ed., *Ethnic Groups in the Republic of Turkey* [Wiesbaden, Germany: L. Reichert,
1989]). Estimates of the Kurdish population range from 7 to 15 million, out of Turkey's
overall population of 60 million. Population figures for Kurds are estimates or extrap-
olations—generally derived from province-by-province birthrates—since questions
about ethnicity are not asked in Turkish censuses. For the most recent detailed study of
this question, see Servet Mutlu, "Ethnic Kurds in Turkey: A Demographic Study,"
International Journal of Middle East Studies 28/4: 517–541.

35. See, for example, (Foreign Minister) Tansu Ciller, "Turkish Foreign Policy in Its
Dynamic Tradition," *Perceptions* 1/3 (September–November 1996): 5–16.

longstanding insistence that "there are no ethnic minorities in Turkey" has largely been dropped.

Implications

The repeal of the 1983 language law was prompted primarily by then President Ozal's belief that Turkey would never gain acceptance in Europe until the Kurdish issue is solved.[36] His view was and remains accurate. Worse for Turkey, the increasing prominence of the Kurdish issue has undermined ties with both Western Europe and the United States, severely tarnishing Turkey's already none-too-pristine human rights image. In the United States, traditionally more forgiving of Turkey's human rights lapses than Western Europe, a 1995 congressionally mandated State Department study raised questions about the possibility that Turkey is turning U.S. arms against its own innocent civilians in the battle against the PKK. In 1996 and 1997, human rights–based opposition from within the executive branch and Congress blocked completion of a major arms deal involving ten Cobra attack helicopters. The growing influence of human rights lobbies suggests the likelihood of further such problems. Turkey's impeded access to U.S. arms markets is particularly significant because defense ties are the traditional foundation of the U.S.–Turkish bilateral relationship. Perhaps as much as any issue, Turkey's approach to the Kurdish issue could widen the growing gulf between Ankara and the West and cause the West to loosen its ties to Turkey.

Establishment of a separate Kurdish state within the territory of what is now Turkey is very unlikely. More probable is a political settlement that affirms a greater level of cultural, linguistic, and political expression for Turkey's Kurds, but this will require a new regime paradigm that fully embraces pluralism or, less likely, binationalism. That will take years, if not decades.

ISLAMIC POLITICS

An even more fundamental question for the future of the Turkish Republic is its political-religious orientation. Of the three sets of issues discussed here, this one is likely to influence most profoundly the future of Western-Turkish ties. The first two problems—civilian control and the Kurdish issue—might affect the West's desire to integrate Turkey into its ranks, but they will have no direct impact on the Turkish establishment's desire to be part of the West. The issue of Islam's role in Turkey and the secular nature of the state may determine less the West's desire for close

36. Fehmi Koru, *Taha Kivanc'in Not Defteri* [*Taha Kivanc's Notebook*] (Ankara, 1996).

relations with Turkey than it does Turkey's fundamental character and its consequent desire for close relations with the West.

Islamic politics in Turkey is complicated by historical tension between secularism and democracy; a succession of governments since the first mulitparty elections in 1950 have modified the state founder Mustafa Kemal Ataturk's secular reforms and enhanced the role of religion in Turkish life in a bid for popular support. Another complication is disagreement within Turkey over the appropriate nature of secularism itself. In the Ataturkist republic, secularism has meant not so much *separation of state and mosque* as *state control of mosque*. State control is exercised through a religious affairs directorate, which appoints mosque personnel and religious instructors and determines the content of Friday sermons. Through state control, Ataturkists have tried to limit the political and social influence of Islam, which they associate with the backwardness of the last centuries of the Ottoman Empire. Islamists and some others say the Turkish system amounts to "oppression of believers" and call for a loosening of or an end to these state controls. This would allow Turkish secularism to more nearly resemble Western- or U.S.–style secularism, which emphasizes total separation of church and state. Ataturkists are convinced that Islamists seek to break down state control so that they, the Islamists, can control the state themselves.

Ataturk's measures in both *disestablishing Islam* and *de-Islamizing Turkish culture* were thoroughgoing. He abolished the caliphate, eliminated the constitutional designation of Islam as the state religion, changed the script for Turkish from Arabic to Latin, closed Islamic schools of learning, banned Sufi brotherhoods (tarikats) and Islamic headgear, and put Islamic clerics strictly under the control of the state, while ending their control of education and religious endowments, a major source of independent wealth.[37] Post-Ataturk democracy widened possibilities for religious expression, however, and revealed that Islam remained a powerful force in Turkish society. Indeed, the nearly half-century history of multiparty democracy in Turkey now appears as a slow-motion erosion of, if not counterrevolution against, Ataturk's austere brand of secularism.

Governments of recent decades have focused on expanding the numbers of mosques and religious schools and expanding state job opportunities for graduates of the religious school system. Since the 1980s especially, the enforcement of bans on tarikats and Islamic headgear have been decidedly relaxed, though not formally repealed.

For the military and many Ataturkists, these trends appeared to reach

37. Bernard Lewis, *The Emergence of Modern Turkey* (London, Oxford, New York: Oxford University Press, 1968). See especially 276–279, 401–442.

frightening proportions during the Erbakan prime ministership. Indeed, Erbakan's ostentatious hosting of more than three dozen traditionally clad Sufi sheikhs for a Ramadan break-the-fast meal at the prime minister's residence in January 1997 was probably an important precipitant in the military's decision to try to topple his government. The NSC's eighteen demands of February 1997—which, if fully implemented, would amount to an Ataturkist "purification" movement—called for full application of Ataturk's "revolutionary" laws, including those proscribing tarikats and Islamic headgear. Convinced that religious schools had become breeding grounds for Welfare Party supporters and activists, the military (via the NSC) also called for dramatic limits on the number of students in religious schools.

The most obvious manifestations of the growth of Islamic consciousness in Turkey is the electoral success of Erbakan's Welfare party, which ran candidates in six nationwide elections since 1984 and increased its vote each time, starting from 4 percent and achieving 21 percent and an unprecedented plurality in the December 1995 parliamentary elections. Welfare "arrived" as an electoral powerhouse in the March 1994 nationwide local elections, when it won 19 percent of the total vote and roughly one-third of major-city mayorships, including those of Turkey's two largest and most internationally prominent cities, Ankara and Istanbul. Erbakan's success in negotiating his way into the senior position in a coalition government in June 1996 was a watershed event for Ataturk's republic, allowing Turkish Islamists to crow that "Turkey" had its first "real Muslim" leader since the Young Turks of the Ottoman empire deposed the pious and pan-Islamist Sultan Abdul Hamid II in a coup in 1908.

Welfare's success is attributable to many factors, aside from religion. The party has vast funds, impressive organization, devoted cadres, and a reputation for clean government in the roughly four hundred large and small municipalities it leads. Moreover, it is the beneficiary of terrible errors made by Turkey's traditional secular politicians, including economic mismanagement, constant squabbling, and seemingly endless scandals involving reports of bribery, kickbacks, and, most recently, lurid links among politicians, internal security forces, and the Mafia. To many Turks, Welfare leaders appear selfless and committed, secular leaders selfish and cynical. Thus, it is difficult to discern how many of Refah's ballots are cast for strictly Islamist reasons.[38]

38. Although the Welfare party does not openly advocate a state based on Islamic law—to do so is unconstitutional and would lead to the party's instant banning—it is widely seen as favoring that course. In the waning days of the Erbakan administration, the Turkish state prosecutor opened a case to ban the party, based on the suspicion that it seeks to establish a state based on religious law.

Implications

The military's success in toppling Erbakan is a setback to Islamists' goal of dramatically transforming Turkish politics and society in the near term. Many Islamists will be expelled from the state bureaucracy,[39] and religious schools are to be reduced in number and more closely monitored. Nevertheless, the continuing societal trend toward greater emphasis on religion—and the ongoing problem that more democracy usually means more Islam, as politicians try to appeal to peoples' core values—suggests that the Islamist-secularist struggle and its unsettling implications for Turkish democracy are far from over.

The focus on these three issues that fundamentally affect the structure of the Turkish state is intended to isolate factors that affect regime stability and future foreign-policy orientation. Of course, other issues also will affect Turkey's future relations with the West. Probably the two most significant are trade, which tends to bind Turkey to the West,[40] and relations with Greece, which, because of EU member Athens's veto over the course of future EU–Turkish relations, tends to drive it away. Yet another is the economy, mainly for its effect on political stability: Both Refah and the PKK draw their strongest support from the poor and the dislocated.

GLOBAL PROCESSES

So-called global processes have an important, if sometimes equivocal, impact on the problems discussed here, particularly on the Islamist and Kurdish issues. Demographic trends, both population growth patterns and internal immigration, are vital elements of these issues. The endless flow of rural inhabitants to the cities has created millions of shantytown dwellers in Turkey. The resultant dislocations, economic and psychological, have helped swell Refah's vote totals by increasing the ranks of those susceptible to the appeal of both religious and populist politics.

Fueling the Kurdish problem and making its solution more urgent is Turkey's differentiated birthrate, far higher in the largely Kurdish-inhabited east than in the non-Kurdish west, giving the Kurds a steadily larger proportion of the population. On the other hand, internal immigration seems also to have dampened Kurdish separatist aspirations. So great has been the movement of Kurds from east to west that it is now estimated

---

39. The military itself expelled over two hundred junior officers on suspicion of Islamist leanings in 1996–1997.

40. Roughly two-thirds of Turkey's trade is with OECD countries.

that over half of Turkey's Kurds now live in the western half of the country, outside traditionally Kurdish areas. Istanbul is said to contain the largest Kurdish population of any city in the world. In a 1992 interview with a Turkish journalist, the PKK leader Abdullah Ocalan said that Kurds might have to be content to solve their problem within the current boundaries of Turkey—that is, without separation and independence—lest their brethren living and working in western Turkey be expelled or need to obtain visas to remain in their current jobs and domiciles.

There is even some evidence that Kurds tend to abandon their nationalism with their homes when they move west. Despite periodically expressed PKK threats, and Turkish fears, that large concentrations of Kurds in the major cities will produce large-scale urban terrorism, this has not happened, at least not so far. Moreover, the 1995 parliamentary vote revealed a surprising disparity in voting patterns between the Kurds of the east and the Kurds of the west. In the east, the pro-Kurdish People's Democracy party, running in an election for the first time, won some 30 percent of the vote, a plurality. In the west, it received only negligible totals. (Its overall national total of 4.4 percent left it well short of the 10 percent threshold required to enter Parliament.) Optimists see this as a hopeful sign that Kurds who live in the west, that is, among Turks, tend to integrate into national life.

Population also plays a role in Turkey's unhappy bid for EU membership. Current EU members fear that were Turkey to gain full EU membership, their societies would be culturally and economically overwhelmed by millions of Muslim Turks exercising their freedom of movement to seek work in more prosperous EU societies. Turkey's population also would make it one of the largest and thus politically powerful states in the EU.

Another "global process" with an impact on crucial political issues in Turkey is the freeing and spread of electronic media. Since legislation ending the state monopoly of radio and television in 1992, some eighteen national private television stations and countless local television and radio stations have been started. At least two stations promote Islam, one of them owned by the Welfare party.

The freeing of the airwaves has allowed Welfare to get its message out far more effectively than before. Islam versus secularism debates have become a staple on the talk shows of virtually every station. One prominent writer for an Islamist newspaper pointed out that the phenomenon of total ignorance of Islam, so common among secularists for decades, has been brought to an end by the combination of mandatory religious education and media discussion of religion.

Discussion of the Kurdish issue in the public media is somewhat more restricted than that of Islam and secularism. That issue, too, has been affected by the media, however. Since 1995, those with satellite dishes have been able to pick up the pro-PKK MED-TV, which broadcasts from Europe and features nearly nightly interviews with PKK leader Ocalan. There are periodic reports of Turkish government efforts to jam its transmission.

Ironically, in 1992, President Ozal urged that Turkish state radio and television stations begin Kurdish-language broadcasts. "If we don't," Ozal prophetically warned, "the other side will." Ozal's suggestion remains unimplemented.

OPTIMISTIC AND PESSIMISTIC SCENARIOS

As Turkey works its way through its problems, a variety of outcomes are possible over the next five to twenty years. In the most optimistic scenario, Turkey will solve its Kurdish problem and its problems with the PKK by establishing a more pluralistic structure with broader cultural and political rights for Kurds and thus undermining support for separatism. Turkey might also move decidedly away from the Islamist path, perhaps as economic growth shrinks the ranks of the unemployed and disaffected from which the Islamists (and the PKK) draw their primary support. These developments might enable Turkey to establish a stable democratic order under clear civilian control. To top off this rosy vision, we might imagine that Turkey and Greece resolve their problems over Cyprus and the Aegean, prompting Greece to cease using its veto to obstruct Turkish–EU relations, and that Turkey manages to bring down its inflation rate to Western standards while maintaining its generally high levels of growth. Even under these circumstances, it is unlikely (but no longer impossible) that Muslim Turkey, by then probably harboring a larger population than any EU state but Germany, would be accorded full EU membership. It might, however, be granted a special status in the EU and would, in any case, remain firmly anchored to the West. It would also be likely to continue to serve as a security asset for the United States and the West.

In the most pessimistic scenario, support for political Islam continues to surge, and Turkey allies itself with one of its rogue neighbors or itself enters the rogue category. It thus becomes an enemy of the West.

It should be pointed out that a successful Islamist takeover of Turkey would not, in and of itself, mean that Turkey would behave like or ally itself with a rogue state. Islamist Saudi Arabia, for example, is strongly pro–U.S. Indeed, given Turkey's geostrategic importance, the United States is likely to try to establish close ties with Turkey, as it has with Saudi

Arabia, whatever its political and religious orientation. But pursuing those ties would be far more difficult with an Islamist regime than it would be with a secular, pro-Western one. And with its large population and relatively powerful military, as well as a relatively strong economy, Turkey would be a far more self-confident power than is Saudi Arabia.

Both outcomes—resolution of all basic problems on the one hand or Islamist takeover on the other—are unlikely. A "middle outcome" resembling the current situation—continued tensions over political Islam, the Kurdish issue, and military-civilian relations—is most likely in the near term and for some time to come. Given demographic trends and Turkey's basic democratic structure, the Kurdish problem may be the issue most amenable to solution in the next one to two decades.

U.S. POLICY RECOMMENDATIONS

In devising its future strategy toward Turkey, Washington should do the following:

1. *Affirm Turkey's importance.* Any lingering question that Turkey's value as an ally has ended with the Cold War should be put to rest. U.S. policy toward Turkey has been on a roller coaster in the roughly eight years since the end of the Cold War. In 1995 Assistant Secretary of State Richard Holbrooke deemed Turkey "a front-line state" and one that "stands at the crossroads of almost every issue of importance to the U.S. on the Eurasian continent."[41] Holbrooke also emphasized that human rights, however important, would not be allowed to "rupture" U.S.–Turkish relations.[42] Holbrooke's departure in February 1996 began a period of drift—to be fair, caused partly by the uncertainties that Turkey's Islamist leadership presented. Only during the brief Holbrooke era has Ankara had a clear sense of how Washington viewed its place in U.S. global strategy and a firm sense of support in working through its human rights problems

2. *Devise a coherent policy that is supportive of a secular, democratic, pro-Western Turkey, and use senior-level public diplomacy to promote it.* The value of public diplomacy is that it clarifies foreign policy priorities for both U.S. and foreign audiences. U.S. support for Turkey should be affirmed by the president and the secretary of state, not merely by lower-level officials. Executive branch leadership is particularly important in convincing Congress about the importance of U.S.–Turkish security ties. Expression of human rights concerns should be an element of U.S. pol-

41. Richard Holbrooke, statement before the House International Relations Committee, March 9, 1995.

42. Richard Holbrooke, press conference, Ankara, Turkey, February 21, 1995.

icy and public diplomacy but—given Turkey's geostrategic importance, the special demands of its region and its war with the PKK, and
its good record for human rights and democracy relative to the rest of
the Islamic world—not the overriding one.

3. *Initiate a supportive, low-visibility dialogue on human rights.* Make sure
   Turkey understands the nature of the problem it faces in U.S. public
   opinion and the U.S. Congress if it fails to undertake further reform
   on the Kurdish issue (and thus how that issue could further corrode
   bilateral ties). The United States might consider setting out a structure
   of political, diplomatic, and/or economic incentives for significant
   Turkish political reform. Nevertheless, there should be no illusions
   that fundamental change will come easily or quickly.

4. *Demonstrate U.S. backing for Turkey and support Turkey's pro-Western forces,
   including the military, by:*
   • Assuring Turkey's access to the U.S. arms market. This is particular-
     ly important, as two congressionally thwarted arms sales in 1996 led
     Turks to suspect that the U.S. has placed an unstated arms embargo
     on Ankara. Defense ties are important both intrinsically and symbol-
     ically.
   • Initiating a dialogue with Turkey on counterterrorism and counter-
     proliferation measures. This is important in view of Turkey's prox-
     imity to Iran, Iraq, and Syria, all terrorism sponsors and
     "proli-ferators."
   • Affirming that cessation of all forms of support to the PKK and other
     anti-Turkish terrorist groups is a prerequisite for Syria's removal
     from the "terrorism state sponsors list," regardless of Damascus's
     actions on Arab-Israeli peace. Ending Syrian support for the PKK
     should be an important element of Washington's agenda with
     Damascus.
   • Vigorously supporting Turkey's deeper economic, security, and, as
     possible, political integration into Western Europe, from which
     Turkey now is increasingly and dangerously alienated. In particular,
     the United States should establish a dialogue with key EU states,
     including Greece, to emphasize the importance of anchoring Turkey
     to the West. Part of this effort should be to keep the door open to
     eventual Turkish membership in the EU. "Keeping the door open"
     does not mean that Turkey should be admitted to full EU membership
     before it meets all the relevant criteria; it now clearly falls short in both
     political and economic qualifications. The United States should, how-
     ever, urge its EU partners to treat Turkey equally with other countries
     on the "waiting list," which includes virtually every European country.
     The EU failed to do this—and angered Ankara in the process—at its

historic 1997 Luxembourg summit, when it established a candidacy process for eleven new potential members while leaving Turkey's application in abeyance. For the EU to continue this policy means to define Europe in a way that excludes the Turks.

Turkey's disaffection from Europe, in significant part, is the result of growing convictions that it has lost all prospect of joining the EU and that its exclusion reflects the religious prejudice of "a Christian club." This disaffection plays into the hands of the Islamists politically. It also decreases the possibility of Turkish flexibility and increases the possibility of aggressive Turkish action in conflicts with Greece.

· Convincing NATO to affirm its Article Five guarantees to Turkey on all of Turkey's borders.[43] Article Five of the NATO charter affirms that any attack on one NATO member state will provoke a response by the entire alliance. That will no doubt be difficult, since few, if any, NATO member states would want to be involved were Turkey attacked by a Middle Eastern state. Nevertheless, they are obligated by treaty to do so, and reaffirmation of the obligation would restore Turkey's confidence in NATO, shaken by the organization's tepid response to the potential Iraqi threat to Turkey during the 1990–1991 gulf crisis.

· Seeking through trade and investment credits to ameliorate the economic losses Turkey has sustained because of sanctions on Iraq, formerly its number-two trading partner.

· Keeping Turkey's Islamist leaders at arm's length. Washington's ability to affect Turkish politics is limited, but U.S. approval is something most Turkish leaders seek. For example, notwithstanding years of anti–U.S. rhetoric, Erbakan hastened to attend the 1996 Fourth of July party at the U.S. ambassador's residence (including a friendly photo op with the ambassador) just a week after taking office as prime minister. The United States should refrain from statements or actions that would redound to the benefit of Turkey's Islamist movement or appear to acquiesce in its antisecular, anti-Western goals.

Whoever rules in Ankara, Turkey's geostrategic importance will remain intact. If, over time, Islamists emerge as clear winners of their tug of war with the secularists for control of Turkish foreign policy and of Turkey itself, the United States will no doubt have to accommodate itself to that reality. Until then, actively supporting a secular Turkey, while pursuing a less than friendly policy toward its Islamist opponents, is the best way Washington can prevent that day from arriving.

43. See a similar (though different) recommendation, as well as other interesting security-related U.S. policy recommendations, in Ian Lesser, "Bridge or Barrier? Turkey and the West after the Cold War," in *Turkey's New Geopolitics*, ed. Graham E. Fuller and Ian O. Lesser (Boulder: Westview Press, 1993), 131.

EGYPT

Roger Owen

Egypt has been a country of international strategic importance since at least the time of Napoleon's expedition in 1798. More recently, and specifically since 1945, it has assumed additional significance as a neighbor of Israel, as the cultural and often the political center of the Arab world, and as one of the Middle East's major military powers. For these and other reasons, it was able to take the lead in the anticolonial movement in the region after the war, to become a primary target for Soviet-American rivalry in the Cold War period and, more recently, to accrue additional significance as the first Arab state to make peace with the Israelis and the one best placed to act as an intermediary between America and Israel, on the one hand, and the rest of the Arab world, including the Palestinians, on the other.

Given all this, Egypt would seem an excellent candidate as a "pivotal" state in both its positive and negative aspects. It is well placed to play a number of regional roles, whether as a potential leader of the Arab world, an ally of the United States and Israel, or an essential component of the burgeoning Euro-Mediterranean partnership. It also has critical interests in demography, land and water use, and the environment, many of which can best be promoted in a regional or international context. By much the same token, it would be a matter of enormous significance if Egypt were to experience a radical change of regime that led either to a sharp reduction in the present limited democracy or to a major shift in its international alignments. This paper explores ways to establish the exact nature of Egypt's pivotalness and how policies pursued by the United States and the rest of the world community might affect this pivotalness.

In this same context, it is also important to note that Egypt has already had a long and particularly intense association with the United States, beginning with the early aid programs of the 1950s with their emphasis on rural development and the building of the Aswan Dam, then as a recipient of large quantities of PL480 (Agricultural Trade, Development and Assistance Act, 1954) wheat and meat in the 1960s. Lastly, once President Anwar Sadat had ousted the Soviet military advisers and made his famous visit to Jerusalem in 1977, Egypt became a key partner in the peace process and so the recipient of very large sums of American military and civilian aid, $46 billion over the past twenty-five years. In addition, ever since the establishment of the USAID office in Cairo in 1975, this aid has been used as a lever to pressure the Egyptian government into liberalizing both its economic and its political systems as well as an encouragement to join in a number of major American Middle Eastern initiatives, such as the organization of the gulf war coalition and the fight against international terrorism.

Certain major consequences follow and must give pause to anyone who seeks to approach the American-Egyptian relationship anew. Given the length and significance of this relationship, it is no surprise to find that the two bureaucracies are intricately entwined at any number of levels on the basis of a long history of joint projects and repeated interaction and negotiation. Nor is it a surprise to find that, over such a long time, almost every type of initiative has been suggested at one point or another, every type of persuasion attempted. This makes the task of the analyst doubly difficult: there is so much detail to master, so little that has not yet been thought about or put on the table. Nevertheless, however complex the analysis, one thing remains abundantly clear: The relationship between the two countries is too crucial for either of them to put it in any real danger.

For the rest, I will begin by looking at Egypt today in its international and domestic context and then in its present-day relationship with the United States, before attempting to isolate those major themes that seem to me key to any discussion of possible future directions. I should also note that in the first section I will try to present the situation as it is seen in Cairo and through the eyes of the policy making elite.

EGYPT TODAY

Population, Income, and the Environment

Egypt's population was estimated to be 57.6 million in mid-1994 and has now almost certainly reached 60 million.[1] It is presently growing at

---

1. All figures are from World Bank publications, including *Claiming the Future: Choosing Prosperity in the Middle East and North Africa* (Washington, D.C.: The World Bank, 1995), especially the Statistical Appendix.

an annual rate of 2 percent, as opposed to 2.7 percent in the mid-1980s. This reduction is believed to be due to a combination of structural features affecting the women of childbearing age, notably urbanization and better education, as well as an active government policy of increasing access to means of birth control. Nevertheless, the World Bank estimates that Egypt's population will more or less double itself to 118 million by the year 2050.

Nearly half (45 percent) of Egyptians live in urban areas, including the 12 million or so who inhabit Greater Cairo itself. Cairo is one of the most densely populated cities in the world, with little difference between the rich and the poorer quarters.[2] Moreover, perhaps half its inhabitants live in over one hundred "squatter" communities around its periphery. Almost all of these people are in unofficial (and therefore technically illegal) housing, but most are slowly being provided with minimal public services.[3] Contrary to popular mythology, Cairo now has quite a stable population, with only 13 percent of those counted in the 1986 census having been born outside the city itself.[4]

Most of the remainder of the Egypt's inhabitants live either in the Delta area or in a narrow strip of land along the Nile. However, in recent years, strenuous efforts have been made to encourage people to live in new towns and cities established in the desert, first around Cairo itself and then in a number of satellites established between 30 to 70 kilometers away. Efforts have also been made to increase the amount of cultivable land including, most recently, President Mubarak's scheme, the NPDUE (National Project for Developing Upper Egypt), which involves channeling water from the Aswan Dam to the New Valley in the Western Desert so as to allow the irrigation of 50,000 hectares of arid land.

As far as the World Bank is concerned, Egypt is classified as a low-income country with a per capita income of only $710 a year. But given the size and vitality of the informal economy, in which most transactions go unrecorded, there is reason to believe that the actual figure might be anything up to double this small amount.[5] In addition, many families survive on the remittances sent back by the some 3.7 million Egyptians

2. Cairo's population density is 170 persons/hectare. Mexico City has only 30. See Eric Denis, "Urban Planning and Growth in Cairo", *Middle East Report* 27/1, no. 242 (winter 1997): 7.
3. See Asaf Bayat, "Cairo's Poor: Dilemmas of Survival and Solidarity," *Middle East Report* 27/1, no. 242 (winter 1997): 3.
4. Denis, "Urban Planning," 10.
5. For example, Ibrahim Oweiss, *The Underground Economy with Special Reference to the Case of Egypt* (National Bank of Egypt, Commemoration Lecture Programme, Cairo, December 19, 1994), 18–20.

working abroad. The official economy grew fast enough to produce growth in per capita income of some 5.9 percent a year from 1974 to 1985, as a result of a huge increase in the revenues from tourism, workers' remittances and the export of the country's own oil. But the rate then slowed to 1.6 percent a year from 1985 to 1994 and is only just beginning to improve.

A significant proportion of the windfall revenues accruing to the government during the boom years were invested in infrastructural projects (sewage, water, garbage collection, and so on) as well as in housing. Nevertheless, Hosni Mubarak's regime has been forced to abandon many of the "universalistic" aspirations of the Nasser period, particularly insofar as the provision of public services such as health and education is concerned, as well as the automatic access to government jobs once provided for school and university leavers. The regime has also presided over a period that has seen a real decline in the value of official salaries. To make matters worse, it has been estimated that some two hundred fifty to three hundred thousand public-sector jobs will be lost as a result of the promised policies of privatization, although some of this impact will be lessened by newly instituted programs of small redundancy payments to those who agree to voluntary retirement.[6] Job losses of this size will certainly increase the unemployment problem, particularly among those with a secondary or higher education.[7]

The foregoing analysis should be enough to highlight the existence of Egypt's major social problems: poverty and lack of urban amenities, a high rate of illiteracy among the adult population (52 percent), serious unemployment and a poorly resourced system of secondary and university education that produces students with few of the skills needed outside government service. Nor, given the regime's focus on carrying through its program of structural adjustment, is there much hope of amelioration in the near future.

Indeed, this is explicitly recognized by government policy itself, for example by its strong stand against political Islam, which it believes could profit from further poverty and unemployment, and by its justification of yet another period of "emergency rule" by reference to the need to protect its own economic reforms.[8]

Turning lastly to questions of geography and the environment, Egypt's major concerns involve the management of the Nile, the ecological health of the Mediterranean and the Red Sea (which is especially vital for

6. "Egypt: Retirement", Reuters (Cairo), March 23, 1997.
7. One estimate puts 60 percent of the present unemployed in this "educated" category. "Education Proves a Poor Investment," *Financial Times*, March 27, 1997.
8. "Martial Law Extended," *Financial Times*, February 25, 1997.

tourism), and the pollution to be found in its major cities. The division of
the Nile waters is still regulated by a 1959 agreement that specified the
relative shares of Egypt and Sudan but left nothing at all to Ethiopia. Since
then, it has not been in the Egyptian interest to renegotiate this agreement, as any modification would inevitably lead to a reduction in its own
quota. Nevertheless, the day is fast approaching when Ethiopia will have
to be included. Beyond that lie huge problems consequent to the fact that
the number of people living along the valleys of the Blue and White Niles
are projected to increase from their present 250 million to a probable 1
billion by 2050.[9] Water will inevitably become more scarce, posing an
enormous challenge to Egyptian diplomacy as well as, inevitably, neces-
sitating major efforts to reduce water usage in Egypt.

Other local ecological concerns involve the continued impact of the
new system of water storage made possible by the Aswan High Dam.
While there no evidence that this problem has been nearly as serious for
the country itself as many feared, it has had powerful effects along the
Mediterranean coast, including increased salination and a reduction in the
numbers of saltwater fish.[10] Such concerns will have to be dealt with, in
part, through cooperation with Egypt's neighbors, perhaps through joint
action coordinated with those European states along the northern
Mediterranean littoral. As for the problems of urban pollution specified
in a recent USAID report, *Comparing Environmental Health Risks* (Cairo,
1994), these will remain subject to purely national initiatives and are
unlikely to promote an internationalist approach in a country where the
population has shown little interest in the larger questions of environmental degradation so far.[11]

Egypt's International Environment

Egypt's most important international relationships are with the United
States and Israel, all three bound together in the Arab-Israel peace process
begun at the Madrid conference in late 1991. President Mubarak's government began by playing a vital role in establishing one of the necessary
preconditions for Palestinian participation—Yasir Arafat's renunciation
of violence—and has remained a key player ever since. Indeed, one could
well argue that this role has become even more important since Prime

9. "Nile States Look to New Division of Waters," *Financial Times,* February 27, 1997.
10. For a sound analysis of the evidence (or lack of it) regarding the possible negative impact
    of the Aswan Dam, see Robert C. Hunt, "Agricultural Ecology: The Impact of the
    Aswan Dam So Far," *Culture and Agriculture* 31 (winter 1987): 106.
11. This is the conclusion to be found in Nicholas Hopkins and Sohair Mehanna, "Pollution,
    Popular Perceptions and Grassroots Activism," *Middle East Reports* 27/1, no. 242 (win-
    ter 1997): 22.

Minister Benjamin Netanyahu's electoral victory in May 1996, after which Egypt became Arafat's major intercessor in his struggles with the new Israeli government.

The rules of this particular relationship are well understood in Cairo and Washington: Mubarak must be as helpful as possible but without ever becoming a direct party to the Israeli-Palestinian negotiations or taking any unilateral initiatives himself. Any movement outside these narrow parameters is the subject of an immediate reprimand. This happened during one stage of the Hebron negotiations in December 1996 when the Egyptians were accused of introducing "major amendments" to an American document.[12] Given the constellation of forces involved, such reprimands can just as easily be initiated in Tel Aviv as they can by either the White House or the Congress. But whatever the original source, all parties are well aware that what is really at stake is Egypt's annual $2 billion in military and civilian aid from the United States and the threat that it could either be reduced or in some way put at risk.

One central issue yet to be resolved between Egypt and Israel is the question of whether relations should be institutionalized within a framework of alliance that extends beyond the original 1979 peace treaty to something larger, embracing the Jordanians, the Palestinians, and even the Syrians and Lebanese as well. Such an idea seemed to be at the root of Shimon Peres's strategic vision of a new Middle Eastern order anchored in a set of Arab-Israeli agreements involving such matters as disarmament and the creation of a Middle Eastern common market. But it seems that both President Mubarak and his foreign minister, Amr Moussa, had decided, well before the Netanyahu victory in May 1996, that such a tight relationship with Israel was not in Egypt's best interest. Just why they made this decision remains unclear, but my own belief is that the turning point was the failure of the Egyptian initiative to pressure Israel into signing the Nuclear Nonproliferation Treaty in April 1995. The lesson drawn in Cairo from this somewhat humiliating event was that an institutionalized political alliance with the Israelis could never be a partnership of equals, given Israel's close association with the United States. The regime turned instead toward the exploration of alternative sets of relationships that could strengthen Egypt without putting its peace treaty with Israel at risk.

Other sets of considerations pointed in the same direction. One was the general realization that, in a post–Cold War world of large economic blocs, Egypt needed to take immediate action either to join one such bloc or to try to create its own. A second, which gained greater force after the Likud victory in May 1996, was an understanding that Netanyahu's seem-

12. "Egypt's Input in Peace Talks Irritates," Reuters (Jerusalem), December 11, 1996.

ing lack of interest in building better relationships with the Arab states not only let Egypt off the hook as far as its involvement in schemes for insti-tutionalized Israeli-Arab cooperation were concerned, but also provided a perfect opportunity for an Egyptian effort to try to reorganize the Middle East along other, more congenial, lines. This, in turn, meant cap-italizing on its improving relationships with the rest of the Arab world.

As is well known, Egypt has for some years been slowly making its way back to the position of influence and importance it enjoyed among the Arab states before it was ostracized as a result of the Camp David Agreement of 1979. This process was much assisted by its role as a sup-porter of Iraq in the first gulf war (1980–1988), which resulted in its readmittance to the Arab League in November 1987, and again in the sec-ond gulf war (1990–1991), when the crisis facilitated the return of the Arab League headquarters to Cairo after a ten-year sojourn in Tunis. The Arab perception that Egypt was needed as a counterweight to Iran at this time was the main factor underlying the reestablishment of good relations with the gulf Arab states. Indeed, for a brief moment it seemed distinct-ly possible for Egypt to create a profitable strategic alliance in which the Egyptians and the Syrians would provide military security in exchange for financial assistance. In the end, however, this notion, set out in the Damascus Declaration of March 1991, never came to fruition, as the gulf states preferred to buy their security from the United States, Britain, and France. But it helped to create a situation in which Egypt could begin to try out various policy initiatives designed to recreate for itself a central role in Arab affairs. These efforts culminated in its calling the June 1996 Arab Summit to consider a common strategy in regard to the Netanyahu government, and then in its use of the MENA III conference in Cairo in November 1996 to distance itself from official cooperation with the Israelis and to float alternative projects for greater Arab economic coop-eration, including a renewed interest in the creation of a purely Arab Free Trade Area, plans for which were completed by the end of 1997.

Mention should now be made of a third possible partnership, that with the European Union and, more specifically, with the Euro-Mediterranean scheme announced at the Barcelona conference in November 1995.

Europe is important to Egypt for two different sets of reasons. First, at the political level, the EU is a useful alternative to the United States–Israeli axis and can on occasion be persuaded to put pressure on the Israelis or, at the very least, reinforce the international consensus concerning such vital principles as the exchange of land for peace. Successive European declarations have made this same point, most recently after the EU summit meeting in Florence in July 1996. European activity in support of a continued peace process has also become much more insistent since the Netanyahu victory. There are also signs that the EU is using its economic relationship with Israel to make the same point. The main problem remains as it has always been: how to play the European card in such a way that it actually puts pressure on Israel without irritating the United States. But other problems may certainly arise over time, for example, in devising an Egyptian response to the new European initiative involving the creation of a proposed European Rapid Deployment Force (EUROFOR), the aim of which would be to carry out limited peacekeeping and humanitarian missions south of the Mediterranean. Although Egypt is quite well integrated into the Western military alliance through joint exercises and so on, its response to schemes of this type, with their obvious neocolonial overtones, and their possible use against its maverick neighbors, Libya and Sudan, will require very careful diplomatic management.

The second set of reasons involves the economic sphere, and it is here that Egypt faces a difficult choice. One possibility would simply be to join the Euro-Mediterranean Free Trade Area as a way of attaching the Egyptian economy on a permanent basis to the world's largest economic bloc. Such a step would have considerable advantages in ensuring markets for Egyptian goods and increased European assistance in the form of investment, aid, and technical help in reorganizing the country's foreign trade regime to meet the substantial commitments already entered into as a result of participation in the GATT, the Uruguay Round, and the new World Trade Organization. Furthermore, it would lead to participation of an association in which Israel is also a member, but only one among a number of Mediterranean states and without the special clout that its alliance with Washington allows. For these and other reasons, negotiations for upgrading Egypt's existing bilateral treaty with the EU have already begun, although subject, so far, to serious difficulties concerning Egypt's demands for better market access for its food products.

The major problem with this strategy, and one faced by all the other Mediterranean states as well, is that the Euro-Mediterranean formula forces Egypt to negotiate bilaterally on a take-it-or-leave-it basis. Moreover, the whole scheme is based on the notion that Europe is creating a new structure for Middle Eastern regional cooperation, not the states of the region itself. In such circumstances, members of the Egyptian political elite have begun to make renewed calls for turning the present Free Trade Area into an Arab common market that would then negotiate its own relationship with Europe, just as the Gulf Cooperation Council has been encouraged to do. Indeed, the Europeans themselves are anxious for something like this to happen because, in their estimation, foreign capital will be attracted to the Middle East in any large quantity only if the region itself is seen to be united and increasingly integrated from an economic point of view.

Whether or not the Arabs can, in fact, create such an organization is another matter, particularly in the light of the various failures to achieve institutionalized cooperation in the 1950s and 1960s. However, from a purely Egyptian point of view, it has so many obvious attractions that it is certainly worth a considerable diplomatic effort. Of the advantages, clearly the most important is membership in an Arab common market in which Cairo would play a leading role. This would give it a much more powerful bargaining position in negotiations both with the Israelis—about a possible Arab-Israeli market—and with the Europeans. Nevertheless, Egypt has a number of fall-back positions as well. Even without any institutionalized form of regional cooperation, a huge number of projects can still make use of what might be called the local geographical "economies of scale" at the eastern end of the Mediter-ranean, involving such schemes as the present plans to link Egypt's electricity grid with those of Syria, Jordan, Turkey, and Iraq by the year 1998. There is room for project-by-project cooperation with Israeli private capital as well. The Midor partnership, for example, has just completed the financing for a proposed $1.3 billion refinery at Alexandria. Progress in this direction would not only be helpful in its own right but would also fit nicely with the larger American–World Bank and European agendas for the region. It has the added attraction of helping to undermine public perceptions that Israel is playing a central role in the creation of a new economic order in the Middle East.

It follows, I would argue, that the dominant view in Cairo is that it is in Egypt's present interest to create a network of different economic and political alliances, encompassing America and Israel, the Arab states, and Europe in such a way that they all reinforce each other rather than creating contradictions between them. I would also argue that as a result of Netanyahu's accession to power this task has become significantly less difficult in a number of important ways, most notably by making it easier to explore the Arab option without running the risk of alienating the Americans (or those Israelis) committed to the creation of an Israeli-Egyptian strategic alliance. Of almost equal importance is the fact that Egypt's management of its relations with both the Europeans and the United States has been made easier as well. Whereas before May 1996 Egypt found itself in the middle of major disputes, for example over the proposed Middle Eastern Development Bank, these have become much less significant in recent months and no longer pose the problem of having to choose sides. In other words, the bank can open in Cairo when political circumstances allow but with a very reduced role that neither duplicates other international organizations nor forces it to act as the major facilitator for an American-inspired Arab-Israeli economic cooperation.

All this is not to say that there will not be problems ahead. No one can predict what will happen next as far as the peace process is concerned. No one can say how well the Mubarak regime will be able to grapple with the complex problems posed by having to define, and then pursue, national economic goals in a way very different from that long used in Egypt's more conventional political and strategic diplomacy. But for the moment, and perhaps as long as Mr. Netanyahu remains in power, Egypt will be able to operate in a more favorable context in which U.S. political aims in the Middle East seem to be more or less complementary with European economic ones and in which President Mubarak will be left to explore his Arab options free from either commitment to an Israeli alliance or from any need to assist in the creation of an Israeli-Palestinian-Jordanian common market.

Egypt's Domestic Policy Environment

The word *liberalization* is certainly the right one to describe the major programs of political and economic change that have taken place in Egypt since President Sadat first spelled out his notion of *infitah* in detail in April 1974. However, it would clearly be wrong to take this as a guide to where the whole process will end. In Egypt, just as elsewhere, there is no guarantee that anything like a fully fledged democracy or a market economy will ever be put in place. Indeed, if the experience of most other countries can be taken as a guide, we can be sure that a number of other destinations are also possible, some of which are being actively canvassed by different groups in Egypt itself under such titles as the Asian or the Islamic model.

One other caveat is also necessary: Although Egyptian life has certainly become a great deal more *free* since the early 1950s (in terms of ability to invest, to move, to read what you like, and so on), it would be difficult to say that it has become noticeably more *democratic* in any meaningful sense of that term. It is true that there have been a series of contested general elections in the late 1970s and again from 1984 onward. But far from there being a perceptible movement toward a situation in which one of the opposition parties might develop sufficient strength to defeat the government NDP (National Democratic Party), the reverse seems actually to have been the case, with most of the opposition parties boycotting the 1990 election and then the whole group gaining only 13 seats among them in 1995 (against 416 to the NDP and 15 independents). Just as important, this latter election was the subject of more than the usual number of complaints about intimidation and other mal-practices, many of which remain before both the courts and the NDP-controlled National Assembly.

Two other considerations also militate against any easy optimism about future political progress. One is the growing power of President Mubarak himself, reinforced by his decision to run for a third six-year term in 1993. The other is the legacy of the Islamic militancy that began in 1992 and which, though now largely contained, has helped to justify the con-tinued management of the electoral process and the regime's refusal to allow any religious group to organize itself as a party and to put forward candidates in its own right. Hence the opportunity to incorporate the moderate elements among the Muslim Brothers as a stable element with-in the political system has been lost, in the short term at least, while repression and intimidation have been allowed to do their usual work, which is to split the leadership of the Brotherhood itself into rival factions and groups.

In these circumstances, there seems little likelihood of any significant political advance in Egypt during the remainder of President Mubarak's present term of office. Indeed, judging from present trends, the future seems to be one in which a combination of presidential power and tight government control over the National Assembly will provide the condi-tions for what might be called the continued "regeneration" of authori-tarian rule rather than its eventual transformation to something more liberal. There are, however, two significant qualifications. First, in Egypt, as in many other countries, the combination of a lack of govern-ment resources and, on occasion, a retreat from the obligation to pro-vide free public services to all has meant that many areas of social and economic life are outside any system of formal regulation and can be controlled only through a process of negotiation and occasional police intervention. Hence the government may decree that all private mosques must be managed in a particular kind of way, but no one in the administration knows how many such mosques there are. Hence tax col-lection becomes a series of bargains between collectors and private-sec-tor entrepreneurs. Hence building regulations and zoning laws are only fitfully obeyed.

Second, a great deal of public space is occupied not by competition between rival interest groups but by a type of domestic "cultural war" in which people of various Islamic tendencies seek to promote a whole vari-ety of different agendas. These range from changing the laws of personal status, to censoring supposedly "immoral" books and films, to targeting particular intellectuals like the unfortunate Professor Abu Zeid, accused of apostasy and so under threat of being forcibly divorced from his wife.

Meanwhile, different government agencies, as well as (sometimes) the courts, attempt to hold some kind of line. But, given the fact that a sense of Islamic identity is now so much part of middle-class life, it is difficult to see how any consensus can be achieved by either side as to what is or is not to be allowed. To make matters still more complex, this type of cultural war involves organized Coptic Christian groups as well. All this will certainly remain a central feature of Egyptian life for the rest of this century, and probably well beyond. And it follows that any attempt to exclude such religiously motivated groups from a working definition of "civil society" clearly misses a very important part of contemporary reality.

As regards the economy, Egypt has been officially committed to a policy of "structural adjustment" since the 1980s. But this has always proceeded in fits and starts, dominated by domestic political considerations and involving lengthy negotiations at every stage with the World Bank and the IMF. There is general agreement that the regime only acted in real earnest as a result of the promises of substantial debt forgiveness following its participation in the second gulf war. However, even then, there were years of slow progress toward the targets set in such key areas as the privatization of state-owned enterprises. Only with the appointment of Kamal El Ganzoury as prime minister in January 1996 has the program been pursued with real energy and dispatch.

All this was skillfully done. Mr. Ganzoury was able to use the months just before the 1996 MENA III conference to persuade the IMF and then the Club of Paris that sufficient progress had been made to write off the last $4.2 billion of the promised debt forgiveness in October. Even so, difficult problems remain. Although the Ganzoury government succeeded in selling off eight more public companies in the first ten months of 1996—as opposed to the three sold by its predecessor in 1994 and five in 1995—there seems to have been a perceptible slowing down toward the end of the same year, with one sale (of the Amariya Cement Company) called off in November and renewed skepticism as to whether the government's revised target of ninety-one companies to be sold by June 1998 was any more realistic than the others set before.[13]

Some of the lessons to be drawn from all this are not peculiar to Egypt. As elsewhere in the world, there has been powerful opposition to privatization from local vested interests. Like governments elsewhere, the

---

13. "Egypt: Debts Written Off," *Middle East International*, October 25, 1996; "Banks Stand Out Among Cairo's Privatisation Candidates," *Financial Times*, November 5, 1996; and "Egypt Cancels Cement Sell-Off," *Financial Times,* November 27, 1996.

Mubarak regime has been worried about the threat of increased unemployment as well as accusations that it was asking too low a price for valuable state assets and that control of these same assets was in danger of
passing into foreign hands. Indeed, what is now becoming more and more
clear is that the whole process of structural adjustment itself can no longer
be conceived of as a once-and-for-all process by which markets are created anew in only a few years. Rather, it must be viewed as a continuous,
probably irreversible, but necessarily zigzag progress toward distant goals
that may never be fully attained.

There are, however, two important qualifications in the Egyptian case,
as in many others as well. The first is that a myopic focus on the speed of
privatization often obscures quite substantial progress in a host of other,
equally important, aspects of economic life. These include the revivifica-
tion of such key institutions as the stock exchange, the deregulation of the
banking system, and the enactment of new laws more congruent with a
liberalizing economy in the area of trade unions, employer-employee
relations, and property in both its urban and agricultural aspects. These
are major achievements in spite of the fact that they often manage to reim-
pose a much larger degree of state control than would be thought proper
in Western Europe or North America.

The second qualification involves the point that, quite apart from the
targets set in association with the World Bank and the IMF, Egypt is also
locked into a set of much more rigorous timetables consequent on its
obligations (mentioned above) to the WTO and the European Union.
These involve not just a regular reduction of tariffs and quotas but also
new legislation designed to bring local laws, if they existed at all, in line
with best international practice concerning such matters as copyright, the
protection of the environment, and unfair competition. The huge implications of all this for Egyptian economic life cannot be over stressed. Just
as the local economy is being opened up more and more to foreign trade
and finance, the rules governing their practice are being changed in ways
that, in the short run at least, are both difficult to predict and difficult to
manage. A few entrepreneurs such as Mahmoud Wahba, who succeeded
in cornering a large part of the newly deregulated 1995 cotton crop, seem
able to thrive in such an atmosphere. But others can be forgiven for continuing to cling close to the state and its bureaucracy as the only way of
protecting their present interests until they can more clearly see the road
ahead.

This, then, has been the context in which U.S. policy toward Egypt has
been forced to operate. I will now examine the major principles on which
this same policy has been based before attempting to evaluate its overall
effectiveness.

UNITED STATES POLICY TOWARD EGYPT

The basic aims of American policy toward Egypt since the mid-1970s have been, first, to encourage it to make peace with Israel and, second, to preserve and then expand this peace by drawing in other Arab regimes as well as the PLO. More recently, and especially since the first gulf war, the United States has also begun to view Egypt as a major strategic ally in its own right, both in terms of helping to preserve Western access to gulf oil and in the maintenance of a general, American- and Israeli-inspired Middle Eastern security system. In this system the major threats are perceived to derive from a combination of state terrorism, nuclear proliferation and the activities of rogue regimes such as the Libyan, the Sudanese, and, increasingly, the Iranian. All this, in turn, has been viewed as contingent on the successful preservation of the strength and stability of the Egyptian regime itself, something best achieved by persuading it to transform the country's economic and political system in a liberal direction. Whether all these aims are in fact compatible is a subject to which we must necessarily return.

America's principal weapon in pursuing these goals has been the creation of a close relationship with the upper echelons of the regime, underpinned by the provision of economic and military aid at levels equaled only by those given to Israel. However, unlike the case of the Israelis, this aid is not simply handed over directly to the government but administered by what is the largest U.S. diplomatic complex in the world, including the biggest USAID program in the world, with a budget of nearly $1 billion a year and the services of some two hundred employees—all justified in terms of the need to monitor and to control such large expenditures of money and to avoid waste and corruption.[14] This too is a subject that requires careful evaluation.

As far as the military aid is concerned, its main uses have been twofold. First, it has been given out in a series of five-year cycles beginning in 1983 to replace the previous Soviet equipment with American materiel, a process that has worked its way through the Egyptian army and is now focused mainly on the navy and air force. Second, it has involved a process of military reorganization designed to make the armed forces more professional, more mobile, and so better able to respond to a variety of dif-

---

14. Denis J. Sullivan, "American Aid to Egypt: Peace without Development," *Middle East Policy* IV/4 (October 1996): 37. I have drawn extensively on ideas and information from this article.

ferent situations. An essential ingredient in this same process has been a series of combined exercises with British and French as well as American forces.

Where this leaves the Egyptian army in terms of military effectiveness is difficult for a nonexpert to say. Looked at in general terms, and in relationship to possible threats from Egypt's immediate neighbors, the picture must be much the same as it was before the whole process of reequipment began: That is to say, Egypt could easily defend itself against either the Sudan or Libya but would still be no match for the Israelis. But seen from a larger Middle Eastern perspective, Egypt's ability to project its military power some way beyond its borders has clearly been greatly improved. It would seem, *a priori*, that such a situation must be in America's interest as well, the more so as it also gives the U.S. armed forces access to Egyptian bases and equipment in a place close to other areas in which it might want, one day, to intervene.

A final point about military aid concerns its relationship with Egypt's defense expenditures in general. These have continued to rise in recent years and by 1995 had reached $2.96 billion or about 5 percent of GDP, a proportion which is, of course, very high by contemporary European (though not Middle Eastern) standards. Nor is it likely to be much reduced in the immediate future, at least not before the present reequipment cycle (1993–1998) is complete. What happens then is impossible to say but a plausible scenario would be one in which a combination of continued American aid and President Mubarak's own close association with the military makes significant cuts in this area unlikely.

U.S. economic aid is provided through the Economic Support Fund (ERF). Its importance can be measured on two different scales. First, in terms of the Egyptian economy itself, the activities of USAID reach throughout the county, affecting people in rural and urban areas alike not only in terms of income and employment but also education, health, and access to birth control. As such, it also plays an enormously important role in Egyptian bureaucratic life, with different ministries and agencies of government competing with each other for money, advice, and assistance. Second, in the larger context of international aid, the American contribution—no less than 30 percent of all Egypt received in 1994 from both bilateral and multilateral resources—tends to dwarf all the others and so provide the dominant voice when it comes to planning the overall thrust of development.[15] What makes this position still more significant is the fact that the American administration also enjoys such a close rela-

15. Denis J. Sullivan, "Introduction: Re-inventing American Assistance," *Middle East Policy* IV/4 (October 1996): 2.

tionship with the World Bank and the IMF, both of which share its general commitment to structural adjustment and the opening up of the Egyptian economy to outside competition.

Nevertheless, the situation is not without serious problems. For one thing, the U.S. program is so large and possesses so high a profile that it cannot avoid serious criticism both from Egyptians who see it as too intrusive and from Americans who see it as having failed in its primary stated task of transforming the country's economic prospects. As Denis Sullivan points out, for all the good work that may have been done in Egypt, the country cannot be considered one of the international success stories.[16] For another, USAID itself is beset by critics in and out of Congress and has been the subject of repeated attempts to reshape it in such a way that it can better perform the new tasks thought appropriate to the post–Cold War world. In Denis Sullivan's account, both problems have now come together with a vengeance as critics in Washington point to failures in Egypt, while employees in Cairo seek either to thwart directives coming from headquarters or to impose their own spin on them.[17]

Just how to deal with all this in a paper focused on "pivotal" Egypt presents problems of its own. Clearly the future direction of the whole USAID program under its new director, H. Brian Atwood, is a subject more usefully addressed elsewhere and by the appropriate experts. It is also exceedingly difficult for a writer to find a neutral position in a situation in which not only is there no present consensus about how USAID's activities ought properly to be evaluated but also, given the nature of Washington politics and the many unresolved questions about future funding and future direction, it is impossible to conceive of such a consensus developing in the near future if at all.

Three more general comments close this section. First, given the strategic importance of Egypt, it seems unlikely that the absolute level of American aid will be much reduced for some years to come. Indeed, it is significant that, in the last year or so, no leading figure in either country has suggested such a possibility, as Senator Robert Dole did in 1990 and President Mubarak in 1995.[18] If I were an Egyptian, I would be tempted to thank Mr. Netanyahu for this. Second, given the general agreement in Washington, the foundations, and the universities as to the broader aims that should underlie American policy at this time, it would seem reasonable to assume that aid to Egypt will continue to be directed toward Atwood's four principle targets of economic growth, population stabilization, environmental protection, and the promotion of democracy.

16. Sullivan, "American Aid to Egypt," 39–40.
17. Sullivan, "American Aid to Egypt," 46–47.
18. Sullivan, "American Aid to Egypt," 36–37.

Third, given that so many United States companies and institutions benefit directly from the fact that the projects to be financed by USAID are jointly identified by the Egyptians and Americans, any move that might threaten to undermine this privileged position by reducing American input would be seriously resisted in Congress.

It is now necessary to return to the question of the *effectiveness* of American aid, a subject which, in this context, cannot be separated from a second question of whether it has helped or hindered the pursuit of the larger U.S. interests involved. The subject is a difficult one and it might be useful to approach it by starting with three general propositions:

1. As a result of the various policies pursued since the mid-1970s, Egypt has become one of the firmest allies of the United States in the world.
2. President Mubarak and his regime remain firmly in power.
3. Egypt is not seen as an international success story in terms of its progress toward either sustained economic development or a vibrant multiparty democracy.

It is this last proposition which, in my opinion, accounts for the repeated bouts of frustration on the American side, something well illustrated by the appearance of the pseudonymous article by "Cassandra" in the *Middle East Journal* (49/1, winter 1995) entitled "The Impending Crisis in Egypt" and the nervous reaction it inspired among the aid community in Washington. Talk of a "crisis" in Egypt is, of course, nothing new, the term being regularly used by officials in both countries whenever they want to grab the attention of policy makers in either capital. But in this case, the writer's assumption that U.S. policy had managed neither to engineer substantial political and economic progress nor to build up assets for itself in the shape of "dedicated, reliable and powerful supporters"[19] caused a brief panic in the aid community itself, already under attack from Congress and engaged in fierce internal turf wars as it adjusted to the changes brought in by the Clinton administration.

More generally, such comments raise the whole question of how policies are to be judged and of how to evaluate the links between their various components. On the one hand are those who judge matters purely in terms of the stability and the pliability of the regime in question without worrying too much how the aid money has been spent. On the other are the Cassandras who assert that the aid money itself has not only failed to achieve its objectives but may even have helped to undermine them by raising hopes that have not been met and so failing to build up the solid core of support on which the future of the relationship must depend.

19. "Cassandra," "The Impending Crisis in Egypt," *Middle East Journal* 49, no. 1 (winter 1995): 24–26.

None of this is at all unusual. But what gives it significance in the Egyptian case is the very high levels of aid involved, the enormous importance attached to the alliance in Middle Eastern terms and, I would argue, an image of Egypt that has remained unchanged throughout the twentieth century as a country with unmanageable demographic and other social problems.

Let us now look at the history of the American-Egyptian relationship from a somewhat different perspective. A first point is that, given the political situation in Egypt itself, the process of economic restructuring has probably gone just about as fast as could be imagined without stirring up dangerous domestic repercussions. Indeed, one could argue that the Egyptian government has protected USAID (as well as the World Bank) from some of the more dangerous consequences of following its own advice, for example by limiting cuts in subsidies and social welfare at the time when Islamic militancy was most widespread. Second, the process of economic change looks largely irreversible, at least in any foreseeable future. What also looks irreversible is the process of the creation of ever-expanding links of all types between Egyptians and Americans: business, educational, medical, military, and so on. Third, the activities of USAID have been greatly hampered by the lack of consensus within the Egyptian government about how the reforms should proceed, an aspect well captured by many internal confrontations, for example, the current one between a protectionist minister of industry and a liberal minister of finance.[20] As Denis Sullivan points out, probably the only agreement which all share is the need for gradualism.[21] Fourth, in spite of all these problems, it should not be forgotten that an estimated 80 percent of American economic aid returns to the United States for the purchase of goods and services. It is also remarkable that the huge American aid administration has been allowed to go about its business for twenty years without sustained attack or overt interference.[22]

An essential last point is that, ever since notions of aid and development became popular after World War II the issue itself has been a contentious one, subject to sudden changes of direction, fashion, and mood, and still remains without any consensus about how its effects can properly be judged. Indeed, the politics of the whole process seem to demand just such inconsistency, as one set of experts seeks to succeed another by the well-tried method of proclaiming all previous policies to have been a waste of money, the better to justify whatever new initiative they have in

20. "Egypt Confronts Car Tariff Dilemma," *Financial Times*, January 9, 1997.
21. Sullivan, "American Aid to Egypt," 43, 48.
22. Sullivan, "Introduction: Reinventing U.S. Foreign Assistance," 9.

mind. The result is a deliberate suppression of historical memory and the necessary belief that, at any moment, it is possible to start again completely free from past constraints on the basis, more or less, of a *tabula rasa*. It is vital to bear all this in mind when considering whether other policies might be more effective from now on.

U.S. POLICY IN THE FUTURE

It is reasonable to assume that Egypt will remain a vital United States ally over the next ten years or so. This itself is a function of the continued uncertainty of the peace process, America's interest in encouraging the integration of Israel into the Middle East and in protecting regional oil supplies, and a shared interest in confronting Islamic militancy, whether from groups or states. Clearly the overlap is not complete: Egypt is less committed to an enlarged Israeli role than the United States, more worried about relations with such neighbors as Libya and Sudan, and openly competitive when it comes to policies aimed at containing Iraq or assisting the gulf states to develop a more Arab-oriented security umbrella. But for the immediate future, such tensions seem very unlikely to affect the foundations of the relationship.

How, then, can this relationship be best managed? It is useful to begin thinking about future policy directions by trying to identify what will be the most important elements driving events over the next few years. In the case of Egypt, the major feature will be the continuation of the Mubarak presidency along the lines suggested by previous presidencies, that is, toward an ever more authoritarian style of government, an increasing disinclination to tolerate dissent, and, equally inevitably, more and more accusations of corruption leveled against members of his entourage and the political elite in general. This has always been a function of the longevity of a regime, its manipulation of what, in effect, remains a one-party system, and a lack of rotation at the top.

It follows that, once again in the late twentieth century, the United States will be faced with a situation in which it is closely associated with an increasingly dictatorial regime against which charges of human rights abuses, corruption, and other kinds of malpractice are as commonplace as they are embarrassing. And, once again, it will certainly try to limit the damage by constant pressure on the president himself to stick to the rule of law, to prosecute wrongdoers, and to keep censorship and other restraints on freedom to a minimum—as the United States is also trying to do with other pivotal states such as Indonesia and Turkey. Beyond that, there will be particular challenges to American policy, notably the combination of an Egyptian national and a presidential election in 1999. In ideal circumstances, the United States should work to ensure that President Mubarak does not stand for a fourth term, that a successor (or better still, a choice of successors) is in place and that the opposition is much better represented in the National Assembly than it is now. Whether it is willing to push these hopes to a satisfactory conclusion is quite another matter: History shows how difficult it has been to curb the dictatorial tendencies of powerful leaders on whom the United States has chosen to rely.

Turning now to the military side of the equation, the United States will certainly want to complete the present process of retraining and reequipping Egypt's armed forces. But what for? From Washington's point of view, the optimal situation must be that Egypt has a good, well-equipped army that could join it in any major Middle Eastern war as well as defend Egypt from attack by one of its Arab neighbors. But that is about as far as it goes. Although the United States may find it useful from time to time to see units from such an army participate in small-scale peacekeeping or rescue operations, it certainly does not want to see that army used in support of Egyptian policies independent of its own. Nor does it have an interest in the maintenance of the present high levels of military spending well into the twenty-first century. Nevertheless, from a political point of view, this may be the price that will have to be paid for the preservation of the present system, in which a military president ensures the political neutrality of a large and well-paid army.

The future of economic aid is more problematic. Whereas any drastic reduction in military aid would be regarded as a serious blow to Mubarak's own prestige, a phased reduction in economic and technical assistance would be much easier to arrange. Senator Dole's 1990 suggestion of a 5 percent cut in the sums sent to both Israel and Egypt has much to recommend it as a way of making a start, provided it also includes his suggestion that the money saved be redirected toward some of the poorer and less fortunate of the world's emerging democracies.[23] More generally, it seems that the Egyptian-American alliance would benefit if the United States was not seen to be so closely involved in the making of economic policy and thus implicated in what will almost certainly be seen by some as its failure.

A reduction in the size of the USAID team might also be considered a way of putting its local practice more on a par with that in Israel. Certainly, the American attempt to monitor the use of this aid in the interests of preventing mismanagement and corruption is as ineffective as

23. Bob Dole, "To Help New Democracies, Cut Aid to Israel, 4 Others," *New York Times*, January 16, 1990.

it is offensive. Lastly, we can ask for continued U.S. sensitivity in those areas in which the Mubarak regime is using its own pivotal position to improve its domestic economic circumstances, for example, linkages with both the planned Euro-Mediterranean free trade area and the putative Arab common market.

PIVOTAL EGYPT: SOME CONCLUSIONS

The Present

Egypt is a prime candidate for "piviotalness" on many grounds. It lies at the center of the Arab world; it is a neighbor of Israel; it has a stable, relatively well-organized government that allows it to formulate coherent policies and to exercise a regular influence on regional affairs. In addition, it has gone some way in solving a number of the political problems besetting the Arab world, notably those of providing mechanisms for popular representation and the orderly transfer of power. Meanwhile, its program of structural adjustment has proceeded far enough to provide a foundation for moderate, but not spectacular, economic growth in the decades to come. All this gives Egypt considerable power for good or bad. If its present policies continue on track, Egypt will provide encouragement to other Arab countries embarking on the same course. But if they come unstuck and, in particular, if their failure leads to a period of prolonged instability or even a radical change in regime, this is likely to have dramatic repercussions throughout the Middle East.

These same factors have made Egypt such a valuable ally of the United States for the past twenty years. Presidents Sadat and Mubarak used their country's power and influence to make, and then maintain, peace with Israel, to confront threats to the present regional order and, in general, to demonstrate the tangible advantages of putting itself so firmly in the American camp. Nevertheless, the alliance has not been without its problems. U.S. officials have had to learn to recognize the dangers of interfering too closely in a country where much of the population is highly sensitive to threats to Egypt's independence, its culture, and its support for Arab or Islamic causes such as Palestine and a Palestinian East Jerusalem. As for the future, these same officials will have to learn that Egypt must be allowed to develop its own regional role in whatever way suits its interests. They will also have to take care not to be identified too closely with what seems likely to be an increasingly authoritarian regime during the remainder of the Mubarak presidency. They will also have to recognize—and if possible challenge—those forces within the regime which argue that Egypt should follow what they take to be the "Asian" model, in which political freedom is sacrificed to economic success.

Recognition of the limits of American involvement in Egypt will also include allowing Egypt to find its own place in the wider international community outside the Middle East. It has a legitimate interest in nuclear nonproliferation. It has an even more pressing interest in the management of the Nile waters and in its own regional environment. However, the amount of American diplomatic effort put into these and other global issues will probably remain small for some time to come. No domestic constituency exists for such initiatives. More important, Egypt, as a still relatively poor country, has neither the resources nor the combination of economic and political power needed to translate regional influence into a larger world role.

Thinking about the Next Ten Years

Two views of Egypt's future generally vie with each other in books and articles about the Middle East. One paints a dismal scenario in which overpopulation, increasing poverty, environmental pollution, and other scourges provide a potent recipe for popular discontent leading, almost inevitably, to an overthrow of the present regime by radical Islamic forces. The other, so much more benign, is of an Egypt well embarked on the road to a market economy and a liberal democratic political system in tune with the global formula for twenty-first-century success. To these might be added a third, somewhat glib, response that the future must inevitably lie somewhere between these two extremes.

Such an approach needs to be challenged on the grounds that it serves to obscure the real issues that face Egypt over the next decade. Rather than simply talking generally about the threat of overpopulation, it would be more sensible to divide Egypt into its urban and rural components, the better to identify the challenges that each faces as space gets more and more limited and resources shrink. As far as the former is concerned, cities such as Cairo face problems that are roughly similar to those confronting other large Third World conurbations: the provision of services, proper zoning, difficulties in maintenance of its infrastructure, localized pollution, and so on. But where Cairo falls behind is in the fact that it has no proper system of representative municipal government, few channels for popular activism, and a huge gap between formal rules and regulations and the constant encroachment on public space by a population seeking better accommodation, employment, and facilities for recreation. This will all have to be changed if the quality of urban life is not to decline still further.

In the countryside, the demand for water will almost certainly have at least one positive effect, which is to encourage measures for its better use, including a shift in cropping patterns toward the optimal use of Egypt's rich soil: its conversion, now well advanced, from a source of field crops to a producer of vegetables and fruits for the region and for Europe.

A similar approach can be applied to the problems in the political, economic and legal spheres. As far as the political is concerned, the choice of Mubarak's successor will be of great importance, particularly with respect to whether or not he comes from the army. Some Egyptians argue that having an officer as president is the only assurance that the military itself will stay clear of day-to-day politics, confident, as it is today, that its vital interests are being properly protected. Others believe that civilian control can only be properly exercised by a civilian chief executive. A second area of great concern is the present tendency of the official opposition to simply replicate many of the worst features of the official government party, the NDP: its top-down leadership, its inability to formulate a distinct agenda, and so, more generally, its inability to generate real popular support. This, too, will have to be remedied if Egypt is to have a healthy political future.

Basic questions about the future of the economy also remain to be answered. What lies beyond structural adjustment? Can Egypt find the right balance between the public and the private sectors? How will Egypt best protect its economic interests while accommodating itself to a world of common markets and globalized rules governing national foreign trade and investment regimes? As elsewhere, such questions will be best answered in an atmosphere of free discussion and popular participation, supported by a high level of institutionalized research and international exchange. So far, both Egypt's overcrowded and poorly resourced universities and its official research organizations have failed lamentably to contribute to this much-needed national debate. In some cases the creation of new, private institutions may help answer these questions better. But for the most part, it is the public universities that need serious attention rather than the present benign neglect.

Finally, the Egyptian legal system, with its huge accumulation of statutes, rules, and regulations, its overworked courts, and its shortage of qualified judges, also has to receive serious attention if civil life is to flourish and rights are to be properly protected.

It follows that those anxious to help to shape Egypt's future should do so by schemes that address real, rather than imaginary, problems. There is plenty of scope for official, government-to-government assistance. But equally, there is much scope for private and business assistance as well.

American Policy: A Last Word

American policy toward Egypt has been largely successful in meeting its diplomatic and political goals over the past twenty years. The two governments may need each other just as much in the future, given the problems posed to the Middle Eastern peace process by the election of the Netanyahu government.

Nevertheless, it is still worth asking the question, Just because it has worked so well in the past, does that mean that it can continue along the same path in the future? Or to put the question the other way around: What, if any, are the dangers ahead and how can they best be prevented?

The major problem facing the present U.S. administration is not the potential instability of the regime but the fact that, in President Mubarak, it has an ally who is too well entrenched in power to recognize the need for further political reform. The result will be one of those familiar situations in which Washington will want to be able to maintain a certain distance from Mubarak's domestic policies, both to avoid the appearance of responsibility for them and to be in a position to criticize them in a positive way when necessary.

It would be wrong, however, to exaggerate the problems involved: President Mubarak is too aware of the importance of his working relationship with the United States to want to harm it in any serious way. He is also well aware of the way in which the Israelis can make trouble for him on Capitol Hill through criticism of his domestic policy, as a way of putting pressure on him not to support either the Palestinians or the Syrians beyond a certain point. In such a contest, his reputation as a democrat remains a significant asset.

America's policy toward the Egyptian economy is quite another matter. Given the present winds of change in Washington concerning aid, this could well be just the moment not only to reevaluate its efficacy but also to reduce it in both volume and ambition in ways that I have suggested above. This means, among other things, the creation of better mechanisms for ensuring that both USAID and its Egyptian ministerial counterparts share the same aims and are able to cooperate on their achievement. It should also include dropping American support for some of the more controversial policies pursued by the Egyptian government, such as its use of the World Bank's Social Fund to create new jobs for unemployed graduates rather than to serve as a general safety net for Egypt's poor, as was its original intention.

For the rest, it must be assumed that there are no magic answers to Egypt's pressing social problems. Nor do we have some magical formula that will somehow make the economy grow at a much faster rate than at present. Hence it would be wrong to allow USAID to continue to be closely identified with the establishment of targets that raise expectations but have no realistic possibility of attainment. Nevertheless, this should not be cause for alarm. If recent history tells us anything, it is not poverty that has been the cause of political disturbance in Egypt but misguided policy.

SOUTH AFRICA

Jeffrey Herbst

South Africa dominates the southern Africa region and, at least statistically, the entire African continent. This dominance, combined with the remarkable transition from apartheid to nonracial rule, has already caused a debate on how much attention the United States should devote to South Africa as opposed to other African countries in a time of scarce resources for the foreign-assistance budget and when the attention devoted to any foreign issue by senior American foreign policy leaders is limited. This essay will examine the extent to which South Africa is to the United States a "pivotal state" as defined by Robert S. Chase, Emily B. Hill, and Paul Kennedy.[1]

POSTAPARTHEID SOUTH AFRICA

South Africa is entering the post-heroic phase of its history.[2] President Mandela gave up his leadership of the African National Congress (ANC) at the end of 1997 as a prelude to his leaving office at the end of his five-year term in 1999. In many ways, South Africa is becoming a normal country: it is now moving away from its "constitutional moment" and the government is increasingly focusing on the mundane, but critical, issues of how to promote economic growth and restore order.

Of course, due to its unique history of institutionalized white rule and apartheid, South Africa will never be like any other country. However, arguably the greatest success over the past three years has been to move a whole set of monumental questions about the future *off* the agenda. The country no longer obsesses about political crises and imminent race wars: Labor unions are free to be labor unions rather than political movements,

1. Robert S. Chase, Emily B. Hill, and Paul Kennedy, "Pivotal States and U.S. Strategy," *Foreign Affairs* 75, no. 1 (January–February 1996).
2. This section is based partly on Antoinette Handley and Jeffrey Herbst, "South Africa: The Perils of Normalcy," *Current History* 96 (May 1997): 222–226.

nongovernmental organizations can be NGOs rather than an alternative government, and foreign donors can give money to the government to solve social ills rather than working around the state.

What is most notable in South Africa is what has not happened: there has been virtually no violence from the right wing that was once viewed as militant and highly militarized. Before the 1994 nonracial election, at least some South Africans believed that the Mandela administration would have to deal with a terrorist threat that rivaled the Irish Republican Army, given the hostility of some Afrikaners to majority rule. Instead, there have only been a few widely scattered attacks that do not even amount to a nuisance. The threat from the white right dissolved for several reasons: Nelson Mandela's adeptness in addressing the concerns of the whites, the willingness of some respected conservative politicians, notably General Constand Viljoen, to participate in multiparty politics, and a fragmentation of the right itself. Finally, the Truth and Reconciliation Commission—the major effort by the government to uncover the crimes of the past—seems unlikely to aggravate racial tensions unduly because it stresses confession and amnesty rather than Nuremberg-style war crimes and vindictiveness. South Africa has committed itself to a one-person, one-vote order with no special privileges for particular racial groups in a centralized political system and has described a comprehensive set of rights to be enjoyed by all. Although domestic military threats against the new rule are still possible, every day that the new South Africa operates in peace increases the probability that the postapartheid order has been institutionalized.

Nor will the departure of Nelson Mandela from the political scene destabilize the new order. Mandela may well have been indispensable to create the new order but, once the rules and accepted practices are in place, his presence will not be necessary to ensure stability. Whites have been given as much assurance as possible that they have a place in the new South Africa and most have accepted, however grudgingly, the new order. The transition to Mandela's chosen successor, Vice President Thabo Mbeki, began early in Mandela's term. Mbeki is closely associated with all of Mandela's policies. He certainly will never have the legitimacy of Mandela and will have many of the ordinary problems most leaders face (some committed enemies, some ungrateful allies, his fair share of bad luck). However, part of South Africa's inevitable normalization will be to have a man, rather than a saint, as president.

THE ECONOMY

Rather than dramatic armed threats, the major problems that the new South Africa increasingly faces come from more mundane issues familiar

to citizens in many countries: promoting economic growth and preserving law and order. The economic problems are certainly daunting. South
Africa is one of the most unequal societies on earth. In 1994, 53 percent
of Africans lived below the poverty line compared with 2 percent of all
whites. There were immediate demands to do something about the millions unemployed; institute supplemental feeding programs for the 2.3
million people, including 1 million children, who were malnourished;
begin programs to help the estimated 12 million people without adequate
water supplies; and help electrify the homes of the 80 percent of all
Africans without power.[3] The economy experienced negative growth
between 1990 and 1992, and businesses were barely investing enough to
replace their capital stock. In the decade before the 1994 transition, South
Africans had divested from their own economy through continual capital
flight. At the same time, it was expected that the ANC would restructure
the economy to be more outward looking and efficient.

Economic growth during 1994 and 1995, at roughly 3 percent, was a
marked improvement compared with the previous years of economic
decline. However, by the middle of 1996, the government had become
convinced that even the improved economic trajectory was inadequate.
Costings of the expensive new social agenda suggested that on the current
growth path, the government would not be able to deliver on its promises. Most important, after a brief spurt of giddiness about growing again,
it became obvious that 3 percent was not good enough for South Africa.
The government came to understand that if the economy grew by only 3
percent, unemployment would rise by an additional 5 percentage points
to 37 percent in the year 2000.[4] Also, the rand experienced a series of
crises during 1996 that saw its value against the U.S. dollar depreciate by
more than 20 percent. The devaluation started as a normal correction to
what had become a somewhat appreciated currency, but turned into a
rout as investors suddenly became nervous about the underlying fundamentals of the economy and the will of the government to implement
reform quickly.

In June 1996, the government formalized its commitment to growth
through market-based measures with the release of a document entitled
Growth, Employment and Redistribution: A Macroeconomic Strategy (GEAR).

3. Poverty figures from Margie Keeton and Gavin Keeton, "Gearing up for the Long Road:
   The Challenges of Poverty in South Africa," *Optima* 38 (November 1992): 129, and
   Francis Wilson, "Poverty, the State and Redistribution: Some Reflections," in *The Political Economy of South Africa*, ed. Nicoli Nattrass and Elisabeth Ardington (Cape Town:
   Oxford University Press, 1990), 235.
4. South Africa, *Growth, Employment and Redistribution*, June 14, 1996, p. 4. The document
   can be found at http://www.polity.org.za/govdocs/policy/growth.html.

The document, with its emphasis on the need to achieve 6 percent annual growth and further reform the economy, was a sharp break in both tone and substance from the election rhetoric of 1994. If the document was not written by the International Monetary Fund and the World Bank, it was certainly designed to gain their approval.

The GEAR document, as it quickly became known, also marked a change in the relationship between the ANC and its junior coalition partners, the Congress of South African Trade Unions (COSATU) and the South African Communist Party (SACP). Gone was the commitment to consultation that was a key feature of the liberation struggle and the immediate posttransition period. Instead, the change in strategy was announced without much in the way of prior consultation and the minister of finance proclaimed that much of the document was simply "nonnegotiable." The response, both to the changes in form and in process, was quick in coming. COSATU complained that the alliance "seems to be paralyzed by the threat of globalization and the investment strike of business." The unions implied that Mandela's program was "Thatcherite," a fighting word in South Africa.[5]

It would be unfair to say that the government had abandoned its effort to redress past inequalities. In his address to Parliament in February 1997, Nelson Mandela was able to point to programs that provide school lunches for 3 million children, celebrate the fact that seven hundred thousand people had been provided with potable water with 6 million more to benefit soon, and announced that more houses were being built than at any time in the country's history.[6] Still, the GEAR document was deliberately aimed at lowering expectations and marked, as Mandela and Finance Minister Trevor Manuel both suggested, a maturing of the government's approach after the ebullience of the transition.

Indeed, the economy has not done as well as even the downbeat GEAR document projected. In 1996, the government assumed that the economy would be growing at a rate of 6 percent by the year 2000. This would have been an extraordinary performance, given that the economy was essentially stagnant in the 1980s. However, after only slightly more than a year of GEAR, the government was forced to make more modest projections when it released the *Medium Term Budget Policy Statement* in December 1997. Now the government projects that, at best, the economy will be growing at only 5 percent by the year 2000. The government

5. See COSATU, *A Draft Programme for the Alliance*, November 22, 1996, p. 4. Found at http://www.anc.org.za:80/cosatu/docs/discuss.html.

6. Nelson Mandela, Opening Address to Fourth Session of Parliament, Cape Town, February 7, 1997, p. 2. Found at http://www.polity.org.za/govdocs/speeches/1997/sp0207.html.

apparently was forced into this downward revision because the structural problems of the economy are becoming more noticeable, there is concern about drought due to El Niño, and the plummeting price of gold casts even more doubt on the viability of significant portions of the mining industry. Even this new projection is probably too optimistic. Given low savings and investment rates in South Africa, the most credible projection is that the economy will grow by no more than 3 percent a year through 2001.

Table 1. PROJECTIONS OF ECONOMIC GROWTH

Document	1998/99 Projected Growth Rate (%)	1999/00 Projected Growth Rate (%)
GEAR (June 1996)	4.9%	6.1%
Medium Term Budget Plan (December 1997)	3.0%	4.0%

Sources: Government of South Africa, *Growth, Employment and Redistribution: A Macroeconomic Strategy.* Found at www.polity.org.za/govdocs/policy/growth.html; Government of South Africa, *The Medium Term Budget Policy Statement 1997.* Found at www.polity.org.za/govdocs/policy/medium.html.

The rift between the ANC and its allies highlights what is in many ways the fundamental question of South Africa's political economy: Can the organizations that fought apartheid together now govern together? The ANC is inevitably pulled in the direction of a low-wage economy that will benefit the millions of South Africans in the townships and the rural areas who are unemployed. In contrast, COSATU represents almost 2 million workers who, though hardly doing well, are actually highly paid by South African standards and who are not, by international standards, particularly productive.

To date, the unions have nowhere to go, and there are few indications that they would risk, in the immediate future, running against the still very popular ANC as a new social democratic party. Also, the fifty most capable unionists became members of Parliament in 1994, a decapitation from which labor is still trying to recover. It does appear inevitable that union protest will become an increasing problem for the ANC in the years to come, with the potential to disrupt the economic plans designed to convince investors, both foreign and domestic, that the country is stable and will yield high returns to new business. There may also be more populist pressures to spend more, although the Mandela government has been determined in its efforts to manage government spending in a conservative manner. Indeed, Mandela has a much better record than the previous white governments in terms of reducing the government deficit.

There is no evidence that unhappiness with the government's ability to *deliver the goods* in postapartheid South Africa will lead, in the short to medium term, to extraconstitutional threats to the new order. Signs of an immediate crisis of expectations are few, and the government has gone out of its way since 1996 to stress that delivering the goods will take some time. There is no organized group with a coherent critique and an alternative to the current regime's policy. Finally, the African National Congress has an enduring support base earned over decades in the struggle against apartheid. This base will not evaporate simply because fewer houses are built over a few years than was originally expected. True, setbacks might lead to the creation of another party or parties to challenge the Congress, but that would be a healthy development for South Africa's fledgling democracy.

ORDER

The other major issue that South Africa must face immediately is crime. The murder rate is ten times that of the United States, nearly half of large businesses have had a delivery vehicle hijacked, and robbery is a constant concern. Vigilantes who publicly execute drug dealers are widely applauded. Fear of crime is deterring foreign investment, and there is evidence that South Africa's reputation as a violent country is hurting the tourist industry. The Olympic selection committee noted crime as a key problem in Cape Town's application to host the 2004 games.

The causes of the current crime wave in South Africa are complex. Especially in the urban areas, very poor black populations, often without adequate food, water, and shelter, coexist with a white society whose life-style is modeled on those of Europe and the United States. South Africa is also very much a society in transition in which the old institutions and notions of order have been overthrown but new norms of legitimacy are only slowly being created. Add the almost ubiquitous presence of guns, available at very low prices now that the wars around South Africa have ended and the borders have become more open, and it would be surprising if South Africa did not face a significant crime problem.

Finally, lawlessness is, in many ways, nothing new in South Africa. The old white regime was totalitarian but in a particular way. The apartheid governments ruled whole areas of the country, especially black urban areas with a high number of migrants, by simply withdrawing and containing the inhabitants so that they would not pose a threat to the nearby white areas. These "no-go" zones, as they were formally known, were run in large part by gangsters who could easily outgun the police. In other areas, evidence is emerging that the police cut deals with criminal gangs in order to keep public threats to a minimum. The Mandela government, in some ways, is simply confronting the lack of order in these areas that the previous government was willing to ignore as long as the associated problems did not affect the whites.

Some aspects of the crime wave will be addressed once the transformation of the police is completed and the government gets serious enough to allocate the resources necessary to fight increasingly sophisticated crime syndicates. However, the government also faces some unique problems to which it has no ready-made answers. Most of all, the Mandela administration must restore an ethic of lawfulness after many years in which the African National Congress encouraged people not to obey the white authorities. The early results are not good. For instance, the Mandela government has not fully convinced many in urban areas to pay their rents, after encouraging rent avoidance for many years as a way to fight apartheid. Indeed, in some areas rent collections are actually lower than during white rule. Such a general ethic of disobedience creates an encouraging climate for crime.

However, although crime is a significant issue that will increasingly burden the government if not resolved, criminals do not pose a threat to the new order. Even a high number of car-jackings or murders is not, absent an alternative leadership set with another agenda, enough to overturn what has been constructed since 1994. In fact, the government has so far resisted calls to impinge on the enumerated rights of the new democracy to fight crime, an unpopular stance but one that is possible in the new order. The previous government was not threatened by the ANC's own military campaign. The ANC will not be physically threatened by crime without a political agenda now that it controls South Africa's security forces.

THE NEW SOUTH AFRICA AS A PIVOTAL STATE

South Africa has made a miraculous escape from the abyss of race war. However, it faces grave structural problems in many areas that, although not threatening to the new order, suggest that growth will be slow, politics will be contested, and legitimacy must still be won. Given the inheritance of the past, the Mandela administration has done well in its first years in power. Whether even the best of all governments (which the Mandela administration is not) could solve South Africa's problems is not clear. Certainly, South Africa will not be a newly industrializing country or even one with a very vibrant economy, and it will have a nagging problem with order. It will certainly not be able to operate confidently on the world stage given its still great domestic problems. In the words of this project, South Africa is not "tippy." It faces little prospect of instability; indeed, it has a more stable order now than at any time in the last few decades. Nor, however, is South Africa bound for imminent greatness.

SOUTH AFRICA AND THE U.S.

There is no doubt that South Africa dominates its region and, indeed, Africa in terms of its economic clout, technological prowess, and, especially since 1994, the efficiency and success of its transition to democracy.[7] In 1995, South Africa accounted for roughly 84 percent of southern Africa's gross domestic product and about 44 percent of all of sub-Saharan Africa's economic product. Not surprisingly, it accounts for 92 percent of the energy used in the region (59 percent of all that is consumed in sub-Saharan Africa) and for 76 percent of the region's exports (37 percent of all goods coming from Africa).[8] South Africa's miraculous transition has made it a seemingly unambiguous success amid the confusion and "fragmenting" of Africa's thirty other democratic experiments.[9]

Equally important, the United States has a much stronger emotional and political investment in South Africa than in any other African country. Americans have always had a problem relating to foreign countries if domestic metaphors do not apply. However, apartheid was an issue, and a struggle, that Americans could relate to since it seemed to resonate with the American civil rights struggle. Indeed, in their effort to gain support, the ANC and its allies constantly made analogies between apartheid and segregation in the U.S. In the mid-1980s, how at least some in Congress stood on sanctions toward South Africa was taken as a proxy for positions on U.S. civil rights issues. The long domestic debate within the United States about how to confront apartheid also created relatively strong ties between many Americans and South Africa's new leaders. Although the

7. What countries constitute Southern Africa is somewhat unclear. I will use the membership of the Southern African Development Community (Angola, Botswana, Lesotho, Malawi, Mozambique, Namibia, Swaziland, Tanzania, Zambia, Zimbabwe), before the island of Mauritius joined, as the basic region. Of course, as the presence of Nigerian, Zaïrois, and, due to the latest disasters in the Great Lakes region, Rwandan traders on the streets of Johannesburg testifies, South Africa has increasing links with all of Africa.
8. All statistics exclude Angola and Swaziland, although their inclusion would not change the numbers appreciably. Calculated from World Bank, *World Development Report 1996* (Washington, D.C.: The World Bank, 1996), 202–219.
9. See Thomas Carothers, "Democracy without Illusions," *Foreign Affairs* 76, no. 1 (January–February 1997): 87.

end of apartheid inevitably loosens the metaphor with the United States, there is still much in South Africa that Americans instinctively understand and are sympathetic to, given the long American struggle to come to grips with civil rights since the 1960s. By the standards of post–Cold War America, the South African experiment in nonracial rule is being closely watched. As Warren Christopher correctly noted in a major speech in South Africa, "Your example has inspired America and the world. Today, people look at South Africa and say: If this diverse, once-divided nation can be united by common values and aims, then so can any multi-ethnic nation in Africa and the world."[10]

The rise of South Africa has also fed the American view, especially strong after Somalia, that Africa, led by the new government in Pretoria, can solve African problems. Indeed, when I asked a very senior State Department official in 1995 what the United States would do if the remnants of the Hutu army tried to cross the Rwandan border to finish the genocide they began in 1994, he replied that he hoped that South Africa and the Southern African Development Community (SADC) would respond. Of course, neither South Africa nor the SADC has the capability necessary to project the force needed to stop such an attack. In some circles, South Africa is now seen as a kind of "Mr. Fix-It," both able, and because of the sacrifices made by many countries during the liberation struggle, obliged to address Africa's problems. The debate within South Africa about what its role in Africa should be has, perhaps ironically, given new impetus to the idea that the solutions to regional conflicts can be subcontracted.[11] Indeed, President Nelson Mandela has encouraged this optimism. Writing in *Foreign Affairs* he stated that:

> South Africa cannot escape its African destiny. If we do not devote our energies to this continent, we too could fall victim to the forces that have brought ruin to its various parts.[12]

As a result, there is little doubt that American policy makers already see South Africa as a critical state. As Christopher noted: "South Africa is an important global partner for the United States. . . . When I look around the world . . . I see few relationships as vital as [sic] advancing our

10. Warren Christopher, Address at the South African Institute of International Affairs, October 12, 1996, p. 1. Available at http://www.state.gov/www/regions/africa/tripuniv.html.

11. For a general review of South Africa's new foreign policy, see Department of Foreign Affairs, *South African Foreign Policy: Discussion Document*, July 1996. Available at http://www.polity.org.za/issues/foreign.html.

12. Nelson Mandela, "South Africa's Future Foreign Policy," *Foreign Affairs* 72 (November–December 1993): 89.

common interests as the U.S.–South Africa relationship."[13] With roughly one-tenth of sub-Saharan Africa's population, South Africa now receives approximately one-third of American aid to the continent, although that percentage will decrease in the future. South Africa is one of only a handful of countries in the world that has a binational commission with the United States that allows top foreign policy makers to have privileged access to American leaders. Indeed, Vice President Al Gore and South African Vice President Mbeki have become close friends partly as a result of their joint leadership of the binational commission, whose American offices are controlled by the vice president rather than by the State Department.

Given that the basic notion of South Africa as a critical state is not contested, I will examine to what extent it is a pivotal state in that its success or failure will have a critical effect on the southern African region. I will try to specify the different types of linkages between a dominant state and a region and describe the reality of these links in Southern Africa. Finally, I will examine what the United States could do better, in conjunction with other donors, to promote stability in South Africa and, in turn, help the region, if not all of Africa.

PIVOTAL STATES AND THEIR REGIONS

It is only a gentle criticism of the Chase, Hill, and Kennedy article to say that exactly how pivotal states affect their regions was underspecified. They wrote:

> A pivotal state is so important regionally that its collapse would spell transboundary mayhem; migration, communal violence, pollution, disease, and so on. A pivotal state's steady economic progress and stability, on the other hand, would bolster its region's economic vitality and political soundness and benefit American trade and investment.[14]

This is true, as far as it goes, but it does not actually allow for the real identification of pivotal states and does not specify the critical linkages between those states and their regions. For instance, the collapse of Liberia (usually not considered a pivotal state) has caused chaos throughout a significant portion of West Africa. Indeed, the civil war in Sierra Leone, the coup in Gambia, and the (largely ignored) political disturbances in western Côte d'Ivoire can all be traced to the collapse of the state in Monrovia. The region has also seen the accompanying movements of people within and between states as well as the significant environmental decay that

13. Christopher, Address at the South African Institute, 6.
14. Chase, Hill, and Kennedy, "Pivotal States," 37.

Chase, Hill, and Kennedy suggest is typical when a pivotal state collapses. Similarly, the collapse of Rwanda has led to a series of coups in Burundi, the loss of Zaire's territorial integrity (at least in the eastern portion of the country), instability in western Tanzania and southern Uganda, mass movements of people, a spread of disease, and environmental decay. The same story could be told about Somalia and the Horn of Africa. The collapse of almost any country has an important impact on its region.

Correspondingly, it is not immediately clear that a successful state can serve as a locomotive for its region, no matter how great its dominance. The success of Japan did not immediately lead to prosperity in East Asia. Rather, a series of by now well-documented internal reforms in Korea and Taiwan, and later in the countries of Southeast Asia, were responsible for the rise of the varying tiers of newly industrializing countries. Indeed, both Korea and Taiwan grew by trading with distant countries, particularly the United States. Neither Korea nor Taiwan was particularly integrated with the other economies of the region and both were cut off from what should have been one of their largest markets: China. Similarly, interregional trade has not been that noticeable an aspect of the development of Indonesia and Thailand, despite the fact that the economic activity in the surrounding area is many times that of southern Africa. Both of these Southeast Asian countries still send more than 60 percent of their exports to developed countries outside of Asia.[15] The World Bank's major study of Asian success makes no mention of regional trade, stressing instead that Asian countries have succeeded largely because of good domestic economic policies.[16]

It is thus important to understand with some degree of specificity how an important country can affect its region. Of course, a dominant country's ties with its region are by necessity complex. Some are concrete and formal, such as trade and investment relations. Others are material but either informal and/or illegal: the flows of guns, peoples, and drugs all affect relations among countries in a region. Finally, the example of a dominant country may have important, albeit unquantifiable, effects on the region. South Africa's ties with the southern Africa region will be examined in each of these areas.

TRADE AND INVESTMENT

Table 2 provides a review of the evolution of the regional economy since 1960. South Africa's share of economic activity in the region was

15. International Monetary Fund, *Direction of Trade Statistics*, 1994 (Washington, D.C.: IMF, 1994).

16. World Bank, *The East Asian Miracle* (Washington, D.C., 1993).

Table 2. SHARE OF GROSS REGIONAL PRODUCT

Country	Percentages			
	1960	1970	1980	1993
Angola	6	N.A.	3	5
Botswana	N.A.	0.4	1	3
Lesotho	0.3	0.3	0.3	0.5
Malawi	2	1	1	1
Mozambique	8	N.A.	2	1
Namibia	N.A.	N.A.	2	2
South Africa	65	77	77	79
Swaziland	N.A.	N.A.	1	1
Tanzania	5	6	5	2
Zambia	6	8	4	3
Zimbabwe	7	7	4	4

Note: Percentages have been rounded to the nearest integer (except when the number was below 0.5) in order to emphasize the problematic nature of many of these statistics. Data are for the year closest to that actually reported. Data for Angola are, even by southern African standards, problematic. The 1993 figure was generated by guessing that Angola's per capita income is at the bottom of the lower-middle income category—the World Bank's current classification for it ($696)—and then multiplying it by the population.

Source: World Bank, World Development reports, various years.

about 79 percent in 1993, a significant increase over the 1960 figure of 65 percent. The increase in South Africa's share between 1980 and 1993 is particularly noticeable because its own economy was only growing at an annual rate of 0.9 percent during this period.[17] However, South Africa still performed relatively well because of the collapse of the Mozambican, Tanzanian, and Zambian economies and the poor performance experienced by Zimbabwe. Of course, Angola's economy also collapsed between 1960 and 1993; however, the dominance of oil (the one sector that has not suffered from the almost constant warfare in the country) in its measurable national accounts has meant that in statistical terms its economy seems relatively robust. Of the countries in the region, only Botswana, which increased its share of the regional economy by almost an order of magnitude between 1970 and 1993, performed well in both relative and absolute terms.

The fundamental problem now confronting southern Africa is that the regional economy is simply so small that South Africa in particular will

17. World Bank, World Development Report 1995 (Washington, D.C., 1995), 165.

benefit little from regional trade, and the prospects for greater interregional trade are extremely limited. Over the last twenty-five years, the region as a whole performed poorly, with its share of the global economy decreasing from 0.76 percent in 1970 to 0.58 percent in 1993.[18] Southern African countries would be far better served by reforming their economies to take advantage of the roughly 99.4 percent of the world economy that is outside their region. Indeed, there is so little economic activity in Southern Africa that significant efforts to promote trade within the region could quickly become counterproductive. It is true that there are over one hundred million people in the southern African region; however, their extraordinarily low per capita income means that the effective market they represent is minuscule.

The value of greater regional trade is especially limited to South Africa. The region's total economic product without South Africa amounted to only 0.13 percent of the global economy in 1993.[19] The absolute size of the regional economy without South Africa is roughly equivalent to the economy of the Czech Republic or Romania. Hong Kong's economy alone is approximately three times larger than the regional economy excluding South Africa.[20] Indeed, the regional economy is even less attractive to South Africa than if it bordered Romania or the Czech Republic because the market, such that it is, is divided among ten countries. The most important segment is Angola, partially due to the statistical artifact explained above but also due to the constant stream of oil revenue that is a source of wealth unmatched throughout the region. Of course, as long as Angola is in turmoil, oil will be very difficult to export to Luanda. The remainder of the region's wealth is divided among many different markets, with Zimbabwe, Zambia, and Botswana accounting for approximately 43 percent of the remaining economic activity. Obviously, if South Africa hopes to develop, especially by exporting more, the regional economy will be of only marginal help.

The nature of the region's economies also limits the degree to which South Africa can act as a locomotive. Table 2 illustrates that South Africa already accounts for between 34 and 52 percent of total imports in Malawi, Zambia, and Zimbabwe; this figure is probably higher in neighboring countries. It is hard to believe that South Africa will be able to increase these market shares significantly, especially given that in all of the countries in the region imports of fuel, which South Africa cannot meet, probably account for a substantial portion of the import profile.

18. World Bank, *World Development Report 1995*, 167.
19. World Bank, *World Development Report 1995*, 166–167.
20. World Bank, *World Development Report 1995*.

Table 3. DIRECTION OF TRADE

	Exports going to South Africa	Imports from South Africa
Malawi	9	36
Zambia	2	34
Zimbabwe	13	52

Source: International Monetary Fund, *Direction of Trade Statistics Yearbook 1997* (Washington, D.C.: IMF, 1997).

Countries in the region have also not been able to increase exports to South Africa because of a *fundamental mismatch in their development profiles.* As is typical for middle-income countries, South Africa imports mostly capital goods and manufactured products. In 1992, machinery and transport equipment alone accounted for 40 percent of total imports; chemicals, manufactured goods, and miscellaneous manufactured goods accounted for another 22 percent of the total import bill.[21] On the other hand, the countries of the region export mainly a few raw materials. South Africa simply does not need that much of Zambia's copper (79 percent of total exports), Malawi's tobacco (67 percent of total exports), or Zimbabwe's tobacco, gold, or ferro-alloys (48 percent of total exports).[22] What it does need in terms of basic raw materials it probably buys already, suggesting that the immediate scope for increased regional exports to South Africa will be chiefly a function of economic growth rather than increasing market share.

Indeed, given the fundamental mismatch between South Africa's import profile and what the countries in the region are currently exporting, the critical question becomes whether southern African countries can transform their economies so that they are more than mere raw-material producers and can actually manufacture products that South Africa will buy. Thus, prospects for increased exports from the region to South Africa, which would be an important component of any regional economic resurgence, hinge far less on growth in South Africa than on the fate of domestic economic reform. Economic progress in even a pivotal state will only take a region so far.

21. Calculated from South Africa, *South African Statistics 1994* (Pretoria: South Africa, 1994), 16.6–16.8.
22. Statistics are from the Economist Intelligence Unit reports *Zambia and Zaire*, fourth quarter 1995, 3; *Mozambique and Malawi*, fourth quarter 1995, 17; and *Zimbabwe*, fourth quarter 1995, 5.

Trade is not the only way in which a newly transformed South Africa could affect southern Africa. Indeed, one of the more dramatic developments since the April 1994 election has been the appearance of South African businessmen in a large number of African capitals investing funds in new or existing businesses. Although South African investment in a large number of African countries during the apartheid period was an open secret, the enthusiasm of the South African companies for Africa stands in marked contrast to the allergy that the rest of the world has toward investing there. Companies such as Engen (formerly Mobil's subsidiary in South Africa) see themselves as African companies and believe that they have a comparative advantage in investing in Africa because of their location and their greater knowledge of local conditions.

Data on capital flows between African countries is so poor that nothing definite can be said at the moment. However, it does seem reasonable to make some tentative points. First, South African investment is extremely welcome in Africa, given the capital drought the continent faces and its generally poor reputation in international financial circles. It is probably not the case, as some of the more ambitious rhetoric from Cape Town and Johannesburg suggests, that South African companies are investing in Africa because they have different profit calculations than western companies. Rather, it is likely that even the tentative economic reforms that many African countries have undertaken have created, in almost every country, some very attractive investments that are not being recognized by western multinationals who do not want to work in Africa and who are not observing local conditions in a thorough manner. South Africans are therefore essentially cherry-picking the best investment opportunities.

Second, the regional framework for a significant increase in capital flows is lacking. National capital controls in many countries, notably South Africa, restrict the ability of funds to flow freely. There has also been relatively little work by SADC on how to increase capital flows formally. Of course, the lack of administrative work to some degree reflects suspicions that will always haunt South African investment in southern Africa. For instance, Botswana's vice president and minister for finance and development planning, Festus Mogae, recently asked, "Is it necessary for every Botswana company to have some association with a South African corporation to be economically viable?"[23]

Finally, South Africa, a savings-starved country with a low investment rate, is hardly in the position to become the financier of African develop-

23. Barry Baxter, "Botswana Debates South Africa's Investment Role," Reuters, December 20, 1995.

ment. Indeed, the current apparent surge in Africa will probably level off once the best opportunities are taken and when it becomes more attractive to invest in South Africa. Still, there is little doubt that any investment from South Africa would be helpful to Africa and that more emphasis should be placed on increasing regional capital mobility, especially as this issue has been slighted compared with the emphasis on trade. South African investment in the region may also have an important spin-off effect by demonstrating to western multinationals that it can be safe, and profitable, to invest in Africa.

After only three years of the new South Africa, it can be said that although Pretoria dominates the region, the relationship between growth in South Africa and growth in the region as a whole is a complicated issue. Should South Africa manage to start to grow at a considerable rate, it is not clear that it could serve as the locomotive for the region. It is even less clear that significant growth in the region, coming off a tiny economic base, would be consequential for South Africa. In the very long term, of course, sustained growth anywhere in the southern Africa region will be helpful to all of the neighbors, and there have already been some positive investment spillovers. However, the positive spin-off effects may be much slower in coming than is commonly expected.

MOVEMENTS OF PEOPLE

As in any other region, in southern Africa a whole series of transactions and flows on an informal and/or illegal basis are critical to the relationship between a major state and its region. A particularly important issue in Southern Africa is the movement of people. Again, the evidence is largely anecdotal, but trends are becoming evident. Indeed, the largest negative effect on the region from South Africa's democratic transition has been an apparent brain drain as skilled people, especially from the Anglophone countries, are attracted to relatively high salaries and good professional conditions in South Africa. South Africa has an absolute shortage of skilled people across the economy, a continuing flight of skilled whites, a particular shortage of skilled people in areas ignored by previous white governments (such as low-cost housing, peasant agriculture, rural health care), and a need felt by business and other institutions in society to have a work force that more accurately reflects the racial diversity of the country. The long-term solution is obviously to fill these needs with South Africans, but the poor state of education for Africans means that there will be no sudden increase in trained blacks to run the economy. As a result, it is hardly surprising that business and other institutions in South African society (for example, universities) have begun to poach talent from the rest of Africa. Of course, given that African countries themselves face tremendous skill problems, the brain drain southward promises to aggravate already grave economic problems. Thus, prosperity in a pivotal state, given relatively free flows of high-powered labor, can be problematic for a region unless the other countries can make it equally attractive so their citizens will stay.

South Africa also faces the real prospect, especially if the economy does begin to make significant advances, of large flows of unskilled people crossing the border in search of a better life. The presence of Zairian traders on the streets of Johannesburg symbolizes how much has changed in a country that once practiced "influx control" in a fairly successful manner. Further, the boundaries are indefensible given that during the apartheid era even the military was unable to prevent cross-border movement, the country has a history of labor migration that was encouraged by successive white regimes, and ethnic ties across borders in a number of areas make migration even more likely.

Indeed, sitting in Union Building in Pretoria and looking out across the region, a South African leader might perceive not trade opportunities but a sea of poor people who could move to South Africa and abort the improved delivery of social services to citizens and greatly complicate the already depressing employment picture. Significant migration could also aggravate ethnic politics and increase tensions with neighboring countries. It is interesting to note that the Asian tigers largely did not face this problem: Japan, Korea, and Taiwan were largely able to control migration due to their geography and the security situation in the region. There seems to be little prospect of a country experiencing high economic growth with a hinterland of exceptionally poor people and not experiencing high levels of illegal migration.

DEMONSTRATION EFFECTS

As Secretary Christopher pointed out, the South African example could be very important given that most of the countries in the region are trying to democratize. When then President F. W. De Klerk lifted the state of emergency in South Africa in 1991, Zimbabwe and Zambia were forced to lift their own domestic states of emergency, despite their leaders' desires to retain the extraordinary powers, because citizens in both countries would not understand why they should be less free than in South Africa. More generally, across Africa, the release of Nelson Mandela profoundly embarrassed many authoritarians who suddenly found themselves behind South Africa in the extent of political liberties enjoyed.

Once again, however, the demonstration effect is a difficult one to understand fully. Everyone's favorite example of South Africa's effect on the region—the effort led by President Nelson Mandela and other southern African leaders in 1994 to prevent the royal coup by Lesotho's King Letsie III—should not be read as an easily transferable example of how the new South Africa will promote democracy. That effort was remarkably successful because Lesotho is a landlocked country unusually vulnerable to outside pressure. Mandela was simply continuing an old South African practice of dictating to Lesotho what could and could not be done.

Indeed, the effect of South Africa's example, or even its diplomacy, on its neighbors in many situations is extremely limited. Rather than the happy Lesotho story, more usual will be Zambia's President Frederick Chiluba's mocking letter in response to calls from regional leaders for consultations over Zambia's remarkably foolish moves to keep the opposition leadership, including former President Kenneth Kaunda, from running for president. Chiluba called outside pressure "indecent curiosity" and then went on to ask, "Are we also going to discuss the crisis between Botswana and Namibia, President Nelson Mandela's problems in Kwa-Zulu Natal, how [President Robert] Mugabe ran against himself in Zimbabwe's last elections or the definitely volatile situation in Angola?"[24]

In the long term, it is probably the case that a well-institutionalized democracy in South Africa will be a boon to the region. However, as with trade, the exact linkages between issues and countries make the demonstration effect less immediately powerful than is commonly assumed. Robert Mugabe and Frederick Chiluba have adopted authoritarian policies because of their own tactical judgment about their political environment and because of their own individual preferences. The fact that South Africa has a well-functioning Constitutional Court that routinely challenges the executive on critical constitutional issues is not going to inspire those two leaders to immediately change their practices.

South Africa as Regional Policeman

As noted above, another way that South Africa may affect the southern Africa region is as regional policeman.* This is seen as a desirable goal by many in Africa tired of foreign meddling and by many in the United States wishing to disengage from as much of Africa as possible. However, it appears that, at present, the new South Africa has neither the resolve nor

---

24. Joe Chilaizya, "U.S. Cuts Aid, While Japan Steps in," Inter Press Service, July 18 1996.

* [Editors' note: Since Professor Herbst composed this chapter, there have been calls for a "Mandela Doctrine," akin to the Monroe Doctrine, for sub-Saharan Africa: see the *Wall Street Journal*, July 25, 1997, p. A8.]

the institutional capabilities to face the challenge of African peacekeeping in a manner that will allow it to become a regional policeman or for the international community to plausibly say that African problems can be left to the Africans led by Mandela. First, foreign policy writ large is certainly not a priority in South Africa, especially given its rather impressive list of domestic problems. Thus, in Nelson Mandela's opening address to the third session of the first postapartheid Parliament, foreign policy was not mentioned until page eleven of his twelve-page speech, after speaking on the importance of the youth and gender equality commissions. Mandela noted that, although South Africa wanted to contribute to the building of a better world, "we should always be mindful of limitations we have as a nation, as well as the constraints of the real world we have to deal with."[25] Also, southern Africa, where the new South Africa has the most clearly defined set of interests, appears less likely to experience failed states in the near future (the exception is Angola) than other parts of Africa where South Africa's own interests are less compelling. For instance, South Africa made no effort to try to contribute combat units to the recent proposals for intervention in Burundi and eastern Zaire. The new South Africa will undoubtedly contribute to peacekeeping in the future, given the domestic realities that Mandela is conscious of, but there is no evidence that Pretoria will materially change the fact that the resources available on the African continent to address this task are inadequate and that peacekeeping will remain dependent on resources from the international community.

Although its contribution to peacekeeping may be very slow, South Africa is poised to play a significant role in selected international issues. South Africa was exceptionally helpful to the United States in getting the non-proliferation treaty ratified, since the country had enormous credibility as the first nation to renounce nuclear weapons. Because of the prominence of Mandela in particular, it is likely that, on selected other issues, South Africa could be an important opinion leader among developing nations. For instance, intellectual property rights, given South Africa's own relatively sophisticated software and services industry, is the type of issue where Pretoria might have a comparative advantage in lobbying the developing world for positions that the United States might feel comfortable with. When Mandela passes from the scene, some of this legitimacy with the developing world will pass. Also, as noted above, South Africa will have only limited resources to use on the world stage.

25. Nelson Mandela, Opening Address to the Third Session of Parliament, February 9, 1996. Available at: http://www.polity.org.za/govdocs/speeches/parlopen.96.html.

Still, it is likely that Pretoria's opinion and favor should be cultivated carefully by the United States for selected multilateral issues.

THE FUTURE OF U.S.–SOUTH AFRICA RELATIONS

Although there is no doubt that South Africa is the critical state in southern Africa, this paper has argued that the ties between the countries in the region are complex and that, in particular, spillovers from South Africa to the rest of the region will only develop slowly. At the same time, the region itself is already having a profound, and in many ways negative, impact on South Africa. Thus, the first lesson for American foreign policy makers is not to overestimate the leverage (to mix metaphors) that can be gained from South Africa as a pivotal state. Many American goals in southern Africa, and the rest of Africa, will only be achieved if a number of difficult domestic decisions are taken by individual policy makers in a large number of African countries. If decisions regarding domestic and economic and political reform, for instance, are not taken in Zambia, Zimbabwe, and the rest of the region, the positive effects from even a successful South Africa will be slow in developing. Similarly, the idea of South Africa as regional policeman is simply not viable.

Perhaps most important, the United States needs to be patient about developments in South Africa and how even a very successful South Africa will affect southern Africa. In many ways, the United States is still getting over the Civil War and slavery. It would not be at all unreasonable for the new South Africa to wrestle with the economic, political, and social inheritance of apartheid for a generation or more before its politics could even come close to becoming institutionalized. Such patience is a rare commodity in the United States, where a quick up-or-down reading on how a country is doing is by now a common part of what used to be called profound debate over foreign policy. In particular, the United States should focus on policies, such as continuing to have good trade relations with South Africa, when economic success in that country will inevitably generate pressure for the imposition of American antidumping laws and other short-term measures.

The current U.S. fixation with South Africa while ignoring much of the rest of Africa is a mixed blessing. On one hand, it is a positive development that senior American policy makers and, to a small extent, the American public are focusing on a country that has gone through a difficult transition and are trying to be as helpful as circumstances allow. On the other hand, Americans are increasingly ignoring even the positive developments in the rest of Africa. It is probably not the case that the attention focused on South Africa comes at the expense of the rest of

Africa. If Americans paid less attention to South Africa, they would probably not become obsessed with Burundi. However, the idea that developing a relationship with South Africa is a substitute for having a substantial relationship (that includes devoting the necessary resources and attention) with the rest of Southern Africa, or even Africa, should be dispelled. Unfortunately, such a notion is implicit in the notion of South Africa as a pivotal state. This analysis has suggested that there is still no substitute for understanding, and relating to, the dynamics of each country even within the Southern Africa region. South Africa is not strong enough to determine, in either a positive or negative way, the fate of its region. Indeed, although it has avoided disaster, its own fate is yet to be decided.

BRAZIL

Jean Krasno

Brazil, with a population of about 160 million people,[1] is the fifth most populous nation in the world, just behind Indonesia and with slightly more people than Russia's 150 million. At current rates, it is projected that Brazil's population will increase to about 200 million by 2020, increasing the gap with a demographically stagnant Russia.[2] Interestingly, Brazil is also the fifth-largest country in the world in terms of geographic size and would be larger than the fourth-ranking United States without Alaska. Its immense landmass, stretching from about 5 degrees north of the equator to just below the tropic of Capricorn, dominates South America, bordering on ten other countries to the north, west, and south. Brazil's Atlantic coastline, covering 7,400 kilometers, marks its easternmost border.[3]

Unlike the rest of Latin America, which was dominated by Spain, Brazil was colonized by the Portuguese in the 1500s and thus its language and culture reflect Portuguese influence. In fact, the Portuguese monarchy moved to Brazil when Napoleon's forces conquered Portugal. A portion of the royal family stayed on to rule Brazil when the monarchy returned home. Thus, Brazil gained its independence from the mother country peacefully, in dramatic contrast to the rest of Hispanic America, which suffered wars and instability throughout much of the nineteenth century.[4] The other major impact of the Portuguese was their deep involvement in the slave trade, bringing thousands of Africans to Brazil to work on the plantations. Today, Brazil's population is predominantly a mixture of southern Europeans, black Africans, and Brazilian Indians with, by some

1. *Brazil: Country Report*, 2nd quarter 1997 (London and New York: *The Economist* Intelligence Unit Ltd.), 5.
2. *World Almanac and Book of Facts* (Mahwah, N.J.: World Almanac Books, 1997), 746.
3. *New York Times Atlas of the World* (London: Times Books, 1991).
4. Ronald M. Schneider, *Order and Progress: a Political History of Brazil* (Boulder: Westview, 1991), 7.

estimates, about two-thirds being "people of color." About 70 percent of Brazilians are Roman Catholic, but alternative Christian religious sects are growing. A strong African presence is felt through the widely spread practice of Candomblé, religious rituals brought from Africa.

In the north, the Amazon River cuts through the heavily wooded Amazon Basin, covering half the country and rich with biologically diverse wildlife. Traveling along the river, one can still see evidence of the rubber boom of the late nineteenth and early twentieth centuries, which developed cities such as Manaus at midriver and Belém at the mouth. As rubber production declined, coffee and sugar became Brazil's leading exports by midcentury in a predominantly agricultural society. Today, only about 11 percent of Brazil's gross domestic product (GDP) is agricultural. Industry now accounts for 42 percent of Brazil's output, with services making up the remaining 47 percent.[5]

Brazil, like the rest of Latin America today with the exception of Cuba, is a democracy. President Fernando Henrique Cardoso, who serves a term of four years, took office in January 1995. In direct elections Cardoso took nationwide, taking 54 percent of the vote in the first round, a major accomplishment in a country with about eighteen parties. The bicameral national congress is also elected and has an 81-seat Senate and a 513-member Chamber of Deputies. Brazil emerged from twenty-one years of military rule in 1985 with a congressionally elected civilian president and completed a new constitution in 1988. Traditionally, the military, as in many of the other eight pivotal states, has always been a strong force in Brazil and continues to occupy significant political space.[6] But the success of the Cardoso presidency and Brazil's vigorous economy have solidified civilian control, and the military is taking a less visible role.

IS BRAZIL PIVOTAL?

Brazil is clearly a pivotal state by the definition used in the thesis put forth by this volume. Brazil fits most of the criteria that define the pivotal nature of any one country. Geographically, Brazil's sheer size and position make its impact on the region extremely important. Of primary importance, Brazil's economic stability is pivoting between success and failure. Through mid-1977, it looked as though Brazil was on the threshold of successfully overcoming its economic problems. However, when the Asian economic crisis deepened in October 1997, Brazil's overvalued curren-

---

5. *Brazil: Country Report*, 5.
6. Alfred Stepan, *Rethinking Military Politics: Brazil and the Southern Cone* (Princeton, N.J.: Princeton University Press, 1988).

cy, the *real*, was also attacked and prices on the São Paulo stock market dropped. Cardoso managed to defend the real with the country's foreign reserves, but some critics believe Brazil's currency is still overvalued by about 30 percent. Brazil's economy is the eighth largest in the world in terms of 1996 GDP figures.[7] In 1996 Brazil exported about $30 billion in manufactured goods, making it a key player both in the region and around the world. It bought roughly $13 billion worth of goods in 1996 from the United States and is therefore an important market for U.S. products. Currently Brazil's trade with the European Union is slightly higher than its trade with the United States. However, 50 percent of U.S. trade is manufactured goods, which represent only 20 percent of trade with the European Union.[8]

Jeffrey Garten, former undersecretary of commerce for international trade (1993–1995), names Brazil as one of the ten "big emerging markets."[9] Its participation in and creation of Mercosur as a trade group in the southern cone has stimulated an economic integration of South America that benefits the entire continent, making it less dependent on the whims of the north. Brazil is key to the success of Mercosur, which could not exist without the dynamic infusion supplied by Brazil's growing industrial base and huge market. If the United States wants to continue to export to the Mercosur countries, it will have to deal with Brazil.

In terms of the environment, Brazil is absolutely pivotal. Its rain forest holds the greatest collection of biodiversity in the world. The forest itself absorbs significant amounts of carbon dioxide and produces oxygen, playing an important role in the balance needed to control global warming. Deforestation, in combination with burning, is now worse than before the 1992 Earth Summit. This is a very serious concern not only because of the fires, which warm the globe,[10] but also because of the loss of the breathing forest. Relative to its geographic size, Brazil's population is not reaching a crisis stage as in India or Pakistan. But much of Brazil's population is centered in the south. Most of the Amazon Basin is very sparsely inhabited, with few negotiable roads. Such cities as Rio de

7. World Bank, *World Development Indicators 1997* (Washington, D.C., 1997). Available on CD-ROM. China is 7; Canada is 9.
8. This information is taken from an interview with the Brazilian ambassador to the United Nations, Celso Amorim, in his office in New York on June 10, 1997.
9. Jeffery E. Garten, *The Big Ten: The Big Emerging Markets and How They Will Change Our Lives* (New York: Basic Books, 1997).
10. Daniel C. Esty of the Yale School of Forestry and Environmental Studies claims, as stated in his chapter for this book, that the amount of carbon dioxide released from the fires in Brazil could raise the total of global CO_2 emmissions by as much as 20 percent.

Janeiro and São Paulo have experienced massive influxes from the poorer regions of northeast Brazil who crowd into squatter slums, putting pressure on the governability of these key cities. The fastest population growth is among the very poor, which exacerbates the already huge gap between rich and poor, one of the worst in the world and the greatest in Latin America.[11] Therefore, population growth, including internal migration and a disproportionate bulge in the number of people under fifteen years old, presents problems that Brazil must address if it is to raise its standards of living to be comparable to those in the large economies of the industrialized world. Brazil's population growth, in world terms, however, is not a key issue and thus is less of a factor in Brazil's pivotal role.

In terms of human rights, Brazil as a new democracy is emerging out of a murky era under military rule, when repression and human rights violations reached an alarming level, particularly during Emilio Medici's presidency in the early 1970s.[12] Although they did not reach those experienced in Argentina and Uruguay[13] during the same period, human rights violations in Brazil pushed the Brazilian Catholic Church to take a stand against the military regime and call for a return to civil rights and the rule of law.[14] Human rights were a key issue in the pressure to return to democracy and the movement termed "abertura," which called for the "opening" of the political sphere to civil society. It is, therefore, important for democracy and civil society in Brazil to stabilize and develop deep roots so that military rule does not return. If the Brazilian military were to take over the government in a coup, as it did in 1964 and various other times in Brazilian history, the leadership role that Brazil has played in such organizations as the Rio Group, the Organization of American States (OAS), and others[15] could change, and other Latin American militaries with a history of repression might be emboldened to follow Brazil.

11. Riordan Roett, *Brazil: Politics in a Patrimonial Society*, 4th ed. (Westport, Conn.: Praeger, 1992), 159.
12. Evidence of torture in Brazil was gathered by several international human rights groups. Amnesty International listed 1,076 cases of torture in Brazil as of September 1972. See Amnesty International, *Report on Allegations of Torture in Brazil* (London: Amnesty International Publications, 1972).
13. Stepan, *Rethinking Military Politics,* 69.
14. Ralph Della Cava, "The 'People's Church': The Vatican and Abertura," in *Democratizing Brazil: Problems of Transition and Consolidation,* ed. Alfred Stepan (New York: Oxford University Press, 1989), 143–167.
15. Brazil has been slow in taking any leadership role in the UN and has only recently been more active in sending peacekeeping troops on UN missions. Brazil is starting to play a more active role in the hope of gaining a permanent seat on the UN Security Council.

CURRENT DOMESTIC CONDITIONS

The Economy

The key to Brazil's future is its economy. As stated, Brazil has one of the world's largest economies, with a GDP of about $750 billion in 1996.[16] Industrial output is about four times agricultural production. The primary products are steel, autos, textiles, shoes, chemicals, and machinery. The main agricultural goods are coffee, cotton, soybeans, and sugar. Yet the growth rate for 1996 was a slow 2.9 percent by Brazilian standards, even though the year ended with 5.4 percent growth for the fourth quarter. At about $5,580 (1994 figures for purchasing power parity, or PPP), per capita income is low in comparison with other major economies. Brazil still lags behind other emerging markets in competitiveness, with an overall ranking of 48 by the Global Competitiveness Report. (The United States ranked 4, Malaysia 10, Argentina 37.) Corruption is also still a major problem that Brazil must overcome.[17] To understand Brazil's potential for growth, it is important to go back to at least the 1960s, when the Brazilian economy under military rule began to take off. By 1968, Brazil entered what has come to be known as the "economic miracle" with growth rates as high as 13 percent per year.[18]

Unfortunately, in the 1970s Brazil got pummeled from all sides, with the oil shocks of that decade hitting Brazil's growing industries very hard. "With the consumption of about 1 million barrels of oil per day, Brazil was importing 900,000 [barrels] at what suddenly became a staggering and impossible cost in dollars."[19] Brazil began borrowing at a massive rate, believing that its economic growth would make up for the temporary setback and that it would be able to pay back its debt. Also, banks were eager to lend money deposited by suddenly oil-rich OPEC countries, and loans were flowing out to the developing world at a rapid pace. But loans that began at seemingly affordable interest rates soon became more and more expensive as rates in the industrialized North rose higher and higher. On top of the oil and debt

16. *Brazil: Country Report,* 5. Estimates for 1997 suggest a GDP of about $800 billion, indicating a positive 7 percent growth for the year.

17. The Transparency International Corruption index gives Brazil a rating of about 2.5, with 1 equaling high corruption and 10 equaling low corruption. Argentina has a 5; New Zealand has the best, 9.5.

18. Frank J. Devine, "The Dynamics of Today's Brazil," in *Brazil's Economic and Political Future,* ed. Julian M. Chacel, Pamela S. Falk, and David Fleischer (Boulder: Westview, 1988), 86.

19. Devine, "Dynamics of Today's Brazil," 87.

problems, Brazil then faced a global recession in which it was unable to earn revenues on its export goods to meet both its internal and external debts.

Brazil reached a crisis in which it could no longer borrow its way out of trouble, neither outside nor inside the country. Its strategy was to build up its exports to earn more hard currency, and by 1984 it had achieved a record $13 billion trade surplus.[20] But Brazil also had to meet the very large government payroll built up over the years by its nationally owned industries, and so it began to print more and more money. With currency flooding the market, domestic prices rose higher and higher. The cycle continued even after the end of military rule and into the civilian-led governments of the late 1980s and early 1990s. By 1994, hyperinflation had reached an astronomical 2,502.5 percent for the year.[21] Investors were moving their money around on a daily basis in what were called "overnight" accounts. These accounts paid up to 49 percent interest a month, with the rates changing daily. People who had money to invest were moving their cash every day to take advantage of competitive higher interest rates. They were making money faster than inflation was rising, but these investments were not producing anything and they became a cancer on the system. Some people were clearly profiting from inflation, but the economy was obviously out of control.

Then Foreign Minister Fernando Henrique Cardoso was named finance minister and introduced the Real Plan. The Brazilian currency unit, the cruzeiro, was changed to the *real* and was locked into a rate of exchange that made it roughly equal to the dollar, that is, one *real* equaled one U.S. dollar. This was very similar to the plan President Carlos Saul Meném had introduced in Argentina and which had successfully brought inflation under control in that country.[22] Cardoso introduced other stiff measures to control inflation and reform the banking system, and the public was willing to go along. Privatization of national industries was also begun, albeit slowly, and federal payrolls reduced, shrinking monthly government expenditures. A year later in 1995, the first year of Cardoso's presidency, the annual inflation rate was brought down to a manageable 76.8 percent and in 1996 to a mere 16.5 percent.[23] 1997 figures show inflation coming in under 5 percent.

20. Devine, "Dynamics of Today's Brazil," 87.
21. *Brazil: Country Report,* p.5.
22. There were some differences between the Real Plan and the Argentine Peso Plan: The Peso was controlled at a fixed rate of one dollar to one peso whereas the real was allowed to fluctuate within a small $+/-$ range. Also, the Argentine government was not allowed to circulate more pesos than the number of dollars held in reserve; the Real Plan had no such restrictions.
23. *Brazil: Country Report,* 5. These figures published by *The Economist* are higher than those released by Brazilian sources, which were quoted by President Cardoso in a speech in Brasília on December 12, 1996, as 23.17 percent for 1995 and 10.03 percent for 1996.

With the GDP gradually rising and inflation well under control, the picture should look good. But the serious impact of the 1997–1998 Asian crisis shows that Brazil is still vulnerable. Cardoso successfully defended the real at the end of 1997 against speculators but used over $10 billion of its $62 billion in reserves to do it. Brazil's total external debt is now over $170 billion, one of the world's largest and up from 1992, when it was high at $129 billion. Even though banks and other lenders agreed to restructure Brazil's loans in 1992, servicing the current debt places an overwhelming burden on the state, and paying off the loans looks close to impossible in the near future.

The 1995 Cardoso plan also lowered tariffs on imported goods to open trade and force domestic prices down. This led to a flood of buying foreign products, driving up imports. The government began to reverse the policy, but in the last two years Brazil's trade surplus has disappeared, creating in 1997 a record trade deficit of about $33 billion. This trade deficit puts a strain on Brazil's stock of hard currency, which is intended to back the real against the dollar.

Pegging the real to the dollar is also creating problems for Brazil, as it has for all the emerging markets that have adopted this mechanism. The real has depreciated in actual terms in relation to the dollar, and the appreciation of the dollar against other major currencies since the first half of 1996 forced Brazil to devalue the real in July 1997.[24] By keeping the real as high as the dollar, Brazil was losing its competitiveness in pricing its goods in the global market. It was forced to devalue in order to boost its exports.

Watching Indonesia's currency lose 80 percent of its value within a few weeks in the fall of 1997, Brazil scrambled to shore up its economy on various fronts: raising interest to a 40 percent annual rate to attract investors, pushing through social security reform to cut government costs, and stepping up privatization by moving ahead with the scheduled sale of the telecommunications industry. While Cardoso continued his resolve to defend the real, the Brazilian government announced in January 1998 it would set a "maxi band" in which the real would trade against the dollar, allowing a 7 percent depreciation over the next ten to twelve months. This could ease the threat of future currency speculation, but some fear it is not enough.[25] By the beginning of 1998, Brazil seemed to

24. The real was valued slightly higher than the dollar in 1995, trading at about one real to $1.08. During 1996 the real was holding at about equal to the dollar, but after July's devaluation, one real was worth about 92 cents. (See *Wall Street Journal,* exchange rates on a daily basis from July 21 through August 21, 1997.)

25. *Brazil Watch* 15, no. 5 (Washington D.C.: Orbis Publications, January 26–February 9, 1998), 5.

be holding its own. Without the banking and budget reforms Cardoso had forced through in the first years of his administration, Brazil would have been hit much harder by the Asian Crisis.[26]

Cardoso's tight fiscal policy may be risky in an election year, but reducing the deficit through tightening social security outlays, privatization, and holding down inflation is key to Brazil's economic security. Brazil cannot afford to return to the previously expedient policy of printing more money to meet expenses, a practice that led ultimately to hyperinflation in the not-too-distant past.

Politics

As stated earlier, Brazil's political history of Portuguese colonization is unique in Latin America. Although the rest of Latin America was torn by bloody wars with Spain, Brazil's transition to independence was peaceful. However, the political-cultural legacy left by the Portuguese was very similar to that imprinted by its Iberian partner on the rest of the continent. Riordan Roett describes three important aspects of Brazilian sociopolitical life that persist today:

> Among the most important of these are (1) the concept of elite rule, (2) the maintenance of a state bureaucracy at the service of the patrimonial order, and (3) the persistence of a social dualism—a gap between the standard of living of the richest and poorest Brazilians that is as pernicious as it is endemic.[27]

The elite Brazilian oligarchy and its regional power bases never really succumbed to the centralized authority of the monarchy. Emperor Don Pedro I was succeeded by Don Pedro II, but by the 1880s the crown was seriously weakened. In 1889, the armed forces, in cooperation with the elites, overthrew the monarchy in a bloodless coup and established the "Old Republic," which lasted until 1930. This move began the long association in Brazil between the upper class and military. "The military was never far from politics and power in the Old Republic."[28]

The other defining factor of Brazilian politics is the dominance of the political system by the two rival regions: São Paulo, the industrial and agricultural center, and Minas Gerais, the gem and mineral mining center. The leadership of the Old Republic alternated between the top political figures of these two states, and the national government tended to serve in large part the interests of the region that was in control. In 1930,

26. "Brazil's Brighter Future," *New York Times,* February 19, 1998, editorial.
27. Riordan Roett, "Brazilian Politics at Century's End," in *Brazil under Cardoso,* ed. Susan Kaufman Purcell and Riordan Roett (Boulder: Lynne Rienner, 1997),15.
28. Roett, "Brazilian Politics at Century's End," 21.

Getulio Vargas, the governor of the emerging power base in the state of Rio Grande do Sul, ended this rivalry and led a civil-military movement that quickly overthrew the government and established an authoritarian regime.[29] The Vargas era contributed to the solidification of Brazil as a nation through the building of a centralized and institutionalized governmental structure. Vargas promised to end authoritarian rule, and in 1945 elections took place. The years from 1946 through 1964 marked a turbulent democratic period, with elections interrupted by military coups and attempted coups. As Kenneth Erickson explains:

> If Brazil proved ungovernable in these years, it was because of contradictions among the principles and interests shaping the national political process. Corporatism, an elitist principle, limited political participation, while populism expanded it. Structural dependency aggravated class conflict. . . . Left-wing groups hoped to establish some form of socialism, but they lacked effective power because both corporatism and populism had undermined their institutional autonomy. When a real confrontation came in 1964, the forces of the right easily seized power, ended the populist era, and shaped the Brazilian polity so it would serve their interests.[30]

From the time of the military coup in 1964 until 1985, the military ran Brazil. A series of military presidents controlled Brazilian politics and the economy. State-sponsored development in this era produced amazing growth, and the armed forces gained enormous respect for their ability to turn the economy around with such success. But authoritarian rule, with no mechanisms for accountability, led to the gradual abuse of power. Impunity began to permeate the system. Leaders succumbed to the temptation to exterminate any opposition, and it gradually dominated political motives. Human rights abuses mounted, and the elite who had once sponsored military rule were now questioning it. The worst abuses took place under President Medici in the early 1970s. By the mid-1970s, the authoritarian state was challenged by new movements within civil society such as the church, new labor groups, lawyers, the press, new entrepreneurs, and even artists' groups. Labor and the church, along with these other groups, began to demand a return to democracy. Eventually a deal was struck to grant amnesty on abuses in return for a peaceful transition to democracy.[31]

It is important to acknowledge that Brazil has a history of political par-

---

29. Kenneth Erickson, "Brazil: Corporative Authoritarianism, Democratization, and Dependency," in *Latin American Politics and Development*, ed. Howard J. Wiarda and Harvey F. Kline (Boulder: Westview, 1979),160–211.

30. Erickson, "Brazil," 179.

31. Stepan, *Rethinking Military Politics*, 3–12.

ticipation by civil society and that even during the military regime (1964–1985) there were limited elections to public office, especially on the local level. Although all other parties were outlawed during the regime, the military party did allow one opposition party to exist and run candidates for seats in the national congress. The expectation that Brazil would return to democracy was always present, and the military took some limited steps to at least keep the appearance of participation. State governors and local mayors began to be elected freely several years before the 1985 transition.

In 1985, the civilian candidate Tancredo Neves was elected by the national congress to become president. But before he could take office Neves died, and his vice president, José Sarney, was sworn in. Ironically, the first democratically elected president after the military regime never took office and the nonelected, fairly obscure Sarney had the task of launching the new democratic era. Everyone held their breath. But Sarney quietly supervised the transition, and a new constitution was completed under his tenure in 1988. The first nationally elected president, Fernando Collor de Mello, took office in January 1990, but was later charged with widescale influence peddling worth millions of dollars. His impeachment was a setback to Brazil as it tried to set a steady course toward democratic rule. However, because the military did not stage a coup as it had done in the past, the peaceful transition of power to Vice President Itamar Franco was a sign that Brazil could handle the blow and still keep democracy on track. Nevertheless, President Franco's appointment of certain former military officers to high-level positions gave the impression that the military was still operating behind the scenes.[32] Military pressure was evident when a Brazilian newspaper revealed that in the fall of 1993 three military ministers backed President Franco in an unsuccessful coup attempt by mid-level military officers and business leaders from São Paulo.[33]

Here, it is important to understand the role that the military in Brazil has traditionally played in terms of national security. Military culture has been quite clear in this regard. The military is responsible not only for defense against external threats but also for the maintenance of internal order. That premise is also written into the new constitution of 1988. In an interview conducted by the author with a member of the Brazilian armed forces in 1991, it was explained: "The military serves the nation and defends the state, but first it defends the nation, meaning the history, the culture, the language, and the tradition." What this means is that the

32. *New York Times*, May 27, 1993, p. A9.
33. *Journal do Brasil*, January 6, 1994.

military is given the task of defending the nation and its culture, not necessarily a particular government. If there is a threat to the country, the military has the right to take over the government to save the nation. Although some Brazilians do not agree with this premise, this definition of the role of the military is a part of Brazilian political culture and remains in the constitution.

Fernando Henrique Cardoso, the foreign minister and then the finance minister under Itamar Franco, was elected president and took office in January 1995. He serves through the end of 1998. The constitution stated that a president can only serve one term, but Cardoso successfully garnered enough support to amend the constitution in June 1997 and will run again in the fall 1998. If the economy remains stable and inflation stays under control, Cardoso has a good chance of serving a second term. The left seems to be disorganized, and no strong opponent is on the horizon.

Social Factors

Brazil remains an elite-dominated society in which most of the wealth is concentrated in the upper 1 to 2 percent of the population, families who have accumulated their wealth through industry and agribusiness. The landed elite makes up a smaller class but retains certain privileges from an earlier era when it dominated Brazilian politics. The government at various times has passed agrarian reform bills, but these laws have rarely been enforced. The gap between rich and poor in Brazil is one of the largest in the world, and this disparity between the haves and have-nots is also reflected in the distribution of land. Some families hold huge tracts of land equal in size to some of the smaller and medium-size states in the United States. The large landowners represent only 1 percent of the population but possess about 46 percent of the total land.

The issue revolves around what are called the *latifúndios*, or large tracts of land, totaling some 33 million hectares, which are held by a few individual families but not cultivated. Well-organized groups who call themselves Movemento Sem Terra, or the "landless movement" continue to bring pressure on the landowners and the state to break up these landholdings and distribute some of the land to the disenfranchised poor.[34]

Confrontations between the landholders and the peasants have at times been violent. (Peasants here are broadly defined as landless rural workers, poor tenants, and owners of small plots.) The peasants began to build an organization before the 1964 coup but were wiped out by the military regime. Since democratization peasant organizations have resurfaced but

34. João Pedro Stedile and Frei Sergio, *A Luta Pela Terra no Brasil* (São Paulo: Editora Pagina Alberta Ltda.,1993), 40–41.

face powerful landlords who control local water supplies, bank credit, feed, and seed supplies, as well as local police forces. These elites have often hired their own gunmen to control land protesters and local land sit-ins. Peasant protests have usually only occurred when forces from outside the locality, such as Movemento Sem Terra, have done the organizing, brought in the media, and offered leverage against the power of the local landlords. Peasant workers demonstrating in Brasilia have displayed long lists of those who have been killed in these disputes. The Base Church (Igreja de Base) segment of the Catholic Church has also supported the local peasants but with limited success, except to divide up some church-held lands for the poor.

The landless issue plays a greater role in Brazil's problems than might first meet the eye. Much of the internal migration that has brought about the city slums (favelas) is by poor peasants fleeing the northeast, where they cannot own land for subsistence farming or find jobs. In most cases they remain unemployed or underemployed in the cities in the south, but end up creating a day-to-day life in these squatter shanties and don't go back home. Family structure has broken down, and crime and poor health and sanitation surround these people's lives. Their needs put enormous pressure on cities such as Rio de Janeiro and São Paulo, and the poverty and crime that have grown in these cities are often blamed on these migrants. Children are often sent out to beg from cars or passersby on busy streets. Some of these children return home to their families in the favelas at night, but others stay on the streets and end up being organized by criminal elements who force them to work on their behalf. With no one to protect them, the lives of these children have little or no value. They are often found murdered on the streets, and the cases often go uninvestigated. A study by the National Chamber of Deputies in 1992 stated that in the three years leading up to the study, some forty-six hundred children had been murdered in Brazil, approximately four "assassinations" per day. About 82 percent were black and 23 percent were girls. Children most at risk were those between fifteen and seventeen years old.[35] The Brazilian media at times have referred to these street killings as clean-up operations (limpezas). Reports of these murders have reached the international media and are an indication of the poverty and misery that still remain unaddressed by the Brazilian power elite.

Labor has been an important force in Brazil, organizing waves of strikes in the late 1970s to protest the military regime and its tight control on labor and its interests. These campaigns clearly established the metal-

---

35. Câmara dos Deputados, Comissão Parlamentar de Inquérito, *O Extermínio de Crianças e Adolescentes no Brasil* (Brasília, 1992).

workers, especially the auto workers and other metalworkers around São Paulo, as the leaders of the labor militancy.[36] Luis Inacio Lula da Silva, president of the Metalworkers' Union of São Bernardo and Diadema, became an important national figure and the leading presidential candidate for the Workers' Party (the PT) in 1989 against Collor and again in 1994 against Cardoso. Lula plans to run against Cardoso again in 1998. With the new constitution, labor has won the autonomy, for the most part, that it wanted from the state. But as Margaret Keck points out, Brazilian culture, built on elite norms, does not have a tradition of direct bargaining with laborers, who are expected to know their place. Bargaining among elites, which has taken place in Brazil over the years, is not translated into conciliation or bargaining "between elites and the great mass of the population."[37] With the new economic success and control of inflation carried out by the Cardoso administration, labor has lost much of its galvanizing force. Strikes have been barely visible since the 1994 election. Yet unemployment is high, reaching 16 percent by the end of 1997 in the state of São Paulo, which is the engine of the country's industrial base. Official national unemployment figures, hovering around a very decent 5 percent for the last five years, are misleading.

> To measure employment, the government asks whether someone has had any income over the past month. Thus the hundreds of thousands of people who sell candy from makeshift stands on the sidewalk or watch parked cars for spare change are counted as employed. . . . In recent polls by Gallup and other institutions, Brazilians cited unemployment as the biggest problem facing the country in 1996, outpacing crime and under-funding of social services.[38]

1997 estimates show national unemployment figures reaching 7 percent.[39] Labor complains that although inflation has been low by Brazilian standards, dropping under 5 percent for 1997,[40] the real value of earnings has gone down.[41] Yet labor seems to be at a disadvantage. No one

36. Margaret E. Keck, "The New Unionism in the Brazilian Tradition," in *Democratizing Brazil: Problems of Transition and Consolidation,* ed. Alfred Stepan (New York: Oxford University Press, 1989), 262.
37. Keck, "The New Unionism," 285.
38. Laurie Goering, "Jobs Dearth Casts Pall in Latin America," *Chicago Tribune,* March 25, 1996, business section, 1.
39. Eliana Simonetti and Ricardo Grinbaum, "Assombração nacional," *Veja,* February 11, 1998, p. 70
40. Economic summary, in *Brazil Watch* (Washington, D.C.: Orbis Publications, January 26–February 9, 1998), 1. There is no author listed: exec editor is Richard Foster.
41. "The Acceleration of Unemployment in Greater São Paulo and Reports by FGTS of the Real Losing Its Value," *Boletin Diese* 194 (May 1997).

wants the return of hyperinflation, and so laborers are discouraged from striking over wages. Also, because of unemployment or underemployment, workers fear going on strike because other laborers will simply move in and take their jobs. Lula, whose charismatic leadership once mobilized action among workers, is now launching a renewed presidential campaign for 1998, but the left as a whole appears disorganized.

Clearly, the economic growth that Brazil has demonstrated to the world has not reached the poor and the working classes. The 1997 Human Development Report, by combining various indicators, ranks Brazil sixty-eighth in the world in terms of the human condition of its citizens, down from 58 the year before. As the world's eighth largest economy, a ranking of 68 suggests that income distribution is sorely lacking. Costa Rica, Chile, and Argentina are all ranked higher. The infant mortality rate, considered an important indicator of the health of a society, is 55 per one thousand births.[42] This is very high considering rates of 6 to 9 per thousand for the industrialized countries.

Per capita income among workers remains low while prices are relatively high in dollar/real terms, leaving the working class without the means to buy the goods one would normally consider within the domain of the normal lower- to-middle-class life-style. For example, although 73 percent of Brazilians have safe drinking water, only 44 percent have access to sanitation, the same rate as sub-Saharan Africa.[43] Now with inflation under control, people have an incentive to save, and there is evidence that a middle class in Brazil is growing. But many complain that the gap is widening, as some are able to move up into the middle, while others are losing ground. The middle class is often credited with providing stability to society as they strive to protect the status quo. So Brazil will need to provide measures that will allow the middle class to expand and more workers to move up.

Education is a major factor in impeding Brazil's progress. With about 17 percent illiteracy,[44] Brazil has one of the least-educated populations among the emerging market nations. As Amoury de Souza explains, "About half of Brazil's labor force either has no formal schooling or did not complete primary school, and only 37 percent of the population ages

42. Central Intelligence Agency, *CIA World Factbook 1996*. Available at http://www.odci. gov/cia.
43. *Human Development Report 1997*, published for the United Nations Development Programme (New York: Oxford University Press, 1997).
44. *CIA World Factbook 1996*; also, the *Human Development Report 1997* lists Brazil with 83 percent literacy.

sixteen to eighteen is enrolled in secondary schools."[45] For Brazil to compete with other industrialized nations, it will have to show major improvements in education and literacy levels.

The Environment

Environmental issues in Brazil, as in the other pivotal states as well as the United States, are integrated into the economic, social, and political struggles in society. Human rights concerns are also interwoven into disputes over land use. The legacy of a statist society in Brazil, with a short history of democracy from 1945 to 1964, also embedded in a patrimonial order controlled by the Brazilian elite, means that bargaining over policy is conducted by a small group at the top of the political hierarchy. The business interests of this privileged group generally lie in exploiting the environment for development purposes. In this emerging democracy, where voting rights do not automatically translate into power, public interests are often left out of the equation. Since the 1970s, a number of governmental bodies have been created to address one aspect or another related to the environment, but conflicts over environmental policy are frequently left unresolved, and the sheer number of bureaucratic actors dealing with environmental issues precludes any cooperation.[46] This disarray benefits those interests that can move ahead unencumbered by the lack of cooperation in the environment bureaucracy.

The history of environmental exploitation begins with the early extraction policies of the Portuguese, whose primary products included the rosewood trees, mahogany, and brazil wood (after which the country was named) that were cut and sold into Europe. Early sugar plantations established by the land barons and worked by slaves brought from Africa required clearing the forests. Soil depletion through the overproduction of cane brought desertification and drought across much of the northeast, forcing plantation owners to expand and cut more forest.

The policy to develop the Amazon Basin began with the military regime under President Emilio Medici in the early 1970s. The Amazon Basin covers 60 percent of Brazil, including some 5 million square kilometers (about one half the size of the United States) that had been relatively untouched. Medici intended to colonize and develop this vast resource by building a trans-Amazon highway and attracting migrants and

---

45. Amoury de Souza, "Redressing Inequalities: Brazil's Social Agenda at Century's End," in *Brazil under Cardoso*, ed. Susan Kaufman Purcell and Riordan Roett, (Boulder: Lynne Rienner, 1997), 65.
46. Roberto P. Guimarães, *The Ecopolitics of Development in the Third World: Politics and Environment in Brazil* (Boulder: Lynne Rienner, 1991), 189.

big business to settle the region and expand the nation. Settlement of the Amazon rain forest was also seen as an antidote to the drought and desertification of the northeast. Peasants were encouraged to emigrate from the more densely populated northeast, where highly unequal land ownership patterns and the drought had contributed to growing social unrest. Many of the unskilled migrants had ended up in squatter shanties in the big cities of the south. With little hope of reforming the agrarian structure in the northeast, the government intended to defuse the problem by encouraging the move westward.[47]

The Medici government enacted a two-pronged policy that instead of alleviating the misery of the landless migrants simply spread the same two-class system into new territory. While promoting the migration of peasants from the northeast, the government offered enormous land concessions to Brazilian and foreign corporations. Other incentives included a 50 percent reduction of corporate income taxes on funds destined for Amazon investment, full tax exemption for approved projects up to 1982, exemption from import duties for raw materials, exemption from export duties for certain commodities, special credit arrangements, and matching funds.[48] Some large corporations that took up the offer were Volkswagen, Nestlé, Mitsubishi,[49] and McDonald's. The poorer migrant laborers were offered none of these incentives and, for example, in the state of Mato Grosso in the Amazon area, small farmers received no government support.[50] The result was that the big corporations took most of the land, absorbing the migrants as slavelike laborers, bonding them through systems of manipulated debt. The other human tragedy that resulted from building the highway and settling the virgin territory was the effective genocide of the native peoples, whose habitat was destroyed.

After the marketable wood had been harvested, the highly efficient slash-and-burn method—traditional on the large sugar plantations—was used to clear the forest and prepare the soil for pasture land. But the soil that makes up the floor of the rain forest is not suitable for supporting grassland, and after a few years the fields became useless. Each year cattle ranchers had to clear more forest in order to create more grazing area for their cattle. In the early 1970s, the state of Rondônia in the Amazon region lost forests covering an area equal to the size of the state of Massachusetts. By the late 1980s, the Brazilian Amazon Basin had lost to

47. Judith Lisansky, *Migrants to Amazonia: Spontaneous Colonization in the Brazilian Frontier* (Boulder: Westview, 1990), 1–18.
48. Lisansky, *Migrants to Amazonia*, 9.
49. Guimãres, *The Ecopolitics of Development*, 121.
50. Lisansky, *Migrants to Amazonia*, 10.

deforestation an area equivalent to California and New England com-bined.[51]

Deforestation and desertification are not limited to the northeast and the Amazon Basin. They are also spreading in the south in the states of Paraná and Rio Grande do Sul. In the 1800s, natural forest covered 82 percent of the state of São Paulo, but by the 1970s this area had shrunk to under 9 percent.[52] The irony is that most analysts agree that the Amazonian cattle ranches have been economic failures. Cattle production was less than anticipated, and the predicted ecological consequences of deforestation (erosion, degraded soil, loss of carbon absorption) have taken place. Misappropriation of investment monies also meant less development than original plans had promised.[53]

Over the past five to six years, under various democratic administra-tions, government policy on the environment has been in a state of disar-ray.[54] Brazil lost $80 to $90 million in funds in 1996 and 1997 from the United Nations Development Programme because the government was too disorganized to administer the grants.[55]

The results have been an alarming renewal of deforestation, which had slowed around the time of the 1992 Earth Summit in Rio de Janeiro, Brazil. In 1995, the National Institute for Space Research detected through its weather satellites 72,200 fires in the first half of the month of August, up from 61,000 fires in the whole month of August in 1994.[56] The Brazilian National Institute for Space Research reported that during the period 1991–1994, deforestation in Brazil increased by 33 percent.[57] While the world's attention was focused on Indonesia's record forest fires in the fall of 1997, Brazil had one of the worst burning seasons in memory. U.S. satellite data showed fires in Brazil up 28 percent from 1996.[58] This

51. Guimarães, *The Ecopolitics of Development*, 221.
52. Guimarães, *The Ecopolitics of Development*, 134.
53. Lisansky, *Migrants to Amazonia*, 149.
54. The Secretário Especial do Meio Ambiente (SEMA), created in 1973 under military President Medici, had a depressing performance of environmental protection. President Sarney established the Brazilian Institute of the Environment and of Natural Resources (IBAMA) to oversee SEMA and other bodies; President Collor set up the Secretary of the Environment (SEMAN) without dismantling IBAMA or SEMA. The current system appears to be unmanageable; see Guimarães, *The Ecopolitics of Development*, 199, 200, 227.
55. From an interview with Frank Pinto of UNDP on July 30, 1997, at the UN.
56. In clearing the forest, usable wood is cut and removed first, then what remains is burned to clear away the rubble and prepare the land for some kind of cultivation. So, techni-cally, the rain forest trees are not all being burned, but the fires indicate that the forest is gone.
57. Laurie Goering, "Blazes Char Amazon Forest: A Burning Season Is Expected, but This Year Is Out of Control," *Chicago Tribune*, October 17, 1997, p. 1.
58. Reported by the Rainforest Action Network, San Fransisco, California.

increase came after claims by the Brazilian Congress that the burning had slowed. An account of what was happening on the ground was impossible because the Congress had stopped allocating the $500,000 needed to pay the scientists to do the analysis.[59] In recent years, Southeast Asian logging firms from Indonesia and Malaysia, after having exhausted their own forests, have acquired large tracts of rain forest, clearcutting the land and sending the logs back home to be processed.

The burning of the forest not only contributes to global warming, but the elimination of the forest also prevents the absorption of carbon dioxide and the production of oxygen by the vegetation, as well as destroying the habitat of one of the largest sources of biodiversity in the world. Also, the rain in the Amazon basin is created by the cycle of evaporation and release produced by the jungle growth. When this rain cycle is curtailed, desertification sets in.

It doesn't look as though this policy will end anytime soon. During 1997 and 1998, foreign companies, especially in the United States and Canada, have committed to investing about $2.5 billion in exploring untouched reserves, mostly in Brazil's Amazon, according to Carlos Oiti Berbert, president of the Brazilian Geological Service. Recent finds, including a gold mine with reserves of about 500 tons in the state of Pará, are expected to bring a total investment of around $12.5 billion by the year 2000. Oiti claimed that "next to South Africa, this is the richest area in the world."[60] The 1988 Brazilian constitution allowed for foreign investment in Brazilian mines, but only through forming joint partnerships with Brazilian companies that would hold the controlling interest. However, in 1994, the law was changed to allow foreigners to control mining firms as long as they maintained offices in Brazil. Companies seeking to avoid environmental restrictions in other countries are moving to Brazil, which already produces about 30 percent of the world's gold each year.[61] The government may feel it needs to compromise its environmental policy in order to raise the necessary funds to service its $170 billion debt. Some figures suggest that government land distribution programs are also accelerating the destruction of the Amazon where almost three quarters of authorized resettlements are located.[62]

Human rights concerns are also intertwined with land use and the environment. At the time of Portuguese colonization in the 1500s, it was estimated that there were from two to five million Indians in Brazil. Now

59. "Amazon Is Burning Again, as Furiously as Ever," *New York Times,* October 12, 1995.
60. "Mines Get Ready for New Boom," *Chicago Tribune,* February 22, 1997, p. 3.
61. "Mines Get Ready for New Boom."
62. "Brazil Report," in *Latin American Regional Reports* (London: Latin American Newsletters, January 6, 1998), 3.

about 200,000 are left. Many died of diseases brought from the outside world. Others were killed over the years in the process of taking and clearing the forest where they lived, most recently during the building of the trans-Amazon highway. As explained earlier, there is also the issue of debt peonage, instituted by the large landholding mining and cattle-ranching corporations. Migrants have been forced into hard labor under miserable conditions and are told they cannot leave because they owe the company for transportation, food, or housing costs. Companies often create and enforce these indebted conditions to hold on to cheap labor. Some of these conditions have been alleviated in recent years, but stories of similar slave-labor situations are reappearing.

The assassination of Chico Mendes in 1988 is another example of human rights violations as a direct result of environmental conflict. Mendes's chief purpose was to protect his fellow rubber tappers' right to earn their living by extracting products from the forest without destroying it. He became involved in the environmental movement to show that an intact-forest management system could sustain workers and their families while preserving the environment. His murder was the result of his outspoken protests against the slash-and-burn tactics of the cattle ranchers. A father and son, both cattle ranchers and members of the right-wing Rural Democratic Union (RDU), were convicted of the murder and are now in a high-security prison in Brasília, after having escaped the local jail. The RDU is suspected of being involved in a number of murders of rural leaders throughout the country.

The struggle over environmental issues is a complex process involving power politics, economics, bureaucratic organizations, and social and human rights issues. Protecting the environment for future generations in Brazil and for the planet will require thoughtful adjustments in all these areas. Not addressing even one of these components could have disastrous results.

BRAZIL AND THE REGION

Brazil is certainly a pivotal state in South America. Its sheer size and the fact that it borders ten other countries is an indication of its natural influence. Its role covers many issues including the resurgence of democracy, the role of the military and the acquisition of weapons, diplomacy and cooperation, economic and trade issues, and human rights.

Democracy

All the countries of Latin America with the exception of Cuba are now democracies. But equally important to consider is that most have gone through periods of military rule interrupted by periods of limited democracy. Military coups were common occurrences and are still a real threat in most of Latin America. Democracy remains fragile and depends on the organizational skills of civil society, and success at stabilizing the economy and other social factors. Brazil's leadership role as the largest democracy in the region is important. The historic military style of authoritarian control is the antithesis of a system based on individual rights and private enterprise. If democracy were to fail in Brazil and the military were to step in, civil society in the rest of Latin America would suffer the loss of open interaction with their counterparts in the most populous and largest economy in the region. Military regimes could be emboldened to take over in other countries, perhaps even with the tacit support of Brazil.

The Military

Military rule in Brazil, as in the rest of Latin America, has in the past been credited with state development. The military has been the one institution in Brazil that has continued to be organized and structured and to provide a system of education and employment for a significant proportion of the population. The military as an institution has been able to bridge the regional rivalries within Brazil and offer leadership when conflict among elites or between classes threatened to become chaotic. However, the military's hierarchical power structure, combined with a lack of supervision, led to repression, human rights violations, and other abuses of power that occurred during the period of military rule. These abuses, coupled with economic pressures, brought the regime's downfall. But many people still see the military as a kind of savior when events get out of control.

Besides human rights violations and repression, military rule in Brazil brought about other dangers. During the military regime of the mid-1970s to mid-1980s, the armed forces—all three forces, but particularly the navy—conducted a secret program to develop a nuclear weapons capability. With covert help from the West Germans, Brazil reached a status of technical sophistication capable of enriching uranium to weapons-grade level. A secret test site was built by the air force at Cachimbo in the state of Pará; it was later disclosed and formally shut down by President Collor in the fall of 1990. Although President Cardoso has renounced nuclear weapons aspirations and asked the Senate to approve adherence to the Nonproliferation Treaty in 1997, the military has never been forced to dismantle its nuclear research facilities. Brazil's current policy is not to have nuclear weapons, but should the military retake control, that could change.[63]

---

63. Jean Krasno, "Brazil's Secret Nuclear Program," *Orbis* 38, no. 3 (summer 1994): 425–437.

In terms of Brazil's relations outside the region, prior to the 1991 gulf war a team of Brazilian engineers under the direction of retired General Hugo Oliveira Piva, former head of the secret nuclear weapons program in Brazil,[64] was helping Iraq build a high-tech air-to-air missile. The program was abandoned as a result of the war but Brazilian nuclear material was found in Iraq by United Nations inspectors.[65] Brazil has also been one of the world's largest exporters of conventional weapons, particularly to the Third World, including Iraq and Libya.

Diplomacy and Cooperation

Progress in regional cooperation has grown significantly since the end of military rule. The Treaty of Tlatelolco, which creates a nuclear-free zone in Latin America, finally went into force in 1994. The treaty could not take effect until every Latin American country had signed. Some countries had waived that condition, but Brazil had continued to avoid that step. By 1994, Brazil had not only waived that condition but had also taken the initiative to bring the last holdout, Cuba, into the accord. The Brazilian foreign minister at the time, Celso Amorim, traveled to Cuba and convinced Castro to join on the grounds that it benefited Latin America, irrespective of United States' interests. This was a major achievement for nonproliferation and for Latin America.

Brazil and Argentina, which have both developed secret nuclear weapons programs under military rule, have taken additional steps to remove the nuclear threat in the region by establishing the Argentine-Brazilian Agency for Accounting and Control of Nuclear Materials (ABACC). The agency is a mechanism for mutual inspections to ensure that neither country is pursuing nuclear weapons and that nuclear research facilities are not diverting nuclear material for weapons use. The United Nations International Atomic Energy Agency (IAEA) has also been included in the inspection process.

Regional security cooperation also developed as a part of the Central American peace process with the start of the Contadora Group (Mexico, Venezuela, Panama, and Colombia), which sought a nonmilitary solution to the crisis of civil wars in the region. Four more Latin American countries, including Brazil, joined the Contadora as a "support group." The meetings of these eight countries evolved into what is known today as the Rio Group, which has its secretariat in Brazil and has declared its commitment to peace, development, and democracy in the region. Brazil also

---

64. José Goldemberg, secretary of science and technology at the time, stated formally that the two principal officials who carried out the project were Rex Nazareth Alves and Air Force Brigadier General Hugo de Oliveira Piva. See *New York Times*, October 9, 1990, p. A1.

65. Krasno, "Brazil's Secret Nuclear Program," 435–436.

plays a leadership role in a bloc of countries making up the Portuguese-speaking world, including Portugal and the former Portuguese colonies of Africa and Asia.

The Brazilian foreign relations community, often referred to as Itamaraty, has a cultural tradition of seeking peaceful solutions to disputes. This tradition was established by one of Brazil's highly revered cultural heroes, Rio Branco, who was foreign minister from 1902 to 1912 and who successfully settled several of Brazil's border disputes through negotiation and bargaining. Brazil has now begun to expand that tradition outside its own borders. Recently Brazil successfully intervened diplomatically in Paraguay, preventing a military coup. In addition, Brazil sent peacekeeping personnel to monitor the border between Ecuador and Peru after a crisis broke out between the two countries over a long-standing border dispute. Brazil initiated a treaty on regional cooperation among the nations that share the Amazon Basin; the treaty was signed by the eight foreign ministers in 1978.[66]

For Brazil as well as Argentina, and to a certain extent the rest of Latin America, two significant events since the early 1980s have shaped thinking on international relations and security issues in the region: the 1982 Falklands/Malvinas war and the 1991 gulf war. Both events dramatically demonstrated the dominant power of the first world and the large gap between the military capacity of the highly industrialized countries and the middle powers of the developing world.

Though the north considered it a victory for democracy, the humiliating defeat of the Argentine military by the British (over 11,000 kilometers from home) not only ended military rule in Argentina but left a pall of impotence across the continent. Brazil particularly was frustrated by the inability to stop the impending crisis because of its own weakness in the face of U.S. control in such bodies as the Organization of American States (OAS) and American support for the British. As much as Argentina and Brazil had developed industrially and technologically, they were no match for the superior technological base of the northern powers. This was reinforced in the Gulf War as daily television coverage displayed the bombing campaigns against Iraq. Brazilian engineers had been trapped in Iraq until the days of the initial bombing. Military industrial sales to the Third World, once an important source of revenue for Brazil, plummeted as a result.

Argentina and Brazil saw the nuclear-powered submarines used by the

66. Roett, *Brazil: Politics,* 193.

British in 1982 as a particular threat,[67] and both countries sought to intensify their nuclear research. The Brazilian navy cites the Malvinas war as a reason for Brazil's need to have nuclear-powered submarines.[68] With the onset of democracy, Argentina adopted a policy of "if you can't beat them, join them" and was eager to engage the first world by joining the Nonproliferation Treaty. Brazil took a much more independent stand and held out on joining the NPT until June 1997, when President Cardoso stated that Brazil would become a party to the treaty on approval by the Senate. By March 1998, the Congress still had not ratified the treaty, but there did not seem to be any clear opposition mounted against accession.

Economic and Trade Issues

The creation of Mercosur is the most significant regional effort at economic cooperation in recent years. It began through meetings between the newly elected Presidents of Argentina, Raúl Alfonsin, and Brazil, José Sarney, at the end of military rule. The historic meeting of the two presidents in 1986 at the Iguaçu River, which divides the two countries, marks the beginning of normalization between them and the strengthening of civilian rule. In the same year, President Sarney visited Buenos Aires and signed a twelve-point protocol creating a regional common market (Mercosur). The planning began immediately and moved ahead of schedule. Brazil encouraged Uruguay and Paraguay to join and by 1990 the four countries were part of the agreement.[69] Brazil wanted to avoid Mercosur's being a strictly bipolar arrangement. The strategy included building a regional bloc so as to be more attractive to the United States for future free trade and leverage in getting better trade arrangements in the region and with the industrialized countries. Bolivia and Chile are now associate members of Mercosur. Brazil is key to the success of Mercosur because it has about 80 percent of the total population of the four countries and also about 80 percent of their combined GDP. There has been a large upsurge in trade as well as cooperation in the private sectors among all four partners since the creation of the common market.[70]

---

67. The submarines used by the British did not carry nuclear missiles, but being nuclear powered, they could stay under water for much longer periods of time than a diesel-powered submarine, which has a combustion engine and requires oxygen to operate, forcing the vessel to surface periodically. Nuclear power makes a submarine a better predator and therefore a greater threat. However, some of the British surface ships did carry nuclear weapons because they didn't have time to get rid of them when they left the Mediterranean Sea before heading far into the South Atlantic.
68. Krasno, "Brazil's Secret Nuclear Program," 426.
69. Roett, *Brazil: Politics*, 195.
70. Roett, *Brazil: Politics*, 197.

Human Rights

Since the return to democracy throughout Latin America as well as Brazil, incidents of human rights violations and disappearances have dramatically decreased. But issues of impunity and unequal justice bogged down by inefficient and inadequate justice systems still persist. At the 1997 OAS General Assembly meeting, Brazil "urged that the summit agree on cooperative actions to advance human rights, including prison and judicial reform and proposed international cooperation to combat corruption, for example through agreements to provide access to bank accounts." Brazil also proposed "that the Inter-American Development Bank (IDB) consider opening a window to support regional integration efforts, including assistance to retrain and relocate displaced workers [a creative idea that failed to win support in the U.S. government or elsewhere]."[71] Brazil could provide an important leadership role in continuing to improve human rights conditions in the region.

THE YEAR 2020: OPTIMISTIC AND PESSIMISTIC PROJECTIONS FOR THE FUTURE

Optimistic

Brazil's democratic institutions continue to solidify; successful transitions of power are the norm at the local and national levels. Through privatization, reduction of state corruption, better management, and improved tax collection, Brazil has reduced its debt and kept inflation under control. It has continued to promote trade and joint ventures through Mercosur, which has increased its trade with the European Union and the United States. In addition, American markets have been opened up to products from the region through reciprocal agreements. Brazil has completed the gas pipeline from Bolivia to Argentina with connections to Paraguay and Uruguay, bringing an important regional source of energy and decreasing dependence on oil.

With economic stabilization and democratic solidification, the military has receded and civilian supervision has reduced military prerogatives. The World Bank, the Inter-American Development Bank, and the United States, after years of trading debt relief for environmental protection measures, have worked with Brazilian scientists and ecological experts in almost eliminating slash-and-burn deforestation and replaced it with sus-

---

71. Richard E. Feinberg, *Summitry in the Americas: A Progress Report* (Washington, D.C.: Institute for International Economics, April 1997), 115.

tainable forest management and harvesting processes. Debt relief tied to successful fulfillment of grants for rural development has decreased migration to the urban areas and into Amazonia. Brazil has continued to support cooperation among the nations that share the Amazon Basin and has established a multilateral commission to oversee the elimination of deforestation and enforce environmental laws.

Brazil has gained a permanent seat on the United Nations Security Council and has used this position to help the UN mediate an agreement between India and Pakistan to eliminate their nuclear arsenals, using the Brazilian-Argentine agreement and inspection mechanisms as a model. With reduced costs servicing the debt, increased revenues from trade through Mercosur expansion, and reduced military spending, Brazil has channeled more resources into health and education. A better-educated work force has improved the overall infrastructure of the country.

Pessimistic

Social unrest due to unalleviated poverty and nationwide strikes brought on by losses in real earnings among the working poor has created a crisis leading to a military coup. The social crisis was exacerbated by a return to hyperinflation and the collapse of the Real Plan. A return to democracy does not look promising for the near future. Military repression and human rights violations have reached a level comparable with that of the early to mid-1970s. A degradation of sanitation has led to an outbreak of cholera; a repeat of the meningitis epidemic of the mid-seventies has hit the major cities. Furthermore, mutations in malaria migrating from portions of Africa to the Amazon are resisting treatment. With the depressed situation in Brazil, Mercosur has weakened, and Argentina and Chile have returned to a system of high tariffs to protect national industries. Brazil can no longer invest in regional projects, and the Bolivian gas pipeline was never completed. Efforts to earn greater revenues to service the debt have led to agreements with multinational companies to strip mine gold reserves in the Amazon, and deforestation is continuing.

Brazil has been unable to stop the spread of drug trafficking across its borders with Colombia and Peru. The Brazilian military, formerly reluctant to get into drug enforcement, is now conducting military raids against drug warlords who have moved into positions along the borders with Brazil and into the state of Acre in Brazilian territory. Other bad news is the discovery that Brazil had been stockpiling enriched uranium from its Aramar research facility. Argentina has broken off its nuclear agreement with Brazil in protest. Brazil refuses to let the IAEA investigate the allegations, citing issues of sovereignty. The discovery has also weakened Brazil's credibility in its other treaty obligations, and the sense of distrust in the region is growing.

PROPOSALS FOR A UNITED STATES STRATEGY TOWARD BRAZIL

U.S. Interests

The United States has multiple interests in Brazil, not only economic and political ones but also the environment, human rights, and nonproliferation of weapons of mass destruction. Brazilian markets are important to the United States and should increase with the growing Brazilian middle class. About $13 billion worth of U.S. goods were purchased in Brazil during 1996, making up just under one quarter of all Brazilian imports.[72] The inflow of direct foreign investment was $9 billion in 1996, second only to China. That figure doubled in 1997.[73] With privatization in Brazil, the U.S. has an interest in investing in companies previously owned by the state, such as electric power and telecommunications, particularly cellular telephones. Such investments can be mutually beneficial if managed carefully. U.S. companies can profit from the sale and service of these products and at the same time offer Brazilians high-technology systems and service training. By selling off these companies, Brazil can reduce spending on government payrolls. Government revenues could then be used to address social needs and reduce the government deficit. The U.S. also purchases a number of Brazilian products—about $9 billion worth in 1996—including iron and steel, chemicals, machinery, footwear, fruits and vegetables, wood and wood pulp, and so on.

Important as a trading partner, Brazil can also be a key political partner. Historically, Brazil has been an ally of the West during the two world wars and on significant issues in intergovernmental bodies such as the United Nations. As an important leading member of the Organization of American States, Brazil can influence a large bloc of votes (some thirty countries) and is being considered as a permanent member of the UN Security Council. When the United States needs international political support from the developing world as it did in the 1991 gulf war, Brazil can be an important friend.

---

72. The second-largest source of imports was from Germany at roughly $6 billion, Argentina was third with about $5 billion, and Japan was fourth with about $2.6 billion. This data is from *Brazil: Country Report*, 2nd quarter, 1997, 5.
73. Melvyn Levitsky, "Progress in Brazil Is Impressive," *Miami Herald*, January 28, 1998, Viewpoints.

Brazil is also a pivotal nation in curbing environmental degradation, preventing climate change, and in preserving biodiversity. The United States has a strong interest in helping Brazil manage sustainable development and reduce deforestation in the Amazon Basin, the world's largest single concentration of biodiversity.[74] In addition, the American public's interest in environmental issues in Brazil is closely linked to human rights, as conflicts over resources and poverty are played out in disputes over land use. The U.S. government has also named nonproliferation as a high priority. Brazil's renunciation of its nuclear weapons program, its cooperation with Argentina and the IAEA on inspections of its nuclear material, its leadership role in the Treaty of Tlatelolco, and its recent intentions to join the Nonproliferation Treaty, all contribute to making Brazil an important partner in halting the spread of nuclear weapons.

Although it seems clear that the United States has key interests in Brazil, Brazil does not appear to be on the front burner for the State Department. According to Washington officials, U.S. policy makers tend to feel that Brazil has not shown much interest in a closer relationship compared with Argentina, which has been actively working to create greater ties to the United States and Europe. Brazil is seen as seeking a more independent role and as being more absorbed in its own internal issues. Argentina joined the Nonproliferation Treaty (NPT) several years ago, gaining friends in the West by doing so, and recently achieved recognition as a "non-NATO ally" of the United States, a status that the Brazilians have missed out on. Brazil had been much more reluctant to join the NPT and its Congress only recently is considering ratification. Brazil's military rulers were highly nationalistic and mistrustful of its large neighbor to the north. In truth, Brazil has been much more focused on itself and its own problems. Even after the end of military rule in 1985, Brazil went through a succession of weak leaders, and the country was not in a position to reach out from a position of strength. Only in the last three years, since President Cardoso has been able to stabilize the economy, has Brazil has been able to think about a coordinated foreign policy and stake its claim for recognition by the first world.

Rather than its overall impact on the region, how much effort a particular country makes, in this case Argentina, determines whether its issues get on the State Department agenda. Argentina's size, economy, and population are only a small portion of Brazil's, and yet, for the moment, it has gained a greater hold on U.S. thinking. Policy makers in Washington are also reluctant to openly single out any country in South America for special attention, fearing that would jeopardize other rela-

74. Lester Brown et al., *State of the World 1997* (New York: W. W. Norton, 1997), 15.

tionships in the region. Yet special relationships grow anyway as certain countries demand attention, but the State Department does not seem to follow any particular strategy. As Don Daniel and Andrew Ross point out in their essay for this book, the Pentagon feels that South America as a whole is not a priority for U.S. strategy, and Brazil is therefore off the radar screen as well.

Brazil's Needs

Brazil's strengths are its natural resources, industrial base, creative ingenuity, a highly educated elite, and a growing educated middle class. But Brazil is also plagued by a number of major threats to its ultimate success. It has the largest gap between rich and poor in Latin America and one of the worst in the world.[75] Land distribution is also an important indicator of imbalances. In Brazil, the "top 5 percent of landowners control at least 70 percent of the arable land, the bottom 80 percent have only 13 percent of the cultivable area."[76] Social unrest could threaten Brazil's governability. Land occupation campaigns organized by the Sem Terra movement have induced violent reactions by landowners. An estimated thirty thousand to fifty thousand people marched in Brasília in April 1997 to protest the plight of the 4 million landless families and delays in land reform.[77]

Brazil's need to address the misery of its poor population is in direct competition with its need to increase exports and service—let alone pay off—its huge and growing $170 billion external debt. It must also keep its deficit within a manageable range by continuing to press for privatization and reducing expenditures. How Brazil balances these constraints will determine its success or failure.

A Convergent Strategy for Brazil

Brazil and the United States primarily share common interests. The successful scenario for Brazil outlined above also benefits the United States. But Brazil is often frustrated by America's inconsistent policy toward it, featuring a series of constant reversals, now embracing this Latin American giant and then ignoring it. A case in point is the recent debacle over visas for Brazilians traveling to the United States. Within a few months' period, U.S. visa policy changed drastically three times. First a visa was good for three years, then without any notice good only for three months, followed by a complete reversal, changing the duration

---

75. *Human Development Report 1997.*
76. Brown et al, *State of the World 1997*, 122.
77. *Country Report: Brazil*, 2nd quarter 1997, 12.

to ten years. Brazil would like simply to be recognized for its weight in the world and be treated accordingly and consistently by the United States.

Primarily, the United States needs to support the democratization process in Brazil. In this case, not only is what the United States does important, but also what it does *not* do. During the 1964 military coup, the United States played an important catalytic role:

> U.S. military aid helped to set the stage for the coup, according to testimony by a U.S. army general. Brazilian officers kept the U.S. military attaché's office informed of their plans, and the attaché offered material help. In case heavy assistance was needed, the U.S. ambassador had a naval task force, including an aircraft carrier, a helicopter carrier, six destroyers, and four oil tankers, move into position off the coast.[78]

In light of the military's record on human rights, nuclear policy, environmental degradation, and so on, the United States should *not* support a military takeover in Brazil as it has done in the past.

The United States can support democracy in Brazil by helping the government alleviate social problems that could lead to unrest. Grants to education, job training, rural development, and small-business creation would help. Even though Brazil, with its large economy, may not seem to need aid, USAID should continue to target social concerns that the government may be too overstretched to address or that may be ignored by the controlling elites.

The United States does not have to do this alone. It can work with intergovernmental bodies like the United Nations Development Programme and the World Bank as well as nongovernmental organizations. Support for World Bank reform under its director, James Wolfensohn, who has been working to change the bank,[79] would encourage the bank to be more responsible to environmental and social concerns. Recent loans under consideration by the World Bank to alleviate rural poverty, help build the Bolivia–Brazil gas pipeline, and aid privatization would be steps in the right direction. Resources to support institution building in the justice system would offset claims of impunity and help to address the sense of injustice that is often reported in the media. Debt relief is also an important consideration. The pressure on Brazil to meet its debt demands takes away from its capacity to resist big business investors who could devastate the rain forest through clear-cut logging and strip mining. It also reallocates resources away from the social sector

78. Erickson, "Brazil," 192.
79. James D. Wolfensohn, "The Challenge of Inclusion," address to the Board of Governers, Hong Kong, China, September 23, 1997.

and may force Brazil to privatize national enterprises that might better serve the people through public ownership. Trading debt relief for environmental preservation and rural development or land reform might help manage a number of these problems at the same time.

Some specific recommendations can be made. A high-level bilateral commission between the U.S. and Brazil could be established on the order of the commission set up under Secretary of State Henry Kissinger through an agreement signed between Brazil and the United States in February 1976 but never fully implemented. The commission could formulate a joint plan on areas of common interest, such as protecting forests and biodiversity in the two countries, job creation, and joint investments. USAID could focus on improving levels of education as a whole and particularly in the work force. Increased joint effort could be put into improving the rate of access to sanitation from the current very low 44 percent. Another important contribution to the relationship between the two countries would be to formulate a treaty of commerce and navigation with Brazil. Both Argentina and Honduras have such treaties with the United States, but Brazil has no such arrangement. By offering special visa privileges, the treaty would open up avenues for Brazilians who want to invest in the United States and do business here. Right now, Argentines have these privileges. With Brazil's huge potential markets and large economy, Brazilians ought to be entitled to this kind of priority access.

A successful and sustainable economy and social structure in Brazil are clearly in the best interests of the United States, not only because they build broader markets for U.S. goods but also because democracy in Brazil would be severely threatened by economic and social failure. Democracy in Brazil is the key to alleviating concerns for human rights and nonproliferation as well as building cooperation in Latin America. These are common interests for the United States and the Brazilian people.

ALGERIA

William B. Quandt

On the rare day that Algeria is featured in the American press, it is usually in conjunction with some particularly atrocious act of violence in the long-running conflict between the country's military-dominated regime and its radical Islamist opponents. Algiers sounds increasingly like Beirut in the 1980s, with car bombs and assassinations becoming a part of everyday life. In the past four years, more than sixty thousand Algerians have died in this internecine struggle, an average of nearly three hundred each week. Hardly a family has been spared—and this in a country that paid an inordinately high price in blood and treasure to win its independence from France just thirty-five years ago.

But as with Lebanon during its much more destructive civil war, reports of the demise of Algeria as a functioning society or state are premature. In large parts of the country life goes on quite normally; the economy registered a modest upturn in 1996; oil companies are scrambling to invest in what seem to be promising new regions; a major gas project has just been completed, linking Algeria closely to Europe for years to come; and even Algerian political and intellectual life has a surprising vitality, reflected in one of the freest presses in the Arab world. Several political parties, including moderate Islamists, compete for support, albeit under tight controls from the government.

So which image is more compelling—that of Algeria on the verge of civil war, or an Algeria on a path toward recovery, merely struggling with what the regime calls "residual terrorism"? Neither picture is quite satisfactory, and any honest assessment will have to admit that the situation in Algeria as of 1997 is extremely complex and fluid, and could significantly improve or deteriorate in the next few years. In short, choices remain to be made by the regime, by its opponents, by ordinary Algerians who have tended to stand on the sidelines, and by foreign creditors and partners. Out of this mix of contingent choices will come a future Algeria that could well play a significant part in the North African and Middle Eastern region: as a country deserving to be considered pivotal in the positive sense, or quite possibly as a country that fails to achieve its potential, remains deeply troubled by violence and corruption, and whose problems infect the surrounding region to one degree or another.

ALGERIA'S PRESENT CRISIS

To gain some perspective on Algeria's uncertain present, we need a quick look at the recent past. From its independence in 1962 until the early 1980s, Algeria was ruled by a series of authoritarian regimes, in which the military, the single party, and the bureaucracy were the key players. Populism and nationalism, coupled with a degree of romantic "Third Worldism," provided the ideological matrix of politics.[1] Oil and gas revenues allowed some significant modernization. Education, health care, and cheap housing were provided in return for political passivity on the part of the people in whose name the regime governed. The system did not work very well; all the expected problems accompanied this model of development; but life did improve for the bulk of the rapidly growing population. By the early 1980s, however, the ruling party was widely seen as corrupt and unresponsive to popular needs, and pressures for change were mounting. Some gradual liberalization of the economy began, which tended to benefit those with connections to the regime, thus deepening the alienation of those on the margins of society—the young, unemployed, recent migrants from the rural areas who found themselves without much hope and without much education in crowded suburbs around Algiers and other large cities.[2]

When international oil prices collapsed in the mid-1980s, Algeria was one of the countries that was hardest hit. Never one of the big oil exporters, Algiers had gambled on continued high prices through the 1980s to finance the construction of light and heavy industries. Enormous sums were spent on expensive factories that produced goods for which there was little obvious demand.[3] Algeria went heavily into debt, but the managers assumed that rising oil prices would make it easy to repay the debts when they came due. Yet that was not to be. Instead, oil revenue plummeted, just as heavy demands for repayment hit in the late 1980s.

1. Robert Malley, *The Call From Algeria: Third Worldism, Revolution, and the Turn to Islam* (Berkeley: University of California Press, 1996), 115–156.
2. Reporters sans Frontières, *Le Drame algérien: un peuple en ôtage* (Paris: La Découverte, 1995), 11–45.
3. Smaïl Goumeziane, *Le mal algérien: économie politique d'une transition inachevée, 1962–1994* (Paris: Fayard, 1994), 33–138.

The government of the day had to do something to make ends meet. Removing part of the social safety net might save money, but risked a social explosion.

And that is precisely what happened in October 1988.[4] Throughout the country there were demonstrations demanding the removal of the government. Who organized them, and even what caused them, is still debated—but the regime was threatened, for the first time since independence, by massive protests. The army was called in, hundreds of civilians were killed, and Algerians were stunned that violence of this sort had erupted after nearly twenty-five years of relative security and domestic stability.

The regime responded, remarkably, by adopting a policy of rapid political and economic liberalization. Within months, freedom of the press and of association had been secured with a new constitution, and Algerian political life changed dramatically. Dozens of associations were formed; a whole range of publications appeared; and one new mass movement emerged to speak for the marginalized and dispossessed. The new movement was called the Islamic Salvation Front, or FIS (using its French acronym).[5] Islam had always been a part of the Algerian national identity, though until now there had not been a strong Islamist party. But political liberalization in these circumstances produced a dominant opposition whose liberal credentials were highly suspect.

In 1990 the FIS won municipal elections with an impressive 4 million plus votes (out of a total eligible electorate of nearly 13 million). The FIS immediately demanded presidential elections and was offered instead parliamentary ones in 1991. After a great deal of maneuvering within the regime and within the FIS, those elections were held in late 1991 and once again the FIS was headed toward victory—albeit with a million fewer votes than the previous year.[6] The military, however, stepped in and cancelled the second round of balloting, outlawed the party, arrested its leaders, and declared a state of emergency A transitional period of several years began during which Algeria was ruled essentially by the military.

Somewhat surprisingly, the regime that canceled the elections did not try to return to a totally authoritarian model. The period of democratic experimentation from 1988 to 1991 left some residues, especially in the form of a relatively free press and acceptance of the idea of a plurality of

4. M'hammed Boukhobza, *Octobre 1988: Évolution ou rupture?* (Algiers: Éditions Bouchene, 1991).

5. Severine Labat, *Les islamistes algériens: entre les umes et le maquis* (Paris: Seuil, 1995).

6. Lahouari Addi, *L'algérie et la démocratie: pouvoir et crise du politique dans l'algérie contemporaine* (Paris: La Découverte, 1994), 174–180.

political parties. In short, the old populist one-party model could not be revived; but at the same time, democracy seemed too risky, as if it might open the floodgates to Islamist opponents of the regime.[7]

Insofar as the regime had a coherent strategy, it seemed to consist of trying to restore "law and order," then revive the economy, then reestablish a measure of legitimacy through a controlled series of political reforms. Efforts were made—with what degree of sincerity is hard to say—to find an accommodation between the regime and the jailed leaders of the FIS. But by mid-1995 these efforts were abandoned, with the regime charging that the FIS would not condemn the use of violence, and the FIS claiming that the regime itself was relying on violence to stay in power. From this point on, the imprisoned FIS leadership was placed in solitary confinement and the FIS as an organized movement began to fall apart. It was replaced on one extreme by the much more militant Armed Islamic Group (GIA) and on the moderate wing by Hamas, an Islamist movement that was willing to renounce violence and work on building grass-roots support through welfare and educational work. Meanwhile, the death toll continued to rise.

By 1995, it was becoming clear that the Islamist opposition would not be able to overthrow the regime. Algeria was not destined to follow the path of Iran. At the same time, the radical Islamist opposition was not about to lay down its arms and surrender. Equally striking was the seeming indifference on the part of most Algerians to both the appeals of the regime and its Islamist critics. There were few demonstrations of support for one side or the other in this deadly quarrel.

In November 1995, presidential elections were held. Unusual in the Arab world, a number of candidates were allowed to run, but the victory of General Liamine Zeroual was a foregone conclusion. Still, a very large number of Algerians did actually turn out to vote—the official returns said 75 percent, of whom 61 percent voted for Zeroual. Even if the figures were inflated and the elections far from fully democratic, it seemed clear that many Algerians had cast their votes for Zeroual in the hope that he would use his new legitimacy to find a way out of the crisis.

Since the election, there has been a great deal of political activity in Algeria, but it has not had the effect of ending the crisis. Indeed, much of it has seemed formulaic—endless consultations, proposals, debates—but the regime all the while has proceeded with a plan to strengthen the insti-

---

7. The regime rejected "in detail" a set of proposals put forward by most of the opposition parties, including the FIS, negotiated under the auspices of the religious community of Sant'Egidio in January 1995. For the text, see Andrew Pierre and William B. Quandt, *The Algerian Crisis: Policy Options for the West* (Washington, D.C.: Carnegie Endowment for International Peace, 1996), 59–63.

tution of the presidency, at the same time making it difficult for any of the parties to mount an effective challenge.

The first step toward rebuilding a strong presidency after the election was to oust the reformist leadership of the old nationalist party, the FLN, and to try to reconstitute it as the president's party. After 1992, it had joined the ranks of the legal opposition parties and had called for legalizing the FIS. But in mid-1996, the Central Committee of the FLN met and returned an old-guard loyalist, forcing the reformers to the sidelines. Then the regime proposed a platform for national discussion, the centerpieces of which were a revision of the constitution and new parliamentary elections. Consultations, dialogue, and a national congress all took place, but essentially the regime's project was hardly affected. In November 1996, a referendum was held on new constitutional provisions. In essence, the new constitution would give the president more power and it would create a second chamber of parliament, one third of whose members would be appointed by the president. A new electoral law would prevent parties from basing themselves on religion, region, or language. The regime claimed that the vote was overwhelming in favor of the proposed changes, but many doubted the accuracy of the official figures, and election monitors had not been allowed to check the polls. Nearly all the parties had opposed the referendum and had urged abstention or a negative vote.

With the referendum behind it, and a constitution that ensured a strong presidency, the regime pressed ahead to carry out parliamentary elections in June 1997, to be followed by municipal elections in October 1997. Since the FLN remained divided and unpopular, the regime encouraged a new party, the Democratic National Rally (RND), to represent the regime's views. What genuine support it had was in the trade unions. Although many were skeptical that the parliamentary elections would be honest, most of the parties agreed to participate. Some thought the regime might well permit free elections, since it had already assured itself that real power would remain in its hands.

Meanwhile, the GIA seemed determined to show that the regime's claims that the armed opposition has been defeated were false. During much of 1997, the GIA carried out a series of atrocious attacks, the only point of which seemed to be to show that it could still strike terror in downtown Algiers and in surrounding villages, and even in the eastern part of the country. No political agenda accompanied the terror, and the other Islamist groups, including the remnants of the FIS, were quick to denounce such senseless killing. The regime, though hardly popular, seemed to hope that the excesses of the GIA would work to its advantage (which led some conspiracy-minded Algerians to believe that the regime was actually behind some of the GIA atrocities).

When parliamentary elections were held in June 1997, the results did not create a particularly clear picture. About two-thirds of the eligible voters actually showed up at the polls, more than in 1991 but fewer than in 1995. According to official statistics, the pro-government party, the RND, won about 40 percent of the seats, with about 34 percent of the vote. Two Islamist parties managed to win 27 percent of the seats, with 24 percent of the vote. The government was assured a comfortable, but not overwhelming majority, and a three-party coalition government was formed that included ministers from one Islamist party.

Many accused the government of manipulating the results of the elections, and no doubt there were some abuses. International observers under United Nations auspices were unwilling to declare the elections "free and fair," but in private they were willing to say that the margin for manipulation was unlikely to have been more than 5 to 10 percent. In any event, the point of the elections was to create an institution by which Algerians could resolve conflicts peacefully, and it would take time to see whether that might eventually be an outcome of the series of elections in recent years.

Local and provincial elections were then held in October 1997, but this time the accusations of fraud were much more widespread than in the previous June. Still, the regime proceeded to create pseudo-democratic institutions, but without winning much credit from an increasingly weary and frustrated populace. The violence, after all, was subsiding, so what was the point of all the so-called political reforms? Even a truce of sorts negotiated with the armed wing of the FIS failed to reduce the scale of the killings. The GIA, in fact, seemed to be resorting to increasingly brutal attacks on isolated rural villages. The regime either could not, or chose not to, do much to protect these vulnerable populations.

How might Algeria emerge from its current turmoil? Although the regime has little credibility and modest political skills at best, one cannot dismiss entirely the possibility that it will forge ahead with its preferred scenario and will retain its grip on power. In this version, elections will continue to be held (relatively freely, with substantial participation), thereby showing that the Algerian people are allowed a voice in governing themselves and have turned their backs on the extremists; the economy may pick up in the next several years; the GIA may be marginalized and other Islamists coopted. In this optimistic scenario, Algeria might begin to resemble Turkey (a semidemocratic regime with the military as the ultimate guardian of order and legitimacy); or one of the formerly dictatorial regimes of Latin America (Chile, Peru, Argentina) that eventually made a transition to democracy. What seems missing in the Algerian case is a cadre of committed leaders who see the need for change and have the credentials to convince the public that they are heading in that direction.

The alternative, more pessimistic vision for Algeria sees an isolated military dictatorship squandering the resources of the country, cut off from popular support, running a "predatory" state based on the collection of oil and gas rents. Civil society will weaken as the small middle class chooses to emigrate, and the large number of young, alienated youths will continue to provide recruits for the most extreme Islamists. A prolonged period of domestic turmoil might ensue: Some have imagined a wealthier version of Afghanistan or Somalia, with endless clan and tribal warfare. Central America may provide other depressing models of prolonged civil strife; Guatemala, El Salvador, and Nicaragua come to mind.

Between these two scenarios one can find a picture of an Algeria in which the main political forces of the country—the military, the trade union, the legal political parties, and the less extreme among the Islamists—reach a political understanding on a new political pact. The military would be acknowledged as the ultimate arbiter of the system (as in Turkey), but would withdraw from day-to-day management of the country; a centrist coalition of democrats, secularists, and moderate Islamists would be given the chance to govern; economic reforms would continue, permitting the emergence of new, independent social actors; and eventually the violence would end through fatigue and political accommodation. This is doubtless the most desirable of the three scenarios for the small group of committed democrats in Algeria, and the one that holds the brightest promise for the future. We will discuss later whether outsiders can do much to increase its chances of being realized.

Is Algeria Pivotal?

At first glance, Algeria is a somewhat surprising choice to include in a discussion of pivotal states.[8] Of the nine countries thus designated by Chase, Hill, and Kennedy, Algeria is the smallest in population and gross domestic product (GDP).[9] It ranks seventh in exports, fourth or fifth in per capita income, and third in size of territory.

8. Robert S. Chase, Emily B. Hill, and Paul Kennedy, "Pivotal States and U.S. Strategy," *Foreign Affairs* 75, no. 1 (January–February 1996): 33–51.

9. Based on data from the CIA *World Factbook 1995* and from *Human Development Report 1995,* published for the UNDP (New York: Oxford University Press, 1995). The UNDP used PPP dollars for purchasing power parity measurements, an attempt to provide a common standard for judging the value of income across countries. The CIA data places Algeria fifth among the nine "pivotal" states in terms of GNP per capita; the UNDP places it fourth.

In more precise terms, Algeria has a population of about 30 million; a GDP of around $36 billion; a gross national product (GNP) per capita of around $1,500 ($3,480 in purchasing power parity—PPP—dollars); annual exports of about $10 billion; and a land mass of more than 2,330,000 square kilometers. It borders Morocco, Mauritania, Mali, Niger, Libya, and Tunisia. An important source of energy for Europe, it produces about 1.2 million barrels per day of oil and lease condensates (of total world consumption of about 63.7 million b.p.d.) and has the potential for modest increases in coming years. Its gas reserves are enormous— the fifth largest in the world—and it has just opened a pipeline across the Strait of Gibraltar that can carry 9.5 billion cubic meters of gas per year to Spain. Eventually, that amount may be doubled. Algeria also has a small 15 megawatt heavy water nuclear reactor, ostensibly for research purposes.

If Algeria is indeed to be considered a pivotal state, it is not because of any one of these factors taken in isolation. Other countries in the developing world have larger populations (Bangladesh), export more oil (Libya, Nigeria, Venezuela, and Iran), and seem to be more reliable partners of the Western democracies (Chile, Argentina). But Algeria does occupy an important geostrategic space, and that, taken together with its resources, probably does place it in contention for being considered a pivotal state. Its proximity to Europe, as well as its position as a major Arab state, mean that what happens in Algeria will have repercussions beyond its borders.

We must be careful, however, not to exaggerate Algeria's influence. At one time, of course, Algeria symbolized a certain kind of revolutionary Third World nationalism. It led the call for a new and more equitable international economic order, promoting the interests of the south against the north. But those days are gone, and Algeria is no longer looked to as a positive model of development or leadership, either in Africa or the Arab world. Instead, Algeria is more often mentioned as an example of the dangers of precipitous democratization. (The Egyptian and Tunisian regimes are among those that make this point to justify their own harsh approach to Islamist movements.) Although Algeria may no longer serve as a model to others, events in Algeria could still have regional consequences, both negative and positive.

In North Africa and the Middle East, events in Algeria are followed closely. By and large, the regimes in power are hoping that the government will win out in its struggle with the Islamists. By contrast, Islamist groups are cheering on their ideological brethren. If the Islamists were to come to power, they would have some effect well beyond Algeria's borders. After all, the Islamist wave seems to be receding—some have spoken of the "failure of political Islam"[10]—and a victory in a significant Arab country such as Algeria would give Islamists everywhere a sense of renewed possibilities. Similarly, if the regime manages to marginalize the Islamist radicals and coopt the moderates, that will also be seen as a significant development. But no mechanistic domino effect is at work here. If Algeria, for example, were to succumb to the Islamists, that does not mean that Tunisia and Morocco would follow suit. Indeed, they might adopt even stricter policies toward their own opposition movements and begin to provide help to dissident Algerians as well. Somewhat surprisingly, Libya might also oppose an Islamist regime in Algeria.

The European perspective on developments in Algeria is important, since one reason for concern over the situation in Algeria is its potential to affect conditions in France in particular. Already several million Muslims live in France, most originally from North Africa. The French have become very sensitive to the prospect of additional waves of illegal immigrants crossing the Mediterranean to join family members already in Europe and to find jobs. With the openness of borders within Europe, it may become quite difficult to prevent substantial illegal immigration. If the Algerian conflict spills over into France, it can bring with it episodes of violence and terrorism.

In the worst of circumstances, a future Algeria might turn some of its oil wealth to the development of weapons that could conceivably threaten Europe. For the moment, there is not much concern with Algeria's military power—the country spends less than 3 percent of its GDP on the military—and few are really worried about Algeria developing nuclear capabilities anytime soon. But any move in that direction would obviously set off alarm bells in Europe and in the Middle East as well.

Though unlikely, a scenario of growing chaos and violence in Algeria could demonstrate the negative sense in which Algeria may be seen as pivotal. A large flow of refugees to neighboring countries could be destabilizing; a radical Algeria could find itself in a state of confrontation with Morocco and Tunisia; France might try to help non-Islamist Algerians constitute a resistance movement, leading to Algerian support for terrorism in France. Various militant Islamist movements might take up residence in Algiers, drawing Algeria into a web of regional conflicts, including the Arab-Israeli dispute. An embattled, threatened regime might begin to think seriously about the nuclear option, raising fears in Europe and sparking scenarios for preemptive military action. Investments in Algeria's oil and gas sectors could then plummet, creating short-

10. Olivier Roy, *The Failure of Political Islam* (Cambridge, Mass.: Harvard University Press, 1994).

ages in energy supplies, especially for southern Europe. In this worst-case scenario, a radical Algeria in turmoil could be very bad news indeed for the West and for other moderate states in the region. To prevent such an outcome is principally up to the Algerians themselves, but Europe, the United States, and others in the Middle East will have a strong interest in seeing that Algeria does not go down that path.

Algeria, then, seems to qualify as at least a marginally pivotal state for two main reasons: Events in Algeria can influence, for better or worse, a wide range of countries in the Middle East and Europe, both regions of importance to the United States; and Algeria is likely to be a major source of energy for Europe in the future, with all that implies for investment opportunities in Algeria for Western companies. On balance, the United States and Europe have every reason to hope that Algeria will follow a stable, positive course in the future and should be prepared to help it where possible. How that might be done will be addressed later in this paper.

THE IMPACT OF GLOBAL CHANGE

In many ways, Algeria is typical of Mediterranean countries. Even a casual visitor will notice the layers of civilization that have been left by succeeding waves of immigrants and colonizers. A Berber-speaking minority still lives in the mountains. Alongside is the Arabic-speaking majority (mostly of Berber origins), some with names that also show Ottoman influence. Roman remains dot the countryside, just as French architecture dominates the urban and small-town landscape. Europe and the Middle East have deeply influenced this land, and the pulls from both are still felt. Perhaps ironically, modern Algerian nationalism was first given voice by Algerian workers in the suburbs of Paris after World War I, articulating ideas of patriotism and Islamic reform that were being propounded in Cairo and Damascus.

Not surprisingly, Algerians, who were once told by their French teachers that their country did not exist, feel somewhat uncertain about the components of their national identity. Nearly all Algerians are Muslims of the Sunni Maliki rite, but the reality of Islam in Algeria is much more complex. One can find Sufi brotherhoods, moderate reformists, strident fundamentalists, and secularists all claiming to represent a legitimate face of Islam. The early years of independence saw a premium placed on the notion of a unified people all sharing an Arab, Islamic, Algerian identity. Arabization of the educational system was a major state policy from the late 1960s on, and early in 1997 a decree was issued banning the use of French by government officials. Despite such homogenizing efforts, the reality of Algeria has remained much more diverse, politically, culturally, and socially. The Islamists regularly attack the "Party of France," as they call the regime; clannish politicians from one region form coalitions against others; the military has a subculture of its own; Berber-speakers resent the attempts at forced Arabization; Algerian dialect, far from standard Arabic, includes a rich mixture of words from Arabic, Berber, and European languages; the press includes a dozen newspapers, some in French and some in Arabic—but the French papers regularly outsell those in Arabic.

The point of this sketch of Algerian culture is to show that it is much more diverse than propagandists have portrayed. Algeria absorbs political currents from the east, but also from the north. It is very much a part of the Middle East–North Africa cultural region but also has deep ties across the Mediterranean. And for all that, it is very inward looking. It is a Third World country with first-world aspirations. Many Algerians have been to France to work and watch French television at home by means of satellite dishes. The young dream of the comforts of Europe while sometimes supporting the most extreme of Islamist groups.[11]

With its history and its social makeup, Algeria does not seem destined to become an Islamic state on the model of Iran or Sudan. But even if Islamists were to come to power, some have argued, they would be obliged to nurture ties to the West because of the many economic networks that exist across the Mediterranean.[12] There is something to this argument, although it may be a bit sanguine. Still, the economic reality of Algeria does predispose it to maintain close ties with Europe. The top five trading partners of Algeria are France, Italy, Spain, Germany, and the United States, with not a single Arab or Muslim country on the list. Algeria basically exports its energy supplies—over 95 percent of total exports—and imports almost everything, including some $3 billion worth of food, from the West.

Although education in Arabic had made remarkable headway in the past generation, the elite still makes sure that its children learn French, and often English as well. Indeed, English is becoming a very popular language of study. Many Algerians still manage to go abroad—to France, Britain, or the United States—for some of their schooling. In fact, the leader of the FIS, Abbassi Madani, received a Ph.D. in education in Britain. And for those who cannot go abroad, the Internet is now available on university campuses. Messages pass back and forth between Algerians at home and abroad by phone, e-mail, and fax. Islamists and sec-

---

11. Meriem Vergès, "Genesis of a Mobilization: The Young Activists of Algeria's Islamic Salvation Front," in *Political Islam: Essays from* Middle East Report, ed. Joel Beinin and Joe Stork (Berkeley: University of California Press, 1997), 292–305.
12. Graham Fuller, *Algeria: The Next Fundamentalist State?* (Santa Monica: Rand, 1996).

ularists alike use these modern technologies. There is no way of cutting Algeria off from the rest of the world.

As much as proud Algerian nationalists might like to run a totally autarchic state, they have finally come to the realization that they cannot. Faced with mounting repayment obligations on some $30 billion in external debt in recent years, Algerian leaders have reluctantly concluded that they must deal with the IMF and the World Bank. As a result, in recent years Algeria has adopted a liberalization program that has won praise from the head of the IMF. The exchange rate for the dinar has been unified and allowed to float; the budget deficit has been reduced, and with it inflation; subsidies have been removed from most food items; and a few small steps have been taken to privatize state-owned companies. The regime, of course, continues to receive the rents from oil and gas sales, so the public sector is bound to remain quite large. But the move toward a liberal economy was very much the result of Algeria's heavy dependency on its creditors. This is just one graphic example of the extent to which Algeria can be influenced by global trends.

As Algeria has liberalized its economy and opened the door to foreign investment, a number of large companies have made substantial investments, including British Petroleum, Anadarko, Bechtel, Brown and Root, and Total. One might think that the appalling security situation in and around Algiers would deter businesses, and to some extent this has been true. But where profits can be made, businesses are quick to adapt. It is now possible to fly directly to the oil fields from Europe on regularly scheduled flights, bypassing Algiers. The oil-producing areas are protected by fairly effective security measures. Throughout all of Algeria's internecine fighting, there have been frequent predictions that oil installations would be targeted, but to date no serious threat to the energy sector has occurred.

However, Algeria's connections to the West cut more than one way. Many Algerians have learned to live with the complexities of a dual culture, but others have not. They see the materialism of the West but realize that they cannot hope to enjoy such a standard of living. Their appetites have been whetted but cannot be satisfied. They see the wealth of their own elite—often earned through dubious links to western businesses—and they conclude that power and corruption are the means to prosperity in contemporary Algeria. These Algerians live on the margins, often in appalling housing conditions, and see in the Islamist opposition a means of ousting the corrupt establishment, removing the privileges of the French-educated elite, and opening the way for a more equitable distribution of wealth. Ironically, much of Algeria's apparent "modernization" has fueled the turn to Islam by youths who cannot hope for much from the system that has ill prepared them for productive employment.

The pool of alienated, unemployed young men who have made up the bulk of the Islamists' most militant constituency will remain large for years to come. It will pose a challenge to any government, secular or Islamic. The simple demographic facts are these: Population growth rates are beginning to decline and sometime between 2000 and 2005 will probably be under 2 percent annually. Demand for jobs by new entrants into the labor force will peak around 2005, but for the next fifteen years thereafter, until around 2020, more Algerians will be seeking to enter the labor force than will be leaving it through retirement. This unavoidable reality means that any regime will have to be particularly attentive to finding a job-intensive growth trajectory. Unfortunately, oil and gas do not provide vast numbers of jobs. Already Algeria has one of the highest percentages of the population working in the public sector and should be trying to reduce those numbers for the sake of greater economic efficiency. But if this means more unemployment, there is little incentive to go ahead with privatization. So the bad news is that demography has saddled Algeria with a generation-long problem of finding productive outlets for its young people in the national economy. The good news is that the trend toward lower population growth has begun, and the country can anticipate a time a generation from now when the demographic transition will have essentially been completed and a more stable society, and most likely polity, can be envisaged.[13]

Islamism, the language in which opposition to the regime is most likely to be expressed for the foreseeable future, is not just an Algerian phenomenon. It is very much a global trend wherever substantial Muslim communities are found. Anyone who reads the writings of Algerian Islamists will appreciate the extent to which they quote from radical thinkers such as the Egyptian Sayyid Qutb and the Pakistani Abd al-Ala al-Mawdudi. FIS representatives operate all over Europe, in the United States, in Turkey, and elsewhere in the Middle East. Although the extent of foreign financing has been exaggerated by some, there seems little doubt that the FIS and other Islamic movements get some help from other Islamist movements.

Often in Algeria today one hears of the influence of the "Afghans," Algerians who went to Peshawar and on into Afghanistan during the struggle against the Soviets. They came home crowned with the prestige of victorious fighters in a holy war, wearing distinctive garb, and trained

---

13. Much of this analysis is derived from Philippe Fargues, "Demographic Explosion or Social Upheaval?" in *Democracy Without Democrats? The Renewal of Politics in the Muslim World*, ed. Ghassan Salamè (New York: I. B. Tauris, 1994), 156–179.

in the use of arms and explosives, sometimes, it is believed, by western intelligence sources. How much these "Afghans" really played a part in the emergence of a radical brand of Islamism in Algeria is not clear, but there is no reason to doubt that there was some influence. And this, too, is a sign of how global developments can work their way back to Algeria.

Algerians who are proud of their own distinctive revolutionary past have tended to think that they are unique in other dimensions of their national experience as well. National pride has seemed to preclude much interest in the political and economic experiments of other countries. For example, Algerians have looked down on Egypt and other Arab models; they have had little good to say about Tunisia or Morocco; and the Asian "tigers" have been dismissed with a blunt "We are not Chinese." But now many more models suggest comparison, and Algerians are beginning to look to Latin America and Eastern Europe for examples of how to balance political and economic change. This too is a sign of globalization, although there is still no consensus on what lessons might be learned. But the idea of borrowing from the experiences of others is less and less a taboo.

Algeria, like most other countries, is subject to a wide variety of influences from beyond its borders—economic, cultural, social. Algerians do not want to turn their backs on the West, but they do not want to lose their own identity in the process. The forces for change that come from the global economy and from the information revolution are fully felt in Algeria, but it is still not clear exactly how Algerian society and the political system will respond. The one option that seems excluded is a sharp break with the outside world, a complete turning inward, the reinvention of a more "authentic" Islamic community rooted in the past. True, Algerians are Muslim, and that component of their identity is likely to remain strong, but Algeria seems an unlikely candidate for the next fundamentalist state in the region.

U.S. INTERESTS IN ALGERIA

It would be hard to make the case that Algeria is a pivotal state for the United States simply in terms of direct American interests in the country. Of course the United States has some tangible economic interests, but of a modest sort. But there is no formal alliance, as with Turkey; there is no strong interest, as with Egypt; and there is not much of an American presence or a developed political relationship with Algerians in any walk of life. American diplomats have relatively little contact with the reclusive political establishment in the country; only a modest number of Algerian students study in the United States; very few Americans, whether tourists, diplomats, or business people, ever set foot in the country; and there is no sizable Algerian-American community in the United States. By all these measures, the relationship is minimal.

However, America has substantial derivative interests related to Algeria's links to Europe and to the broader Middle East and North Africa region. After all, if Europe is still important to the United States, and if Algeria is important to Europe (which it is), then simple logic suggests that Washington should not be indifferent to developments in Algeria. But such a connection says little about how the United States should conduct its relationship with Algiers.

Because of Europe's overriding interest in North Africa, the United States could be tempted to defer to European, especially French, leadership in the conduct of relations with Algiers. But that stance assumes that Europe has a coherent policy on how to deal with Algeria, and that it makes some sense. If not, then the United States, even if its interests in Algeria are partly derived from those of Europe, has every reason to take an independent look at its relations with Algeria.

What are the American interests in the Middle East and North Africa that might be affected by developments in Algeria? At the top of any list of U.S. interests in the region is the Arab-Israeli peace process. Algeria has largely been a bystander, but it can throw its weight in inter-Arab circles either with those who support peace or against them. A genuinely radical regime, similar to that of present-day Iran, could actively support groups that oppose the peace process. An Islamist victory in Algiers would certainly strengthen Islamists everywhere. It is not surprising, therefore, that many Israelis (and their supporters in the United States) are urging Washington to pay more attention to what is happening in Algiers.

Making Arab-Israeli peace the central focus of the U.S. dialogue with Algiers is likely to be counterproductive, however, as will be argued in the next section. Still, we have no interest in seeing Algiers join the antipeace camp. As is often the case, the interest here may be a "negative" one—warding off an unpleasant development—but that, after all, is a good part of what diplomacy is all about.

What happens in Algiers can also have an immediate impact on Morocco and Tunisia. The United States has significant interests in both countries, including military access agreements with Morocco and some joint training and exercises with Tunisia. Although these are not vital interests, they are taken seriously by the U.S. military and serve a useful purpose. If Algeria were to become stridently antiwestern, it might pressure both neighbors to end such military cooperation.

Less tangible but very important is the symbolic role that Algeria could still play depending on whether it moves along a promising course of development and democratization, or turns toward a strict Islamist agenda, or simply continues to wallow in its internal crisis. It is not too much to argue that Algeria's path will be influential, for better or worse, elsewhere in the region. This is an important sense in which Algeria may indeed be pivotal. Already its troubles with rapid democratization and managing a militant Islamist movement have given rise to a whole range of supposed lessons that other regimes in the region are paying heed to. So, on balance, Algeria stands out as a country in which the United States has modest direct interests, but significant indirect ones. What, then, should Washington do to protect its interests there?

CURRENT AMERICAN POLICY AND
OPTIONS FOR THE FUTURE

When the military canceled the second round of parliamentary elections in January 1992, the United States adopted a somewhat ambivalent position. Initially the State Department spokesman seemed to endorse the decision, then, the following day, restated the American view in less categorical terms. This uncertainty has characterized policy ever since. On the one hand, it has been hard to work up much enthusiasm for the various ruling bodies that have governed Algeria in recent years. At the same time, the Islamist opposition seems to have become increasingly radical and prone to violent actions. The middle-of-the-road political groups have had a hard time organizing and building popular support.

One must be careful not to overinterpret American policy. At no time in recent years has Algeria been the subject of a full-scale policy review. A relatively small number of people in the State Department and the National Security Council set the tone for policy. Few members of Congress are interested or informed. Algerian diplomats in Washington have adopted a low profile. Still, one can identify two distinctive trends in American thinking about Algeria.

The first school of thought argues that the Algerian regime is bound to fail in its effort to crush the Islamist opposition. It sees the Algerian public as largely behind the Islamists and believes that Algeria, somewhat like Iran, will eventually be ruled by a government that is more or less Islamist. Remembering the price paid by American diplomacy for excessive identification with the Shah, those who follow this line of thinking argue that the United States should remain aloof from the current regime, should maintain discreet contracts with the Islamist opposition, and should wait for the dust to settle. They point to the fact that thus far no Americans have been killed in Algeria as evidence that a posture of maintaining some distance from the regime has helped protect American interests. This line of thinking had some support in the bureaucracy in 1993–1994, and a low-level dialogue was maintained during those years with FIS leaders in exile.

The alternative school of thought in Washington has argued that an Islamic revolution in Algeria is not inevitable; that an Islamist regime, whatever our stance toward it, would probably be hostile to many of our broader interests in the region, such as the Arab-Israeli peace process; that Islamist moderates are likely to be swept aside by radicals if there is an Islamic victory; and that an authoritarian nationalist regime can be more readily urged to reform itself both economically and politically than a religious fundamentalist regime. This line of thinking, which has prevailed in the last few years, urges a cautious engagement with the regime, relying primarily on positive inducements rather than pressures to bring about economic and political change.

Proponents of both the first and second school of thought were able to agree that the United States should support the Sant'Egidio platform, which was done. Where they have disagreed is on the wisdom of the dialogue with the FIS and the merits of higher level engagement with the regime.

A stronger version of the second view has maintained that the current regime deserves more open support; that Zeroual was elected in November 1995 in a legitimate election; and that American interests would be best served by stronger backing for the regime. This version sees Islamists of all stripes as unacceptable partners and argues that the United States should support Zeroual precisely because his regime is waging a fierce battle against the Islamists. Much will hinge, this school of thought maintains, on whether the Algerian regime wins or loses this battle.[14]

After Zeroual's election, President Clinton sent a letter of congratulations to him that held out the prospect of a more active American role in Algeria as the country moved forward with its reforms and returned to stability. This message was carried directly to Zeroual—and to the Algerian public—when Assistant Secretary of State Robert Pelletreau visited Algiers in March 1996. There he laid out the logic of "positive conditionality," an offer to match steps of reform and democratization with concrete assistance of an unspecified nature. He specifically urged a political settlement to the Algerian crisis and spoke of the importance of including all groups, including Islamists, that renounce the use of violence

14. Of thirty-two participants in the study group on Algeria that served as a basis for Pierre and Quandt, *The Algerian Crisis*, one favored the first view, twenty-nine supported the recommended second view, and two supported the third.

to attain and hold on to power. No high-level meeting between an American official and Zeroual has taken place since spring 1996. In fact, Americans have very little contact with the highest levels of the Algerian government.

It is probably fair to say that as of early 1998 Washington's hopes that Zeroual would turn out to be an effective president and a capable reformer have been disappointed in the past year. The constitutional referendum, with the strong suspicion of a manipulated vote, the problematic parliamentary elections, the questionable local elections, and especially the inability of the Zeroual regime to bring an end to the violence, have led to a loss of optimism about the near-term future of Algeria. And there is a pervasive belief in Washington that the United States can do little to influence the course of events in Algeria. This lack of belief that the United States can do much about the situation in Algiers has been a major reason for the absence of serious debate over policy. But is it really true that the United States has such limited influence?

Algerians are notoriously touchy about foreign interference in their affairs, especially coming from France. Spokesmen for the regime regularly hint that any effort to pressure Algeria will be counterproductive. But Algerians know they do not live in a vacuum, and the regime has responded to pressures for economic reform without undue complaining. Algeria's internal politics is, no doubt, a sensitive area for outsiders to address. Yet without political reform, it is hard to see how Algeria can find its way toward peace and stability.

American views are certainly listened to in Algiers. Even the softest comment from Washington receives top billing in the Algerian media. That does not mean, of course, that Algerians will acquiesce to whatever the United States asks of them. But it does ensure that American views will be heard and treated seriously. So the first item of business for Americans is to decide if they want to engage in a dialogue with the Algerian regime (and with various segments of Algerian society as well), and if so, to what end. A second decision to make is whether to act alone or in coordination with Europeans. Finally, Americans must decide what resources to bring to the discussion.

If Algeria is as important as we have maintained, it certainly makes sense to try to raise the level of political dialogue. Some in Washington in early 1998 were beginning to ask how this might be done. This would mean trying to develop ongoing contacts at the highest level and with the major actors in Algerian society. The thrust of the message should be clear: The United States wants to see an end to the violence in Algeria and believes that some form of political accommodation among the significant political groupings of the country will be the key to civil peace. In brief, we will support a program of economic and political reform but will find it difficult to back a purely military solution to the problem of internal violence. The more Algeria moves toward democratization, the more it can count on American support.[15]

To be effective, this theme needs to be conveyed privately and often to Zeroual and his closest associates. They need to be reassured that the United States is not working to bring the Islamists to power, as some suspect. But they also need to hear encouragement for a political settlement. At a minimum, this might help strengthen the hand of moderates within the regime.

Given our regional interests and Algeria's role in the Arab world, it makes sense to discuss the Arab-Israeli conflict with Algerian authorities. But it is not wise to pressure the Algerians to move rapidly toward peace with Israel, as we have at times in the past. They have made it clear that once an agreement has been reached between Israel and the Palestinians and Israel and Syria, they will be prepared to normalize their own relations with the Jewish state—but not before. It will do little good to push on this issue, and if the regime is seen as too compliant to American pressure, it will be vulnerable to strong criticism from its Islamist opponents. In the past, Washington has seen too much of the U.S.–Algerian relationship through the lens of the Arab-Israeli conflict.

Second, the United States should try to coordinate its moves with Europe. Washington has very little direct leverage, but it does have a voice that will be heard. Europe, especially France, has the big guns of financial aid. Europe offers over $1 billion in credit to Algeria each year. And Europeans hold most of the Algerian debt (along with Japanese and American banks). So if the United States wishes to amplify its message, it should do so in coordination with Europe. But if that proves impossible, the United States still has a role to play alone.

Finally, we need to think of the instruments of policy that will be most useful. For example, it does not seem realistic to consider a substantial aid program. Algeria does not need money per se to solve its problems. It does need to attract technology and investment, and here the United States can be helpful. The United States can help to guarantee American investors against losses (OPIC guarantees); it can guarantee, at very little cost, credit to the Algerian government to cover some of its imports; it can support debt rescheduling in the Paris Club when those negotiations

15. Chase, Hill, and Kennedy, "Pivotal States," 35, argue that the interests of the United States "lie in the status quo." But when the status quo is untenable, as seems likely in Algeria, U.S. interests would seem to call for change that might help to ensure stability over the long term.

come up in 1999; the Export-Import Bank can become more actively involved; and it can use its influence in the World Bank and IMF to be helpful to Algeria as it proceeds with its economic reforms.[16]

Some would argue that a policy of supporting economic development will simply make it easier for the regime to ignore the need for political reforms. Such a risk does exist. But the United States and its partners can make a positive link between various forms of assistance to Algeria and reform measures in both the economic and political spheres. For example, it might be possible to convey to Algerian authorities that free and fair presidential elections in 2000 will be seen as an important indicator of whether Algeria is serious about democratization. Americans and Europeans should be prepared to participate on a substantial scale in future international monitoring of elections if legal opposition parties are allowed to participate. If the elections turn out to be reasonably fair, we should proceed with a number of positive programs; if they are not, we should hold back for a while.

Meanwhile we should consider small steps that might increase the capabilities of those who look like the best bet for Algeria's future. We should try to find ways to encourage Algerian students to learn English and study in the United States and ways generally to enhance cultural and academic exchanges. In addition, we should try to encourage ties with journalists, union organizers, small business owners, and political party leaders. All of this can be done at little cost and often with the involvement of nongovernmental organizations.

None of these steps alone will have much impact on developments in Algeria. At most, they can be effective at the margin. But at a time when so much is in flux in Algeria, and so much is at stake, even marginal moves in the direction of a political solution and a return to civil order are worth the effort. And if Europeans can be persuaded to work for the same outcome, then there is a real chance of having some influence. The alternatives of doing nothing, or blindly supporting an unpopular regime, are likely to be costly to American interests.

---

16. Although the International Monetary Fund attaches explicit economic conditions to its aid, it is forbidden by statute to attach political conditions.

MEXICO

Peter H. Smith

The end of the Cold War has everyone guessing. The collapse of
European communism and the implosion of the Soviet Union brought a
sudden end to the postwar international system, but have not (yet)
bequeathed a new world order. Among global actors, a disjuncture in the
distribution of economic and military power has created confusion and
uncertainty. Also unclear is the role and importance of the developing
world—perceived during the Cold War as a geopolitical battleground in
the contest between East and West, now regarded in many quarters as
irrelevant and insignificant. Now that the communist threat has disappeared, it is often said, Washington can safely ignore the Third World.

Chase, Hill, and Kennedy have sharply challenged this interpretation.
Conceding that U.S. priorities will necessarily focus on such major world
players as Europe, Russia, and Japan, they argue forcefully that "America's
national interest also requires stability in important parts of the developing world." Yet the United States should exercise discrimination: Instead
of giving equal weight to every nation-state or reacting in ad hoc fashion
to crises wherever they occur, Washington should concentrate its efforts
on "pivotal states" whose destiny will be crucial to world politics. As these
countries go, so go surrounding regions—and, by extension, the international system as a whole. Stability within these countries will therefore
assure regional and global stability and thus advance the interests of the
United States, which has "the most to lose from global instability. . . .
[T]he interests of the United States lie in the status quo."[1]

Pivotal states share two key characteristics. First, they can affect the
course of regional and international events. Second, they are "hot spots,"
countries that face serious threats of instability. The principal challenge,
however, is not from without but from within: "the danger is that they will

1. Robert S. Chase, Emily B. Hill, and Paul Kennedy, "Pivotal States and U.S. Strategy,"
Foreign Affairs 75, no. 1 (January–February 1996): 33–51, with quotes from 33–35.

fall prey to internal disorder," and this could prove to be "a greater and more insidious threat to American interests than communism ever was."[2] As of the mid-1990s, the Yale team identified nine pivotal states: Mexico, Brazil, Algeria, Egypt, South Africa, Turkey, India, Pakistan, and Indonesia.

How well does this analysis fit Mexico? What guidelines might it yield for U.S. policy? To approach these questions, I begin by discussing the applicability of the "pivotal states" concept to Mexico.[3] I analyze recent political, economic, and social trends in Mexico and their implications for the future. I then examine critical issues on the U.S.–Mexican bilateral agenda—drugs, migration, and environmental protection. I conclude with suggestions and guidelines for U.S. policy.

MEXICO: PIVOTAL OR CRITICAL?

By any conceivable criterion, Mexico is certainly a crucial state. It has a large territorial expanse, with a population of more than 90 million. It possesses key natural resources, including petroleum. It has strong economic prospects, having been heralded by Wall Street and the international community as one of the world's most promising "emerging markets." It also shares a 3,200-kilometer border with the United States. Unlike Brazil, in fact, Mexico stands on the northern fringe of Latin America, not in its heartland, which makes the country especially significant to the United States.

Mexico has played key roles in Latin America. In August 1982 the threat of default by Mexico provoked the decade-long "debt crisis" that eventually afflicted almost the entire region. Perhaps ironically, too, it was Mexico's implementation of orthodox "structural adjustment" measures that stamped the nation as an exemplary model for economic reform. Also during the 1980s, Mexico took the lead in forming the Contadora Group, which sought to broker a peaceful settlement to political and military conflicts in Central America. In these and other ways Mexico has exerted major influence on Latin America, especially on nearby countries in Central America and the Caribbean, and would thus appear to satisfy criteria for classification as a "pivotal state."

At the same time, Mexico's strategic position—and its "pivotal" role— have been severely restricted by the hegemonic power of the United States. The simple fact is this: Those places where Mexico might exert the

---

2. Chase, Hill, and Kennedy, "Pivotal States," 34.
3. An earlier version of this essay included a commentary and critique about the overall notion of "pivotal states." Most of my concerns are addressed in the conclusion to this volume.

most impact are also well within the U.S. sphere of influence, so Mexico's performance as a "pivotal" state is continually subordinate to the overwhelming presence of the United States. Indeed, Mexico has sometimes attempted to employ its pivotal status in order to challenge U.S. preeminence, as in the case of Contadora, but these efforts have not altered the basic power equation. It is the United States, not Mexico, that predominates throughout the region.[4]

Such complexities underlie the North American Free Trade Area (NAFTA), the free trade zone linking Mexico, Canada, and the United States. Unveiled in August 1992, the original NAFTA pact was signed that October by leaders of the three countries in the midst of the U.S. presidential campaign. Its stated goal was to promote the free flow of goods between member countries by eliminating duties, tariffs, and nontariff barriers to trade over a period of fifteen years, with implementation to begin in January 1994. NAFTA thus created one of the largest trading blocs in the world: With a population of 370 million and combined economic production of approximately $6 trillion as of 1992, North America would be a worthy rival to competitors in Europe and the Asia-Pacific region.[5] From the outset, it was predicted that the integration of technology, capital, and natural and human resources would enhance the competitiveness of the entire region, especially of the United States. For Mexico, NAFTA would attract direct investment from all parts of the world, stimulate development, and assure social peace; it would extend the process of economic liberalization, strengthen the cause of political reform, and draw the country into the highly prized ranks of the first world. As officials and pundits repeatedly proclaimed, NAFTA would create a "win-win-win" situation.[6]

For the United States, NAFTA has had a clear political consequence: Washington cannot permit "collapse" in Mexico. The U.S. government, and especially the Clinton administration, invested too much capital in debates over NAFTA ratification to permit disintegration of its neighbor. Chaos in Mexico would vindicate opposition to NAFTA, emphasize the fallibility of the Clinton team, and throw confusion into U.S. relations with trading partners around the world. Collapse in Mexico has thus become unthinkable in Washington.

4. See Peter H. Smith, *Talons of the Eagle: Dynamics of U.S.–Latin American Relations* (New York: Oxford University Press, 1996).
5. Comparison of the economic size of these two blocs was highly contingent on exchange rates for the U.S. dollar; according to some calculations (at some moments) NAFTA was larger than the European Union, according to others it was smaller.
6. See M. Delal Baer and Sidney Weintraub, eds., *The NAFTA Debate: Grappling with Unconventional Trade Issues* (Boulder: Lynne Rienner, 1994).

Mexico is therefore of great importance to the United States—but more because of *bilateral* connections than because of its regional position as a pivotal state. (Indeed, long-cherished notions of exceptionalism suggest that Mexico has been untypical of Latin America in many ways.) What makes Mexico so crucial to U.S. interests is the fact of geographical proximity. Because of the border, and because of multiple linkages between the two nations, whatever happens in Mexico has a direct impact on the United States. Mexico may or may not qualify as a "pivotal state" in the strict sense of the term, in other words, but it is undoubtedly a critical state.[7]

HEADING FOR CHAOS? CURRENT TRENDS IN MEXICO

The Mexican political system finds itself in the midst of long-term evolution. From the late 1920s to the 1980s, an authoritarian regime marked by a close alliance between technocrats, politicians, and leaders of key groups—especially labor and the peasantry—successfully imposed social and political stability. These coalitions were frequently sealed in explicit compacts, or *pactos*, that achieved and implemented consensus on economic policy. Key decisions were made at the top, behind closed doors, as an official party (the Partido Revolucionario Institucional, or PRI) routinely and regularly triumphed in not-very-contested elections. Opposition voices were muted, the media conspired openly with the ruling establishment, instances of rebellion and protest were sparse. From the 1940s onward, even the armed forces accepted a civilian monopoly on the presidential office. Turbulent Mexico, land of the first major social revolution in the twentieth century, thus succumbed to forces of political domination. With traces of envy and admiration, the Peruvian novelist-politician Mario Vargas Llosa once christened Mexico's system as "the perfect dictatorship."

Starting as far back as the 1970s, however, the dominant-party system began a gradual evolution. First the historic coalition started to weaken: The peasantry no longer represented a significant resource; organized labor lost authority; and although small and medium business remained a fragile sector, large-scale business was accumulating power and independence from the government. Second, the party system shifted: Though still strong, the PRI came to stand at the center of a three-party system, with the Partido Revolucionario Democrático (PRD) on the left and the Partido de Acción Nacional (PAN) on the right, both of which were

---

7. The distinction is not merely semantic: Whereas "pivotal" status might come and go for individual nation-states, "critical" status is permanent.

attracting considerable support from the urban middle class. At the same time, traditional fiefdoms reemerged: Old-time politicians (*dinosaurios*) found refuge in state governorships, for instance, and in niches within the party apparatus of the PRI.

What might be called a "familial" crisis has also appeared—that is, profound schisms within Mexico's political elite, once regarded as the "revolutionary family." For decades, the coherence (and internal discipline) of this ruling elite formed a central foundation for political stability.[8] Although the 1940s through the 1980s saw stresses and strains, and occasional cracks in the edifice of power (including the split-off of the *corriente democrática* against the PRI in 1986), nothing would compare to the fissures of the 1990s.

Pressures also welled up from below. On January 1, 1994—the day that NAFTA went into effect—a guerrilla movement in the poverty-stricken state of Chiapas rose up to denounce the NAFTA accord, the neoliberal economic model, and the undemocratic character of the political regime. With colorful and able leadership, the Zapatista National Liberation Army (EZLN) captured national and international attention during the course of highly publicized negotiations with governmental authorities.

A deadly spiral of violence then followed. On March 23, 1994 an assassin's bullet struck down Luis Donaldo Colosio, Carlos Salinas de Gortari's hand-picked successor and the presidential candidate of the PRI. Salinas hastily chose another candidate, the forty-two-year-old Ernesto Zedillo Ponce de León, who scurried to develop a credible campaign for the upcoming August election. On September 28, another shooting took the life of José Francisco Ruiz Massieu, the number-two leader of the PRI and one of Zedillo's most trusted political allies.

These shocking developments inflicted a devastating blow to Mexico's international image. Mexico could no longer be seen as an up and coming country on the brink of joining the first world; it looked, instead, like a Third World society threatening to come apart at the seams. A temporary respite came from the August 1994 presidential elections, by all accounts the cleanest in Mexican history, in which Zedillo triumphed with 48.8 percent of the vote (compared with 26.0 percent for the right-

8. See Peter H. Smith, *Labyrinths of Power: Political Recruitment in Twentieth-Century Mexico* (Princeton, N.J.: Princeton University Press, 1979); Miguel Angel Centeno, *Democracy within Reason: Technocratic Revolution in Mexico* (University Park: Pennsylvania State University Press, 1994); and Roderic Ai Camp, *Political Recruitment Across Two Centuries: Mexico, 1884–1991* (Austin: University of Texas Press, 1995).

ist PAN and only 16.6 percent for the populist PRD).[9] His capacity to govern nonetheless remained open to doubt.[10]

In effect, Mexico has been witnessing political disintegration at two distinct levels—among its uppermost institutions and within the political class. There is less power at the center of the system, even in the presidency, than there used to be. To be sure, Carlos Salinas de Gortari was able to impose his will in an exceptional way, partly through personal guile and partly as a result of his lifelong immersion in the system, but Zedillo has neither the resources nor the opportunity to demonstrate such authority. Forever resistant to facile nomenclature, Mexico's political regime might now be thought of as "neo-authoritarian."[11]

Economic Crisis

It didn't take long for trouble to arrive. Laden with pageantry, the inauguration of Ernesto Zedillo Ponce de León as president of Mexico on December 1, 1994 attracted throngs of dignitaries from home and abroad. The outgoing president, Carlos Salinas, received a thunderous ovation in honor of his remarkable *sexenio* (six-year term). A sympathetic audience listened to the earnest but untested new president offer pledges of honesty, reform, expanded political opening, and, the following day, "stability, stability, stability." The chorus of praise then moved to Miami, where U.S. President Bill Clinton hosted on December 9–11 a resplendent gathering of hemispheric heads of state (except Fidel Castro) known as the "Summit of the Americas." Characteristically effusive about prospects for democracy and prosperity throughout Latin America, Clinton repeatedly extolled NAFTA as an exemplary case of economic integration and praised Mexico for its performance as a strong and dependable partner.

Suddenly the wheels came off. On December 19, as foreign reserves were rapidly dwindling, the Zedillo administration unexpectedly widened the band for trading pesos with dollars from 3.47 to 4.00—in effect, permitting a 15 percent devaluation of the peso and violating Zedillo's heartfelt pledge about stability. This prompted a speculative run against the

---

9. Discounting invalid (*nulos*) ballots, Zedillo received 50.2 percent of the vote—just enough to claim a majority.
10. For thoughtful analysis see Denise Dresser, "Five Scenarios for Mexico," *Journal of Democracy* 5, no. 3 (July 1994): 57–71.
11. See Denise Dresser, "Twilight of the Perfect Dictatorship: The Decline of Dominant-Party Rule in Mexico" (paper presented at Latin American Studies Association, Washington, D.C., September 1995); Gabriel Zaid, *Adiós al PRI* (México, D.F.: Oceano, 1995); and Juan Pablo González Sandoval and Jaime González Graf, eds., *Los límites rotos: anuario político* (México, D.F.: Oceano, 1995).

peso; within two days the government was obliged to abandon its position, letting the peso float freely against the dollar. Unable to persuade foreign investors of Mexico's trustworthiness, the newly installed secretary of the treasury—Jaime Serra Puche, the secretary of commerce under Salinas who had played a key role in the NAFTA negotiations—submitted his resignation after merely three weeks on the job. One of the most judicious and knowledgeable U.S. experts on Mexico, Sidney Weintraub, arrived at a gloomy conclusion: "Ernesto Zedillo is off to a horrible start as president of Mexico."[12]

By late January the Clinton administration managed to put together a multilateral package of nearly $50 billion, including $20 billion from the U.S. government, but the peso continued to slide. To combat inflationary pressures (and meet the demands of international creditors) the government adopted rigorous adjustment programs. Stringent measures eventually stabilized financial and foreign-exchange markets, but at a staggering cost: output contracted, unemployment increased, and real wages fell. The combination of recession and high interest rates threatened the financial health of numerous companies and jeopardized the solvency of the entire banking system. Overall, the Mexican GDP declined by nearly 7 percent in 1995—and crime rates rose to record levels.

Accused of grotesque irresponsibility, Carlos Salinas lost all prestige in Mexico and went into self-imposed exile. In February 1995 governmental authorities arrested his brother Raúl Salinas de Gortari in connection with the Ruiz Massieu assassination (plus illicit enrichment). Such humiliating treatment of an ex-president's family was utterly without precedent, at least in recent times, and it revealed sharp cleavages within the ruling class.

The crisis had international repercussions as well. As a result of the "tequila effect," Brazil and other emerging markets suffered large losses of reserves; in Argentina, capital flight caused the central bank's reserves to fall from $16 billion to $11 billion by May 1995. The Mexican debacle had little effect on such countries as Chile or Peru, however, and Brazil and Argentina both managed to adjust before the end of the year. As Albert Fishlow has written, "the net consequences of the subsequent substantial decline of the peso and associated retraction of demand have remained primarily a Mexican problem. The so-called tequila effect in the end had little impact. That is one of the remarkable features of this crisis: unlike its historical predecessors it did not simply expand."[13]

12. Sidney Weintraub, "Mexico: Honeymoon From Hell," *Hemisfile* 6, no. 1 (January–February 1995), 1.
13. Albert Fishlow, "Foreword," in *The Mexican Peso Crisis: International Perspectives*, ed. Riordan Roett (Boulder: Lynne Rienner, 1996), ix.

In the meantime, Zedillo struggled to consolidate his hold on power. His government foundered on numerous fronts. The adjustment measures of 1995 inflicted enormous pain on large sectors of the population, making little or no headway against poverty and income maldistribution. Government investigators failed to solve either the Colosio murder or the Ruiz Massieu assassination. Prolonged negotiations with the Chiapas guerrillas resulted in stalemate, while a new uprising broke out in the state of Guerrero. As Zedillo completed his first year in office, Miguel Pérez offered a retrospective assessment in the respected newspaper *Reforma*:

> With an unprecedented economic crisis, with inflation about to surpass official estimates, with a high rate of unemployment, without any progress [*claridad*] on investigations of the assassinations of Luis Donaldo Colosio and José Francisco Ruiz Massieu, and with the sewer of official corruption wide open, President Ernesto Zedillo today completes one year at the head of the government of Mexico.
>
> In merely 365 days, the country's GDP fell by more than 7 percent; inflation rose from 7 to 49 percent; and the rate of [open] unemployment climbed to more than 6 percent, which means that there are 2.5 million people without work.[14]

It was a devastating summation of a devastating year.

Ultimately, the harshness of such judgments on Zedillo implies that Mexicans are becoming disenchanted with the nation's entire political elite, including its technocratic cadres. Vilification of Salinas is understandable enough. Denunciations of the well-intentioned Zedillo are more significant because they seem to suggest that, in the eyes of many Mexicans, little hope remains for honest and effective leadership. There are no good guys anymore.

Future Prospects

Mexico's political system is thus traversing a period of upheaval and instability. But this does not necessarily mean that it is on the brink of "chaos" or "collapse."[15] Indeed, Mexico has frequently been the subject of hyperbolic exaggeration and apocalyptic fantasy.[16] During the Cold War, conservative writers often asserted that Mexico stood on the brink of Communist takeover.[17] During the 1980s there were frequent warnings

---

14. Miguel Pérez, "El Presidente y sus 365 días," *Reforma*, December 1, 1995.
15. One of my initial concerns about the *Foreign Affairs* article on "pivotal states" was that it failed to define the notions of "chaos" or "collapse."
16. Observe the title of Andrés Oppenheimer, *Bordering on Chaos: Guerrillas, Stockbrokers, Politicians, and Mexico's Road to Prosperity* (Boston: Little, Brown, 1996).
17. See Sol Sanders, *Mexico: Chaos on Our Doorstep* (Lanham, Md.: Madison Books, 1986).

that Mexico could become "another Iran." And more recently, former U.S. defense secretary Caspar Weinberger has spelled out a fanciful scenario whereby Mexico's submission to drug cartels would lead to U.S. military intervention.[18]

Mexico's future is far from clear. Over the foreseeable term—let us say, the next ten to fifteen years—three potential resolutions of the current political uncertainty loom large:

- First, and most favorable, would be an acceleration of the processes of liberalization and democratization. The ongoing crisis of authority could lead to replacement of the long-standing system by truly democratic politics. The ultimate test of such a transition cannot occur until the elections of 2000, at which point it would have to be genuinely possible for an opposition candidate to win the presidency. (One difficulty inherent in this criterion is that the only credible proof of such a possibility would be an opposition victory.)
- Second would be an authoritarian throwback, a return to populist and nationalist politics engineered by, perhaps, an alliance of old-line party *dinosaurios* with segments of the Mexican military. This could occur in response to mounting social disorder, mass protest (especially in major cities), and continued evidence of the disintegration of power.
- Third might be a fragmentation and dispersion of power, a redistribution of power among a congeries of regional and bureaucratic fiefdoms. According to this scenario, processes of disintegration would continue apace. Power would reside in pockets: Some might follow democratic practices, others would be blatantly authoritarian. Contests among these fiefdoms would be chronic, continuing, and probably brutal. The future of Mexico might thus lie in contemporary Russia and the former Soviet Union.

All in all, the political consequence of economic crisis has been to generate uncertainty and instability. The traditional system is on the way out, but it is by no means clear where Mexico is heading.[19]

Longer-term developments are likely to result from the interplay of demographic change, resource management, and economic development. Mexico's population will approach or surpass 100 million by the

18. Caspar Weinberger and Peter Schweizer, *The Next War* (Washington, D.C.: Regnery, 1996), 161–213.
19. See also Gerardo Otero, ed., *Neoliberalism Revisited: Economic Restructuring and Mexico's Political Future* (Boulder: Westview, 1996), especially ch. 12; and Wayne A. Cornelius, *Mexican Politics in Transition: The Breakdown of a One-Party-Dominant Regime* (La Jolla: Center for U.S.–Mexican Studies, University of California, San Diego, 1996), especially 115–119.

year 2000. According to World Bank projections, it is likely to reach 135 million in the year 2025 and about 160 million by the mid-twenty-first century. This expansion will naturally place increasing demands on the nation's resources. By the same token, one of the country's most pressing current problems—the conspicuous "youth bulge" resulting from high rates of birth in the 1960s and 1970s—is likely to decline over time. As of the year 2000, according to the World Bank data, over 44 percent of the national population will be under the age of twenty; by 2025 this proportion will drop to just over 30 percent, and by 2050 it could be as low as 26 percent.[20] Indeed, Mexico has substantially reduced its population growth rate from around 3.6 percent annually in the 1960s to less than 2 percent in the early 1990s. As a result, the principal challenge is not so much to feed the children of the distant future; it is to provide gainful employment for young people who are now entering the job market at the rate of a million per year.

A related issue concerns environmental degradation. Haphazard economic growth and ineffective planning have inflicted serious damage on Mexico's natural resources. According to some studies, nearly a third of the country's over 20 million hectares of farmland have been eroded, and 86 percent is suffering erosion to some observable degree. Government-promoted colonization has turned more than 1 million hectares of the Lacandón rain forest into cornfields and cow pastures (leaving just 134,000 hectares as a reserve). Logging and other activities have led to the wholesale destruction of plant and animal species in the Sierra Madre Occidental and other regions of the country. Tourist developments have produced pollution along some beaches and destroyed underwater reefs. Then there is Mexico City, which takes most of its water from an underground aquifer whose life span can be measured in decades, and where 3 to 4 million automobiles burn 19 million liters of gas every day, spewing over 8,000 metric tons of pollution into the air, mostly in the form of carbon monoxide, nitrogen oxides, and hydrocarbons. In consequence, ozone levels in Mexico City exceed international norms during nine out of every ten days.[21]

In view of these trends, it is entirely possible to imagine that population growth plus resource depletion in Mexico could eventually lead to intensified social strife, zero-sum (or negative-sum) politics, and the kind of "chaos" that the Yale team has in mind. There is little doubt that such

20. Edward Bos, My T. Vu, Ernest Massiah, and Rodolfo A. Bulatao, *World Population Projections, 1994–95 Edition* (Baltimore: Johns Hopkins University Press [for the World Bank], 1996), 342–343.

21. Joel Simon, *Endangered Mexico: An Environment on the Edge* (San Francisco: Sierra Club, 1997).

developments would have negative systemic consequences and that they would, in the long run, heighten the prospects for political disintegration and authoritarian repression. Before leaping to such dire conclusions, however, it is important to remember that Mexico still has significant natural resources, that structural effects of hitherto unfettered growth can be mitigated by enlightened resource management,[22] and that economic development could yield expanding employment for workers and public revenues that could be used for environmental protection. And if population-versus-resources pressures accelerate in the future, the effects will appear not only within Mexico itself, but also in the country's relationship with the United States.

MEXICO AND THE UNITED STATES

The U.S.–Mexican relationship has long been complex. It is intense, in view of proximity and interdependence; it is asymmetric, in view of the preponderance of U.S. power; and it has been fraught with misunderstanding, in view of cultural and developmental differences. As the post–Cold War agenda has emerged, three issues have come to the fore: drugs, migration, and the cross-border environment. All have regional implications, but they are essentially bilateral in nature.

Illicit Drugs

A thriving international commerce in illicit drugs has claimed attention at the highest levels in both Mexico and the United States. From the 1930s through the 1970s, Mexico occupied a straightforward role in the international market, supplying some of the heroin and most of the marijuana imported by the United States. Both crops were raised by small-scale farmers: Opium poppies were cultivated in the north-central states of Sinaloa, Durango, and Chihuahua, and to a lesser extent in Sonora; cannabis (for marijuana) was grown throughout the country, not only throughout the northwest but also with notable concentrations in Michoacán, Jalisco, and Nayarit.[23]

Much of the processing and transportation of final products rested in the hands of fewer than a dozen large and illegal organizations, although

22. See Lane Simonian, *Defending the Land of the Jaguar: A History of Conservation in Mexico* (Austin: University of Texas Press, 1995). See also Gordon J. MacDonald, Daniel L. Nielson, and Marc A. Stern, eds., *Latin American Environmental Policy in International Perspective* (Boulder: Westview, 1997).
23. Miguel Ruiz-Cabañas I., "Mexico's Changing Illicit Drug Supply Role," in *The Drug Connection in U.S.–Mexican Relations*, ed. Guadalupe González and Marta Tienda (La Jolla: Center for U.S.–Mexican Studies, University of California, San Diego, 1989), 48–50.

the marijuana industry was less centralized than the opium/heroin business. As a rule, these groups maintained close relations with local farmers, from whom they regularly purchased crops; they kept their headquarters in key production areas; and although they earned substantial profits, they did not expand their operations to reach new markets with new goods. They resorted to bribery and intimidation, of course, but mostly on the local and regional level, and they maintained relatively low political profiles.[24] Although they exercised effective control over the Mexican narcotics trade, in other words, they did not constitute "cartels" in the same way as their Colombian counterparts.[25] They were local organizations dealing in locally grown products.

This situation underwent major changes in the 1980s, when *narcotraficantes* from Colombia began seeking new routes for shipping cocaine into the United States. As U.S. law enforcement agencies cracked down on shipments through the Caribbean and South Florida, Colombian entrepreneurs—especially leaders of the sophisticated Calí cartel—turned their attention toward Mexico. Initially, they ferried relatively small shipments of cocaine in small planes from Colombia to Mexico and then, with the aid of Mexican collaborators, sent them overland to the United States. In the early 1990s, as operations matured, Colombians began to fly their merchandise to central and southern Mexico in converted 727s and Caravelles capable of handling multi-ton loads; Mexican carriers would then take them north in trucks, small planes, and trains across the border to the United States, where operatives under the Colombians would break down the shipments for wholesale and retail distribution. As of 1989, the U.S. State Department estimated that 30 percent of U.S.–bound cocaine passed through Mexico; by 1992, the estimate surpassed 50 percent; for other years, the estimate has been as high as 75 to 80 percent.[26]

Mexico's entry into the cocaine trade reshaped both the structure and the power of trafficking organizations. Where the Colombians forged

24. See José Luis Trueba Lara, *Política y narcopoder en México* (México, D.F.: Editorial Planeta, 1995), 54–56; and Peter A. Lupsha, "Drug Lords and Narco-Corruption: The Players Change but the Game Continues," *Crime, Law and Social Change* 16 (1991): 41–58, especially 44–48.

25. Peter A. Lupsha, "Drug Trafficking: Mexico and Colombia in Comparative Perspective," *Journal of International Affairs* 35, no. 1 (spring–summer 1981): 95–115, especially 100–102.

26. See U.S. State Department, Bureau of International Narcotics Matters, *International Narcotics Control Strategy Report, March 1989* (Washington, D.C., 1989), 92; *International Narcotics Control Strategy Report, March 1992* (Washington, D.C., 1992), 167; and Bureau of International Narcotics and Law Enforcement Affairs, *Strategy Report, March 1996*, 141.

joint partnerships with Mexican traffickers, as in Guadalajara, they expanded and strengthened their economic base; and where the Colombians enticed other smuggling gangs into the cocaine trade, as in the state of Tamaulipas, it led to the emergence of new contenders. Second, the profitability of the cocaine trade greatly augmented the economic resources of trafficking groups. According to Thomas Constantine, the head of the Drug Enforcement Administration, annual earnings for Mexican *traficantes* now approach $7 billion per year (on gross proceeds of $27–$30 billion per year). Third, the emphasis on cocaine has severed the long-standing relationship between farmers and distributors. Mexican traffickers have less allegiance than before to local areas, less reason to concentrate their attention on the local scene; they all compete against each other for the same goods and the same market.

Mexico currently has at least five drug cartels of world-class stature and scope: the Guadalajara cartel, strengthened and refurbished by recent alliances with Colombian suppliers; the Tijuana cartel, which handles most northward shipments into the lucrative California market; the Sinaloa cartel, a traditional grouping fortified by leaders who broke off from the Tijuana group; the Ciudad Juárez (or Chihuahua) cartel, which dominates traffic from east of Tijuana to Ciudad Juárez–El Paso; and the Gulf cartel, based in the state of Tamaulipas, which has controlled trafficking along the U.S. border from Matamoros to Brownsville down the eastern coast of Mexico and around the Yucatán peninsula.[27] A half dozen or more additional groups play significant roles in the drug trade, and many other minor participants, but it is the "big five" cartels that dominate the market, cultivate connections with upper echelons of Mexican politics, and maintain key links to South America.[28]

This restructuring of the drug trade in the late 1980s and early 1990s exerted profound impacts on Mexico's political regime. One has entailed an escalation of corruption. To be sure, Mexico has a long history of political corruption, often tacitly accepted as a necessary evil, but the windfall of cocaine profits brought this practice to entirely unprecedented levels. According to some calculations, Mexico's *nouveaux riches* cartels can afford to spend as much as $500 million per year on bribery—more

27. In reference to illicit drugs, the term "cartel" commonly applies to participation in an effective oligopsony/oligopoly. Unlike "trusts" or classic "cartels," drug organizations do not normally engage in collusion to establish market prices, though they sometimes reach tacit agreement on market boundaries.

28. Peter A. Lupsha, "Mexican Narco-Trafficking: The Dark Side of NAFTA," *Encuentros* (Latin American Institute, University of New Mexico) 1, no. 1 (fall 1994): 10. Partly because conditions change so rapidly, there is inconsistency and uncertainty in the designation of Mexico's leading cartels.

than twice the total budget of the attorney general's office.[29] Shrewdly, and characteristically, they have disbursed these funds among: (1) top-level *políticos* who could provide protection, (2) heads of agencies engaged in antidrug activities, and (3) rank-and-file foot soldiers in Mexico's antidrug units. A conspicuous target of such efforts has been the federal judicial police force.[30]

Second has been an escalation of violence. Some of this reflects tension and rivalry between opposing gangs: Throughout the mid-1990s, for instance, the Tijuana and Sinaloa cartels have been locked in a bitter struggle for control of the Pacific corridor. This violence may have resulted from expansion in the economic stakes involved, as the dollar volume of Mexico's drug trade swelled rapidly in the late 1980s and early 1990s. The increase in violence may also demonstrate the influence of Colombians, especially former associates of the rough-and-tumble Medellín group, which unleashed a civil war in its own country for several excruciating years. Further, the rise in violence may represent a response by traffickers to heightened law enforcement, which has multiplied the number of clashes and raids. (Mexico's antidrug budget tripled between 1987 and 1989.) But whatever the cause, the effect has been to produce a string of high-level assassinations, morbidly known within the trade as "excellent cadavers": the former state attorney general of Sinaloa, murdered while jogging in a Mexico City park; a Roman Catholic cardinal, Juan Jesús Posadas Ocampo, assassinated (either on purpose or as a result of mistaken identity) at the Guadalajara airport in May 1993; and numerous police officials, especially those responsible for law enforcement in the Tijuana area. (A federal chief of police, appointed by Zedillo, was also poisoned in his sleep and temporarily paralyzed as a result.) It is widely assumed, in addition, that the assassinations of Luis Donaldo Colosio and of José Francisco Ruiz Massieu were related to drug trafficking in one way or another.

The escalation of corruption and violence has contributed to the broadest and farthest-reaching challenge to Mexican politics: maintenance of law and order and, more generally, the capacity to govern. Soon after taking office, in fact, President Zedillo received an official report warning:

> The power of the drug-trafficking organizations could lead to situations of ungovernability, using whatever political or economic space in which institutions show weakness or inattention; the advance of drug-trafficking

29. Mark Fineman and Sebastian Rotella, "The Drug Web That Entangles Mexico," *Los Angeles Times,* June 15, 1995.

30. Lupsha, "Drug Lords," especially 48–55.

promotes impunity and uncertainty in the institutions, justifies violence and increases intimidation of the authorities.[31]

This threat to legal authority takes multiple forms. One is brazen defiance of the government, most spectacularly through assassination. Another comes from the replacement of de jure constitutional rule by de facto informal authority, especially in poppy-growing regions and in host cities for the top cartels; in such areas drug kingpins wield supreme power, much in the manner of traditional *caciques* in eras past. A third kind of threat, perhaps the most effective and sinister of all, results from the entanglement of political leaders within the drug-trafficking network itself. The logic of the traffickers is disarmingly straightforward: If top-level politicians stand to benefit from *narcotráfico,* they will not take serious action against it. And the result, as Eduardo Valle Espinosa has said, is that Mexico's *traficantes* have been able "to create a state within a state."[32]

Taken together, all these consequences for the political system—violence, corruption, abuse of power—have helped generate widespread skepticism within civil society about the Mexican regime and its leaders. As a result of these developments (plus other disappointments, such as the peso crisis), Mexican citizens have come to assume the worst about the motivations, integrity, and capability of their political leaders. Such disbelief undercuts support for the country's weakening authoritarian system and may hasten its collapse, but it does not necessarily create civic foundations for political democracy. The progressive alienation of Mexican society from its leadership represents an unnerving and potentially troublesome trend.

Yet the power and role of drugs and drug traffickers in Mexico do have limits. The country has not so far fallen prey to "Colombianization." The government has continued to wage a vigorous (if not always successful) campaign against *narcotraficante* groups, and it has not formed a semipublic working partnership with cartel leaders. Nor has drug money had a major distorting impact on the national economy. Despite the threats and challenges, Mexico has so far managed to contain (if not control) its drug industry.

Even so, drug trafficking has had pernicious effects on U.S.–Mexican relations. Especially during election cycles, U.S. politicians have succumbed to the temptation of charging Mexico with responsibility for drug-related problems in American society: indeed, "Mexico-bashing" has become a lamentably predictable element in public discussions of narc

31. Fineman and Rotella, "Drug Web."
32. Eduardo Valle, *El segundo disparo: la narcodemocracia mexicana* (México, D.F.:, 1995).

throughout the United States. In contrast, Mexicans tend to focus on the presence of the U.S. demand for illicit drugs. More than a decade after the initial proclamation of the "war on drugs," they point out, more than 12 million Americans continue to use illicit drugs of one type or another. As of 1994 approximately 9.8 million Americans were making regular use of marijuana; about 1.3 million were taking cocaine on a monthly basis, more than half of whom (700,000) qualified as a heavy users; many others were steadily consuming heroin and/or synthetic drugs.[33] Moreover, the use of illicit drugs—especially marijuana—among U.S. high school seniors was continuing to rise.[34] In this perspective, the fundamental problem is not *supply* from Mexico; it is *demand* in the United States. The drug issue thus creates conditions and incentives for mutual recrimination.

Adding to this tension is a difference in policy goals. According to official pronouncements, the primary motivation for the U.S. government is "to reduce illegal drug use and its consequences in America." For the United States, drug consumption represents a threat to public health, claiming twenty thousand lives per year; it spawns crime, including violent crime; it encourages delinquency and gang membership in inner-city ghettos; and, in general, it imposes yearly "social costs" of around $67 billion, "mostly from the consequences of drug-related crime." To combat this situation, the U.S. government has increased its annual antidrug budget from $4.7 billion in fiscal year 1988 to $13.8 billion in FY 1996 (and a requested $15.0 billion for FY 1997). About one-third of these expenditures go toward demand reduction, including prevention and treatment; fully two-thirds are dedicated to law enforcement, including interdiction and international programs designed to "break foreign and domestic drug sources of supply."[35] Ever since Ronald Reagan declared a "war on drugs" in the early 1980s, in fact, Washington has resolutely persisted in its efforts to reduce the importation of illicit drugs from foreign countries.

Mexico faces very different challenges. Although drug use is growing in some areas, especially along routes of transit, the country does not have a major problem of illicit drug consumption (there is excessive use of inhalants, especially by street children, but that is another story).[36] As

---

33. e House, *The National Drug Control Strategy: 1996* (Washington, D.C., 1996), 79.
34. ne Cimons, "Teen-Agers' Marijuana Use Nearly Doubles," *Los Angeles Times*, mber 13, 1995.
35. House, *Drug Control Strategy: 1996*, 11–12, 20–21, 35–37; and supplementary *The National Drug Control Strategy, 1996: Program, Resources, and Evaluation* (gton, D.C., 1996), especially 298.
36. M.na Medina-Mora and María del Carmen Mariño, "Drug Abuse in Latin A in *Drug Policy in the Americas*, ed. Peter H. Smith (Boulder: Westview, 1992), ch

described by María Celia Toro, the most pressing concerns for Mexico are fundamentally political. One has been "to prevent drug traffickers from directly confronting state authority," to obstruct the formation of "states within the state," and to diminish the threat of narcoterrorism. A second goal, "equally important," has been "to prevent U.S. policy and judicial authorities from acting as a surrogate justice system in Mexico."[37] Mexico has thus sought to assert and maintain its sovereignty in the face of Washington's war on drugs. In other words, U.S. policy itself poses a significant danger to Mexican national interests.[38]

Friction became especially apparent in 1995, as Mexico faced the "certification" process created by an amendment to the Foreign Assistance Act of 1986. Frustrated by the continuing flow of drugs (especially cocaine) from Mexico to the United States, American politicians—liberal and conservative alike—called for "decertification" of Mexico. Amid this swirling controversy, the State Department (in consultation with other government agencies) approached the Mexican issue cautiously. "Entering office in December 1994," the official report began,

> President Ernesto Zedillo declared drug trafficking the principal threat to Mexico's national security and promised a major offensive against the drug cartels and drug-related corruption. He and Mexican Attorney General Antonio Lozano recognized that Mexico's law-enforcement efforts were being seriously undercut by narco-corruption and intimidation and by the high-tech capabilities of the trafficking organizations. They intensified the counternarcotics effort, prosecuted corrupt officials, and sought to expand cooperation with U.S. and other governments.

On balance, the State Department concluded, Mexico deserved full certification. Continued the report:

> Even with positive results and good cooperation with the U.S. and other governments, Mexico has a number of obstacles to overcome. The Zedillo Administration has set the stage for action against the major drug cartels in Mexico, and for more effective cooperation with the U.S. and other international partners, but it will need to equip its investigators and prosecutors with the appropriate legal tools to combat modern organized crime and provide adequate material resources. It will need to pass and implement proposed legislation to establish controls on money launder-

37. Toro, *Mexico's "War,"* 2. See also María Celia Toro, "The Internationalization of Police: The Case of the DEA in Mexico" (paper presented at meeting of the International Studies Association, San Diego, California, April 16–20, 1996).

38. "More than any other nation," William O. Walker III has said, "Mexico has been the object of coercive diplomacy by the United States." Walker, "International Collaboration in Historical Perspective," in *Drug Policy in the Americas*, ed. Peter H. Smith (Boulder: Westview, 1992), 273.

ing and chemical diversion. It must move forcefully to dismantle major drug trafficking organizations. Above all, it will have to take serious, system-wide action against endemic corruption.[39]

This was a highly qualified endorsement. The issue was and is far from resolved.[40]

Illegal Migration

The United States developed as a nation of immigrants. From the 1950s through the 1980s the volume of legal migration increased steadily, from 2.5 million in the 1950s to 6.0 million in the 1980s—the highest absolute figure in the world, it might be said, but well below proportional levels of the early 1900s. A precipitous decline in the share of immigrants from Europe and Canada (mostly Europe) also occurred, from 66 percent in the 1950s to 14 percent in the 1980s, and a concomitant rise in Asian immigration from 6 percent to 44 percent. Legal immigration from Mexico held steady, around 12 to 14 percent of the total, whereas flows from elsewhere in Latin America increased sharply during the 1960s and subsequently hovered around 26 to 27 percent of the total.

These trends underline important points. First, there was—and continues to be—a significant volume of legal migration from Mexico and Latin America to the United States. Second, alterations in the composition of the immigrant stream—especially the relative decline of the component from Europe—have prompted xenophobic and nativistic reactions among the U.S. public. Third, the establishment of numerical quotas has proven to be an illusory exercise. Even the increase in legal entries—which nearly doubled between the 1960s and the 1980s—could not accommodate growing pressures for migration to the United States. As a result many people have chosen to enter the United States without official authorization, in violation of U.S. law. It is by definition impossible to gauge the magnitude of this population with much precision, but responsible demographers have settled on a rough estimate of a stock of 2.5 to 4 million "illegal aliens" from all parts of the world as of 1992. Particularly conspicuous was illegal migration from Mexico, estimated to account for 55 to 60 percent of unauthorized residents in the United States.

U.S. immigration policy has long devoted special attention to Mexico. The underlying goals have been sharply contradictory: One has been to assure a continuous flow of cheap and desirable labor, another to stanch the flow of "illegal aliens." A culmination of these efforts came with the

39. U.S. Department of State, *Strategy Report*, 1996, xli–xlii.
40. As shown by events in early 1997, when Mexico narrowly escaped decertification again.

Immigration Reform and Control Act of 1986. Passage came amid a national clamor to "take control of our borders," in President Reagan's telling phrase, and as persistent unemployment fueled public resentment against workers from Mexico and other countries. Attorney General Edwin Meese III also proclaimed, in the face of both logic and fact, that restrictions on illegal immigration would reduce the flow of illicit drugs to the United States. Sponsored by Alan Simpson (R.-Wyoming) and Peter Rodino (D.-New Jersey), the bill contained four principal provisions:

- economic sanctions against U.S. employers who "knowingly employ, recruit, or refer for a fee" undocumented workers;
- permanent amnesty for undocumented workers who could prove continuous residence in the United States since any time prior to January 1, 1982;
- partial amnesty for undocumented workers in the agricultural sector who had worked for at least ninety consecutive days in the three consecutive years prior to May 1986 (SAW I) or during the year between May 1985 and May 1986 (SAW II);
- the readmission of "replenishment agricultural workers" (RAWs) in 1990–1992.

Ultimately, IRCA represented a compromise between those political forces opposing unauthorized migration (from organized labor to racist reactionaries), those who benefited from its existence (mostly employers), and Hispanic leaders expressing concern about the potential aggravation of ethnic prejudice.

IRCA achieved mixed results. The employer-sanctions portion of the law showed itself to be toothless. It remained possible for employers to comply with the law and still hire undocumented workers, who could make use of counterfeit documents. In contrast, the amnesty portion of IRCA turned out to be highly effective. Approximately 1.7 million applications were submitted under the "pre-1982" program and 1.3 million under the SAW program. More than 90 percent of the pre-1982 applicants had their status adjusted from temporary to permanent residency. All SAWs approved for temporary residence automatically received permanent resident status. In other words, nearly 3 million people acquired legal status in the United States as a result of Simpson-Rodino.

In the meantime a historic shift continued in the nature and composition of *indocumentados* from Mexico, away from the temporary or seasonal migration of single working-age men toward the longer-term settlement of families, women, and children. But as Wayne A. Cornelius concluded in the early 1990s, "There is no evidence that IRCA has reduced the total pool of Mexican migrants employed or seeking work in U.S. labor markets."[41] Though sharpening the distinction between migrant workers with and without legal status, in fact, IRCA might even have served to increase the size of the overall pool and, in so doing, it may have exacerbated social and political tensions within American society over unauthorized immigration.

Since then the U.S. government has redoubled its efforts. A tough stand against undocumented migration has in fact become a hallmark of the Clinton administration, which took office in the midst of a crisis over an influx of immigrants from Haiti.[42] Encouraged by reports from the U.S. Commission on Immigration Reform (established by the Immigration Act of 1990 and chaired by the late former Congresswoman Barbara Jordan), the Clinton administration has given high priority to immigration control, increasing the INS budget from $1.4 billion in FY 1992 to $1.85 billion in FY 1995 and proposing a 24 percent increase to $2.6 billion for FY 1996. As Attorney General Janet Reno declared in a September 1994 speech: "We *are* securing our nation's borders, we are aggressively enforcing our nation's borders, and we are doing it *now*. We will not rest until the flow of illegal immigrants across our nation's border has abated."

In keeping with this commitment, the Clinton administration increased the overall size of the Border Patrol by 51 percent from 1993 to 1995, bringing the number of agents to more than forty-five hundred and establishing a target of seven thousand for 1998. And it was not just a matter of adding more agents. In September 1993 the administration proclaimed Operation Hold-the-Line in El Paso, Texas (formerly known as Operation Blockade), an effort to curtail illegal entrants by deploying Border Patrol agents at close intervals along the border itself, and in September 1994 Attorney General Reno proclaimed the initiation of Operation Gatekeeper in San Diego. In 1996 the Republican-led Congress increased the INS budget yet again, authorized construction of a triple fence in the San Diego area, and approved measures for swift deportation of criminal aliens and asylum seekers.[43] An INS strategic plan called for a long-term, phased effort to extend concentrated enforcement operations to encompass the entire southwestern border. By mid-1997 it

41. Wayne A. Cornelius, "From Sojourners to Settlers: The Changing Profile of Mexican Immigration to the United States," in *U.S.–Mexico Relations: Labor Market Interdependence*, ed. Jorge A. Bustamante, Clark W. Reynolds, and Raúl A. Hinojosa Ojeda (Stanford: Stanford University Press, 1992), 184.
42. On this episode see Smith, *Talons of the Eagle*, 284–290.
43. Patrick J. McDonnell, "Deportation of Criminals, INS Fugitives at New High," *Los Angeles Times*, June 23, 1997.

appeared that the White House would propose a ten-year increase in the Border Patrol from around 6,200 agents to 20,000 or so.[44]

Even so, it remained unclear whether such efforts could ever be effective, or whether they would simply encourage would-be entrants to seek new modes of access.[45] Data on INS apprehensions of illegal aliens along the U.S.–Mexican border from January 1990 through August 1995 reveal substantial continuity in overall levels of migration and in seasonal cycles.[46] The first semester of 1995 showed a marked increase, on the order of 30 percent, apparently in response to the peso crisis of December 1994 and the ensuing depression in Mexico. (Popular opinion in Mexico increasingly holds NAFTA to blame for the crisis, which would indicate an indirect causal relationship between free trade and emigration; in view of the complex origins of the peso crisis, however, I tend to discount this argument.[47]) Mexico's economic collapse has driven more people to make the attempt, but the doomsaying forecasts of a mass exodus have not materialized. "We don't see the signs of a huge shift to the north, of Depression-era movements of people," said Robert Bach of the INS.[48]

There was, however, one clear-cut effect of such stepped-up operations as Gatekeeper and Hold-the-Line: relocation of routes of access into the United States. In the San Diego area, for instance, Gatekeeper slowed transit through long-standing avenues and pushed migration eastward.[49] Within a year or so, apprehensions dropped by nearly 20 percent along

44. Jesse Katz, "A Good Shepherd's Death by Military," *Los Angeles Times*, June 21, 1997.

45. For an excellent discussion of these initiatives see Wayne A. Cornelius, "Appearances and Realities: Controlling Illegal Immigration in the United States," in *Immigration, Refugees, and Citizenship: Japanese and U.S. Perspectives*, ed. Myron Weiner and Tadashi Hanami (New York: New York University Press, 1997).

46. INS data supplied by Charles W. Haynes and Gordon Hanson, both of the University of Texas at Austin. It must be said, of course, that the number of arrests provides a less than perfect guide to the number of illegal entries. Apprehension statistics refer to the frequency of *events* (arrests), rather than number of people; they make no allowance for multiple detentions; they make no adjustment for voluntary returns to Mexico; and they respond to the intensity and magnitude of enforcement by the U.S. Border Patrol (the correlation between agent hours and apprehensions over the sixty-eight-month span from January 1990 through August 1995 is +.299).

47. Except insofar as NAFTA encouraged large sums of portfolio investment, which may have created a false sense of confidence within Mexican policy making circles—and which abruptly fled the country in November–December 1994.

48. Patrick J. McDonnell, "Fears of the Border Run Fall Short," *Los Angeles Times*, June 18, 1995.

49. See San Diego Dialogue, "Enforcement and Facilitation: An Analysis of the San Ysidro Port of Entry and the Implementation of Gatekeeper Phase II" (La Jolla: San Diego Dialogue, University of California, San Diego, 1996).

the coastal area of Imperial Beach[50] but more than doubled along the twenty-mile stretch of inland border between Otay Mesa and Tecate. As INS officials have explained, this was precisely the point: "Operation Gatekeeper has made it more difficult than before for aliens to get across the San Diego section of the Southwest Border illegally. Forced out of Imperial Beach, potential illegal crossers encounter considerable personal adjustments as they move eastward toward Tecate or Mexicali."[51] The presumption is that the added hardship (and potential expense) of traversing unfamiliar and dangerous terrain would provide an effective deterrent against illegal crossing.

The experience of 1995 suggests that there is likely to exist an upper ceiling on Mexican migration. Visions of "chaos" in Mexico often yield predictions of manifold increases in undocumented migration, with millions upon millions fleeing disorder and despair in search of economic and/or political refuge in the United States.[52] The reaction to the peso crisis indicates that such fears are greatly exaggerated. My own judgment is that Mexican migration obeys fairly consistent economic and social dynamics and is relatively resistant to law enforcement efforts or to short-term pressure. Upheaval in Mexico might produce temporary increases but not permanent waves of cross-border migrants.

Throughout the debates on this issue, scant attention has focused on the underlying contradiction between NAFTA and the anti-immigration movement. On the one hand, the Clinton administration (and the U.S. government in general) has been reaching out to Mexico with an expansionist, inclusive economic policy; on the other hand, it has been containing Mexico with a restrictive, exclusive social policy. The resulting contradiction has emerged on three levels. One is symbolic (and hence political): The construction of a wall along the U.S.–Mexican border seems utterly inconsistent with the spirit of a newfound economic partnership. A second is procedural and institutional: Although NAFTA made no provision for labor migration, the U.S. emphasis on unilateral assertion appears to undermine the principles of cooperation and consultation enshrined in the free trade agreement. The third is substantive: Experience around the world has shown that economic integration tends to foster social integration. Freer trade encourages transnational investment,

---

50. It has been charged, however, that Border Patrol agents were encouraged to undercount arrests around Imperial Beach in order to exaggerate the success of Operation Gatekeeper. *Los Angeles Times*, July 6 and 9, 1996.

51. U.S. Immigration and Naturalization Service, *Operation Gatekeeper: Landmark Progress at the Border* (Washington, D.C.: Immigration and Naturalization Service, October 1995).

52. Ronald Reagan often used this argument in order to justify his Central American policies. See also Sanders, *Mexico: Chaos on Our Doorstep*.

which generally stimulates cultural interaction and, ultimately, labor migration. By endorsing anti-immigration measures, the Clinton administration is tacitly attempting to restrict and curtail the social consequences of the economic policy that it has so strongly endorsed. Eventually, if not immediately, this inconsistency is bound to become self-evident: You cannot have it both ways.

Environmental Protection

The U.S.–Mexican border area has long been a site for environmental degradation. It has a total population of more than 10 million, with about 45 percent concentrated in the San Diego–Baja California region. The San Diego border crossing is the busiest in the world. And the *maquiladora* program, started in the 1960s, has allowed U.S. and transnational firms to operate under much more lax (and more laxly applied) antipollution standards than those in the United States. Indeed, *maquiladora* industries pose multiple threats through pollution of air and water, and through the occurrence of industrial emergencies (spills, explosions, fires, and so on). In addition, the northern border region has suffered from improper use of agricultural chemicals, particularly herbicides and pesticides.

As a result, the frontier region has for decades confronted serious environmental hazards, including renegade sewage (mainly from Tijuana toward San Diego), industrial pollution (especially in the "gray triangle" of southern Arizona–northern Sonora), air contamination (as in the twin cities of El Paso and Ciudad Juárez), and water pollution (in rivers and underwater aquifers). Dumping of industrial waste by U.S. firms has added to these problems.[53]

These challenges create substantial incentives for cross-border collaboration. El Paso and Ciudad Juárez share a common air basin, for instance, and both cities need to reduce air pollution. Both Tijuana and San Diego suffer from the pollution of rivers flowing from Mexico into the San Diego and Imperial Valley areas of California; the same applies to pollution of the Rio Grande and overuse of transboundary aquifers between Texas and Chihuahua. Indeed, as one expert has written, "The water supply and quality is a major, if not the essential, issue for successful growth along the border."[54] Simply put, the problem is that there is no more water to be found: Conservation, reclamation, and cooperation are vital to the interests of both nations.

53. See Simon, *Endangered Mexico*, ch. 8.
54. Clifton G. Metzner, "Comments Related to U.S.–Mexican Free Trade Agreement and the Border Environmental Agreement," in *The Mexican–U.S. Border Region and the Free Trade Agreement*, ed. Paul Ganster and Eugenio O. Valenciano (San Diego: Institute for Regional Studies of the Californias, San Diego State University, 1992), 70.

In this context, NAFTA negotiations led to public concern over the relationship between environment and trade. Many analysts maintained that export-oriented development would accentuate abuse of natural resources in Latin America. They further insisted that economic liberalization, including privatization and foreign investment, would promote the formation of "pollution havens" (analogous to tax havens) in countries of the region. In contrast, trade advocates argued that economic opening and international competition would lead to widespread adoption of "clean" technologies and improved production techniques. They also charged that excessive concern for the environment could furnish a transparent disguise for economic protectionism on behalf of selfish interest groups.

As originally drafted, NAFTA made only passing reference to environmental concerns, as in the provision that its member countries "recognize that it is inappropriate to encourage investment by relaxing domestic health, safety or environmental measures." Like GATT, NAFTA was not intended to be an ecological charter, but environmental groups protested that the so-called green language in NAFTA was vague and inadequate. In keeping with his campaign pledge, President Clinton then supervised the initiation of negotiations on a supplementary NAFTA accord on environmental protection in March 1993. After months of strenuous deliberation, the parties reached an agreement that was "significantly narrower" than the original U.S. position.[55] An environmental secretariat was established as subordinate to the ministerial council, rather than as a truly independent entity, without the power to initiate dispute settlement and sanction procedures. Private groups were authorized to submit complaints within carefully specified limits, but they could not initiate legal action on their own; they could also press their views before a Commission on Environmental Cooperation, an officially recognized forum for lobbying. A violation of standards was ultimately defined as a "persistent pattern of failure . . . to effectively enforce" domestic environmental law. (Even so, the accord explicitly acknowledged the need for "reasonable" discretion in the application of laws; the starting point for tracing violations would be January 1, 1994, which meant that it would take substantial time to accumulate a record of "persistent" transgression.) Penalties could be imposed on an offending party only by an arbitration panel established by a ministerial decision of two countries out of three, and only after a lengthy and cumbersome quasi-legal process.

55. Gilbert R. Winham, "Enforcement of Environmental Measures: Negotiating the NAFTA Environmental Side Agreement," *Journal of Environment and Development* 3, no. 1 (winter 1994): 35.

The U.S.–Mexican border received special attention as a consequence of NAFTA. The United States and Mexico developed an Integrated Environmental Plan for the U.S.–Mexico Border Areas, a multiyear program of intensified cooperation under the direction of a Border Environmental Cooperation Commission (BECC) composed of twenty-four members representing various districts of the border region. To assist these efforts, Mexico committed $460 million for border cleanup during 1993–1995 and the United States pledged $379 million.

Whatever its practical outcome, negotiation of the NAFTA side agreement made one point clear: By the 1990s, trade and environment were inextricably intertwined. As one analyst has written, these developments forcefully demonstrated

> that the environment has become a staple of trade politics in the 1990s, for it was politically impossible to contemplate the completion of the NAFTA trade accord without a complementary agreement on the environment. Thus, trade liberalization became dependent on parallel efforts to protect the environment. However, it could also be argued that environmental progress became dependent on trade liberalization, in that NAFTA focused attention on problems such as pollution along the U.S.–Mexico border—problems that would have been less visible without a trade agreement.[56]

The terms of debate thus took shape. Instead of focusing on the potentially deleterious effects of untrammeled commerce and export promotion, attention now fastened on the potentially constructive consequences of the government-to-government *negotiation* of free trade agreements. In this connection, the Mexico–NAFTA process may well provide a model for subsequent trade negotiations between industrialized and developing countries, especially in the Americas.

It should be noted, however, that the principal U.S. concern with environmental protection in Mexico relates to cross-border issues. Unlike Brazil, Mexico is not the site of an Amazon forest that is seen (and claimed) as a critical global resource; it does, however, possess one of the world's largest endowments of biodiversity. And Mexico faces serious environmental challenges throughout its territory, not least in Mexico City. But the central focus of the NAFTA discussions and subsequent actions dealt with transboundary problems affecting key Southwestern states. Once again, it is the bilateral relationship that has given shape to underlying U.S. interests in Mexico.

56. Winham, "Enforcement," 30.

CONCLUDING REMARKS

Mexico has been and will be critical to the United States. Of that there can be little doubt. However, this importance derives not so much from its role as a "pivotal state" within Latin America as from its location as an immediate neighbor. It is the bilateral relationship, with all its complexities, that makes Mexico so significant for the United States.

A hypothetical exercise might illustrate the point. If Mexico were located in sub-Saharan Africa, for example, would the Clinton administration have rushed to provide a rescue plan in 1994–1995? It is to be observed, in this respect, that there were no discussions of bailouts for Argentina or Brazil (a pivotal state in the more genuine sense). Mexico is simply different from other developing nations, and what makes it different is not so much its effect on surrounding countries or on the international system at large, but its impact on the United States.

Yet there remains at least one way in which Mexico could (or has already) become a pivotal state in the strict sense: in regard to NAFTA expansion and/or the possible creation of a Free Trade Area of the Americas. The likelihood that other Latin American countries will be able to enter free trade agreements with the United States will depend to a crucial degree on Mexico's performance as a NAFTA partner. If Mexico enjoys economic recovery and political stability (plus opening), it will be conceivable for other Latin American nations—individually or collectively—to acquire membership in NAFTA (or in an FTAA). If Mexico founders, however, prospects for other countries will sharply decline. Stability and prosperity in Mexico thus constitute a necessary but not sufficient condition for hemispheric free trade. To this extent, all other countries in the region are held hostage to Mexico.

Policy Implications

Whether Mexico is seen as "critical" or "pivotal," it deserves careful attention from Washington. As Chase, Hill, and Kennedy noted in *Foreign Affairs*, NAFTA already represents acknowledgement of Mexico's unique importance to the United States.[57] Yet with regard to policy, there still is more to be done.

Caveats are necessary here. First, Washington has no single or coherent "Mexico policy" but a plethora of policies—some made by bureaucratic agencies, some made in deference to electoral considerations, still

---

57. Chase, Hill, and Kennedy, "Pivotal States," 40.

others made by local and state authorities (especially in border states). Nor is it self-evident that, given the range of interests involved, it would ever be possible to forge a coherent policy toward Mexico.[58]

Second, there are limits on possible change. If the central goal of U.S. policy toward Mexico was to promote stability and development, for instance, one might consider two proposals: (1) lift all restrictions on cross-border labor migration, and (2) legalize the sale and use of drugs. In the current (and foreseeable) political climate, however, mere mention of such alternatives underlines their total impossibility. We must work within some serious constraints.

That said, focus on Mexico as a critical (or pivotal) state yields several guidelines for U.S. policy:

1. *Give special attention to Mexico.*

It seems neither appropriate nor necessary to treat Mexico the same as Colombia, Honduras, Nigeria, or Bangladesh. This is consistent with the pivotal states argument. Mexico is a neighboring country with deep historic ties to the United States and, even more to the point, a member of NAFTA. These facts alone provide ample justification for uniquely tailored policies.

2. *Stick with NAFTA.*

Over the long term, NAFTA offers the best available hope for sustained development in Mexico. It may have ambiguous effects, and numerous uncertainties remain. But a U.S. rejection of NAFTA, or failure to follow through on its provisions, would have devastating consequences on political stability and economic development in Mexico. It would also inflict irreparable damage on the bilateral relationship. NAFTA is here to stay.

We also have to make it work. This means that the U.S. and Mexican governments should take every possible step to ensure long-term economic development and social peace in Mexico. At some point, this may require assistance for those Mexicans who are displaced as a result of NAFTA—farmers and *campesinos* in grain-growing areas, for example, and/or entrepreneurs and workers in small- and medium-size businesses. Ultimately, NAFTA may need the kind of "social fund" that was so essential and effective in the European Union. Ultimately, such a fund would prove to be a bargain.

3. *Anticipate disagreement and uncertainty.*

The United States has a paramount interest in a relatively smooth transition to democracy in Mexico. Almost by definition, however,

---

58. Some have even argued that a single, coherent policy would not be desirable, since it might reduce Mexico's ability to take advantage of the contradictions.

democratization involves instability. And as pluralization (or at least decentralization) proceeds in Mexico, it will create more space for disagreement and debate. In consequence, the bilateral relationship is likely to become more difficult to manage, more resistant to control, more subject to unpredictability. The voices of Mexican nationalism, more or less silent in the early 1990s, are almost certain to make themselves heard. Having long promoted the cause of political stability in Mexico, Washington must now become responsive to forces and factors for change.

4. *Revise migration policy.*

The United States has loudly asserted its sovereign right to make and enforce its own laws. That is not in dispute. The question is how best to manage (or control) migration from Mexico to the United States. Evidence and *a priori* logic suggest that this requires bilateral cooperation and consultation at the highest levels of government. As a beginning, three subjects could provide bases for negotiation: (1) creation of a guest-worker program for Mexican nationals in the United States; (2) apprehension and repatriation of smugglers, or *coyotes*; and (3) promotion of economic development and job creation in traditional areas in Mexico from which migrants come (perhaps through tax incentives for investments or other opportunities that might be made available through NAFTA). In addition, the U.S. federal government should rigorously apply employer sanctions in the United States. Nothing would be gained from pressuring the Mexican government to prevent its citizens from leaving the country, as many U.S. citizens demand, since that would constitute flagrant infringement of a fundamental human right.

5. *Reconcile immigration policy with trade policy.*

The United States should undertake to make its immigration policy compatible with the spirit as well as the letter of NAFTA. Operations Hold-the-Line and Gatekeeper do not meet this test. This does not mean that it is illegitimate or inappropriate for the United States to enforce its own laws; it means that immigration and trade policy are currently at cross-purposes. Washington should make serious efforts to resolve this inconsistency at distinct levels—political, institutional, and substantive. Otherwise there remains the danger that anti-immigrant sentiment and policy in the United States will undermine the promise and purpose of NAFTA.

6. *Revamp drug control policies.*

Legalization is not the only alternative to current policy on drugs. As many experts have argued, the U.S. government should restructure its priorities so as to give primary emphasis to the reduction of demand, rather than curtailment of supply. Extensive research has yielded two major findings: (1) interdiction of shipments and eradication of crops have negligible impacts on the availability of illicit drugs in the U.S. market, and (2) preventive and therapeutic efforts can effectively reduce the level of demand.[59] With regard to Mexico (and other supplier/transit countries), the primary emphasis should be on maintaining governability, rather than on waging war on producers and/or smugglers. Recognizing that U.S. market demand is the driving force behind supply, Washington should seek genuine cooperation from Mexican authorities. One positive step in this direction would be to rescind the legislative provision for certification.

7. _Intensify cooperation on environmental issues._

Measures to improve the cross-border environment have so far been disappointing. It would serve the interests of both Mexico and the United States to accelerate these efforts. In addition, the two countries should seek ways to combat environmental hazards in other parts of Mexico (including the capital city). Although Mexico has neither an Amazon forest nor a Chernobyl, it has natural resources that merit effective protection.

8. _Lower the political heat._

There is an understandable (if unpraiseworthy) temptation for U.S. politicians to seek advantage by blaming Mexico for trade deficits, joblessness, crime, drugs, and other social ills in the United States. This should be stopped. Otherwise resentments are liable to grow and bilateral cooperation will become all the more difficult. Political leadership, from the highest office in the land, would have the most effect in this regard. In the vast majority, U.S. citizens are fully capable of responding constructively to public information and to education on key issues. Mexico should be seen not as a perpetual source of bothersome problems or sinister threats, but as the critical state that it is.

---

59. For example, see Smith, _Drug Policy._

CROSSCUTTING ISSUES

POPULATION AND PIVOTAL STATES

Jack A. Goldstone

In matters of global population, some states clearly are pivotal. States with large populations, or those with moderately large populations and extremely high growth rates, will dominate the pattern of future global population increase. Of the projected increase in the world's population from 1995 to 2010—an increase from 5.7 to 6.9 billion people, thus an addition of 1.2 billion—seventeen of the world's 192 states will contribute 775 million, or two-thirds of the total. These are, in order of their contribution, India, China, Pakistan, Nigeria, Indonesia, the United States, Brazil, Bangladesh, Ethiopia, Iran, Mexico, the Philippines, Vietnam, Egypt, South Africa, Turkey, and Tanzania. India alone will contribute 503 million, or over 40 percent of the entire world's growth. If some states are pivotal for influencing the world's population, surely, it seems, they would be the ones on this list.[1]

Yet the connection between population and security issues is not merely a matter of overall population growth. Some states whose population growth is significant may not contribute greatly to security concerns: Although the United States and Ethiopia are both forecast to gain 30 million in the next dozen years, in neither case is that growth likely to pose a security issue to the world. In contrast, states that will not contribute greatly to global population increase may suffer internal economic and political strains from demographic growth that outpaces their resources; if financial and political chaos results, that outcome may pose a substantial security threat to the United States or its allies. Algeria may increase in population by only 8 million in the next twelve years; however, if it is not able to peacefully absorb and employ that 30 percent increase in its population, any ensuing political breakdown would entail massive emigration to France, possible disruptions of energy supplies to the world market, and a follow-up effect of increased Islamic fundamentalist political strength throughout the Middle East.

---

1. World Bank, *World Development Indicators 1997* (CD-ROM), Table 2.1.

The connections between population and international security, therefore, cannot be summed up simply by adding mounting population totals.
What matters is how various aspects of a population—its size, age distribution, urbanization, and growth rate—interact with its economic and
political institutions and resources to shape its likely future. To understand which states have population issues that are pivotal for U.S. and
world security concerns, we must combine attention to the "new" security issues of population and political stability, with an appreciation of the
"old" security issues of the geopolitical significance (in terms of vital raw
materials, strategic location, or geographic proximity) of particular
states.

There are three critical areas of interaction among population, the
economy, and politics:

1. *Consumption:* How do population and consumption trends combine to
   shape a country's demand for raw materials and imports from the global
   economy and that country's load of pollution and waste on the
   global environment?

2. *Economic stability:* How do labor-force growth and urbanization match
   up with the productive and financial resources of the country? High
   rates of un- and underemployment, and excessive borrowing to meet
   the needs of a population that is not producing enough to supply its
   own needs, can both contribute to political and fiscal disasters.

3. *Political stability:* What impact will urbanization, a "youth bulge" in age
   distribution, growing demands for government services, and the
   expansion of middle classes have on political institutions? Political
   institutions that fail to accommodate to these demographic changes
   may be overwhelmed by dissent and protest, leading to political weakness or even (as in Iran and Nicaragua in 1979, and the Philippines in
   1986) political collapse.

Let us consider each of these patterns of interaction in turn, and then
return to the issue of which are the world's "pivotal" states in terms of the
relationship between population and security.

CONSUMPTION

Growth in consumption is generally healthy for the world's economy;
increases in trade and output usually follow increases in demand, allowing all trading nations to increase their wealth. However, growing consumption can have its downside, as well. If consumption of key
commodities traded on world markets—such as food and energy supplies—surges beyond increases in supply, sharp price increases and local
shortages can easily arise. Also, if growth in consumption launches rapid-

ly developing nations on certain paths—for example low energy-
efficiency dependence on coal, instead of on natural gas or nonfossil fuels;
or land-intensive agriculture that degrades soil and forest cover—then
consumption growth can have negative long-term consequences on the
environment, and on global resources.

The largest impact on consumption will come from some, but not all,
of those countries listed above as contributing the most to world increases in population. Some countries will not contribute greatly to world consumption growth because they are, and are likely to remain, at relatively
low levels of income and consumption; these include Ethiopia, Bangladesh, Nigeria, and Vietnam. Others will not contribute greatly to consumption growth, despite being at high levels of consumption per capita,
because they are increasing their own energy efficiency (like the United
States), or increasing consumption per capita at a relatively modest pace.
For example, Canada and China in 1995 both had private consumption of
just over $330 million (in current U.S. dollars). Yet the *annual increase* in
consumption in China is nearly *ten times greater than in Canada,* because
China combines an immense population, a faster population growth rate,
and a much faster rise in per capita consumption.

The commodities that are most likely to be security concerns for the
United States and the world in the years immediately ahead are food and
energy. Indeed, Lester Brown has already raised the specter of China's
demand for food placing enormous strains on the grain markets of the
world early in the next century, with soaring prices and major shortfalls
leading to famines in poorer nations, higher prices for consumers everywhere, and possible strategic hoarding and diplomatic conflicts over
access to food supplies.[2] Energy supplies have been plentiful in recent
years; however, doubts are increasingly being raised about the environmental and safety risks of megadam projects, coal-burning plants, and
nuclear plants. If all of these sources of electric power generation are
restricted in growth, demands for the remaining fossil fuels, namely oil
and natural gas, could again result in shortfalls and rising prices.

Food Consumption and Supply

Recent studies suggest that, contrary to Lester Brown's worst case scenarios, China has adequate land to feed its population.[3] However, China's
ability to use this land effectively depends on several factors that remain
uncertain. The first is an adequate supply of irrigation water; this will
require immense new engineering works, as major aquifers are already

2. Lester R. Brown, *Who Will Feed China?* (New York: W. W. Norton, 1995).
3. Vaclav Smil, "Feeding China," *Current History* 94 (September 1995): 280–285.

being overtapped, and surface irrigation channels are already succumbing to siltation and salt deposition on soils. The second is continuing agricultural research to reduce losses to pests and weeds, to increase resistance to disease, and to improve yields of major grains. In the United States, the steady and spectacular increase in yields throughout the twentieth century has depended heavily on investments in agricultural research, as well as diffusion of the best techniques for production and of the latest hybrid seed strains. Similar research lay behind the green revolution of the 1960s and 1970s in Asia. Yet if progress in yields and output efficiency are to continue for another generation in China and India and not plateau at current levels, a further period of intensive research and diffusion of the latest techniques is vital. Third, China (and India) need to feel confident enough to utilize their agricultural land to produce the crops of highest local value and to rely on international trade in foodstuffs for their other needs, rather than aiming at complete food self-sufficiency. For example, as China and India urbanize and diversify their diets, it will be important to devote far more crop land to high-value fruits, nuts, and vegetables, high-quality rice for human consumption, and local poultry and meat production, while relying on imports for coarse and feed grains.[4]

For all three of these avenues to balancing food output with rising consumption, foreign policy coordination with the United States will be crucial. Foreign investment and engineering support may be needed to help China make more efficient use of its limited freshwater supplies. Foreign advice and cooperation (for example, respecting patents on hybridized seeds) will be essential in helping China improve its agricultural research and extension programs, as will diffusing global best practices in seed selection, integrated pest management, and soil conservation. Further, without confidence in the international grain market and secure trading rights and access to global markets, China cannot embark on the rationalization of its agricultural investment to make best use of its agrarian resources. Without such foreign assistance and integration in improving its agriculture, China's galloping consumption may yet give rise to Brown's international security nightmares of global food scarcity.

To a greater or lesser extent, all three of these issues that face China—water management, agricultural research, and integration of national and local agricultural markets—are important for the major food-consuming countries of the developing world and will require significant international cooperation to avoid disastrous outcomes. Yet these issues are often poorly understood in the United States. Farm groups sometimes argue

---

4. Organization for Economic Co-operation and Development, *Agricultural Policies, Markets and Trade in Transition Economies* (Paris: OECD, 1996).

that providing assistance to foreign agricultural production will reduce markets for U.S. farmers. And the specter of using U.S. food production as a strategic weapon against China is sometimes raised. Yet both such policies are bound to backfire and create new security problems for the United States. Providing assistance to China, India, and other nations to increase their output of fruits, nuts, vegetables, and meats at lower prices is likely to *increase* the market for U.S. feed grains. As China's and other nations' income and demand for meat consumption grows, demands for those crops that dominate U.S. food exports will also rise; withholding assistance is more likely to create eventual chaos and price controls in a world market attempting to cope with food shortages. Furthermore, threats to use food as a weapon are likely to lead China and other nations to seek alternate sources of supply, perhaps to turn inward and seek food self-sufficiency, again at the cost of lower efficiency and slower growth of food imports from the United States and more disruptive and autarkic global food markets.

Two kinds of countries bear watching for an adverse impact on world grain supplies: those countries that in recent years have been significantly expanding their demand for imported grains, and those countries that, although currently not experiencing major increases in grain imports, could well see such a change in the future if their domestic production lags behind their future growth in consumption.

In the first category, the developing countries showing major increases in imports between 1980 and 1994 were (with the increase in million metric tons [mmt] shown in parentheses): Algeria (4.3), Egypt (3.2), Saudi Arabia (3.1), Iran (2.7), Brazil, (2.2), Malaysia (2.2), Indonesia (1.6), Pakistan (1.3), Colombia (1.3), the Philippines (1.2), and Mexico (0.9).[5] All of these countries have recently shown considerable declines in their rate of population increase; thus, all of them are likely to increase their demands for food imports either more slowly, or only slightly faster (allowing for increases in income and consumption), than in the previous decade. Much larger demands for increased food imports came from the developed world—for example, Japan (5.5 mmt) and South Korea (6.8 mmt).

In 1994, the ten largest cereal importers in the developing world (including China) imported a total of 71.6 mmt; this was only 3.8 percent of total world cereal production and 34 percent of total world imports of cereals.[6] The world grain market is thus highly disaggregated, and no truly "pivotal" states currently dominate the world demand for imported grain.

5. World Bank, *Indicators 1997,* Table 4.4.
6. World Bank, *Indicators 1997,* Table 4.4.

Notice that both India and China—the countries most commonly discussed as sources of disruption to world food markets—are not on the list of countries experiencing major increases in grain imports. India is basically self-sufficient in food. And although China is currently the world's second-largest grain importer after Japan (which imports twice as much grain as China), China's cereal imports in 1994—16.3 mmt—were actually slightly *less* than they had been in 1980. Although China and India can make major demands on global food production in bad years, they have shown no long-term tendency to encroach on global grain supplies. Only if future population growth should consistently outrun domestic food production—something that is possible, but likely only if international cooperation on agricultural issues is not forthcoming—are these countries likely to become massive food importers. Indeed, future U.S. food security policy could well be thought of in terms of trying to make sure that these countries, each of which is experiencing a combination of large population increases and fast-rising private consumption, do *not* land on the list of countries that have experienced rapidly increasing grain imports.

From 1980 to 1995, China and India both increased their cereal consumption and production by about one-half. China's cereal consumption rose from 280 million metric tons in 1980 to 433 mmt in 1995, while India's consumption rose from 140 to 215 mmt over the same period. But China's cereal imports in 1995 were only 16 mmt, and India's imports were nil. Thus in both countries production rose at virtually the same rate as consumption. Together, China and India consumed about 648 mmt per year of cereals in 1995 (about one-half of total world cereal production), and yet they imported only about 2.5 percent of their annual needs.[7]

China is expected to add 147 million to its population between 1995 and 2010; India should add 198 million. What will be the impact of this population increase on their demand for grain? In 1995, China's per capita grain consumption was .36 metric tons per year. This was about equivalent to that of Japan (.34), which relies much more on fish for protein than does China, and somewhat less than South Korea (.422), whose diet is closer to that of the Chinese. India's per capita grain consumption was far less, at .23 metric tons per year. Let us say that over the next fifteen years, a richer China would increase its per capita grain consumption to the level of South Korea today, and that a richer India—most of whose inhabitants do not eat beef—would increase its per capita grain consumption to a level somewhat less than that of China today, say, to .30 metric tons per year. Combining current population growth projections

7. The data in this section are from World Bank, *Indicators 1997,* Tables 2.1, 4.13, and 4.4.

with these increases in per capita consumption leads to a forecast demand for grain in 2010 of 568 mmt per year for China and 338 mmt per year for India, or a total demand of 906 mmt per year. This represents an increase of 258 mmt a year, or about 40 percent, over current demand.

The key question is how much of this increase in consumption will have to be supplied by imports. Since both China and India increased their cereal output by 50 percent between 1980 and 1995, a continuation of this growth rate in output (about 2.5 percent per year) would more than meet their increased demand, and eliminate any need for large grain imports. Even if cereal production growth rates should fall to 2 percent per year, this would increase China and India's grain output to 850 mmt per year by 2010, leaving about 56 mmt per year to be supplied by imports. Although this is a considerable increase over current import levels of 16 mmt per year, this import level in 2010 for China and India combined would be only somewhat more than the combined 1995 grain imports of Japan and South Korea (42 mmt per year), and should not press greatly on world grain supplies. In other words, as long as India and China continue to meet 95 percent of their cereal needs by domestic production, then even though their grain imports would also increase—from 16 mmt in 1995 to over 50 mmt in 2010—this would not present a security concern.

However, if China and India were unable to increase their own output to keep pace with demand, so that they had to shift an increasing fraction of their grain consumption to imports, problems could arise. For example, if China's and India's cereal production rose only 1 percent per year in the next fifteen years, so that in 2010 they could produce only 80 percent of their domestic needs, then imports could conceivably rise by a factor of ten or more. At this point, Lester Brown's nightmare scenarios—with China's and India's import demands requiring as much as all the cereal traded on world markets today—start to become plausible.

It is thus critical, in order to preserve the stability of world cereal markets, that China and India continue to improve their agricultural output to meet their needs. The steady, incremental progress of U.S. farmers in raising output over the past century shows what can be done. There is no reason that India and China cannot achieve similar gains *if* investments and international support are given as readily as they were in the past.[8]

In sum, population and consumption data suggest that among the developing countries that have recently seen the largest increases in cere-

8. Vaclav Smil, "How Many People Can the Earth Feed?" *Population and Development Review* 20 (June 1994): 255–293.

al imports, none is truly "pivotal" for world grain markets. Only two countries are "pivotal" for keeping world demand for cereal imports on an even, moderately upward path: China and India. It should be a priority of U.S. and world agricultural policy to ensure that they do not join the ranks of those countries with a large and rapidly increasing dependence on imports for their basic foodstuffs.

Energy Consumption and Supply

Despite concerns about rising energy use in the developing world, it is difficult to make a case that population expansion and consumption growth will have a significant impact on world energy security in the near future. The United States and Japan currently each import energy resources of roughly 400 thousand metric tons of oil equivalent (MTOE) annually; by comparison, the largest energy importer among developing nations is India, which imported only 47 thousand MTOE in 1994. India's total growth in commercial energy use is 11.8 thousand MTOE per year; at that rate, even if all additional use is fueled by imports, it will be decades before India's oil import needs become significant compared with those of the developed nations. Brazil imports roughly as much energy as India, but its total energy use is growing much more slowly at only 4.18 thousand MTOE per year. Turkey and Thailand are the only other significant energy importers among developing nations, and their imports, at roughly 30 thousand MTOE and growing at one to four MTOE per year, are also minor on the world scene.[9]

Among developing nations, only China's growth in commercial energy use, at 36.4 thousand MTOE per year, is comparable with that of the developed nations (annual growth of energy use in the United States is 30.5 thousand MTOE per year).[10] Yet China is currently able to supply almost all of its own energy needs, and with its huge reserves of coal, its planned expansion of nuclear power, and the hydroelectric resources of the Three Gorges and other major dam projects, it is likely to continue to do so.

If growing population and consumption of energy in the developing world pose any security concern to the United States, it is not in the area of energy consumption itself but in the environmental damage that accompanies energy production and use.

Pollution and Waste

The developing nations of the world can impose major security concerns on the United States and the developing world with regard to two

9. World Bank, *Indicators 1997*, Tables 3.4 and 3.5.
10. World Bank, *Indicators 1997*, Tables 3.4 and 3.5.

major concerns: carbon dioxide (CO_2) emissions, which contribute to global warming through the "greenhouse effect"; and rain forest deforestation, which has the dual impact of reducing habitats for species diversity and further contributing to global warming by reducing the considerable CO_2 absorption capacity of the rain forests' rich foliage.

With regard to CO_2 emissions, developing nations are increasingly significant contributors to the global load of greenhouse gases. In 1992, China and India together released 3,437 million metric tons (mmt) of CO_2 to the atmosphere, about 15 percent of the world's total, although still considerably less than the United States, whose release was 4,881 mmt. No other developing nation except Mexico (at 333 mmt per year) emitted even as much as 300 mmt. Judging from current trends, however, things will change rapidly in the future. If one extrapolates from current per capita levels of CO_2 emissions and allows for energy use per capita to increase at the 1980–1994 rate to the year 2010, then one can estimate that by that year China alone will emit 5,397 mmt, almost the same amount of CO_2 as the United States (5,593 mmt). India will add 2,071 mmt, and six other developing nations—Iran (615 mmt), Indonesia (587), Saudi Arabia (511), Mexico (469), South Africa (431), and Brazil (337)—will contribute yet another 2,950 mmt. In other words, in 1992, the United States' CO_2 emissions were as large as those of the eight other largest CO_2 emitters in the developing world *combined*. However, if current trends continue for roughly another decade, U.S. emissions will increase by only about 15 percent, whereas emissions from the developing countries with the most substantial emissions will increase 116 percent; by 2010 those eight developing nations will be emitting almost twice as much CO_2 as the U.S.[11]

Clearly, if action is to be taken on global CO_2 emission, China, India, Iran, Indonesia, Saudi Arabia, Mexico, South Africa, and Brazil are the "pivotal" states. Not only will these states provide the largest increase in CO_2 emission, but because each is a regional leader in economic growth, the pathways that they find are likely to be widely imitated by other economies in their region. If these nations can find and agree on a pathway to economic growth that provides lower energy intensity and lower CO_2 emissions, it would be the single most important step in preventing the more rapid accumulation of greenhouse gases in the near future.

With regard to rain forest and habitat destruction, the list of "pivotal" states is slightly smaller. In a number of nations, population expansion and clearing of land for agriculture, forestry, and settlement is destroying forest and habitat at notable rates. The most dramatic loss of forest land is

11. World Bank, *Indicators 1997,* Tables 2.1, 3.4, and 3.5.

occurring in Brazil and Indonesia; between 1980 and 1990, Brazil is estimated to have lost 36.7 thousand square kilometers of forest, and
Indonesia to have lost 12.1 thousand square kilometers. However, significant losses of forest also occurred in this period in China (loss of 8.8
thousand sq. km), Zaire (7.3), Mexico (6.8), Venezuela (6.0), Bolivia
(6.3), and Thailand (5.2).[12]

In regard to habitat destruction, there is some overlap with this list, but
also some changes. The number of threatened plant and animal species
considered "threatened" is highest in Australia, Brazil, Canada, China,
Costa Rica, Cuba, Greece, India, Japan, Malaysia, Mexico, Panama,
South Africa, Spain, Sri Lanka, Tanzania, Turkey, and the United States.[13]
Clearly, species preservation is an issue for which both developed and
developing nations bear responsibility. Also, many species that are
"threatened" in developing nations may not be on this list, as they are yet
unknown. However, it is interesting that a large number of the develop-
ing nations that appear as "pivotal" for species conservation—Brazil,
India, Mexico, South Africa, and Turkey—are among those that Chase,
Hill, and Kennedy have selected as pivotal for geopolitical reasons.[14]

Among the developing nations of the world, the two that will by far
add the most people to the globe in the next decade—India and China—
have already dramatically slowed their growth rates. Their projected
growth rates for the years 1995–2010, 0.8 percent per year for China,
and 1.3 percent for India, are tributes to the success of family planning
and government population policies. Not much can be done to decrease
their rates of growth further. Low rates of population growth (under 1.5
percent per year) are also likely in the coming decade in Brazil, Indonesia,
Mexico, and Turkey. Some large or strategically important developing
nations, however, remain with very high growth rates. Estimated growth
rates for 1995–2010 in Pakistan, Nigeria, Iran, and Ethiopia range from
2.4 to 2.8 percent per year, and estimated growth for Saudi Arabia,
although it has slowed greatly from the preceding decade, is still reckoned
to be 3.3 percent per year.

Nonetheless, for none of these nations are population growth and the
ensuing consumption of resources likely to pose a security threat to the
United States or the world. Neither India nor China needs to make threatening assaults on world food markets; China is self-sufficient in energy,
and India's energy imports are modest and not growing at alarming rates.

12. World Bank, *Indicators 1997*, Table 3.1. We should note that there was a substantial
    loss of forest in Russia, where 15.5 thousand sq. km of forest were lost.
13. World Bank, *Indicators 1997*, Table 3.2.
14. Robert S. Chase, Emily B. Hill, and Paul Kennedy, "The Pivotal States and U.S.
    Strategy," *Foreign Affairs* 75, no. 1 (January–February 1996): 33–51.

A failure to cooperate in improving the agricultural capacities of developing nations *could* lead to turmoil in world food markets, but this outcome should be avoidable if a solid foundation of agricultural research and open markets for international food trade can be built and maintained. Of course, these are no small goals and high priority should be given to committing the modest resources necessary to ensure that China and India do not become dramatically dependent on imported food supplies for their basic needs.

The notion of "pivotal states" makes rather more sense for dealing with the impact of growing population and consumption in developing countries on the production of greenhouse gases, deforestation, and species conservation. Eight developing nations—China, India, Iran, Indonesia, Saudi Arabia, Mexico, South Africa, and Brazil—will dominate global increases in CO_2 emissions in the next decade. Helping these nations find a less energy-intensive, less emissions-producing growth path will be the major requirement of an effective global policy to curb greenhouse gases. A similar list of developing countries is "pivotal" for dealing with major deforestation—Bolivia, China, Mexico, Thailand, Venezuela, and Zaire—and for helping threatened plant and animal species—Brazil, China, Costa Rica, Cuba, India, Malaysia, Panama, South Africa, Sri Lanka, Tanzania, and Turkey. The countries that appear on at least two of these lists—China, India, Mexico, South Africa, and Brazil—would seem to merit special attention as developing countries that, in a variety of ways that reflect the impact of increases in population and consumption on the environment, are "pivotal" to U.S. interests.

ECONOMIC STABILITY

The impact of population and consumption growth is not limited to strains on global resources and the environment. Indeed, the interaction of population changes with more traditional security concerns—economic and political stability—is likely to prove more vexing to U.S. security interests.

Economic stability is most likely to be affected by two factors: jobs and state finances. Growing populations need employment; particularly if the population is extremely young, the rate of entry into the labor market will far exceed the rate of total population growth. This age-driven employment pressure will be compounded further if the population is also experiencing a shift to the cities as a result of more efficient agriculture displacing labor from rural areas. The combination of population increase, an age distribution that amplifies the demand for entry-level employment, and a large-scale migration that focuses job demands on urban areas, can lead to extremely high rates of un- and underemployment in developing nations.

A population that is not productively employed can also lead state finances into a "scissors" crisis, in which the government budget is squeezed between rising real costs and stagnant or declining real revenues. A growing and urbanizing population that is not employed does not pay taxes, contributing little to state resources. But at the same time, such a population requires government services—sanitation and health, education, provision of justice and law enforcement, housing, food supplies—if riots and health disasters are to be avoided. A lag between growth in the labor force and urbanization, and the provision of productive jobs in sufficient numbers, can force governments into borrowing or inflation to meet short-term needs. If such measures are sustained for too long, they can push governments over the brink of financial crisis.

For example, Mexico from 1980 to 1994 had a labor-force growth rate of 3.2 percent per year, one of the highest in the world. Mexico is also highly urbanized; its urban population of 69 million (1995) is the fourth largest in the developing world, behind only China, India, and Brazil. Throughout the early 1990s, Mexico experienced a modest economic "boom," foreign investment poured in, and government spending provided expanded services and infrastructure.

But prosperity was neither widespread nor solidly grounded. In 1992, 15 percent of the population still earned less than $1 per day.[15] In the southern province of Chiapas, population growth had led indigenous farmers to claim lands in the forest areas, land also coveted by cattle ranchers and large commercial farms.[16] Government attempts to disperse the indigenous farmers produced a small-scale rebellion by the "Zapatistas." The rebellion sapped the government's credibility and exposed strains on support for the ruling PRI regime. Foreign investors began to take flight and, as they did, they in turn exposed the degree to which the government had relied on short-term foreign funds, rather than taxation of its own domestic production, to pay its bills. In the ensuing peso crash, not only did the Mexican government require an international assistance package; the fright to foreign investors also unsettled markets throughout Latin America, inflicting serious damage on economies throughout the region.

In Egypt, Algeria, Brazil, Turkey, South Africa, and Iran, similar pressures from rapidly expanding and urbanizing labor forces can be found.

15. World Bank, *Indicators 1997*, Tables 2.3, 3.6.
16. Joseph Whitmeyer and Rosemary L. Hopcroft, "Community, Capitalism, and Rebellion in Chiapas," *Sociological Perspectives* 39 (winter 1996): 517–539.

High rates of un- and underemployment, and governments that depend on combinations of inflation, borrowing, and other financial chicanery to maintain themselves, continue to create conditions of financial uncertainty for both foreign and domestic investors. Without solid employment for its labor force, a solid foundation of prosperity is difficult for any country to establish.

Let us, for the moment, take the Chase-Hill-Kennedy list of "pivotal states" and several other regionally significant nations, and inquire as to how they look from the point of view of labor force growth and urbanization (Table 1).

Table 1. ANNUAL GROWTH RATES: LABOR FORCE
AND URBAN POPULATION

	Labor Force (1980–1995)	Urban Population (1990–1995)		Labor Force (1980–1995)	Urban Population (1990–1995)
Algeria	3.8	4.0	South Africa	2.6	2.9
Brazil	2.6	2.5	Turkey	2.6	4.7
Egypt	2.6	2.5	Iran	3.3	4.0
India	1.9	2.9	Saudi Arabia	5.4	4.0
Indonesia	2.2	3.9	Nigeria	2.7	5.3
Mexico	3.2	2.7	China	0.8	3.8
Pakistan	3.1	4.7			

Source: World Bank, *World Development Indicators 1997* (CD-ROM), Tables 2.3 and 3.6.

Of all the countries on this list, only one—India—is low on *both* labor force growth (below 2.0 percent per year) and urban growth rate (less than 3 percent per year). It seems clear that of the countries that Chase, Hill, and Kennedy feel are "pivotal," almost all are facing unusually high pressures from rapid labor force growth and urbanization. They are not the only countries in the world that face such strains of course; they are common to most developing nations. However, many of the other large developing nations that face similar strains—Iran, Saudi Arabia, and Nigeria—have oil revenues to shore up their government's finances. Among the countries on the "pivotal" list, only Algeria, Indonesia, and Mexico have oil resources, and Mexico and Indonesia are much more diversified economies, far less dependent on oil revenues than Iran, Saudi Arabia, or Nigeria.

These data suggest that a faltering in economic growth, as occurred in Mexico, could leave any of the "pivotal states," with the exception of India, exposed to powerful labor force and urbanization pressures that can create "scissors" crises for state finances.

To sustain stability in Mexico, the United States needed to lead an international effort to rescue the peso. The effort was successful, and the costs were minimal compared to what a full-fledged collapse of the Mexican economy would have entailed. Yet if problems in finding employment for its labor force and in coping with the rapidly growing demands for services for a rapidly urbanizing population played any role in the Mexican crisis, the presence of this pattern throughout most of the "pivotal" states is cause for concern. It suggests that financial crises will be a recurrent threat until these states establish a solid basis of employment and taxation to support their services, and that the U.S. and international financial agencies will need to keep a reserve fund available for the next "pivotal" state that requires major financial assistance to avoid a sustained crisis.

At present Indonesia is suffering from the financial crisis in Asia, with huge currency devaluations and stock market declines. If these conditions produce a rapid rise in unemployment, a classic "scissors" squeeze on state finances is likely to ensue, producing further demands on the West for financial support. Precisely such pressures have already led to the abrupt departure of President Soeharto.

POLITICAL STABILITY

A financial crisis is not the only way that employment and revenue strains may play out. Things may unravel further, leading to state collapse. Indeed, it is striking that of the developing nations that experienced population growth rates of over 3 percent per year from 1980 to 1990, a large number—including Iran, Nicaragua, Ethiopia, Afghanistan, Angola, Algeria, Tajikistan, the Yemen Republic, Rwanda, and Zaire—suffered major revolutions or civil wars.

Population change can affect the political stability of a regime through several pathways. First, the "scissors" of rising demands for government services and inadequate government revenues can bring financial stress to a regime. Whether the regime responds by seeking to increase revenues, borrowing from abroad, permitting spreading corruption, or allowing currency inflation, unless the problems are quickly resolved the long-term effect is to erode the confidence of both elites and the general population in the competence of the regime.

Second, the growth of urbanized, educated middle classes can bring strong demands for greater participation in government. Regimes that lack the inclination to incorporate rising middle classes into the political system have, sooner or later, come to grief. It is one of the paradoxes of authoritarian regimes that in seeking to develop the economy and create a cadre of professionals, managers, businessmen, engineers, and teachers, they create a constituency for opposition to their regime.[17] Democracy cannot be imposed on autocrats; attempts of U.S. policy makers to encourage the shah of Iran, Somoza in Nicaragua, and Marcos in the Philippines to be "more democratic" led to shams of democratic practices that only further undermined support for their regimes. However, the United States can prepare for the passing of autocrats from the scene in developing nations by maintaining contacts with groups across the political spectrum and being ready to support a moderate opposition once an autocrat is clearly faltering.

Such efforts require a deft touch; Jimmy Carter's fumbling support and retreat from the shah of Iran earned the United States only enmity from the shah's opponents. Ronald Reagan's decisive abandonment of Marcos and support for Corazón Aquino came too late to save the United States' air and naval bases in the Philippines; however, it did come in time to shore up the Aquino government and prevent a further breakdown of order in the Philippines. In countries facing demand for broader political inclusion in the face of opposition from autocrats or closed regimes— Egypt under Mubarak, Indonesia under Soeharto, Algeria under military rule, Mexico under the PRI party-state, and Saudi Arabia under its royal family—the United States must walk a fine line between support for stability and maintaining friendly relations with the existing regime, and preparing for the day when a majority of the population will demand a more inclusive and open government.

Finally, widespread popular opposition to a regime can arise from frustrations over unemployment, or ethnic or religious favoritism in the economy and politics. Regimes in which a particular ethnic group dominates the economy or political power are vulnerable to mass protests over those conditions. Such protest becomes all the more likely when high unemployment makes political or economic exclusion increasingly bitter to endure.

Popular opposition is particularly easy to mobilize among the young, those who are not yet attached to families and careers, and who have the idealism and energy to seek radical change. Revolutions have historically occurred in societies that had a marked "youth bulge"—that is, a relatively high proportion of the population age fifteen to twenty-five compared with the population age twenty-five and older.[18] A recent study of demographic, economic, and political causes of state failure from 1950 to 1990

---

17. Tim McDaniel, *Autocracy, Modernization, and Revolution in Russia and Iran* (Princeton, N.J.: Princeton University Press, 1991).

18. Jack A. Goldstone, *Revolution and Rebellion in the Early Modern World* (Berkeley and Los Angeles: University of California Press, 1991).

similarly found that major ethnic conflicts were far more likely to break out in countries with a marked "youth bulge" in their population.[19]

Looking again at the "pivotal" states, and other major states, we can assess how "young" their population is by looking at what portion of their population is under age fifteen (Table 2).

Table 2. PERCENTAGE OF POPULATION UNDER AGE 15, 1990

Algeria	41.6	Mexico	38.9	Iran	45.9
Brazil	34.4	Pakistan	44.2	Saudi Arabia	45.4
Egypt	39.4	South Africa	38.3	Nigeria	47.7
India	36.0	Turkey	34.7	China	26.9
Indonesia	36.6				

Source: World Bank, World Development Indicators 1997 (CD-ROM).

Clearly, these are all very young populations, with the exception of China, where the one-child policy has drastically reduced the population under fifteen. (China's population age 15–25 during the Tiananmen Square uprising, however, was probably considerably higher than these figures imply, as that cohort would have reflected population growth in the 1970s, before the one-child policy went into effect.) Several of the Muslim countries—Algeria, Pakistan, Iran, Saudi Arabia, and Nigeria— have the very youngest populations and therefore may be the most volatile; however, every country listed except for China has a youth population large enough to be considered vulnerable to mass mobilization.

Singly, any one of these factors—state financial strain, elite discontent, popular grievances, urbanization, and the youth bulge—may create some unrest but is unlikely to pose a severe threat to the political stability of a regime. Such threats arise only when several of these factors converge at a single time in a particular state.[20] Clearly, for most of the "pivotal" states, as well as for other states with strategic resources or locations, rapid urbanization and a youth bulge are present. State financial strain, elite discontent, and popular grievances can be monitored through diplomatic channels. When all coincide, it would be well to place policy makers on alert.

19. Daniel C. Esty, Jack A. Goldstone, Ted Robert Gurr, Barbara Harff, Pamela Surko, and Allan Unger, Workshop on Risk Assessment and Crisis Early Warning System, ed. John Davies and Ted Robert Gurr (Boulder: Rowman and Littlefield, forthcoming).
20. Jack A. Goldstone, "Population and Revolution in the Developing World," in Theorizing Revolution, ed. John Foran (London: Routledge, 1997).

Currently, the "pivotal" states closest to calling for alarms on all counts are Mexico, Indonesia, and South Africa. In Mexico several regional rebellions are in fact already under way and the ruling PRI regime is on the verge of losing power. Whether it does so gracefully through elections, or more chaotically through protests and rebellion, remains to be seen. In the next decade, Mexico's stability will depend on whether it can maintain sufficiently rapid economic growth to absorb its rapidly growing labor force and underwrite its government's expenditures, and on whether it enjoys sufficiently rapid political reform to satisfy the claims for greater political power from its fast-growing urban professional and middle classes.

Indonesia is, as this is written in early June 1998, on the verge of collapse. Although President Soeharto has already been forced from power, his departure will not alleviate the long-term stresses due to the past two decades' rapid population growth and urbanization. While the economy was robust, these trends could be absorbed. However, the downturn in Asia has exposed the degree of debt and duplicity involved in the economic and financial system under Soeharto, leaving a rapid increase in unemployment, an unstable financial system, and difficult negotiations over Indonesia's debts to his successors. It therefore seems unlikely that stability will be easily restored. Conflicts over control of the country's resources, and over the country's currency and unemployment crises, will most likely continue.

South Africa also faces an exceptionally difficult conjuncture of population and economic problems as part of its legacy from the era of apartheid. During the apartheid years, state policy prevented Africans from settling in the major cities; this "displaced urbanization" created artificially low rates of urbanization for Africans—about 50 percent compared with 80–90 percent for whites, Asians, and coloureds. Perhaps 1 million Africans who would prefer to live and work in cities thus live in rural areas immediately adjacent to cities. With the end of apartheid's artificial barriers will come an enormous demand for migration and residence in the major cities, a demand that will place extraordinary pressures on the state to assist with housing and relocation.[21]

The apartheid regime also made a substantial investment in providing manufacturing and service employment in the artificial "homelands," in order to lure Africans away from the white population centers. With the

21. Richard Tomlinson, *Urbanization in Post-Apartheid South Africa* (London: Unwin Hyman, 1990); Colin Murray, "Displaced Urbanization: South Africa's Rural Slums," in *Segregation and Apartheid in Twentieth-Century South Africa*, ed. William Beinart and Saul Dubow (London: Routledge, 1995), 231–255.

end of apartheid, the rationale and funding for these projects ceased, leaving tens of thousands of Africans without work. Add to this the decline of gold prices, the devaluation of the South African currency, and the consequent slowdown of the economy, and the ability of South Africa to provide formal employment for its growing labor force has almost ceased—by one estimate, the fraction of South Africa's labor force without regular jobs has grown from 46 percent in 1985 to 57 percent in 1995.[22] The current leadership of South Africa enjoys enormous popular support due to its struggle and victory against apartheid. However, unless it can begin to reverse the steady rise in un- and underemployment and make some progress on the problem of housing the displaced urban population, that support may wane, leading to another, perhaps more violent, struggle for leadership in this racially and ethnically divided nation.

Other states on the list of "pivotal states" show these dangerous characteristics to various degrees. Closer monitoring of these conditions over the near term seems likely to be helpful, if these states are indeed considered to be "key" to U.S. security interests.

POPULATION, PIVOTAL STATES, AND U.S. POLICY

A survey of the role of population in security analysis can contribute to the discussion of the "pivotal states" thesis in two ways: one is by asking whether attention to population and related issues helps to identify a set of "pivotal" states on which policy makers can focus; and a second is by examining population dynamics in states that are alleged to be "pivotal" and see if they do indeed raise security concerns regarding those states.

With regard to the first issue, it seems clear that no single list of "pivotal" states will embrace all significant issues. Costa Rica and Sri Lanka are important states for species conservation, but they are too small to be of global significance in addressing deforestation. Saudi Arabia is a "pivotal" state in dealing with the emission of greenhouse gases; yet it is not on the Chase-Hill-Kennedy list.* For the issue of global food supply, only two states are pivotal—India and China—and what is pivotal for these states is keeping them *off* the list of rapidly growing importers of basic foodstuffs. As long as India and China increase their imports by no more than their overall rates of consumption growth, the world should be able to meet global cereal export needs without major disruptions.

Nonetheless, a number of states do emerge as repeated concerns in

---

22. Christian M. Rogerson, "The Employment Challenge in a Democratic South Africa," in *The Geography of Change in South Africa*, ed. Anthony Lemon (New York: Wiley, 1995), 172–173.

* [Editors' note: Because the United States regards it as vital for other reasons.]

matters related to population and consumption: Among all the world's nations, China, India, South Africa, Mexico, and Brazil all will be crucial for dealing with CO_2 emissions, deforestation, and species and habitat protection. Inasmuch as Chase, Hill, and Kennedy already have identified all of these states as "pivots" for geostrategic reasons, their prominence in matters of global population, consumption, and pollution matters reinforces the argument for concentrating executive and congressional expertise, and diplomatic and financial resources, on a relatively small number of "pivotal" states.

However, for many of the other states considered in this essay—Saudi Arabia, Iran, Turkey, Egypt, Indonesia, Nigeria, Pakistan, Algeria—there will be much debate about which, if any, are truly "pivotal." Interestingly, they are all Islamic states and five of the eight are significant energy exporters. I find it hard to believe that all eight Islamic states, and even all five energy producers, are equally "pivotal" in U.S. interests or in global affairs. I would think it preferable to focus on one state that has great influence in each major geographic area (Nigeria in sub-Saharan Africa; Egypt in the Middle East; and Indonesia in Southeast Asia) and the largest energy exporter (Saudi Arabia), and take those as "pivotal," assigning lower priority to the other states. Other scholars and policy makers may choose differently. Still, I believe the general principle that a relatively small number of states will be key to diplomatic efforts in a number of different areas, and therefore deserve special attention, is fundamentally sound.

Yet these states are indeed, as Chase, Hill, and Kennedy imply, "wobbly" pivots. Almost all of them, excepting only India with its low urbanization and labor-force growth rates, suffer from what we might call a "population pressure" syndrome: a combination of high urbanization rates, high labor force growth rates, a marked youth bulge, and un- and underemployment of a large fraction of the work force. These pressures threaten considerable difficulties in the near term: financial strains and crises; discontent of a growing urban middle class; popular discontent and protests; and, if all of these should coincide and grow, the collapse of the existing regimes. If these states are indeed deemed to be of geopolitical importance, then devoting scarce resources to understanding better conditions in these specific states and establishing ties with a wide range of actors in these societies to better prepare for an uncertain future, would be a most sensible investment.

What can be done to help avoid or react constructively to the threat of instability in these states? In the past, United States policies toward the developing nations has often been a reward-or-reaction policy. The U.S. has attempted to reward regimes, however small or distant, if they followed policies that conformed to its interests, particularly during the

Cold War. The regimes of the shah of Iran, Marcos in the Philippines, Pinochet in Chile, and Somoza in Nicaragua, however distasteful, were shored up on the basis of concerns about repelling communism. Yet it can hardly be believed that any of these regimes were significant in the eventual winning of the Cold War.

The second wing of U.S. policy toward the developing world has been reactive. Whether responding to humanitarian crises in Africa or to threats by rogue states in the Middle East, the United States has done a quick study, marshaled its military and area experts, and swooped in with mobile forces to try to rectify the situation on the ground. Although these tactics have often done much good, they have also left U.S. forces exposed and without a clear mission. This pattern of events has played itself out in Somalia and Ethiopia, in East and Central Africa, in Lebanon, and now, perhaps, in Bosnia. It has become clear that although rapid-response interventions can accomplish their immediate mission, it is impossible to achieve long-range diplomatic goals without a long-range diplomatic plan and adequate preparation for its implementation.

A "pivotal states" policy that identifies a small number of developing nations important in a number of ways—demographic, environmental, geostrategic—and that makes preparations to advance U.S. long-range goals in those states would be a more coherent, and probably far more efficient, foreign policy plan than the current reward-or-reaction scheme.

One area in which improvements could readily be made is in U.S. population policy toward the developing world, which has been remarkably inconsistent. At the most recent United Nations Population Conference in Cairo in 1994, the United States took the lead in fashioning an agreement among most of the world's nations and major nongovernmental organizations (NGOs) on the basic principle that voluntary family limitation leads to increased health, better education, and better employment prospects (especially for women), and can help reduce environmental degradation and risks of political instability. Yet at the same time that the Clinton administration was endorsing these goals and the conference was finding that there is "an urgent need to mobilize substantially increased donor and developing country resources on behalf of population stabilization," the U.S. Congress was in the midst of drastically *reducing* U.S. assistance for overseas family planning, cutting the 1996 budget allocation for population assistance by 35 percent from the previous year. The result is the lowest level of family assistance provision per woman in the developing world since 1968. With a foreign aid budget of 1 percent of total federal spending and a population assistance budget now reduced to .03 percent of federal spending, support in the

Congress for U.S. overseas family assistance programs has clearly declined.[23]

Part of the reason for this failure to maintain consistency in U.S. population policy stems precisely from the inability of the U.S. policy makers to focus on any "pivotal" states for the purpose of managing such assistance. The U.S. government has been the largest supporter of global family planning assistance, but that support is widely diffused. Roughly one-half of U.S. population planning assistance is disbursed through bilateral agreements with thirty-six different countries, often countries that are also receiving far larger U.S. inflows of economic and military assistance; the other half contributes to fifty-nine regional or global programs, often in conjunction with NGOs or global bodies such as the United Nations Population Fund. Administrative support is also isolated. At the State Department, population planning comes under the direction of the Office of Global Affairs, not under any major regional or state desks, and is implemented by the independent Agency for International Development. As a vaguely global program not directly linked to geostrategic interests in any particular region or nation, population assistance becomes an easy target to disregard or reduce.

In many of the "pivotal" states named by Chase, Hill, and Kennedy, as well as a few other key regional states such as Nigeria and Saudi Arabia, there is a vast unmet need for family planning services as well as for the female health and education facilities that amplify their effects. Meeting those needs aggressively would likely further reduce population growth and the potential for economic and political difficulties stemming from that growth in these key countries. If population planning assistance were integrated into a "pivotal states" strategy focused on a few countries that were large and/or geostrategically significant and showed rapidly growing labor forces; rapid urbanization; weak education infrastructures; and potential security difficulties including fiscal problems, political unrest and/or large-scale emigration, then the link between population policy and U.S. security interests would be far more apparent.

Of course, targeting population assistance to these states would *not* be satisfactory as a substitute for existing global programs; doing so would strip away a major support for women's health and education around the globe. However, clearly demonstrating that family planning assistance is part of an integrated approach to U.S. security concerns in regard to a modest number of "pivotal" states could provide an anchor for U.S. pop-

23. "U.S. Funding for International Population Programs," *Population and Development Review* 23 (March 1997): 213–218. Available at USAID Web site: Population and Health Programs (www.info.usaid.gov/pop_health/infopack.htm).

ulation assistance and perhaps spur new funding for those states, thus reversing the major across-the-board reductions in funding for family planning assistance.

CONCLUSION

In combination with urbanization, changes in the age structure of populations, and various aspects of development, population growth in developing nations poses a number of potential security challenges for those nations *and* the United States. These include managing global food supplies to avoid massive local shortages, finding paths to development that do not greatly increase CO_2 emission and its greenhouse effects, limiting the impact of growing human populations on the viability of diverse species and ecosystems, and absorbing rapidly growing labor forces without severe fiscal dislocations, mass migrations, or rebellions.

A focus on "pivotal states" will not adequately deal with all of these challenges; different states will emerge as key players on different issues. And certain crucial policy problems—such as the refugee troubles and political reconstruction of Bosnia and Rwanda—would neither be anticipated nor facilitated by a focus on "pivotal states." Clearly, U.S. foreign policy makers must hold some resources in reserve to deal with specific states as problems germane to them arise.

Nonetheless, keeping such a "reaction reserve" is not a substitute for an overall foreign policy framework; it is rather a means to deal with the inevitable shortcomings of any such framework. Standing alone, a reaction reserve simply denotes the absence of an overall foreign policy plan and provides no way to diminish or ameliorate future foreign policy burdens. In the area of population policy in particular, the failure to tie spending on population planning assistance for foreign nations to any clear set of national or regional security goals has left this vital, and relatively inexpensive, element of reducing future security problems vulnerable to sharp attacks and cutbacks.

Although the attention being paid to the "new" security issues of population, environment, migration, and refugees has greatly increased,[24] these concerns are often raised as additions or alternatives to existing geopolitical security concerns, leading to an awkward and unwieldy piling up of security issues. A pivotal states framework that includes an appreciation of the multiple impacts of population growth on consump-

---

24. Norman Myers, *Ultimate Security* (New York: W. W. Norton, 1993); Thomas Homer-Dixon and Valerie Percival, *Environmental Scarcity and Violent Conflict: Briefing Book* (Washington, D.C.: AAAS, 1996).

tion, pollution, and economic and political stability, and treats these not simply as "global" problems but focuses on their geostrategic implications for specific states, would go far to overcome the obstacles that policy makers face in incorporating these "new" security concerns to their existing agendas.

If the goals of a foreign policy for the next century are to bring greater coherence to the diversity of concerns pressing on U.S. policy makers, to anticipate change more promptly, and to foster a stable and supportive world for the growth of U.S. trade and the U.S. economy, a pivotal states strategy would be a fine place to start crafting it.

INTERNATIONAL MIGRATION AS A PIVOTAL ISSUE[1]

Michael S. Teitelbaum

To what extent is it appropriate to consider international migration—both into and out of the pivotal states—a phenomenon of high salience to the national interests of the United States? The effects of such migrations could be either *direct*, insofar as they could be judged to have straightforward impacts (positive or negative) on the welfare and security of the United States; or *indirect*, if they were to affect (positively or negatively) the well-being and security of other states (including pivotal states) in a manner that affected U.S. interests in that state or world region.

To be sure, physical contiguity has some relevance here, and of course of the pivotal states only Mexico shares a border with the United States. For such geographical reasons, in addition to matters of history and culture, the direct impacts of Mexico–U.S. migration—actual, potential, and perceived alike—are likely to be far more obvious than those of distant pivotal states such as India or South Africa. Any impacts on the United States of migration into or from such distant pivotal states are more likely to be indirect in form. However, it is also worth noting that the rapid advances of international travel and communication have diminished the force of geography. As a result, it now is far more difficult to

1. Some sections of this essay draw on the introductory chapter to a previous publication prepared jointly with Myron Weiner: *Threatened Peoples, Threatened Borders: World Migration and U.S. Policy* (New York and London: The American Assembly and W. W. Norton, 1995). This material has, however, been very substantially revised and augmented, and hence Professor Weiner bears no responsibility for any errors of fact or interpretation that may appear. The interpretations expressed are the author's and not necessarily those of the Alfred P. Sloan Foundation.

   The author also gratefully acknowledges the assistance of Dr. Hania Zlotnik, Chief, Mortality and Migration Section, Population Division, United Nations, New York. Dr. Zlotnik kindly provided unique data on international migration that are available to the United Nations but not yet published.

imagine a United States that is able to insulate itself from any future chaotic migration waves that might emanate even from very distant states, pivotal or not.

This essay deals with the dynamic and complex phenomenon of international migration in relation to U.S. foreign policy. Its basic propositions are:

First, that the very conceptualization of U.S. foreign policy interests in international migration has undergone a profound shift, a virtual sea change, over the past ten to fifteen years. Rather than assessing migrations as they arguably might promote U.S. Cold War interests by stabilizing strategic regions and countries, U.S. foreign policy now more often perceives large-scale international migrations as contributing to instability in countries and regions of U.S. foreign policy interest.

Second, that the domestic politics surrounding U.S. immigration and refugee policy has been radically transformed in recent years in a direction that has produced heightened public interest in U.S. foreign policy in general, and more specifically toward a number of the pivotal states. Indeed, migration questions have risen near the top of the U.S. agenda related to some of the pivotal states.

And third, that although international migration is a global phenomenon, the pivotal states under scrutiny in this volume include a number for which such migration is of very high salience, in some cases a dominant and even transcendent concern.

The past decade has seen the unleashing of torrents of people moving from or within Rwanda, Burundi, Zaire, Somalia, Sudan, Algeria, Bosnia, Croatia, Iraq, Afghanistan, Tajikistan, Azerbaijan, Armenia, Sri Lanka, Bangladesh, Burma, China, Indonesia, Haiti, Cuba, Mexico, Guatemala, Nicaragua, and El Salvador—and this is by no means a complete listing. In most cases, the destinations have been other developing countries nearby, but more distant, industrialized countries (often those with former colonial ties) have also been goals. In many cases, such movements have produced palpable perceptions of threat. The turmoil and alleged massacres in the former Zaire, following the mass entry of millions from Rwanda and Burundi, is a most evocative recent example. Within only the past few years, very considerable foreign policy interests have attached to actual or threatened migrations of Iraqi Kurds into Turkey, of Russians escaping harsh treatment by minorities in some successor states of the former Soviet Union, of Bosnians seeking refuge from civil war, and of Mexicans, Central Americans, Cubans, and Haitians pursuing opportunity in the United States.

Western industrialized countries have been not only important migration destinations, but also the locus of rising anxieties. The United States has been concerned with migration, much of which is unlawful, from Mexico, Central America, the Caribbean, and China. Concern in Japan has arisen about much smaller movements from China and Southeast Asia. And in Western Europe, anxiety about international migration has risen to the top of the political agendas of countries such as France and Germany.

This essay deals first with the perspectives about international migration that prevailed in U.S. foreign policy from the 1940s to the 1980s, and then with the evolution of these views since the end of the Cold War. It then turns to the rise of domestic political concerns about immigration, including issues of credibility and the yawning gap between public and elite opinion. These U.S. anxieties and responses are then compared and contrasted with those in Europe and elsewhere. The limited data currently available on internal migration and urbanization in the pivotal states are summarized. Finally, a series of brief vignettes on the significance of international migration for particular pivotal states is presented.

CHANGING U.S. FOREIGN POLICY PERSPECTIVES ON INTERNATIONAL MIGRATION

Cold War Views

Following the end of World War II, the return and resettlement of the millions displaced and scattered by its violence, persecutions, and privations were seen as essential steps toward reestablishment of stability in Europe. Moreover, the forcible "repatriation" of ethnic Germans from regions of long-standing settlement in Eastern Europe was accepted and assisted by the U.S. in its role as an occupying power of postwar Germany.

For much of the Cold War that ensued, the conventional U.S. position was that the flight of refugees from communist countries was a phenomenon to be welcomed, indeed promoted, as a palpable demonstration of the political illegitimacy and/or economic failure of communist regimes. Under this policy, the United States pressed communist countries to permit freedom of exit; sought via propaganda to encourage departures from countries such as Hungary; and readily admitted individuals from Vietnam, Laos, Cambodia, Nicaragua, Cuba, the Soviet Union, and the countries of Eastern Europe. This position was infrequently challenged and to a great extent formally embodied in U.S. refugee law and practice.

The framers of American foreign policy during that period paid little attention to the ways in which such outmigrations may also have benefited their declared Cold War adversaries. Certainly the departure of political dissidents weakened opposition to communist regimes. Perhaps their departure made political change less rather than more likely. Moreover, communist regimes were strengthened by the flow of remittances from refugees settled abroad, in some instances (as in Cuba) providing millions of dollars annually to improve their balance of payments. Paradoxically, while policy makers argued that refugee flows undermined the regimes of America's adversaries, they also reasoned that migration and refugee flows strengthened the regimes of America's friends. The government of El Salvador, for example, convinced several U.S. adminstrations that the roughly one-sixth of Salvadoran citizens residing irregularly in the United States should be allowed to stay on, so as to restrain labor market pressures in El Salvador and provide needed foreign exchange. Similarly, the Mexican government persuaded some Americans that Mexico's economic and political stability was enhanced by lax enforcement against irregular migration flows across the Mexico–U.S. border.

Shifting Post-Cold War Perspectives

In recent years the view that migration to the United States could both weaken American adversaries and strengthen its friends has received more thoughtful scrutiny. The result has been a clear shift toward a new view that a large influx of asylum claimants, refugees, and illegal migrants can be a threat to U.S. interests by imposing unacceptably high costs on receiving countries that are of special foreign policy concern, and indeed on the domestic sectors of the United States itself. This new perspective has been driven by strong evidence from the 1980s that large-scale human movements can produce social and political turbulence and even destabilization in regions as diverse as the Middle East, South Asia, Western Europe, and south Florida.

No one would describe such shifts as coherent, or consistent, or orderly. A major source of incoherence has been the palpable momentum of the past—immigration and refugee policies that were created under circumstances now transformed beyond recognition. The hallowed assumptions of more than four decades of the Cold War die hard. Moreover, some provisions (for example, the Cuban Adjustment Act of 1966) have been formalized in law or judicial interpretation, making change more easily blocked by focused interest groups.

Yet responses there have been, in recent years rising to the very highest governmental levels in both administrative and political terms. For reasons perhaps best explained by psychologists, migrations by boat seem to evoke the greatest perception of threat, and hence the highest political levels of attention. Certainly it is not because the numbers involved are higher than those crossing land borders; the reverse is true. It may be due to the greater concentration, vulnerability, and "televisibility" of migrants in small boats and homemade rafts. Meanwhile, unregulated movements by equal or larger numbers of people via land or air have not evoked the same level of threat perception.

U.S. DOMESTIC DEBATES ABOUT IMMIGRATION: SHIFTING POLITICS

The domestic politics and public discourse about immigration have become increasingly raucous and divisive in recent years. This transformation of the domestic debate has served to increase public interest in some of the pivotal states producing significant migratory movement. For some of these countries, such as Mexico, migration issues are now at or near the top of the bilateral agenda and present an important convergence of domestic and foreign policy concerns and a significant source of bilateral tension.

The emphasis of recent U.S. debates about immigration has been on the illegal or undocumented category. Although some Americans willingly employ illegal immigrants, others regard them as interlopers or as competitors for jobs who are prepared to work at low wages and for employers who violate labor standards. Were the government willing and able to stop employers from hiring them, the critics say, there would be more opportunities for unemployed Americans, especially for those who belong to minority communities. Beyond the issue of employment, American fears of a large influx of asylum claimants, refugees, and illegal migrants have deeper roots in the structure of the welfare state; the distribution of financial resources among local, state, and national governments; uncertainties over the prospects for immigrant integration; and concern over loss of control—the apparent inability of government to manage the flows in an orderly manner.

In regions of the country with large numbers of children who are illegal migrants or asylum claimants, local communities resent federal requirements that they use property taxes to pay for the costs of those children's schooling. Similarly, some state governments view migrants as unwarranted financial burdens on public services. Texas, California, Arizona, Florida, and New Jersey all have filed so-far unrequited lawsuits against the federal government, seeking financial redress for the billions of dollars they have spent on educating illegal aliens, paying their Medicaid costs, and imprisoning those convicted of crimes. They argue that by failing to control borders, to punish employers who hire illegal workers, and to deport aliens, the federal government has permitted more than 5 million illegal aliens to stay in the United States—but passed on much of the welfare cost to state governments.

Finally, in the minds of some Americans migration is also linked to crime, drug traffic, and terrorism. Little hard evidence supports these alleged linkages to immigrants and refugees in general, but the particular case of the World Trade Center bombing did involve a group of Middle East immigrants and asylum claimants and seems to have played an important role in increasing public anxieties over immigration. Ample evidence does link drug trafficking and migration, especially along the U.S.–Mexico border and in the involvement of migrants (a minority to be sure) from countries such as Colombia, Mexico, and the Dominican Republic. Finally, hard evidence also shows that some of the illegal migration to the United States (and elsewhere) is now part of a worldwide trafficking business, with very substantial fees paid for forging documents and arranging illegal entry and employment of migrants. (Press reports indicate that upward of $30,000 fees are being paid by Chinese illegal migrants who are then forced to repay their loans by bonded employment in restaurants, sweatshops, or prostitution.)[2]

Some of the special volatility of recent immigration debates may be attributed to widespread perceptions that previous policies have lacked credibility. Past policies intended to reassure the public that migrants do not constitute a threat, that illegal migration has been contained, and that refugee and asylum flows can be managed have indeed proved to be notably ineffective. The sanctions against employers of illegal aliens adopted in 1986 legislation were so emasculated and constrained by their opponents that it is no surprise that they have not been effectively enforced. Credibility was similarly strained by the experience with hundreds of thousands of irregular migrants from El Salvador and Nicaragua, who were granted "temporary protected status" when they did not qualify for asylum but then were not repatriated when political and economic conditions in their home countries improved. Finally, in 1990 Congress passed legislation sharply increasing the number of legal migrants admitted each year on the basis of "needed skills" in response to demands by some employers alleging "labor shortages" that did not subsequently appear, just as large numbers of Americans were being laid off or facing increasingly chilly labor market conditions.

Public and Elite Opinion

Opinion polling data suggest that American public concern over legal immigration, refugees, and illegal migration is substantial and perhaps even growing. The concerns are particularly great in certain regions of the

---

2. See Paul J. Smith, ed., *Human Smuggling: Chinese Migrant Trafficking and the Challenge to American Immigration Tradition* (Washington, D.C.: Center for Strategic and International Studies, 1997).

country and among certain social classes and ethnic groups. Generally speaking, public opinion polls since the 1960s have shown that between one-third and two-thirds of respondents would like to see the volume of legal immigration decrease, whereas less than 10 percent would like to see it increase. (The remainder indicate the numbers should stay the same or have no opinion.) Meanwhile, elite opinion is far more positive about the admission of large numbers of immigrants and refugees. All available evidence suggests that "if public opinion polls dictated U.S. immigration policy, much of the restrictionist legislation of the 1920s would have remained in place, and refugee programs would probably have never been enacted."[3] At the same time, respondents are more favorable to immigrants as individuals, and hence more positive about immigrant admissions if they are couched in terms of particular human-interest cases.[4]

Immigration issues resonate loudly in recent gubernatorial and congressional elections in California and Florida in particular, and in a 1994 California ballot referendum (known as Proposition 187) designed to change that state's policies regarding public benefits for illegal aliens. It is far too early to say whether these effects are merely temporary reactions to recession and unemployment or reflect longer-term misgivings about cultural, social, economic, and financial costs. All we can do is note that such effects have begun to register, and flag the issue for an assessment that may become more feasible years hence.

EUROPEAN AND INTERNATIONAL RESPONSES[5]

Domestic political concern over the effects of unwanted migrant and asylum flows is even greater in Europe than in the United States. Virtually every country of Western Europe has an anti-immigration political party, and the leaders of all the major parties are acutely aware of growing public opposition not only to continuing migration, but against the very presence of migrants and their children who have been living in Europe for several decades. The French are particularly concerned that growing Islamist influence in north Africa will result in an exodus to France by

---

3. Rita J. Simon, "Immigration and American Attitudes," *Public Opinion,* July–August 1987: 50.

4. The data are summarized usefully in Rita J. Simon and Susan H. Alexander, *The Ambivalent Welcome: Print Media, Public Opinion and Immigration* (Westport: Praeger, 1993), Table 3.1.

5. This section draws upon the discussion in Michael S. Teitelbaum and Myron Weiner, "Introduction: Threatened Peoples, Threatened Borders," in *Threatened Peoples, Threatened Borders: World Migration and U.S. Policy*, ed. Michael S. Teitelbaum and Myron Weiner (New York: W. W. Norton, 1995).

many secular middle-class Algerians, and by the growth of Islamic fundamentalism among Arabs presently living in France. German policy makers regard their country as a front-line state, no longer standing against Soviet tanks but against asylum seekers and illegal migrants from Eastern Europe and the successor states to the Soviet Union. There has been increasing cooperation at the European level in approaches aimed at regulating international migration movements into the European region.

It is common for political debates in some European countries (especially in Germany) to reflect denial that substantial international migration is allowed or occurring, often in the face of clear evidence to the contrary. American, Canadian, and Australian commentators increasingly have been urging their colleagues in these countries to be more open and explicit about the reality that substantial levels of immigration are taking place. But many in these countries demur, noting (sometimes politely, sometimes passionately) that they do not wish to see their societies become more like those of the United States, Canada, and Australia.

Some member states of the European Union have focused especially on legal, constitutional, and foreign policy measures designed to insulate themselves from the refugee flows that result from internal disputes and violent conflict within other countries. Germany, for example, went through the politically divisive process of amending its constitution (Basic Law), and indeed the flow of refugees and asylum seekers to Germany has markedly declined. Other Western European governments have followed a similar strategy, with the result that the refugee flows from Eastern Europe, the former Soviet Union, and the Third World have decreased. These policies are, in effect, the European equivalent of U.S. interdiction policies directed toward Haitian and Cuban migrants.

Concern about sudden and unanticipated refugee flows has also been a focus in other countries and world regions. Governments can regard refugee flows as a humanitarian issue if the refugees are going to another country, but as a security issue if the refugees are crossing their own borders. The views of the Italian government toward recent episodes of migration by Albanians across the Adriatic is but one relatively small example. Were the Baltic states, Ukraine, Georgia, Kazakhstan, or any of the other former republics of the Soviet Union to engage in "ethnic cleansing" of their Russian minorities, and were there to be a Russian military response, the United States and its European allies surely would perceive the matter in security terms. Similarly, the forcing of non-Russians out of Russia by ultranationalists would raise the prospect of internal and international conflicts within a critical region of the world of great security concern to the West.

REDUCING THE PRESSURES FAVORING DEPARTURE

In both Europe and North America, growing if sometimes naïve interest has been expressed in measures aimed not at deterring departure of migrants per se, but instead at changing the circumstances in their countries that motivate them to seek to leave. These have taken economic form (trade, investment, and aid aimed at increasing employment and wages in the sending country), and politico/military form, as in the U.S. military intervention in Haiti.

An example of the economic form is represented by the arguments emanating from proponents of the North American Free Trade Agreement (NAFTA) that its adoption would reduce unauthorized migration from one of the pivotal states, Mexico. These were largely rhetorical points, since proponents were well aware of strong evidence that any such effects could not be expected to emerge for decades. Nonetheless they indicate a political judgment by NAFTA proponents that such migration-restraining effects would be perceived as an important positive contribution of the proposed NAFTA agreement.

It is important to recognize, however, that in no cases have trade, investment, and aid policies yet been driven mainly by migration concerns. Trade policies especially are motivated by other economic and political forces, led by regions and industries that see themselves as economic beneficiaries or victims of such measures. As this is the case in the United States, so too is it true in Europe, where public alarm about migration influxes is combined with trade restrictions on exports from the countries of migrant origin, restrictions that are demanded by agricultural and industrial interest groups.

IS MIGRATION A PIVOTAL ISSUE IN THE PIVOTAL STATES?

The list of pivotal states was developed largely on criteria unrelated to international migration. To what extent, one might ask, is migration nonetheless an important issue for this set of states? Indeed, are there pivotal states in which international migration might be seen as a pivotal issue? We approach these questions in two steps: first, with brief vignettes on migration issues as they appear in each of the pivotal states; and second, in a more general discussion of the degree to which international migration may properly be linked to the pivotal states.

Migration Vignettes on Pivotal States

MEXICO   Mexico has long been a country of substantial outmigration.

Almost all emigration from Mexico flows in the direction of its northern neighbor the United States, with which Mexico shares a 3,200-kilometer border.

Mexican migration to the United States includes large numbers of both legal and illegal migrants. Mexico is at once by far the largest single source country of legal immigrants and the predominant origin country of illegal immigrants to the United States. As of 1994, approximately 17.1 million Mexican-origin people were resident in the United States, of whom about 6.3 million were born in Mexico. Of the latter group, nearly 60 percent had arrived in the fourteen years since 1980, and only 14 percent had become naturalized U.S. citizens.[6]

The above estimates are based on data derived from the U.S. Current Population Survey. More recent estimates have been developed from coordinated analyses of both U.S. and Mexican data collected by the Binational Study of migration between Mexico and the United States, sponsored by the governments of both countries:

> the total size of Mexican-born resident population in the United States in 1996 (both enumerated and unenumerated, legal and unauthorized) was 7.0–7.3 million persons. Of this population, legal residents accounted for about 4.7–4.9 million persons, about 0.5 million of whom were naturalized U.S. citizens. Unauthorized migrants accounted for 2.3–2.4 million persons.[7]

If the Binational Study estimates are roughly correct, this would mean that the total Mexico-born population numbered about 101–102 million in 1996, of which some 7 percent had taken up residence in the United States, mostly during the 1980s and 1990s. Of these, approximately one in three were resident in the United States in an unlawful or unauthorized manner. Finally, Mexican-born persons made up nearly half of the 5 million illegal migrants estimated by the U.S. Immigration and Naturalization Service to be resident in 1996 (other plausible estimates run somewhat higher).

Immigration issues, along with those of drug trafficking, have been

6. Calculated from Current Population Survey data in Alene H. Gelbard and Marion Carter, "Mexican Immigration and the U.S. Population," in *At the Crossroads: Mexico and U.S. Immigration Policy*, ed. Frank D. Bean, Rodolfo O. de la Garza, Bryan R. Roberts, and Sidney Weintraub (Lanham, Boulder, New York, London: Rowman & Littlefield, 1997), Table 4.1.
7. Mexico/United States Binational Study on Migration, *Migration between Mexico and the United States* (Mexico City and Washington, D.C.: Mexican Ministry of Foreign Affairs and U.S. Commission on Immigration Reform), 7.

a source of substantial tensions between the governments of Mexico and the United States. In recent years, there have been very large increases in resources allocated to the U.S. Border Patrol, which is deployed principally along the U.S.–Mexico border. Long-neglected border fences in urban areas such as San Diego have been reconstructed and reinforced, and substantial investments have been made in technological aids such as night scopes, seismic sensors, and computers.

Over the same period, Mexico, the United States, and Canada jointly negotiated the North American Free Trade Agreement (NAFTA), intended to accelerate trade among the three signatory countries. For this and other reasons there has also been substantial investment in enhancing the capacities of border crossing points to facilitate legal entry of both goods and persons.

In the multilateral political realm, the Mexican government has devoted very considerable efforts to migration issues. It has been the energetic leader of several efforts to frame new international conventions at the United Nations and its specialized agencies, with the declared intention of enhancing and protecting the political and economic rights of all migrant workers, both lawful and unlawful. To date such efforts have attracted the support of only a few other countries, mostly developing countries with large numbers of their workers abroad.

SOUTH AFRICA[8]   The economic prosperity of the Republic of South Africa has long been a magnet attracting migrant workers from neighboring countries in southern Africa, especially in the direction of the mining industry. Around two hundred thousand foreign workers were formally recruited to work in the gold and coal mines of South Africa each year during the 1980s. Though substantial, this represented a considerable decline in numbers from the preceding decade, even as the total number of workers employed increased. Hence the proportion of mine workers who were foreign declined markedly, from around 75 percent in the early 1970s to about 40 percent in the early 1980s. These declines were due both to decisions by South Africa to reduce its dependency on migrant workers and to restrictions on the emigration of workers imposed by some countries of origin such as Malawi and Mozambique. South Africa also received modest flows of permanent immigrants from other African countries, from Latin America, and from Asia.

8. United Nations, Commission on Population and Development, *World Population Monitoring, 1997* (New York: United Nations, draft 96-37712).

The abolition of apartheid and the change to majority rule has been accompanied by an influx of undocumented migrant workers from other poorer African countries. The wage gap between South Africa and neighboring Mozambique, for example, is estimated at 10 or 15 to 1.[9]

As with most other undocumented migration movements, no well-founded statistical evidence is available. Estimates of the undocumented population cited in the press range from 2 to 8 million, though most experts tend to favor the lower number. If true, this would mean that such migrants constitute 5 percent of South Africa's population of about 40 million. Immigration has become a hot political issue in South Africa, with black trade unions demanding more effective enforcement and public opinion polls showing majority support for such measures. The home affairs minister, Chief Mangosuthu Buthelezi, has blamed illegal immigrants for the crime wave in South Africa, which he said has reached "almost unmanageable proportions."[10] However, the governing African National Congress is divided on the issue, seeking to avoid alienating neighboring African countries that provided safe haven for its guerrillas during the struggle against apartheid. In 1994, the South African government deported ninety to a hundred thousand illegal aliens, stepped up patrols along the Zimbabwe border, turned the electric fence on the Mozambique border up to the "warning" power level, and instituted random ID checks and raids on suspected "safe houses."[11]

Recent reports suggest a dramatic increase in outmigration by South Africans with professional or technical skills, estimated to have risen by 27 percent between comparable quarters in 1995 and 1996. The increase is attributed by some observers to rising concerns about rampant violent crime and deteriorating education standards in South African cities.[12]

INDIA[13]   It may be surprising to learn that the migrant stock of India has been the second largest in the world over the past three decades, second only to that of the United States. Most, however, are persons who were born within the territory of what is now Pakistan and Bangladesh,

---

9. Judith Matloff, "Flood of Illegals Stymies a New South Africa," *Christian Science Monitor*, January 5, 1995, p. 7.
10. Christopher Munnion, "Immigrants Blamed for S. African Crimewave," *Daily Telegraph* (London), December 6, 1994, p. 15.
11. *Migration News* 2, nos. 1, 2, and 5 (1995).
12. *Migration News* 3, no. 11 (November 1996).
13. United Nations, *World Population Monitoring 1993* (New York: United Nations, 1996). (sales no. E.95.X111.8).

before the partition of British India and the secession of Bangladesh from Pakistan. (The 1981 Indian census shows 7.9 million foreign-born persons, of whom 4.2 million were born in Bangladesh and 2.7 million in Pakistan.) Although all other countries accounted for relatively small numbers of the foreign born, there have been substantial increases in persons born in Sri Lanka (from 27,000 in 1961 to 212,000 in 1981); in Burma (doubling from 62,000 in 1961 to 135,000 in 1981), and China (a tripling from 8,000 to 27,000).

Substantial unlawful migration from Bangladesh to the northeastern Indian state of Assam has been under way for the past two decades, with unofficial reports suggesting that almost 2 million Bangladeshi nationals are unlawfully resident in that state. By some estimates, 35 percent of Assam's residents are foreigners, mostly from Bangladesh. This migration has provoked considerable political violence and instability in Assam and has forced the Indian government to assert central government authority over the state. An estimated seven thousand persons have been killed in clashes between natives and immigrants since the 1980s. In 1985, the Indian Government pledged to remove all Bangladeshis who had immigrated illegally after 1971. In 1993, the Indian Election Commission struck 3 million alleged Bangladeshis from Assam's voting rolls, but an Indian court later overturned this action. Press reports in 1995 indicated that Indian authorities had begun not only to emphasize the need to reduce immigration pressures from Bangladesh, but also to push those they deemed to be illegal immigrants back across the border. In response, the Bangladesh government had ordered its troops to shoot on sight any "illegally entered foreigners" who violate its night curfew along the 4,200-kilometer border with India.[14]

Though the growth of the foreign-born population from other than Pakistan and Bangladesh might be considered related in some way to strife and persecution in origin countries, India has generally been reluctant to acknowledge the presence of "refugees" in its territory. Thus, in 1985 the country reported to the United Nations High Commission on Refugees (UNHCR) that there were only 7,200 refugees in its territory, mostly from Afghanistan. In 1991 the figure reported was still low (13,000). However, a substantial change in official perspectives apparently occurred shortly thereafter, since by 1993 the Indian Government was reporting 113,000 refugees from Sri Lanka, 80,000 from Tibet and 53,000 from Bangladesh, raising the total to 259,000.[15] Most of the new refugees

14. Sanjoy, Hazarika, "India Weighs New Approach to Immigration," *New York Times,* February 12, 1995, p. A6; "Bangladesh Orders Shoot-on-Sight to Stop 'Illegal Entry' from India," *Agence France Press,* May 28, 1995; "Bangladeshi Illegals Seek a New Life in India," *Swiss Review of World Affairs,* August 2, 1996.

15. Hania Zlotnik, United Nations, personal communication, 1996.

appearing in the statistics did not arrive in India during the 1990s but had been there earlier. In fact, Tamils from Sri Lanka had already begun returning to their country under repatriation drives organized by the government of India and the UNHCR.

India also produces substantial numbers of out-migrants. According to one estimate, some 15 million ethnic Indians are scattered around the world, with more than a million each in the United States, South Africa, and Burma, 700,000 in Canada,[16] and 800,000 in the United Kingdom.[17] In addition, during the 1980s hundreds of thousands of Indians were able to find contract employment in the booming economies of the Persian Gulf, and the hard currency remittances to their families in India constituted an important component of total foreign currency flows entering India. The political and military crises caused by the Iraqi invasion of Kuwait left many of these Indian nationals stranded in dire straits, and the Indian Government found itself forced to mobilize emergency airlifts and sea transport. Notwithstanding these reversals, remittance inflows to India in 1995 exceeded official development assistance by a substantial margin.[18]

PAKISTAN   The largest number of persons originating in Pakistan is found in neighboring India. They have been there probably since partition. More recent outmigrations have been to the Middle East and the United Kingdom. Pakistan granted over a million clearances to work abroad during 1980–1989 and granted 715,000 during 1990–1994. However, in 1995 Saudi Arabia announced plans to eliminate foreign workers from the public sector by the year 2000, and in 1996 the United Arab Emirates expelled an estimated 145,000 illegal residents from India, Pakistan, Bangladesh, the Philippines, Sri Lanka, and Iran.[19] In the United Kingdom the number of persons enumerated as born in Pakistan was 234,000 in 1991, and the number of ethnic Pakistanis was considerably higher at 477,000 residents. (The 1990 U.S. census did not list separately the number of persons born in Pakistan.) As in the case of India, foreign currency remittances from Pakistanis working abroad exceeded official development assistance provided to Pakistan in 1995.[20]

16. Rahul Jacob, "Passage from India: 15 Million Expatriates Have Made Their Mark around the Globe," *Time*, March 25, 1996.
17. Haskey, John C., "Demographic Characteristics of the Ethnic Minority Populations of Great Britain," in *Minority Populations: Genetics, Demography and Health*, ed. A. H. Bittles and D. F. Roberts, (Basingstoke, England: Macmillan, 1992), 183–184.
18. *Migration News* 3, no. 9 (September 1996).
19. *Migration News* 3, no. 11 (November 1996).
20. *Migration News* 3, no. 11.

On the receiving side, Pakistan has long provided refuge to hundreds of thousands of Afghans fleeing internal strife. Estimates vary significantly as to the numbers currently resident in Pakistan, but one respected source estimates 865,000 as of the end of 1995.[21] Surprisingly, the Karachi police reportedly estimate that up to 2 million persons in that city of 10 million are illegal aliens, mostly from Bangladesh and Burma.[22] This can hardly contribute to the country's prospects of ensuring long-term stability.

BRAZIL   There is little doubt that emigration from Brazil increased during the 1980s, but it is still small relative to the population size of the country. Comparisons between the 1981 and 1991 censuses of Brazil (the latter still unpublished) created a stir when Brazilian demographers estimated that about 1 million persons were unaccounted for, more men than women. Although some commentators attribute this gap to increased emigration from the country, it is possible that it is due in part to changes in the rate of census underenumeration.

Nontheless, data from the main receiving countries indicate that the population of Brazilian expatriates did indeed grow markedly during the 1980s, especially in Japan, the United States, and certain European countries (for example, Spain and Portugal). The 1990 U.S. census does not list the number of Brazilians separately (that is, they numbered less than 100,000); Japan had 56,000 Brazilians in 1990; the numbers in Spain and Portugal are in the same range or lower; and Italy regularized 14,000 Brazilians in 1990. There has been some mention of Brazilians migrating illegally to neighboring Bolivia or Paraguay, but as is usual for such irregular flows, no reliable numbers are available.

From within the pivotal states framework, it is worthy of note that although international migration from and to Brazil has not yet reached high levels of salience, there is widespread international interest in the large and growing internal migration of Brazilians. These movements have emanated largely from densely populated coastal areas, especially in the relatively poor northeast, and toward the land-rich and sparsely populated Amazon Basin regions. These migrations have raised concerns among environmentalists and other governments about the destruction of the Brazilian rain forest that has resulted.

INDONESIA   Indonesia was late in joining the group of countries sending workers to the Middle East, but nonetheless is the origin of a sub-

---

21. U.S. Committee for Refugees, *World Refugee Survey 1996* (Washington, D.C.: Immigration and Refugee Services of America, 1996), Table 1.

22. Hasan Jobal Jafri, "Government Claims Two Million Illegal Immigrants in Karachi," *Deutsche Presse-Agentur*, February 22, 1995.

stantial number of migrant women working as domestic workers in other Muslim countries.

Part of Indonesian territory on the island of Borneo borders the provinces of Sabah and Sarawak of Malaysia, and the booming Malaysian economy (up to 1997, at least) has attracted substantial undocumented migration of Indonesians, initially to Malaysian plantations to replace Malaysian workers attracted by higher pay in the cities. As usual, reliable data on the number of such undocumented migrants are scarce. A figure that began to be widely cited in the 1990s was 1 million. The Malaysian government has carried out several regularization programs. In 1992 this produced 320,000 applications for temporary work permits;[23] another concluded in 1995 but the number of persons applying for regularization is not known as yet.

In 1996, the Malaysia government described foreign workers as "a security threat." At the same time, Chinese-Malaysians believe that the government tolerates the influx of illegal migrants from Indonesia because it bolsters the hold on power of the Malay ethnic groups.[24] At the beginning of 1997, the Malaysian government implemented new laws and procedures and threatened to deport up to 1 million illegal migrants, of whom most are thought to have come from Indonesia.[25] The economic crises that began in late 1997 may increase political support for such measures. Moreover, in early 1998 *The Economist* magazine reported in a cover story that "Asia's most senior statesmen are issuing dark warnings about the tragedy they see emerging in [Indonesia]. . . . They fear millions of Indonesian refugees turning up on their shores. . . ."[26]

TURKEY Turkish migrants are found in nontrivial numbers in almost every Western European country. The process of Turkish labor migration began with the recruitment of Turkish workers by German employers during the late 1960s. Even today, the largest number of emigrant Turks is found in Germany (1.9 million in 1993). In addition, however, France was hosting a further 200,000; the Netherlands another 200,000; Belgium 88,000; and Switzerland, 76,000.

A key feature of Turkish migration is that it did not decline after the

23. Peter Stalker, *The Work of Strangers: A Survey of International Labour Migration* (Geneva: International Labour Office, 1994).

24. *Migration News* 3, no. 5 (May 1996).

25. "Illegal Workers Try to Flee Malaysia," *Reuters World Service,* December 29, 1996; "New Agency to Tackle Foreign-Worker Issues," *Straits Times,* December 19, 1996; "Malaysia to Begin Deporting 8,000 Illegal Foreign Workers," *Deutsche Presse-Agentur,* December 17, 1996.

26. "Asia's Coming Explosion," *The Economist,* February 21, 1998, p. 15.

halt of labor recruitment by the receiving countries around 1973–1974. Through family reunification and claims for political asylum, the Turkish population in Germany continued to increase. Between 1980 and 1993 it rose from 1.5 million to 1.9 million. In other countries (for example, Austria and Switzerland) the mechanisms allowing the population to grow may also have included the selective importation of labor. Although some return migration to Turkey occurred, that part of the migration process has not been properly quantified.

The large population of expatriate Turks resident in Western Europe has made Turkish migration a sensitive political issue for all concerned. Turkey is an active member of NATO, but its strenuous efforts to gain admission to the European Community/Union have been rebuffed repeatedly, in substantial measure due to the unwillingness of Germany and other European governments even to contemplate the free cross-border movement of Turkish workers.

Turkey was also the destination for a substantial inflow of ethnic Turks from Bulgaria during the late 1980s. On one day alone in July 1989, about 105,000 Bulgarians crossed the border into western Turkey. By August 320,000 Bulgarian Turks had moved to Turkey, although at least 65,000 returned to Bulgaria during 1990. Turkey does not report these ethnic Turks as refugees.

In 1991, Turkey refused to allow the entry of Iraqi Kurds as they sought to flee attacks by the Iraqi army. The Turkish position led to military intervention by the U.S. and other NATO forces to create "safe areas" for the Kurdish population within Iraq itself. During 1996, strife between contesting Kurdish factions produced renewed fighting in these protected areas, culminating in Iraqi military intervention and the flight of several thousand Kurds endangered by their ties to the U.S. protection force. The situation remains clouded and unstable.

ALGERIA   Whereas Turkish migrants have migrated to many countries in Europe, Algerian migrants resemble Mexicans in having only one destination country: France. The 1982 census of France enumerated 805,000 Algerians. The 1991 census enumerated 614,000, but this apparent decline is due to changes of citizenship and not to a real reduction of the population of Algerian origin in France. Moreover, it is possible that the 1982 census overestimated the number of persons of Algerian citizenship in France because some French-born children of Algerians were erroneously declared as Algerian instead of correctly as French citizens.

Data on the flow of Algerians to France are scarce and of poor quality, partly because a French-Algerian treaty exempted Algerians from French immigration controls for many years. Since political turmoil began in Algeria, French policy toward Algerian migration has become more strict, and probably fewer Algerians have been admitted as legal migrants. Algerians wishing to travel to France need a visa, and because French consulates in Algeria no longer process visas, Algerians must travel first to another country to obtain a visa.

Undocumented migration from Algeria to France allegedly has increased, but as usual there are no reliable data. Income gaps between France and Algeria are large and growing: In 1992, the per capita gross domestic product (GDP) in France was $22,260 as opposed to $1,840 in Algeria[27]—more than a 10 to 1 ratio, and roughly equivalent to the gap between the U.S. and Mexico. Moreover, there is widespread alarm in French political circles as to the migration consequences should a fundamentalist government gain power in Algeria, with predictions that several million Algerians would attempt to migrate to France. The foreign policy of the French government toward the civil strife within Algeria has been substantially affected by such concerns.

EGYPT   There is very meager information about emigration from Egypt. Many Egyptians were reported to be working in Iraq when the latter invaded Kuwait, but no reliable statistics are available. Egyptians were also well represented among the foreign workers in the Middle Eastern oil-producing countries such as Kuwait, but reliable data on their numbers also are unavailable.

Following the conclusion of the gulf war, it seems likely that Egyptian migration to Kuwait and Saudi Arabia increased. Egyptians were among those recruited to take the jobs left vacant by the hundreds of thousands of Palestinians and Yemenis who were deported as a result of perceptions that they supported the Iraqi invasion. Egyptians have also migrated to some European countries. The United Kingdom enumerated 22,000 in 1991, and they are said to be well represented among undocumented migrants in Greece, but no data on them are available. Italy regularized 20,000 in 1990.

SUMMARY AND CONCLUSIONS

Migration was not a central element among the criteria used to develop the set of pivotal states. What can now be said, after the fact, as to the utility of the concept of the pivotal states with respect to migration patterns and trends? From the perspective of U.S. foreign policy formulation, does it make sense to pay special attention to migrations that are taking

---

27. *Migration News* 2, no. 3 (March 1995).

place to and from a set of fewer than ten of 130 developing countries? At first glance, international migration is such a large and global phenomenon that affirmative responses to these questions might seem unlikely.

Yet, perhaps surprisingly, the particular set of states designated as pivotal include a surprising number for which migration phenomena turn out to be quite central issues. For some pivotal states—Mexico, for example—international migration is at or near the very top of the policy agenda, a transcendent matter that dominates the way it conducts its most important bilateral relationships. For others—South Africa, India, Pakistan, Egypt, Turkey, and Algeria—international migration issues are not so dominant but are seen as significant matters for public policy and often closely linked to matters of internal stability. For still others—Brazil, Indonesia—international migration per se is a matter of only occasional public policy significance, but internal migration is an issue of considerable international and foreign policy interest. Surprisingly enough, many of the pivotal states are at one and the same time experiencing both substantial in-migration of foreigners and substantial out-migration of their own nationals. This is true of Mexico, India, Turkey, and South Africa at least.

Many of the pivotal states also have become deeply entwined in an international market for labor, and hence their balances of payments are heavily affected by remittance income from workers overseas. Such a characterization can be applied to at least Mexico, India, Pakistan, Indonesia, Turkey, Algeria, and Egypt. These countries are therefore quite sensitive to economic and political trends in destination countries, and especially to political movements against immigration that have emerged in many of them.

Finally, in some of the pivotal states—notably Brazil and perhaps Indonesia—internal movements toward undeveloped regions has provoked substantial domestic and international concerns about consequent destruction of tropical rain forests and other environments of regional and even global interest.

To summarize: The list of countries designated as pivotal states turns out to be a set in which migration trends are widely seen as of great political and economic significance. In addition, however, there are some other countries not included among the pivotal states but for which actual or potential migration forces loom large. These include:

- China, with a exceptionally large demographic and economic potential for emigration, and already the venue of highly profitable networks of migration traffickers dominated by organized crime;
- the Philippines, a country somewhat akin to Mexico, with a long tradition of emigration for work and very substantial migrant outflows;

- the Dominican Republic, a smaller country with a substantial and long-standing outmigration, mostly to the United States;
- countries such as Haiti and Bosnia, with intractable and long-standing political and economic problems that have generated very substantial flows of outmigration;
- Russia and the former Soviet republics, characterized by varying levels of political and economic instabilities, accompanied by simmering ethnic tensions that can on occasion produce large-scale flight.

The high salience of migration questions among the pivotal states has been mirrored in many of the industrial countries that the pivotal states see as having great significance. These include the United States, Germany, France, the United Kingdom, and Australia, among others. In many of these countries, immigration is a volatile and unpredictable subject that can evoke wildly diverse reactions within their populaces, with passion and dissonance tending to overwhelm reason and consensus. At the same time, international migration serves to bring "home," in quite concrete ways, the realities of global trends from which even prosperous industrial countries may not be able to insulate themselves. Perhaps paradoxically, concerns about the potential negative implications of international migration may lead some otherwise insular voters to become less resistant to involvement by their governments in activities such as peacekeeping, overseas development assistance, and trade liberalization.

Overall, then, an assessment of the pivotal states framework through the lens of migration issues suggests that *pivotal states* is a rubric that offers real intellectual and policy potential.

PIVOTAL STATES AND THE ENVIRONMENT

Daniel C. Esty

One important dimension of a pivotal states strategy in foreign policy is the capacity to integrate "new" issues into national security analysis. In many respects, the prototypical new issue is the environment.[1] This chapter explores the linkage between U.S. foreign policy interests, environmental threats, and a pivotal states approach to setting international affairs priorities.

Three important and distinct aspects of the relationship between environmental protection and a pivotal states security strategy deserve attention. First, environmental issues affect U.S. security interests when public-health or ecological harms undermine or threaten the stability of regimes that the United States considers central to its security interests. Haiti, once known as the "Pearl of the Antilles," now suffers from such severe deforestation and soil erosion that the country cannot feed itself. The resulting political chaos, which has caused thousands of boat people to leave for the United States, is a classic example of an indirect environmental effect on U.S. national security.[2] The first part of this essay thus examines how resource- and pollution-based stresses might affect pivotal states. In looking at the range of public-health and ecological harms that could contribute to state failure, this chapter seeks to develop a better understanding of the role of the environment as a security issue.[3]

Second, some overseas environmental harms are of interest and concern because they directly affect the welfare—and in some sense, the security—of the people of the United States. Traditional national security analysts, of course, reject the notion of *environmental security* threats.

1. Richard H. Ullman, "Redefining Security," *International Security*, summer 1983: 129–153; Norman Myers, "Environment and Security," *Foreign Affairs,* spring 1989: 23–41.
2. Jessica Mathews, "Redefining Security," *Foreign Affairs,* spring 1989: 162–177.
3. Robert S. Chase, Emily B. Hill, and Paul Kennedy, "Pivotal States and U.S. Strategy," *Foreign Affairs* 75, no. 1 (January–February 1996): 33–51.

They reserve the security rubric for military and political risks to the territorial integrity of the nation. It is unlikely that invading armies will attack the United States as a result of environmental problems. But such a narrow definition of "security" misunderstands the nature of the twenty-first-century foreign policy challenge. In fact, the dictionary definition of security is "freedom from danger or risk." In this respect, environmental harms may well rise to the level of security issues in the years to come. Indeed, although they are less visible than an invading army and the harm they inflict may be slower and more subtle than that of gunfire or bombs, global environmental problems such as ozone layer depletion and climate change represent a real and not inconsequential invasion of the territorial integrity of the United States and an assault on the well-being of its citizenry.[4] The second part of this essay thus explores the range of direct environmental threats to the United States. It examines the various types of spillover harms that might be visited on U.S. citizens by: (1) activities in neighboring countries such as Mexico, Canada, or those of the Caribbean islands; and (2) global environmental harms such as ozone layer depletion and climate change as well as the loss of resources in the "global commons" such as depleted fisheries. The third dimension of the environment–pivotal states relationship involves the application of a pivotal states strategy to international environmental affairs. The third part of this essay therefore examines the hypothesis that certain nations have such size, demographic weight, and resource richness or pollution-causing potential that they should be given special focus in U.S. environmental diplomacy. The prospect of achieving successful and workable

4. The seriousness of future harms varies by issue, as does the certainty of adverse effects arising. In some cases, as with ozone layer thinning, the science is quite clear and the risks are relatively well understood. Ozone layer depletion may lead to increased cancer rates, changes in agricultural productivity, and changes in disease vectors. See Duncan Brack, *The Montreal Protocol and International Trade* (London: Chatham House, 1996). In other cases, the science is less certain, and the spectrum of potential future results is correspondingly wider. Climatic change poses a risk of more severe wind storms and rises in sea levels. See Intergovernmental Panel on Climate Change (IPCC), *Second Scientific Assessment of Climate Change* (New York: Cambridge University Press, 1995). Climate change also could have effects on rainfall patterns and result in the loss of arable land to desertification. See Joel Smith and Dennis Tirpak, "The Potential Effects of Global Climate Change on the United States," Pub. No. EPA-230-05-89-050 (Washington, D.C.: EPA, 1989). One study estimates that the costs of climate change could top $20 billion. See William R. Cline, *Global Warming: The Economic Stakes* (Washington, D.C.: Institute for International Economics, 1992). Other studies offer a more skeptical perspective about the severity of the harms that will arise and the expense of adaption to the changes that will occur. See William Nordhaus, "An Optimal Transition Path for Controlling Greenhouse Gases," *Science*, November 20, 1992; Richard Cooper, *Environment and Resource Policies for the World Economy* (Washington, D.C.: Brookings Institution, 1994).

international pollution control or resource management agreements by means of negotiation with all of the nearly two hundred countries in the world seems increasingly remote. Recent climate change and biological diversity negotiations have been hampered by the large number of parties engaged in the process.[5] The interests of the United States might be better advanced through a policy of negotiating with a smaller number of pivotal states and concentrating U.S. environmental assistance on a core set of countries that have the "capacity to affect regional and international stability" with regard to pollution and resource issues.[6]

The fourth part of this essay examines the Chase-Hill-Kennedy list of pivotal states through an environmental lens. It analyzes, in particular, the prospect that environmental factors will threaten the governmental stability of these nations. In addition, it reviews the potential for environmental spillovers from these pivotal states that will affect the United States. Finally, the importance of each of the countries on the Chase-Hill-Kennedy list is examined from an environmental diplomacy perspective. Notably, this part asks whether these are the states that must be brought together to achieve success in advancing international environmental protection.

The final part of this essay draws some conclusions about the value of the pivotal states approach to international affairs from an environmental point of view. It also assesses the value of a pivotal states priority setting as part of a framework for international environmental policy.

ENVIRONMENTAL EFFECTS ON PIVOTAL STATE STABILITY

Looking beyond the traditional politico-military threats to national security is controversial, but no longer really new. Environmental issues emerged on the foreign affairs scene with the UN–sponsored 1972 Stockholm Conference on the Human Environment. In the years that followed, a series of observers drew attention to the prospect of international conflict over environmental harms and resource tensions.[7] Some of these studies, such as the work of Gurr and that of Timberlake and Tinker,

---

5. Daniel C. Esty, "Rio Revisited: Turning the Giant's Head," *Ecodecision*, September 1993.
6. Chase, Hill, and Kennedy, "Pivotal States."
7. Lester R. Brown, *World Without Borders* (New York: Random House, 1972); Norman Myers, *Not Far Afield: U.S. Interests and the Global Environment* (Washington, D.C.: World Resources Institute, 1987); Michael Renner, "National Security: The Economic and Environmental Dimensions," Worldwatch Paper No. 8 (Washington, D.C., 1989); Lloyd Timberlake and Jon Tinker, "The Environmental Origins of Political Conflict," *Socialist Review*, November–December 1985: 57; Ted Robert Gurr, "On the Political Consequences of Scarcity and Economic Decline," *International Studies Quarterly*, March 1985: 51–75; Ullmann, "Redefining Security"; Matthews, "Redefining Security."

raised the prospect that resource scarcities and tensions would lead to traditional national security conflicts.[8] Others focused on a broader understanding of the concept of U.S. security interests. Ullman, for example, argued that national security should encompass events that threaten to "degrade the quality of life for the inhabitants of a state," or "to narrow the range of policy choices available to the government."[9] Similarly, Myers called for a new definition of security focused on the loss of arable land, access to fresh water, diminished fishery resources, and other aspects of the planetary habitat.[10] Recent scholarship has added even more careful and subtle arguments in favor of adding an environmental dimension to security. Goldstone suggests, for example, that we must not think about security issues as inherently involving military conflict but rather must develop an understanding of the concept that incorporates a variety of strands, including those related to economic and environmental policy.[11]

A number of those arguing for a broadened definition of security that includes an environmental dimension have undertaken case studies to prove their point. Myers reviews the pattern of deforestation, soil erosion, and declining food supplies in the 1960s and argues that the 1974 overthrow of Haile Selassie in Ethiopia occurred "for primarily environmental reasons."[12] In addition to the Ethiopian case study, Myers examines environmental sources of instability in the Middle East, Mexico, India, and Africa. Homer-Dixon has undertaken case studies of Bangladesh, India, Chiapas, Gaza, Pakistan, Rwanda, Senegal and Mauritania, South Africa, El Salvador, Honduras, Haiti, Peru, the Philippines, and Israel's West Bank.[13] Based on this work, Homer-Dixon and Percival argue that "scarcities of renewable resources, such as crop land, forests, and water produce civil conflict and instability."[14] They go on to suggest that environmental factors affect state stability "mainly by generating social effects, such as poverty and migrations" but conclude that "the causal linkages are

8. Timberlake and Tinker, "Environmental Origins"; Gurr, "On the Political Consequences."

9. Ullman, "Redefining Security."

10. Norman Myers, *Ultimate Security: The Environmental Basis of Political Stability* (New York: W. W. Norton, 1993).

11. Jack A. Goldstone, "Saving the Environment and Political Stability," *Environmental Change and Security Report* (Washington, D.C.: Woodrow Wilson Center, 1996), 33–34.

12. Myers, *Ultimate Security*, 60.

13. Thomas Homer-Dixon, "Project on Environment, Population, and Security: Key Findings," in *Environmental Change and Security Report* (Washington, D.C.: Woodrow Wilson Center, 1996), 45–48.

14. Thomas Homer-Dixon and Valerie Percival, "Environmental Scarcity and Violent Conflict: Briefing Book" (paper of the Project on Environment, Population, and Security, The Peace and Conflict Studies Program, Toronto, 1996) (Washington, D.C.: University of Toronto Academy of Arts and Sciences), 6.

often indirect" because environmental scarcity interacts with political, economic, and social factors.

The U.S. Central Intelligence Agency has also supported attempts to analyze rigorously the connections between regime failure and resource scarcity, population growth, pollution, and other environmental stresses.[15] This effort, involving several dozen academic experts, sought to correlate "state failures"—broadly defined to include ethnic and civil wars, as well as various forms of regime collapse—over the past forty years with hundreds of theoretically important political leadership, demographic, economic, and environmental variables. Using standard regression analysis and neural net analysis (a sophisticated pattern recognition technique), the State Failure Project identified several dozen nontraditional security variables that were highly correlated with political instability. The most robust model focused on three critical variables: the vitality of democratic institutions, the openness of the regime to international trade, and "quality of life" (best measured by infant mortality but also reflecting a number of environmental factors).

Interest in the connection between environmental degradation and national security expanded in the wake of Robert Kaplan's 1994 *Atlantic Monthly* article "The Coming Anarchy."[16] Kaplan's grim picture of life in Africa marked by violence, misery, and conflict —which he believes can be traced to environmental causes—captured the attention of political leaders at the highest levels. His conclusion that resource conflicts and environmental degradation will be the "national security issue of the early twenty-first century" has not, however, gone unchallenged.[17]

Questions about the relevance of environmental issues to national security abound. The Dabelko literature survey reviews the arguments against making environmental issues part of national security analysis.[18] Dunlap and other environmental security skeptics suggest that a narrow, military-based definition of security has ongoing utility.[19] Levy argues that claims about the importance of indirect environmental threats to U.S. security are largely unsubstantiated empirically. He further observes that the case studies conducted so far assign an arbitrarily high weight to envi-

15. Daniel C. Esty et al., *State Failure Task Force Report* (McLean, Va.: Science Applications International Corporation, 1995). Note that the State Failure Report is not based on intelligence reporting and reflects the thinking of the authors.

16. Robert D. Kaplan, "The Coming Anarchy," *Atlantic Monthly,* February 1994, 44–76.

17. Kaplan, "The Coming Anarchy," 45.

18. Geoffrey D. Dabelko and David D. Dabelko, "Environmental Security: Issues of Conflict and Redefinition," *Environmental Change and Security Report* (Washington, D.C.: Woodrow Wilson Center, 1995), 3–13.

19. Charles Dunlap, "The Origins of the Military Coup of 2012," *Parameters,* winter 1992–1993: 2.

ronmental causes of violence and governmental crises without considering whether other forces, such as political institutions, might be more
important causes of the problems identified.[20] Other skeptics, such as
Deudney, argue that the concept of environmental security establishes a
context of confrontation when cooperation is what is needed.[21] Deudney
further notes that much of the debate about environmental security has
been muddled.[22] And Finger suggests that the use of the term *security* is
simply a bureaucratic strategy for extracting greater funding for environmental policies.[23]

While the debate rages over the wisdom of broadening the concept of
security to include environmental variables, the fact that ecological and
public-health harms can contribute to state failures and security tensions
that affect the United States cannot be doubted.[24] Some of the Chase-
Hill-Kennedy pivotal states face particular environmental challenges.
Although these challenges may not directly affect the stability of governments, the indirect effects of pollution and resource problems may be
substantial. In particular, when environmental stress arises in conjunction
with population pressures and demographic strains (significant unemployment, high degrees of inequality of access to resources, and so on),
the combination may result in social and political crises that translate into
regime instability—and thus quite traditional national security problems.

Mexico

Political instability arising from environmental causes has certainly
affected Mexico. With a population that has grown from 67 million in
1980 to 89 million today, Mexico's land and water resources are under
considerable demand pressures.[25] Although the total fertility rate has
dropped from 4.5 percent in 1980 to 3.2 percent in 1996, the addition
of tens of millions of new mouths to feed has put considerable stress on

20. Marc A. Levy, "Is the Environment a National Security Issue?" *International Security* 20,
    no. 3 (winter 1995–1996): 35–62.
21. Daniel Deudney, "The Case Against Linking Environmental Degradation and National
    Security," *Millennium,* winter 1990: 461–476.
22. Daniel Deudney, "Environment and Security: Muddled Thinking," *Bulletin of Atomic
    Scientists,* April 1991: 22–28.
23. Matthias Finger, "The Military, the Nation State and the Environment," *The Ecologist,*
    September 1991: 220–225.
24. Indeed, some of the sharpest critics of making the environment a *security* issue recognize
    the potential for significant environmental effect on the welfare of the United States.
    Daniel Deudney argues, for instance, that environmental harms are best understood as
    global problems that go beyond conceptions of national security. See Daniel Deudney,
    "The Case against Linking," 461.
25. World Bank, *World Development Report 1996* (New York, 1996).

Mexico's food supply.[26] Dry to begin with, Mexico has suffered from considerable desertification over the last several decades. Thousands of acres of farmland have been swallowed up by spreading deserts.[27] The growing population also has increased the strain on water resources that are already subject to salinization and pollution.[28] In the last twenty-five years, Mexico's supply of crop land has increased considerably, but much of this new agricultural land is of marginal quality. Moreover, yields on this land have fallen steeply in recent years due to overuse.

Mexico's basic demographic pressures are exacerbated in some areas by unstructured development and urbanization. Along the U.S.–Mexico border, for example, basic air and water pollution have become critical problems. The 1992 Border Plan developed by the U.S. Environmental Protection Agency and its counterpart in Mexico (then called SEDUE) chronicles a range of environmental threats to public health and ecological vitality.[29]

The accumulation of air, water, waste, and land use problems is of great concern to the Mexican public. Recent opinion polls have suggested that Mexicans rank their deteriorating environment as a very serious problem, second only to crime in most studies. The government has responded to the public's environmental concerns with reforestation plans and major funding commitments to environmental infrastructure projects. Nevertheless, environmentally induced social strains continue to threaten the government. For the last several years, the government has been threatened by insurgents based in Chiapas, one of the most environmentally degraded parts of the country. The Chiapas population has been growing at a 3.6 percent annual rate, rising from 1.6 million in 1970 to nearly 4 million in 1996.[30] The population growth rate among the indigenous population is even more dramatic, rising 4.6 percent per year.[31] Food and water supplies are falling increasingly short. The amount of cultivated land in Chiapas has grown over the last twenty years but not at a rate that keeps pace with the rising population. Per capita cultivated land therefore has fallen sharply.[32]

The resource strain in Chiapas has been exacerbated by a variety of fac-

26. World Bank, *World Development Report 1996.*

27. Norman Myers, "Environment and Security," *Foreign Affairs*, spring 1989: 36.

28. Robert Farvolden, "Water Crisis: Inevitable or Preventable?" *Geotimes*, July 1990: 4.

29. Environmental Protection Agency (EPA), "Integrated Environmental Plan for the Mexican–U.S. Border Area" (Washington, D.C., 1992).

30. Philip Howard and Thomas Homer-Dixon, "Environmental Scarcity and Violent Conflict: The Case of Chiapas, Mexico" (paper of the Project on Environment, Population and Security, The Peace and Conflict Studies Program, Toronto, 1995).

31. Howard and Homer-Dixon, "Environmental Scarcity," 4.

32. Howard and Homer-Dixon, "Environmental Scarcity," 7.

tors, both natural and humanmade. In 1983, the Chicon volcano in the northern central highlands displaced thousands of people and disrupted farming in many areas. Hydroelectric projects flooded other farmlands, particularly in the Grijalva Basin.[33] In addition, the past practice of cutting down forests to create new cropland is reaching its limit as nearly every potentially cultivable acre has been pressed into agricultural service.

Land degradation, especially from agricultural practices such as overgrazing, has sharply reduced the capacity of many of the inhabitants of Chiapas to sustain themselves. Deforestation has also contributed to significant soil erosion. Much of the tree cutting has occurred in the highlands where soils are on steep grades and so particularly vulnerable to erosion. The loss of soil cover has reduced topsoil depth, the diversity of soil biota, and the capacity of the land to filter and hold water.[34] The increased pressures on the land have been aggravated by what Howard and Homer-Dixon call "structural scarcity." In particular, they cite the concentrated nature of land ownership in Chiapas and the marginal subsistence agriculture it imposes on many people as sources of further environmental stress that has erupted in violence.[35]

It is impossible to determine whether the political strains that have emerged in Chiapas would have arisen under other environmental circumstances. Nevertheless, environmental factors clearly seem to have contributed to political instability in the region. More broadly, Mexico appears vulnerable to social strains brought on by the pressures of population growth and intensified land use. To avert food and water shortages, Mexico's leadership seems to be betting on industrial growth and expanded trade to generate resources to permit the country to import food and to invest in improved water supply systems and other environmental infrastructure projects. Given Mexico's proximity, environmental stress there has particularly direct impacts on the United States. Indeed, in the last decade, millions of Mexicans have fled across the border in search of better jobs and life prospects. Despite many contributions to American life, these migrants can also be seen as a strain on social services, public tolerance, and political will across the United States.

Egypt

Like Mexico, Egypt has a rapidly growing population and a series of resource constraints that may prove destabilizing. Egypt's population has

33. Howard and Homer-Dixon, "Environmental Scarcity," 8.
34. Howard and Homer-Dixon, "Environmental Scarcity," 10.
35. Howard and Homer-Dixon, "Environmental Scarcity," 13–15.

grown from 41 million fifteen years ago to 57 million today.[36] Although the nation was once self-sufficient in food production, it now imports millions of tons of grain.[37]

Egypt would be environmentally challenged under the best of circumstances. Within a desert setting, the nation has only about 4,000 arable hectares lying in a thin strip on either side of the Nile River. In recent years, some expansion of the food supply has been achieved through expanded irrigation. But in other parts of the country, salinization of agricultural land has occurred because of an inadequate supply of fresh water.[38] In 1996, Egypt announced plans for a $223 million canal designed to bring water to the country's arid Western Desert. This new project, which will divert water from the Nile River, may hold the key to Egypt's prospects for feeding its burgeoning urban population.[39]

Water disputes in the Middle East are, of course, legendary. In 1980, President Anwar Sadat threatened Ethiopia with war if it tried to divert the waters of the Blue Nile.[40] The Western Desert Canal may well create new security tensions, especially since Egypt remains vulnerable to water claims from upriver nations including Sudan, Uganda, Kenya, Tanzania, Zaire, Rwanda, Burundi, and Ethiopia.[41] Water shortages in Egypt, moreover, affect not only food production but also the power-generating capacity at the Aswan Dam.

Egypt and Sudan have a Nile River water-allocation agreement in place, but Sudan is agitating for a larger allotment, arguing that its current share is insufficient to meet anticipated needs. Ethiopia, the source of the Nile (and not a party to the Sudan-Egypt water-sharing agreement), has recently begun to demand its "rightful" portion of the Nile.[42] In 1996, Sudan charged that Ethiopia was sponsoring Sudanese opposition forces as part of a scheme to deprive Sudan and Egypt of the waters of the Nile.[43] Ethiopia denied the charges, but the incident illustrates the depth of tensions over shared resources in this region.

In addition to significant regional environmental problems, Egypt is also especially vulnerable to global environmental harms. If the more serious predictions for climate change prove correct, Egypt may suffer

36. World Bank, *World Development Report 1996*.
37. Myers, "Environment and Security."
38. Howard and Homer-Dixon, "Environmental Scarcity," 30.
39. "Nile States Look to New Division of Water," *Financial Times*, February 27, 1997, p. 3.
40. Peter H. Gleick, "Environment and Security: The Clear Connections," *Bulletin of the Atomic Scientists,* April 1991: 16–21.
41. Myers, "Environment and Security."
42. Howard and Homer-Dixon, "Environmental Scarcity."
43. "Egypt Calls for Cooperation Between Nile States," Reuters World Service, February 25, 1997.

some of the gravest consequences of any country in the world. In particular, it is likely to see changes in rainfall and water flow patterns that will further reduce its capacity to produce food.[44] Already facing pressure from Islamic extremists, the Mubarak regime could come unglued under these environmentally derived demographic strains.

India

Nowhere are the pressures of population and the related environmental stresses more evident than in India. Although the inevitability of mass death from starvation that Paul Ehrlich predicted in *The Population Bomb* has not come to pass, India's rapid population growth has created serious and potentially destabilizing demographic and environmental stress.[45] In fact, India stands out as a veritable model of the interplay of economic and ecological pressures. These strains, of course, are not new. A generation ago, the Second India Study, sponsored by the Ford Foundation, predicted crises for India in the provision of fresh water, sanitation, and other basic environmental services to its growing urban population. Although disaster has been largely averted, these demands remain pressing.

Nevertheless, in many parts of India, the number of people living below the poverty line has decreased over the past several decades.[46] Although the amount of agricultural land per person has fallen steadily, India's green revolution increased agricultural yields per acre and has therefore achieved somewhat of an improved picture with regard to food supply. Thus, although the population growth rate in 1990 is 2.1 percent—down only a bit from the 2.2 percent level of 1970—resource and environmental crises have not led to massive political instability as some predicted.

In important respects, however, India's environment has deteriorated and resource strains remain a potential tinderbox for political instability. Much of India's irrigation system is silting up because of deforestation in upland areas. Millions of acres of farmland have become flooded or salinized because of improper irrigation practice,[47] and water tables in many parts of the country are falling. Along the coast, salt water is penetrating aquifers, increasing the number of Indians who do not have adequate fresh water supplies.[48]

44. J. Broadus, "Possible Impacts of and Adjustments to Sea Level Rise: The Cases of Bangladesh and Egypt," *Woods Hole Oceanographic Contribution No. 7147* (Woods Hole, Mass., 1990).

45. Paul R. Ehrlich, *The Population Bomb* (New York: Ballantine Books, 1968).

46. Robert Repetto, *The Second India Revisited: Population, Poverty, and Environmental Stress over Two Decades* (Washington, D.C.: World Resources Institute, 1994).

47. Repetto, *The Second India Revisited.*

48. Repetto, *The Second India Revisited,* 6.

Deforestation and devegetation, estimated at 330,000 hectares per year, undermine the quality of life in many parts of rural India. Overharvesting of wood for fuel and overgrazing of livestock have led to soil erosion on a massive scale.[49] Land conversion threatens not only subsistence agriculture but also India's once abundant biodiversity. Deforestation in the Himalayas has resulted in downriver silting and rising riverbed levels. This, in turn, expands floodplains and increases the number of areas vulnerable to floods. Even if India's environmental degradation does not lead directly to security problems, the stress imposed on hundreds of millions of already impoverished people could become a flashpoint for unrest that might have an impact on regional security.

In addition to local environmental issues such as deforestation, falling water tables, and exposure to air and water pollution, India appears especially vulnerable to global environmental problems such as climate change.[50] A small rise in sea levels would affect millions of Indians, and could also displace tens of millions of people living in flood-prone Bangladesh, possibly creating a refugee crisis in India.[51] In fact, it is estimated that nearly 20 million Bengali refugees and migrants already live in India, having fled their native land because of floods and food shortages.[52] Climate change could increase the weight of India's burden.

Pakistan

Like India, Pakistan has experienced rapid population increases over the last generation. At the current annual growth rate of 3.1 percent, Pakistan's population will double in just over twenty years.[53] Pakistan's population growth means that limited resources must be stretched further. And although Pakistan has averted food crises over the last several decades by adding new agricultural land, crop land per capita is now falling rapidly.[54]

Pakistan's stability is threatened not only by the increased demand for resources by its growing population but also by the degradation of land, water, and other critical resources. Gizewski and Homer-Dixon identify

49. H. E. Dregne, "Erosion and Soil Productivity in Asia," *Journal of Soil and Water Conservation*, January–February 1992: 8–13.
50. Kurt Kleiner, "Climate Change Threatens Southern Asia," *New Scientist*, August 27, 1994.
51. Thomas Homer-Dixon, Jeffrey Boutwell, and George Rathjens, "Environmental Change and Violent Conflict," *Scientific American*, February 1993: 38–45.
52. Homer-Dixon, "Project on Environment," 15.
53. Peter Gizewski and Thomas Homer-Dixon, "Environmental Scarcity and Violent Conflict: The Case of Pakistan" (paper of the Project on Environment, Population and Security, The Peace and Conflict Studies Program, Toronto, 1996).
54. Gizewski and Homer-Dixon, "Environmental Scarcity: Pakistan."

a number of reasons for falling agricultural productivity in Pakistan: water and wind erosion, salinization, waterlogging, flooding, and loss of organic material.[55] Pakistan faces critical water quality and quantity problems as well. Naturally arid, the country must irrigate 65 percent of its agricultural land. Lack of rain or poor water management translate quickly into surface water shortfalls and then into food shortages. Pakistan has also seen the water levels in its underground aquifers falling sharply.[56] In addition to irrigation and drinking water shortages, water supply problems have also resulted in hydroelectric power generation problems.

The Indus River represents a particular focus of the water resource tensions. Shared among four Pakistani states as well as with India, the Indus and its tributaries are under constant pressure from increased demands for water. To alleviate this source of security stress, the waters of the Indus are today physically divided so that India and Pakistan each get a guaranteed share of the water.

Like its neighbors, Pakistan has suffered from severe deforestation over the past century. Forest cover has fallen from 14 percent of the land area seventy-five years ago to about 5 percent today.[57] The demand for timber for building and fuel wood, as well as the pressure to clear forests for the purposes of establishing new agricultural and grazing lands, has put natural habitats under strain across the country. The high levels of deforestation translate into serious soil erosion, sedimentation, and desertification problems in many upland areas and the siltification of downriver water bodies. The once significant Warsak Reservoir, for example, is now nearly useless because of the buildup of silt.[58]

In addition to demand and supply pressures, Pakistan's environment and resource picture is made worse by what Homer-Dixon calls structural scarcities.[59] In particular, the economic domination of the country by a small elite and the privileged position of the military have resulted in a small number of people controlling most of the land and other resources. The result has been the economic and ecological marginalization of the great masses.[60] A tradition of corruption exacerbates this problem.

Pakistan has witnessed considerable unrest and political instability over the last several years. Although the troubles cannot be blamed directly on environmental problems, resource and ecological difficulties certainly

55. Gizewski and Homer-Dixon, "Environmental Scarcity: Pakistan," 12-13.
56. Gizewski and Homer-Dixon, "Environmental Scarcity: Pakistan," 14.
57. Gizewski and Homer-Dixon, "Environmental Scarcity: Pakistan," 15.
58. Gizewski and Homer-Dixon, "Environmental Scarcity: Pakistan," 1.
59. Homer-Dixon, "Project on Environment."
60. Gizewski and Homer-Dixon, "Environmental Scarcity: Pakistan," 17.

contribute to the underlying social tensions, and worsening environmental conditions could lead to more serious future troubles. Its proximity to other population-challenged and resource-constrained nations such as India marks Pakistan as a particularly significant security problem. Pakistan's role as a regional environmental "hot spot" that could quickly ignite conflicts across borders gives the country a pivotal position in South Asian regional stability.

Other Pivotal States and the Environment

Environmental issues and resource conflicts are a potential source of political strain in a number of the other pivotal states identified by Chase, Hill, and Kennedy. Brazil, for example, continues to face questions not only about the development of the Amazon but also about the severe public-health issues created by the high degree of pollution in São Paulo and its other cities. Similarly, Indonesia's development prospects are sharply defined and constrained by the rate and form of natural resource exploitation. Unrest has broken out in response to environmental degradation at the massive gold mine run by the New Orleans–based Freeport McMoRan in Irian Jaya.[61] Some analysts have also concluded that the unsustainable rate at which Indonesia's forests have been cut would actually, if properly accounted for, leave the country with a negative growth rate in recent years.[62] More dramatically, smoke from Indonesian forest fires (deliberately set to clear and enrich the land) choked much of Southeast Asia for months in 1997—causing severe respiratory problems in Indonesia and several nearby countries and leading to serious political friction within Indonesia and between Indonesia and its downwind neighbors. The ongoing political unrest in the Middle East is exacerbated by the existence of a number of shared vital resources. Water rights in the Jordan and the Euphrates River basins, for example, are a source of endless jockeying.[63] Turkey's dams on the Euphrates have created tension.[64] Of course, in all of these cases, it is not clear whether environmental factors are playing a driving role or whether poor societies and poorly governed countries face crises for other reasons, and environmental problems are just a manifestation of these other issues.

61. Eyal Press, "Jim Bob's Indonesian Misadventure: a U.S. Mining Company Clashes with Indigenous Peoples," *Progressive*, June 1996: 32–35.
62. Robert Repetto et al., *Wasting Assets: Natural Resources in the National Income Accounts*, (Washington, D.C.: World Resources Institute, 1989).
63. Miriam R. Lowi, "Rivers of Conflict, Rivers of Peace," *Journal of International Affairs*, summer 1995: 123–144.
64. "Drip-Feed from the Euphrates," *Middle East*, September 1992: 32.

DIRECT ENVIRONMENTAL SPILLOVERS

Some environmental problems threaten the United States not because of their potential for causing political instability in other countries, but rather because they risk spilling over onto the United States. In analyzing these threats, it is useful to distinguish between harms from neighbors that might be considered *regional* and global environmental problems.

Regional pollution spillovers include Canadian toxic emissions into the Great Lakes, Mexican air pollution along the Texas and California borders, and marine resource issues with our Caribbean neighbors. Of course, the flow of harms in these circumstances is not necessarily one way. Canada has long complained about acid rain from sulfur dioxide emitted by power plants in the American Midwest, and Mexico has expressed concerns about toxic waste shipped across the border from the United States for disposal in Mexico. Likewise, a number of Caribbean islands have argued that the United States underattends to the environmental impacts of shipping (for example, tankers spilling oil or wastes at sea), which can have a devastating effect on tourism.

From a traditional international relations point of view, these relatively "local" environmental effects do not rise to the level of a security issue. Who can imagine the United States going to war over transboundary pollution?[65] To the extent, however, that management of foreign affairs today requires consideration of an array of issues beyond traditional and narrow politico-military concerns, environmental harms affecting the quality of life in the United States do matter.

The threat to territorial integrity becomes more vivid in the context of global environmental problems such as climate change and ozone layer depletion. Emissions from one country inevitably spill across borders and, in some cases, blanket the earth; these inherently worldwide problems demonstrate the ecological interdependence of the planet.[66] It is impossible physically to protect one's borders against such invasions. Even, for example, if the United States stops all of its releases of chlorofluorocarbons (CFCs) and other chemicals that harm the earth's protective ozone layer, but other countries fail to follow suit and end

---

65. But note that Canada has fired on Spanish fishing vessels in the Atlantic in a dispute over depleted fisheries. So the slide from environment and resource issues to armed conflict may not be that far.

66. Daniel C. Esty, "Environment and Security: Borders and the Biosphere," in *The Convergence of US National Security and the Global Environment*, ed. Dick Clark (Washington, D.C.: Aspen Institute, 1996).

their releases of CFCs, the ozone layer will still thin, cancer rates will rise, and thousands of Americans will die as a result.[67] Although these deaths may not be as dramatic as those suffered in wartime, they are just as real.

Climate change represents the most potentially serious global environmental challenge.[68] The full dimensions of this threat—especially the size, timing, and regional distribution of the anticipated global warming and other effects[69]—are not yet clear, but the levels of carbon dioxide and other greenhouse gases in the atmosphere have been rising steadily since the dawn of the industrial age. If, however, climate change harms emerge toward the greater end of the scale of current predictions, the economic impacts could amount to 20 percent of world gross domestic product (GDP).[70] Economic disruption of this magnitude might convince even the most dogged environmental security skeptics of the need to think about ecological harms in a security context.

For the purpose of fashioning a response to global environmental issues, certain countries are unequivocally more important than others. Pivotalness in the environmental domain turns on a number of factors. Some countries require attention because of their demographic heft. No solution to the problem of climate change can be achieved, for example, without the cooperation of China and India.[71] Because the growth in emissions rather than the current level of greenhouse gases will likely spur climatic changes, the policy challenge can be viewed as a matter of controlling emissions from the developing world where most of the growth is occurring. Indeed, the United States, Europe, Japan, and most other Organization for Economic Cooperation and Development (OECD) countries have had nearly stable greenhouse gas emissions over the past twenty-five years. In the developing world, however, greenhouse gas emissions—which are closely tied to energy consumption and thus to

67. Brack, *The Montreal Protocol*.
68. One of the effects of a buildup of greenhouse gases in the atmosphere is "global warming." We now know that other impacts such as more severe windstorms and changes in rainfall patterns may be even more significant than temperature increases. Hence, the term *climate change* rather than "global warming." IPCC, *Second Scientific Assessment*.
69. Intergovernmental Panel on Climate Change (IPCC), *Scientific Assessment of Climate Change* (New York, 1990); IPCC, *Second Scientific Assessment*.
70. Cline, *Global Warming*.
71. Chase, Hill, and Kennedy exclude China and Russia from their list of pivotal states, noting that these two countries must be U.S. foreign policy priorities and that their analysis is meant to help discriminate among the next tier of nations that might arguably be important to U.S. security.

economic growth—are rising rapidly.[72] Developing countries already contribute more than 45 percent of current worldwide emissions of greenhouse gases.[73] China, now the number two emitter behind the United States, will become the largest source of greenhouse gas emissions in the world early in the next century.[74] And if India's economic growth continues on its current track, it too will be a leading producer of greenhouse gases by the middle of the next century.

Other countries are pivotal in the environmental context because of their particular natural endowments. Brazil, for example, is home to one of every five trees on the planet. Deforestation in Brazil, therefore, has significant global impacts. Perhaps more important, when the land is cleared by burning the trees, massive amounts of carbon dioxide are released. It has been estimated that the burning forests of the Brazilian Amazon could raise the global total of CO_2 emissions by 20 percent.[75] This would be a significant step toward the doubling of greenhouse gas levels that climate scientists believe might induce harmful changes in global temperatures, sea levels, the frequency and severity of windstorms, and rainfall patterns.

Similarly, China and India are environmentally pivotal because they sit on vast supplies of coal. All fossil fuels emit greenhouse gases, but coal produces the largest amount of carbon dioxide per unit of energy produced. Thus, whether and how countries exploit their coal reserves dramatically affects climate change scenarios. A shift in energy consumption away from coal to less carbon-intensive natural gas could produce significant reductions in the world's greenhouse gas trajectory. In this regard, countries that are rich in natural gas, such as Russia, are also pivotal states.

Nations may also be pivotal because of their "positive" environmental spillovers. Brazil's Amazonian and coastal rain forests, for instance,

72. Of course, those in the developing world will argue that there is no reason to "grandfather" the large base of emissions that currently come from the OECD countries. As the Malaysian prime minister, Mahathir bin Mohamad, frequently notes, the industrialized world has gotten wealthy through economic activities that have caused much of the past pollution, and it is now the developing countries' turn to pollute and grow. Mahathir expresses further outrage at the suggestion that the developing world limit its emissions when the developed countries, especially the United States, do nothing to address their resource-intensive, consumption-oriented life-styles. Mahathir bin Mohamad, Honorable Dr. Datuk Seri (prime minister of Malaysia), speech at the U.N. Conference on Environment and Development (Rio de Janeiro, June 13, 1992).

73. World Bank, *World Development Report 1992* (New York, 1992).

74. Daniel C. Esty, D. Rosen, and S. Dunn, "A Difficult Position: China, Climate Change, and Joint Implementation," *China Review*, summer 1996: 16–17.

75. Philip Fearnside, "Environmental Destruction in the Brazilian Amazon," in *The Future of Amazonia,* ed. David Goodman and Anthony Hall (Basingstoke: Macmillan, 1990).

are a huge "sink" that absorbs carbon dioxide and reduces the risk of climate change. Maintaining Brazil's forests is therefore of interest to the world community, not only because clearing there would generate additional carbon dioxide emissions, but also because the standing trees "sequester" carbon. In addition, the Brazilian rain forest is an enormous storehouse of biological diversity with potentially important medicinal and other resources. More than half the species known to exist on the planet live in tropical forests.[76] Although they provide carbon sequestration and biodiversity protection services to the world, Brazil and other forested countries are not currently compensated for their positive externalities.

From an environmental perspective, countries may be pivotal not only because of their demographic heft or special resource endowments, but also because of their rogue behavior. Iraq's intentional release of oil into the Arabian Sea during the Gulf War shows how an environmentally badly behaved country can inflict devastating ecological harms on others. The continued use of inherently unstable nuclear reactors in Russia and other parts of the former Soviet empire, which creates the risk of another Chernobyl-type nuclear accident, might similarly pose a threat to the safety and well-being of the United States and its allies. Russia's failure to abide by the Montreal Protocol's phaseout of chlorofluorocarbons (CFCs), thereby undermining global efforts to protect the ozone layer, is another example of a global environmental risk created by an out-of-control state.[77]

A final category of environmental spillovers deserves brief mention. Notably, some countries may strategically choose to carry out their environmental policies in ways that grossly underattend to *localized* pollution harms. Although the inadequate domestic air and water pollution or toxic waste management programs of others may not seem to be a threat to the United States because there is no physical spillover, the competitive advantage gained by industries operating in these low-standards jurisdictions may have consequences for U.S. industry. In particular, in an increasingly globalized marketplace, how other countries handle their local environmental problems will affect the relative competitiveness of U.S. companies. Alternatively, the prospect of having to compete with companies in other jurisdictions where environmental costs are lower may lead U.S. companies to lobby for less strict standards or enforcement

76. John Terborgh, *Diversity and the Tropical Rain Forest* (New York: Scientific American Library, 1992).
77. Brack, *The Montreal Protocol.*

in the United States—which could result in suboptimal domestic environmental policies.[78]

A major political and academic debate rages over the seriousness of this potential race to the bottom.[79] Economists argue that lower standards reflect differences in developmental or environmental circumstances between the United States and other countries, and consequently any competitive disadvantage that U.S. companies face is not unfair but simply a product of naturally varying competitive advantages.[80] A number of other observers have noted, however, that where low standards represent the decision by a nation's political or business elite to subject its citizenry to environmental conditions that they have not and would not have chosen, the competitive advantage obtained might well be viewed as an inappropriate subsidy and a threat to U.S. economic interests, especially the existence of a fair and open world trading system.[81]

78. In the context of the NAFTA debate, Ross Perot raised the prospect, for example, of a "giant sucking sound" as U.S. factories moved to Mexico to take advantage of lower environmental standards and thus lower production costs. Empirical studies suggest that such industrial migration occurs only rarely. Patrick Low and Alexander Yeats, "Do Dirty Industries Migrate?" in *International Trade and the Environment*, ed. Patrick Low (Washington, D.C.: World Bank, 1992); Adam Jaffe, Steven Peterson, Paul Portney, and Robert Stavins, *Environmental Regulation and International Competitiveness: What Does the Evidence Tell Us?* Resources for the Future Discussion paper 94-08 (Washington, D.C.: RFF, 1994). But critics argue that what matters is not what happens to industry but rather the effect on environmental policy making. In this regard, there is strong evidence, albeit anecdotal, that all governments set their environmental standards with an eye on competitiveness impacts. Daniel C. Esty, *Greening the GATT: Trade, Environment, and the Future* (Washington, D.C.: Institute for International Economics, 1994); Alvin Klevorick, "Reflections on the Race to the Bottom," in *Fair Trade and Harmonization*, ed. Jagdish Bhagwati and Robert Hudec (Cambridge, Mass.: MIT Press, 1996).

79. Wallace Oates and Robert Schwab, "Economic Competition among Jurisdictions: Efficiency Enhancing or Distortion Inducing?" *Journal of Public Economy 35* (April 1988): 333; Richard Revesz, "Rehabilitating Interstate Competition: Rethinking the 'Race-to-the-Bottom' Rationale for Federal Environmental Regulation," *New York University Law Review*, December 1992: 1210–1254; Daniel C. Esty, "Revitalizing Environmental Federalism," *Michigan Law Review* 95, no. 3 (1996): 570–653. Ultimately, whether a regulatory "race toward the bottom" is likely, and thus whether policy makers are justified in varying standards depending on what competing jurisdictions are doing, depends on the specific policy making context.

80. Jagdish Bhagwati and T. N. Srinivasan, "Trade and Environment: Does Environmental Diversity Detract from the Case for Free Trade?" in *Fair Trade and Harmonization: Prerequisites to Free Trade*, ed. Jagdish Bhagwati and Robert Hudec (Cambridge, Mass.: MIT Press, 1996).

81. Richard Stewart, "Environmental Regulation and International Competitiveness," *Yale Law Journal*, June 1993: 2039.

PIVOTALNESS AND INTERNATIONAL ENVIRONMENTAL POLICY

The pivotal states strategy may have application as a framework for constructing an optimal international environmental policy for the United States. Negotiating international and environmental agreements is never easy,[82] especially when trying to work through the complexities of a problem such as climate change with over 190 nations at the bargaining table.[83] Identifying a subset of pivotal states—regional leaders—as a focus for U.S. environmental diplomacy therefore makes considerable practical sense.

The Chase-Hill-Kennedy approach to pivotal states could be interpreted as trying to identify a comprehensive list of countries that are more important to the United States than the rest in the security context.[84] But in the environmental domain, a floating set of pivotal states, varying by issue and evolving over time, seems more likely to produce a viable policy framework. For example, with respect to nuclear safety, Ukraine and the Baltic states are even more important than Russia. Moreover, the pivotal environmental states with which the United States needs to work might well be different from those identified from a traditional national security point of view.[85]

As noted before, pivotalness in international environmental negotiations will arise from a variety of circumstances. Countries with demographic heft cannot be ignored. In addition to China and India, countries with large populations such as Indonesia, Brazil, Pakistan, and Nigeria will likely be key participants in negotiations. Nations with particular resource endowments central to the issue at hand may also be pivotal. With respect to climate change, one cannot imagine a successful negoti-

82. Richard Gardner, *Negotiating Survival: Four Priorities After Rio* (New York: Council on Foreign Relations, 1992); Peter Haas, Robert Keohane, and Marc Levy, *Institutions for the Earth: Sources of Effective International Environmental Protection* (Cambridge, Mass.: MIT Press, 1993); Lawrence Susskind, *Environmental Diplomacy: Negotiating More Effective Global Agreements* (New York: Oxford University Press, 1994).

83. Daniel Bodansky, "The United Nations Framework Convention on Climate Change: A Commentary," *Yale Journal of International Law* 18 (summer 1993): 451.

84. Chase, Hill, and Kennedy seek to avoid this critique and to indicate that the list of pivotal states will change over time. See also Howard and Homer-Dixon, "Environmental Scarcity."

85. Even within the "environmental" category, the critical nations on any particular issue might vary. For example, if the issue is climate change, then the demographic heft of India and China and the resource endowments of Russia and Brazil make them central players. If, however, the focus is on fisheries, then another set of countries, perhaps including Taiwan and Korea but not Russia and Brazil, might be central to an agreement.

ation that does not reflect the interests of Brazil, China, and Russia. Undoubtedly, successful environmental negotiations must also include all of the world's major economic powers. Thus, any "executive committee" convened to advance on an international environmental agreement should include Japan and the European Union.[86]

One of the central arguments of the pivotal states theory is that certain countries act as regional leaders or "first dominoes." Interestingly, only some of the Chase-Hill-Kennedy pivotal states perform this role in the environmental domain. Latin American countries have long looked to Mexico as a spokesperson in international environmental negotiations. Brazil has also played a very important role in a number of international environmental agreements. In other parts of the world, however, the regional leaders are not the Chase-Hill-Kennedy pivotal states. Indonesia, for example, has played a relatively modest role in international environmental affairs. Although it lacks the large population and broad resource base of a number of its neighbors, the Southeast Asia leadership role has actually been seized by Malaysia. Malaysia's pivotal position clearly reflects, in part, the personal qualities and leadership of Prime Minister Mahathir bin Mohamad. Though circumstances may change, if one wants today to make progress on international environmental issues over the next few years, Malaysia must be included on the list of key players.

In Africa, neither Algeria nor Egypt has played a particularly central role in recent international environmental negotiations. Nevertheless, in constructing a set of states considered pivotal for their trendsetting and leadership potential, either Egypt or Algeria should be included because of their capacity to influence others in the Arab world. In sub-Saharan Africa, South Africa plays a regional leadership role, but one might also conclude that Nigeria is a more likely domino and better represents this part of the world.

For the purpose of environmental diplomacy, issue-specific considerations must be taken into account in choosing pivotal states. On wildlife protection, for instance, Kenya is an essential player. Likewise, the particularly significant impact of global-warming-induced sea level rise on low-lying countries and island states would argue for including an activist island nation on the list of countries to which extra attention would be devoted in the climate change context.

---

86. The Chase-Hill-Kennedy discussion of pivotal states takes for granted that Europe, Japan, China, and Russia will be U.S. international affairs priorities. However, in applying the pivotal states model to environmental affairs per se, it seems useful to reiterate the central role that these countries must play to any successful negotiation. Indeed, Russia and China are, in many respects, *the* pivotal states.

PIVOTAL STATES FROM AN ENVIRONMENTAL PERSPECTIVE

This chapter has identified three critical connections between environmental policy and a pivotal states approach to international affairs: (1) the prospect that environmental and resource problems will spill over into political instability in states deemed pivotal for other reasons; (2) the need to deem certain countries pivotal because of their potential to inflict environmental harms on the United States; and (3) the value of identifying a subset of nations that will be central to achieving success in international environmental diplomacy. Table 1 attempts to assess whether the Chase-Hill-Kennedy pivotal states are "more important than the others" from this environmental perspective.

Table 1. RANKING ENVIRONMENTAL PIVOTAL STATES

	Capacity for environmental issues to affect state and regional stability	Potential for environmental spillovers onto the United States	Centrality to global environmental negotiations
Mexico	yes	yes	yes
Brazil	yes	yes	yes
Algeria	no	no	maybe
Egypt	yes	no	maybe
South Africa	maybe	no	maybe
Turkey	yes	no	no
India	yes	yes	yes
Pakistan	yes	no	no
Indonesia	yes	yes	maybe
China	yes	yes	yes
Russia	yes	yes	yes

Mexico fits the definition of a pivotal state according to all of these criteria. Resource strains are part of the current difficulties the Mexican government faces. Environmental security issues in Mexico also have the potential to broaden into regional concerns since water and food shortages might well result in migration north to the United States or south into neighboring Central American nations. As a U.S. neighbor, Mexico has as great a potential as any country in the world to cause direct environmental harms to the United States.[87] Moreover, because of its leadership position within Latin America, Mexico is critical to the success of any international environmental negotiation.

Similarly, Brazil has a range of environmental resource issues that are of considerable importance to its political stability. Its position as the leading forest country in the world creates the potential for significant global environmental effects on the United States. Brazil's demographic heft and particular resource endowments make it pivotal in almost any international environmental negotiation.

In contrast, Algeria does not seem to fit as a pivotal state from an environmental point of view. Environmental threats are not central to the Algerian government's stability. Other than its role as an oil producer, Algeria has no special potential for inflicting environmental harms on the United States. To date, Algeria has not played a particularly important role in environmental diplomacy.

Egypt has, perhaps, a stronger environmental claim to pivotalness. The government in Egypt faces real challenges from resource issues, especially in water management. Because the Nile is shared with other countries, Egypt's environmental problems have the potential to spill over and become regional security crises as well. On the positive side, Egypt has played something of a leadership role in past environmental negotiations and could become a regional model and leader in the future.

Although some analysts see resource use playing a role in South Africa's current violence, the claim that environmental effects are a major contributor to political instability in South Africa seems strained.[88] South Africa has little potential for causing environmental spillovers onto the United States. Its environmental pivotalness therefore must rest on its potential as a regional model and leader.

Turkey faces regional "shared resource" stability issues, especially with respect to Syria. It does not, however, play a particularly important role as a source of global environmental problems or as a contributor to international environmental negotiations. Thus, from an environmental perspective, Turkey's claim to pivotalness is limited.

India, in contrast, is unequivocally an environmentally pivotal state. India's stability rests on important resource and environmental questions. Governmental crises derived from shortages of water, food, or other demographic strains might well create serious regional instability. Moreover, the country's size, expanding population, and economic growth (and particularly its dependence on coal) give India a very signif-

87. Farvolden, "Water Crisis."
88. Homer-Dixon and Percival, "Environmental Scarcity."

icant potential for causing environmental spillovers that would affect the
United States. In this regard, India must be taken seriously as a key participant in international environmental negotiations. Although Pakistan
has a similar set of environmental threats to its stability and could create
some degree of regional instability, it does not seem to present the same
level of risk to the United States as a source of environmental spillovers.
Nor does Pakistan have much potential as a central participant in international environmental negotiations.

Indonesia does have a set of environmental issues, especially related to
the management of natural resources and the control of population
growth, that makes it vulnerable to environmentally induced state failure.
The risk of Indonesia's problems becoming regional issues is limited by
the country's geography, particularly the fact that it is an island nation.
But Indonesia's size and rapid growth give it some potential for causing
global environmental spillovers that would affect the United States.
Although it has not played a particularly important role in past environmental negotiations, Indonesia's demographic position and capacity for
regional leadership might be important in the future.

Although Chase, Hill, and Kennedy put China and Russia in a special
category, from an environmental perspective these two countries stand
out as *the* pivotal states. As noted earlier, China will soon be the world's
largest emitter of greenhouse gases, and its rapid economic growth is
causing a range of other environmental harms to its neighbors. Thus, the
country's potential for causing serious transboundary environmental
spillovers is unmatched. China's unique position as the world's most populous country and as the possessor of vast coal reserves gives it an indisputably central role in international environmental affairs.

Russia faces a range of environmental issues central to its potential for
stability and steady growth. The communist legacy of toxic contamination significantly limits the nation's potential for economic revitalization.[89] Not only do vast portions of the country suffer from severe air and
water pollution, but a number of industrial sites are so contaminated that
potential Western investors will not consider putting money into them.
Russia's potential for environmental spillovers is also dramatic. Not only
is it a large and therefore politically important country, it also holds the
most extensive energy reserves of any nation in the world. Whether
Russia sells its coal or its natural gas to others will have a profound effect
on the planet's future greenhouse gas levels. In addition, Russia's nuclear

89. Daniel C. Esty, "Environmental Protection during the Transition to a Market Economy,"
    in *Economies in Transition: Asia and Europe*, ed. Wing Woo, Stephen Parker, and Jeffrey
    Sachs (Cambridge, Mass.: MIT Press, 1997).

power plants pose a constant threat of radiation contamination to the rest of Europe and perhaps to broader areas as well. For all of these reasons, Russia is an environmentally pivotal state.

CONCLUSION

In restructuring America's international affairs around a select group of pivotal states, there is much to be gained by considering environmental issues. Resource and pollution problems threaten the stability and security of a number of nations that might be considered pivotal. Environmental issues, moreover, may help to define which states are pivotal. Some countries are particularly important to U.S. interests because of their capacity to inflict environmental harms on Americans. In some cases, proximity leads to these spillovers. In other cases, the risk arises from global environmental problems.

If the pivotal states strategy provides a framework for making American foreign policy, then it has application within the environmental domain. Specifically, the prospect of achieving "collective action" in response to inherently worldwide environmental challenges may be enhanced by focusing attention on a small set of countries that have the potential to determine the success or failure of international collaborative efforts. Just as the pivotal states approach provides an opportunity to target foreign assistance and to improve its efficacy, concentrating U.S. assistance in the environmental realm on a small set of pivotal states might yield similar results.

The ecological interdependence of the countries of this planet is becoming increasingly apparent and widely accepted. The presence of inescapable linkages argues for an international environmental policy that is attentive to the potential certain countries have to inflict environmental harms and significant welfare losses on U.S. citizens. No matter how politically unattractive from our current perspective it may be to invest U.S. resources overseas, it seems clear that in some circumstances, *domestic* environmental protection can be most cheaply purchased abroad. Indeed, to the extent that the most cost-effective ways of mitigating climate change lie with investments in improved energy efficiency in the developing world (especially in China), we must reconfigure our thinking about how we deploy our environmental protection resources.

The United States needs to develop a capacity to set priorities and to leverage its inevitably limited investments in assisting developing countries. In the post–Cold War era, U.S. interests abroad have become more diverse and complicated. To the extent that we must now factor environmental concerns into our security calculations, we need to restructure our foreign policy making apparatus to facilitate consideration of pollution and resource issues. The Clinton administration's appointment of an undersecretary of state for environmental issues represents a step in the right direction, as was former Secretary of State Warren Christopher's commitment (in the waning days of his tenure) to making the environment a more central element of U.S. foreign policy. But integrating the work of the State Department's Oceans, Environment, and Science Bureau into the policy thinking of the State and Defense Department analysts who attend to more traditional politico-military matters would be even more important. Making the intelligence community aware of the range of environment and related demographic issues that may affect the stability of foreign governments and regions is another critical step that should be taken. Developing a better capacity to monitor environmental data, track shared resource conflicts, and analyze public health and ecological threats to governmental stability would also be useful. This type of environmental security program would likely require closer collaboration among officials in the State and Defense Departments, the CIA, the EPA, NASA, and other agencies with relevant data-gathering capacities and policy mandates.

Of course, better focused and coordinated U.S. policy making will not be enough to address the panoply of international environmental challenges we face. Even if the United States were to engage in a large-scale program of data and analytic support, technology assistance, policy design sharing, and environmental training aimed at helping a set of pivotal states with their pollution and resource problems, the lack of a functioning international environmental regime would make success in reducing environmental security pressures elusive. The weakness of the UN Environment Programme and the diffusion of international environmental responsibilities across a dozen other UN bodies and a growing number of treaty secretariats makes it nearly impossible to overcome the special difficulties of organizing an adequate response to global-scale environmental harms.

A pivotal states approach to international affairs would nevertheless help us to understand the vulnerability of key countries to pollution and resource crises and to better manage our own exposure to environmental threats that arise from other countries. The value of a pivotal states framework would be even greater to the extent that the categorization is nuanced enough to recognize that states may be pivotal for different reasons, that *the* pivotal states on any single issue may deviate from the baseline list, and that the priorities for U.S. foreign affairs will evolve over time as new issues become salient.

A PIVOTAL STATES
HUMAN RIGHTS STRATEGY

Charles H. Norchi

In 1964 Senator J. William Fulbright observed, "We are handicapped by foreign policies based upon old myths rather than current realities. There is an inevitable divergence, attributable to the imperfections of the human mind, between the world as it is and the world as men perceive it."[1] At the end of our century many human rights policy makers, advocates, and scholars are trapped by old myths rather than confronting current realities. And the rhetoric of human rights has failed to inspire a real global and penetrating application of human rights norms. Despite a universal language of dignity and rights, for vast numbers of human beings basic dignity is beyond reach. Whereas the human rights "movement"—the large nongovernmental organizations (NGOs) in London, New York, and Geneva, and the many small though effective grass-roots groups of the developing world—fights the human dignity battles on the front lines *wherever* those lines and battles emerge, this strategy has been a less than effective human rights policy for *states*. Applying national human rights resources too broadly and too thinly has yielded uneven outcomes. There is an embarrassing discrepancy between human rights goals and human rights achievements. Five years after the United Nations World Conference on Human Rights convened at Vienna in 1993, the human rights regime is experiencing overstretch. This is not so much a problem of inadequate policy formation for nonstate regime participants as of ineffective strategy of the most politically relevant states. A pivotal states strategy would address this international human rights *problematique*.

If America were to adopt a pivotal states strategy and "focus its efforts on a small number of countries whose fate is uncertain and whose future will profoundly affect their surrounding regions,"[2] what would this mean

---

1. J. William Fulbright, speech before the U.S. Senate, May 27, 1964.
2. Robert S. Chase, Emily B. Hill, and Paul Kennedy, "Pivotal States and U.S. Strategy," *Foreign Affairs* 75, no. 1 (January–February 1996): 33.

for international human rights? The nine pivotal states account for one-half of the developing world's population. Six of the nine are significant participants in nonwestern civilizations holding varying perspectives of "universal" human rights, and all of the nine are regionally influential—capable of affecting the lives of vast numbers of human beings beyond their own borders. Thus *any* advance in the human rights of the people living in these states would elevate the global human dignity index. And if these states functioned as human dignity platforms, the prospect of fulfilling the human rights promise made to all the world's people in the United Nations Universal Declaration a half century ago would be closer than at present.

However, there is a potential pitfall. A pivotal states strategy, as a policy of states, risks being horizontal, that is, a policy of states conducted between state capitals. But human rights problems are vertical. They are less about power among states than they are about power between states and people, and increasingly between people and nonstate entities. Human rights problems demand anthropological approaches that reach *into* societies. Thus it is critical that although the structure of the platforms may be states, the strategy must be to fulfill the human dignity of the people on and around the platforms. The pitfall is avoided to the extent that the strategic focus on these states enables a vertical commitment to the people living within the nine, and potentially beyond.

To appraise the pivotal states strategy as a foreign policy guide in navigating some of the critical human rights challenges that plague the post–Cold War international system, one must first understand the contemporary human rights system and something of its antecedents. What is the origin of human rights and the wider institutional regime? What are the principal challenges to the international human rights system? Might a human rights pivotal states strategy meet those challenges?

PIVOTAL STATES IN THE INTERNATIONAL HUMAN RIGHTS SYSTEM

Before 1945 no recourse was available to remedy deprivations of fundamental rights. Tensions between the individual and the state necessitated a set of external arrangements and procedures to which a person could appeal. In the immediate post–World War II environment, norms were codified, governmental and nongovernmental international organizations and institutions were established, and in the wake of the Nuremberg trials nation-states became increasingly concerned with international human rights. Soon the beginnings of an international human rights program, or regime, were in place.

But the aspirations of international human rights and resulting prescriptions had arisen in response to claims relating to the deprivation of basic human dignity. Throughout the world people were asserting claims to a broad spectrum of basic values; to respect, to well-being, to power, wealth, rectitude, skill, and enlightenment. These claims transcended national borders and indigenous cultures and were asserted in both the developed and the developing world, in peace and in war. Human rights practitioners and scholars have termed these "rising common demands."[3]

The contemporary human rights system took form when the United Nations Human Rights Commission held its first plenary session in January 1947. The commission comprised eighteen nations, and its chairwoman was Eleanor Roosevelt. The task was to draft an international bill of human rights. American policy "was to get a declaration which was a carbon copy of the American Declaration of Independence and Bill of Rights."[4] When finally drafted a year later, the Universal Declaration of Human Rights was presented to fifty-five member states of the United Nations and adopted.

Prior to the advent of an international system for the protection of the rights of individual human beings, it was assumed that what a government did to its own people within its own territory was its own business. Because of the experience of the Nazi Holocaust, human rights norms were aimed at restraining the use of a government's power. The basic proposition of the international law of human rights was that a government could no longer utilize *any* means against its own people even while acting within its own territory.

From the halcyon days of the immediate post–World War II period through the end of the Cold War, the evolution of the human rights system was marked by standard setting and institution building. Despite the politics of the Cold War, the Universal Declaration of Human Rights was followed by other international instruments: the International Covenant on Civil and Political Rights, the International Covenant on Economic, Cultural and Social Rights, and specialized international instruments notably devoted to the rights of the child and to the human rights of women. Cumulatively, these legal instruments are termed the "International Bill of Human Rights." From successive meetings of the United Nations Human Rights Commission new mechanisms and institutions emerged. Regional institutions having varying degrees of efficacy took

---

3. See Myres S. McDougal, Harold D. Lasswell, and Lung-chu Chen, *Human Rights and World Public Order* (New Haven and London: Yale University Press, 1980), 7.

4. Joseph P. Lash, *Eleanor: The Years Alone* (New York: New American Library, 1972), 62. This was the view of James P. Hendrick, then chief of the International Affairs Division of the State Department.

form in Western Europe, the Americas and Africa. World conferences designed to appraise the entire human rights system were held. The 1993 World Conference on Human Rights convened in Vienna produced a new human rights mechanism, the office of the United Nations High Commissioner for Human Rights.

These are the contours of the human rights system. But what are human rights? The fundamentals of human rights are these: individual human beings and the values they seek. The whole system is driven by individual claims to the fulfillment of human values. International human rights law, its mechanisms and institutions are vehicles for the achievement of those values. Thus "individual human beings, affected by constantly changing environmental and predispositional factors, are continuously engaged in the shaping and sharing of all values, with achievement of many different outcomes in deprivation and fulfillment. It is these outcomes in deprivation and fulfillment in the shaping and sharing of values which constitute, in an empirical and policy-oriented conception, the human rights which the larger community of humankind protects or fails to protect."[5] Human rights means securing the dignity of people in a world of states.

This concern about "people" was long revolutionary to those who applied or appraised international law. Human rights is a subset of international law. And from the advent of seventeenth-century Grotian[6] principles well into the Cold War period, only states were considered subjects of international law. Only states appeared before the International Court of Justice, and the point of international law was the maintenance of order in a community of states.

It is relevant to consider what international law is and what it is not. Law is a mode of decision making by which members of a community manage their relations. In the international system the essential community members have been states. Law might be, but is not necessarily, words on paper—whether that paper is called a contract, a United Nations resolution, or even a treaty. These are often *lex simulata* or *lex imperfecta*. International lawmaking, including the international law of human rights, is a process of communication in which a prescription is conveyed to a target audience. That prescription is accompanied by an authority signal and conveys control intention and a policy content. In a critical feedback loop in this communication, the targeted audience legitimates the signaled prescription and makes claims both formally and

5. McDougal, Lasswell, and Chen, *Human Rights and World Public Order.*
6. The Dutch jurist Hugo Grotius, also called Hugo de Groot, published his influential *De jure belli ac pacis* in 1625.

informally.[7] As international law increasingly attended to the fulfillment of individual claims through this process of communication, human beings became subjects of a legal order that transcended states.

A pivotal states strategy must not be purely a policy of states. Those who apply the strategy must be careful not to neglect the dynamic of complex normative signaling that animates human rights and protects people. As the subject of international law, the human dignity of individuals residing within those pivotal states must be of primary concern. Fulfilling human dignity might require the targeted signaling of prescriptions to particular elites. Remedying severe deprivations might require appraising claims of individuals and nonstate entities operating within pivotal states. The reality is that an effective human rights policy operates despite, not because of, national borders. The state gave rise to the need for a human rights system in the first place.

Another context affects a pivotal states human rights strategy. That is the geometric rate by which global telecommunications are accelerating increasingly common perspectives. Digital technology, the key feature of our information age, has brought the international human rights system to the brink of great advances in securing human dignity. Because of international communications, rapid transnational signaling of expected international norms occurs continuously. An expanding and "unceasing homogenization of a global culture . . . tends to shape, within its domain, essentially similar conceptions of past and future, and of human possibility, remarkably similar value demands, and in a more limited fashion, awareness of and identification with an inclusive environmental system."[8] This startling outcome of our digital age is doing more for international human rights than the slow and often unresponsive United Nations human rights program. Using information appliances, people struggling in the human rights trenches can communicate reports of substandard behavior to the UN Human Rights Centre, to international news organizations, and to national foreign ministries. A pivotal states human rights policy should enable the *people* of those states to participate in late-twentieth-century communications advances, thereby sharing in the values of the human rights regime.

Human rights has evolved to express authoritatively an entire range of

7. See W. Michael Reisman, "International Lawmaking as a Process of Communication," in *Proceedings of the American Society of International Law* (1981), 101; Myres S. McDougal and W. Michael Reisman, "The Prescribing Function in the World Constitutive Process: How International Law is Made," in *International Law Essays*, ed. Myres S. McDougal and W. Michael Reisman (New York: The Foundation Press, 1981) .

8. Myres S. McDougal, W. Michael Reisman, Andrew R. Willard, "The World Community: A Planetary Social Process," in *U.C. Davis Law Review* 21, no. 3 (1988): 834.

values demanded by all human beings. Although not all communities agree on the clarification of those values that amount to human rights, no elite rhetoric denies the existence of human rights. And every individual makes demands and claims by invoking human rights standards. Never before in the history of the planet has so much transnational activity been devoted to the intelligence, promotion, invocation, prescription, application and appraisal of human rights.

HUMAN RIGHTS CHALLENGES AND A PIVOTAL STATES POLICY

The critical challenges to international human rights are: (1) the challenge of promotion; (2) the challenge of application; and (3) the challenge of the particular. This is not to suggest the human rights movement does not face other difficulties. For example, Aryeh Neier has deplored the "new double standard" of the current American administration, whereas Jeffrey Garten has written of the "need for pragmatism" in human rights policy.[9] And other serious problems plague international human rights: weak international institutions; insufficient resource allocation, an inability or unwillingness to connect human rights and development; devotion to civil and political rights to the exclusion of economic, cultural, and social rights; failed states; and a wide range of humanitarian law (human rights in armed conflict) issues. But broad systemic challenges are at the roots of these problems. In the current state of human rights system overstretch, a strategy to confront these problems is sorely needed. Let us consider the challenges with reference to two designated pivotal states, India and Pakistan.

The Challenge of Promotion

The contemporary human rights program owes much of its success to the promotion of standards and policies. International lawyers conceive of promotion as "processes by which consciousness of a discrepancy between a desirable state and one that is or is about to take place gradually leads to a demand for some type of community intervention and regulation."[10] In organized communities this function is performed by lobbyists, agitators, and lawyers. Actors in less organized communities or in non-Western cultures and developing states are more varied and often dimly aware of their promotional roles. The promotion of human rights

---

9. See Aryeh Neier, "The New Double Standard," *Foreign Policy* no. 105 (winter 1996–1997): 91–101; Jeffrey E. Garten, "Comment: The Need for Pragmatism," *Foreign Policy* no. 105 (winter 1996–1997): 103–106.

10. W. Michael Reisman, *Jahrbuch 1989/90* (Berlin: Institute for Advanced Study), 239.

standards and policies has been successful indeed—or, rather, successful in Geneva, New York, and London, less so in Islamabad, Jakarta, and Algiers.

A case for the concentrated promotion of human rights standards and machinery can be made for each designated pivotal state and should be a centerpiece of American pivotal state policy. Effective promotion would require financial and technical assistance to primarily non-governmental organizations. The promotional goal should be to build in every pivotal state a human rights culture that is sufficiently vibrant to infect the region.

Promoting respect for human rights can go a long way toward alleviating conflict in societies racked by violence. Such states are inherently unstable. Violence is often a symptom of extreme human rights deprivation and can spill over into neighboring states or the region. Mass violence can engender state disintegration. The pivotal states of Pakistan and India face acute problems connected to communal violence and extrajudicial killing. Some violence is centered in contentious border areas over which these states have fought three wars. The dispute over Kashmir could spark a fourth. The resulting chaos would be decidedly detrimental to human dignity.

Both India and Pakistan are experiencing enormous and uncontrolled population growth, and desperate poverty. Three hundred fifty million people live in abject poverty despite advances in certain economic sectors in India. Western policy makers and Western members of the human rights movement must come to understand what every human being living in the Third World knows: that a child dying of starvation is as much a human rights abuse as an adult being tortured. A human rights policy devoted to the focused application of human rights law in pivotal states could ensure the fulfillment of *all* rights, economic and social as well as political.

United States human rights policy toward Pakistan should place promotion of respect for the integrity of the person at the center. The policy should also assist nongovernmental organizations within Pakistan. Human rights institutions and organizations exist, but they are weak owing to a paucity of resources. Children's and women's rights organizations are desperately in need of technical and financial assistance. Along with the Pakistani Lawyers' Committee for Human Rights, they have been attempting to redress child labor, deprivation of women's rights, and discrimination against minorities. Slowly, increasing numbers of Pakistani lawyers are taking public interest cases. Although cases have been registered and litigated to advance the rights of women, children, and minorities, advocacy organizations lack the funds and training to function effectively. A sustained program to teach and support public-interest civil rights litigation is greatly needed.

The National Human Rights Commission (NHRC) of Pakistan holds great promise for the advancement of human rights, but it too is in need of financial and technical assistance. An independent entity, the NHRC has begun to place human rights monitors throughout the country to collect evidence of abuses and report to the commission's headquarters. But the monitors need training in collection procedures and standards. The NHRC is embarking on a project to bring Pakistani laws into conformity with the Convention on the Elimination of Discrimination Against Women (CEDAW). Again, training and funding are needed. It would be inexpensive and beneficial to both sides for the United States to export a few of its surplus lawyers to Rawalpindi, Lahore, and Karachi. And the nascent human rights movement of a key pivotal state would benefit.

If Pakistan becomes a pivotal platform for the promotion of human rights, efforts there could benefit neighboring Afghanistan. Millions of Afghan refugees find themselves in Pakistan's Northwest Frontier Province and in the province of Baluchistan. They have been there since the early 1980s, victims of chaos across the border. They are viewed with increasing animosity by Pakistani officials and citizens, who perceive the refugees as a resource drain on a poor country. The Afghan people's right to self-determination should be promoted to the government of Pakistan, which intermittently engages in covert operations north of its border.

Promoting human rights in pivotal India is more complicated because vast problems and deep divisions conflict with a long civil rights tradition. The Indian Constituent Assembly in 1947 adopted an "Objectives Resolution" stating ideals to guide the founding of the Union:

> This Constituent Assembly declares its firm and solemn resolve to proclaim India as an Independent, Sovereign Republic and to draw up for her future governance a Constitution . . . wherein shall be guaranteed and secured to all the people of India justice—social, economic and political; equality of status, of opportunity and before the law; freedom of thought, expression, belief, faith, worship, vocation, association and action, subject to law and public morality.

The ensuing Indian Constitution reflects many aspirations of the major international human rights instruments. India has a political tradition of forming commissions to advance human rights policies, as well as an active community of nongovernmental human rights organizations. Some operate countrywide, others operate at the village level. Human rights in India also benefit from growing public-interest litigation and a free and critical press. In 1990 Acts of Parliament amended the Indian Constitution to establish a National Commission for Scheduled Castes and Scheduled Tribes and a National Commission for Women. In 1992 an act of Parliament established a National Commission on Minorities. In 1993, the Protection of Human Rights Act created the National Human Rights Commission (NHRC).[11] The commission was born of some controversy and remains, in effect, an arm of the government. But prodded by the NGOs and the press it has achieved some notable successes. NGOs were critical of the idea of a governmental national human rights institution from the beginning, but a working relationship is evolving.

Since its formation, the National Human Rights Commission has taken its promotional tasks seriously. It has sought to operate small community human rights workshops, to disseminate human rights literature, and to train and sensitize the police to respect human rights. The latter is especially important because torture and custodial deaths are rampant. But a United States human rights policy toward India could prod the commission to do more. The commission should actively promote human rights standards in Kashmir, particularly among military and paramilitary forces operating in Kashmir and in other border areas.

The promotion of human rights is highly dependent on engagement and on exchange. Exchanges in commerce, in education, with NGOs, accompanied by new communication technologies that now make possible follow-through and sustainable relationships, all serve to promote human rights. Through focused constructive engagement, the United States could promote the fulfillment of a human rights system in India, Pakistan, and other pivotal states at minimal cost.

The Challenge of Application

Standard setting and institution building have been the hallmarks of the contemporary human rights system. As the post–Cold War world prepares for the twenty-first century, human rights will turn on application. Application is "the specification of law to a particular set of events and the determination of a sanction."[12] How will human rights law be applied in pivotal states? If United States human rights policy is concentrated on select states, application may be more achievable. International human rights law is applied through the domestic legal systems of states, in bilateral and multilateral state relations, and through international organizations.

A government committed to human rights norms, and a strong and independent judiciary that is willing to apply those norms, is critical to the achievement of human rights. In Pakistan the judiciary is scarcely

---

11. The case load of the NHRC has primarily accrued from excesses of the police and armed forces, custodial deaths, custodial rape, dowry deaths, and torture.

12. W. Michael Reisman and Aaron M. Schreiber, *Jurisprudence: Understanding and Shaping Law* (New Haven, Conn.: New Haven Press, 1987), 15.

independent, although independence is provided for in the Constitution. Pakistan has a civil judicial system, special terrorism courts, and religious courts—the Federal Shari'a Court and the Shari'a bench of the Supreme Court. Judges serve pursuant to short contracts at the sufferance of the government. This is part of a broader problem of widespread corruption. The desire of judges for reconfirmation has resulted in few rulings against the government.

Although the government of Pakistan regularly speaks in favor of international human rights standards, the application of many of those standards has been uneven at best. United States human rights policy should focus on the judiciary and the legal system, key appliers of human rights law. It should also support and encourage the development of parallel systems for the application of human rights law, such as quasi-governmental commissions.

The obstacles to the application of human rights law in India are as complex as India's society itself. The courts are enormously backlogged, and access to the courts can be problematic. The National Human Rights Commission has emerged as a kind of parallel system to which a person can appeal, and which can apply the law when moved to do so. But there is skepticism in India about the role of the NHRC as a genuine applier of human rights norms. This skepticism can be traced to the institution's birth.

By the time the Congress (I) Party actively considered the establishment of a National Human Rights Commission in 1991, India was increasingly subject to international criticism for its military activities in the Jammu-Kashmir region. The government had implemented draconian security-related legislation, the Terrorist and Disruptive Activities Prevention Act (TADA) and the Armed Forces Special Powers Act (AFSPA). TADA mandated minimal automatic prison sentences of five years for activities including speech or actions that might disrupt or challenge the sovereignty or territorial integrity of India. The AFSPA accorded army officers the power to search, arrest, and shoot in order to maintain public order. In international forums, the government found itself under high-profile attack, often instigated by the government of Pakistan but also increasingly by international human rights groups, including Human Rights Watch and Amnesty International. An internal Government of India Ministry of Home Affairs report noted:

> There has been growing awareness in the country and abroad about issues relating to Human Rights. National and international organizations in this field have been highlighting alleged violations of human rights by various Government functionaries. There is a growing feeling that the

Government is not serious about such violations and excesses and in bringing the guilty persons to book.[13]

The noted human rights advocate Ravi Nair observed, "It's clear that the Government is responding to international criticism, to Amnesty International, Asia Watch and U.S. Congressional criticism."[14] Many Indian human rights advocates believed the government was attempting to "circumvent international scrutiny by stating they have adequate national institutions to investigate these charges."[15] An internal Government Home Ministry report noted:

> Against this background, any impression of Government's lack of seriousness on the issue of Human Rights is a matter of serious concern and needs to be dispelled. It is, therefore, necessary to consider whether institutional arrangements need to be further strengthened through which human rights issues could be addressed in their entirety in a more focussed manner, and allegations of excesses could be looked into independently of the government, in a manner that would serve, not only to underline the commitment of the Government but also help to complement, and further strengthen the efforts that have already been made in this direction. One of the proposals in this regard pertains to setting up of a Human Rights Commission at the national level.[16]

Indian human rights advocates continued to express skepticism:

> Pronouncements prior to the establishment of the Human Rights Commission shed light on the motivating factors in the setting up of the Commission. The proposed Commission was seen as an instrument to blunt or deflect the increasing international criticism of India's human rights practice rather than creating accountability processes. In another attempt to deflect international criticism, the government has time and again refused to allow international human rights groups to conduct on the spot research in India.[17]

India, like most developing countries, could not simply ignore independent international human rights reports. The Tamil Nadu–based lawyer Rajeev Dhavan is convinced the decision to establish the National

---

13. Government of India, Ministry of Home Affairs, "Background Note on Setting Up of a National Commission on Human Rights—Issues and Tentative Frame Work" (undated).
14. *New York Times*, October 14, 1992.
15. *New York Times*, October 14, 1992.
16. Government of India, Ministry of Home Affairs, "Background Note on National Commission."
17. South Asia Human Rights Documentation Centre, *Commission Yes—Human Rights No: The Human Rights Commissions Bill, 1993*, 1.

Human Rights Commission had nothing to do with "the quest for truth."[18]
He noted, "What has pressurised India is its diplomatic reverses abroad,
and the threat that international economic decisions will carry human
rights conditionalities." [19]

But the National Human Rights Commission does have teeth. It can
issue summonses to enforce the attendance of witnesses to its proceedings and examine those witnesses under oath.[20] It can conduct the discovery and production of documents, receive evidence through affidavits,
and requisition public records. The NHRC has the capacity to engage the
application of human rights law. As an arm of the government, it may also
have motivations not to apply human rights standards. It would be greatly detrimental to human rights in India if, as expectations for the NHRC
as an applier of human rights prescriptions rise, it fails to meet those
expectations. Whether that failure was accidental or deliberate, it would
be a setback for human dignity in India. This is where a concentrated U.S.
policy effort would be critical.

There is another reason to include support of national human rights
institutions such as the NHRC as an element of United States human
rights policy. As distinct from Europe, Latin America, and Africa, a
regional mechanism for the protection of human rights has eluded Asia.
The diversity of Asia includes diverse perspectives about the nature and
meaning of human rights and differences over the rigor with which
"Western" human rights norms should be applied. But government-sponsored institutions, "national human rights institutions," are emerging
from India to the Phillippines to Indonesia. These may provide the foundation for a pan-Asian regional human rights institution.

The Challenge of the Particular

At the end of the Cold War the global expectation of violence which,
for most people, had obscured the idea of universal human rights, seemed
largely removed. But in the wake of the bipolar order, the fragmentation
of states and societies suggests less is shared, less is universal than the
architects of an earlier age appear to have thought. In 1997, the "personal insecurity" that the policy scientist Harold Lasswell ingeniously connected to world politics sixty years earlier hardly ebbs.[21] Human rights is

18. Rajeev Dhavan, "More Is Not Always More: Unto Us a Human Rights Commission Is
    Given—But Why?" New Delhi: Public Interest Legal Support and Research Centre,
    Working Paper no. 18, 14.
19. Dhavan, "More Is Not Always More."
20. India, Protection of Human Rights Act (1993), III.13.
21. See Harold D. Lasswell, *World Politics and Personal Insecurity* (New York: McGraw-Hill,
    1935).

subject to the culture and power topography of the planet in new and profound ways. The earlier anticipated age of universalism appears in brutal relief as an age of particularism.

The challenge of the particular to the presumed universal was anticipated by the historian Ada Bozeman, who warned that "between the poles of the contemporary cultural and political map of the world, there are numerous well-defined civilizations as well as many others that are just beginning to define themselves."[22] In the late 1950s Professor Bozeman wrote:

> Behind the screen of an official accord upon Occidental interpretations of such values as tyranny and freedom, power and law, ignorance and knowledge, discords grew in the field of intercultural relations. The Africans and Asians proceeded, both consciously and unconsciously, to reinstate their native modes of thought and behavior, while continuing to pay obeisance to Western words and forms. . . . An intense, albeit little-noticed, dialogue between substratal or residual non-Western values on the one hand, and the classical Occidental on the other, had thus been in progress for some time when the encounter of civilizations was further complicated by Russia's propagation of the communist doctrine.[23]

With the intense and potentially massively lethal competition between two major systems of world order gone, the operational codes of heretofore lesser systems are clearly visible.

On the cusp of the twenty-first century we find cleavages among cultures and polities, between those who do not rely on revealed truth, which cannot be subjected to tests of reason, and those for whom revelation is paramount despite its inaccessibility to reason. Nietzsche believed the religious impulse would dissipate and leave a tremendous vacuum, and in place of religious belief secular ideology would triumph. Indeed, this is the way the planet looked when the Cold War world was in the throes of two ideological camps. But with apologies to Nietzsche, religion is back with a vengeance. God's comeback in the post–Cold War world is as historical an event as was his death.

Another schism has arisen between those who believe ideas and institutions are *nomos,* or made by man, and those who believe our ideoethnemes are *physis,* or imposed by nature or divine will. The former view engendered Western civilization from the Enlightenment to the present, and with it human rights. In its extreme form, the latter view is a crucial challenge. Its triumph would amount to one of the most profound value

22. Ada Bozeman, *Politics and Culture in International History* (Princeton, N.J.: Princeton University Press, 1960), 6.

23. Bozeman, *Politics and Culture,* 5.

shifts since the Age of Reason. And its impact on the planet would be no less significant than when God first spoke to Muhammad.

In a widely cited article in the journal *Foreign Affairs*, the political scientist Samuel P. Huntington wrote, "the principal conflicts of global politics will occur between nations and groups of different civilizations. The clash of civilizations will dominate global politics. The fault lines between civilizations will be the battle lines of the future."[24] To term the sound of cultural tectonic plates grating against one another a "clash" is overstating the case. But fault lines do exist. Some states designated as "pivotal" are on those fault lines; others are marked by furrows of several civilizations. Although our global order is not jarred by the sounds of civilizations clashing, voices from diverse perspectives are speaking up about the promotion, application, and evolution of human rights norms. These voices are genuine. They are not always the haranguings of Third World dictators but are more often a plea for full participation on respectful terms. If neglected, certain states, including some pivotal, could become "spoilers" for the broader international human rights agenda.

Anwar Ibrahim, the deputy prime minister of Malaysia, noted:

> Not so long ago, all the world was under the spell of the modern West. But today the spell has been broken, and its moral and political ideas are no longer seen as universal. . . . For the debate on Western values has become the dominant discourse of our time, having been preceded by a sustained and devastating critique of the Enlightenment by the West's own leading thinkers. They are disenchanted with reason and modernity, and they attribute the malaise of their society—moral decadence, rising crime and the disintegration of the family—to the fatal mistake of exalting human reason as the sole guide in civilization. . . . Unlike the West since the Enlightenment, which severed itself from the dominant world view of the Age of Faith, Asia, despite centuries of change, still preserves its essential religious character. Faith and religious practice are not confined to the individual; they permeate the life of the community. It is religion that makes Asia a continent of infinite diversity. Western man, on the other hand, in his arrogance and intolerance toward the unfamiliar, sought to fashion the world according to his egocentric vision through the instrument of natural reason founded on the forces of modernity. This self-centered preoccupation was the root of imperialism.[25]

These are not isolated views. They are widely held and expressed by elites in Pakistan, India, Indonesia, Algeria, Egypt, and Turkey—six of

---

24. Samuel P. Huntington, "The Clash of Civilizations?" *Foreign Affairs* 72, no. 3 (summer 1993).

25. Anwar Ibrahim, "Religion and Politics, East and West," *Wall Street Journal*, June 6, 1996, p. A14.

the nine states designated as pivotal. Thus it is vital that American policy engage these states in respectful dialogue in order to avert either a "clash of civilizations" or the more likely spoiler effect for the achievement of international human rights. Cultural and regional particularities do not necessarily mean that human rights standards will be flouted. But it is unrealistic to expect that human rights will be either promoted or applied at the expense of centuries-old, genuinely held beliefs. This is why vertical, in addition to horizontal, engagement is critical.

Pakistan is at the center of a resurgence of Islam[26] as the most powerful myth of identification on the planet. Islam is not only a religion, rather it defines a particular community and a *total* way of life.[27] A "Muslim" is one who submits, or surrenders to Allah.[28] The Islamic faithful have come to accept total submission to the will of God, "which determines the ultimate values and purposes of human life."[29] Islamic law shapes much of what Muslims expect out of life, and that law, in essence, is God's divinely ordained command. But reducing Islamic jurisprudence to a direct application of Qur'ānic prescriptions would be a simplification of reality. As one scholar has put it, "jurisprudence in Islam is the whole process of intellectual activity which ascertains and discovers the terms of the divine will and transforms them into a system of legally enforceable rights and duties."[30] Any discussion of rights or duties occurs within the context of a divinely imposed law. Fundamental tenets are not subject to amendment. How do Muslims conceive of "rights"? One Islamic scholar explains, "a right is an interest which the revealed law does not preclude."[31] In fact, rights are not primarily due human beings, they are owed to God.

Militant fundamentalism has become a late-twentieth-century reality.[32] This phenomenon is usually equated with Islam, but Hindu funda-

26. The Taliban forces that have recently swept through Afghanistan emerged from refugee camps in Pakistan. They issued fatwahs, declared jihads, and established schools and mosques in Pakistan (headquartered in Lahore) and taught in the madrassas, or mosque schools, of the Afghan refugee camps in Pakistan during the 1980s.

27. Ahmad Farrag, "Human Rights and Liberties in Islam," in *Human Rights in a Pluralist World*, ed. Jan Berting (Westport, Conn.: Meckler Ltd., 1990), 133.

28. *Shari'a* means "the well-worn path made by camels, leading to the watering place." Thus *Shari'a* is the path Muslims follow in the conduct of their lives. See John Bowker, *Voices of Islam* (Oxford: One World Publications, 1995), 21.

29. Neil J. Coulson, *Conflicts and Tensions in Islamic Jurisprudence* (Chicago: University of Chicago Press, 1969), 1.

30. Coulson, *Conflicts and Tensions*, 2.

31. Coulson, *Conflicts and Tensions*, 133.

32. *The Economist* presents this view: "Islamic fundamentalism has become the principal threat to the survival of regimes throughout the Arab world. . . . This is an argument about how people think and live, not merely about lines on maps." *The Economist*, March 13–15, 1993, p. 25.

mentalism is equally destructive. Broadly, fundamentalism defines the fundamentals of a religious system and the efforts toward adherence. "One of the cardinal tenets of Islamic Fundamentalism is to protect the purity of Islamic precepts from the adulteration of speculative exercises."[33] Fundamentalism is "a certain intellectual stance that claims to derive political principles from a timeless divine text."[34] It is a reaction to the modern state and more particularly to secular Western civilization. Its followers are often rural migrants to urban areas who belong to lower or declining socioeconomic strata. What adherents to Islamic radicalism fear is "the total eclipse of Islam, brought about by the ungodly innovations of the secular state. . . . [S]o long as a revealed text is constantly judged to be the final arbiter of human affairs, or of truth and falsehood, fundamentalism is bound to appear under various labels and systems of thought."[35]

In many pivotal states and in their regions, discussion of human rights never occurs far from the perspective of revealed text. Intensely held beliefs can be the ultimate arbiter of human rights. That is true in the Islamic world; it is also true in India. In India, increasing numbers of senior civil servants, intellectuals, and journalists have begun to talk the language of Hindu fundamentalism. Observers fear that Hindu fundamentalism will sound the death knell of secularism in modern India and cause the breakup of the Union. Khushwant Singh, a columnist for the *Hindustan Times*, writes:

> In India, secular has always meant two slightly different things. One is the separation of church and state. This Western sense of the word was how Jawaharlal Nehru, India's founding Prime Minister, understood it. The second meaning is Mohandas K. Gandhi's concept of equal respect for all religions. Nehru's notion of secularism died with him. Thereafter politicians openly displayed their religiosity. . . . India may retain its secular facade but the spirit within will be that of militant Hinduism."[36]

Fundamentalism aside, Hinduism has core concepts, beliefs, and customs, with which Hindus identify and upon which their expectations and demands in life are based. These identifications, expectations and demands shape Hindu views of human rights. In the Hindu cosmos one's station in

---

33. Dilip Hiro, *Holy Wars: The Rise of Islamic Fundamentalism* (New York: Routledge, 1989), 2.
34. Youssef M. Choueiri, *Islamic Fundamentalism* (Boston: Twayne Publishers, 1990), 10.
35. Choueiri, *Islamic Fundamentalism*, 12.
36. Khushwant Singh, "India, the Hindu State," *New York Times*, March 26, 1994.

this life is a function of one's deeds in a prior life.[37] If one's caste or one's deprivation of human dignity in this life is a result of actions taken in a previous life, why promote human rights? What is the government to do? Why should the National Human Rights Commission of India do anything? A noted Hindu scholar writes, "We have no right to curse anything or anybody for our own griefs and ailments. But we can do one thing. We can make our future lives happy. That depends on our present efforts."[38]

A cursory exploration of "the particular" as manifested in two pivotal states, Pakistan and India, reveals the complexity of squaring a horizontal policy with vertical challenges. A pivotal states human rights policy must not confine policy makers to a horizontal optic. Yet one of the strengths of the policy could be in facilitating an intense vertical observational standpoint capable of resolving previously intractable dilemmas. Though our world can hardly be characterized by a "clash of civilizations," there is the prospect of what might be called "garrison cultures." Cultures predisposed to an inward orientation could "garrison" and not participate in a perceived secular, Western-shaped world order—one in which the West sets the rules. That is why the West, and Americans in particular, must not freeze the Universal Declaration of Human Rights in time, influenced by some notion of original intent or swayed by the myth of a constitutional moment. The very concept of human rights must be "dynamic, responsive and adaptable. . . . [W]e must be culturally sensitive in our interpretation and application of some of the norms, while being more inventive in devising measures for the promotion and implementation of human rights which are less Western, more diverse, and more closely tailored to meet local cultures and traditions."[39]

Would a pivotal human rights strategy allay the "universal versus particular" stress affecting the promotion and the application of international human rights law? It could go a long way toward alleviating tensions while

---

37. "Each deed (*karma*) is destined to bear a fruit (*karma-phala*), sooner or later. A good or meritorious deed (*shubha karma*) brings pleasure as its effect and an evil deed (*ashubkha karma*) brings pain." Thus the *karma-phala* are the consequential pleasure and pain one accumulates owing to the performance of meritorious and evil deeds. "During each lifetime we exhaust only a portion of our past *karma-phala*. This portion is called *prarabdha*. The remainder that has to be tasted in future lives is called *samchita*. The fruits of our present deeds will lie stored up as *kriyamana*. Hence, for reaping the fruits of our own actions, we have to go from birth to birth. . . . We cannot avoid the pleasure and pain caused by our own acts (*karma*) during past lives." Swami Nirvedananda, *Hinduism* (Calcutta: Ramakrishna Mission, 1984), 39.

38. Nirvedananda, *Hinduism*, 40.

39. Philip Alston, "The Fortieth Anniversary of the Universal Declaration of Human Rights: A Time More for Reflection Than for Celebration," in *Human Rights in a Pluralistic World*, ed. Jan Berting (Westport, Conn.: Meckler Ltd., 1990), 7.

making possible the task of clarifying a shared common interest. What the human rights community decries as the challenge to universal human rights is in reality a plea for a place at the Western-arranged table and attention to a distinctive voice. A policy that affirmatively places the developing world within U.S. global strategy would make a place at the table for and respect non-Western voices. It is imperative that the United States not surrender its commitment to international human rights. But a pivotal states human rights policy must be sensitive to cultural variation and not insist on standards to which only advanced industrial societies can be held. In those pivotal states whose "fate is uncertain and whose future will profoundly affect their surrounding regions,"[40] the United States must be prepared to act on serious human rights deprivations where and when they occur. This will be difficult so long as many states of our planet are confined to marginal participation in the international human rights system because they have been relegated to Professor Huntington's camp of clashing civilizations.

PIVOTAL POLICY AND HUMAN RIGHTS OUTCOMES

What is the American interest in any human rights policy? American foreign policy must safeguard and improve the welfare of the American people. A pivotal state is identified by "the capacity to affect regional and international stability. . . . [I]ts collapse would spell transboundary mayhem. . . . [A] pivotal state's steady economic progress and stability . . . would bolster its region's economic vitality and political soundness and benefit American trade and investment."[41] Stability and growth are at risk absent the fulfillment of basic human dignity. The range of values amounting to human rights will never be uniformly fulfilled across the planet, but there must be a minimal floor while admitting of a contextual ceiling. Minimum guarantees of human dignity with a commitment to the continually expanding promotion and application of human rights standards is in the American interest.

A pivotal states human rights strategy does not address the difficult task of sorting and responding to claims and demands to elevate the conditions of being human in places where the human condition is at its lowest ebb. But with policy clarity and the integration of human rights issues with security issues, policy makers would be more attentive to claims from pivotal states, and responses would be measured against accepted international human rights standards.

This strategy would produce a beneficial human rights outcome if piv-

40. Chase, Hill, and Kennedy, "Pivotal States," 37.
41. Chase, Hill, and Kennedy, "Pivotal States," 37.

otal states became *human dignity platforms*, meaning sustained promotion of human rights norms within the nine states, a commitment to invoke as unacceptable behavior falling below standards established by the major international human rights instruments, sustainable application of human rights law within pivotal states, and the sustained promotion of human rights norms in areas contiguous to the pivotal states, utilizing resources within the pivotal states.

The mix and intensity of implementing each measure will depend on the human rights condition of each platform. The annual U.S. Department of State Country Reports on Human Rights Practices, the Amnesty International Annual Human Rights Report, the Human Rights Watch Report, the many smaller nongovernmental organization reports, and the mechanisms associated with the United Nations Human Rights Commission are all good indicators of the current human rights platform viability of pivotal states. Some platforms are sturdy, potential buttresses of human rights activity in neighboring states. Others are shaky. Their weaknesses range from the political rot that comes with the deprivation of human dignity over time to near collapse.

Algeria is in desperate need of assistance in the application of international human rights standards. It is the shakiest pivotal platform, on the brink of collapse. Algerian society is racked by fundamentalism. The government has responded by curtailing a range of human rights, causing more incidents of fundamentalist violence. Since 1992 more than sixty thousand people have been killed. During one summer night in 1997 between one hundred and three hundred people were massacred, decapitated, and burned in the village of Sidi Rais, thirty miles south of Algiers.[42] If Algeria collapses as a human rights platform, neighboring states could crumble, Europe will shake, and Islam will tremble to its core. Of the four components of the human dignity platform outlined above, implementation of the first three is urgently required.

At the other end of the spectrum is the sturdiest platform, South Africa. American policy ought to assist this pivotal state to yield positive human rights outcomes regionally, thus implementing the fourth component of the human dignity platform. Nelson Mandela's South Africa is the most promising country in the human dignity platform vision of a pivotal states strategy. The other states lie in between.

Egypt, Turkey, Indonesia, and Pakistan are currently less capable of functioning as human dignity platforms. In Egypt, human rights have been curtailed in an effort to combat Islamic militancy. Torture of political

42. BBC World Service, August 29, 1997; Radio France Internationale, August 29, 1997; *New York Times,* August 30, 1997, p. 3.

prisoners is systemic. Violence between armed opposition groups and security forces continues. Applying international norms internally would promote a human rights culture. In Turkey, torture remains commonplace, and prisoners of conscience can be held indefinitely. Yet with concentrated promotion and application efforts, Turkey, astride Europe and Islam, could become a positive human rights platform to the Islamic world.

Indonesia remains rigidly authoritarian. Serious human rights abuses continue. The government cracks down regularly on the activities of domestic human rights organizations. Foreign nongovernmental organization monitoring of human rights is considered interference with the internal affairs of the government. The government and elites tend to view the international human rights program as a manifestation of Western values. The immediate strategy should be to weave Indonesia more fully into the international human rights system. A much needed positive human rights platform for Islamic Asia may later emerge. A spotty human rights record and regular outbreaks of mass violence generally preclude Pakistan from functioning as a human dignity platform, with one exception. Pakistan, a once and current weapons funnel to Afghan groups north of its border, could be a platform for the disintegrated state of Afghanistan.

India is capable of functioning as a human dignity platform for states throughout the region, Pakistan excepted. As a regional power, India should be encouraged to export its National Human Rights Commission model via technical assistance to neighboring states. Brazil and Mexico, although perhaps closest to South Africa in human dignity platform capacity, require a nuanced policy approach. Each state has human rights difficulties. In Brazil, extrajudicial killings and torture still occur. The poor, landless workers, indigenous people, and street children are regularly deprived of their human dignity. Brazil also has problems of forced labor and racism. Mexico faces poverty, politically motivated violence, extrajudicial killings of peasants and peasant squatters, and forced labor. But each state has adopted measures to forge a human rights culture. Their ability to influence the development of human rights bilaterally and through the inter-American human rights system is profound.

Human rights deprivations produce stress, crisis, and weakened platforms. The human dignity dimensions of collapse can be far reaching. Specific measures should enhance stability and prevent collapse. The following are policy components by which the United States could implement a pivotal states human rights strategy, thereby spawning human dignity platforms.

1. Identify and support governmental and nongovernmental human rights–enhancing institutions.

2. Strengthen the United States Agency for International Development (USAID) and the United States Information Agency (USIA) human rights programs. A promising new mechanism is the USAID Office of Transition Initiatives; its mission is to assist countries at a turning point in governance to recover from political crisis.

3. Use human rights programming in pivotal states to promote neighboring-states initiatives and regional initiatives.

4. Apply small amounts of targeted assistance to selected "value-creating institutions." Such institutions operate at the grass roots or village level and include rights groups, women's organizations, and educational groups.

5. Launch concentrated human rights monitor training for grass-roots organizations.

6. Support government-sponsored national human rights institutions where they exist. Where they do not exist, their development should be promoted, depending on the context.

7. Ensure that United States policy promotes and increases exchanges and ties to American private citizens' organizations, human rights organizations, universities, bar associations, unions, trade groups, and women's organizations.

8. Promote the growth and preservation of independent media, including journalist training and international exchanges.

9. Assist in the development of public-interest litigation.

10. Promote strong and independent judiciaries.

11. Promote chambers of commerce and business and trade group exchanges. International market participation can remove barriers that give rise to garrison states and cultures.

12. Press the United Nations human rights machinery to be actively engaged in pivotal states, beginning with the UN High Commissioner for Human Rights.

13. Promote development objectives as human rights goals.

14. Assist and promote human rights training for police, border forces, and state paramilitary units.

15. Promote and support individual participation on the information superhighway within pivotal states.

A platform requires legs. If the pivotal states are to become human dignity platforms, the foregoing would be a solid first set of legs. Attention focused on the structure over time would bring more legs, a sturdier platform, and a more effective pivotal states strategy. A good, solid platform would reinforce its neighboring states, enhancing the human dignity index for an entire region.

However, a pivotal states human rights strategy does entail an ethical dilemma. Vast communities of human beings in the nonpivotals could be left out of any strategy for the fulfillment of human dignity. Special state interests could be placed ahead of the common interests of people, with unintended consequences. A focus on the club of pivotal states only could inflict a myopia of neglect, resulting in the sacrifice of truly desperate nations to the marginally desperate. This has less to do with the policy than with the principles that would guide it. That is why, for human rights, a pivotal strategy must be conducted according to *first principles.* The first principle is human dignity. "The essential meaning of human dignity . . . can be succinctly stated: it refers to a social process in which values are widely and not narrowly shared, and in which private choice, rather than coercion, is emphasized as the primary modality of power."[43] For Americans, identifying first principles is easy, since they are enumerated in our Bill of Rights. For the wider international community first principles are found in those provisions of the Universal Declaration of Human Rights binding on all states as customary international law.

These principles have sprung from the common interest. "The effective authority of any legal system depends in the long run upon the underlying common interests of the participants in the system and their recognition of such common interests, reflected in continuing dispositions to support the prescriptions and the procedures that comprise the system."[44] This is why it is so important that large-scale challenges to the rights system are engaged and resolved. Appreciating the common interest is fundamental to navigating the tides of uncertainty that increasingly characterize international human rights. A pivotal states strategy must spring from the American interest, but it must recognize the broader common interest of which the American interest is a part.

The measure of a successful human rights policy is the condition of those who, in the words of James Joyce, are outcast from life's feast. Many such people live in pivotal states, but many others live in states that dream of becoming pivotal. A pivotal states strategy would bring useful direction to human rights policy by setting discriminative parameters. The danger would be in excluding states that are far from pivotal, states bordering on chaos, where human suffering is bleakest. But an ethically conducted pivotal states policy would include a springboard to assisting those states.

The human rights "movement"—comprising the NGOs, the policy makers and wonks, the international civil servants—is stalled. The focus

43. Myres S. McDougal and Harold D. Lasswell, "The Identification and Appraisal of Diverse Systems of Public Order," in *Studies in World Public Order,* ed. Myres S. McDougal et al. (New Haven and London: Yale University Press, 1960), 16.
44. McDougal and Lasswell, "Identification," 9.

is increasingly on big issues (for example, Most Favored Nation status and China), while lower-profile issues that affect larger numbers of people (population, health care, and so on) are neglected. A cynic might conclude that the human rights agenda is increasingly driven by what can be funded rather than by a sensible strategy of what might improve the lives of the greatest number of human beings.

For humanity, human rights is a pivotal enterprise. Our shared future depends on it. The values we expect to fulfill at home depend on what others achieve abroad. Power, wealth, health and a range of other values are interdeterminate. Fulfilling values for a geometrically exploding global population is a struggle. Yet no war is fought on all fronts, and victory depends on choosing one's battles well. In a milieu of limited resources and program overstretch, choices have to be made. *Any advancement of international human rights into the next century will depend on appraising priorities and arriving at difficult policy decisions.* Human rights victories will depend on continuity and intensity of commitment. If an American partnership were to help pivotal states become platforms in the shared achievement of human rights, we might finally achieve the goal of the early architects of our human rights system—a world order of human dignity.

ETHNIC CONFLICT AND THE PIVOTAL STATES

*Eileen F. Babbitt**

If the pivotal state strategy is to be useful, it must give effective guidance to American policy makers about current and future policy priorities. One of the most important questions involved in establishing these priorities is whether to intervene (politically, economically, or militarily) in foreign ethnic conflicts. These internal conflicts now pervade the international system, and at present, the U.S. government does not have a coherent policy on when and how to intervene.

Unlike the issues of overpopulation and environmental degradation, the problem of ethnic conflict does not easily allow one to pinpoint key states that could help to contain its incidence globally. Every country is a unique case, with its own complex history and current conditions. More important, each country *believes* its ethnic problems to be different from those of any other country. Although trends can be identified, and lessons from one context can be instructive in another, the solution to one state's internal intergroup conflicts may not be suitable in another state. And unlike the human rights movement, which focuses on protecting the individual, there are no agreed-on universal norms for acknowledging and protecting group identity.[1]

This leaves each instance of ethnic conflict to be managed ad hoc by both local and international actors. Because of the strength of America's resources and standing in most of the world, it is often called on to help in some way. Obviously, the United States cannot be everywhere at once, and the electorate would not tolerate such a broad commitment even if boundless resources were available. The government, therefore, needs to set priorities for its potential involvement in foreign countries. The piv-

---

* Note: The author would like to thank Tozun Bahcheli, Antonia Hadler Chayes, and Timothy Sisk for their insightful comments on this chapter.
1. The 1992 UN General Assembly Declaration on the Rights of Persons Belonging to National or Ethnic, Religious and Linguistic Minorities begins to address these issues.

otal states strategy could lend clarity to the United States intervention[2] dilemma; that is, if the strategy holds, U.S. policy should make a priority of involvement in the pivotal states to prevent or manage destabilizing internal conflict over involvement in other states that may be experiencing similar tensions. This chapter argues that the United States *should* adopt the pivotal states strategy as an organizing principle for its involvement in ethnic conflict, in addition to its existing obligations under international conventions and treaties. However, to be viable as an organizing principle, the strategy must be expanded to incorporate multilateral as well as unilateral action.

THE IMPERATIVE OF ETHNIC AND OTHER IDENTITY CONFLICTS

Ethnic and other identity conflicts are primarily *internal* conflicts, that is, they take place within the borders of a state. We can no longer view them through a Cold War lens, and without the Cold War lens they have become increasingly visible since the fall of the Soviet Union. From 1989 to 1996, of the 101 conflicts taking place in the world, 99 were internal.[3] As in Angola, the superpower rivalry during the Cold War exacerbated the animosities, but obviously there were real conflicts between local groups that had little to do with the United States and the Soviet Union. Suppression of intergroup conflicts was also common in the Soviet Union and the Warsaw Pact during the Cold War, and such tensions have risen to the surface now that the authoritarian regimes have fallen. These ethnic and other intergroup cleavages are one of the most serious threats to the stability and governability of states in the post–Cold War international system.

Why should the United States care about these disputes, most of which are occurring in the developing world? There are several reasons. First, developing countries matter in terms of markets, migrations into first world countries, cooperation on global issues such as environmental protection, and the potential for violence due to arms proliferation. Strong ethnic and other intergroup conflicts in these countries severely strain the ability of a government to function. If the conflict has become violent, the government must maintain a large internal army to counter the insur-

2. *Intervention* here is meant to include a range of policy options, not only military force. Thus, intervention could include preventive diplomacy, economic assistance or sanctions, technical assistance, support for financial aid or the development of democratic institutions, and so on.
3. Peter Wallensteen and Margaret Sollenberg, "The End of International War? Armed Conflict 1989–1996," *Journal of Peace Research* 34, no. 3 (1997): 339–358.

gents, which is very expensive and drains resources from other enterprises. It also eats away at the credibility of the existing government if the government cannot or will not respond to a large segment of its population. In this technological world, news of repression and internal violence are spread abroad instantly. Such governments are therefore under pressure not only from within but also from other governments, international organizations and lenders, and nongovernmental organizations (NGOs). Resisting such pressure also drains resources by taking the attention of decision makers away from more constructive political and economic activity. Most of the pivotal states are currently or potentially at risk in these ways.

A second reason for concern is the potential spillover to other neighboring states, especially if they are "kin" states (that is, home to a majority population of the same ethnicity as the minority population in the conflict) or if they contain a similar minority population. The Kurds are an example of a group with multiple minority status who reside in Turkey, Iraq, and Syria. Other examples include Albania as a kin state to the Albanians in Macedonia and Serbia, Hungary as the kin state to the Hungarians in Slovakia, and India as the kin state to the Tamils in Sri Lanka. States outside a region may also be brought into a conflict because of perceived ties to either the majority or the minority group's interests, which could serve to escalate or expand the conflict. Russian involvement in the Caucasus is an example.

Third, ethnic and other intergroup conflict creates potential long-term problems because it poisons the political and social environment. Once the "other side" has been vilified and dehumanized, as so readily happens in such conflicts, it is difficult to reverse the process psychologically and politically. The "us versus them" mentality is often institutionalized in the state structures, with political parties and government agencies deriving their role and identity from preserving the conflict.[4] This may erode the governability of the state over time, as happened in South Africa and may be happening currently in Algeria. The enormous challenge then becomes not only restructuring such institutions, but also changing the attitude and relationship between the conflicting groups.

WHAT CAN BE DONE ABOUT ETHNIC CONFLICTS?

In order to understand the options available to the United States in dealing with ethnic conflict in pivotal states or elsewhere, the nature of

---

4. James Notter and Louise Diamond, "Building Peace and Transforming Conflict: The Practice of the Institute for Multi-Track Diplomacy," Occasional Paper no. 7 (Washington, D.C.: Institute for Multi-Track Diplomacy, 1996).

the problem must be understood. This chapter cannot address that question fully, but a brief summary is important.

THE NATURE OF ETHNIC CONFLICT

Ethnic conflict is a term that refers to many different types of phenomena. It has become a conceptual proxy for any type of *internal* conflict (within the borders of a state) that violates or challenges the *identity* of a group, including religious and racial groups. It has become the catch-all label for any conflict that appears "irrational," in which the disputants seem willing to fight to the death to avenge historical grievances rather than to better their current status, and in which civilian populations bear the brunt of the harm.

Ethnic conflict is a special case of intergroup conflict in which the parties are groups or peoples rather than states, and the salient feature of the group's identity is its ethnicity. Ethnic and other identity conflicts have two major components: psychological and structural. To be sustainable, any resolution of these conflicts must address both aspects.

The psychological component is due to the kinship qualities of ethnicity, in which people feel connected to some common history or family.[5] These ties are subjective in nature; whether or not descent and bloodlines are in fact shared is not the issue. As Walker Connor states, "[I]t is not *what is,* but *what people believe is* that has behavioral consequences. A nation is a group of people characterized by a myth of common descent."[6] Examples include the indigenous peoples of North America and the Quebecois of Canada.

In addition to this myth of common descent, ethnic groups often share what some analysts have called "chosen traumas" and "chosen glories."[7]

---

5. Donald L. Horowitz, *Ethnic Groups in Conflict* (Berkeley: University of California Press, 1985), 52; Max Weber, "Ethnic Groups," in *Max Weber, Economy and Society: An Outline of Interpretive Sociology,* ed. G. Roth and C. Wittich (New York: Bedminster Press), 389; Walker Conner, *Ethnonationalism: The Quest for Understanding* (Princeton, N.J.: Princeton University Press, 1994), 74.

6. Connor, *Ethnonationalism,* 75.

7. Vamik D. Volkan and Norman Itzkowitz, *Turks and Greeks: Neighbours in Conflict* (Cambridgeshire, England: The Eothen Press, 1994), 7–10. A chosen trauma is an event that "invokes in the members of one group intense feelings of having been humiliated and victimized by members of another group. A group does not, of course 'choose' to be victimized and, subsequently, to lose self-esteem, but it does 'choose' to psychologize and mythologize—to dwell on the event. . . . Once a trauma becomes a chosen trauma, the historical truth about it does not really matter." Likewise, a chosen glory is an event that brings up feelings of having been successful or having triumphed over another group. "Chosen glories serve to bolster a group's present self-esteem and, like chosen traumas, are heavily mythologized."

Both become part of the group's identity and are passed along from generation to generation via stories, communal festivals, and history lessons. Because one, in effect, grows up with such myths, they are not easily relinquished.[8]

In addition to the psychological dimensions of ethnicity structural factors are also at work. These include competition and inequality among groups,[9] which can result in real or perceived disparities in privileges and access to political and economic resources. They may also come from new or continuing forms of discrimination whereby access to political or economic advancement is systematically blocked or one's group is actively persecuted, including prohibitions on the use of language, religion, or other cultural practices that are different from those of the dominant group.

A review of the scholarship on ethnic and other identity conflicts reveals several important insights. The first is that ethnicity, though defined by one's heritage and culture, is not necessarily the most salient aspect of one's identity at every moment in time. It can be subsumed by other factors, such as class or religion or even profession, until something occurs that causes one to feel threatened because of one's ethnic affiliation. Such affiliation may be self-defined or may be attributed by other groups. In the face of such threats, it is difficult to opt out of identity with your ethnic group because you are forced to choose sides; in an "us versus them" environment, the maxim "you are either for us or against us" is strongly upheld.

The second is that the threats to the survival of one's ethnic group may take many forms, real or perceived. When threatened, members of the same ethnic group will usually band together for either offensive action or defensive protection. It is worth noting that, even in situations like that in the former Yugoslavia where the role of the manipulative leader has

---

8. The Protestant marches in Northern Ireland to commemorate William of Orange and the Serbs' remembrance of their defeat at Kosovo in 1389 are examples of such chosen glories and traumas. A dramatic demonstration of how these past events can be interpreted differently by different groups and encroach on current events occurs on July 20 each year in Cyprus. That is the date when Turkish troops landed on the island in 1974. On the Greek Cypriot side of the island, it is a day of mourning. At 10 a.m. and then again at 10 p.m., church bells ring and people stop for five minutes of silence in remembrance of the Greeks who are still "missing" and unaccounted for from the Turkish "invasion." On the Turkish side, there is festivity and celebration as they commemorate their "liberation" from the Greek oppressors. Tension is highest at the Green Line, where the two groups face each other across the physical barriers and dramatize their separate and antagonistic interpretations of the day's meaning.

9. Ted Robert Gurr, "Minorities, Nationalists, and Ethnopolitical Conflict" in *Managing Global Chaos*, ed. Chester Crocker et al. (Washington, D.C.: United States Institute of Peace, 1996), 53–77.

been extensively described, such a leader has to have some basis on which to build his or her manipulation of fear. Thus, real or perceived threats become the basis for stirring the group to action.

Finally, when studying ethnic conflict we are more likely to focus on the threat to the lower power group because of concerns for protecting minority rights. But from a conflict resolution perspective, it is important to recognize that the higher power group may also feel threatened; this mutual fear creates a dynamic that is very difficult to diffuse. Intervention efforts that aim to resolve the conflict must attend to the fears of both groups, or the conflict, even if settled temporarily, will recur with the same vehemence at some point in the future.

The Nature of Intervention in Internal Identity Conflicts

The UN Charter established the principle of nonintervention[10] in the internal affairs of other countries. In Article 2.7, countries are instructed that "Nothing contained in the present Charter shall authorize the United Nations to intervene in matters which are essentially within the domestic jurisdiction of any state . . ."[11] But the same Article contains a caveat: "[T]his principle shall not prejudice the application of enforcement measures under Chapter VII." Chapter VII, of course, allows for intervention "to maintain or restore international peace and security." Even at its inception, the UN was authorized, under certain conditions, to interfere in the internal affairs of states, although such intrusions were rare. However, sovereignty was never an iron-clad constraint, even during the Cold War.

In addition, the Universal Declaration of Human Rights, the Helsinki Final Act, and the establishment of the Conference on Security and Cooperation in Europe were all steps to set standards and monitor human rights activity within state borders, especially in the countries dominated by the Soviet Union. But responses to such abuses were limited to exposing them publicly and trying to shame the host governments into changing their policies. In extreme cases, such as in dealing with the apartheid regime in South Africa, more drastic measures like economic sanctions were imposed to put pressure on the offending government.

Since the end of the Cold War, with the increase in intrastate conflicts, the international community has begun more explicitly to revisit the rules and norms regarding sovereignty and intervention. Confusion has arisen because the norms are sometimes in conflict: support for national self-determination without also inadvertently supporting "tyranny of the

10. This refers to the more traditional, limited definition of intervention as the use of force.
11. The Charter of the United Nations, in *Everyone's United Nations: A Handbook on the Work of the United Nations* (New York: United Nations), Appendix.

majority"; support for human rights principles while also respecting governments' needs to provide barriers against aggressive or imperial forces; concern for the rights of individuals versus the rights of peoples and groups; and acknowledging the need for order in the international system while supporting the principle of self-determination.[12] The Cold War muted these issues somewhat, but ethnic conflicts bring them all squarely to the fore in questioning when and how to intervene.

So far, two trends are emerging from the confusion. The first is the move away from sovereignty as defined by control over territory and borders and toward sovereignty as the legitimacy conveyed by links to a defined population.[13] This is historically depicted as the difference between a "state" and a "nation." The international recognition since 1991 of Eritrea, the Czech Republic, Slovakia, and the successor states of the Soviet Union and Yugoslavia illustrates this trend.

The second trend is the powerful and moral imperative of humanitarian intervention. Even after the perceived failure of the Somalia mission, the human tragedies in Rwanda, Bosnia, and Zaire prompted international cries for more than humanitarian assistance. Nongovernmental organizations and the United Nations High Commissioner for Refugees (UNHCR), along with the International Committee of the Red Cross (ICRC), will always show up as states are disintegrating, thousands are dying, and refugees are on the move. The question is, who else should be there to help create order out of the chaos? It may be politically risky for the United States to get involved in such crises, but it may become equally difficult to stay out.

The Purpose and Timing of Outsider Involvement

The questions of purpose and timing are intimately related, as the goal of any intervention depends to a large extent on the phase or stage of the conflict.[14] *Conflict prevention* occurs before a conflict escalates to violence. The purpose of such an intervention is to stop the escalation. Scholars and practitioners have identified early warning signs that indicate when escalation is beginning. In situations of ethnic conflict, these can include the passage or increased enforcement of discriminatory language or employ-

---

12. Stanley Hoffmann, "The Crisis of Liberal Internationalism," *Foreign Policy*, March 22, 1995: 159.

13. J. S. Barkin and B. Cronin, "The State and the Nation: Changing Norms and the Rules of Sovereignty in International Relations," *International Organization* 48, no. 1 (winter 1994): 108.

14. Boutros Boutros-Ghali, *An Agenda for Peace* (New York: United Nations, 1992); Michael Lund, *Preventing Violent Conflict* (Washington, D.C.: United States Institute of Peace Press, 1996).

ment laws; increases in human rights abuses of minority groups; inflammatory rhetoric that demonizes another group; or establishment or increased activity of ethnically based political parties. Preventive diplomacy should aim to reverse these provocative trends and to understand and address the underlying concerns that motivated them.

Another view on prevention is that ethnic conflict is a by-product of a disintegrating state, not the cause of such disintegration.[15] If one takes this view, the early warning indicators become a bit different, requiring forecasting of state collapse rather than of increasing ethnic cleavage. At least two of the indicators are similar to those of impending ethnic violence: uneven economic development along ethnic lines and a legacy of vengeance-seeking group grievance or group paranoia.[16]

Conflict management is the goal when conflict has already escalated to violence. The aim is to stop the violence and to get the parties to the negotiating table to construct an agreement that ends the conflict. At this stage, sometimes a painful trade-off must be made between waiting to get the best possible agreement (that is, one that meets the most important needs of the parties and satisfies international norms of justice and fairness) and getting a suboptimal agreement that at least stops the killing and allows a peace-building process to begin. Bosnia is the most recent example of such a trade-off. The Dayton Accord was probably the best deal that could be struck as of 1995 when it was negotiated, and it did stop the war and end the violence. But it is far from clear that the parties to the conflict feel that their interests were sufficiently met, or that the peace building taking place under the guidelines of Dayton provides a just and secure basis for stable governance and refugee return.

Post-settlement peace building occurs after an agreement has been reached between the parties in conflict. Its goals are multiple and usually include establishing or reestablishing the rule of law; jump-starting economic development, including rebuilding of infrastructure; encouraging political development, including the organizing of multiparty elections and movement toward democratic institutions; and building or rebuilding a functioning civil society. Though discussed so often they can sound like clichés, these steps are very complex and take a long time to achieve. Bosnia is again the telling example. If done well, these steps lay not only the structural but also the psychological foundation necessary for peace to be sustained. They determine whether peace will hold or unravel to reproduce the ethnic tensions that could once again escalate into violence.

15. Pauline H. Baker and John A. Ausink, "State Collapse and Ethnic Violence: Toward a Predictive Model," *Parameters*, spring 1996: 19–31.
16. Baker and Ausink, "State Collapse," 26.

At all three of these phases, any intervention should therefore ensure that the grievances behind the conflict are acknowledged and addressed in both psychological and structural ways. Structural change includes looking at possible new approaches to power sharing within the country, whether through restructured executive and parliamentary bodies; the creation of multiple political parties where only one existed before; election rules that are more balanced; or more equitable distribution of access to economic resources. Alternatively, it could mean increased separation of the groups through autonomy or independence. In addition, standards of justice and adherence to human rights norms should be established and maintained.

The other dimension of prevention, management, and peace building that must accompany the structural changes is psychological. The parties in an ethnic conflict don't have to love each other, but they do have to accept the reality of living together in an interdependent way. This means forging some kind of working partnership, whether in the same country or in adjacent countries. Since the essence of intergroup conflict is the construction of an "us versus them" mentality, this attitude must shift or soften sufficiently so that trust is established and functional cooperation, at the very least, is possible.[17] This is not an easy or instantly achievable outcome, but it is essential to sustainable peace. Useful approaches have included the design of development projects that foster collaboration across ethnic lines and nonofficial meetings of influential members of each group who can discuss the difficulties of changing the political relationship and design strategies for doing so.

Types of Intervention

There are many important dimensions that a potential intervenor must consider before deciding on the most effective type of intervention: to be an advisor or advocate for one party, or to be a neutral intermediary; if acting as an intermediary, whether to offer good offices, facilitation, or mediation (reflecting ascending levels of involvement in the substance and process); to use economic, political, or military resources (or some combination or sequencing of the three); to offer carrots or sticks (incentives or disincentives), or a combination or sequencing of both; to act alone or in concert with other intervenors. The choice of the type of intervention will depend, to a large extent, on the purpose and timing, as discussed above, and on the resources and stature of the intervenor.

---

17. Herbert C. Kelman, "Social Psychological Dimensions of International Conflict," in *Peacemaking in International Conflict*, ed. I. William Zartman and J. Lewis Rasmussen (Washington, D.C.: United States Institute of Peace), 191–237.

In addition to governments and intergovernmental organizations, nonofficial actors are increasingly intervening in ethnic conflicts. These include eminent persons (former diplomats and heads of state, such as Jimmy Carter); business leaders; scholars; and nongovernmental organizations with expertise in conflict management. The advantage of such nonofficial intervenors is their ability, in some cases, to convene parties off the record and to meet with parties that cannot be "recognized" by official actors.

THE PRIORITY OF PIVOTAL STATES IN THE GLOBAL MANAGEMENT OF ETHNIC OR IDENTITY CONFLICT

The pivotal states strategy recommends a focus on nine states as a priority for United States foreign policy in the developing world. The question is, does this make sense in terms of managing ethnic conflict? As stated above, such conflicts and related internal divisions are the predominant disputes in the world and promise to be so for the coming decades. The relaxing of nonintervention norms and the imperatives of impending or occurring conflict could put pressure on the United States to become involved. The conflict analysis framework discussed above provides guidance on appropriate intervention points and strategies. It does not, however, help with the question of *where* to step in. Should these nine states receive special attention in this context?

On the one hand, the strategy cannot wholly dictate where the United States may commit its resources regarding ethnic conflict. As a signatory to the 1948 Convention on the Prevention and Punishment of the Crime of Genocide, for example, the United States is obligated to prevent the crime of genocide.[18] And domestic constituencies, CNN broadcasts, international and alliance pressures, and other political dynamics will always create "situationally" pivotal states. Bosnia and Somalia were examples of these.

But there are also powerful reasons why the pivotal states identified in this volume *should* be given priority, all things being equal. The first is that, taken together, they comprise half the population of the developing world and one-third of the total world population (see p. 7). Arguably, if the stability of these countries reflects justice and power sharing, their example will go a long way toward creating a climate for similar dispute settlement around the world. For a brief period in 1994, major strides were taken in Northern Ireland, South Africa, and in the Israeli-

---

18. Convention on the Prevention and Punishment of the Crime of Genocide, 78 UNTS, December 1948, 277.

Palestinian conflict. In many other conflict-ridden parts of the world, people were saying, "If they can do it, maybe we can too." The impact would be even greater with the combined influence of the nine pivotal states.

A second reason is that, as individual states, they could be major *bell-wethers* of internal conflict in several strategic regions. As bellwether states, they would indicate the direction that ethnic or identity issues could take, either constructive or destructive, in their region or in other states experiencing similar kinds of internal conflict.

In looking at the pivotal states, we can group them in terms of the kinds of identity conflicts they contain and the phase in which each conflict currently sits (Table 1).

Table 1. IDENTITY CONFLICTS IN THE PIVOTAL STATES

Phase of Conflict	Type of Conflict		
	Ethnic/Racial	*Religious*	*Class*
Prevention	Indonesia	Indonesia	Brazil
	Pakistan	Egypt	Mexico
	India	Turkey	
Management	Turkey	Algeria	
	India	Pakistan	
	Pakistan	India	
Peace building	South Africa		

Two examples from the table will serve to illustrate the ways such states can be used as bellwethers and the challenges to the United States in determining whether to be involved.

Turkey and the Kurds

The primary ethnic conflict in Turkey concerns its Kurdish minority population. It is estimated that there are about 12 million Kurds in Turkey, making up roughly 19–20 percent of the population.[19] They have historically lived in the high mountains in the southeast of the country, and the population extends also into Iraq, Iran, and Syria, bringing the total number of Kurds to an estimated 25 million.[20] However, the Turkish government has acknowledged their existence as a distinct non-Turkish group only since 1991, having banned their language at the formation of

19. David McDowall, "The Kurdish Question," in *The Kurds: A Contemporary Overview*, ed. P. G. Kreyenbroek and S. Sperl (London and New York: Routledge Press, 1992), 32.
20. Gerard Chaliand, *The Kurdish Tragedy* (London: Zed Books, 1992), 14.

the secular state in the early 1920s and having tried unsuccessfully to assimilate them into an overarching Turkish identity.

In the 1970s, a number of clandestine Kurdish political parties emerged, specifically dedicated to Kurdish self-determination and secession from Turkey. In 1984, one of these, the Kurdistan Workers Party (PKK), undertook a campaign of violence in order to secure Kurdish rights. Although most Kurdish people abhorred the PKK's tactics, the draconian countermeasures often used by government forces has increased the support (or at least the noninterference) of most of the Kurds in eastern Turkey. In addition, the Kurdish expatriate community in Western Europe has been growing, and their location in urban centers has increased their political sophistication and their organizing on behalf of Kurdish rights. The Turkish government can no longer pretend that there is no "Kurdish problem."

The Turkish government's concern is the identity of the Turkish state and the preservation of Ataturk's edict that all citizens of the state must adopt a Turkish identity. The military in particular has taken on the role of protecting and defending this definition of Turkish identity and sees the Kurds as a threat to the integrity of the state. On the Kurdish side, many have, in fact, assimilated. But there is a strong desire for recognition of the Kurdish language and culture as distinct from those of the Turks and, in the Kurdish area of Turkey's southeast, still a demand for devolution of power and the establishment of an autonomous region.

The nature of the two entities that would have to negotiate a way out of this dilemma makes a constructive outcome more difficult to achieve. The PKK, unlike the Palestinian Liberation Organization (PLO) in the Palestinian community, is not considered the sole legitimate representative of the Kurdish people. Although their activities are not denounced by many Kurds, their leader, Abdullah Ocalan, has no authority to negotiate on their behalf. In any event, the government has adamantly insisted that no such negotiation can take place with the PKK because of its terrorist activities. Still, the PKK is the strongest group by far in the fragmented Kurdish community. Several more moderate political parties have emerged, but they have been attacked by the PKK and squelched by the Turkish government as well, with many of their leaders arrested.

On the government side, the 1995 elections brought a shaky coalition to power, headed by the Islamist Welfare Party. The coalition lost a no-confidence vote in the Parliament in the spring of 1997, and as of this writing another coalition government has been formed under the leadership of Prime Minister Mesut Yilmaz, with new elections to be held on a yet-to-be-determined date. The instability of the ruling coalitions within Turkey does not bode well for managing the Kurdish problem. On the one hand, the Welfare Party courted the Kurds in the 1995 elections, and though the party has now been officially banned, a possible successor Islamist party may still draw support from Kurds in the upcoming elections. On the other hand, any new prime minister, even one with Kurdish support, may not be strong enough politically to risk the integrity of the government by negotiating with even the moderate Kurds and appearing "soft" on the PKK. Also, the acquiescence of the military to any political settlement will be needed, and that will be hard to obtain.

The costs to Turkey of continuing its Kurdish policy are great. "Indeed, the Kurdish problem has become the Achilles' heel of an otherwise promising Turkish future."[21] The conflict is undermining Turkey's economy directly, with the PKK threatening that " 'no oil pipelines [from the Caspian Sea region] can be laid without an agreement with us, and if they are laid it will not be possible to operate them.' Turkish officials themselves admitted that revenue losses due to PKK attacks and threats against the tourism industry have contributed to the current deficit, while Morton I. Abramowitz, the U.S. ambassador to Turkey from 1989 to 1991, wrote that 'the war against the PKK absorbs perhaps as much as 30 per cent of military forces and a substantial though undisclosed portion of the state budget.' "[22]

If Turkey is considered as a bellwether, its ability to come to terms with its Kurdish population could set the tone for settlement with the Kurds in neighboring countries and serve as an important lesson for governments in other young and emerging democracies (such as those in the Caucasus) to deal fairly with their minority populations before violence and costs escalate and the only acceptable outcomes are autonomy or secession. Like the Oslo Accord between Israel and the Palestinians, a settlement could also, depending on its stability, lower the temperature in the Middle East region due to decreased military activity and terrorism. Continuation of the conflict provides an ongoing demonstration of the problems created by ignoring minority claims and disallowing the expression of group identity. It also tests the patience of Western states for human rights abuses, especially if arms purchased from countries such as the United States are shown to have been used against Kurdish citizens.

Washington has discussed these issues with Turkish officials in Ankara and has let them know of U.S. misgivings. Some arms sales have been subject to review because of these concerns.[23] And the European Union has

21. Michael M. Gunter, *The Changing Kurdish Problem in Turkey* (London: Research Institute for the Study of Conflict and Terrorism, 1994), 1.

22. Gunter, 22.

23. Phone interview with Steve Klemp, U.S. State Department desk officer for Turkey, July 1997.

cited the Kurdish issue as one of the reasons for refusing Turkey admission. However, no sanctions or more serious measures are being contemplated, either by the United States or Europe. The primary reasons are: no strong public outcry, in the United States or Europe, against repression of the Kurds, as there was against apartheid in South Africa; a reluctance on the part of the United States to confront the Turkish government, especially when its ruling coalition is shaky, because of the American strategic relationship with Turkey as a NATO member and as a perceived bulwark against Islamic fundamentalism in southeastern Europe and southwest Asia; and no real European champions of Turkey's candidacy for the EU. In addition, the United States views the PKK as a terrorist organization and does not object to the Turkish military's attempts to squelch it.[24]

However, the United States *is* concerned about spillover, as is evident from its decision to send forces to northern Iraq for Operation Provide Comfort. In the aftermath of the gulf war in 1991, the Kurds in Iraq responded to U.S. encouragement to rise up against a weakened Saddam Hussein. They were brutally crushed, and many fled into neighboring countries. Turkey closed its border, and many thousands of Iraqi Kurds were stranded in the high mountains that separate the two states. The decision to send in U.S. forces was a difficult one, with many arguments against such a move. However, one of the factors that tipped the balance in favor of U.S. involvement was the fear that the Kurdish refugees could destabilize Turkey. Thus there *is* an awareness on the part of the U.S. government that the Kurdish situation could threaten Turkey's integrity.

Nongovernmental efforts to bring the moderate Kurds together with government officials have been initiated by both local and U.S.–based organizations. Such meetings have been useful in exploring possibilities for a more constructive relationship between the two sides, but so far have not translated into significant political action on the part of the Turkish government.

South Africa

South Africa is an example of a bellwether state that tests the possibilities of power sharing after an extreme asymmetry of power between internal groups, and the ability of a "young" democracy to manage the significant threat of ethnic conflict.[25]

Since its inception as a dominion, South Africa had been governed by

---

24. Klemp phone interview.
25. Donald Horowitz, "Democracy in Divided Societies," *Journal of Democracy* 4, no. 4 (1993): 18–38.

its white minority population. In 1948, with the ascendance of the Afrikaner National Party, the government began the construction of the apartheid apparatus, which institutionalized the separation of the South African population into white, black, Asian/Indian and Coloured groupings. Now notorious for their terrible discrimination against the non-white population, the governments that upheld and enforced apartheid were pariahs in the world community. In 1990, South Africa's government finally bowed under the weight of sanctions, internal resistance, and violence to recognize the African National Congress (ANC). In 1994 it proceeded to a transitional government, a new constitution, and finally to multiparty elections, which ultimately brought the first majority-rule government to power.

Ethnic cleavages in South Africa played out most notably in the prelude to elections; the most reactionary Afrikaner groups wanted to stop the transition altogether, and the Zulu Inkatha Freedom Party (IFP) sought to ensure a more decentralized power structure out of fear that an ANC sweep would push them to the margin. A large number of the Coloured population, who had been opposed to the National Party, supported the change in government but were unsure what treatment to expect under black majority rule. Currently, ethnic cleavages in South Africa manifest in several ways:[26] continuing intergroup tensions between ANC supporters and the Inkatha Freedom Party in KwaZulu Natal; African-Coloured tensions in the Western Cape; campus conflicts at all of the major universities along racial and ethnic lines; and ethnic conflicts within the workplace, particularly at some mines and within the South African Police Services. However, the predicted escalation of ethnic and racial tensions sufficient to derail the transition did not take place. In fact, the power-sharing arrangements established in the transitional constitution have proven very successful so far in moving South Africa toward its goal of a "nonracial" society.[27]

Several factors have mitigated against ethnic tensions. The first is the leadership of Nelson Mandela and F. W. de Klerk. Mandela is unique both in the authority and respect he commands and in his commitment to inclusion and national unity. He reflects the original ANC commitment to a nonracial country in which people are not rewarded or punished because of their race. He has reached out to include Chief Mangosuthu Buthelezi of the Inkatha Freedom Party into his political circle, recently

26. Timothy Sisk, "Sustaining a Culture of Bargaining: Political Institutions and Ethnic Conflict Management in Post-Apartheid South Africa," unpublished discussion paper for the U.S. State Department (1997).
27. Timothy Sisk, *Power Sharing and International Mediation in Ethnic Conflicts* (Washington, D.C.: United States Institute of Peace, 1996).

appointing him as acting president while Mandela was out of the country. And Mandela has established his credibility with the Afrikaners as well as with the black and Coloured populations because of his vision of a nonracial society and his political skill. His leadership has been key to the success of the transition and the early years of the new government.

Former president de Klerk has also helped to diffuse tensions. His political skill in bringing along the Afrikaner population and the National Party has been exemplary; he has also succeeded in neutralizing the Afrikaner far-right wing.

Second, the apartheid regime fostered a society systematically structured around racial and ethnic exclusion. Most South Africans want to avoid continuation of that policy in any form. To this end, the peace process has included both structural and psychological dimensions.

Structurally, the constitution allows the citizens of the state to participate directly in electing the four-hundred-person National Assembly (according to party list proportional representation), and to participate indirectly through the nine newly created provinces in electing the ninety-person Council of Provinces. The National Assembly then elects, by majority, the executive president, who is the head of state.[28] Any party obtaining more than eighty seats in the National Assembly is also entitled to nominate a deputy president.[29] This connection between the electorate and the leadership is crucial, because so many have been disenfranchised in the past. It also protects minority parties and provides for their continued participation.

In addition, traditional leaders have been accommodated at all three levels of government (national, provincial, and local) through provincial legislatures and autonomous, third-tier local governmental bodies in which traditional leaders are to be ex officio members. This could meet a "key requirement for strengthening the state: that existing rules of social control be made compatible with and supportive of those prescribed by the state."[30]

In psychological terms, the process of arriving at the transitional constitution and the accounting for grievances under the apartheid regime were carefully crafted to elicit maximum inclusion and open discussion, and to begin to heal the wounds created by apartheid. The National Peace

28. Pierre DuToit, *State Building and Democracy in Southern Africa* (Washington, D.C.: United States Institute of Peace, 1995), 210–211.
29. The ANC and the National Party each nominated a deputy president, Thebo Mbeki and F. W. de Klerk, respectively. The National Party pulled out of the government of national unity in mid-1996, to form what it called a true opposition party.
30. DuToit, *State Building*, 210.

Accord, signed on September 14, 1991, by the leaders of all political groups in the country (except three white right-wing groups), established the basic principles that would govern the transition and beyond. It succeeded in "developing a 'peace culture,' in securing an ideological commitment from the principal political actors to 'political tolerance,' and in being able to establish procedures and mechanisms for crisis management."[31]

Equally powerful is the Truth and Reconciliation Commission, which is soliciting testimony from perpetrators of political violence and granting amnesty in exchange for coming forward. Unlike the tribunals in Rwanda and Bosnia, the commission will not punish offenders, but will instead decide who warrants amnesty of those who come forward, and what reparations may be due the victims. The hope is that this will provide "restorative justice," such that reconciliation and not revenge will prevail.[32]

There are, however, incidents indicating that ethnic and racial tensions are not completely absent and could resurface. Localized intra-Zulu confrontations in Natal still occur, as do isolated bombings by radical Afrikaner groups. The crime rate has also skyrocketed, especially in the major cities, causing fears to rise among the white population in particular. Finally, new illegal immigrants from other African states are creating tensions due to squatting and perceived involvement in crime.[33]

It seems unlikely that ethnic tensions will escalate to violent conflict in the near future. However, several possible flashpoints in the coming months and years should be anticipated. The first is the election scheduled for 1999, which will decide on a permanent constitution. The test of any new democracy is not its first election, but its second, when the international community is no longer a big presence. The second election demonstrates the extent to which democratic principles have taken root. Thebo Mbeki is in line to take Mandela's place in the ANC but it is not clear what the opposition parties will look like then or how strongly they will play on ethnic and racial divisions to garner votes. In addition, the absence of Mandela from the political scene will be a great loss. His stature is unparalleled, even though Mbeki is well respected. Mandela is a strong force behind reconciliation, and it's not clear who else could play that role when necessary.

The last issue concerns economic opportunity and access. The people of South Africa have, so far, been patient with the difficulties in trying to

31. International Alert, quoted in Peter Gastrow, *Bargaining for Peace: South Africa and the National Peace Accord* (Washington, D.C.: United States Institute of Peace, 1995), 93.
32. Timothy Garton Ash, "True Confessions," *New York Review of Books* XLIV, no. 12 (1997): 33.
33. Interview with Timothy Sisk, United States Institute of Peace, February 1997.

rectify decades of discrimination. If the economy should take a major downturn, and the black population feels it is not achieving promised adjustments, racial division could reopen as each group tries to get a larger share of the pie.

So far, South Africa appears to be a success story, unlike the more unfortunate postsettlement cases of Bosnia and Cambodia. The world will watch its progress intently, as a test case for power sharing and conflict resolution. It has become a beacon in the dark for many countries still struggling with intergroup violence; people from South Africa are now traveling to other parts of Africa and the rest of the world (Northern Ireland, Cyprus, Bosnia, Rwanda, Nigeria, and so on) to tell their stories and provide examples of both structural and psychological processes that others may follow.

A BRIEF COMMENT ON THE REMAINING PIVOTAL STATES

Brief comments on the remaining pivotal states will round out the discussion. Identification of the major identity conflicts within each are drawn from the country profiles contained in this volume.

Algeria

As of this writing, Islamist groups are opposing the government, primarily through terrorism. The government is seeking to delegitimize this opposition and consolidate its own power. Algeria could be seen as a bellwether for diffusing militant and opposition groups in North Africa and the Middle East.

Brazil

Conflicts are primarily class based, relating to concentrations of wealth and land. Some racial overtones exist, as many blacks are poverty stricken. Brazil could be a bellwether for addressing such inequities in all of Latin America.

Egypt

Egypt is engaged in an ongoing "cultural war," in which various Islamic and Coptic Christian groups compete to control social norms and laws governing personal behavior and cultural practices. This is a bellwether for the potentials of liberalization and pluralism in North Africa and the Middle East.

India

The dominant conflict is the ongoing one with Pakistan over Kashmir. Also notable are the internal separatist movements, such as the Sikhs in

Punjab. India is a bellwether for Hindu-Muslim reconciliation and for management of diversity in a large, multiethnic state.

Indonesia

Tensions between the devout Muslim community and Christians, and in some regions between natives and migrants, are growing. The conflict with East Timor over its independence also continues. In addition, the Chinese minority often elicits envy and suspicion because of their great wealth. Indonesia is an Asian bellwether for managing incipient disputes in a pluralistic and democratizing society.

Mexico

Conflicts take the form of disputes over land tenure and other resources between the majority population and the Indian population. Mexico could be a bellwether for dealing with indigenous claims.

Pakistan

Because of Pakistan's failure to accommodate ethnic, linguistic, regional, and cultural diversity in a pluralistic and democratic framework, it is a bellwether for the ability of a newly democratizing state to institute such accommodation. The ongoing conflict with India over Kashmir, as stated above, is a bellwether for Hindu-Muslim reconciliation.

IMPLICATIONS FOR UNITED STATES POLICY

This analysis leads to several recommendations for American decision makers:

1. *In the absence of other pressures, focus on pivotal states.*

At present, the United States lacks an organizing principle for determining where and how to intervene in ethnic and other intergroup conflicts. All things being equal, and recognizing that situational pressures might dictate otherwise at any given moment, the United States should focus its attention on the pivotal states, asking what appropriate action might be taken in each, either bilaterally or multilaterally, to prevent or manage existing ethnic conflicts.

This contrasts with another proposed strategy, which might involve the United States in an ideological conflict with Islam.[34] Rather than perpetuate a siege mentality and another "us versus them" struggle akin to the Cold War, the pivotal states strategy would have the United

---

34. Samuel Huntington, *The Clash of Civilizations and the Remaking of World Order* (New York: Simon and Schuster, 1996).

States engaged with strategically important regional and global bell-wether states in a positive and proactive way.

2. *Conflict prevention should be pursued whenever possible.*

Rather than waiting for conflicts to escalate to violence, the United States should engage in preventive action in the pivotal states where appropriate (see Table 1). Preventive action can include diplomatic initiatives to bring potential disputants into discussion, or encouragement of, or sometimes pressuring for, the protection of minority rights and acknowledgment of grievances. Such action can also include economic incentives, both unilateral and multilateral, for political liberalization and support for NGO activity to develop civil society.

To return to the example of Turkey, the United States should be alert to how it might support the prodemocracy factions in Turkey and to how it might provide aid that helps raise the standard of living for the millions of poor Turkish citizens susceptible to influence by radical Islamic factions. The United States should also work slowly but steadily with the Turkish military to balance civil-military relations in the country.

The United States should also support "Track II" diplomacy efforts between the Turkish government and the Kurdish community. It is not appropriate for official parties to convene such discussions at this stage. But nonofficial groups can assist the parties in exploring options, with the hope that a future, more stable government might move the conflict toward settlement.

In some cases, the relationship with a particular country may be such that American carrots or sticks will encourage preventive action. Other cases will require multilateral efforts. Each case should be analyzed to determine the most effective approach. For example, indirect U.S. influence can be exercised through international lenders as well as through intergovernmental organizations.

3. *Multilateral action is a necessary component of prevention, management, and peace building. The United States should build the coalitions and support the international institutions that make such multilateral efforts possible.*

The pivotal states strategy rests on the notion of unilateralism, of the United States acting in the context of its bilateral relationship with each of the nine states to enhance their stability and influence their trajectory of development in a variety of ways. The days of unlimited unilateral reach, however, are over. The problems of policy posed to the American government by internal identity conflicts, just as with issues of environment and human rights, pointedly demonstrate that the United States simply lacks both the leverage and the legitimacy, in many cases, to take effective unilateral action on these critical issues.

The United States is currently the world's only superpower, which means that its leadership is needed and its resources, particularly militarily, are unique and likely to stay that way. However, the United States by its very strength is perceived as a bully unless it is part of a multilateral military effort. And economic unilateralism is ineffective; in particular, any independent efforts to use economic sanctions can be nullified by other economically powerful states. Even U.S. diplomatic pressure will be insufficient to prevail in many of these pivotal states without assistance from other international actors.

For example, the Kurdish issue is an extremely sensitive one in Turkey. Given the weakness of the present coalition government and the military's resistance to find a political solution, only with a concerted effort by the United States *and* European institutions (the EU, NATO, OSCE [Organization for Security and Cooperation in Europe], and so on) to offer both carrots and sticks to the Turkish government will any progress be possible. As mentioned above, official and nonofficial efforts must be coordinated to bring the parties together for discussion.

What does this say for the pivotal states strategy? Its unilateral emphasis must be broadened, because the United States has to be prepared to enlist allies in whatever efforts it proposes. The nine states must therefore be seen as pivotal to others as well, in order for the American government to build consensus and coalitions for international action.

4. *Internal coordination of U.S. policy making on ethnic conflict should be strengthened.*

The U.S. government will be in no position to execute effectively either unilateral or multilateral efforts to prevent or manage ethnic conflicts unless its own house is in order. At present, bureaus and other subunits within several government agencies[35] have pieces of the action, but no one place exists in which all these separate activities are coordinated.

A standing group on conflict prevention and management should be established, under the leadership of either the State Department or the National Security Council. It should be convened at the Deputy Assistant Secretary (DAS) level, to provide sufficient senior status so that its deliberations will carry weight. Membership should include representatives from the relevant government agencies and bureaus mentioned above.

35. This includes the Departments of State and Defense, the National Security Council, USAID, the Departments of Justice and Health and Human Services, and the intelligence bureaus.

The group's purpose would be to share information and coordinate preventive efforts, and to avoid humanitarian emergencies and government collapse created by intergroup violence. This group would take a longer-range view than is normally the case in government analysis, looking for the early warning signals of escalation and taking coordinated action to forestall such escalation. In cases where violence has already erupted, it could continue to function as the crucial link and bridge between the activity of separate agencies. In addition to its own operational expertise, the group should draw upon regional specialists and conflict resolution experts in analyzing information and in designing intervention strategies.

As stated above, such action may be more effectively taken multilaterally, but the United States is often in the position to lead these efforts. If such a coordinating body is established, the combined expertise of many government agencies could be brought to bear in a timely way and could establish the effectiveness of the United States as a leader in both preventing and managing ethnic conflicts.

INTERNATIONAL FINANCE, TRADE, AND THE PIVOTAL STATES

Robert Chase

Of all the "crosscutting" international trends that link events in the pivotal states to U.S. interests, perhaps none has such a dramatic impact as transnational financial and trade flows. Although the rapidly changing dynamics of economic interdependence have brought prosperity to many people, they have also introduced financial volatility and economic insecurity, which overshadow future prospects for stable growth. After a decade of breathless enthusiasm for global deregulation and integration, economists, bankers, and politicians are beginning to appreciate the ways in which interdependence is a double-edged sword.

If this wary interpretation is justified, it suggests the Mexican peso crisis of 1994 and 1995 was a harbinger of things to come rather than a freakish aberration in an otherwise healthy global economy. Obviously, that particular crisis captured the attention of U.S. policy makers. The United States' new NAFTA trade partner suffered through a currency crisis that led to severe currency devaluation, massive outflows of portfolio investment, and a general loss of confidence in the viability of emerging market investments. In skittish response to economic difficulties in Mexico, capital evacuated otherwise strong emerging economies in what has come to be known as the "tequila effect." To shore up the Mexican economy and inspire greater confidence in the financial system, the U.S. government acted boldly to organize the IMF and the international community to offer Mexico a generous bailout program. The Mexico crisis vividly illustrated how promising economic prospects can reverse themselves with startling capriciousness and far-ranging effect on today's global financial system.

Three years later, economic turmoil engulfed another pivotal state. With Indonesia's difficulties at its epicenter, the Asian financial crisis has shaken global economic prospects so severely that the aftershocks may be felt for years. With almost no warning, Indonesia pivoted from being a potential wellspring of growth for Southeast Asia to becoming that region's economic sinkhole. The U.S. and the international community have not decided how to respond to challenges the crisis presents, but some sort of systematic response is needed. As our original article highlighted,[1] issues of economics and finance are now a central concern of U.S. foreign policy. Further, United States policy needs to pay particular attention to pivotal states such as Mexico and Indonesia because of the joint opportunities and perils those economies present.

The peso and Asian crises could not have occurred twenty-five years ago. Since the Second World War, the economies of the United States, Europe, and Japan (the G-7 countries) have become well integrated, rarely involving the developing world in the process. Because they shared levels of development, economic policy institutions, and Cold War objectives, these industrial countries could build profound trade and financial linkages. But in recent years economic relations between the G-7 countries and some developing nations have also broadened and deepened. This increase in interdependence of financial and trade flows beyond the United States' traditional economic partners allowed the crises in Mexico and Indonesia to occur and to reverberate around the globe.

Fearing just such crises, many people are wary of interdependence and globalization. However, interdependence has positive effects that are often discounted. It allows those select few developing economies that become integrated through financial and trade flows to grow quickly, offering promising investment opportunities and export markets for industrialized countries. Unmistakably, the U.S. economy can gain from the prosperity of these developing countries. International economic integration can be mutually beneficial.

In the recent histories of the pivotal states, overall economic prospects have fluctuated between quite promising and rather grim. Looking ahead in these countries, optimistic analysts see enthusiastic booms where pessimistic analysts see listless stagnation. As the Mexico and Indonesia crises show, economic prospects for these economies can pivot dramatically, for these economies rest on narrow fulcrums. Though even the most careful observers have difficulty identifying them beforehand, seemingly insignificant events can tip the balance in the pivotal states. In addition, because of integration, economic booms or busts will spill over to the industrialized countries. These spillovers mean that the economic futures of the

---

1. Robert S. Chase, Emily B. Hill, and Paul Kennedy, "Pivotal States and U.S. Strategy," *Foreign Affairs* 75, no. 1 (January–February 1996): 33–51.

pivotal states matter to the United States. Thus, although the economic dimension is not the only factor to identify which states are pivotal, it is certainly crucial.

CHANGED ECONOMIC LANDSCAPE

For most of the post–World War II era, the United States could divide its economic relations into three categories. According to a scheme referred to elsewhere in this volume, in the economic realm countries fell into groups of "Friends," "Enemies," and "the Rest." With its select group of Friends, the United States had deep economic linkages so that investment and trade flowed liberally. Comprising the Western European countries, Japan, and Canada, these economic allies had comparable levels of development as measured by GNP per capita. They also followed broadly similar approaches to economic policy. As a result of their common development state and outlook, they shared leadership of Western international economic institutions. Although internal tensions certainly arose, it was easy to recognize the economic allies of the United States.

Tensions among Friends remained under control because, for much of the last fifty years, Enemies in the economic realm were also starkly apparent. Throughout the Cold War, the United States had very limited economic interactions with the Soviet Union and members of the Council for Mutual Economic Assistance. Though similar levels of economic development between East and West might have allowed deeper economic linkages, East and West did not exchange goods or investment because of the fundamentally different approaches to how an economy should operate.

Beyond solidifying the United States' primary economic alliances, the Cold War sparked competition between West and East for allegiances with the Rest. Both the United States and the Soviet Union built economic links with developing countries, based not on economic but on political considerations. Having much lower per capita income, more scarce human and physical capital, and rudimentary economic institutions, the less-developed countries were dissimilar to the United States and its primary OECD allies. Because of these differences, neither the United States nor the less-developed countries themselves saw their economic relationship as one between equals. Development assistance was the primary economic link between OECD countries and the developing world. Trade and investment often reflected colonial patterns. When the United States expended foreign policy energy building connections in the developing world, those connections did not create deep economic interdependence.

Distinctions between Friends, Enemies, and the Rest have disintegrated in recent years. Now that the Soviet Union has collapsed and its economic approach is discredited, the United States no longer has clear-cut ways to distinguish economic friends from enemies. Without a capitalist/communist axis around which to organize economic relations, tensions among the United States' erstwhile friends have sprung to the surface. As Friends and Enemies have fallen out of focus, the Rest have ceased to capture much foreign policy attention. If economic aid once was the primary policy instrument in U.S. relations with these countries, the steady decrease in official bilateral assistance indicated policy makers' parallel loss of interest in the developing world.

But the developing world has changed since the idea of the Rest was formed. In the 1950s, countries of the Third World seemed economically remote from the United States and its primary allies. Large gaps in economic development existed between the least well off of our Friends and the most well off of the Rest. In the intervening years, although progress has not been uniform and some countries are arguably worse off, there have been some outstanding development successes. For example, although they have recently fallen on hard times, the East Asian newly industrialized countries achieved startlingly high growth in per capita GNP, in the range of 6 to 9 percent per year.[2] Sustaining this growth for years on end, the GNP per capita of these emerging markets was converging toward that of the OECD countries.

The factors that propel countries to emerge from the economic "rest" are varied and complex. They include high domestic savings rates, effective human capital development strategies, resource endowments, and pure luck. But one policy theme runs through the narrative of their catch-up with the OECD: All have opened their economies to international investment and trade. Openness may not ensure convergence with the developing countries, but an inward-looking economic approach certainly precludes it.

Since the nineteenth century, when the United States was an emerging market, economic openness has had an important effect on a developing country's growth. However, recent international economic transformations make the effects of openness increasingly profound. In the second half of the twentieth century, advances in information technology and telecommunications have had sweeping effects, effectively eliminating the costs of moving information around the world. As a result, the speed with

---

2. For example, between 1965 and 1995 South Korea's average annual per capita growth rate in real GDP was 7.2 percent, Taiwan's 6.2 percent, Malaysia's 4.8 percent, and Indonesia's 4.7 percent. *Emerging Asia: Changes and Challenges* (Manila: Asian Development Bank, 1997).

which people communicate and the volume of information flowing around the globe have both increased.[3]

With information moving more readily, international financial transactions have become more fluid. Electronic networks allow traders to exchange currencies across borders with astounding ease. Those same networks provide more information about potential disparities in exchange rates across countries. With more information and lower exchange costs at their disposal, currency traders can identify and exploit arbitrage opportunities to a degree not possible even a few years ago. If the search were limited to the developed nations, information technology changes would not lead to such a drastic increase in currency arbitrage. OECD economies have relatively similar financial systems and present similar financial risks. However, as this technology spreads to developing markets rather different from the United States, Europe, and Japan, opportunities for currency arbitrage increase exponentially.

Compared with the situation twenty-five years ago, capital now flows at much higher volume to a much broader swath of countries. Seeking higher rates of return than industrialized countries can offer, international investors now include emerging markets in their portfolios. In these markets, lower capital-to-labor ratios offer higher returns. But, as always, higher returns carry higher risks. Emerging market risks result from differences in economic institutions, legal and political uncertainty, a lack of fully transparent presentation of financial information, and less vibrant internal competition. In an attempt to balance risk and returns, investors have so far explored only a few large emerging markets. While total investment in emerging markets has grown tremendously since the late 1970s, most of it is concentrated in a few countries. Many other economies in the developing world have been bypassed.

As a complement to this flood of new financial flows sweeping the world in general and the emerging markets in particular, the volume of international trade has also increased. Over the last forty years imports and exports have grown dramatically as a percentage of GDP in essentially all more-developed and emerging economies. For example, between 1965 and 1995, U.S. exports as a percentage of GDP more than doubled. In addition, the character of trade has changed.[4] In the first decades after the Second World War, most international trade consisted of essentially finished products. Now, more and more unfinished goods within industries are moving across borders.

---

3. See W. Bowman Cutter, "A New International Economic Order?" Woodrow Wilson International Center for Scholars Working Paper (Washington, D.C.: October 1996).
4. Cutter, "A New Order?"

This increase in intra-industry trade reflects, among other factors, the growth of multinational corporations. In an effort to take advantage of lower unit labor costs beyond their traditional homes in the developed north, industries have increasingly moved some of their operations to less-developed countries. The growth of intra-industry trade and multi-national corporations has also contributed to the increase in capital flows to emerging markets, not just through portfolio investment, but also through direct investment.

In summary, the volume of both trade and financial flows has increased and now reaches beyond OECD countries to a select group of emerging markets. This represents a profound change in the pattern of global economic relations. As observers of international relations have discussed at great length,[5] these factors have led to increased international interdependence. That interdependence has not only sewn the developed countries more tightly together, it has also incorporated a few large developing countries with high growth potential.

But why are some developing countries able to join this network of international economic interdependence while others are excluded? What characteristics explain this distinction? An outward economic orientation is obviously essential. Although several of the emerging markets have at times (or for certain sectors) adopted inward-looking, import-substitution policies,[6] only when a country allows or encourages trade and financial openness can it become fully involved in the international economy. And only those economies that have chosen to throw themselves into that economic group have been able to achieve sustained growth, growth which in turn allows their incomes to converge toward OECD levels.[7]

Beyond openness, countries that get most involved in the global economy must have human capital or physical resources that interest investors or trade partners. However, there is some evidence that extensive physical resources can backfire on a country's development. Although a few countries have assembled effective development strategies based on their natural resources of raw materials,[8] these assets often attract investment

---

5. For example, writings by Robert Reich (*The Work of Nations,* New York: Knopf, 1991), Kenichi Ohmae (*The Borderless World*, New York: Harper & Row, 1990), and Paul Kennedy (*Preparing for the Twenty-First Century*, New York: Random House, 1993) discuss these themes.

6. South Korea, for example, protected its steel industry, and prior to 1991 India operated according to a stringent import-substitution strategy.

7. Nonetheless, even the fastest-growing countries still lag significantly behind the upper band of the OECD countries with regard to per capita GDP. By 1995 South Korea was able to achieve per capita GDP 48.8 percent of the United States'. Indonesia's per capita GDP in 1995 was only 13.1 percent of the U.S. (*Emerging Asia: Changes and Challenges*).

8 . Botswana's handling of its diamond industry is often cited in this regard.

from strictly extractive industries. In these countries, economic rents accrue to elite groups, leading to unstable political arrangements and development that does not involve a majority of the population. For example, Nigeria's oil resources have enriched a narrow band of the population, but the economy has not been able to translate this oil wealth into broad-based economic development. In contrast, despite the relative lack of physical resources in the newly industrialized countries, these nations have well-educated, industrious populations. Human capital, rather than physical resources and raw materials, has proved essential for their success.

Finally, although a stratospheric growth rate is certain to attract investment and trade attention, so is a large population. Those developing countries that have more than roughly fifty million inhabitants offer the prospect of big potential export markets. When the U.S. Department of Commerce assembled a list of those fast-developing economies worthy of high priority for American businesses, each of the Big Emerging Markets (BEM) it identified had a large population, usually with a potentially significant middle class to which companies could sell their products.

The overlap between the Big Emerging Markets list and the pivotal states is fairly extensive. On both lists are Brazil, Mexico, India, South Africa, and Turkey. The ASEAN region, which includes the pivotal state of Indonesia, is also considered a BEM. The economies that are on the Department of Commerce's list but are excluded from our list of pivotal states are Argentina, South Korea, Poland, and China. Conversely, those pivotal states not on the BEM list are Algeria, Egypt, and Pakistan.

The difference is easily explained. The Commerce Department identifies markets that U.S. businesses could productively enter. However, economic potential is only one of the many factors that make a state pivotal. A pivotal state could become an economic power fully interlinked into the global economy. But it could also flounder. Many pivotal states have endured or are currently enduring difficult economic periods. Either success or failure would have direct effects as it reverberated through international economic linkages. Because of each pivotal state's influence on its region's growth, either outcome could also reach U.S. interests indirectly. For reasons of strategic foreign policy planning, the United States should establish policies that ensure strong economic linkages with these pivotal states the better to ensure their economic success.

A DOUBLE-EDGED SWORD

The transformation of the global economy has led to increased financial and trade flows between developed economies and a select few emerging markets. These flows have generated substantial economic interdependence. Many developing nations, including pivotal states, covet the opportunity to forge links with large industrial economies and gain the very real benefits of access to capital and trade.

One of the scarcest resources in less-developed countries is capital. If development is a process of capital accumulation, then a country will develop more rapidly the more capital it attracts. So long as the real returns on capital to the economy as a whole exceed interest costs, developing countries can grow progressively by attracting investors. Linkages to developed countries and their high-volume financial flows offer opportunities for faster growth. If capital enters in the form of direct foreign investment and if advanced industrialized countries build subsidiaries in developing countries, then they offer more than just capital. They also transfer technology and management systems. This technology transfer can improve the productivity of a developing country's industry and improve that country's welfare.

Trade flows also offer real benefits to pivotal states. To recount the classic arguments: By trading with industrialized economies, developing nations can import products at a lower price than if they were to make the products themselves. Trade increases the volume of goods their earnings can buy. Further, they can export goods in which they have a comparative advantage. Because the world market offers greater demand for these export goods than does the domestic economy alone, the price of their export goods increases, further enhancing the welfare of the developing country. Although a country must confront questions about who suffers income or job losses and who benefits most, aggregate income and welfare increase when a country opens its borders.

Economic interdependence with pivotal states also benefits industrialized nations. In developing nations with scarce capital, investment projects can generate large returns. United States investors benefit from higher returns on investments than they can find in industrial countries, where capital is abundant and returns are generally lower. With nearly 50 percent of the adult population of the United States owning some form of mutual fund, higher investment returns accrue not only to the wealthy, but to a large portion of the economy. In addition, through interdependence, firms can choose to open plants in the developing world, where they enjoy lower labor costs and higher profit margins. These higher profits translate again into higher potential dividends for equity holders.

Just as open trade with the United States can increase purchasing power in the developing world, the U.S. public can also benefit when it imports from and exports to pivotal states. Goods imported from the pivotal states are cheaper than if they were produced inside the United States.

With low-wage labor, pivotal states can produce labor-intensive goods more cheaply than industrialized countries. At the same time, the United Sates has a larger market for its exports. With greater demand for its products, it enjoys higher prices, which result in higher wages for workers producing export goods. Further, if firms can reduce costs by making more, trade with the large markets of pivotal states allows them to produce more goods at a lower per-unit cost and generate a higher profit margin. The entire industrialized country can benefit from liberalized trade so long as these gains from trade are redistributed to compensate groups that suffer, such as those workers who have lost their jobs or whose wages have decreased because their work can be done more cheaply in the developing world.

If we assume, as economists do, that governments distribute the benefits of economic interdependence fairly, then close financial and trade ties appear mutually beneficial for industrialized and emerging countries. Pivotal states enjoy the opportunity to acquire necessary capital through short-term investment, longer-term direct foreign investment, and imports of now-cheaper capital-intensive goods. The United States and the industrialized countries have the opportunity to garner high returns on short-term capital investment, benefit from lower labor costs if they choose to build plants in pivotal states, and enter promising new markets for their exports.

If these rosy aspects of interdependence were the only ones operating, one would expect globalization to spread at an even faster and more profound rate than it has, sewing all developing nations, not just a few large emerging markets, into a tight, secure global network. But economic interdependence is not a free lunch. Enthusiasts of economic interdependence often overlook the necessity of compensating those who suffer from financial and trade linkages. Policy makers must address the problem of winners and losers to allow the potential benefits of interdependence to reach the entire populace of each type of country.[9] In addition to this drawback, interdependence brings significant risks for both pivotal states and industrialized countries. As the Mexican peso crisis of 1994 and 1995 and the Asian crisis of 1997 and 1998 aptly illustrate, financial movements into and out of a pivotal state can be gravely destabilizing.

In the early 1990s the United States and Mexico were strengthening their economic linkages, beyond the many Mexican workers who play a crucial role in U.S. agriculture. It seemed likely that the North American Free Trade Agreement would clear its final political hurdles in Congress.

9. See, for example, Paul Kennedy, "Globalization and Its Discontents" (recorded May 20, 1996, for *Analysis*, Radio 4, U.K.).

U.S. firms were taking advantage of lower operating costs to open subsidiaries in Mexico, offering Mexican workers jobs otherwise hard to come by. U.S. financial markets discovered the high returns resulting from short-term or portfolio investment and poured cauldrons of this "hot money" into the country. Mexico and the United States seemed poised to enjoy many of the benefits of economic interdependence.

However, financial markets picked up rumors that the Mexican international financial position was not as solid as they had previously assumed. Optimism quickly turned to skepticism. Currency speculators began betting against the peso, leading to deeper investigations of previously hidden macroeconomic fundamentals. As the shiny veneer of Mexican stability began to reveal deeper macroeconomic dross, financial players abandoned their investments. Having entered Mexico on only hot-money commitments, they abandoned the country immediately.

The resulting devaluation, stabilization, and economic restructuring generated real difficulties for Mexico. In a story repeated often since the first developing-country stabilization programs of the early 1980s, austerity created a Mexican recession that imposed hardship throughout the economy. Although efforts to restructure have laid the groundwork for longer-term, stable growth in income and welfare, the ferocity of the economic crisis has destabilized the Mexican government and populace alike. Profound financial integration allowed the crisis to develop at a pace terrifying for all involved.

The negative effects of the peso crisis were not confined within Mexico's borders. In a phenomenon termed the "tequila effect," emerging markets suffered throughout the world, but particularly in Latin America. Singed by the Mexican crisis, money managers became wary about their other emerging market holdings. Without carefully analyzing the macroeconomic and financial positions of these other countries, financial actors lost confidence in emerging market investments. Even in solid economies, they unjustly saw potential peso crises. Brazilian, Argentinean, even Asian emerging markets fell as capital retreated to the safety of more familiar investments in major industrialized countries.

Interdependence means that economic difficulties affect all parties. The negative spillovers of the peso crisis were not limited to emerging markets. There was a real danger that Mexican economic collapse would destabilize financial markets in the industrialized countries. More directly, economic chaos in Mexico could send millions of economic refugees across the Rio Grande. However, the Clinton administration acted quickly and boldly to stem any further detrimental effects, so the short-term effects of the crisis in the United States were not so severe as they might have been. If one doubts how seriously the United States took these neg-

ative possibilities, consider the time, effort, and political capital that
senior members of the Clinton administration devoted to the $50 billion
Mexican bailout plan. That effort is particularly remarkable, given the
public's solid opposition to the plan and the president's well-known concern about public opinion when acting in the foreign policy realm.

The Asian crisis offers another example with even more profound and
far-reaching implications. As noted above, the East Asian "tigers" have
been heralded as miracles of economic development. Prior to late 1997,
the economic links between Asian emerging markets and the industrialized nations seemed to generate unalloyed benefits for all. The industrial
policies these countries pursued prompted people around the world to
reconsider the appropriate role of government in the economy. The sustained, spectacular growth of the region's economies offered an "East
Asian model" that both would-be emerging markets and stagnating industrial economies scrambled to emulate.

The Asian crisis seriously dampened this enthusiasm. It started in
Thailand, where international investors had lent heavily to the real estate
market. When that market faltered, investors began to get jittery. Moving
out of the baht, they put pressure on the Thai government to adjust its
peg to the dollar. As Thailand sought to avoid devaluation and defend its
currency, currency speculators discovered the Bank of Thailand's scarcity of international reserves. The ensuing run on the baht prompted the
government to devalue.

The currency crisis in Thailand created "a vortex that quickly sucked
in the rest of East Asia."[10] In a reprise of the peso crisis, financial markets
lost confidence. Having ignored weaknesses in the Thai banking system
and in the country's foreign reserves position when per capita GDP
growth was averaging 4.8 percent, as it had between 1965 and 1995, fund
managers did not want to be caught unawares with similar situations in
other emerging market investments in the region. Scrutinizing more
carefully, they found financial-sector weaknesses that previously they had
either overlooked or ignored. The market herd stampeded, trampling
currencies across the region and increasing the costs associated with for-
eign-denominated short-term loans. Without a steady stream of capital
inflows to allow them to repay these loans, businesses and banks collapsed.

Obviously, the countries of the region suffered from this crisis, which
economic interdependence allowed. Indonesia, the largest Southeast

10. See Nayan Chanda, "Rebuilding Asia" in *Far Eastern Economic Review* (February 12, 1998,
    pp. 46–50) for a more complete analysis. Also, Steven Radelet and Jeffrey Sachs, "Asia's
    Reemergence," *Foreign Affairs,* November–December 1997: 44.

Asian economy and pivotal for the region, has been particularly hard hit. As President Soeharto is succeeded by a new leadership and markets respond accordingly, the Indonesia crisis will unfold for some time to come. However, at this early stage some effects are starkly clear. Decades of hard-won gains in per capita income evaporated. Having reached $1,200 prior to the crisis, annual per capita income fell to $300 with the rupiah's collapse,[11] "only 22 of Indonesia's 286 publicly held companies are considered solvent,"[12] and the IMF's projections for Indonesia's annual GDP growth slipped from 8.2 percent in May 1997 to 5.0 percent in December. Later projections will likely be even more dire.

As discussed throughout this book, one cannot separate economic from political stability, particularly in the pivotal states. Indonesia is a prime example. As Jack Bresnan discusses, fast-paced economic growth masked many of the political and social tensions mounting in this enormous, diverse, disrupted country. Without that economic growth to provide jobs and raise incomes, Indonesia is erupting. As political tensions and food riots spread throughout the country, Indonesia must walk a precarious knife-edge to balance IMF calls for austere restructuring with efforts to maintain political control.

Because economic networks now encircle the globe, the United States cannot isolate itself from the Asian crisis, just as it could not from the peso crisis. Along with all industrial countries, it faces a dangerous situation. Obviously, the United States must first concern itself with the stability of the international financial system. So far, the collapse of banks and businesses has been restricted to East Asia. However, if the primary source of capital for the region, the Japanese banking sector, falters, the direct implications for the United States could be very grave indeed. Many might pass off such worries as doomsterism, but it is again useful to consider the attention that secretary of the treasury William Rubin placed on the Asian crisis. In response to its challenges, Secretary Rubin stressed that "we must . . . modernize the architecture of the international financial markets."[13] If the secretary of the treasury publicly discusses the need for systematic changes, the U.S. government takes seriously indeed the implications of the crisis for international financial stability. At the 1998 meeting of the World Economic Forum in Davos, a central theme of both the planned and spontaneous discussions was appropriate strategies for dealing with the crisis. Obviously, the impact of the crisis extended beyond Asia.

11. John McBeth, "Ground Zero," *Far Eastern Economic Review*, January 22, 1998, pp. 14–17.
12. McBeth, "Ground Zero."
13. William Rubin, address at Georgetown University, Washington, D.C., January 21, 1998.

Although the financial system has weathered the crisis thus far, there will likely be longer-term repercussions. Currency devaluations have left the price of Southeast Asian products extremely low. As these goods flow through the trade linkages that interdependence requires, they could spawn additional protectionist pressures in Europe and the United States.[14] They could tip the balance against free trade in the U.S. polity, where many are already wary of the potential of trade to lower workers' wages, undermine labor standards, and allow lax environmental practices. If the U.S. were to abandon its postwar leadership of free trade, the benefits of its having a broad set of economic partners would vanish.

After discussing some of the perils that accompany economic interdependence, readers might be tempted to discount its benefits. In fact, many sectors of the U.S. populace and many influential Americans are quite wary of the global trade and financial linkages that have developed so rapidly between the industrialized countries and certain pivotal states. Naturally, much of that concern comes from unfamiliarity with these recently developed global processes. Many people are disconcerted that economic events in far-off Indonesia are (rightly) occupying the attention of our nation's leaders. Less isolationist voices are just as rightly concerned about the ability of governments to ensure that those who benefit from interdependence compensate fairly those groups within a country who suffer.

Though some people would like to react to these changes by trying to withdraw economically from the world, economic interdependence is unavoidable for the United States. It results from irreversible technology changes and the long-sought growth of specific pivotal states. In the near future, it may lead to sudden and dramatic financial market movements such as those in Mexico and Indonesia. But because economic interdependence has the potential to increase the prosperity of all Americans as well as people in states around the world, it is in the United States' best interest to act prudently to develop strong economic linkages with promising markets.

The United States must also recognize that as it establishes these linkages, benefits are not evenly spread across the economy, so it must support those who suffer. Further, risks inevitably accompany rapid financial flows, particularly in the short term, while the architecture of international financial dealings adjusts to economic interdependence and establishes ways to deal with these risks. Because it offers real benefits at the same time as it presents real risks, interdependence is a double-edged

14. In his February 4, 1998, column in the *New York Times*, entitled "The Asian Blues," Thomas Friedman explores the possibility of U.S. protectionism resulting from the Asian crisis.

sword that governments in both the United States and the pivotal states must handle carefully. As the United States builds its economic policies toward the pivotal states, it must balance these benefits against these risks.

ECONOMIC PIVOTALNESS

The above discussion of the peso and Asian crises brings to light how Mexico and Indonesia are pivotal to the United States in the economic dimension. However, a state needn't be a seat of global financial crisis in order to be pivotal. As a group, the pivotal states are large, emerging economies whose futures are important to the United States' interests. Economic potential is a crucial characteristic, but that potential can only be realized through extensive economic linkages between industrialized economies and a developing economy. Only through those linkages can a pivotal state have an impact on U.S. interests. Designed to guide American foreign policy and protect those interests, the pivotal states strategy would encourage the United States to build economic linkages with those economies in the developing world that have the most likelihood of affecting U.S. interests and welfare either positively or negatively.

With over 160 million people, vast natural resources, and the eighth-largest economy in the world, Brazil could be the center of successful South American development. Although its average annual growth rate of GNP per capita between 1985 and 1994 wallowed at –0.4 percent, nonetheless it has been able to industrialize: industrial products account for 35 percent of GNP and 60 percent of exports. In the past twenty years its growth outlook has oscillated between dire and promising, and foreign investment has mirrored that fluctuating outlook. Since the 1980s debt crisis it has fought a long battle to stabilize its currency. The Real Plan, which among other things managed to decrease government deficits, seems to be successful. The country has vacillated in its approach to trade policy, having erected and dismantled protectionist barriers in close succession. However, through its leadership of Mercosur and flirtation with a free-trade area of the Americas, Brazil has settled on a reasonable degree of economic openness. As the primary economic power in South America, it has ambitions to assume a larger economic leadership role in the world. Because of the potential for Brazil's economic prospects to swerve and because of its increasing influence, it is imperative that the United States establish strong economic policy linkages with this pivotal state.

Whereas Brazil will likely be an ever-increasing force in the global economy in coming years, Egypt's economic prospects are grimmer. With 96.5 percent of its land desert, few natural resources, and location in the center of the politically unstable Middle East, the country struggles to find promising avenues for growth. Between 1985 and 1994, GNP per capita grew at an average of 1.6 percent per year. Unemployment in the range of 20 percent and high urban growth rates pose economic difficulties that constantly threaten to erupt into social and political conflagration. As discussed more extensively in Roger Owen's essay, the United States has exerted a significant amount of economic policy energy in an effort to help Egypt grow. Egypt's USAID allocation is second only to Israel's and dwarfs nearly all other USAID budgets. While political and strategic dimensions account for these U.S. flows and for its inclusion as a pivotal state, the likelihood of Egypt's becoming a major emerging market on economic grounds alone is remote.

Like Egypt's, Algeria's growth prospects do not inspire confidence. Its economy is based on oil revenues, and nearly all investment and trade linkages with the industrialized world are in the energy sector. However, political instability continues to wrack the country, alienate potential investors, and diminish the prospects that it can diversify out of oil and develop other sectors. Real GNP grew by only 0.6 percent between 1970 and 1995. Again, on purely economic grounds, Algeria does not hold the growth potential of other pivotal states.

One pivotal state in Africa does offer more promising growth than Egypt and Algeria. South Africa is blessed with enormous natural resources, a relatively skilled labor force, and an extensive infrastructure. Following the collapse of apartheid, it has become the darling of the international community. International trade and investment opportunities abound, particularly given government efforts to develop pro-business, pro-investment policies. For example, in 1994 it had over $10 billion in foreign direct investment and $13 billion in portfolio investment. Further, it achieved 3 percent GNP growth in 1995. South Africa's economic role extends beyond its borders, as South African businesses are beginning to invest and export products throughout southern Africa. Because South Africa offers growth potential as a big emerging market, on economic grounds its inclusion as a pivotal state is well justified.

In contrast, Turkey presents a mixed economic picture. Its location gives it relatively easy connections to European markets and Central Asia, though the European Union's continuing rebuff of its membership application may strain the existing customs union. Despite difficulties in stabilizing its currency through the mid-1990s (its GDP fell 6 percent in 1994 as a result), it registered 8 percent growth in 1995 and 7.9 percent growth in 1996. Between these wide fluctuations lies average annual GNP per capita growth of 1.5 percent between 1985 and 1994. The fluctuations also explain the relatively low levels of foreign direct investment, for investors are wary of economic and policy instability. Because Turkey has the potential to grow quite dramatically and offer promising markets but has also shown tendencies to perform quite poorly, in economic terms it is highly pivotal.

Though Pakistan's per capita GDP growth between 1965 and 1995 was also 1.5 percent, these long-term figures make sporadic fluctuations. During the 1980s real GDP grew annually at a 6 percent rate. In the early 1990s, the economy suffered an economic downturn as the government adopted poorly balanced fiscal and monetary policies. In recent years, it has made some efforts to reform and reduce chronic fiscal and foreign-trade deficits, though such efforts have been hindered by corruption and lack of political resolve. Because of that corruption and economic instability, investors judge Pakistan with significant suspicion. If Pakistan were able to reinvigorate growth and regain the confidence of international investors, however, this pivotal state would offer real potential as an emerging market in South Asia.

In South Asia, the largest emerging market is India, the second most populous nation on earth and likely to surpass China in population shortly after the year 2010. With GNP per capita of $310 and distressingly high poverty, India has maintained only sluggish, average per capita growth in GNP of 2.2 percent per year between 1965 and 1995. During much of that period, it supported an insular economic system of import substitution, a high percentage of government ownership, and dizzying regulation. Since the early 1990s, however, it has made major efforts to liberalize, decrease state ownership, and open its economy to international trade and financial linkages. As a result of these changes, the Asian Development Bank projects that over the next thirty years, per capita GDP growth will more than double to 5.5 percent between 1996 and 2025.[15] Particularly because there is some indication that efforts to reform the economy are starting to lag, it is imperative both for South Asia and for United States interests that we build linkages to encourage the continued integration of the Indian economy.

U.S. ECONOMIC POLICY TOWARD THE PIVOTAL STATES

Each of the pivotal states has particular economic circumstances that determine the degree to which its economy prospers. As recent financial crises demonstrate, those circumstances can change rapidly and dramatically. If the United States were to try to fashion careful country-specific economic policies that would deftly respond to each pivotal state's changing circumstances, those policies would likely fail. Economic events

15. *Emerging Asia: Changes and Challenges* (Manila: Asian Development Bank, 1997).

develop too quickly and, except in times of particular urgency, economic policy instruments at the disposal of the United States cannot respond at a sufficiently rapid pace or with adequate influence. Instead, the United States needs to lead the international community to establish a clear, consistent set of standards and policies concerning investment and trade with the pivotal states. Given set rules, all actors in the international economic realm can form reasonable expectations about policy responses by the United States and other countries.

The overall objective of U.S. economic policies in pivotal states should be to promote prudent internal economic policies and openness to international investment and trade. If each of the pivotal states achieves stable, sustainable growth and protects those who suffer as a result, it can improve the welfare of its people. Aside from the inherent attractions of such welfare, solid economic growth can promote political and social stability, which is in America's interest to maintain around the world. Further, growth will offer economic opportunities to the United States through investments and trade. Finally, with stable growth the pivotal states can set examples for their regions and serve as regional hubs for trade within the developing world. Through these regional economic spillovers, economic prosperity in the pivotal states can offer indirect benefits to other U.S. interests in the developing world beyond the pivotal states.

To achieve these objectives, the United States needs to lead the international community in establishing and respecting rules of trade and finance, to create a level playing field for international commerce. The architecture of the international trade system has been evolving over the last half-century and now consists of the General Agreements on Tariffs and Trade, currently adjudicated by the World Trade Organization. The United States needs to respect the outcomes of that body, even when the WTO decides against U.S. businesses. With such respect for hard-won international trade agreements, the United States would establish a common ground for all international trade, including that with the pivotal states. In addition, it needs to support many of the pivotal states in their recent efforts to open up their economies, even when, as in Indonesia, domestic political forces clamor for protectionist policies.

The United States also must promote international investment linkages with the pivotal states. The Department of Commerce's strategy of focusing attention on the Big Emerging Markets and sponsoring trade missions to those states is a valuable element of U.S. policy. More important, however, the United States needs to initiate changes in the architecture of the international financial system, as Secretary Rubin suggested. Those changes would secure the benefits to all of investing in pivotal states and other emerging markets while tempering the risks that the peso and Asian crises illustrated.

Although interdependence lies at the roots of both of these crises, economic integration alone need not lead to financial instability. However, many emerging markets, including Indonesia and Mexico, also lack full financial transparency. Behind a wall of secrecy, banks can make cozy, corrupt investments without regard to careful financial standards. To minimize the risks of financial interdependence, U.S. economic policy must promote financial transparency in the pivotal states. The United States also needs to be diligent in its opposition to corrupt business practices. Finally, it should encourage pivotal states to adopt international financial standards and independent, effective regulation.

Although these rule-based changes will diminish the possibility that financial crises will develop, the international financial system must also augment its ability to respond in the event of a future crisis. As the Asian crisis aptly demonstrated, the International Monetary Fund does not have the resources or the authority to stem the tidal wave of international capital that can be mobilized when financial markets move. As the preeminent economic and political power, the United States should lead the international community in developing some augmented form of financial coordination that can act in the event of future crises.

Some might look first to the Group of Seven major industrialized economies to initiate discussions about appropriate economic standards and augmented crisis response. To explore ideas that would have such international effect, the highest levels of government, like the leaders that make up the G-7, must be involved. But so far this body has shown itself unwilling or unable to tackle difficult structural problems. Because world leaders seek to conclude their economic summits with rosy statements of agreement, the G-7 has shied away from discussing such truly knotty issues as the need for changes in the international financial system. Perhaps the Asian crisis or the one that follows it will prove sufficient to galvanize these leaders' attention.

However, as some emerging economies grow in the next several years, the composition of the G-7 will become increasingly outdated. For example, the economies of China, India, and Brazil will have grown larger than those of several current G-7 members. A serious debate of international coordination should involve nations likely to have an enhanced future role in the global economy, particularly since these international structures will shape the links between emerging and industrialized economies. Thus, a discussion of changing international financial architecture should not be limited to the G-7 but should also include several of the largest non-G-7 countries.

As a result of this inclusion, these economically pivotal states will feel ownership of a revised architecture. Rather than resenting international financial regimes imposed on them, they would respect and adhere to conventions and institutions that they helped design. If major actors agree to establish rules for openness and transparency, all can reap the benefits and minimize the costs of interdependence. However, if rising economic powers continue to feel marginalized by the current international regime, they may choose to establish separate economic or financial standards. As the tensions of the Cold War illustrated, it is in the United States' interest to forestall efforts to develop parallel economic systems.

Whatever the improved international architecture, it is clear that the United States and its economic allies must move toward more inclusive structures to deal with expanding economic interdependence. At the end of World War II, the United States took the lead to establish the Bretton Woods institutions, which have served the international community well for much of the last fifty years. As the United States confronts the changed economic landscape of the twenty-first century, it needs to be equally imaginative and forward looking. Perhaps it could design changes around an existing institution, augmenting the International Monetary Fund, for example. Alternatively, it could lead efforts to create new structures. Both the Commission on Global Governance[16] and the Yale University / Ford Foundation Task Force on the United Nations in Its Second Half-Century[17] proposed that the United Nations create an economic council including the largest industrialized and emerging economies. This council could establish international standards for economic openness and transparency and coordinate efforts to control financial crises. Regardless of the structure's final form, the United States must initiate its creation.

With the rise of international interdependence, economic issues have come to occupy an increasingly central role in U.S. foreign policy. The newest elements of that interdependence are the deep financial and trade linkages that have developed or are beginning to develop with the pivotal states. In general, those linkages have had beneficial effects on U.S. economic interests. However, as the peso and Asian crises demonstrate, they are a double-edged sword with the potential to destabilize the international financial system. Because of both these positive and negative effects, it is essential that the United States devote appropriate attention to developing constructive linkages with the pivotal states through a revised architecture of international economic relations.

16. Commission on Global Governance, *Our Global Neighborhood* (New York: Oxford University Press, 1995).
17. Independent Working Group on the Future of the United Nations, *The United Nations in Its Second Half-Century* (New York: Ford Foundation, 1995).

U.S. STRATEGIC PLANNING AND THE PIVOTAL STATES

Donald C. F. Daniel and Andrew L. Ross*

Defense planners, no less than their counterparts elsewhere in the U.S. foreign affairs arena, are in search of a new Holy Grail. With the end of the Cold War and the consequent early end of the twentieth century (and even, according to some, the end of history), a new geopolitical framework, a new strategic construct, is needed. Neither of the two post–Cold War U.S. administrations has yet developed a suitable successor to containment. The United States thus remains adrift, subject to the vagaries of improvised or narrowly focused decision making. As a former member of the Bush administration's defense planning team observed, "An administration can neither evaluate specific policy decisions adequately, nor reach an effective consensus with respect to them, without first constructing a framework for guiding policy, setting priorities, and deciding what constitutes vital U.S. interests."[1]

There has, of course, been no dearth of geopolitical, and even geoeconomic, proposals intended to help us sort out the uncertainties and ambiguities of the early twenty-first century. Defense planners have been variously attracted to and repelled by visions of Huntington's "clash of civilizations," Mahbubani's "West and the rest," Mearsheimer's journey "back to the future," Kaplan's "coming anarchy," Singer and Wildavsky's "zones

* Note: The views expressed here are those of the authors and do not necessarily reflect the views of the Naval War College, the Department of the Navy, or any other U.S. government department or agency.

1. Zalmay Khalilzad, "Losing the Moment? The United States and the World after the Cold War," *Washington Quarterly* 18, no. 2 (spring 1995): 87. For an assessment of alternative post–Cold War grand strategy frameworks, see Barry R. Posen and Andrew L. Ross, "Competing Visions for U.S. Grand Strategy," *International Security* 21, no. 3 (1996–1997): 5–53.

of peace" and "zones of turmoil," and the Tofflers' first-, second-, and third-wave wars.[2]

In "Pivotal States and U.S. Strategy," Chase, Hill, and Kennedy advanced a less sweeping but nonetheless intriguing and serviceable proposal.[3] Though acknowledging a long history of antecedents, including classical geopolitics and the Cold War domino theory, they see their approach as calling attention to a variety of "new" security issues that "traditional security forces find hard to address" and that "resist the realist emphasis on power and military and political security."[4] These claims raise several questions that Chase, Hill, and Kennedy themselves view as needing investigation: How do their perspectives, framework, and conclusions compare with those of the U.S. defense officials who determine the planning and employment priorities for the nation's "traditional security forces"? Specifically, what criteria do U.S. decision makers apply? What pivotal developing states do they identify? What other pivotal concerns or foci do they identify? How do their list of states and their broader concerns correspond with those of the Yale group? What are the implications of the similarities and differences of perspectives, frameworks, and conclusions between the Chase, Hill, Kennedy team and U.S. defense planners?

In order to address these issues, we summarize the main features of the Chase, Hill, Kennedy proposal; present the approaches of U.S. defense planners from the late Cold War period to today, with particular attention to the Clinton administration; compare the views of the Yale team with those of U.S. planners; and end with our own perspectives on America's national security priorities, pivotal states, and how concerns that transcend or have only transitory ties to any particular state might be dealt with.

THE CHASE, HILL, KENNEDY PROPOSAL

For the purposes of this chapter, we will emphasize three points made by Chase, Hill, and Kennedy. First, they advance a discriminative

---

2. Samuel P. Huntington, *The Clash of Civilizations and the Remaking of World Order* (New York: Simon & Schuster, 1996); Kishore Mahbubani, "The West and the Rest," *The National Interest* 28 (summer 1992): 3–12; John J. Mearsheimer, "Back to the Future: Instability in Europe after the Cold War," *International Security* 15, no. 1 (summer 1990): 5–56; Robert D. Kaplan, "The Coming Anarchy," *Atlantic Monthly*, February 1994: 58; Max Singer and Aaron Wildavsky, *The Real World Order: Zones of Peace/Zones of Turmoil*, rev. ed. (Chatham, N.J.: Chatham House Publishers, 1996); and what is surely one of the most superficial works to attract the attention of defense planners, Alvin and Heidi Toffler, *War and Anti-War* (New York: Warner Books, 1993).

3. Robert S. Chase, Emily B. Hill, and Paul Kennedy, "Pivotal States and U.S. Strategy," *Foreign Affairs* 75, no. 1 (January–February 1996): 33–51.

4. Chase, Hill, and Kennedy, "Pivotal States," 36.

approach to post–Cold War strategic planning that is explicitly conservative, intended to maintain the status quo. The United States is thought to have "the most to lose from global instability."[5] For them, as for mainstream realists, the central strategic priority for the United States as it prepares for the twenty-first century is obvious and unchanged: managing the country's relations with the other major powers. Though the list could conceivably change, for now that means the major European states, Russia, China, and Japan.

Second, even though a conservative focus on the major players is required, the rest of the world cannot simply be ignored. Chase, Hill, and Kennedy call for discriminately, or selectively, engaging in the developing world, which constitutes much of the rest of the world. It is, after all, primarily though not exclusively in the developing world where the new threats of "chaos and instability"[6] are to be found. Yet the United States need not respond to every instance of chaos and instability in Latin America, Africa, and Asia. Limited resources prohibit it from doing so in any case. Instead, the United States should focus on "pivotal states" in the developing world, those "countries whose fate is uncertain and whose future will profoundly affect their surrounding regions."[7]

The characteristics of pivotal states will not surprise those familiar with work on the components of state power.[8] To be pivotal, according to Chase, Hill, and Kennedy, a state must, at a minimum, be physically impressive, have a large population, be strategically located, and possess economic potential. In addition, a pivotal state will have the "capacity to affect regional and international stability."[9] Its collapse would result in "transboundary mayhem," but its prosperity and stability "would bolster its region's economic vitality and political soundness and benefit American trade and investment."[10]

Third, no longer is it communism or external aggression that poses the greatest challenge to the prosperity and stability of these states. Rather, it is disorder brought about by new, nontraditional threats[11]—"overpopula-

---

5. Chase, Hill, and Kennedy, "Pivotal States," 35.
6. Chase, Hill, and Kennedy, "Pivotal States," 34.
7. Chase, Hill, and Kennedy, "Pivotal States," 33.
8. See Klaus Knorr, *The War Potential of Nations* (Princeton, N.J.: Princeton University Press, 1956); Knorr, *Military Power and Potential* (Lexington, Mass: D.C. Heath, 1970); and Knorr, *Power and Wealth: The Political Economy of International Power* (New York: Basic Books, 1973).
9. Chase, Hill, and Kennedy, "Pivotal States," 37.
10. Chase, Hill, and Kennedy, "Pivotal States," 37.
11. On nontraditional threats, see Jessica T. Mathews, "Power Shift," *Foreign Affairs* 76, no. 1 (January–February 1997): 50–66; and Paul Kennedy, *Preparing for the Twenty-First Century* (New York: Random House, 1993).

tion, migration, environmental degradation, ethnic conflict, and eco-nomic instability" and "dirty industrialization," drug cartels, terrorism, and disease[12]—rather than external dangers that may undermine the political stability of the key states once described as dominoes and now labeled "pivotal." These new, and generally transnational, threats are less amenable to traditional military solutions, particularly of the unilateral variety, than the external threats of old.

If we were to be consistently and rigorously discriminatory or selec-tive, few developing countries would qualify as pivotal. There can be only a small number of developing countries whose "success or failure will powerfully influence the future of their surrounding areas *and* affect American interests."[13] Setting aside "rogue states" and special allies (Saudi Arabia, Kuwait, South Korea, and Israel), Chase, Hill, and Kennedy offer as candidates nine countries: Mexico, Brazil, Algeria, South Africa, Egypt, Turkey, Pakistan, India, and Indonesia. The concept of pivotal states, they caution, is dynamic rather than static. Consequently, any list of such states should not, as in the not so distant past, be viewed as carved in stone.

The Yale team identified pivotal developing countries in the context of a broader foreign policy perspective. Yet the perspectives and priorities of the U.S. defense establishment overlap with those of Chase, Hill, and Kennedy only to a limited extent.

U.S. DEFENSE PLANNING PERSPECTIVES AND PRIORITIES

Setting the Stage: Late Cold War Defense Planning[14]

Chase, Hill, and Kennedy's call for a strategy of discriminate engage-ment recalls a late–Cold War defense planning document, *Discriminate*

---

12. Chase, Hill, and Kennedy, "Pivotal States," 36.
13. Chase, Hill, and Kennedy, "Pivotal States," 37. Emphasis added.
14. A note on sources is necessary here. A small number of unclassified published docu-ments lay out U.S. defense strategy and priorities. Near annual reports are issued by the White House (the *National Security Strategy* series) as well as by the secretary of defense and the uniformed military leadership, including the regional commanders in chief. These often appear as published reports or as prepared testimony for Congress. Also, one-off and multiyear studies and reviews often signal or codify turning points in offi-cial policy. An important recent example is Secretary William Cohen's *Report of the Quadrennial Defense Review*; another is the chairman's *Joint Vision 2010*. In this category as well are five regional security reports prepared by the Office of the Assistant Secretary of Defense for International Security Affairs and published in 1995. They lay out the Defense Department's analyses of how to apply regionally the Clinton administration's national security objectives and priorities. Finally, one publication, the yearly *Strategic Assessment*, though formally unofficial is of particular interest because it is prepared at the U.S. National Defense University's Institute for National Strategic Studies in

Deterrence, the report of the Commission on Integrated Long-Term Strategy.[15] Chaired by two experienced Cold War defense planners, Fred Iklé and Albert Wohlstetter, the commission recognized, as do Chase, Hill, and Kennedy today, the need for the United States to focus its strategic resources on the other great powers. For the commission that meant the Soviet Union at the time and, for the future, Japan and China. But the commission, just as Chase, Hill, and Kennedy do now, recognized as well that the Third World matters and called for a more focused and effective strategy—labeled "selective involvement" in a supporting document[16]—for dealing with what was acknowledged to be a diverse group of countries. Though the commission did not systematically disaggregate the Third World, broader regional priorities for the future can be discerned and, surprisingly, evidence of concerns about nontraditional threats is readily apparent.

The commission's awareness of nontraditional threats was most noticeable in its assessment of the security environment. Though a preoccupation with the Soviet Union is evident throughout the report, the

---

Washington, D.C.; its contributors and reviewers include many military officers and civilian officials, and its analyses are relatively detailed.

It should be noted that, except for *Strategic Assessment*, all of the above are official statements. When crafting them, American policy makers are not free to engage exclusively in brand new, top-down analyses. Present realities, including commitments made by predecessors, can limit consideration of new possibilities and what is publicly said about them. Silence and studied ambiguity are frequently employed, not only to paper over differences within the government but also to avoid overcommitment or offense to friends and potential coalition partners who may not be deemed "pivotal."

It must also be noted that the official documents vary considerably as to the degree to which they designate and provide rationale for geostrategic priorities in the developing world, and the only two instances, we believe, when the term "pivotal" was used to described a state were applied to Japan and, ironically enough, to the United States in the context of its role in the Middle East. The Japan remark was contained in the 1997 draft of the annual statement prepared for delivery to Congress by Admiral Joseph Prueher, USN, commander in chief, U.S. Pacific Command, photocopy, 1 [hereafter cited as 97 Pacific Command]. The statement on the United States is in U.S. Department of Defense, Office of International Security Affairs, *United States Security Strategy for the Middle East* (Washington, D.C., May 1995), 15 [hereafter cited as ISA, *Middle East*]. On the other hand, in some documents the term *key* or like reference is applied to so many states or to a group of states as to require judgments or inferences as to which can be most validly characterized as key or pivotal. Nevertheless, even documents that are "ageographic" in perspective, focusing on generic threats, remain quite useful. As will be seen, they provide a window illuminating a growing tendency to see threats as coming from all directions than as grounded in particularly significant states or regions.

15. Commission on Integrated Long-Term Strategy, *Discriminate Deterrence* (Washington, D.C.: U.S. GPO, January 1988).

16. Regional Conflict Working Group, *Supporting U.S. Strategy for Third World Conflict* (Washington, D.C.: Pentagon, June 1988).

commission's view of the international security environment was far from static. Members of the commission were no more prescient than other observers in anticipating the immediacy and extent of the changes about to reshape the world (or at least that part of the world on which U.S. strategists had been fixated), but they believed "that the environment may change dramatically. Twenty years hence America may confront a vastly more complex environment."[17] Some of the anticipated changes reflected familiar "old" concerns: the potential rise of Japan and China and consequent erosion of bipolarity; Soviet economic uncertainties; rapidly evolving military technology; weapons proliferation; and deteriorating access to foreign bases. But a wide array of today's "new" concerns were evident as well. Concern about the implications of rapid population growth, urbanization, migration, pervasive poverty, unemployment, disease, nationalist resentments and ethnic differences, religious conflict, and terrorism for U.S. involvement in Third World conflict was marked.[18] Though these threats were often discussed in the context of Soviet efforts to exploit them, members of the commission's Regional Conflict Working Group recognized that

> most threats to U.S. interests [in the Third World] were indigenous: voracious forces of societal change tearing at the fabric of developing societies; destabilizing overpopulation and overurbanization, coupled with underproductivity; new social, economic, and political ideas contesting with centuries old rigidities; radical nationalism and militant sectarianism; clashes of ethnic and religious prejudices; and stress on educational systems wholly inadequate for dealing with the foregoing or with the onrush of new technologies compressing travel time and opening media vistas of distant lands of unimaginable wealth.[19]

The "new" threats, clearly, have long been with us and are not new to defense planners.[20] What has yet to be agreed on, however, is the significance of these threats for defense planning itself.

The commission and its working groups devoted more attention to functional than to geostrategic priorities. Regional priorities and key states were not systematically identified. An unsurprising Euro- and Soviet-centric orientation is evident in the commission's documents. A case was made, however, for the rising importance of East Asia, particu-

17. *Discriminate Deterrence*, 6.
18. *Discriminate Deterrence*, 5–11; Working Group on the Future Security Environment, *The Future Security Environment* (Washington, D.C.: Pentagon, October 1988).
19. *Supporting U.S. Strategy for Third World Conflict*, 7.
20. This recognition at the White House level goes at least as far back as the Nixon administration. See President Richard Nixon, *U.S. Foreign Policy for the 1970s: Shaping a Durable Peace* (Washington, D.C., May 3, 1973), 207–208, 221–229.

larly Japan and China. The Persian Gulf, Mediterranean, and "Western Pacific" were identified as "the most vital regions" of the Third World.[21] The gulf was featured in a survey of potential "Wars on the Soviet Periphery."[22] Latin America, or, more accurately, Central America, received more attention than it does from today's defense planners. And sub-Saharan Africa essentially dropped off the commission's scope.

Possible pivotal states in the developing world were not often explicitly identified. But a few developing countries merited special attention. The commission's Future Security Environment Working Group called for the development of expertise on future regional powers such as Brazil and India.[23] The defense industrial capabilities of Brazil, India, Turkey, and South and North Korea were highlighted.[24] Turkey was described as "key" and "critical" in the context of NATO's southern flank.[25] In Asia, India—as well as Japan and China—was designated a growing power.[26] Concern was expressed about a potential "Mexico problem": "Political instability in Mexico," according to the Future Security Environment Working Group, "could have substantial repercussions north of the border, while the establishment of a hostile regime in Mexico could introduce new military threats to the United States."[27] Further south, the "fall" of Nicaragua necessitated resurrection of the domino theory: "If the Sandinista regime consolidates its power in Nicaragua and continues to receive Soviet support, hostile Communist regimes might gradually become established elsewhere in Central America—for example, in El Salvador, Honduras, and Panama. Any such trend could be expected to endanger control of the Panama Canal and threaten the political stability of Mexico."[28] Thus several of Chase, Hill, and Kennedy's pivotal states—Mexico, Brazil, Turkey, and India (though not Algeria, South Africa, Egypt, Pakistan, or Indonesia)—were singled out for attention by the commission and its working groups. But the commission also highlighted a few states, most notably North and South Korea and Nicaragua, not identified as pivotal by Chase, Hill, and Kennedy.

The Bush Administration's Attempted Transition

It was the Bush administration that first confronted the challenge of developing a new U.S. grand strategy for the post–Cold War world.

21. *Discriminate Deterrence*, 13

22. *Discriminate Deterrence*, 23–31.

23. *The Future Security Environment*, 67.

24. *The Future Security Environment*, 47–53.

25. *Discriminate Deterrence*, 67–68.

26. *The Future Security Environment*, 43–44.

27. *The Future Security Environment*, 55.

28. *Discriminate Deterrence*, 11.

Unfortunately, it did not advance much beyond what it attempted to portray as an aspiration, what many reacted to as a declaration, but what was in reality little more than a slogan: the notion of a "new world order." In the absence of a strategic successor to containment, defense planners attempted to reorder U.S. functional and geostrategic priorities for the post–Cold War world in a conceptual vacuum.

The principal defense planning documents it issued show the Bush administration to be conservatively oriented and as focused on the major powers as was the Commission on Integrated Long-Term Strategy. The strategic conservatism of the administration is particularly evident in Secretary of Defense Cheney's *Defense Strategy for the 1990s: The Regional Defense Strategy*. In the secretary's view, "America's strategic position is stronger than it has been for decades. Today, there is no challenger to peaceful democratic order similar to the Soviet Union and the Warsaw Pact. There are no significant hostile alliances. To the contrary, the strongest and most capable countries in the world remain our friends."[29] Thus the objective is clear: "We must preserve the extraordinary environment that has emerged from the challenges of the Cold War. . . ."[30] Defense planners had only to "preserve and enhance" the strategic depth that had been "won at such great pains."[31]

Bush administration defense planners, no less than their Cold War predecessors, focused their attentions on the major powers, particularly the Soviet Union and its successor states. In the 1991 *National Security Strategy*, the list of "opportunities and concerns" began with "the Soviet Future." The Soviet Union was still regarded as a superpower with conventional forces that would continue to "dwarf any other national force in Europe."[32] By 1993, the former Soviet Union headed the list of "national security challenges." Indeed, supporting stability and economic and political reform there and in Eastern Europe was designated the "number-one foreign policy priority."[33] Despite recognition of the increasing significance of China, Japan, and a reunited Germany, the Bush administration's Cold Warriors clearly remained fixated on the Soviet Union and its descendants.

The Bush administration, like the Commission on Integrated Long-

29. Secretary of Defense Dick Cheney, *Defense Strategy for the 1990s: The Regional Defense Strategy* (Washington, D.C.: Department of Defense, January 1993), 7.
30. Cheney, *Defense Strategy for the 1990s*, 27.
31. Cheney, *Defense Strategy for the 1990s*, 1.
32. *National Security Strategy of the United States* (Washington, D.C.: U.S. GPO, August 1991), 5.
33. *National Security Strategy of the United States* (Washington, D.C.: U.S. GPO, January 1993), 1, 6.

Term Strategy before it, was aware of nontraditional threats. Narcotics trafficking, terrorism, ethnic conflict, hunger, poor housing, lack of education, immigrant and refugee flows, and environmental depredation all found a place on the administration's agenda. Yet an appreciation of the significance of these and other nontraditional threats was notably more evident in various versions of the administration's *National Security Strategy* than in defense planning documents such as Secretary Cheney's *Defense Strategy for the 1990s* and the 1992 *National Military Strategy*. For military planners, the unknown, uncertainty, and instability, whether generated by traditional or nontraditional means, replaced the Soviet threat.[34]

Despite their obvious preoccupation with first the Soviet Union and subsequently with its successor states, Bush administration planners made an explicit effort to stress the regional reorientation of U.S. strategy. Secretary Cheney, for instance, declared that "Our national strategy has shifted from a focus on a global threat to one on regional challenges and opportunities. We have moved from Containment to the new Regional Defense Strategy."[35] The chairman of the Joint Chiefs of Staff, General Colin Powell, proclaimed that "the threats we expect to face are regional rather than global. . . . [O]ur plans and resources are primarily focused on deterring and fighting regional rather than global wars."[36] One of the administration's central goals was to ensure "that no hostile power is able to dominate or control a region critical to our interests."[37] For Cheney, those critical regions were Europe, East Asia, the Middle East–Persian Gulf region, and Latin America.[38] It was in these regions that it was most important to maintain and nurture alliances and friendships. Europe, the Middle East, and Asia were highlighted in General Powell's call for focusing defense planning efforts "on regions of potential conflict."[39] Only in these three parts of the world was the continued stabilizing influence of a significant U.S. military presence thought to be required.

The identification of regional priorities was not accompanied by the designation of pivotal developing states. In neither the 1991 nor the 1993 versions of the *National Security Strategy* were any developing countries in Europe, Asia, the Middle East, South Asia, Latin America, or Africa depicted as "key" or "critical." Indeed, regional institutions such as the

34. *National Military Strategy of the United States* (Washington, D.C.: U.S. GPO, January 1992), 4.
35. Cheney, *Defense Strategy for the 1990s*, 1. The same declaration appears in the January 1993 *National Security Strategy of the United States*, 13.
36. *National Military Strategy of the United States* (January 1992), 11.
37. *National Security Strategy of the United States* (January 1993), 3.
38. Cheney, *Defense Strategy for the 1990s*, 3.
39. *National Military Strategy of the United States* (January 1992), 11.

North Atlantic Alliance, the Conference on Security and Cooperation in Europe, the Association of Southeast Asian Nations, the Gulf Cooperation Council, the Organization of American States, and the Organization of African States were accorded far more attention than were any developing countries. Secretary Cheney did consistently list Ukraine alongside Russia in references to the states of the former Soviet Union. But it is far from clear that Ukraine was therefore regarded as pivotal. Similarly, the North Korean threat to South Korea was regarded as the "most active regional security concern in Asia," and in Latin America, Cuba was seen as "an area of special concern." But again, neither North Korea nor Cuba appears to have been elevated to the status of pivotal statehood.[40] Early post–Cold War defense planners, it would appear, were even less drawn to the notion of pivotal developing countries than was the Commission on Integrated Long-Term Strategy.

Grappling with the New: The Clinton Administration

Both continuities and discontinuities are evident in the pronouncements and actions of the Bush and Clinton administrations. The continuities are particularly marked. The Clinton administration, for instance, has been every bit as pleased with the U.S. position in the world, and therefore just as conservative, as its predecessor. Its strategic pronouncements are fundamentally conservative. The administration is quite satisfied with the present state of affairs and aims for the United States to be even "safer and more prosperous" than it already is.[41] As the president put it at the beginning of his preface to the 1997 National Security Strategy report, "Our military might is unparalleled; a dynamic global economy offers increasing opportunities . . . and the community of democratic nations is growing, enhancing the prospects for . . . stability."[42] Reflecting on the military dimensions of U.S. security, Defense Department officials predict that the United States will remain the only global military superpower through 2015. They do not foresee a global peer competitor comparable to the Cold War's Soviet Union, nor do they consider it likely that a "regional power or coalition will amass sufficient conventional military strength in the next ten to fifteen years to defeat our armed forces, once the full potential of the United States is mobilized and deployed to the region of conflict."[43]

40. Cheney, Defense Strategy for the 1990s, 19–26.
41. A National Security Strategy for a New Century (Washington, D.C.: U.S. GPO, May 1997), i [hereafter cited as 97 NSS].
42. 97 NSS, i.
43. Secretary of Defense William S. Cohen, Report of the Quadrennial Defense Review (Washington, D.C., May 1997), 5 [hereafter cited as QDR].

Clinton administration defense planners see a broad diversity of threats confronting American interests, including what Chase, Hill, and Kennedy have labeled the "new" security issues. But White House and Pentagon emphases differ.

The 1997 *National Security Strategy* differentiates among "three, often intertwined, categories" of threats to U.S. interests: regional or state centered, weapons of mass destruction, and transnational.[44] The first two in particular refer to "old" security issues. Regional or state-centered threats would arise from "coercion or cross-border" aggression as much against vital allies and friends as against the United States itself. Such threats could come from a rising hostile regional hegemon or a government's acquiring nuclear, chemical, or biological weapons. In addition, "unstable nations, internal conflicts or failed states may threaten to further destabilize regions where we have clear interests." Threats from mass-destruction weapons could arise from potentially hostile or "outlaw" states as well as from nonstate actors such as terrorists and criminal gangs. Finally, transnational threats group together most of the "new" issues: terrorism, drug trafficking, arms flows, international criminal organizations, cross-border refugee movements, and environmental challenges.

Since the end of the Cold War, Pentagon officials have increasingly distinguished between "old" and "new" dangers. But except for terrorism and environmental sabotage (such as Saddam Hussein's setting Kuwaiti oil wells afire and releasing oil into the gulf), they generally pay less attention to them than does the Clinton White House.[45] Instead they emphasize far more the difficulties of predicting the future, and they are especially concerned with how quickly developments in globally available, militarily applicable technology could outpace "compensating political or military countermeasures" and confront the United States with "technological or operational surprise."[46] As a result, they see the world generally becoming "less stable, presenting the Armed Forces with a wide range of plausible futures."[47] From this perspective, there is an intense focus on countering the threat from weapons of mass destruction, on combating terrorist strikes against U.S. military forces, and protecting both military

44. 97 *NSS*, 5–6. This is the source for all the direct citations in the paragraph.

45. On "old" and "new dangers," see Secretary of Defense Les Aspin, *Report on the Bottom-Up Review* (Washington, D.C., October 1993), 1–2 [hereafter cited as *BUR*]. For a present-day listing of threats, see, among others, Secretary of Defense William S. Cohen, *Annual Report to the President and Congress* (Washington, D.C., April 1997), 1–2 [hereafter cited as Cohen, *Annual Report*]. See also *QDR*, 3–5.

46. Office of the Chairman of the Joint Chiefs of Staff, *Joint Vision 2010: America's Military-Preparing for Tomorrow*, as found in *Joint Forces Quarterly*, 12 (summer 1996), 38 [hereafter cited as *JV 2010*]. See also *QDR*, 13.

47. *JV 2010*, 39. See also *QDR*, 49.

and related civilian information hardware and software systems from hostile disruption.[48] A thread running through all of these concerns is that of asymmetric threats, whereby an adversary would use "unconventional approaches to *circumvent* or *undermine* our strengths while *exploiting* our vulnerabilities." The approaches could include "terrorism, NBC [nuclear, biological, and chemical] threats, information warfare, or environmental sabotage."[49]

This concern for threats that may be hard to predict and rapidly evolving is reinforcing the tendency in the U.S. defense establishment to be "ageographic" in perspective, that is, not to tie down U.S. planning too much to specific regional or state-centered contingencies, since threats could arise anywhere. During the Cold War most U.S. military planners were fixated on the "canonical" Soviet threat. But they also believed that they could contend with any other threats, which were labeled "lesser-included cases."

In the Defense Department's 1993 *Bottom-Up Review*, the canonical Soviet threat was replaced with that of a notional regional aggressor whose capabilities loosely correspond to those of Iraq prior to Desert Storm.[50] In addition, both a North Korean attack south and an Iraqi attack into Kuwait and Saudi Arabia became "illustrative" planning scenarios. Both were viewed as plausible in themselves and as "posit[ing] demands characteristic of those that could be posed by conflicts with other potential adversaries." In short, they stood in for the rest of the world because each was considered a "useful representation" of the challenges facing the American military if confronted with "a well-armed regional power initiating aggression thousands of miles from the United States."

Since the *Bottom-Up Review*, increasingly greater emphasis has been placed on the possibility of a notional adversary that might employ unconventional or asymmetric means to outflank the U.S. military. These threats are usually described in *functional* terms—as are proposed solutions—without geographic reference since they are essentially open-ended geographically.[51] Reinforcing this "ageographic" tendency may be a sense as well that the world is still in a period of transition or military transformation and that it will take some time for the loci of future threats to be become clear.[52]

48. *QDR*, 49–51.
49. *QDR*, 4. Emphasis in the original.
50. See, e.g., *BUR*, 13. All citations in the paragraph are drawn from pp. 13–15 of this document.
51. See *JV 2010*, 38–39 and Department of Defense, Commission on Roles and Missions of the Armed Forces, *Directions for Defense* (Washington, D.C., May 1995), 1–9 [hereafter cited as *CORM*].
52. See inset in *CORM*, 1–7.

The *Quadrennial Defense Review* is the latest in a series of comprehensive efforts to evaluate U.S. defense strategy and programs. It is noteworthy for the emphasis it places on how the U.S. military must be ready *for anything, at any time, anywhere*. After referencing all the threats mentioned above, it almost redundantly adds that of unspecified " 'wild card' scenarios":

> Along with these projected trends (continued regional dangers, the proliferation of advanced weapons and technologies, transnational dangers, and the increased danger of asymmetric attacks), there are . . . "wild card" scenarios. . . . [They] range from the unanticipated emergence of new technological threats, to the loss of U.S. access to critical facilities and lines of communications in key regions, to the takeover of friendly regimes by hostile parties. Taken individually, these scenarios are unlikely. But taken together, it is more likely that one or more wild cards will occur than that none will occur. In addition, while the probability of individual wild cards may be low, their consequences may be disproportionately high. Therefore, the United States must maintain military capabilities to deal with such events.[53]

Along with this ageographic inclination defense planners today recognize the need for geostrategic priorities. Some parts of the world matter more than others. A survey of Clinton administration defense planning documents reveals that developments in Europe, the East Asia–Pacific region, and the Middle East–Southwest Asia are considered vital; those in Latin America, Africa, and South Asia are not.

Planners have no doubt as to the primacy of Europe, the East Asia–Pacific region, and the Middle East–Southwest Asia. They are the only areas whose stability and development are characterized as "vital."[54] In addition, only Europe and the East Asia–Pacific region are specifically mentioned by name in the administration's summary of its strategic priorities. And more American forces are deployed in Europe and East Asia (one hundred thousand in each) than anywhere else.[55]

Of the three, it is Europe (still) that appears to be first among equals.[56] Favoring it are its economic power and market potential, its foremost concentration of nations and peoples that share America's commitment to democracy and free markets, and the long-standing Euro-American ties of culture, ancestry, and alliance—with NATO the most important

53. QDR, 5. Emphasis in original.
54. QDR, 8 and ISA, *Middle East*, i.
55. 97 NSS, 2.
56. On Europe, see in particular 97 NSS i, 21–23, and U.S. Department of Defense, Office of International Security Affairs, *United States Security Strategy for Europe and NATO* (Washington, D.C., June 1995) [hereafter cited as ISA, *Europe*].

defense pact for the United States. Europe also draws American attention because it is at a critical period in terms of enlarging the number of states firmly committed to democracy and free markets; ethnic and national rivalries on its periphery significantly threaten stability; and the control of weapons of mass destruction and associated expertise is a major concern in several states at its eastern edge.

The East Asia–Pacific region would seem to be second among equals, but with developments there becoming ever more salient to America's well-being. Its economic potential is vast, and its dynamic rate of economic growth—it will account for 60 percent of global growth over the next decade—gives it not only economic clout but political power as well.[57] The United States also has important security commitments in the region. In language not used in pronouncements on Europe, the U.S. military presence in Asia is described as the "foundation for economic growth" and as the " 'oxygen' for . . . development."[58] On the negative side, however, possible territorial conflicts and sovereignty disputes among indigenous parties threaten to complicate U.S. relations with those parties and others. The proliferation of weapons of mass destruction and delivery systems within the region and to states outside it complicate relations as well. At the heart of the region is China, also a rising major power with which the United States will increasingly have to contend.

In his introduction to the Defense Department's *United States Security Strategy for the Middle East*, former Secretary William Perry most starkly outlined the significance of the region when he wrote that nowhere are U.S. criteria to use force to defend vital interests "more clearly met than in the Middle East."[59] His criteria were threefold: insuring the survival of key U.S. security partners, protecting critical economic interests, and reacting to the emergence of future nuclear threats. The key partners are, as will be discussed later, Israel, Egypt, and Saudi Arabia; the paramount economic interest is, of course, access to the region's oil; and the "pressing" proliferation threats arise from Iran, Iraq, and Libya, all of which virulently oppose U.S. engagement in the region and two of which are regional aspirants that threaten America's friends and the flow of oil.[60]

For the purposes of U.S. defense planning, Latin America, Africa, and South Asia are in another category altogether—essentially, the rest of the

57. See 97 *Pacific Command*, 4.
58. U.S. Department of Defense, Office of International Security Affairs, *United States Security Strategy for the East Asia and Pacific Region* (Washington, D.C., February 1995), 1, 2 [hereafter cited as ISA, *EA*].
59. ISA, *Middle East*, i, 5–8.
60. ISA, *Middle East*, 5–8, 17.

world. The situation in Latin America has improved so much that it is no longer of great interest to defense planners, as it was in the 1980s and even during the early 1990s when Secretary Cheney, as noted earlier, listed it as one of four critical regions. A 1995 Defense Department strategy document for the Americas offered an extremely upbeat picture of an area where "Democracy has become the norm . . . as market-based . . . practice has become the rule."[61] U.S. interests were described as "substantial" but not as vital or critical.[62] At the same time the White House's security strategy reports referred to the Western Hemisphere as "a fertile field for a strategy of engagement and enlargement."[63] Cuba, the reinforcement of democratic practices (with Haiti specifically mentioned), drug trafficking, protecting environmental resources—these and other problems were all referred to, but with no sense of urgency or of potentially disastrous consequences looming on the horizon.[64]

In sharp contrast to Latin America, sub-Saharan Africa seems a region almost overwhelmed with problems, notwithstanding the exceptionally favorable turn of events in the Republic of South Africa. Problems or not, however, it is the one region that is explicitly downplayed in U.S. documents. One cannot be more categorical than was former Secretary Perry when, in his introductory remarks to the *United States Security Strategy for Sub-Saharan Africa,* he wrote, "we have no direct vital security interests in the region."[65] Acknowledging Africa's many challenges and opportunities, the White House's own summary reaction was distinctly lukewarm: "We must identify," it says in its 1997 strategy paper, "those issues where we

61. U.S. Department of Defense, Office of International Security Affairs, *United States Security Strategy for the Americas* (Washington, D.C., September 1995), 33.

62. *United States Security Strategy for the Americas,* 7.

63. These words first appeared in the 1994 report and were repeated verbatim the next two years. All three reports are entitled *A National Security Strategy of Engagement and Enlargement* and were published in July 1994, February 1995, and February 1996. The cites are on pp. 24 (1994), 29 (1995), and 41 (1996).

64. In his 1997 State of the Union address, President Clinton made mention of Latin America only in terms of its market potential, and in her prepared statement for her confirmation hearing to be secretary of state, Madeleine Albright restricted her comments on Latin America until toward the end, when she turned to economic issues. See Bill Clinton's 1997 State of the Union speech, delivered on February 4 to a joint session of Congress. The text is found in the Virtual Library of the White House's Worldwide Web site. As for Secretary Albright's remarks, they are contained in her "Prepared statement before the Senate Foreign Relations Committee," January 8, 1997, *U.S. Department of State Dispatch,* January 1997, p. 13 [hereafter cited as Albright, Confirmation].

65. U.S. Department of Defense, Office of International Security Affairs, *United States Security Strategy for Sub-Saharan Africa* (Washington, D.C., August 1995), I. See also Institute for National Security Studies, National Defense University, *Strategic Assessment 1997: Flashpoints and Force Structure* (Washington, D.C.: U.S. GPO, 1997), 167 [hereafter cited as 97 *SA*].

can make a difference and which most directly affect our interests and target our resources efficiently."[66]

Finally, South Asia seems in a class by itself. Planners sometimes lump it together with the Middle East and Southwest Asia, but it clearly is not accorded the priority of its partners. Indeed, it was not even mentioned in the Defense Department's 1995 regional strategy reports, and the 1997 *Strategic Assessment* bluntly concludes that the "U.S. does not have vital interests to protect in South Asia."[67] As for the White House, it labels only as "important" the maintenance of "[r]egional stability and improved bilateral ties" as well as the "expansion of democracy and economic reform."[68] Noteworthy, however, is that the Pacific commander in chief seems to view India as a very significant state.[69] Perhaps the specter of a South Asian nuclear arms race will force the rest of the U.S. defense establishment to agree.

U.S. defense planning documents do not apply the term *pivotal* to developing states, but they refer to working with "key nations."[70] In Europe, several developing states are viewed as key. But in light of what is said about them, Ukraine and Turkey are the most deserving to be regarded as especially key or "pivotal."

Other than Russia, Ukraine is the only nation regularly singled out by name in policy statements to the effect that developments within and between the former constituent Soviet republics are of profound concern. The White House could not have been more explicit when it declared in 1997 that "the United States has vital security interests in the evolution of Russia, Ukraine, and the other NIS [Newly Independent States] into stable, modern democracies."[71] So too were successive Defense Department reports that pointed out that building cooperative links "with Russia, Ukraine, and the other NIS" was one of the department's highest priorities.[72] In addition, Ukraine is now the third-largest recipient of U.S. foreign assistance (approximately $1.2 billion a year); it was the nation most often visited (at least four times) by William Perry when he was secretary of defense; and it is one of only four countries globally—the others being Russia, South Africa, and Egypt—that has an explicit link or "commission" between the head of state or government, in this case President Leonid

66. 97 *NSS*, 28.

67. 97 *SA*, 130.

68. 97 *NSS*, 27.

69. 97 *Pacific Command*, 13. This may be because, as noted earlier in this volume, India is included in U.S. Pacific Command whereas, grotesquely, Pakistan is located under U.S. Central Command.

70. The term *key nations* is used, for example, in the 1997 *NSS*, 2, 6.

71. 97 *NSS*, 22. See also ISA, *Europe*, 20.

72. Secretary William J. Perry, *Annual Report to the President and Congress* (Washington, D.C., March 1996), 3; and Cohen, *Annual Report*, 3.

Kuchma, and the U.S. vice president. The Gore-Kuchma commission is a high-level vehicle for raising and resolving issues of mutual interest.

Several factors underlie American concerns with all the former Soviet republics, Ukraine included.[73] One is the commitment to enlarging the community of democratic and free market states—axiomatically regarded as having a stake in stability and peaceful change—and an associated worry that such practices are not yet strongly rooted in the former republics. A second is that the "NBC [nuclear, biological, and chemical] proliferation trend is especially worrisome" because of the doubtful ability of some of the states to control the weapons, materials, and technologies they inherited.[74] A third is the prospect of violent conflict within and between any of the states—with the Russian threat being a special concern—since violence would slow or derail desired reform and possibly spill over both within and outside the former republics. A fourth is "bringing Russia, Ukraine, and the other NIS into a new post–Cold War European security order."[75]

In addition to the above, at least four other factors apply specifically to Ukraine. First, it inherited a large number of nuclear weapons and missiles after the Soviet Union's breakup. Second, its relations with Russia have been rocky. Russia has made clear that it is uncomfortable with Ukraine's independence in foreign policy and its overtures toward Western Europe and the United States. Problems have also arisen over the sovereignty of the Crimea, the status of ethnic Russians in Ukraine, the stationing of Russian forces there, and Ukraine's assertion of control over Soviet nuclear weapons, missiles, the Black Sea Fleet, and its ports. Third, "from strategic self-interest . . . Ukraine is a bridge," says Secretary Cohen, "between East and West."[76] Finally, Ukraine seems to be seen as something of a bellwether for the fate of democratic and economic reforms in the area. The western half is clearly oriented toward reform and closer ties with Europe, whereas the eastern half, where most of Ukraine's ethnic Russians live, resists these trends and leans toward reestablishment of formal ties to Russia.[77]

Alongside Ukraine as a perceived pivotal state in Europe is Turkey. The 1997 *National Security Strategy* labels as "critical" Turkey's "continued ties

---

73. Relative to this and the next paragraph, see, among others, 97 *NSS*, 22–23; ISA, *Europe*, 21; 97 *SA*, 15–24; and Office of the Chairman of the Joint Chiefs of Staff, *National Military Strategy of the United States of America* (Washington, D.C., February 1995), 2.

74. *QDR*, 4.

75. 97 *NSS*, 22.

76. Dana Priest, "Ukraine Savors New Ties with NATO," *Washington Post*, July 14, 1997, p. 15.

77. 97 *SA*, 54–57, 62–65.

to the West and its support for our overall strategic objectives in one of the world's most sensitive regions."[78] The Defense Department's strategy review for Europe elaborated on this statement in declaring that "Turkey in particular is now at the crossroads of almost every issue of importance to the United States on the Eurasian continent—including NATO, the Balkans, the Aegean, Iraq sanctions, relations with the NIS, peace in the Middle East, and the transit routes for Central Asian oil and gas."[79] In her confirmation testimony Secretary Albright adopted a narrower but no less definitive focus when she referred to the Greek-Turkish disputes as "affect[ing] European stability and our vital interests."[80]

Heightening the perceived special significance of Turkey is the fear that "of all the NATO allies, [it] is the most vulnerable for . . . domestic and external reasons."[81] External reasons include not only its disputes with Greece but also the rebuff it received to its request for membership in the European Union at a time when the applications of several other states have been greeted more favorably. The rebuff has had internal repercussions, threatening to strengthen those forces which would have Turkey, with its Islamic culture, move away from its secular domestic arrangements and its orientation toward Western Europe and democratic, free-market practices. Other domestic factors are an ongoing internal civil conflict with Kurdish separatists and the difficulty of dealing with associated terrorist bombings. Internal tranquillity could also be disrupted by a breakdown in the Arab-Israeli peace process in light of Turkey's moves to expand relations with Israel.

In the East Asia–Pacific theater, many developing states are referred to as key along one or another dimension. But from a defense planning perspective, the only developing states seen as pivotal would seem to be the two Koreas, with Thailand and Indonesia as possible future candidates. To a great degree, American policy makers view East Asia as a region whose business is business and where indigenous leaders are generally committed to sidestepping confrontation that could seriously jeopardize the conduct of business.[82] The major disruption to that reality is seen as coming from an economic cripple, North Korea. The threat it poses to South Korea, its nuclear capabilities, and the prospect that it may collapse of its own weight hold significant potential to destabilize northeast Asia and

78. 97 NSS, 22.
79. ISA, Europe, 25.
80. Albright, Confirmation, 12.
81. 97 SA, 36.
82. See especially Institute for National Security Studies, National Defense University, Strategic Assessment 1995: U.S. Security Challenges in Transition (Washington, D.C.: U.S. GPO, 1995), 18–20.

draw in three other major powers beyond the United States: Russia, China, and Japan.

South Korea's pivotal position would seem to rest on at least five factors. First, the Republic of Korea (ROK), of course, is intertwined with a regionally troublesome twin. Washington cannot deal with Pyongyang without working with Seoul. Second is its formal defense alliance with the United States. These two factors by themselves make the ROK a "central" feature of the U.S. strategy to maintain regional as well as peninsular stability.[83] Third, the ROK is a nation where democratic habits are taking root and, as such, "a vital component in our national objective of supporting and promoting democracy."[84] Fourth, it is also an Asian economic "tiger" and trading partner. Fifth, the U.S. sees it as having a long-term strategic role: "Even after the North Korean threat passes, the United States intends to maintain its strong defense alliance with the Republic of Korea, in the interest of regional security."[85] The U.S. military presence on the peninsula would then be determined by many considerations, not the least of which would be the "nature of the U.S. relations with Korea, China, Japan, and Russia"—the same states that lie at the heart of U.S. concerns for regional stability should there be a North Korean crisis.[86] This potential future U.S. presence would differ from that of today, with less emphasis on heavy ground units in favor of quick reaction forces, air and naval as well as ground.

Finally, regarding Thailand and Indonesia, their status as possible future pivotal states reflects how they are viewed by the Pacific commander in chief (CINC).[87] The former is described as a "critical" contributor to regional security and stability and a "model for access and training" for U.S. military forces. The latter is said to have a role in the region that "cannot be overstated. Its strategic location, large Muslim population, and well-established regional involvement make closer relations with Indonesia a significant strategic interest." Whether or not the CINC's views will be echoed in future White House or Pentagon policy pronouncements remains to be seen. Thus, despite their present economic crises, it would seem premature to list them as more than possible future candidates at this time.

In the Middle East–Southwest Asia, three states appear to be regarded as friendly pivots—Israel, Egypt, and Saudi Arabia—and two as hostile—Iran and Iraq. The three friendly pivots are the only ones listed in the 1996

83. ISA, *EA*, 10.
84. ISA, *EA*, 10.
85. ISA, *EA*, 10.
86. 97 *SA*, 107.
87. All citations in this paragraph are from *97 Pacific Command*, 13–14.

Strategic Assessment as having de facto alliances with the United States.[88] Egypt and Saudi Arabia were also characterized in the Defense Department's regional strategy document as "our principal Arab partners." And Israel and Egypt have since the Camp David Agreement consistently received the bulk of U.S. foreign assistance—now running at roughly $5 billion a year.[89]

The U.S. commitment to Israel's security is described as "unshakable" and is regularly reaffirmed, including by the White House when it speaks of "ensuring" that nation's well-being as well as its security.[90] Among the reasons for the U.S. position are the circumstances surrounding Israel's founding, the influence of its friends among the U.S. citizenry, and its Cold War strategic location at the eastern end of the Mediterranean.

The commitment to Israel has spilled over to buttress Egypt's position, for the Israeli-Egyptian accommodation has led the United States to see Egypt as the "cornerstone of the American-led effort to achieve a comprehensive Middle East peace."[91] In addition, with Egypt a leader in the Arab world, its support is important on other issues, such as securing Arab League backing for Kuwait after its takeover by Iraq.[92] It would be a major symbolic blow to U.S. prestige and its position in the region should Egypt succumb to anti–U.S. fundamentalism, terrorism, or general unrest. Egypt is struggling economically, and its social cohesion is under strain. Many unemployed or discontented among its burgeoning population find an outlet in antigovernment fundamentalism that could destabilize the region and almost certainly affect the price if not the flow of oil.

That Saudi Arabia owns the world's largest oil reserves would be enough to account for its pivotal status. It is also the largest of the friendly gulf states, and its oil revenues have given it an important leadership

88. Institute for National Security Studies, National Defense University, *Strategic Assessment 1996: Instruments of U.S. Power* (Washington, D.C.: U.S. GPO, 1996), 116–118.

89. ISA, *Middle East*, 8.

90. The term "unshakable" is used by both Secretary Albright and the DoD. See Albright, Confirmation, 12 and ISA, *ME*, 7. The White House statement is in 97 *NSS*, 26. For another recent and prominent example of reaffirmation, see *QDR*, 3. Also note, however, that there may be an increasing trend in U.S. thinking, at least among some, that the threat to Israel has decreased enough as to make it unnecessary to use U.S. forces in its support. See, for example, the carefully worded statements in U.S. European Command, *USEUCOM Strategy of Engagement and Preparedness* (Stuttgart, GE, November 1996), 4, 7. See also 97 *SA*, 115.

91. General J. H. Binford Peay III, "Statement of General J.H. Binford Peay, III, Commander in Chief, U.S. Central Command, before the House Appropriations Committee, Subcommittee on National Security, 5 March 1997," 12–13 [hereafter cited as Peay statement]. See also ISA, *Middle East*, 8.

92. ISA, *Middle East*, 8.

role as a relatively moderate Arab state.[93] It too faces internal pressures from anti-Western groups, and, rich as it is, its ever-increasing population now confronts problems of sustaining the standard of living to which it has become accustomed. In addition, it shares a land border with one hostile pivot, Iraq, and sits astride the western side of the gulf with the other hostile pivot, Iran, on the opposite bank.

Iraq and Iran are like North Korea in that they threaten to be major spoilers. Iraq continues to possess the largest military force in the gulf and, thus, to pose a major military threat to Saudi Arabia and Kuwait that must be deterred. It also remains defiant of UN Security Council resolutions, including those which call on it to account for all of its NBC capabilities and ballistic missiles so that they can be destroyed. Hussein's virulent hatred of Israel and the United States has also led him to sponsor terrorist attacks against their interests.

It is Iran, however, that is regarded—at least by some—as the more serious long-term threat in view of its undiminished ambitions to be a regional hegemon and Islamic leader. A number of factors contribute to its ambitions:[94] It is the most populous state of the region, and many of its people are well educated and technically skilled; it has abundant oil, gas and mineral deposits; it is making a major investment in its military even while its economy is in malaise; it is aggressively pursuing the development of weapons of mass destruction; it is a major champion of Islamic radicalism and a supporter of extremist and terrorist groups operating in the moderate Arab states as well as in developed Western nations; and it can affect the flow of oil not only by threatening or striking at the gulf states but also by acting to close off tanker traffic plying the gulf and the Strait of Hormuz.

THE YALE TEAM VERSUS U.S. PLANNERS: AN ASSESSMENT

The logic that informs the argument advanced by Chase, Hill, and Kennedy is evident in the logic of U.S. defense planning. As do Chase, Hill, and Kennedy, U.S. defense planners have adopted a fundamentally conservative strategic approach. They have also found it useful to distinguish between the "old" and the "new" threats. Nontraditional threats have not escaped their notice, but the White House perspective on them is closer to that of the Yale team than is that of the Pentagon and the regional commanders. The Yale group and the White House can think of the nontraditional threats in terms of trying to lessen them in the first place.

93. ISA, *Middle East*, 8.
94. See Peay statement, 9–10.

This can involve marshaling the State Department, Treasury, Commerce, AID (Agency for International Development), other departments and agencies, and international organizations to work on biodiversity treaties, Uruguay rounds, population control programs, and the like; but defense planners approach nontraditional threats largely in terms of reacting to their effects, which can range from major regional conflicts to ecoterrorism. In the end, Pentagon planners see their primary, though not exclusive or sole, responsibility as ensuring that the country has the means to deter, fight, and win military engagements.

When Pentagon planners think of new threats, they also focus (unlike the Yale team) on the application of globally available, militarily applicable technology that could outflank U.S. military prowess by striking at communication links or other such vulnerabilities. They see this threat ageographically. For the most part, the threat cannot yet be "attached" to a specific region or state. The ageographic perspective may become even more pronounced and thus be at odds with a geographic perspective, but it may also become more geographically focused. Only time will tell.

This is not to say that U.S. defense planners do not have geopolitical priorities. Though they do not refer to "pivotal [developing] states" and do not systematically lay out a globally culled list of such states, they do identify some regions and some states as vital or critical. For strategic planners, the obviously critical, or pivotal, regions are Europe, East Asia and the Pacific, and the Middle East and Southwest Asia. Conflict in these regions has the potential to upset not merely local and regional balances of power but the global distribution of power. Adverse developments in critical regions, furthermore, would seriously undermine what are deemed vital as opposed to major or important U.S. national interests.

To be regarded as pivotal for defense planners, a state must have (or credibly aspire to acquire) the *military* capability to maintain, right, or upset order and stability in its region.[95] It must be located in a region that matters. A state is not pivotal if it is located in a geostrategically insignificant part of the world: hence defense planners' disregard of, say, Brazil and South Africa. The state's policies and actions must at least potentially affect, either positively or negatively, vital U.S. interests.[96] It should be evident that, generally, the criteria for designating a state as pivotal are more restrictive for defense planners than for foreign policy makers. A

---

95. This does not necessarily mean that such a state could not also engage in essentially non-military mayhem, such as ecoterrorism, within a larger military context.

96. Admittedly one must be careful of circular logic here. For example, would Nigeria's becoming a powerful and dominant regional power force the United States to revise the priority assigned to Africa? The answer would have to be "no" as long as African developments did not have a significant impact on American interests.

state may be pivotal for foreign policy makers but not for defense planners. Conversely, defense planners are more inclined to classify rogue states as pivotal, since they may have to confront them militarily, than are their broader foreign policy counterparts or the Yale team.

Chase, Hill, and Kennedy identified nine developing states in five regions where, they argued, the scarce resources of foreign policy makers should be concentrated. Their list is based, correctly, on a multidimensional set of criteria: size, location, economic potential, regional import, and precarious, but consequential, future. For defense planners, pivotal developing countries will be relatively rare. Judging from contemporary defense planning documents, only nine states (Ukraine, Turkey, North and South Korea, Israel, Egypt, Saudi Arabia, Iran, and Iraq) in three regions would seem to qualify as pivotal. The number drops to only three if the rogue states (North Korea, Iran, and Iraq) and special allies (South Korea, Saudi Arabia, Kuwait, and Israel) are eliminated from the list, as Chase, Hill, and Kennedy suggested. This leaves Ukraine, Turkey, and Egypt. Only the last two overlap with the Chase-Hill-Kennedy nine.

Some Implications

Considering the differing perspectives of the Yale team and U.S. planners, the fact that there is so little overlap between their lists of pivotal states should be neither surprising nor upsetting. That Algeria, South Africa, or Mexico, for example, are not pivotal from a defense perspective does not mean that they are unimportant. Considering its size, population, and long border with the United States, Mexico undoubtedly is extremely important and automatically a potentially pivotal state. Mexico can become actually pivotal if its stability becomes so fragile as to warrant major concern about internal conflict, refugee flows, or economic disruption in the southwestern United States. At that point it may (but not necessarily) become pivotal from a defense perspective as well. The same would apply to most of the other states on the Yale list.

In the absence of a comprehensive list, there may well be value in having two lists. One reason is to identify states that should be seen as especially significant—Egypt and Turkey in our analysis—because they appear on both lists. A second reason is to sensitize foreign and defense planners to the importance of a particular state. Defense planners, for example, may not regard Brazil as pivotal, but they may still wish to treat it with extra consideration (when planning military exchanges or seeking allies for a Desert Shield–type operation, for example) by virtue of its otherwise pivotal status (if it indeed rates such a status). Similarly, if the Pentagon is giving increasing relative weight to ageographic threats, the very existence of a geographically oriented list based on broader foreign policy concerns can serve as a useful reminder to planners that some states indeed deserve special attention.

At the end of the day, then, we do not see any significant disadvantage to having two lists. During the Cold War, U.S. foreign policy was driven too exclusively by narrow, or "hard," security concerns. The United States frequently supported deplorable governments and gave in to some states on economic and other issues for the sake of maintaining a solid anti-Soviet front. Had there been a list based on a broader set of concerns, U.S. strategy might have served long-term U.S. interests better.

STRATEGIC PRIORITIES, DEFENSE PLANNING, AND PIVOTAL STATES

Functional and geostrategic priorities must be considered in the broader context of the U.S. post–Cold War role in the world. It is evident that both the Bush and Clinton administrations adopted a fundamentally conservative strategy for dealing with the rest of the world. Not only did they both recognize the advantages of the post–Cold War international status quo for the United States and attempt to maintain it, they also both focused on U.S. relationships with what have been considered the major powers—in Europe, Britain, Germany, and France; elsewhere, Russia, Japan, and China. Both elected as well to maintain high levels of defense spending to support downsized versions of a Cold War military.

Although the United States has consistently acted in a conservative manner since the end of, as well as during, the Cold War, its rhetoric has not been so consistently conservative, particularly during the Clinton administration. It, after all, early on proposed that containment be succeeded by enlargement.[97] The declared objective has never been simply "to secure the peace won in the Cold War." Instead, "our national security," President Clinton has proclaimed, "is . . . based on enlarging the community of market democracies. . . ."[98] The Cold War effort to contain Soviet power and influence was a conservative enterprise. A serious post–Cold War effort to enlarge the community of market democracies would be an extraordinarily ambitious political and economic undertaking. It is only the selective, restrained pursuit of enlargement by the administration that permits us to characterize its strategy as conservative.

97. Anthony Lake, "From Containment to Enlargement," *U.S. Department of State Dispatch* 4, no. 39 (September 27, 1993): 658–664.

98. *A National Security Strategy of Engagement and Enlargement*, (Washington, D.C.: U.S. GPO, February 1996), 2. See also Strobe Talbott, "Democracy and the National Interest," *Foreign Affairs* 75, no. 6 (November–December 1996): 47–63.

Despite its rhetoric, then, the Clinton administration, following in the hesitant footsteps of its predecessor, clearly has opted for the restrained rather than the extraordinary. Short-sighted prudence has won out over vision. From a broader perspective, the United States should seize the unique opportunity it has to promote freedom, and do so vigorously rather than timorously. Since democracies tend not to go to war with each other, the spread of democracy enhances both U.S. security and world order.[99] A democratic zone of peace already encompasses North American and Western Europe. No serious analyst expects these democratic, free-market states to take up arms against each other. Why should other countries not be provided the opportunity to partake of this democratic peace dividend?[100]

The Cold War, it is said, was fought in the name of freedom. Victory in that struggle served to preserve freedom. Now it is time to extend that freedom to others. Political and economic freedom are not uniquely American or even Western values; they are universal values to which even Asian autocrats must yield. Excuses need not be made for the pursuit of U.S. interests, especially when they coincide with those of peoples (though not necessarily those of states) everywhere. The Clinton administration's lofty vision should more fully guide its actions. Hedging, or domestically driven political triangulation, is not always prudent.

The continuing conservative focus on the major powers, evident in both post–Cold War administrations, must be reconsidered as well. Though necessary during the Cold War, America's major power fixation is now somewhat dysfunctional. The United States, of course, cannot ignore the other major powers. But it need not allow them to dominate its strategic agenda. The United States devotes too much attention to the major powers today, more than they deserve. In particular, the major European powers—Britain, Germany, and France —do not now require

99. Thomas Carothers, "Democracy," *Foreign Policy* 107 (summer 1997): 11–18, misguidedly takes issue with what has come to be known as the democratic peace proposition. It is not the proposition that democracies tend not to take up arms against each other that is in dispute but the significance of the proposition and the contending explanations that have been advanced. Carothers and other doubters would do well to read Michael E. Brown, Sean M. Lynn-Jones, and Steven E. Miller, eds., *Debating the Democratic Peace* (Cambridge, Mass.: MIT Press, 1996); Steve Chan, "In Search of Democratic Peace: Problems and Promise," *Mershon International Studies Review* 41, supp. 1 (May 1997): 59–91; and John R. Oneal and Bruce M. Russett, "The Classical Liberals Were Right: Democracy, Interdependence, and Conflict, 1950–1985," *International Studies Quarterly* 41, no. 2 (June 1997): 267–294.

100. The case for promoting democracy is persuasively presented in Tony Smith, *America's Mission: The United States and the Worldwide Struggle for Democracy in the Twentieth Century* (Princeton, N.J.: Princeton University Press, 1994).

the continued sustained attention of U.S. defense planners. Europe would require less attention if NATO expansion were recognized for what it is: a solution in search of a problem. Russia and China do deserve significant attention, but not because they are major powers; they are not. They are barely significant regional powers. (Russia even during the Cold War was merely a Third World country that managed, just barely, to field a first world military. Now it is a developing country with the conventional military of a developing country.) Instead, they require attention because they are large, strategically located, developing states undergoing potentially destabilizing political and economic change. Either or both could be major spoilers. Here, then, are real pivotal developing states, for defense planners and foreign policy makers alike.

Devoting less attention to the "old" concerns of the major powers would allow the United States to devote more attention to the "new" nontraditional threats. Both the Bush and Clinton administrations, and even the Commission on Integrated Long-Term Strategy, exhibited an awareness of nontraditional threats. In neither administration, however, have nontraditional threats been more than a peripheral concern for defense planners. They have not had a real influence on military strategy and have had no more than a negligible impact on force-structure choices. Yet most of the operations in which U.S. military forces have been involved during the 1990s have been what are often referred to as nontraditional missions (or military operations other than war) to deal with the implications of nontraditional threats. Despite the military's often-expressed desire to preserve its capabilities for "real" military tasks, it is likely that the United States will more frequently employ military force to deal with the consequences of nontraditional than with traditional threats. Robert Kaplan has portrayed nontraditional threats as "*the* national-security issue of the twenty-first century. The political and strategic impact of surging populations, spreading disease, deforestation and soil erosion, water depletion, air pollution, and, possibly, rising sea levels . . . will be the core foreign-policy challenge from which most others will ultimately emanate."[101] For Paul Kennedy, similarly, transnational concerns such as "overpopulation, pressure upon the land, migration, and social instability on the one hand, and technology's power both to increase productivity and to displace traditional occupations on the other" confront us with our greatest challenges as we look ahead to the twenty-first century.[102]

These challenges must not be ignored or avoided by defense planners. They deserve more than lip service in the development of U.S. military

101. Kaplan, "The Coming Anarchy," 58.
102. Kennedy, *Preparing for the Twenty-First Century*, 11.

strategy. Force-structure choices should reflect the high level of military involvement in meeting these challenges. So too should force-employment choices, which, after all, affect global perceptions of U.S. willingness to play a leadership role. More serious training regimens to prepare U.S. forces fully to react to these challenges could be instituted as well. Although the U.S. military must be prepared to deter, fight, and win the nation's "real" wars, that will not be its exclusive function. It must also be prepared, when possible, to prevent, manage, and resolve nontraditional conflicts.[103] Ultimately, as former President Bush observed, "security is indivisible. The safety, freedom, and *well-being* of one people cannot be separated from the safety, freedom, and *well-being* of all."[104]

The high level of strategic interdependence President Bush posited and the salience of nontraditional challenges have obvious implications for U.S. geostrategic priorities. There is no significant disadvantage to having two lists of pivotal developing states—a foreign policy list that reflects concerns about nontraditional threats and a defense one that to date does not—but it is possible to develop a broader master list of pivotal concerns. A straw-man matrix on which such a list might be based is presented in Table 1. It is entitled "Pivotal Concerns from the White House Perspective" because the formulation of comprehensive national priorities must be shaped by a broad national security perspective. The left column addresses the interests which should be advanced: the protection of the U.S. homeland from major attack, from other attacks (such as against major electrical generation centers, for example), and from major environmental threats; economic well-being in terms of emerging markets, resource providers and migration to the U.S.; promotion of the democratic way of life; and historical legacy–emotional ties (such as the U.S. relationship with countries to which many citizens feel an especial cultural, ethnic, or religious connection). The columns on the right address entities that would have either a positive or a negative impact on these values, and in both cases the entity could be a state, a group of states, or a nonstate actor. This last category could encompass, among other groups, nongovernmental organizations (NGOs), resource cartels, organized criminal gangs, terrorist organizations, and geographic groups that cut

---

103. If this is "social work," as Michael Mandelbaum characterized it in "Foreign Policy as Social Work," *Foreign Affairs* 75, no. 1 (January–February 1996): 16–32, so be it. The label makes it no less worthwhile. U.S. reluctance to commit to participation in peace support operations is reflected in the development of official policy. See Donald C. F. Daniel, "The United States," in *Challenges for the New Peacekeepers*, ed. Trevor Finlay (Oxford: Oxford University Press for the Stockholm International Peace Research Institute, 1996), 85–98.

104. *National Security Strategy of the United States*, August 1991, p. 33. Emphasis added.

Table 1. PIVOTAL CONCERNS FROM A WHITE HOUSE PERSPECTIVE

Pivotal to What?	*Positive* Potential Sources of Impact			*Negative* Potential Sources of Impact		
	States	*Groups of States*	Non-States	States	*Groups of States*	Non-States
HOMELAND INTEGRITY						
Major attack						
Conventional						
NBC weapons						
Other Attacks						
Against people						
Against infrastructure						
Major environvental degradation						
ECONOMIC WELL-BEING						
Energy Markets						
Resource Providers						
Refugees/migration to U.S.A.						
PROMOTION OF DEMOCRACY						
HISTORICAL LEGACY/ EMOTIONAL TIES						

across national boundaries (such as that formed by Baden-Wurttemberg, Alsace, and Basel, which is said to now form one region for employment purposes).[105] All candidates would be listed in the cells, including major powers, special allies, and rogue states (all of which are explicitly excluded by the Yale team) in order to develop the "big picture" when assessing how the United States should expend its foreign policy resources. From that perspective, some major countries or special allies might come across as relatively more or less important than originally assumed. Certainly some version of a first-among-equals status will have to be given to those entities that show up more than once in the matrix. They clearly would have to be included in any comprehensive list of entities seen as pivotal.

Both the Bush and Clinton administrations had regional priorities. Both focused on Europe, East Asia, and the Middle East (with the Bush people focusing on Latin America as well). South Asia, Central Asia, and Africa tended to drop off the scope. After all, even in the context of a high level of strategic interdependence, some parts of the world and some countries will matter more than others. If not traditional Great Power relationships but nontraditional, transnational challenges are the national

105. John Newhouse, "Europe's Rising Regionalism," *Foreign Affairs* 76, no. 1 (January–February 1997): 71.

security issues of the future, however, the defense planners' list of regional priorities must be recast and expanded. Though nontraditional,
transnational challenges are not absent from Europe, East Asia, and the
Middle East, they are most evident in the rest of the world, precisely those
parts of the world to which defense planners are least attuned. Even if
Latin America, South Asia, Central Asia, and Africa do not make it to the
top of a revised list of regional priorities, they must at least make it onto
the list, even if they are at the bottom. In a world characterized by a high
level of strategic interdependence, no part of the world can be safely
ignored.[106]

Our list of proposed pivotal developing states begins, as already noted,
with Russia and China. The only two countries that made both the
Clinton administration and the Chase, Hill, and Kennedy lists, Egypt and
Turkey, also make it onto our list of pivotal developing states. For the reasons advanced by the Clinton administration, Ukraine belongs on the list
as well.[107] Saudi Arabia, because it is a metaphor for oil, joins Egypt as a
pivotal Middle Eastern state. Our only other candidates are India and
Indonesia.

India is the world's largest democracy (and it must be encouraged to
remain democratic) and a major emerging market. Its population will surpass that of China early in the next century. Most important, it can serve
as a major counterweight to China, a nation that many see as becoming a
potentially significant rival of the United States and its major allies such
as Japan. And we are only now waking up to India's nuclear potential.

John Bresnan has nicely made the case for Indonesia's pivotal status earlier in this volume. But beyond its geographic position astride critical sea
lanes, he did downplay viewing it as pivotal from a "hard" security point
of view. We disagree, for reasons he himself provides when justifying its
status in "soft" security terms. We accept East Asia as vital to U.S. interests and see Indonesia, as he does, as an anchor and leader in Southeast
Asia. Indonesia, we would add, seems as concerned as the United States
is with the long-term implications of growing Chinese military capability.[108] Despite its current economic and political problems, Indonesia's
size, Muslim culture, and leadership role in the Non-Aligned Movement,

106. Both regional priorities and priorities within regions should perhaps be determined not
by any one government department but by interagency working groups. The identification of priorities might also be facilitated by increased cross-departmental regional
coordination and rationalization. Currently the State Department and the Pentagon
define regions differently; and Africa, the Middle East, and South Asia are all split
between different regional commands.

107. On the significance of Ukraine, see John Edwin Mroz and Oleksandr Pavliuk,
"Ukraine: Europe's Linchpin," *Foreign Affairs* 75, no. 3 (May–June 1996): 52–62.

108. See Simon Long's "Survey" on Indonesia in *The Economist*, July 26, 1997, p. 18.

the Organization of the Islamic Conference, and especially in ASEAN and the ASEAN Regional Forum[109] make it a major player in a region where long-term territorial disputes over potentially vast energy reserves could draw in China, Taiwan, Vietnam, the Philippines (with which the U.S. has a formal alliance), and others. As China and the "tigers" continue to grow economically, one or more of them may see those reserves as critical to continued economic growth (comparable to how the United States and others view the gulf area). The reserves could be a catalyst to armed conflict.

The U.S. defense establishment would necessarily play a central role in responding to any "transboundary mayhem" that might result if things go badly in any of our pivotal developing states. But should it also play a role in efforts to prevent a pivotal state from collapsing? The distinction made earlier between the military's proactive and reactive roles in dealing with nontraditional threats should be kept in mind. Any defense role in proactively preventing the downfall of a pivotal state is likely to be limited. The Department of Defense simply is not equipped for these types of preventive efforts. Other U.S. government departments and agencies should be expected to take the lead here.

It could be argued that no list of pivotal states will be sacrosanct, that foreign policy makers and defense planners should emphasize the concept rather than any particular list. Considerable debate will surround any proposed set of candidates. Inevitably, the case will be made for adding or dropping one or another. That would serve to demonstrate the appeal and utility of the concept. But it would also illustrate that the specific choices matter greatly. It is, after all, the actual list of pivotal states, not just the abstract concept, that is intended to shape the choices made by U.S. policy makers.

109. See Michael Leifer, *The ASEAN Regional Forum*, Adelphi Paper no. 302 (Oxford: Oxford University Press, for the International Institute for Strategic Studies, 1996).

LESSONS LEARNED

CONCLUSION

Robert Chase, Emily Hill, and Paul Kennedy

Since we launched out pivotal states thesis three years ago, hardly a week has gone by without one or more of our nine countries grabbing the headlines. Forest fires burn out of control in Brazil and Indonesia; economic crisis in Indonesia brings down Soeharto after over thirty years of rule; and India and Pakistan conduct nuclear tests, raising concerns of a nuclear conflagration in South Asia. All this poses questions about American foreign-policy priorities in the post–Cold War era.

Three years ago, we called for an inquiry into U.S. strategy toward the developing world and into the possibility of setting clearer priorities and better calibrating American policies toward those regions. As described in our Introduction, this call inspired a detailed analysis of nine countries comprising one-half the population of the developing world and of their chances for achieving peace and prosperity in the next several decades. These analyses included a close examination of U.S. policies toward each pivotal state as well as recommendations for ways to improve those policies. This broad effort also enlisted specialists on global trends such as population increases, resource depletion, and financial and commercial transformations. These scholars assessed the likely impacts of these trends on the nine regionally influential countries in question.

The results of this inquiry appear in the preceding chapters. The reader need not agree with each and every part of this multifaceted endeavor to find some value in it. Many critics, for example, accepted the need for the United States to set stringent priorities in its policy toward the developing world, but had different lists of favored states. Others welcomed the emphasis on the nonmilitary global challenges facing developing societies, but rejected our state-centered approach to confronting these challenges. Various officials felt it politically and diplomatically impracticable for the United States to have a publicly announced "preferred list" of states, yet liked the methodology and process of the intellectual undertaking itself. NGO representatives worried that focusing on nine identified special countries could lead to an abandonment of "the rest of the Rest" in the developing world, although some of them admired the interdisciplinary and structured form of the pivotal states exercise. These were only a few of the initial reactions to the project.

Because the pivotal states exploration had such a variety of aims and responses, it has also produced a wide array of conclusions. These include thoughts about process, or methodology, about the substance of the original argument, and about the overall intellectual and policy contributions that might flow from implementing a pivotal states strategy.

PROCESS AND METHODOLOGY

As noted in the Introduction, the debate touched off by the publication of our article in *Foreign Affairs* encouraged us to pursue further our idea for a more focused American strategy toward the developing world. We wanted to push our ideas beyond the level of the merely provocative to test them, to make them more rigorous, and to find out what utility they had in the realm of policy and politics. In making this decision, however, we hoped to take a different path than the one we saw many prominent scholars following at the time. The favorite gambit in advancing a foreign policy idea, we noted, had been to compose a controversial article in a prominent publication such as *Foreign Affairs* or the *Atlantic Monthly* to be the center of attraction during the ensuing heated debate, and then, at the behest of a Manhattan publisher, to write a follow-up book defending and expanding on the original thesis.[1]

At the end of our presentation at the Council on Foreign Relations in January, 1996, one publisher asked us to do just that—that is, to coauthor a 250-page volume on the pivotal states thesis within the year. By that time, however, we had already been working out a different methodology and research plan with the Pew Charitable Trusts. We felt that simply responding quickly in a short book to the criticisms of our thesis would not allow us the time or the objectivity to step back and judiciously assess the merits of the pivotal states concept. We hoped instead to seek feedback from all corners in order to refine our conclusions and to ground them in political reality.

Acting on this inclination, we tried to provoke discussion of and responses to the pivotal states thesis in a wide array of ways. Some of these were traditionally academic, others were not. They ranged from an op-ed piece for the *Los Angeles Times* syndicate suggesting that the United States adopt a pivotal states strategy to an article on foreign aid published in the magazine *Forum*. Our efforts also included sending the original article to numerous scholars and policy makers, talking with members of

1. See the Introduction, p. 11.

Congress, and giving presentations to a wide range of audiences. We spoke before the Council on Foreign Relations, Congress, the State Department, and numerous college and university audiences; but we also gave talks at local high schools, mostly for social studies teachers. Finally, we invited a wide selection of people including scholars, policy makers, and business people to a three-day conference on pivotal states in February 1997. On the whole, we felt, the overall process distinguished itself by the sheer variety of activities and results.

Our primary effort was to enlist the help of experts on each of the pivotal states as well as on the crosscutting, or transnational, issues affecting the future of these states. This effort was the core of what we talk about as our "process" or methodology.[2] In devising this process, we hoped not only to refine our own ideas and to assess their practicality, but also to enhance the current debates on foreign policy. We sought an exercise that could enable scholars and other commentators not only to float useful ideas about American policy, but also to disseminate those ideas beyond an academic audience and to give them political resonance. As a result, the methodological structure of the pivotal states project distinguished it from other recent efforts, discussed earlier, to think broadly about American foreign policy and international relations.

First, the pivotal states project motivated scholars of different disciplines, different areas of expertise, and different levels of experience to interact in a way that directly influenced their conclusions about the pivotal states strategy. It encouraged generalists (us) to talk with specialists; it allowed junior scholars to work with senior scholars; it also required economists to work with historians, and political scientists with demographers. In this way it provided a model for interdisciplinary research.

The process also enabled area specialists to talk with global issues experts. It ensured that "new security" and "old security" scholars interacted. For example, Roger Owen, the author of our chapter on Egypt, found himself discussing threats to the Egyptian state with Dan Esty, our expert on global environmental affairs. Although Owen's first draft of his chapter did not address problems of environmental degradation and its effect on Egypt's stability, his contact with Esty and other scholars led him to do so in his final draft. This kind of revision also happened in the reverse way. It forced authors such as Charles Norchi and Eileen Babbitt to ask themselves tough questions about whether universalistic objectives in the

2. Though the efforts of many social scientists during this century to follow the scientific method employed by the natural and hard sciences have occasionally produced dubious results, the spirit behind this effort should not be discarded. Many scholars in the humanities and social sciences excel at proposing new interpretations of various global phenomena; but few approximate the natural scientists' rigor in testing their hypotheses.

field of human rights or ethnic conflict could be dealt with by working through state governments.

Our methodology also ensured that we sought to understand the point of view of policy makers. William Quandt, Dan Esty, Don Daniel, Andrew Ross, and Alan Makovsky—all contributors to this book—were once or are now government officials in some capacity. Presenting our ideas before government groups and individuals, as noted above, ensured the interaction of academics and policy makers, an exchange often discussed but not so often achieved. Alan Makovsky, for example, who formerly worked in the Department of State on Turkish issues, was able to explain why the United States lacks an intrinsic policy toward Turkey— why it seems always to be "a function of U.S. policy toward somewhere else." Makovsky lists four reasons for this, which he learned from personal experience, among them the bureaucratic structure of U.S. foreign policy agencies, which militates against policy prominence for the Turks.[3]

Finally, the pivotal states project called for a certain amount of feedback from the American public, including the business world. The financial experts Bowman Cutter and Sherle Schwenninger were able to sketch out for us the private-sector view on global financial markets, which added significantly to our own chapter. Since the emerging markets community already takes great interest in the prospects of most of our pivotal states—although Pakistan and Algeria much less so—this information aided the country experts considerably.

Overall, one conclusion about the benefits of this interactive process stood out. We found repeatedly that talking about different kinds of security, not to mention talking about the national interest, works better on a state-specific and concrete level than on the level of general principle. Skeptics of the seriousness of the "new" global challenges became much more intrigued when the debate focused on, say, the demographic and environmental pressures facing Egypt and Mexico. Believers in the overall challenge to humanity posed by ethnic conflicts or migration came to admit the importance of governmental structures in meeting these tests. Through an exercise like the one we conducted, proponents of the new versus the old security issues can usefully remind one another about the range of problems facing developing states while avoiding a long-winded debate on how "security" should be defined.

LESSONS LEARNED

Although the substance of our argument about pivotal states emerged from this process unscathed, the feedback it generated produced a con-

---

3. Makovsky essay, pp. 101–103.

siderably more sophisticated proposal for an American strategy toward the developing world than was contained in the original article. As we had hoped, the criticism and suggestions we received throughout this process led us to modify some of our ideas and to abandon others entirely.

First, we rescinded our early recommendation that a pivotal states strategy would require an overhaul in patterns of American spending on foreign aid. In the original article, and in subsequent public presentations, we suggested that the United States should direct its foreign aid toward the pivotal states. Rather than spread small amounts throughout numerous countries in the developing world as it now does, we argued, it should focus this aid on the states that are most likely to affect international stability and consequently American security. We noted that, "relative to what other states give for development, the American contribution is declining. By continuing to spread those resources across a broad swath of developing countries, the United States might further diminish the impact of its assistance in many countries. In contrast, concentrating on a few pivotal states would increase American influence in them."[4] We also pointed out that, apart from a number of exceptions, the USAID budget is "thinly distributed to the remaining hundred or more developing countries. As a result, U.S. foreign aid is neither focused enough to enhance U.S. national security nor generous enough to make a real contribution to the needs of the poorest developing countries."[5]

As it turned out, our subsequent, more concentrated look at the pivotal states, and at existing patterns of U.S. foreign aid, led us to amend that argument. For the most part, we learned, the pivotal states not only do not need foreign aid per se, but they also do not want it. Rather than seeking a relatively few dollars from USAID, the more developed pivotal states are instead looking for assistance in the form of technology transfers, trade and investment, and high-level political support for their diplomatic initiatives.

Brazil provides a perfect example of the pivotal states' comparative indifference to foreign aid. Direct U.S. foreign assistance to Brazil is at present a drop in the bucket compared with domestically generated capital or foreign private investments. Increasing American aid flows to this large economy at the expense of smaller and more impoverished countries would not particularly enhance American political leverage in Brazil or elsewhere. As Dr. Albert Fishlow pointed out during our three-day conference, the Brazilian government itself believes that Brazil's relative advancement obviates the need for American development assistance.

4. Robert S. Chase, Emily B. Hill, and Paul Kennedy, "Pivotal States and U.S. Strategy," *Foreign Affairs* 75, no. 1 (January–February 1996): 50.
5. Chase, Hill, and Kennedy, "Pivotal States," 50.

Instead it would prefer forms of support commensurate with its global and regional status. Indonesia and India are similar examples of pivotal states that would benefit from a variety of assistance on a par with their level of development. For example, John Bresnan points out that the United States needs to help stabilize Indonesia's economy and assist a peaceful political transition through this fragile period. In fact, this task is so immense that the United States is now forced to seek help from regional powers as well as G-7 members who have the resources to back the IMF and other international bodies that jointly may be able to save the situation in Indonesia. Still, the crisis there is clearly a challenge to the United States's ability to manage a pivotal period in this important country. America's capacity to do so is currently hampered by disorganization and poor communication among the U.S. agencies that set foreign, military, and trade policy and implement it. Yet Indonesia needs this kind of U.S. participation far more than it needs USAID.

In a few cases, we found that a pivotal state was receiving, if anything, *too much* money from USAID. In our original *Foreign Affairs* article, we criticized the U.S. government for spending less than 1 percent of the foreign assistance budget on South Africa. Surely, we argued, such a paltry sum seemed "glaringly inconsistent with U.S. strategic priorities?"[6] Yet as Jeffrey Herbst points out, South Africa currently receives so much monetary assistance, as well as capital inflows from around the globe, that it has little need of American development assistance. Given the postapartheid state's fortunate circumstance, it would be counterproductive to transfer funds from poorer countries in sub-Saharan Africa to the comparatively developed South Africa in the hope of achieving greater leverage for U.S. interests. South Africa, like Brazil, needs American support and assistance on various political and technical fronts, and the assurance of sustained American interest in the country, but not USAID dollars.

Egypt, though certainly not suffering from South Africa's embarrassment of foreign-assistance riches, needs not an increase in U.S. foreign aid but a different kind of support and assistance. As we noted in our article, Egypt is the second largest recipient of American aid after Israel.[7] Yet, as Roger Owen points out in his essay, Egypt is rarely heralded as a success story for American foreign assistance efforts. It is difficult to recommend an improved American policy for helping this state lift itself out of its morass of underdevelopment, resource depletion, and political instability that has not already been attempted.

Yet if we have concluded that directing the majority of foreign-aid

---

6. Chase, Hill and Kennedy, "Pivotal States," 50.
7. Chase, Hill and Kennedy, "Pivotal States," 41.

money to the pivotal states is not the best way to use American taxpayers' moneys, we still feel that patterns of American spending on foreign aid need to be rethought—that they continue to reflect the strategic priorities of the Cold War and other historic anomalies rather than those of the late 1990s. For instance, that so large a percentage of USAID dollars goes to Israel and Egypt makes much less sense in 1998 than it did in 1978. And we continue to feel that American aid is poorly distributed between military and social concerns. As we argued before, "Congress should seriously consider redirecting American aid. F-16 fighters can do little to help Egypt handle its internal difficulties, but assistance to improve infrastructure, education, and the social fabric would ease the country's troubles."

Our investigation also led us to question the initial emphasis on the importance to the United States of maintaining "stability" and defending the status quo around the world. We noted in our 1996 article that, "like the British Empire in the nineteenth and early twentieth centuries, the interests of the United States lie in the status quo." We further emphasized the critical importance of maintaining regional and international stability in order to protect the American national interest. Our inquiry over the last few years has not altered our belief in the fundamental necessity of considering the importance of U.S. security and global stability first and foremost when devising a strategy toward the developing world. Nor have we ceased comparing the American geopolitical position in the 1990s with the British position in the 1890s, and drawing conclusions accordingly.

We have, however, taken to heart the observations by authors such as Peter Smith (on Mexico) and Roger Owen (on Egypt), that "stability" and the "status quo" are not always desirable ends. Do we promote stability in Egypt as the ultimate end, since it is good for American interests, and in so doing prop up the Mubarak regime should it weaken further? Or would it be better to promote democracy and economic liberalization at the expense of this authoritarian regime, and risk the loss of stability in the short term? These complicated questions can only be addressed on the basis of individual cases. The United States is still, in a conceptual and historical sense, a "status quo" power, and its strategy should reflect this position; but American policy makers should avoid falling into the trap, which ensnared them more than once during the Cold War, of bolstering Third World dictators for the sake of stability. On the other hand, Americans should remain equally wary that movement away from an authoritarian yet stable and prosperous regime toward a democratic model may not necessarily enhance U.S. interests, even for the long term. As Bresnan points out with respect to Indonesia, the former Soeharto regime, with all its limitations, "has acted in ways that are consistent with U.S. interests across a wide range of regional and global issues prior to the recent

economic crisis. It is not clear that a more pluralist or populist government in Indonesia would be certain or even likely to improve on this performance," though Bresnan calls for the support of independent-minded
Indonesian business leaders as a way to reduce corruption and contribute
to the peaceful transition of the political system.[8]

A third modification to our pivotal states hypothesis concerned the
issue of regional spillover. Our 1996 article argued that the futures of the
pivotal states—whether successful or disappointing—would critically
affect the futures of their respective regions. Indeed, determinative
regional influence was one of the main attributes that qualified particular
states in the developing world as "pivotal." A pivotal state was "a hot spot
that could not only determine the fate of its region but also affect international stability." We suggested that the pivotal states were the "new
dominoes." How they went, we implied, so would go their regions. Each
pivotal state is so important regionally, we wrote, "that its collapse would
spell transboundary mayhem: migration, communal violence, pollution,
disease, and so on. A pivotal state's steady economic progress and stability, on the other hand, would bolster its region's economic vitality and
political soundness and benefit American trade and investment."[9]

Although this early observation proved generally to be true, the extent
and character of this influence actually varies a great deal, depending on
the pivotal state. For example, Herbst argues that our assumption about
South Africa's regional potential was too facile. Examining the economic
relationship between South Africa and its neighbors, he concludes that
even a booming economy in the former would not necessarily improve
the prospects for its underdeveloped neighbors. Conversely, he suggests
that, were South Africa's political stability and economic progress to
founder, the consequences for the rest of sub-Saharan Africa would not
be so profound as one might assume. Other country experts had similar
doubts about our conception of regional spillover: Quandt thought that
an Algeria falling to radical Islam would produce conservative countermeasures, rather than "dominoes," in Morocco and Tunisia; Smith felt that
a turbulent Mexico would affect the United States more than the rest of
Central America; and Cohen and Ganguly worried about the troubles of
India's neighbors "spilling into India" rather than a reverse process.

On the other hand, many experts persuasively detailed the regional
influence and potential regional spillover effects of the country about
which they were writing. A prosperous and democratic Brazil would significantly affect its neighbors, as it would were it troubled or stagnating.

8. Bresnan essay, p. 36.
9. Chase, Hill, and Kennedy, "Pivotal States," 33, 37.

Algeria's collapse would have considerable impacts in southern Europe. A radicalized or disturbed Turkey could destabilize the Middle East. Pakistan's future, whether promising or not, would significantly affect regional stability. As we write this, Indonesia's spiraling domestic crisis has all its neighbors worried about the possible effects.

Fourth, we realized that our discussion of "collapse" as a possible outcome for many of the pivotal states had been too simple. It was one thing to claim that these states were so important regionally that their "collapse would spell transboundary mayhem," but how catastrophic had that condition to be and what did it mean exactly? Did we really think that Egypt, or Indonesia, or Brazil, for that matter, were in danger of collapsing? Did collapse mean a fall of the current government and a change of regime (which might be welcome) or a lapse into civil war (which no one could desire)? Did we simply mean a reversal of the significant progress these countries have been making in recent times?

To clarify this issue, we asked each of the country experts to describe a "best-case" and a "worst-case" scenario, and then to estimate what was likely to occur during the next ten to fifteen years. In most cases, the authors were open enough to admit a variety of outcomes but felt that a muddling through, rather than a stunning success or an apocalypse, was probable. None of this modifies our original question: How can the United States defend its national interest by better helping these countries handle the strains and challenges of today and tomorrow?

ON LISTS AND LISTING

Perhaps the aspect of the pivotal states thesis that stirred the most controversy was the idea of identifying specific priorities in the developing world. Unsurprisingly, to many people the very notion of distinguishing among foreign countries purely in terms of their importance to U.S. interests causes difficulties. Such cold discrimination has an un-American feel to it. Some dislike a focus on states and prefer either a regional approach (as in a hemispheric policy, or a Pacific Rim policy) or a concentration on transnational issues (such as drugs or climate change). Others zero in, not on the states that are on the list but on the possible implications for the 120 or so developing countries that are *not* on the list ("the rest of the Rest," as Bryan Hehir calls them), a concern we address below. A great number of commentators sought to challenge the appropriateness of certain of our short-listed pivotal states (Algeria is the most frequent here) and to come up with additional candidates, perhaps not realizing that we had hoped to stir up precisely such a debate. Several authors of our chapters on global threats produced their own lists of which countries were "pivotal" from the perspective of their particular crosscutting issue. This suggests possible utility in comparing such lists to discover what they tell us.

Before attempting such a comparison, however, the very idea of publicly designating a list of developing states that require additional U.S. attention merits further consideration. In our original *Foreign Affairs* article, we argued that both an isolationist Congress and an American public reluctant to intervene indiscriminately might welcome the suggestion of focusing on a select few developing countries that deserve special care because their fates will directly affect the U.S. national interest. Though this suggestion had resonance on the Hill, pursuing it would undoubtedly cause political and diplomatic problems at home and abroad. As Congressman Doug Bereuter (Republican from Nebraska) pointed out during one of our presentations, powerful ethnic groups in key constituencies would exert enormous pressure on U.S. representatives were the government to announce a list of the top ten developing countries. Would not Greek-Americans and Armenian-Americans condemn the idea of giving Turkey special treatment? Similarly, how would the State Department representative to OAS meetings ward off trenchant criticism were the U.S. to designate Brazil and Mexico as the most important countries in Latin America? What explanations would our ambassador to Argentina, a country pressing for greater bilateral relations, have to provide?

Yet arguing over whether or not to announce "the list" misses the point. Making lists is a way of setting priorities and developing a global strategy to focus American energies and attention on those countries critical to its national interest. As a Great Power, the United States must occasionally stop and examine whether it is concentrating on the most strategically appropriate places. In fact, some departments, including the Pentagon and the Commerce Department, already *do* set and articulate priorities and believe that it makes sense to do so. Moreover, as we shall discuss below, the United States manages its relationship with certain key states through a small number of special bilateral commissions at the vice presidential level, including two of our "pivotals." As these commissions show, the idea of creating a special category for particular states already exists, although in an unsystematic way.

Whereas many critics found the idea of selecting a few pivotal states unworkable or impolitic, others had the reverse reaction. In particular, observers from inside the Beltway occasionally pointed out that American policy makers *already* do set priorities. Various departments and agencies recognize, for example, that in terms of the American interest, Mexico and Brazil are the two most important players in Latin America. Similarly, policy makers acknowledge the strategic importance of South Africa and

Egypt and consequently privilege these states when formulating policy.

It was precisely because we received such contradictory responses—we *can't* or *shouldn't* focus only on a few key countries, or we *do* already maintain such focus—that we resolved to press ahead with this inquiry. Our hunch was that, though publicly announced lists of pivotal states would probably cause even more fuss than the *US News & World Report*'s annual college rankings, most policy makers and their advisers instinctively recognize a need to discriminate and to set priorities abroad, although there is much less evidence of this practice.

The pivotal states project was intended to generate debate—to goad Americans into thinking strategically about the developing world. In this strategic sense, which developing countries require special U.S. attention? Before attempting to answer that question, let us recall two caveats made in the original article. The first was our warning that no list of pivotal states should be fixed in stone. Over time, any such list will and should change. The general principle of setting U.S. strategic priorities in the developing world does not preclude substituting Nigeria for Algeria at some time in the future. Indeed, some of these countries could become so prosperous and stable in twenty years' time that they will not require a special focus. Alternatively, as in the case of India, Brazil, and Indonesia, these states might by then have become Great Powers in their own right.[10]

The second caveat is that our pivotal states list, by its very nature, does *not* include those countries toward which U.S. strategists and policy makers already, and necessarily, pay the highest attention. This cannot be stressed strongly enough. What one might call "Category A" states from the viewpoint of American national interests include the larger powers of Europe, Russia–Ukraine, China, Japan; U.S. special clients such as Israel, Saudi Arabia–Kuwait, South Korea; and "rogue states" (usually threatening the clients) such as Libya, Iran, Iraq, North Korea, and Cuba.

Regardless of which administration is in the White House in the years to come, there is surely no doubt that the situation in Ukraine, or the Korean Peninsula, or the Persian Gulf, will continue to be closely monitored by U.S. agencies and remain high on the National Security Council's agenda. Our concern, rather, was that there might not be sufficient strategic discrimination in U.S. policies toward the "Category B" states, that is, all the rest of the world, except for a spasmodic response to a CNN-covered atrocity. Some of those 130 countries really *are* more important to the American national interest than others.

10. See Richard W. Stevenson, "World Bank Report Sees Era of Emerging Economies," *New York Times*, September 10, 1997, p. D7, for a summary of the most recent World Bank report.

That said, it is instructive to compare our list with those put forward in some of the chapters on global trends. It will be recalled that these essays were included to provide a check on the adequacy of our initial state-centered list. Depending on the issue (global financial markets, demographic pressures, military strategy), it was likely that each of these authors would put together a somewhat different list of pivotal states. From an environmentalist's perspective, some of our pivotal states—Brazil, India, and Indonesia, certainly—will be key players in any strategy for achieving a slowdown in global warming and the ecological degradation of our planet; but, as Esty points out, any successful international agreement on the global environment will have to include Russia and China. Similarly, in terms of overpopulation as a global issue, the largest (forecast) contributors to world population increases do include most of our pivotal states. Again, however, one would have to add China. Likewise, from an emerging markets perspective, many of our states are important players, but so too are some smaller, vigorous economies such as Malaysia or Hungary.

Daniel and Ross provide perhaps the most significant "counter list" in their subtle analysis of American strategic priorities from the Pentagon's point of view. They observe that, by and large, defense planners designate "Category A" countries as meriting top priority. Their main concern, understandably enough, is with Europe, Russia–Ukraine, China, and Japan, "rogue states" such as Iran, and special client states such as Israel and South Korea. But Daniel and Ross do note, however, that in two cases the Pentagon's priority "list" overlaps with the list of the pivotal states. Turkey and Egypt, no doubt because their geopolitical relationship to America's interests in the Mediterranean, the Middle East, and the Caucasus are central concerns of defense planners. In addition, Daniel and Ross suspect that India and Indonesia should be moved into the first category, a sentiment with which—given the current turbulences in both these giant states—we can only applaud. Had they already been on the United States' priority list, perhaps it might have better anticipated the Indonesian crisis. Had South Asia been given more attention by American strategists, we might not have been so surprised by the India/Pakistan nuclear tests.

Unsurprisingly, such a ranking by military planners reflects the traditional focus on "hard" security issues that our pivotal states project sought to enlarge. It is a good list for the immediate post–Cold War era. As we suspected, however, it is too narrowly focused to account for the potential turbulences and shifts in the strategic balances that will mark the early twenty-first century. For instance, the Pentagon pays little attention to South Africa and Brazil, or even to Mexico. More unnerving is its lack of concern about Pakistan and Algeria, considering their potential to affect war and peace in their respective regions.

The interesting contrast to the Pentagon's point of view is laid out by chapters on such "soft" security concerns as human rights, ethnic conflict, and migration. The NGO community initially reacted to the pivotal states thesis with hostility, probably because (as we suggested) this community tends by its very nature to emphasize grass-roots activism; it often regards "states" as obstacles to providing human security for all in many parts of the world, and often rightly so. Yet Charles Norchi's nuanced counterargument is an intriguing one. The encouragement of large "human rights platforms" in the developing world could boost significantly the presently somewhat uncertain and diffuse human rights movement. Not only would this focus on few but populous "platforms" improve the lot of much of humanity, but their example could also have favorable spillover effects. Such has been the case with Mandela's South Africa and, to some extent, Cardoso's Brazil. Babbitt's chapter on ethnic conflict and Teitelbaum's on migration make much the same point. Both discuss troubling phenomena that have universal manifestations, yet conclude that working to resolve these issues in the nine pivotal states would go a long way toward lessening their incidence and intensity overall.

The setting and listing of priorities provides an excellent means to check the extent to which American policies toward the developing world currently reflect long-term strategic interests, but a nagging doubt remains. Even if the world were fortunate enough to see these nine important countries enjoy rapidly growing prosperity, democracy, and sustainable development, what would that mean for the other 120 developing states, especially the poorest of the poor? Don't we have a special obligation to "the rest of the Rest"? Undoubtedly so, but it should be recalled that this exercise is investigating U.S. *strategy* toward certain key states, not American philanthropy or the pattern of international aid. We have already concluded that diverting the meager amounts of USAID moneys from the poorest countries would be of little use to the pivotal states while provoking unneeded controversy at home.

This does not mean, however, that our present distribution of development aid should not be reexamined. As noted earlier, in the course of asking hard questions about the pattern and purposes of this assistance, we kept coming upon intriguing facts, such as South Africa's rejection of "conditionality"-related aid. Again, when we asked the question, How badly would (say) Kenya be hit by the elimination of U.S. official assistance? we were surprised to learn that American official bilateral funding comprised only 4 percent of the aid Kenya received worldwide; the World Bank, the EU, and Japan were much more important donors.

This kind of statistic, which we came upon again and again, suggests that it might be useful for the various aid donors and recipients to establish an international "division of labor" with respect to development assistance. Tacitly, something like this already exists, as many of our articles confirmed. But why not make it more explicit? Why not produce an annual report on the totality of aid transfers (bilateral, multilateral, charities, NGOs, foundations) and the totality of the recipients (governments, churches, local initiatives, cooperatives, scholarships) that is much more broadly known to politicians and the public than the published but obscure DAC (Development Advisory Commission) data? This would allow people other than development experts to identify disparities of aid flows and to pay more attention to those developing countries that are slipping through the cracks. Publicity over this issue might also remind Americans how little of their GDP is given to official aid, as compared with the rest of the OECD (Organization for Economic Cooperation and Development) countries.

Such knowledge, in turn, could inform a more sophisticated U.S. pivotal states strategy. Identifying countries such as South Africa, Algeria, and Brazil that don't need direct American aid inevitably leads to an investigation of what *really* would help them—assistance from the IMF and World Bank, providing markets for their produce, technical transfers, educational facilities and scholarships, and so on. This sort of nuanced package, together with the provision of security and stability in critical regions through the global reach of American and allied armed forces, would offer a coherent U.S. policy toward the developing world. Such a strategy would attract less criticism than does Washington's present vaguely defined and ill-explained practice and would offer better prospects for both the pivotal states and the "rest" of the countries facing the challenges of global change.

FINAL THOUGHTS

At the end of the day, and while acknowledging all the modifications made to this intellectual hypothesis since floating the original *Foreign Affairs* article, we continue to see considerable benefits for American policy makers and for the larger world community in pursuing a pivotal states strategy during the years to come.

In the first place, this experiment has challenged the claim that America *already* sets clear priorities in the developing world and *already* has coherent policies toward the important states. With one or two exceptions, our authors contend that American policy toward these pivotal states lacks coherence and shows serious deficiencies. This suggests that although the United States may possess enormous military and economic muscle, it has underinvested in diplomatic and political finesse. Improving this situation is a major charge to U.S. policy makers as the nation enters the next century.

In addition, many secondary benefits flow from this investigation. The chapters above offer a plethora of country-specific recommendations for American policy makers, complemented by the various proposals on the crosscutting global issues. These ideas will contribute to the current debates on U.S. strategy in the post–Cold War decades. The two levels of recommendations should not be confused, however. Improving American policies in Indonesia, for example, is certainly necessary, but not sufficient. A better U.S. strategy toward the developing world as a whole will require an overhaul of the structures and processes of policy making.

What would that structural and procedural overhaul consist of? The preceding chapters have provided some possible but potentially misleading clues. For example, Herbst describes the U.S.–South African relationship as the clear exception to this overall pattern of neglect and lack of focus. Yet this exception results from the "special relationship" between the two countries' vice presidents, so it is difficult to ascertain the implications of this fruitful interaction. Does the success of this relationship suggest that every one of our pivotal states should have a special vice presidential link or a bilateral commission, since only this would require Washington to focus consistently on those countries? Would ten or fifteen such high-level linkages ultimately reduce the effectiveness of all of them and overstrain the American personnel involved? Moreover, to what extent is the U.S.–South African relationship an *ad hominem* arrangement resulting from Vice President Gore's personal interest in South Africa, which would not endure a successor's relative neglect? If so, what other, more permanent bureaucratic arrangement would ensure that U.S. policies toward each of the pivotal states received proper scrutiny? Would there not be merit in having a searching, annual, interagency assessment of the United States' relationship with Indonesia, Turkey, and the rest, conducted out of the White House or the NSC? *Whatever* is done, this is clearly not a task for the State Department alone.

Another benefit of the pivotal states project is that it cannot help but reinforce the argument that the U.S. "security community" has to take the newer, nonmilitary threats to international stability more seriously. Any fair-minded reading of the above chapters on Mexico, Indonesia, Turkey, and Pakistan reveals that the precariousness of their present condition could have serious consequences, not only for these states themselves but also for American interests; and yet the sources of such instability lie much more in the realm of the environment, demography, and the fraying of the social fabric than in old-fashioned interstate aggressions. In much the same way, a possible financial meltdown of these overseas markets, which had American officials and senior bankers huddled together in the White House's "situation room" in early 1998, simply confirms that economic dangers can have security implications. This suggests that, even more than the NSC, the Pentagon itself also needs to work together with civilian agencies in formulating policies toward the pivotal states.

Calling for a strategy toward the developing world based on pivotal states has, in our experience, the potential of raising general consciousness about global issues. A serious debate about the nature and focus of American policies in those parts of the world that do not receive the automatic attention of an incoming secretary of state is long overdue, yet the NGOs and other internationalists who urge such a debate have not yet come up with arguments strong enough to attract policy makers' attention. Suggesting that a discrete number of developing states deserve special scrutiny from the American government, calling for a fresh look at U.S. and international aid patterns, and citing the consequences of a failure in any pivotal state all help to provoke reactions and discussion. Periodically, all Great Powers require this sort of debate, precisely to reexamine their priorities or lack thereof. Hasn't the time come again for just such an exercise?

The final and greatest potential benefit of this project is to encourage *proactive* rather than *reactive* American policies toward the developing world. We should not have had to wait for the early 1998 financial crisis in Asia to witness a White House crisis team meeting daily in an attempt to douse the flames. We should not have had to wait until the present implosion of Indonesia to have that country's fate gain the attention of the NSC, the Pentagon, and the president himself. To be sure, a reactive foreign policy is conventional for a superpower that possesses massive retaliatory force and tends naturally toward a conservative strategy of defending the status quo. A century ago Lord Salisbury, the prime minister of Great Britain, described his country's foreign policy as being one of "floating lazily downstream, putting out the boathook to avoid the occasional collision." In its present blessed geopolitical circumstances, the United States could arguably do just the same, pursuing only short-term responses as particular emergencies arise. After reading the detailed assessments of the challenges facing the pivotal states, and of the broader challenges arising from worldwide transformations of human society, however, such a passive, lackadaisical policy is surely no longer feasible or prudent. America needs the sort of intelligent, focused, proactive policies that are suggested in the pages above.

INDEX